THE LIFE OF JOHN MARSHALL

VOLUME IV

JOHN MARSHALL
From the portrait by Henry Inman

THE LIFE
OF
JOHN MARSHALL

BY

ALBERT J. BEVERIDGE

VOLUME IV

THE BUILDING OF THE NATION

1815–1835

BOSTON AND NEW YORK

HOUGHTON MIFFLIN COMPANY

The Riverside Press Cambridge

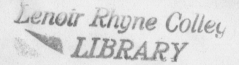

The Riverside Press
CAMBRIDGE · MASSACHUSETTS
PRINTED IN THE U. S. A.

CONTENTS

CONTENTS

and exclusive — Marshall attacks the enemies of Nationalism —
The immediate effect of Marshall's opinion on steamboat transportation, manufacturing, and mining — Later effect still more
powerful — Railway development incalculably encouraged — Results to-day of Marshall's theory of commerce — Litigation in
New York following the Supreme Court's decision — The whole-
hearted Nationalism of Chief Justice Savage and Chancellor
Sanford — Popularity of Marshall's opinion — The attack in Congress on the Supreme Court weakens — Martin Van Buren, while
denouncing the "idolatry" for the Supreme Court, pays an exalted
tribute to Marshall: "The ablest judge now sitting on any judicial
bench in the world" — Senator John Rowan of Kentucky calls the
new popular attitude toward the Supreme Court "a judicial
superstition" — The case of Brown *vs.* Maryland — Marshall's
opinion completes his Constitutional expositions of the commerce
clause — Taney's remarkable acknowledgment.

Marshall's dislike for the formal society of Washington — His
charming letters to his wife — He carefully avoids partisan politics — Refrains from voting for twenty years — Is irritated by
newspaper report of partisanship — Writes denial to the Richmond
Whig — Clay writes Marshall — The Chief Justice explains incident to Story — Marshall's interest in politics — His letter to his
brother — Permits himself to be elected to the Virginia Constitutional Convention of 1829–30 — His disgust at his "weakness"
— Writes Story amusing account — Issues before the convention
deeply trouble him — He is frankly and unshakably conservative
— The antiquated and undemocratic State Constitution of 1776
and the aristocratic system under it — Jefferson's brilliant indictment of both in a private letter — His alarm and anger when his
letter is circulated — He tries to withdraw it — Marshall's interest in the well-being of the people — His prophetic letter to Charles
F. Mercer — Marshall's only public ideal that of Nationalism —
His views on slavery — Letters to Gurley and Pickering — His
judicial opinions involving slavery and the slave trade: The Antelope; Boyce *vs.* Anderson — Extreme conservatism of Marshall's
views on legislation and private property — Letter to Greenhow
— Opinions in Ogden *vs.* Saunders and Bank *vs.* Dandridge —
Marshall's work in the Virginia convention — Is against any reform — Writes Judiciary report — The aristocratic County Court
system — Marshall defends it — Impressive tributes to Marshall
from members of the convention — His animated and powerful
speeches on the Judiciary — He answers Giles, Tazewell, and Cabell, and carries the convention by an astonishing majority — Is
opposed to manhood suffrage and exclusive white basis of representation — He pleads for compromise on the latter subject and
prevails — Reasons for his course in the convention — He probably prevents civil strife and bloodshed in Virginia — The convention adjourns — History of Craig *vs.* Missouri — Marshall's

CONTENTS

Widespread expressions of sorrow—Only one of condemnation—
The long-continued mourning in Virginia — Marshall's old club re-
solves never to fill his place or increase its membership — Story's
"inscription for a cenotaph" and the words Marshall wrote for
his tomb.

ILLUSTRATIONS

LIST OF ABBREVIATED TITLES MOST FREQUENTLY CITED

All references here are to the List of Authorities at the end of this volume

Adams: *U.S. See* Adams, Henry. History of the United States.

Ambler: *Ritchie. See* Ambler, Charles Henry. Thomas Ritchie: A Study in Virginia Politics.

Ames: Ames. *See* Ames, Fisher. Works.

Anderson. *See* Anderson, Dice Robins. William Branch Giles.

Babcock. *See* Babcock, Kendric Charles. Rise of American Nationality, 1811–1819.

Bayard Papers: Donnan. *See* Bayard, James Asheton. Papers from 1796 to 1815. Edited by Elizabeth Donnan.

Branch Historical Papers. See John P. Branch Historical Papers.

Catterall. *See* Catterall, Ralph Charles Henry. Second Bank of the United States.

Channing: *Jeff. System. See* Channing, Edward. Jeffersonian System, 1801–1811.

Channing: *U.S. See* Channing, Edward. History of the United States.

Curtis. *See* Curtis, George Ticknor. Life of Daniel Webster.

Dewey. *See* Dewey, Davis Rich. Financial History of the United States.

Dillon. *See* Dillon, John Forrest. John Marshall: Life, Character, and Judicial Services.

E. W. T.: Thwaites. *See* Thwaites, Reuben Gold. Early Western Travels.

Farrar. *See* Farrar, Timothy. Report of the Case of the Trustees of Dartmouth College against William H. Woodward.

Hildreth. *See* Hildreth, Richard. History of the United States of America.

Hunt: *Livingston. See* Hunt, Charles Havens. Life of Edward Livingston.

Kennedy. *See* Kennedy, John Pendleton. Memoirs of the Life of William Wirt.

King. *See* King, Rufus. Life and Correspondence. Edited by Charles R. King.

Lodge: *Cabot.* *See* Lodge, Henry Cabot. Life and Letters of George Cabot.

Lord. *See* Lord, John King. A History of Dartmouth College, 1815–1909.

McMaster. *See* McMaster, John Bach. A History of the People of the United States.

Memoirs, J.Q.A.: Adams. *See* Adams, John Quincy. Memoirs. Edited by Charles Francis Adams.

Morison: *Otis.* *See* Morison, Samuel Eliot. Life and Letters of Harrison Gray Otis.

Morris. *See* Morris, Gouverneur. Diary and Letters. Edited by Anne Cary Morris.

N.E. Federalism: Adams. *See* Adams, Henry. Documents relating to New-England Federalism, 1800–1815.

Parton: *Jackson.* *See* Parton, James. Life of Andrew Jackson.

Plumer. *See* Plumer, William, Jr. Life of William Plumer.

Priv. Corres.: Webster. *See* Webster, Daniel. Private Correspondence. Edited by Fletcher Webster.

Quincy: *Quincy.* *See* Quincy, Edmund. Life of Josiah Quincy of Massachusetts.

Randall. *See* Randall, Henry Stephens. Life of Thomas Jefferson.

Records Fed. Conv.: Farrand. *See* Records of the Federal Convention of 1787. Edited by Max Farrand.

Richardson. *See* Richardson, James Daniel. A Compilation of the Messages and Papers of the Presidents, 1789–1897.

Shirley. *See* Shirley, John M. The Dartmouth College Causes and the Supreme Court of the United States.

Story. *See* Story, Joseph. Life and Letters. Edited by William Wetmore Story.

Sumner: *Hist. Am. Currency.* *See* Sumner, William Graham. A History of American Currency.

Sumner: *Jackson.* *See* Sumner, William Graham. Andrew Jackson. As a Public Man.

Tyler: *Tyler.* *See* Tyler, Lyon Gardiner. Letters and Times of the Tylers.

Works: Ford. *See* Jefferson, Thomas. Works. Edited by Paul Leicester Ford.

Writings: Adams. *See* Gallatin, Albert. Writings. Edited by Henry Adams.

Writings: Hunt. *See* Madison, James. Writings. Edited by Gaillard Hunt.

THE LIFE OF JOHN MARSHALL

THE LIFE OF JOHN MARSHALL

CHAPTER I

THE PERIOD OF AMERICANIZATION

Great Britain is fighting our battles and the battles of mankind, and France is combating for the power to enslave and plunder us and all the world.
(Fisher Ames.)

Though every one of these Bugbears is an empty Phantom, yet the People seem to believe every article of this bombastical Creed. Who shall touch these blind eyes. (John Adams.)

The object of England, long obvious, is to claim the ocean as her domain.
(Jefferson.)

I am for resistance by the *sword*. (Henry Clay.)

INTO the life of John Marshall war was strangely woven. His birth, his young manhood, his public services before he became Chief Justice, were coincident with, and affected by, war. It seemed to be the decree of Fate that his career should march side by side with armed conflict, and that the final phase of that career should open with a war — a war, too, which brought forth a National consciousness among the people and demonstrated a National strength hitherto unsuspected in their fundamental law.

Yet, while American Nationalism was Marshall's one and only great conception, and the fostering of it the purpose of his life, he was wholly out of sympathy with the National movement that led to our second conflict with Great Britain, and against the continuance of it. He heartily shared the opinion of the Federalist leaders that the War of 1812 was unnecessary, unwise, and unrighteous.

By the time France and England had renewed

hostilities in 1803, the sympathies of these men had become wholly British. The excesses of the French Revolution had started them on this course of feeling and thinking. Their detestation of Jefferson, their abhorrence of Republican doctrines, their resentment of Virginia domination, all hastened their progress toward partisanship for Great Britain. They had, indeed, reverted to the colonial state of mind, and the old phrases, "the mother country," "the protection of the British fleet," [1] were forever on their lips.

These Federalists passionately hated France; to them France was only the monstrous child of the terrible Revolution which, in the name of human rights, had attacked successfully every idea dear to their hearts — upset all order, endangered all property, overturned all respectability. They were sure that Napoleon intended to subjugate the world; and that Great Britain was our only bulwark against the aggressions of the Conqueror — that "varlet" whose "patron-saint [is] Beelzebub," as Gouverneur Morris referred to Napoleon. [2]

So, too, thought John Marshall. No man, except his kinsman Thomas Jefferson, cherished a prejudice more fondly than he. Perhaps no better example of first impressions strongly made and tenaciously retained can be found than in these two men. Jefferson was as hostile as Marshall was friendly to Great Britain; and they held exactly opposite sentiments toward France. Jefferson's strongest title

[1] "The navy of Britain is our shield." (Pickering: *Open Letter* [Feb. 16, 1808] *to Governor James Sullivan*, 8; *infra*, 5, 9–10, 25–26, 45–46.)

[2] *Diary and Letters of Gouverneur Morris:* Morris, II, 548.

to immortality was the Declaration of Independence; nearly all of his foreign embroilments had been with British statesmen. In British conservatism he had found the most resolute opposition to those democratic reforms he so passionately championed, and which he rightly considered the manifestations of a world movement.[1]

And Jefferson adored France, in whose entrancing capital he had spent his happiest years. There his radical tendencies had found encouragement. He looked upon the French Revolution as the breaking of humanity's chains, politically, intellectually, spiritually.[2] He believed that the war of the allied governments of Europe against the new-born French Republic was a monarchical combination to extinguish the flame of liberty which France had lighted.

Marshall, on the other hand, never could forget his experience with the French. And his revelation of what he had endured while in Paris had brought him his first National fame.[3] Then, too, his idol, Washington, had shared his own views — indeed, Marshall had been instrumental in the formation of Washington's settled opinions. Marshall had championed the Jay Treaty, and, in doing so, had necessarily taken the side of Great Britain as opposed to France.[4] His business interests[5] powerfully inclined him in the same direction. His personal friends were the ageing Federalists.

[1] Jefferson to D'Ivernois, Feb. 6, 1795, *Works of Thomas Jefferson:* Ford, VIII, 165.

[2] Jefferson to Short, Jan. 3, 1793, *ib.* VII, 203; same to Mason, Feb. 4, 1791, *ib.* VI, 185.

[3] See vol. II, 354, of this work.

[4] *Ib.* 133-39.   [5] The Fairfax transaction.

He had also become obsessed with an almost religious devotion to the rights of property, to steady
government by "the rich, the wise and good,"[1] to
"respectable" society. These convictions Marshall
found most firmly retained and best defended in the
commercial centers of the East and North. The
stoutest champions of Marshall's beloved stability
of institutions and customs were the old Federalist leaders, particularly of New England and New
York. They had been his comrades and associates
in bygone days and continued to be his intimates.

In short, John Marshall had become the personifi-
cation of the reaction against popular government
that followed the French Revolution. With him and
men of his cast of mind, Great Britain had come to
represent all that was enduring and good, and France
all that was eruptive and evil. Such was his outlook on social and political life when, after these
traditional European foes were again at war, their
spoliations of American commerce, violations of
American rights, and insults to American honor
once more became flagrant; and such continued to
be his opinion and feeling after these aggressions
had become intolerable.

Since the adoption of the Constitution, nearly
all Americans, except the younger generation, had
become re-Europeanized in thought and feeling.
Their partisanship of France and Great Britain
relegated America to a subordinate place in their
minds and hearts. Just as the anti-Federalists and

[1] The phrase used by the Federalists to designate the opponents of
democracy.

their successors, the Republicans, had been more concerned in the triumph of revolutionary France over "monarchical" England than in the maintenance of American interests, rights, and honor, so now the Federalists were equally violent in their championship of Great Britain in her conflict with the France of Napoleon. Precisely as the French partisans of a few years earlier had asserted that the cause of France was that of America also,[1] the Federalists now insisted that the success of Great Britain meant the salvation of the United States.

"Great Britain is fighting our battles and the battles of mankind, and France is combating for the power to enslave and plunder us and all the world,"[2] wrote that faithful interpreter of extreme New England Federalism, Fisher Ames, just after the European conflict was renewed. Such opinions were not confined to the North and East. In South Carolina, John Rutledge was under the same spell. Writing to "the head Quarters of good Principles," Boston, he avowed that "I have long considered England as but the advanced guard of our Country. . . If they fall we do."[3] Scores of quotations from prominent Federalists expressive of the same views might be adduced.[4] Even the assault on

---

[1] See vol. II, 24–27, 92–96, 106–07, 126–28, of this work.

[2] Ames to Dwight, Oct. 31, 1803, *Works of Fisher Ames:* Ames, I, 330; and see Ames to Gore, Nov. 16, 1803, *ib.* 332; also Ames to Quincy, Feb. 12, 1806, *ib.* 360.

[3] Rutledge to Otis, July 29, 1806, Morison: *Life and Letters of Harrison Gray Otis,* I, 282.

[4] The student should examine the letters of Federalists collected in Henry Adams's *New-England Federalism;* those in the *Life and*

the Chesapeake did not change or even soften them.[1]
On the other hand, the advocates of France as
ardently upheld her cause, as fiercely assailed Great
Britain.[2]

Never did Americans more seriously need emancipation from foreign influence than in the early decades of the Republic — never was it more vital to
their well-being that the people should develop an
American spirit, than at the height of the Napo-
leonic Wars.

Upon the renewal of the European conflict, Great
Britain announced wholesale blockades of French
ports,[3] ordered the seizure of neutral ships wherever found carrying on trade with an enemy of
England;[4] and forbade them to enter the harbors
of immense stretches of European coasts.[5] In reply, Napoleon declared the British Islands to be
under blockade, and ordered the capture in any
waters whatsoever of all ships that had entered
British harbors.[6] Great Britain responded with the
Orders in Council of 1807 which, in effect, prohib-

Correspondence of Rufus King; in Lodge's *Life and Letters of George
Cabot;* in the *Works of Fisher Ames* and in Morison's *Otis.*

  [1] See Adams: *History of the United States,* IV, 29.

  [2] Once in a long while an impartial view was expressed: "I think
myself sometimes in an Hospital of Lunaticks, when I hear some of
our Politicians eulogizing Bonaparte because he humbles the English;
& others worshipping the latter, under an Idea that they will shelter
us, & take us under the Shadow of their Wings. They would join,
rather, to deal us away like Cattle." (Peters to Pickering, Feb. 4,
1807, Pickering MSS. Mass. Hist. Soc.)

  [3] See Harrowby's Circular, Aug. 9, 1804, *American State Papers,
Foreign Relations,* III, 266.

  [4] See Hawkesbury's Instructions, Aug. 17, 1805, *ib.*

  [5] Fox to Monroe, April 8 and May 16, 1806, *ib.* 267.

  [6] The Berlin Decree, Nov. 21, 1806, *ib.* 290–91.

ited the oceans to neutral vessels except such as traded directly with England or her colonies; and even this commerce was made subject to a special tax to be paid into the British treasury.[1] Napoleon's swift answer was the Milan Decree,[2] which, among other things, directed all ships submitting to the British Orders in Council to be seized and confiscated in the ports of France or her allies, or captured on the high seas.

All these "decrees," "orders," and "instructions" were, of course, in flagrant violation of international law, and were more injurious to America than to all other neutrals put together. Both belligerents bore down upon American commerce and seized American ships with equal lawlessness.[3] But, since Great Britain commanded the oceans,[4] the United States suffered far more severely from the depredations of that Power.[5] Under pressure of conflict, Great

[1] Orders in Council, Jan. 7 and Nov. 11, 1807, *Am. State Papers, For. Rel.* III, 267–73; and see Channing: *Jeffersonian System*, 199.

[2] Dec. 17, 1807, *Am. State Papers, For. Rel.* III, 290.

[3] Adams: *U.S.* v, 31.

[4] "England's naval power stood at a height never reached before or since by that of any other nation. On every sea her navies rode, not only triumphant, but with none to dispute their sway." (Roosevelt: *Naval War of 1812*, 22.)

[5] See Report, Secretary of State, July 6, 1812, *Am. State Papers, For. Rel.* III, 583–85.

"These decrees and orders, taken together, want little of amounting to a declaration that every neutral vessel found on the high seas, whatsoever be her cargo, and whatsoever foreign port be that of her departure or destination, shall be deemed lawful prize." (Jefferson to Congress, Special Message, March 17, 1808, *Works:* Ford, XI, 20.)

"The only mode by which either of them [the European belligerents] could further annoy the other .. was by inflicting .. the torments of starvation. This the contending parties sought to accomplish by putting an end to all trade with the other nation." (Channing: *Jeff. System*, 169.)

Britain increased her impressment[1] of American sailors. In effect, our ports were blockaded.[2]

Jefferson's lifelong prejudice against Great Britain [3] would permit him to see in all this nothing but a sordid and brutal imperialism. Not for a moment did he understand or consider the British point of view. England's "intentions have been to claim the ocean as her conquest, & prohibit any vessel from navigating it but on . . tribute," he wrote.[4] Nevertheless, he met Great Britain's orders and instructions with hesitant recommendations that the country be put in a state of defense; only feeble preliminary steps were taken to that end.

[1] Theodore Roosevelt, who gave this matter very careful study, says that at least 20,000 American seamen were impressed. (Roosevelt, footnote to 42.)

"Hundreds of American citizens had been taken by force from under the American flag, some of whom were already lying beneath the waters off Cape Trafalgar." (Adams: *U.S.* III, 202.)

See also Babcock: *Rise of American Nationality*, 76–77; and Jefferson to Crawford, Feb. 11, 1815, *Works:* Ford, XI, 451.

[2] See Channing: *Jeff. System*, 184–94. The principal works on the War of 1812 are, of course, by Henry Adams and by Alfred Mahan. But these are very extended. The excellent treatments of that period are the *Jeffersonian System*, by Edward Channing, and *Rise of American Nationality*, by Kendric Charles Babcock, and *Life and Letters of Harrison Gray Otis*, by Samuel Eliot Morison. The latter work contains many valuable letters hitherto unpublished.

[3] But see Jefferson to Madison, Aug. 27, 1805, *Works:* Ford, x, 172–73; same to Monroe, May 4, 1806, *ib.* 262–63; same to same, Oct. 26, 1806, *ib.* 296–97; same to Lincoln, June 25, 1806, *ib.* 272; also see Adams: *U.S.* III, 75. While these letters speak of a temporary alliance with Great Britain, Jefferson makes it clear that they are merely diplomatic maneuvers, and that, if an arrangement was made, a heavy price must be paid for America's coöperation.

Jefferson's letters, in general, display rancorous hostility to Great Britain. See, for example, Jefferson to Paine, Sept. 6, 1807, *Works:* Ford, x, 493; same to Leib, June 23, 1808, *ib.* XI, 34–35; same to Meigs, Sept. 18, 1813, *ib.* 334–35; same to Monroe, Jan. 1, 1815, *ib.* 443.

[4] Jefferson to Dearborn, July 16, 1810, *ib.* 144.

The President's principal reliance was on the device of taking from Great Britain her American markets. So came the Non-Importation Act of April, 1806, prohibiting the admission of those products that constituted the bulk of Great Britain's immensely profitable trade with the United States.[1] This economic measure was of no avail — it amounted to little more than an encouragement of successful smuggling.

When the Leopard attacked the Chesapeake,[2] Jefferson issued his proclamation reciting the "enormity" as he called it, and ordering all British armed vessels from American waters.[3] The spirit of America was at last aroused.[4] Demands for war rang throughout the land.[5] But they did not come from the lips of Federalists, who, with a few exceptions, protested loudly against any kind of retaliation.

John Lowell, unequaled in talent and learning among the brilliant group of Federalists in Boston, wrote a pamphlet in defense of British conduct.[6]

[1] *Annals*, 9th Cong. 1st Sess. 1259–62; also see "An Act to Prohibit the Importation of Certain Goods, Wares, and Merchandise," chap. 29, 1806, *Laws of the United States*, IV, 36–38.

[2] See vol. III, 475–76, of this work.

[3] Jefferson's Proclamation, July 2, 1807, *Works:* Ford, X, 434–47; and *Messages and Papers of the Presidents:* Richardson, I, 421–24.

[4] "This country has never been in such a state of excitement since the battle of Lexington." (Jefferson to Bowdoin, July 10, 1807, *Works:* Ford, X, 454; same to De Nemours, July 14, 1807, *ib.* 460.)

For Jefferson's interpretation of Great Britain's larger motive for perpetrating the Chesapeake crime, see Jefferson to Paine, Sept. 6, 1807, *ib.* 493.

[5] Adams: *U.S.* IV, 38.

[6] Lowell: *Peace Without Dishonor — War Without Hope:* by "A Yankee Farmer," 8. The author of this pamphlet was the son of one of the new Federal judges appointed by Adams under the Federalist Judiciary Act of 1801.

It was an uncommonly able performance, bright, informed, witty, well reasoned. "Despising the threats of prosecution for treason," he would, said Lowell, use his right of free speech to save the country from an unjustifiable war. What did the Chesapeake incident, what did impressment of Americans, what did anything and everything amount to, compared to the one tremendous fact of Great Britain's struggle with France? All thoughtful men knew that Great Britain alone stood between us and that slavery which would be our portion if France should prevail.[1]

Lowell's sparkling essay well set forth the intense conviction of nearly all leading Federalists. Giles was not without justification when he branded them as "the mere Anglican party."[2] The London press had approved the attack on the Chesapeake, applauded Admiral Berkeley, and even insisted upon war against the United States.[3] American Federalists were not far behind the *Times* and the *Morning Post*.

Jefferson, on the contrary, vividly stated the thought of the ordinary American: "The English being equally tyrannical at sea as he [Bonaparte] is on land, & that tyranny bearing on us in every point of either honor or interest, I say, 'down with Eng-

---

[1] See *Peace Without Dishonor — War Without Hope*, 39–40.

[2] Giles to Monroe, March 4, 1807; Anderson: *William Branch Giles — A Study in the Politics of Virginia, 1790–1830*, 108.

Thomas Ritchie, in the Richmond *Enquirer*, properly denounced the New England Federalist headquarters as a "hot-bed of treason." (*Enquirer*, Jan. 24 and April 4, 1809, as quoted by Ambler: *Thomas Ritchie — A Study in Virginia Politics*, 46.)

[3] Adams: *U.S.* iv, 41–44, 54.

land' and as for what Buonaparte is then to do to us, let us trust to the chapter of accidents, I cannot, with the Anglomen, prefer a certain present evil to a future hypothetical one." [1]

But the President did not propose to execute his policy of "down with England" by any such horrid method as bloodshed. He would stop Americans from trading with the world — that would prevent the capture of our ships and the impressment of our seamen.[2] Thus it was that the Embargo Act of December, 1807, and the supplementary acts of January, March, and April, 1808, were passed.[3] All exportation by sea or land was rigidly forbidden under heavy penalties. Even coasting vessels were not allowed to continue purely American trade unless heavy bond was given that landing would be made exclusively at American ports. Flour could be shipped by sea only in case the President thought it necessary to keep from hunger the population of any given port.[4]

[1] Jefferson to Leiper, Aug. 21, 1807, *Works:* Ford, x, 483–84.

Jefferson tenaciously clung to his prejudice against Great Britain: "The object of England, long obvious, is to claim the ocean as her domain. . . We believe no more in Bonaparte's fighting merely for the liberty of the seas, than in Great Britain's fighting for the liberties of mankind." (Jefferson to Maury, April 25, 1812, *ib.* xi, 240–41.) He never failed to accentuate his love for France and his hatred for Napoleon.

[2] "During the present paroxysm of the insanity of Europe, we have thought it wisest to break off all intercourse with her." (Jefferson to Armstrong, May 2, 1808, *ib.* 30.)

[3] "Three alternatives alone are to be chosen from. 1. Embargo. 2. War. 3. Submission and tribute, &, wonderful to tell, the last will not want advocates." (Jefferson to Lincoln, Nov. 13, 1808, *ib.* 74.)

[4] See Act of December 22, 1807 (*Annals,* 10th Cong. 1st Sess. 2814–15); of January 9, 1808 (*ib.* 2815–17); of March 12, 1808 (*ib.* 2839–42); and of April 25, 1808 (*ib.* 2870–74); Treasury Circulars of

Here was an exercise of National power such as
John Marshall had never dreamed of. The effect
was disastrous. American ocean-carrying trade was
ruined; British ships were given the monopoly of
the seas.[1] And England was not "downed," as Jefferson expected. In fact neither France nor Great
Britain relaxed its practices in the least.[2]

The commercial interests demanded the repeal of
the Embargo laws,[3] so ruinous to American shipping,
so destructive to American trade, so futile in re-
dressing the wrongs we had suffered. Massachusetts was enraged. A great proportion of the tonnage of the whole country was owned in that State
and the Embargo had paralyzed her chief industry.
Here was a fresh source of grievance against the
Administration and a just one. Jefferson had, at
last, given the Federalists a real issue. Had they

May 6 and May 11, 1808 (*Embargo Laws*, 19–20, 21–22); and Jefferson's letter "to the Governours of Orleans, Georgia, South Carolina,
Massachusetts and New Hampshire," May 6, 1808 (*ib.* 20–21).

Joseph Hopkinson sarcastically wrote: "Bless the Embargo —
thrice bless the Presidents distribution Proclamation, by which his
minions are to judge of the appetites of his subjects, how much food
they may reasonably consume, and who shall supply them .. whether
under the Proclamation and Embargo System, a child may be lawfully born without a clearing out at the Custom House." (Hopkinson to Pickering, May 25, 1808, Pickering MSS. Mass. Hist.
Soc.)

[1] Professor Channing says that "the orders in council had been
passed originally to give English ship-owners a chance to regain some
of their lost business." (Channing: *Jeff. System*, 261.)

[2] Indeed, Napoleon, as soon as he learned of the American Embargo laws, ordered the seizure of all American ships entering French
ports because their captains or owners had disobeyed these American statutes and, therefore, surely were aiding the enemy. (Armstrong to Secretary of State, April 23, postscript of April 25, 1808,
Am. State Papers, For. Rel. III, 291.)

[3] Morison: *Otis*, II, 10–12; see also Channing: *Jeff. System*, 183.

availed themselves of it on economic and purely American grounds, they might have begun the rehabilitation of their weakened party throughout the country. But theirs were the vices of pride and of age — they could neither learn nor forget; could not estimate situations as they really were, but only as prejudice made them appear to be.

As soon as Congress convened in November, 1808, New England opened the attack on Jefferson's retaliatory measures. Senator James Hillhouse of Connecticut offered a resolution for the repeal of the obnoxious statutes. "Great Britain was not to be threatened into compliance by a rod of coercion," he said.[1] Pickering made a speech which might well have been delivered in Parliament.[2] British maritime practices were right, the Embargo wrong, and principally injurious to America.[3] The Orders in Council had been issued only after Great Britain "had witnessed . . these atrocities" committed by Napoleon and his plundering armies, " and seen the

[1] *Annals*, 10th Cong. 2d Sess. 22.

The intensity of the interest in the Embargo is illustrated by Giles's statement in his reply to Hillhouse that it "almost . . banish[ed] every other topic of conversation." (*Ib.* 94.)

[2] Four years earlier, Pickering had plotted the secession of New England and enlisted the support of the British Minister to accomplish it. (See vol. III, chap. VII, of this work.) His wife was an Englishwoman, the daughter of an officer of the British Navy. (Pickering and Upham: *Life of Timothy Pickering*, I, 7; and see Pickering to his wife, Jan. 1, 1808, *ib.* IV, 121.) His nephew had been Consul-General at London under the Federalist Administrations and was at this time a merchant in that city. (Pickering to Rose, March 22, 1808, *New-England Federalism:* Adams, 370.) Pickering had been, and still was, carrying on with George Rose, recently British Minister to the United States, a correspondence all but treasonable. (Morison: *Otis*, II, 6.)

[3] *Annals*, 10th Cong. 2d Sess. 175, 177–78.

deadly weapon aimed at her vitals." Yet Jefferson
had acted very much as if the United States were a
vassal of France.[1]

Again Pickering addressed the Senate, flatly charging that all Embargo measures were "in exact conformity with the views and wishes of the French
Emperor, . . the most ruthless tyrant that has
scourged the European world, since the Roman Empire fell!" Suppose the British Navy were destrcyed
and France triumphant over Great Britain — to the
other titles of Bonaparte would then "be added
that of Emperor of the Two Americas"; for what
legions of soldiers "could he not send to the United
States in the thousands of British ships, were they
also at his command?"[2]

As soon as they were printed, Pickering sent
copies of these and speeches of other Federalists to
his close associate, the Chief Justice of the United
States. Marshall's prompt answer shows how far he
had gone in company with New England Federalist
opinion.

"I thank you very sincerely," he wrote "for the
excellent speeches lately delivered in the senate. . .
If sound argument & correct reasoning could save
our country it would be saved. Nothing can be
more completely demonstrated than the inefficacy
of the embargo, yet that demonstration seems to
be of no avail. I fear most seriously that the same
spirit which so tenaciously maintains this measure
will impel us to a war with the only power which
protects any part of the civilized world from the

[1] *Annals*, 10th Cong. 2d Sess. 193.   [2] *Ib.* 279–82.

despotism of that tyrant with whom we shall then be ravaged." [1]

Such was the change that nine years had wrought in the views of John Marshall. When Secretary of State he had arraigned Great Britain for her conduct toward neutrals, denounced the impressment of American sailors, and branded her admiralty courts as habitually unjust if not corrupt.[2] But his hatred of France had metamorphosed the man.

Before Marshall had written this letter, the Legislature of Massachusetts formally declared that the continuance of the Embargo would "endanger . . the union of these States."[3] Talk of secession was steadily growing in New England.[4] The National Government feared open rebellion.[5] Only one eminent Federalist dissented from these views of the party leaders which Marshall also held as fervently as they. That man was the one to whom he owed his place on the Supreme Bench. From his retirement in Quincy, John Adams watched the growing excitement with amused contempt.

"Our Gazettes and Pamphlets," he wrote, "tell us that Bonaparte . . will conquer England, and command all the British Navy, and send I know not how many hundred thousand soldiers here and con-

---

[1] Marshall to Pickering, Dec. 19, 1808, Pickering MSS. Mass. Hist. Soc.

[2] See vol. II, 509–14, of this work.   [3] Morison: *Otis*, II, 3–4.

[4] "The tories of Boston openly threaten insurrection." (Jefferson to Dearborn, Aug. 9, 1808, *Works:* Ford, XI, 40.) And see Morison: *Otis*, II, 6; *Life and Correspondence of Rufus King:* King, V, 88; also see Otis to Quincy, Dec. 15, 1808, Morison: *Otis*, II, 115.

[5] Monroe to Taylor, Jan. 9, 1809, *Branch Historical Papers*, June, 1908, 298.

quer from New Orleans to Passamaquoddy. Though
every one of these Bugbears is an empty Phantom,
yet the People seem to believe every article of this
bombastical Creed and tremble and shudder in Consequence. Who shall touch these blind eyes?"[1]

On January 9, 1809, Jefferson signed the "Force
Act," which the Republican Congress had defiantly
passed, and again Marshall beheld such an assertion of National power as the boldest Federalist of
Alien and Sedition times never had suggested. Col-
lectors of customs were authorized to seize any
vessel or wagon if they suspected the owner of an
intention to evade the Embargo laws; ships could be
laden only in the presence of National officials, and
sailing delayed or prohibited arbitrarily. Rich rewards were provided for informers who should put
the Government on the track of any violation of the
multitude of restrictions of these statutes or of the
Treasury regulations interpretative of them. The
militia, the army, the navy were to be employed to
enforce obedience.[2]

Along the New England coasts popular wrath swept
like a forest fire. Violent resolutions were passed.[3]
The Collector of Boston, Benjamin Lincoln, refused
to obey the law and resigned.[4] The Legislature of

[1] Adams to Rush, July 25, 1808, *Old Family Letters*, 191–92.

[2] *Annals*, 10th Cong. 2d Sess. III, 1798–1804.

[3] Morison: *Otis*, II, 10. These resolutions denounced "'all those
who shall assist in enforcing on others the arbitrary & unconstitutional provisions of this [Force Act]' . . as 'enemies to the Constitution of the United States and of this State, and hostile to the Liberties of the People.'" (Boston Town Records, 1796–1813, as quoted
in *ib.*; and see McMaster: *History of the People of the United States*,
III, 328.)

[4] McMaster, III, 329.

Massachusetts passed a bill denouncing the "Force Act" as unconstitutional, and declaring any officer entering a house in execution of it to be guilty of a high misdemeanor, punishable by fine and imprisonment.[1] The Governor of Connecticut declined the request of the Secretary of War to afford military aid and addressed the Legislature in a speech bristling with sedition.[2] The Embargo must go, said the Federalists, or New England would appeal to arms. Riots broke out in many towns. Withdrawal from the Union was openly advocated.[3] Nor was this sentiment confined to that section. "If the question were barely *stirred* in New England, some States would drop off the Union like fruit, *rotten ripe*," wrote A. C. Hanson of Baltimore.[4] Humphrey Marshall of Kentucky declared that he looked to "BOSTON . . the Cradle, and SALEM, the nourse, of American Liberty," as "the source of reformation, or should that be unattainable, of disunion."[5]

Warmly as he sympathized with Federalist opinion of the absurd Republican retaliatory measures, and earnestly as he shared Federalist partisanship for Great Britain, John Marshall deplored all talk of

[1] McMaster, III, 329–30; and see Morison: *Otis*, II, 4.

The Federalist view was that the "Force Act" and other extreme portions of the Embargo laws were "so violently and palpably unconstitutional, as to render a reference to the judiciary absurd"; and that it was "the inherent right of the people to resist measures fundamentally inconsistent with the principles of just liberty and the Social compact." (Hare to Otis, Feb. 10, 1814, Morison: *Otis*, II, 175.)

[2] McMaster, III, 331–32.   [3] Morison: *Otis*, II, 3, 8.

[4] Hanson to Pickering, Jan. 17, 1810, *N.E. Federalism*: Adams, 382.

[5] Humphrey Marshall to Pickering, March 17, 1809, Pickering MSS. Mass. Hist. Soc.

secession and sternly rebuked resistance to National authority, as is shown in his opinion in Fletcher *vs.* Peck,[1] wherein he asserted the sovereignty of the Nation over a State.

Another occasion, however, gave Marshall a better opportunity to state his views more directly, and to charge them with the whole force of the concurrence of all his associates on the Supreme Bench. This occasion was the resistance of the Legislature and Governor of Pennsylvania to a decree of Richard Peters, Judge of the United States Court for that district, rendered in the notable and dramatic case of Gideon Olmstead. During the Revolution, Olmstead and three other American sailors captured the British sloop Active and sailed for Egg Harbor, New Jersey. Upon nearing their destination, they were overhauled by an armed vessel belonging to the State of Pennsylvania and by an American privateer. The Active was taken to Philadelphia and claimed as a prize of war. The court awarded Olmstead and his comrades only one fourth of the proceeds of the sale of the vessel, the other three fourths going to the State of Pennsylvania, to the officers and crew of the State ship, and to those of the privateer. The Continental Prize Court reversed the decision and ordered the whole amount received for sloop and cargo to be paid to Olmstead and his associates.

This the State court refused to do, and a litigation began which lasted for thirty years. The funds were invested in United States loan certificates, and these were delivered by the State Judge to the State Treas-

[1] See vol. III, chap. X, of this work.

urer, David Rittenhouse, upon a bond saving the
Judge harmless in case he, thereafter, should be compelled to pay the amount in controversy to Olmstead.
Rittenhouse kept the securities in his personal possession, and after his death they were found among
his effects with a note in his handwriting that they
would become the property of Pennsylvania when
the State released him from his bond to the Judge.

In 1803, Olmstead secured from Judge Peters an
order to the daughters of Rittenhouse who, as his executrixes, had possession of the securities, to deliver
them to Olmstead and his associates. This proceeding of the National court was promptly met by an
act of the State Legislature which declared that
the National court had "usurped" jurisdiction, and
directed the Governor to "protect the just rights of
the state . . from any process whatever issued out
of any federal court." [1]

Peters, a good lawyer and an upright judge, but a
timorous man, was cowed by this sharp defiance and
did nothing. The executrixes held on to the securities. At last, on March 5, 1808, Olmstead applied to
the Supreme Court of the United States for a rule
directed to Judge Peters to show cause why a mandamus should not issue compelling him to execute
his decree. Peters made return that the act of the
State Legislature had caused him "from prudential
. . motives . . to avoid embroiling the government
of the United States and that of Pennsylvania." [2]

Thus the matter came before Marshall. On February 20, 1809, just when threats of resistance to the

[1] 5 Cranch, 133.   [2] *Ib.* 117.

"Force Act" were sounding loudest, when riots
were in progress along the New England seaboard,
and a storm of debate over the Embargo and Non-
Intercourse laws was raging in Congress, the Chief
Justice delivered his opinion in the case of the
United States *vs.* Peters.[1] The court had, began
Marshall, considered the return of Judge Peters
"with great attention, and with serious concern."
The act of the Pennsylvania Legislature challenged
the very life of the National Government, for, "if the
legislatures of the several states may, at will, annul
the judgments of the courts of the United States,
and destroy the rights acquired under those judgments, the constitution itself becomes a solemn
mockery, and the nation is deprived of the means
of enforcing its laws by the instrumentality of its
own tribunals."

These clear, strong words were addressed to Massachusetts and Connecticut no less than to Pennsylvania. They were meant for Marshall's Federalist
comrades and friends — for Pickering, and Gore,
and Morris, and Otis — as much as for the State
officials in Lancaster. His opinion was not confined
to the case before him; it was meant for the whole
country and especially for those localities where
National laws were being denounced and violated,
and National authority defied and flouted. Considering the depth and fervor of Marshall's feelings on the whole policy of the Republican régime,
his opinion in United States *vs.* Judge Peters was
signally brave and noble.

[1] 5 Cranch, 135.

Forcible resistance by a State to National authority! "So fatal a result must be deprecated by all; and the people of Pennsylvania, *not less than the citizens of every other state*, must feel a deep interest in resisting principles so destructive of the Union, and in averting consequences so fatal to themselves." Marshall then states the facts of the controversy and concludes that "the state of Pennsylvania can possess no constitutional right" to resist the authority of the National courts. His decision, he says, "is not made without extreme regret at the necessity which has induced the application." But, because "it is a solemn duty" to do so, the "mandamus must be awarded."[1]

Marshall's opinion deeply angered the Legislature and officials of Pennsylvania.[2] When Judge Peters, in obedience to the order of the Supreme Court, directed the United States Marshal to enforce the decree in Olmstead's favor, that official found the militia under command of General Bright drawn up around the house of the two executrixes. The dispute was at last composed, largely because President Madison rebuked Pennsylvania and upheld the National courts.[3]

[1] 5 Cranch, 136, 141. (Italics the author's.)

[2] The Legislature of Pennsylvania adopted a resolution, April 3, 1809, proposing an amendment to the National Constitution for the establishment of an "impartial tribunal" to decide upon controversies between States and the Nation. (*State Documents on Federal Relations:* Ames, 46–48.) In reply Virginia insisted that the Supreme Court, "selected from those . . who are most celebrated for virtue and legal learning," was the proper tribunal to decide such cases. (*Ib.* 49–50.) This Nationalist position Virginia reversed within a decade in protest against Marshall's Nationalist opinions. Virginia's Nationalist resolution of 1809 was read by Pinkney in his argument of Cohens *vs.* Virginia. (See *infra*, chap. VI.)

[3] See Madison to Snyder, April 13, 1809, *Annals*, 11th Cong. 2d Sess. 2269; also McMaster, v, 403–06.

A week after the delivery of Marshall's opinion,
the most oppressive provisions of the Embargo Acts
were repealed and a curious non-intercourse law
enacted.[1] One section directed the suspension of
all commercial restrictions against France or Great
Britain in case either belligerent revoked its orders
or decrees against the United States; and this the
President was to announce by proclamation. The
new British Minister, David M. Erskine, now ten-
dered apology and reparation for the attack on the
Chesapeake and positively assured the Administration that, if the United States would renew intercourse with Great Britain, the British Orders in
Council would be withdrawn on June 10, 1809. Immediately President Madison issued his proclamation stating this fact and announcing that after that
happy June day, Americans might renew their long
and ruinously suspended trade with all the world not
subject to French control.[2]

The Federalists were jubilant.[3] But their joy was
quickly turned to wrath — against the Administration. Great Britain repudiated the agreement of her
Minister, recalled him, and sent another charged
with rigid and impossible instructions.[4] In deep
humiliation, Madison issued a second proclamation
reciting the facts and restoring to full operation
against Great Britain all the restrictive commercial and maritime laws remaining on the statute

[1] *Annals*, 10th Cong. 2d Sess. 1824–30.
[2] Erskine to Smith, April 18 and 19, 1809, *Am. State Papers, For.
Rel.* iii, 296.
[3] Adams: *U.S.* v, 73–74; see also McMaster, iii, 337.
[4] Adams: *U.S.* v, 87–89, 112.

books.[1] At a banquet in Richmond, Jefferson proposed a toast: "The freedom of the seas!"[2]

Upon the arrival of Francis James Jackson, Erskine's successor as British Minister, the scenes of the Genêt drama[3] were repeated. Jackson was arrogant and overbearing, and his instructions were as harsh as his disposition.[4] Soon the Administration was forced to refuse further conference with him. Jackson then issued an appeal to the American people in the form of a circular to British Consuls in America, accusing the American Government of trickery, concealment of facts, and all but downright falsehood.[5] A letter of Canning to the American Minister at London[6] found its way into the Federalist newspapers, "doubtless by the connivance of the British Minister," says Joseph Story. This letter was, Story thought, an "infamous" appeal to the American people to repudiate their own Government, "the old game of Genêt played over again."[7]

[1] Proclamation of Aug. 9, 1809, *Am. State Papers, For. Rel.* III, 304.

[2] Tyler: *Letters and Times of the Tylers*, I, 229. For an expression by Napoleon on this subject, see Adams: *U.S.* v, 137.

[3] See vol. II, 28–29, of this work.

[4] "The appointment of Jackson and the instructions given to him might well have justified a declaration of war against Great Britain the moment they were known." (Channing: *Jeff. System*, 237.)

[5] Circular, Nov. 13, 1809, *Am. State Papers, For. Rel.* III, 323; *Annals*, 11th Cong. 2d Sess. 743.

[6] Canning to Pinkney, Sept. 23, 1808, *Am. State Papers, For. Rel.* III, 230–31.

[7] Story to White, Jan. 17, 1809, *Life and Letters of Joseph Story:* Story, I, 193–94. There were two letters from Canning to Pinkney, both dated Sept. 23, 1808. Story probably refers to one printed in the *Columbian Centinel*, Boston, Jan. 11, 1809.

"It seems as if in New England the federalists were forgetful of all the motives for union & were ready to destroy the fabric which has been raised by the wisdom of our fathers. Have they altogether lost the

Furious altercations arose all over the country.
The Federalists defended Jackson. When the elections came on, the Republicans made tremendous
gains in New England as well as in other States,[1]
a circumstance that depressed Marshall profoundly.
In December an acrimonious debate arose in Congress over a resolution denouncing Jackson's circular
letter as a "direct and aggravated insult and affront
to the American people and their Government."[2]
Every Federalist opposed the resolution. Josiah
Quincy of Massachusetts declared that every word
of it was a "falsehood," and that the adoption of
it would call forth "severe retribution, perhaps in
war" from Great Britain.[3]

Disheartened, disgusted, wrathful, Marshall wrote
Quincy: "The Federalists of the South participate
with their brethren of the North in the gloomy an-
ticipations which your late elections must inspire.
The proceedings of the House of Representatives already demonstrate the influence of those elections on
the affairs of the Union. I had supposed that the late
letter to Mr. Armstrong,[4] and the late seizure [by

memory of Washington's farewell address? . . The riotous proceedings in some towns . . no doubt . . are occasioned by the instigation
of men, who keep behind the curtain & yet govern the wires of the
puppet shew." (Story to his brother, Jan. 3, 1809, Story MSS. Mass.
Hist. Soc.)

"In New England, and even in New York, there appears a spirit
hostile to the existence of our own government." (Plumer to Gilman,
Jan. 24, 1809, Plumer: *Life of William Plumer*, 368.)

[1] Adams: *U.S.* v, 158.

[2] *Annals*, 11th Cong. 2d Sess. 481.

[3] *Ib.* 943. The resolution was passed over the strenuous resistance
of the Federalists.

[4] Probably that of Madison, July 21, 1808, *Annals*, 10th Cong.
2d Sess. 1681.

the French] of an American vessel, simply because she was an American, added to previous burnings, ransoms, and confiscations, would have exhausted to the dregs our cup of servility and degradation; but these measures appear to make no impression on those to whom the United States confide their destinies. To what point are we verging?"[1]

Nor did the Chief Justice keep quiet in Richmond. "We have lost our resentment for the severest injuries a nation ever suffered, because of their being so often repeated. Nay, Judge Marshall and Mr. Pickering & Co. found out Great Britain had given us no cause of complaint,"[2] writes John Tyler. And ever nearer drew the inevitable conflict.

Jackson was unabashed by the condemnation of Congress, and not without reason. Wherever he went, more invitations to dine than he could accept poured in upon him from the "best families"; banquets were given in his honor; the Senate of Massachusetts adopted resolutions condemning the Administration and upholding Jackson, who declared that the State had "done more towards justifying me to the world than it was possible . . that I or any other person could do."[3] The talk of secession grew.[4] At

[1] Marshall to Quincy, April 23, 1810, Quincy: *Life of Josiah Quincy*, 204.

[2] Tyler to Jefferson, May 12, 1810, Tyler: *Tyler*, I, 247; and see next chapter.

[3] Adams: *U.S.* v, 212–14; and see Morison: *Otis*, II, 18–19.

[4] Turreau, then the French Minister at Washington, thus reported to his Government: "To-day not only is the separation of New England openly talked about, but the people of those five States wish for this separation, pronounce it, openly prepare it, will carry it out under British protection"; and he suggests that "perhaps the moment has come for forming a party in favor of France in the Central and

a public banquet given Jackson, Pickering proposed the toast: "The world's last hope — Britain's fast-anchored isle!" It was greeted with a storm of cheers. Pickering's words sped over the country and became the political war cry of Federalism.[1] Marshall, who in Richmond was following "with anxiety" all political news, undoubtedly read it, and his letters show that Pickering's words stated the opinion of the Chief Justice.[2]

Upon the assurance of the French Foreign Minister that the Berlin and Milan Decrees would be revoked after November 1, 1810, President Madison, on November 2, announced what he believed to be Napoleon's settled determination, and recommended the resumption of commercial relations with France and the suspension of all intercourse with Great Britain unless that Power also withdrew its injurious and offensive Orders in Council.[3]

When at Washington, Marshall was frequently in

Southern States, whenever those of the North, having given themselves a separate government under the support of Great Britain, may threaten the independence of the rest." (Turreau to Champagny, April 20, 1809, as quoted in Adams: *U.S.* v, 36.)

[1] For account of Jackson's reception in Boston and the effects of it, see Adams: *U.S.* 215–17, and Morison: *Otis*, 20–22.

[2] On the other hand, Jefferson, out of his bottomless prejudice against Great Britain, drew venomous abuse of the whole British nation: "What is to restore order and safety on the ocean?" he wrote; "the death of George III? Not at all. He is only stupid; . . his ministers . . ephemeral. But his nation is permanent, and it is that which is the tyrant of the ocean. The principle that force is right, is become the principle of the nation itself. They would not permit an honest minister, were accident to bring such an one into power, to relax their system of lawless piracy." (Jefferson to Rodney, Feb. 10, 1810, *Works:* Ford, XI, 135–36.)

[3] Champagny, Duke de Cadore, to Armstrong, Aug. 5, 1810 (*Am. State Papers, For. Rel.* III, 386–87), and Proclamation, Nov. 2, 1810 (*ib.* 392); and see Adams: *U.S.* v, 303–04.

Pickering's company. Before the Chief Justice left for Richmond, the Massachusetts Senator had lent him pamphlets containing part of John Adams's "Cunningham Correspondence." In returning them, Marshall wrote that he had read Adams's letters "with regret." But the European war, rather than the "Cunningham Correspondence," was on the mind of the Chief Justice: "We are looking with anxiety towards the metropolis for political intelligence. Report gives much importance to the communications of Serrurier [the new French Minister],[1] & proclaims him to be charged with requisitions on our government, a submission to which would seem to be impossible. . . I will flatter myself that I have not seen you for the last time. Events have so fully demonstrated the correctness of your opinions on subjects the most interesting to our country that I cannot permit myself to believe the succeeding legislature of Massachusetts will deprive the nation of your future services." [2]

As the Federalist faith in Great Britain grew stronger, Federalist distrust of the youthful and growing American people increased. Early in 1811, the bill to admit Louisiana was considered. The Federalists violently resisted it. Josiah Quincy declared that "if this bill passes, the bonds of this Union are virtually dissolved; that the States which compose it are free from their moral obligations, and that, as it will be the right of all, so it will be the duty of some, to prepare definitely for a separation

[1] Adams: *U.S.* v, 346.
[2] Marshall to Pickering, Feb. 22, 1811, Pickering MSS. Mass. Hist. Soc.

— amicably if they can, violently if they must."[1]
Quincy was the embodiment of the soul of Localism: "The first public love of my heart is the Commonwealth of Massachusetts. There is my fireside;
there are the tombs of my ancestors."[2]

The spirit of American Nationalism no longer
dwelt in the breasts of even the youngest of the
Federalist leaders. Its abode now was the hearts of
the people of the West and South; and its strongest
exponent was a young Kentuckian, Henry Clay,
whose feelings and words were those of the heroic
seventies. Although but thirty-three years old, he
had been appointed for the second time to fill an
unexpired term in the National Senate. On February 22, 1810, he addressed that body on the country's wrongs and duty: "Have we not been for years
contending against the tyranny of the ocean?" We
have tried "*peaceful* resistance. . . When this is abandoned without effect, I am for resistance by the
sword."[3] Two years later, in the House, to which he
was elected immediately after his term in the Senate
expired, and of which he was promptly chosen
Speaker, Clay again made an appeal to American
patriotism: "The real cause of British aggression was
not to distress an enemy, but to destroy a rival!"[4]

---

[1] *Annals*, 11th Cong. 3d Sess. 525.

Daniel Webster was also emphatically opposed to the admission
of new States: "Put in a solemn, decided, and spirited Protest
against making new States out of new Territories. Affirm, in direct
terms, that New Hampshire has never agreed to favor political con-
nexions of such intimate nature, with any people, out of the limits
of the U.S. as they existed at the time of the compact." (Webster to
his brother, June 4, 1813, *Letters of Daniel Webster:* Van Tyne, 37.)

[2] *Annals*, 11th Cong. 3d Sess. 542.   [3] *Ib.* 1st and 2d Sess. 579–82.

[4] *Annals*, 12th Cong. 1st Sess. 601; also see Adams: *U.S.* v, 189–90.

he passionately exclaimed. Another Patrick Henry had arisen to lead America to a new independence.

Four other young Representatives from the West and South, John C. Calhoun, William Lowndes, Langdon Cheves, and Felix Grundy were as hot for war as was Henry Clay.[1]

Clay's speeches, extravagant, imprudent, and grandiose, had at least one merit: they were thoroughly American and expressed the opinion of the first generation of Americans that had grown up since the colonies won their freedom. Henry Clay spoke their language. But it was not the language of the John Marshall of 1812.

Eventually the Administration was forced to act. On June 1, 1812, President Madison sent to Congress his Message which briefly, and with moderation, stated the situation.[2] On June 4, the House passed a bill declaring war on Great Britain. Every Federalist but three voted against it.[3] The Senate

[1] Adams: *U.S.* v, 316.

[2] Richardson, I, 499–505; *Am. State Papers, For. Rel.* III, 567–70.

[3] *Annals*, 12th Cong. 1st Sess. 1637. The Federalists who voted for war were: Joseph Kent of Maryland, James Morgan of New Jersey, and William M. Richardson of Massachusetts.

Professor Channing thus states the American grievances: "Inciting the Indians to rebellion, impressing American seamen and making them serve on British war-ships, closing the ports of Europe to American commerce, these were the counts in the indictment against the people and government of Great Britain." (Channing: *Jeff. System,* 260.) See also *ib.* 268, and Jefferson's brilliant statement of the causes of the war, Jefferson to Logan, Oct. 3, 1813, *Works:* Ford, XI, 338–39.

"The United States," says Henry Adams, "had a superfluity of only too good causes for war with Great Britain." (Adams: *Life of Albert Gallatin,* 445.) Adams emphasizes this: "The United States had the right to make war on England with or without notice, either for her past spoliations, her actual blockades, her Orders in Council other than blockades, her Rule of 1756, her impressments, or her

made unimportant amendments which the House accepted;[1] and thus, on June 18, war was formally declared.

At the Fourth of July banquet of the Boston Federalists, among the toasts, by drinking to which the company exhilarated themselves, was this sentiment: "*The Existing War* — The Child of Prostitution, may no American acknowledge it legitimate."[2] Joseph Story was profoundly alarmed: "I am thoroughly convinced," he wrote, "that the leading Federalists meditate a severance of the Union."[3] His apprehension was justified: "Let the Union be severed. Such a severance presents no terrors to me," wrote the leading Federalist of New England.[4]

While opposition to the war thus began to blaze into open and defiant treason in that section,[5] the

attack on the 'Chesapeake,' not yet redressed, — possibly also for other reasons less notorious." (Adams: *U.S.* v, 339.) And see Roosevelt, chaps. I and II.

[1] *Annals*, 12th Cong. 1st Sess. 1675–82.

[2] Salem *Gazette*, July 7, 1812, as quoted in Morison: *Otis*, I, 298.

[3] Story to Williams, Aug. 24, 1812, Story, I, 229.

[4] Pickering to Pennington, July 12, 1812, *N.E. Federalism:* Adams, 389.

[5] Of course the National courts were attacked: "Attempts .. are made .. to break down the Judiciary of the United States through the newspapers, and mean and miserable insinuations are made to weaken the authority of its judgments." (Story to Williams, Aug. 3, 1813, Story, I, 247.) And again: "Conspirators, and traitors are enabled to carry on their purposes almost without check." (Same to same, May 27, 1813, *ib.* 244.) Story was lamenting that the National courts had no common-law jurisdiction. Some months earlier he had implored Nathaniel Williams, Representative in Congress from Story's district, to "induce Congress to give the Judicial Courts of the United States power to punish all crimes .. against the Government. . . Do not suffer conspiracies to destroy the Union." (Same to same, Oct. 8, 1812, *ib.* 243.)

Jefferson thought the people were loyal: "When the questions of separation and rebellion shall be nakedly proposed .. the Gores and

old-time Southern Federalists, who detested it no less, sought a more practical, though more timid, way to resist and end it. "Success in this War, would most probably be the worst kind of ruin," wrote Benjamin Stoddert to the sympathetic James McHenry. "There is but one way to save our Country .. change the administration — .. this can be affected by bringing forward another Virgn. as the competitor of Madison." For none but a Virginian can get the Presidential electors of that State, said Stoddert.

" There is, then, but one man to be thought of as the candidate of the Federalists and of all who were against the war. That man is John Marshall." Stoddert informs McHenry that he has written an article for a Maryland Federalist paper, the *Spirit of Seventy-Six*, recommending Marshall for President. "This I have done, because .. every body else .. seems to be seized with apathy .. and because I felt it sacred duty." [1]

Stoddert's newspaper appeal for Marshall's nomination was clear, persuasive, and well reasoned. It opened with the familiar Federalist arguments against the war. It was an "*offensive* war," which meant the ruin of America. "Thus thinking .. I feel it a solemn duty to my countrymen, to name JOHN MARSHALL, as a man as highly gifted as any other in the United States, for the important office of Chief Magistrate; and more likely than any other to com-

the Pickerings will find their levees crowded with silk stocking gentry, but no yeomanry." (Jefferson to Gerry, June 11, 1812, *Works :* Ford, XI, 257.)

[1] Stoddert to McHenry, July 15, 1812, Steiner: *Life and Correspondence of James McHenry*, 581–83.

mand the confidence, and unite the votes of that description of men, of all parties, who desire nothing from government, but that it should be wisely and faithfully administered. . .

"The sterling integrity of this gentleman's character and his high elevation of mind, forbid the suspicion, that he could descend to be a mere party President, or less than the President of the whole people: — but one objection can be urged against him by candid and honorable men: He is a Virginian, and Virginia has already furnished more than her full share of Presidents — This objection in less critical times would be entitled to great weight; but situated as the world is, and as we are, the only consideration now should be, who amongst our ablest statesmen, can best unite the suffrages of the citizens of all parties, in a competition with Mr. Madison, whose continuance in power is incompatible with the safety of the nation? . .

"It may happen," continues Stoddert, "that this our beloved country may be ruined for want of the services of the great and good man I have been prompted by sacred duty to introduce, from the mere want of energy among those of his immediate countrymen [Virginians], who think of his virtues and talents as I do; and as I do of the crisis which demands their employment.

" If in his native state men of this description will act in concert, & with a vigor called for by the occasion, and will let the people fairly know, that the contest is between John Marshall, peace, and a new order of things; and James Madison, Albert Gallatin and war, with war taxes, war loans, and all the other dreadful evils of a war in the present state of the world, my life for it they will succeed, and by a considerable majority of the independent votes of Virginia."

Stoddert becomes so enthusiastic that he thinks victory possible without the assistance of Marshall's own State: "Even if they fail in Virginia, the very effort will produce an animation in North Carolina, the middle and Eastern states, that will most probably secure the election of John Marshall. At the worst nothing can be lost but a little labour in a good cause, and everything may be saved, or gained for our country." Stoddert signs his plea "A Maryland Farmer." [1]

In his letter to McHenry he says: "They vote for electors in Virga. by a general ticket, and I am thoroughly persuaded that if the men in that State, who prefer Marshall to Madison, can be animated into Exertion, he will get the votes of that State. What little I can do by private letters to affect this will be done." Stoddert had enlisted one John Davis, an Englishman — writer, traveler, and generally a rolling stone — in the scheme to nominate Marshall. Davis, it seems, went to Virginia on this mission. After investigating conditions in that State, he had informed Stoddert "that if the Virgns. have nerve to believe it will be agreeable to the Northern & E. States, he is sure Marshall will get the Virga. votes." [2]

[1] "To the Citizens of the United States," in the *Spirit of Seventy-Six*, July 17, 1812.

[2] Stoddert refers to this person as "Jo Davies." By some this has been thought to refer to Marshall's brother-in-law, "Jo" Daveiss of

Stoddert dwells with the affection and anxiety of parentage upon his idea of Marshall for President: "It is not because I prefer Marshall to several other men, that I speak of him — but because I am well convinced it is vain to talk of any other man, and Marshall is a Man in whom Fedts. may confide — Perhaps indeed he is the man for the crisis, which demands great good sense, a great firmness under the garb of great moderation." He then urges McHenry to get to work for Marshall — "support a cause [election of a peace President] on which all that is dear to you depends." [1] Stoddert also wrote two letters to William Coleman of New York, editor of the *New York Evening Post*, urging Marshall for the Presidency.[2]

Twelve days after Stoddert thus instructed McHenry, Marshall wrote strangely to Robert Smith of Maryland. President Madison had dismissed Smith from the office of Secretary of State for inefficiency in the conduct of our foreign affairs and for intriguing with his brother, Senator Samuel Smith, and others against the Administration's foreign

Kentucky. But the latter was killed in the Battle of Tippecanoe, November 7, 1811.

While the identity of Stoddert's agent cannot be established with certainty, he probably was one John Davis of Salisbury, England, as described in the text. "Jo" was then used for John as much as for Joseph; and Davis was frequently spelled "Davies." A John or "Jo" Davis or Davies, an Englishman, was a very busy person in America during the first decade of the nineteenth century. (See Loshe: *Early American Novel*, 74–77.) Naturally he would have been against the War of 1812, and he was just the sort of person that an impracticable man like Stoddert would have chosen for such a mission.

[1] Stoddert to McHenry, July 15, 1812, Steiner, 582.
[2] See King, v, 266.

policy.[1] Upon his ejection from the Cabinet, Smith proceeded to "vindicate" himself by publishing a dull and pompous "Address" in which he asserted that we must have a President "of energetic mind, of enlarged and liberal views, of temperate and dignified deportment, of honourable and manly feelings, and as efficient in maintaining, as sagacious in discerning the rights of our much-injured and insulted country."[2] This was a good summary of Marshall's qualifications.

When Stoddert proposed Marshall for the Presidency, Smith wrote the Chief Justice, enclosing a copy of his attack on the Administration. On July 27, 1812, more than five weeks after the United States had declared war, Marshall replied: "Although I have for several years forborn to intermingle with those questions which agitate & excite the feelings of party, it is impossible that I could be inattentive to passing events, or an unconcerned observer of them." But "as they have increased in their importance, the interest, which as an American I must take in them, has also increased; and the declaration of war has appeared to me, as it has to you, to be one of those portentous acts which ought to concentrate on itself the efforts of all those who can take an active part in rescuing their country from the ruin it threatens.

"All minor considerations should be waived; the lines of subdivision between parties, if not absolutely effaced, should at least be convened for a time;

[1] Adams: *U.S.* v, 375–78.
[2] Smith: *An Address to the People of the United States*, 42–43.

and the great division between the friends of peace & the advocates of war ought alone to remain. It is an object of such magnitude as to give to almost every other, comparative insignificance; and all who wish peace ought to unite in the means which may facilitate its attainment, whatever may have been their differences of opinion on other points." [1]

Marshall proceeds to analyze the causes of hostilities. These, he contends, were Madison's subserviency to France and the base duplicity of Napoleon. The British Government and American Federalists had, from the first, asserted that the Emperor's revocation of the Berlin and Milan Decrees was a mere trick to entrap that credulous French partisan, Madison; and this they maintained with ever-increasing evidence to support them. For, in spite of Napoleon's friendly words, American ships were still seized by the French as well as by the British.

In response to the demand of Joel Barlow, the new American Minister to France, for a forthright statement as to whether the obnoxious decrees against neutral commerce had or had not been revoked as to the United States, the French Foreign Minister delivered to Barlow a new decree. This document, called " The Decree of St. Cloud," declared that the former edicts of Napoleon, of which the American Government complained, "are definitively, and to date from the 1st day of November last [1810], considered as not having existed [*non avenus*] in regard to American vessels." The "decree" was dated April 28,

---

[1] Marshall to Smith, July 27, 1812, Dreer MSS. "American Lawyers," Pa. Hist. Soc.

1811, yet it was handed to Barlow on May 10, 1812. It expressly stated, moreover, that Napoleon issued it because the American Congress had, by the Act of May 2, 1811, prohibited "the vessels and merchandise of Great Britain . . from entering into the ports of the United States." [1]

General John Armstrong, the American Minister who preceded Barlow, never had heard of this decree; it had not been transmitted to the French Minister at Washington; it had not been made public in any way. It was a ruse, declared the Federalists when news of it reached America — a cheap and tawdry trick to save Madison's face, a palpable falsehood, a clumsy afterthought. So also asserted Robert Smith, and so he wrote to the Chief Justice.

Marshall agreed with the fallen Baltimore politician. Continuing his letter to Smith, the longest and most unreserved he ever wrote, except to Washington and to Lee when on the French Mission,[2] the Chief Justice said: "The view you take of the edict purporting to bear date of the 28th of April 1811 appears to me to be perfectly correct. . . I am astonished, if in these times any thing ought to astonish, that the same impression is not made on all." Marshall puts many questions based on dates, for the purpose of exposing the fraudulent nature of the French decree and continues:

"Had France felt for the United States any portion of that respect to which our real importance entitles us, would she have failed to give this proof of it? But

---

[1] *Am. State Papers, For. Rel.* iii, 603; and see Channing: *U.S.* iv, 449.
[2] See vol. ii, 243–44, 245–47, of this work.

regardless of the assertion made by the President in his Proclamation of the 2ᵈ of Novʳ 1810, regardless of the communications made by the Executive to the Legislature, regardless of the acts of Congress, and regardless of the propositions which we have invariably maintained in our diplomatic intercourse with Great Britain, the Emperor has given a date to his decree, & has assigned a motive for its enactment, which in express terms contradict every assertion made by the American nation throughout all the departments of its government, & remove the foundation on which its whole system has been erected.

"The motive for this offensive & contemptuous proceeding cannot be to rescue himself from the imputation of continuing to enforce his decrees after their formal repeal because this imputation is precisely as applicable to a repeal dated the 28ᵗʰ of April 1811 as to one dated the 1ˢᵗ of November 1810, since the execution of those decrees has continued after the one date as well as after the other. Why then is this obvious fabrication such as we find it? Why has Mʳ Barlow been unable to obtain a paper which might consult the honor & spare the feelings of his government? The answer is not to be disguised. Bonaparte does not sufficiently respect us to exhibit for our sake, to France, to America, to Britain, or to the world, any evidence of his having receded one step from the position he had taken.

"He could not be prevailed on, even after we had done all he required, to soften any one of his acts so far as to give it the appearance of his having advanced one step to meet us. That this step, or rather the appearance of having taken it, might save our reputation was regarded as dust in the balance. Even now, after our solemn & repeated assertions that our discrimination between the belligerents is founded altogether on a first advance of France—on a decisive & unequivocal repeal of all her obnoxious decrees; after we have engaged in a war of the most calamitous character, avowedly, because France had repealed those decrees, the Emperor scorns to countenance the assertion or to leave it uncontradicted.

"He avers to ourselves, to our selected enemy, & to the world, that, whatever pretexts we may assign for our conduct, he has in fact ceded nothing, he has made no advance, he stands on his original ground & we have marched up to it. We have submitted, completely submitted; & he will not leave us the poor consolation of concealing that submission from ourselves. But not even our submission has obtained relief. His cruizers still continue to capture, sink, burn & destroy.

"I cannot contemplate this subject without excessive mortification as well at the contempt with which we are treated as at the infatuation of my countrymen. It is not however for me to indulge these feelings though I cannot so entirely suppress them as not sometimes though rarely to allow them a place in a private letter." Marshall assures Smith that he has "read with attention and approbation" the paper sent him and will see to its "republication."[1]

[1] Marshall to Smith, July 27, 1812, Dreer MSS. "American Lawyers," Pa. Hist. Soc.

A single quotation from the letters of Southern Federalists will show how accurately Marshall interpreted Federalist feeling during

From reading Marshall's letter without a knowledge of the facts, one could not possibly infer that America ever had been wronged by the Power with which we were then at war. All the strength of his logical and analytical mind is brought to bear upon the date and motives of Napoleon's last decree. He wrote in the tone and style, and with the controversial ability of his state papers, when at the head of the Adams Cabinet. But had the British Foreign Secretary guided his pen, his indictment of France and America could not have been more unsparing. His letter to Smith was a call to peace advocates and British partisans to combine to end the war by overthrowing the Administration.

This unfortunate letter was written during the long period between the adjournment of the Supreme Court in March, 1812, and its next session in February of the following year. Marshall's sentiments are in sharp contrast with those of Joseph Story, whose letters, written from his Massachusetts home, strongly condemn those who were openly opposing the war. "The present," he writes, "was the last occasion which patriotism ought to have sought to create divisions." [1]

Apparently the Administration did not know of Marshall's real feelings. Immediately after the declaration of war, Monroe, who succeeded Smith as Secretary of State, had sent his old personal friend,

the War of 1812: "Heaven grant that .. our own Country may not be found ultimately, a solitary friend of this great Robber of Nations." (Tallmadge to McHenry, May 30, 1813, Steiner, 598.) The war had been in progress more than ten months when these words were written.

[1] Story to Williams, Oct. 8, 1812, Story, I, 243.

the Chief Justice, some documents relating to the war. If Marshall had been uninformed as to the causes that drove the United States to take militant action, these papers supplied that information. In acknowledging receipt of them, he wrote Monroe:

"On my return to day from my farm where I pass a considerable portion of my time in *laborious relaxation*, I found a copy of the message of the President of the 1st inst accompanied by the report of the Committee of foreign relations & the declaration of war against Great Britain, under cover from you.

"Permit me to subjoin to my thanks for this mark of your attention my fervent wish that this momentous measure may, in its operation on the interest & honor of our country, disappoint only its enemies. Whether my prayer be heard or not I shall remain with respectful esteem," etc.[1]

Cold as this letter was, and capable as it was of double interpretation, to the men sorely pressed by the immediate exigencies of combat, it gave no inkling that the Chief Justice of the United States was at that very moment not only in close sympathy with the peace party, but was actually encouraging that party in its efforts to end the war.[2]

Just at this time, Marshall must have longed for seclusion, and, by a lucky chance, it was afforded him. One of the earliest and most beneficial effects of the Non-Importation, Embargo, and Non-Inter-

[1] Marshall to Monroe, June 25, 1812, Monroe MSS. Lib. Cong.

[2] Marshall, however, was a member of the "Vigilance Committee" of Richmond, and took an important part in its activities. (*Virginia Magazine of History and Biography*, VII, 230–31.)

course laws that preceded the war, was the heavily
increased migration from the seaboard States to the
territories beyond the Alleghanies. The dramatic
story of Burr's adventures and designs had reached
every ear and had turned toward the Western country the eyes of the poor, the adventurous, the aspiring; already thousands of settlers were taking up
the new lands over the mountains. Thus came a
practical consideration of improved means of travel
and transportation. Fresh interest in the use of
waterways was given by Fulton's invention, which
seized upon the imagination of men. The possibilities of steam navigation were in the minds of all who
observed the expansion of the country and the
growth of domestic commerce.

Before the outbreak of war, the Legislature of Virginia passed an act appointing commissioners "for
the purpose of viewing certain rivers within this
Commonwealth," [1] and Marshall was made the head
of this body of investigators. Nothing could have
pleased him more. It was practical work on a matter
that interested him profoundly, and the renewal of
a subject which he had entertained since his young
manhood. [2]

This tour of observation promised to be full of va-

[1] *Report of the Commissioners appointed to view Certain Rivers within
the Commonwealth of Virginia, 5.*

[2] A practicable route for travel and transportation between Virginia and the regions across the mountains had been a favorite
project of Washington. The Potomac and James River Company,
of which Marshall when a young lawyer had become a stockholder
(vol. I, 218, of this work), was organized partly in furtherance of this
project. The idea had remained active in the minds of public men in
Virginia and was, perhaps, the one subject upon which they substantially agreed.

riety and adventure, tinged with danger, into forests, over mountains, and along streams and rivers not yet thoroughly explored. For a short time Marshall would again live over the days of his boyhood. Most inviting of all, he would get far away from talk or thought of the detested war. Whether the Presidential scheming in his behalf bore fruit or withered, his absence in the wilderness was an ideal preparation to meet either outcome.

In his fifty-seventh year Marshall set out at the head of the expedition, and a thorough piece of work he did. With chain and spirit level the route was carefully surveyed from Lynchburg to the Ohio. Sometimes progress was made slowly and with the utmost labor. In places the scenes were "awful and discouraging."

The elaborate report which the commission submitted to the Legislature was written by Marshall. It reads, says the surveyor of this division of the Chesapeake and Ohio Railway,[1] "as an account of that survey of 1869, when I pulled a chain down the rugged banks of New River." Practicable sections were accurately pointed out and the methods by which they could best be utilized were recommended with particular care.

Marshall's report is alive with far-seeing and statesmanlike suggestions. He thinks, in 1812, that steamboats can be run successfully on the New River, but fears that the expense will be too great. The

[1] Much of the course selected by Marshall was adopted in the building of the Chesapeake and Ohio Railway. In 1869, Collis P. Huntington made a trip of investigation over part of Marshall's route. (Nelson: *Address — The Chesapeake and Ohio Railway*, 15.)

velocity of the current gives him some anxiety, but "the currents of the Hudson, of the Mohawk, and of the Mississippi, are very strong; and . . a practice so entirely novel as the use of steam in navigation, will probably receive great improvement."

The expense of the undertaking must, he says, depend on the use to be made of the route. Should the intention be only to assist the local traffic of the "upper country down the James river," the expense would not be great. But, "if the views of the legislature shall extend to a free commercial intercourse with the western states," the route must compete with others then existing "or that may be opened." In that case "no improvement ought to be undertaken but with a determination to make it complete and effectual." If this were done, the commerce of Kentucky, Ohio, and even a part of Southwestern Pennsylvania would pour through Virginia to the Atlantic States. This was a rich prize which other States were exerting themselves to capture. Moreover, such "commercial intercourse" would bind Virginia to the growing West by "strong ties" of "friendly sentiments," and these were above price. "In that mysterious future which is in reserve, and is yet hidden from us, events may occur to render" such a community of interest and mutual regard "too valuable to be estimated in dollars and cents."

Marshall pictures the growth of the West, "that extensive and fertile country . . increasing in wealth and population with a rapidity which baffles calculation." Not only would Virginia profit by opening a great trade route to the West, but the Nation

would be vastly benefited. "Every measure which
tends to cement more closely the union of the eastern with the western states" would be invaluable to
the whole country. The military uses of "this central channel of communication" were highly important: "For the want of it, in the course of the last
autumn, government was reduced to the necessity of
transporting arms in waggons from Richmond to
the falls of the Great Kanawha," and "a similar
necessity may often occur."[1]

When Marshall returned to Richmond, he found
the country depressed and in turmoil. The war had
begun dismally for the Americans. Our want of
military equipment and training was incredible and
assured those disasters that quickly fell upon us.
The Federalist opposition to the war grew ever
bolder, ever more bitter. The Massachusetts House
of Representatives issued an "Address" to the people, urging the organization of a *"peace party,"* ad-
juring "loud and deep . . disapprobation of this war,"
and demanding that nobody enlist in the army.[2]
Pamphlets were widely circulated, abusing the
American Government and upholding the British
cause. The ablest of these, "Mr. Madison's War,"
was by John Lowell of Boston.

The President, he said, "impelled" Congress to
declare an "offensive" war against Great Britain.
Madison was a member of "the *French* party."
British impressment was the pursuance of a sound
policy; the British doctrine — once a British subject,

[1] *Report of the Commissioners appointed to view Certain Rivers
within the Commonwealth of Virginia*, 38-39.

[2] Niles: *Weekly Register*, II, 418.

always a British subject — was unassailable. The
Orders in Council were just; the execution of them
"moderation" itself. On every point, in short, the
British Government was right; the French, diabol-
ical; the American, contemptible and wrong. How
trivial America's complaints, even if there was a
real basis for them, in view of Great Britain's unselfish struggle against "the gigantic dominion of
France."

If that Power, "swayed" by that satanic genius,
Napoleon, should win, would she not take Nova
Scotia, Canada, Louisiana, the Antilles, Florida,
South America? After these conquests, would not
the United States, "the only remaining republic,"
be conquered. Most probably. What then ought
America to do? "In war offensive and unjust, the
citizens are not only obliged not to take part, but
by the laws of God, and of civil society, they are
bound to abstain." What were the rights of citizens
in war-time? To oppose the war by tongue and pen,
if they thought the war to be wrong, and to refuse to
serve if called "contrary to the Constitution." [1]

Such was the Federalism of 1812–15, such the arguments that would have been urged for the election
of Marshall had he been chosen as the peace candidate. But the peace Republicans of New York
nominated the able, cunning, and politically corrupt

[1] Lowell: *Mr. Madison's War:* by "A New England Farmer."
A still better illustration of Federalist hostility to the war and the
Government is found in a letter of Ezekiel Webster to his brother
Daniel: "Let gamblers be made to contribute to the support of this
war, which was declared by men of no better principles than them-
selves." (Ezekiel Webster to Daniel Webster, Oct. 29, 1814, Van
Tyne, 53.) Webster here refers to a war tax on playing-cards.

De Witt Clinton; and this man, who had assured the
Federalists that he favored an "honourable peace"
with England,[1] was endorsed by a Federalist caucus
as the anti-war standard-bearer,[2] though not without a swirl of acrimony and dissension.

But for the immense efforts of Clinton to secure
the nomination, and the desire of the Federalists and
all conservatives that Marshall should continue as
Chief Justice,[3] it is possible that he might have been
named as the opponent of Madison in the Presidential contest of 1812. "I am far enough from desiring
Clinton for President of the United States," wrote
Pickering in the preceding July; "I would infinitely
prefer another Virginian — if Judge Marshall could
be the man."[4]

Marshall surely would have done better than Clinton, who, however, carried New York, New Jersey,
Delaware, Maryland, and all the New England
States except Vermont. The mercantile classes
would have rallied to Marshall's standard more
enthusiastically than to Clinton's. The lawyers
generally would have worked hard for him. The
Federalists, who accepted Clinton with repugnance,
would have exerted themselves to the utmost for
Marshall, the ideal representative of Federalism. He
was personally very strong in North Carolina; the
capture of Pennsylvania might have been possible;[5]
Vermont might have given him her votes.

[1] Harper to Lynn, Sept. 25, 1812, Steiner, 584.
[2] See McMaster, IV, 199–200.   [3] Morison: *Otis*, I, 399.
[4] Pickering to Pennington, July 22, 1812, *N.E. Federalism:* Adams,
389.
[5] The vote of Pennsylvania, with those cast for Clinton, would
have elected Marshall.

The Federalist resistance to the war grew more de- termined as the months wore on. Throughout New England the men of wealth, nearly all of whom were Federalists, declined to subscribe to the Govern- ment loans.[1] The Governors of the New England States refused to aid the National Government with the militia.[2] In Congress the Federalists were ob- structing war measures and embarrassing the Gov- ernment in every way their ingenuity could devise. One method was to force the Administration to tell the truth about Napoleon's pretended revocation of his obnoxious decree. A resolution asking the Presi- dent to inform the House "when, by whom, and in what manner, the first intelligence was given to this Government" of the St. Cloud Decree, was offered by Daniel Webster,[3] who had been elected to Con- gress from New Hampshire as the fiercest youthful antagonist of the war in his State.[4] The Republi- cans agreed, and Webster's resolution was passed by a vote of 137 yeas to only 26 nays.[5]

In compliance the President transmitted a long re- port. It was signed by the Secretary of State, James Monroe, but bears the imprint of Madison's lucid mind. The report states the facts upon which Con- gress was compelled to declare war and demonstrates

[1] Babcock, 157; and see Dewey: *Financial History of the United States*, 133.

[2] For an excellent statement of the conduct of the Federalists at this time see Morison: *Otis*, II, 53–66. "The militia of Massachu- setts, seventy thousand in enrolment, well-drilled, and well-equipped, was definitely withdrawn from the service of the United States in September, 1814." (Babcock, 155.) Connecticut did the same thing. (*Ib.* 156.)

[3] *Annals*, 13th Cong. 1st Sess. 302.

[4] See McMaster, IV, 213–14.   [5] *Annals*, 13th Cong. 1st Sess. 302

that the Decree of St. Cloud had nothing to do with our militant action, since it was not received until more than a month after our declaration of war. Then follow several clear and brilliant paragraphs setting forth the American view of the causes and purposes of the war.[1]

Timothy Pickering was not now in the Senate. The Republican success in Massachusetts at the State election of 1810 had given the Legislature to that party,[2] and the pugnacious Federalist leader was left at home. There he raged and intrigued and wrote reams of letters. Monroe's report lent new fury to his always burning wrath, and he sent that document, with his malediction upon it, to John Marshall at Richmond. In reply the Chief Justice said that the report "contains a labored apology for France but none for ourselves. It furnishes no reason for our tame unmurmuring acquiescence under the double insult of withholding this paper [Decree of St. Cloud] from us & declaring in our face that it has been put in our possession.

"The report is silent on another subject of still deeper interest. It leaves unnoticed the fact that the Berlin & Milan decrees were certainly not repealed by that insidious decree of April since it had never been communicated to the French courts and cruizers, & since their cruizers had at a period subsequent to the pretended date of that decree received orders

---

[1] *Am. State Papers, For. Rel.* iii, 609–12.
[2] The Republican victory was caused by the violent British partisanship of the Federalist leaders. In spite of the distress the people suffered from the Embargo, they could not, for the moment, tolerate Federalist opposition to their own country. (See Adams: *U.S.* v, 215.)

to continue to execute the offensive decrees on American vessels.

"The report manifests no sensibility at the disgraceful circumstances which tend strongly to prove that this paper was fabricated to satisfy the importunities of Mr. Barlow, was antedated to suit French purposes; nor at the contempt manifested for the feelings of Americans and their government, by not deigning so to antedate it as to save the credit of our Administration by giving some plausibility to their assertion that the repeal had taken place on the 1st of Nov^r — But this is a subject with which I dare not trust myself."

The plight of the American land forces, the splendid and unrivaled victories of the American Navy, apparently concerned Marshall not at all. His eyes were turned toward Europe; his ears strained to catch the sounds from foreign battle-fields.

"I look with anxious solicitude — with mingled hope & fear," he continues, "to the great events which are taking place in the north of Germany. It appears probable that a great battle will be fought on or near the Elbe & never had the world more at stake than will probably depend on that battle.

"Your opinions had led me to hope that there was some prospect for a particular peace for ourselves. My own judgement, could I trust it, would tell me that peace or war will be determined by the events in Europe."[1]

[1] Marshall to Pickering, Dec. 11, 1813, Pickering MSS. Mass. Hist. Soc.

The "great battle" which Marshall foresaw had been fought nearly eight weeks before his letter was written. Napoleon had been crushingly defeated at Leipzig in October, 1813, and the British, Prussian, and other armies which Great Britain had combined against him, were already invading France. When, later, the news of this arrived in America, it was hailed by the Federalists with extravagant rejoicings.[1]

Secession, if the war were continued, now became the purpose of the more determined Federalist leaders. It was hopeless to keep up the struggle, they said. The Administration had precipitated hostilities without reason or right, without conscience or sense.[2] The people never had favored this wretched conflict; and now the tyrannical Government, failing to secure volunteers, had resorted to conscription — an "infamous" expedient resorted to in brutal violation of the Constitution.[3] So came the Hartford

[1] Morison: *Otis*, ii, 54–56.

[2] "CURSE THIS GOVERNMENT! I would march at 6 days notice for Washington . . and I would swear upon the *altar* never to return till Madison was buried under the ruins of the capitol." (Herbert to Webster, April 20, 1813, Van Tyne, 27.)

[3] The Federalists frantically opposed conscription. Daniel Webster, especially, denounced it. "Is this [conscription] . . consistent with the character of a free Government? . . No, Sir. . . The Constitution is libelled, foully libelled. The people of this country have not established . . such a fabric of despotism. . .

"Where is it written in the Constitution . . that you may take children from their parents . . & compel them to fight the battles of any war, in which the folly or the wickedness of Government may engage it? . . Such an abominable doctrine has no foundation in the Constitution."

Conscription, Webster said, was a gambling device to throw the dice for blood; and it was a "horrible lottery." "May God, in his compassion, shield me from . . the enormity of this guilt." (See

Convention which the cool wisdom of George Cabot saved from proclaiming secession.[1]

Of the two pretenses for war against Great Britain, the Federalists alleged that one had been removed even before we declared war, and that only the false and shallow excuse of British impressment of American seamen remained. Madison and Monroe recognized this as the one great remaining issue, and an Administration pamphlet was published asserting the reason and justice of the American position. This position was that men of every country have a natural right to remove to another land and there become citizens or subjects, entitled to the protection of the government of the nation of their adoption. The British principle, on the contrary, was that British subjects could never thus expatriate themselves, and that, if they did so, the British Government could seize them wherever found, and by force compel them to serve the Empire in any manner the Government chose to direct.

Monroe's brother-in-law, George Hay, still the United States Attorney for the District of Virginia, was selected to write the exposition of the American

Webster's speech on the Conscription Bill delivered in the House of Representatives, December 9, 1814, Van Tyne, 56–68; see also Curtis: *Life of Daniel Webster*, I, 138.)

Webster had foretold what he meant to do: "Of course we shall oppose such usurpation." (Webster to his brother, Oct. 30, 1814, Van Tyne, 54.) Again: "The conscription has not come up — if it does it will cause a storm such as was never witnessed here" [in Washington]. (Same to same, Nov. 29, 1814, *ib.* 55.)

[1] See Morison: *Otis*, II, 78–199. Pickering feared that Cabot's moderation would prevent the Hartford Convention from taking extreme measures against the Government. (See Pickering to Lowell, Nov. 7, 1814, *N.E. Federalism:* Adams, 406.)

view. It seems probable that his manuscript was carefully revised by Madison and Monroe, and perhaps by Jefferson.[1] Certainly Hay stated with singular precision the views of the great Republican triumvirate. The pamphlet was entitled "A Treatise on Expatriation." He began: "I hold in utter reprobation the idea that a man is bound by an obligation, permanent and unalterable, to the government of a country which he has abandoned and his allegiance to which he has solemnly adjured." [2]

Immediately John Lowell answered.[3] Nothing keener and more spirited ever came from the pen of that gifted man. "The presidential pamphleteer," as Lowell called Hay, ignored the law. The maxim, once a subject always a subject, was as true of America as of Britain. Had not Ellsworth, when Chief Justice, so decided in the famous case of Isaac Williams? [4] Yet Hay sneered at the opinion of that distinguished jurist.[5]

Pickering joyfully dispatched Lowell's brochure to Marshall, who lost not a moment in writing of his admiration. "I had yesterday the pleasure of receiv-

[1] Some sentences are paraphrases of expressions by Jefferson on the same subject. For example: "I hold the right of expatriation to be inherent in every man by the laws of nature, and incapable of being rightfully taken from him even by the united will of every other person in the nation." (Jefferson to Gallatin, June 26, 1806, *Works:* Ford, x, 273.) Again: "Our particular and separate grievance is only the impressment of our citizens. We must sacrifice the last dollar and drop of blood to rid us of that badge of slavery." (Jefferson to Crawford, Feb. 11, 1815, *ib.* xi, 450-51.) This letter was written at Monticello the very day that the news of peace reached Washington.

[2] Hay: *A Treatise on Expatriation*, 24.

[3] Lowell: *Review of 'A Treatise on Expatriation'*: by "A Massachusetts Lawyer."   [4] See vol. iii, chap. i, of this work.

[5] See *Review of 'A Treatise on Expatriation,'* 6.

ing your letter of the 8th accompanying Mr Lowell's very masterly review of the treatise on expatriation. I have read it with great pleasure, & thank you very sincerely for this mark of your recollection.

"Could I have ever entertained doubts on the subject, this review would certainly have removed them. Mingled with much pungent raillery is a solidity of argument and an array of authority which in my judgement is entirely conclusive. But in truth it is a question upon which I never entertained a *scintilla* of doubt; and have never yet heard an argument which ought to excite a doubt in any sound and reflecting mind. It will be to every thinking American a most afflicting circumstance, should our government on a principle so completely rejected by the world proceed to the execution of unfortunate, of honorable, and of innocent men." [1]

Astonishing and repellent as these words now appear, they expressed the views of every Federalist lawyer in America. The doctrine of perpetual allegiance was indeed then held and practiced by every government except our own,[2] nor was it rejected by the United States until the Administration became Republican. Marshall, announcing the opinion of the Supreme Court in 1804, had held that an alien could take lands in New Jersey because he had lived in that State when, in 1776, the Legislature passed a law making all residents citizens.[3] Thus he had declared that an American citizen did not cease to be

[1] Marshall to Pickering, April 11, 1814, Pickering MSS. Mass. Hist. Soc.

[2] See Channing: *Jeff. System*, 170–71.

[3] M'Ilvaine *vs.* Coxe's Lessee, 4 Cranch, 209.

such because he had become the subject of a foreign power. Four years later, in another opinion involving expatriation, he had stated the law to be that a British subject, born in England before 1775, could not take, by devise, lands in Maryland, the statute of that State forbidding aliens from thus acquiring property there.[1] In both these cases, however, Marshall refrained from expressly declaring in terms against the American doctrine.

Even as late as 1821 the Chief Justice undoubtedly retained his opinion that the right of expatriation did not exist,[2] although he did not say so in express terms. But in Marshall's letter on Lowell's pamphlet he flatly avows his belief in the principle of perpetual allegiance, any direct expression on which he so carefully avoided when deciding cases involving it.

Thus the record shows that John Marshall was as bitterly opposed to the War of 1812 as was Pickering or Otis or Lowell. So entirely had he become one of "the aristocracy of talents of reputation, & of property," as Plumer, in 1804, had so accurately styled the class of which he himself was then a member,[3] that Marshall looked upon all but one subject then before the people with the eyes of confirmed reaction. That subject was Nationalism. To that supreme cause he was devoted with all the passion of his deep and powerful nature; and in the service of that cause he was soon to do much more than he had already performed.

---

[1] Dawson's Lessee *vs.* Godfrey, 4 Cranch, 321.

[2] Case of the Santissima Trinidad *et al.*, 1 Brockenbrough, 478–87; and see 7 Wheaton, 283.

[3] Plumer to Livermore, March 4, 1804, Plumer MSS. Lib. Cong.

Our second war with Great Britain accomplished none of the tangible and immediate objects for which it was fought. The British refused to abandon "the right" of impressment; or to disclaim the British sovereignty of the oceans whenever they chose to assert it; or to pay a farthing for their spoliation of American commerce. On the other hand, the British did not secure one of their demands.[1] The peace treaty did little more than to end hostilities.

But the war achieved an inestimable good — it de-Europeanized America. It put an end to our thinking and feeling only in European terms and emotions. It developed the spirit of the new America, born since our political independence had been achieved, and now for the first time emancipated from the intellectual and spiritual sovereignty of the Old World. It had revealed to this purely American generation a consciousness of its own strength; it could exult in the fact that at last America had dared to fight.

The American Navy, ship for ship, officer for officer, man for man, had proved itself superior to the British Navy, the very name of which had hitherto been mentioned only in terror or admiration of its unconquerable might. In the end, raw and untrained American troops had beaten British regulars. American riflemen of the West and South had

---

[1] For example, the British "right" of impressment must be formally and plainly acknowledged in the treaty; an Indian dominion was to be established, and the Indian tribes were to be made parties to the settlements; the free navigation of the Mississippi was to be guaranteed to British vessels; the right of Americans to fish in Canadian waters was to be ended. Demands far more extreme were made by the British press and public. (See McMaster, IV, 260–74; and see especially Morison: *Otis*, II, 171.)

overwhelmed the flower of all the armies of Europe. An American frontier officer, Andrew Jackson, had easily outwitted some of Great Britain's ablest and most experienced professional generals. In short, on land and sea America had stood up to, had really beaten, the tremendous Power that had overthrown the mighty Napoleon.

Such were the feelings and thoughts of that Young America which had come into being since John Marshall had put aside his Revolutionary uniform and arms. And in terms very much like those of the foregoing paragraph the American people generally expressed their sentiments.

Moreover, the Embargo, the Non-Intercourse and Non-Importation Acts, the British blockades, the war itself, had revolutionized the country economically and socially. American manufacturing was firmly established. Land travel and land traffic grew to proportions never before imagined, never before desired. The people of distant sections became acquainted.

The eyes of all Americans, except those of the aged or ageing, were turned from across the Atlantic Ocean toward the boundless, the alluring West — their thoughts diverted from the commotions of Europe and the historic antagonism of foreign nations, to the economic conquest of a limitless and virgin empire and to the development of incalculable and untouched resources, all American and all their own.

The migration to the West, which had been increasing for years, now became almost a folk movement. The Eastern States were drained of their young men and women. Some towns were almost depopulated.[1] And these hosts of settlers carried into wilderness and prairie a spirit and pride that had not been seen or felt in America since the time of the Revolution. But their high hopes were to be quickly turned into despair, their pride into ashes; for a condition was speedily to develop that would engulf them in disaster. It was this situation which was to call forth some of the greatest of Marshall's Constitutional opinions. This forbidding future, however, was foreseen by none of that vast throng of home-seekers crowding every route to the "Western Country," in the year of 1815. Only the rosiest dreams were theirs and the spirited consciousness that they were Americans, able to accomplish all things, even the impossible.

It was then a new world in which John Marshall found himself, when, in his sixtieth year, the war which he so abhorred came to an end. A state of things surrounded him little to his liking and yet soon to force from him the exercise of the noblest judicial statesmanship in American history. From the extreme independence of this new period, the intense and sudden Nationalism of the war, the ideas of local sovereignty rekindled by the New England Federalists at the dying fires that Jefferson and the Republicans had lighted in 1798, and from the play of conflicting interests came a reaction against Nationalism which it was Marshall's high mission to check and to turn into channels of National power, National safety, and National well-being.

[1] McMaster, IV, 383–88.

CHAPTER II

MARSHALL AND STORY

Either the office was made for the man or the man for the office.
(George S. Hillard.)

I am in love with his character, positively in love.   (Joseph Story.)

In the midst of these gay circles my mind is carried to my own fireside and to my beloved wife.   (Marshall.)

Now the man Moses was very meek, above all the men which were upon the face of the earth.   (Numbers XII, 3.)

"IT will be difficult to find a character of firmness enough to preserve his independence on the same bench with Marshall."[1] So wrote Thomas Jefferson one year after he had ceased to be President. He was counseling Madison as to the vacancy on the Supreme Bench and one on the district bench at Richmond, in filling both of which he was, for personal reasons, feverishly concerned.

We are now to ascend with Marshall the mountain peaks of his career. Within the decade that followed after the close of our second war with Great Britain, he performed nearly all of that vast and creative labor, the lasting results of which have given him that distinctive title, the Great Chief Justice. During that period he did more than any other one man ever has done to vitalize the American Constitution; and, in the performance of that task, his influence over his associates was unparalleled.[2]

[1] Jefferson to Madison, May 25, 1810, *Works:* Ford, XI, 140.

"There is no man in the court that strikes me like Marshall. . . I have never seen a man of whose intellect I had a higher opinion." (Webster to his brother, March 28, 1814, *Private Correspondence of Daniel Webster:* Webster, I, 244.)

[2] "In the possession of an ordinary man . . it [the office of Chief

When Justices Chase and Cushing died and their successors Gabriel Duval[1] and Joseph Story were appointed, the majority of the Supreme Court, for the first time, became Republican. Yet Marshall continued to dominate it as fully as when its members were of his own political faith and views of government.[2] In the whole history of courts there is no parallel to such supremacy. Not without reason was that tribunal looked upon and called "Marshall's Court." It is interesting to search for the sources of his strange power.

These sources are not to be found exclusively in the strength of Marshall's intellect, surpassing though it was, nor yet in the mere dominance of his will. Joseph Story was not greatly inferior to Marshall in mind and far above him in accomplishments, while William Johnson, the first Justice of the Supreme Court appointed by Jefferson, was as determined as Marshall and was "strongly imbued with the principles of southern democracy, bold, independent, eccentric, and sometimes harsh."[3] Nor did learning give Marshall his commanding influence. John Jay and Oliver Ellsworth were his superiors in that respect; while Story so infinitely surpassed him in erudition that, between the two men, there is nothing but contrast. Indeed, Marshall had no "learning"

Justice] would be very apt to disgrace him." (Story to McLean, Oct. 12, 1835, Story, II, 208.)

[1] Justice Duval's name is often, incorrectly, spelled with two "l's."

[2] "No man had ever a stronger influence upon the minds of others." (*American Jurist*, XIV, 242.)

[3] Ingersoll: *Historical Sketch of the Second War between the United States and Great Britain*, 2d Series, I, 74.

at all in the academic sense;[1] we must seek elsewhere for an explanation of his peculiar influence.

This explanation is, in great part, furnished by Marshall's personality. The manner of man he was, of course, is best revealed by the well-authenticated accounts of his daily life. He spent most of his time at Richmond, for the Supreme Court sat in Washington only a few weeks each year. He held circuit court at Raleigh as well as at the Virginia Capital, but the sessions seldom occupied more than a fortnight each. In Richmond, then, his characteristics were best known; and so striking were they that time has but little dimmed the memory of them.

Marshall, the Chief Justice, continued to neglect his dress and personal appearance as much as he did when, as a lawyer, his shabby attire so often "brought a blush" to the cheeks of his wife,[2] and his manners were as "lax and lounging" as when Jefferson called them proofs of a "profound hypocrisy."[3] Although no man in America was less democratic in his ideas of government, none was more democratic in his contact with other people. To this easy bonhomie was added a sense of humor, always quick to appreciate an amusing situation.

When in Richmond, Marshall often did his own marketing and carried home the purchases he made. The tall, ungainly, negligently clad Chief Justice, ambling along the street, his arms laden with pur-

---

[1] "He was not, in any sense of the word, a learned man." (George S. Hillard in *North American Review*, XLII, 224.)

[2] See vol. I, 163, of this work; also *Southern Literary Messenger*, XVII, 154; and Terhune: *Colonial Homesteads*, 92.

[3] See vol. II, 139, of this work.

chases, was a familiar sight.[1] He never would hurry, and habitually lingered at the market-place, chatting with everybody, learning the gossip of the town, listening to the political talk that in Richmond never ceased, and no doubt thus catching at first hand the drift of public sentiment.[2] The humblest and poorest man in Virginia was not more unpretentious than John Marshall.

No wag was more eager for a joke. One day, as he loitered on the outskirts of the market, a newcomer in Richmond, who had never seen Marshall, offered him a small coin to carry home for him a turkey just purchased. Marshall accepted, and, with the bird under his arm, trudged behind his employer. The incident sent the city into gales of laughter, and was so in keeping with Marshall's ways that it has been re-told from one generation to another, and is to-day almost as much alive as ever.[3] At another time the Chief Justice was taken for the butcher. He called on a relative's wife who had never met him, and who had not been told of his plain dress and rustic manners. Her husband wished to sell a calf and she expected the butcher to call to make the trade. She saw Marshall approaching, and judging by his appearance that he was the butcher, she directed the servant to tell him to go to the stable where the animal was awaiting inspection.[4]

It was Marshall's custom to go early every morning to a farm which he owned four miles from Richmond. For the exercise he usually walked, but, when he

---

[1] Mordecai: *Richmond in By-Gone Days*, 64.   [2] Terhune, 91.
[3] *Ib.* 92; and see Howe: *Historical Collections of Virginia*, 266.
[4] *Green Bag*, VIII, 486.

wished to take something heavy, he would ride. A stranger coming upon him on the road would have thought him one of the poorer small planters of the vicinity. He was extremely fond of children and, if he met one trudging along the road, he would take the child up on the horse and carry it to its destination. Often he was seen riding into Richmond from his farm, with one child before and another behind him.[1]

Bishop Meade met Marshall on one of these morning trips, carrying on horseback a bag of clover seed.[2] On another, he was seen holding on the pommel a jug of whiskey which he was taking out to his farm-hands. The cork had come out and he was using his thumb as a stopper.[3] He was keenly interested in farming, and in 1811 was elected President of the Richmond Society for Promotion of Agriculture.[4]

The distance from Richmond to Raleigh was, by road, more than one hundred and seventy miles. Except when he went by stage,[5] as he seldom did, it must have taken a week to make this journey. He traveled in a primitive vehicle called a stick gig, drawn by one horse which he drove himself, seldom taking a servant with him.[6] Making his slow way

[1] Personal experience related by Dr. William P. Palmer to Dr. J. Franklin Jameson, and by him to the author.

[2] Meade: *Old Churches, Ministers and Families of Virginia*, II, 222.

[3] *Magazine of American History*, XII, 70; also *Green Bag*, VIII, 486.

[4] Anderson, 214.

[5] The stage schedule was much shorter, but the hours of travel very long. The stage left Petersburg at 3 A.M., arrived at Warrenton at 8 P.M., left Warrenton at 3 A.M., and arrived at Raleigh the same night. (Data furnished by Professor Archibald Henderson.) The stage was seldom on time, however, and the hardships of traveling in it very great. Marshall used it only when in extreme haste, a state of mind into which he seldom would be driven by any emergency.

[6] Mordecai, 64–65. Bishop Meade says of Marshall on his trips to Fauquier County, "Servant he had none." (Meade, II, 222.)

through the immense stretches of tar pines and sandy
fields, the Chief Justice doubtless thought out the
solution of the problems before him and the plain,
clear, large statements of his conclusions which, from
the bench later, announced not only the law of particular cases, but fundamental policies of the Nation.
His surroundings at every stage of the trip encouraged just such reflection — the vast stillness, the deep
forests, the long hours, broken only by some accident
to gig or harness, or interrupted for a short time to
feed and rest his horse, and to eat his simple meal.

During these trips, Marshall would become so
abstracted that, apparently, he would forget where
he was driving. Once, when near the plantation of
Nathaniel Macon in North Carolina, he drove over
a sapling which became wedged between a wheel
and the shaft. One of Macon's slaves, working in
an adjacent field, saw the predicament, hurried to
his assistance, held down the sapling with one hand,
and with the other backed the horse until the gig
was free. Marshall tossed the negro a piece of
money and asked him who was his owner. "Marse
Nat. Macon," said the slave. "He is an old friend,"
said Marshall; "tell him how you have helped me,"
giving his name. When the negro told his master,
Macon said: "That was the great Chief Justice
Marshall, the biggest lawyer in the United States."
The slave grinned and answered: "Marse Nat., he
may be de bigges' lawyer in de United States, but he
ain't got sense enough to back a gig off a saplin'." [1]

[1] As related by M. D. Haywood, Librarian of the Supreme Court
of North Carolina, to Professor Archibald Henderson and by him to
the author; and see *Harper's Magazine*, LXX, 610; *World's Work*, I, 395.

At night he would stop at some log tavern on the route, eat with the family and other guests, if any were present, and sit before the fireplace after the meal, talking with all and listening to all like the simple and humble countryman he appeared to be. Since the minor part of his time was spent in court, and most of it about Richmond, or on the road to and from Raleigh, or journeying to his Fauquier County plantation and the beloved mountains of his youth where he spent the hottest part of each year, it is doubtful whether any other judge ever maintained such intimate contact with people in the ordinary walks of life as did John Marshall.

The Chief Justice always arrived at Raleigh stained and battered from travel.[1] The town had a population of from three hundred to five hundred.[2] He was wont to stop at a tavern kept by a man named Cooke and noted for its want of comfort; but, although the inn got worse year after year, he still frequented it. Early one morning an acquaintance saw the Chief Justice go to the woodpile, gather an armful of wood and return with it to the house. When they met later in the day, the occurrence was recalled. "Yes," said Marshall, "I suppose it is not convenient for Mr. Cooke to keep a servant, so I make up my own fires."[3]

The Chief Justice occupied a small room in which were the following articles: "A bed, . . two split-bot-

---

[1] Judge James C. MacRae in *John Marshall — Life, Character and Judicial Services:* Dillon, II, 68.

[2] As late as April, 1811, the population of Raleigh was between six hundred and seven hundred. Nearly all the houses were of wood. By 1810 there were only four brick houses in the town.

[3] *Magazine of American History*, XII, 69.

tom chairs, a pine table covered with grease and ink, a cracked pitcher and broken bowl." The host ate with his guests and used his fingers instead of fork or knife.[1] When court adjourned for the day, Marshall would play quoits in the street before the tavern "with the public street characters of Raleigh," who were lovers of the game.[2]

He was immensely popular in Raleigh, his familiar manners and the justice of his decisions appealing with equal force to the bar and people alike. Writing at the time of the hearing of the Granville case,[3] John Haywood, then State Treasurer of North Carolina, testifies: "Judge Marshall . . is greatly respected here, as well on account of his talents and uprightness as for that sociability and ease of manner which render all happy and pleased when in his company."[4]

In spite of his sociability, which tempted him, while in Richmond, to visit taverns and the law offices of his friends, Marshall spent most of the day in his house or in the big yard adjoining it, for Mrs. Marshall's affliction increased with time, and the Chief Justice, whose affection for his wife grew as her illness advanced, kept near her as much as possi-

[1] Account of eye-witness as related by Dr. Kemp P. Battle of Raleigh to Professor Henderson and by him to the author.

Another tavern was opened about 1806 by one John Marshall. He had been one of the first commissioners of Raleigh, serving until 1797. He was no relation whatever to the Chief Justice. As already stated (vol. i, footnote to 15, of this work) the name was a common one.

[2] Mr. W. J. Peele of Raleigh to Professor Henderson.

[3] See *infra*, 154–56.

[4] Haywood to Steele, June 19, 1805. (MS. supplied by Professor Henderson.)

ble. In Marshall's grounds and near his house were several great oak and elm trees, beneath which was a spring; to this spot he would take the papers in cases he had to decide and, sitting on a rustic bench under the shade, would write many of those great opinions that have immortalized his name.[1]

Mrs. Marshall's malady was largely a disease of the nervous system and, at times, it seemingly affected her mind. It was a common thing for the Chief Justice to get up at any hour of the night and, without putting on his shoes lest his footfalls might further excite his wife, steal downstairs and drive away for blocks some wandering animal — a cow, a pig, a horse — whose sounds had annoyed her.[2] Even upon entering his house during the daytime, Marshall would take off his shoes and put on soft slippers in the hall.[3]

She was, of course, unequal to the management of the household. When the domestic arrangements needed overhauling, Marshall would induce her to take a long drive with her sister, Mrs. Edward Carrington, or her daughter, Mrs. Jacquelin B. Harvie, over the still and shaded roads of Richmond. The carriage out of sight, he would throw off his coat and

---

[1] *World's Work*, I, 395. This statement is supported by the testimony of Mr. Edward V. Valentine of Richmond, who has spent many years gathering and verifying data concerning Richmond and its early citizens. It is also confirmed by the Honorable James Keith, until recently President of the Court of Appeals of Virginia, and by others of the older residents of Richmond. For some opinions thus written, see chaps. IV, V, and VI of this volume.

[2] *Green Bag*, VIII, 484. Sympathetic Richmond even ordered the town clock and town bell muffled. (Meade, II, 222.)

[3] Statements of two eye-witnesses, Dr. Richard Crouch and William F. Gray, to Mr. Edward V. Valentine and by him related to the author.

vest, roll up his shirt-sleeves, twist a bandanna hand-kerchief about his head, and gathering the servants, lead as well as direct them in dusting the walls and furniture, scrubbing the floors and setting the house in order.[1]

Numerous incidents of this kind are well authenti-cated. To this day Marshall's unselfish devotion to his infirm and distracted wife is recalled in Rich-mond. But nobody ever heard the slightest word of complaint from him; nor did any act or expression of countenance so much as indicate impatience.

In his letters Marshall never fails to admonish his wife, who seldom if ever wrote to him, to care for her health. "Yesterday I received Jacquelin's let-ter of the 12th informing me that your health was at present much the same as when I left Richmond," writes Marshall.[2] "John [Marshall's son] passed through this city a day or two past, & although I did not see him I had the pleasure of hearing from Mr. Washington who saw him . . that you were as well as usual." [3] In another letter Marshall says: "Do my dearest Polly let me hear from you through someone of those who will be willing to write for you." [4] Again he says: "I am most anxious to know how you do but no body is kind enough to gratify my wishes. . . I looked eagerly for a letter to day but no letter came. . . You must not fail when you go to Chiccahominy [Marshall's farm near Richmond]

[1] Accounts given Professor J. Franklin Jameson by old residents of Richmond, and by Professor Jameson to the author.
[2] Marshall to his wife, Washington, Feb. 16, 1818, MS.
[3] Same to same, March 12, 1826, MS.
[4] Same to same, Feb. 19, 1829, MS.

. . to carry out blankets enough to keep you comfortable. I am very desirous of hearing what is doing there but as no body is good enough to let me know how you do & what is passing at home I could not expect to hear what is passing at the farm." [1] Indeed, only one letter of Marshall's has been discovered which indicates that he had received so much as a line from his wife; and this was when, an old man of seventy-five, he was desperately ill in Philadelphia. [2] Nothing, perhaps, better reveals the sweetness of his nature than his cheerful temper and tender devotion under trying domestic conditions. [3]

His "dearest Polly" was intensely religious, and Marshall profoundly respected this element of her character. [4] The evidence as to his own views and feelings on the subject of religion, although scanty, is definite. He was a Unitarian in belief and therefore never became a member of the Episcopal church, to which his parents, wife, children, and all other relatives belonged. But he attended services, Bishop Meade informs us, not only because "he was a sincere friend of religion," but also because he wished

[1] Marshall to his wife, Washington, Jan. 30, 1831, MS.

[2] See *infra*, chap. x.

[3] Mrs. Marshall did not write to her children, it would seem. When he was in Richmond, the Chief Justice himself sent messages from her which were ordinary expressions of affection.

"Your mother is very much gratified with the account you give from yourself and Claudia of all your affairs & especially of your children and hopes for its continuance. She looks with some impatience for similar information from John. She desires me to send her love to all the family including Miss Maria and to tell you that this hot weather distresses her very much & she wishes you also to give her love to John & Elizabeth & their children." (Marshall to his son James K. Marshall, Richmond, July 3, 1827, MS.)

[4] See vol. i, footnote to 189, of this work.

"to set an example." The Bishop bears this testimony: "I can never forget how he would prostrate his tall form before the rude low benches, without backs, at Coolspring Meeting-House,[1] in the midst of his children and grandchildren and his old neighbors." When in Richmond, Marshall attended the Monumental Church where, says Bishop Meade, "he was much incommoded by the narrowness of the pews. . . Not finding room enough for his whole body within the pew, he used to take his seat nearest the door of the pew, and, throwing it open, let his legs stretch a little into the aisle."[2]

It is said, however, that his daughter, during her last illness, declared that her father late in life was converted, by reading Keith on Prophecy, to a belief in the divinity of Christ; and that he determined to "apply for admission to the communion of our Church . . but died without ever communing."[3] There is, too, a legend about an astonishing flash of eloquence from Marshall — "a streak of vivid lightning" — at a tavern, on the subject of religion.[4] The impression said to have been made by Marshall on this occasion was heightened by his appearance when he arrived at the inn. The shafts of his ancient gig were broken and "held together by withes formed from the bark of a hickory sapling"; he was negligently dressed, his knee buckles loosened.[5]

In the tavern a discussion arose among some young men concerning "the merits of the Christian reli-

[1] In Leeds Parish, near Oakhill, Fauquier County.
[2] Meade, ii, 221–22.
[3] *Green Bag*, viii, 487.
[4] Howe, 275–76.   [5] *Ib.*

gion." The debate grew warm and lasted "from six
o'clock until eleven." No one knew Marshall, who
sat quietly listening. Finally one of the youthful combatants turned to him and said: "Well, my old gentleman, what think you of these things?" Marshall
responded with a "most eloquent and unanswerable
appeal." He talked for an hour, answering "every
argument urged against" the teachings of Jesus. "In
the whole lecture there was so much simplicity and
energy, pathos and sublimity, that not another word
was uttered." The listeners wondered who the old
man could be. Some thought him a preacher; and
great was their surprise when they learned afterwards that he was the Chief Justice of the United
States.[1]

His devotion to his wife illustrates his attitude
toward women in general, which was one of exalted
reverence and admiration. "He was an enthusiast
in regard to the domestic virtues," testifies Story.
"There was . . a romantic chivalry in his feelings,
which, though rarely displayed, except in the circle
of his most intimate friends, would there pour out
itself with the most touching tenderness." He loved
to dwell on the "excellences," "accomplishments,"
"talents," and "virtues" of women, whom he looked
upon as "the friends, the companions, and the
equals of man." He tolerated no wit at their expense, no fling, no sarcasm, no reproach. On no
phase of Marshall's character does Story place so

[1] This story was originally published in the *Winchester Republican*.
The incident is said to have occurred at McGuire's hotel in Win-
chester. The newspaper account is reproduced in the Charleston
(S.C.) edition (1845) of Howe's book, 275–76.

much emphasis as on his esteem for women.[1] Harriet Martineau, too, bears witness that "he maintained through life and carried to his grave, a reverence for woman as rare in its kind as in its degree."[2] "I have always believed that national character as well as happiness depends more on the female part of society than is generally imagined," writes Marshall in his ripe age to Thomas White.[3]

Commenting on Story's account, in his centennial oration on the first settlement of Salem, of the death of Lady Arbella Johnson, Marshall expresses his opinion of women thus: "I almost envy the occasion her sufferings and premature death have furnished for bestowing that well-merited eulogy on a sex which so far surpasses ours in all the amiable and attractive virtues of the heart, — in all those qualities which make up the sum of human happiness and transform the domestic fireside into an elysium. I read the passage to my wife who expressed such animated approbation of it as almost to excite fears for that exclusive admiration which husbands claim as their peculiar privilege Present my compliments to Mrs Story and say for me that a lady receives the highest compliment her husband can pay her when he expresses an exalted opinion of the sex, because the world will believe that it is formed on the model he sees at home."[4]

Ten children were born to John Marshall and

---

[1] Joseph Story in Dillon, III, 364–66.
[2] Martineau: *Retrospect of Western Travels*, I, 150.
[3] *North American Review*, XX, 444–45.
[4] Marshall to Story, Oct. 29, 1828, *Proceedings, Massachusetts Historical Society*, 2d Series, XIV, 337–38.

Mary Ambler, of whom six survived, five boys and one girl.[1] By 1815 only three of these remained at home; Jacquelin, twenty-eight years old, James Keith, fifteen, and Edward, ten years of age. John was in Harvard, where Marshall sent all his sons except Thomas, the eldest, who went to Princeton.[2] The daughter, Mary, Marshall's favorite child, had married Jacquelin B. Harvie and lived in Richmond not far from Marshall's house.[3] Four other children had died early.

"You ask," Marshall writes Story, "if Mrs Marshall and myself have ever lost a child. We have lost four, three of them bidding fairer for health and life than any that have survived them. One, a daughter about six or seven . . was one of the most fascinating children I ever saw. She was followed within a fortnight by a brother whose death was attended by a circumstance we can never forget.

"When the child was supposed to be dying I tore the distracted mother from the bedside. We soon afterwards heard a voice in the room which we considered as indicating the death of the infant. We believed him to be dead. [I went] into the room and found him still breathing. I returned [and] as the pang of his death had been felt by his mother and [I] was confident he must die, I concealed his being alive and prevailed on her to take refuge with her

[1] Thomas, born July 21, 1784; Jacquelin Ambler, born December 3, 1787; Mary, born September 17, 1795; John, born January 15, 1798; James Keith, born February 13, 1800; Edward Carrington, born January 13, 1805. (Paxton: *Marshall Family*, Genealogical Chart.)

[2] Edward Carrington was the only son to receive the degree of A.B. from Harvard (1826).

[3] Paxton, 100.

mother who lived the next door across an open square from her.

"The child lived two days, during which I was agonized with its condition and with the occasional hope, though the case was desperate, that I might enrapture his mother with the intelligence of his restoration to us. After the event had taken place his mother could not bear to return to the house she had left and remained with her mother a fortnight.

"I then addressed to her a letter in verse in which our mutual loss was deplored, our lost children spoken of with the parental feeling which belonged to the occasion, her affection for those which survived was appealed to, and her religious confidence in the wisdom and goodness of Providence excited. The letter closed with a pressing invitation to return to me and her children." [1]

All of Marshall's sons married, settled on various parts of the Fairfax estate, and lived as country gentlemen. Thomas was given the old homestead at Oak Hill, and there the Chief Justice built for his eldest son the large house adjacent to the old one where he himself had spent a year before joining the army under Washington.[2] To this spot Marshall went every year, visiting Thomas and his other sons who lived not far apart, seeing old friends, wandering along Goose Creek, over the mountains, and among the haunts where his first years were spent.

Here, of course, he was, in bearing and appearance, even less the head of the Nation's Judiciary than he

[1] Marshall to Story, June 26, 1831, *Proceedings, Mass. Hist. Soa* 2d Series, XIV, 344–46.

[2] See vol. I, 55–56, of this work.

was in Richmond or on the road to Raleigh. He was emphatically one of the people among whom he so-journed, familiar, interested, considerate, kindly and sociable to the last degree. Not one of his sons but showed more consciousness of his own importance than did John Marshall; not a planter of Fauquier, Warren, and Shenandoah Counties, no matter how poorly circumstanced, looked and acted less a Chief Justice of the United States. These characteristics, together with a peculiar generosity, made Marshall the most beloved man in Northern Virginia.

Once, when going from Richmond to Fauquier County, he overtook one of his Revolutionary com-rades. As the two rode on together, talking of their war-time experiences and of their present circum-stances, it came out that this now ageing friend of his youth was deeply in debt and about to lose all his possessions. There was, it appeared, a mortgage on his farm which would soon be foreclosed. After the Chief Justice had left the inn where they both had stopped for refreshments, an envelope was handed to his friend containing Marshall's check for the amount of the debt. His old comrade-in-arms quickly mounted his horse, overtook Marshall, and insisted upon returning the check. Marshall refused to take it back, and the two friends argued the mat-ter, which was finally compromised by Marshall's agreeing to take a lien upon the land. But this he never foreclosed.[1]

This anecdote is highly characteristic of Mar-shall. He was infinitely kind, infinitely considerate.

[1] Howe (Charleston, S.C., ed. of 1845), 266.

Bishop Meade, who knew him well, says that he "was a most conscientious man in regard to some things which others might regard as too trivial to be observed." On one of Meade's frequent journeys with Marshall between Fauquier County and the "lower country," they came to an impassable stretch of road. Other travelers had taken down a fence and gone through the adjoining plantation, and the Bishop was about to follow the same route. Marshall refused — "He said we had better go around, although each step was a plunge, adding that it was his duty, as one in office, to be very particular in regard to such things." [1]

When in Richmond the one sport in which he delighted was the pitching of quoits. Not when a lawyer was he a more enthusiastic or regular attendant of the meetings of the Quoit Club, or Barbecue Club, [2] under the trees at Buchanan's Spring on the outskirts of Richmond, than he was when at the height of his fame as Chief Justice of the United States. More personal descriptions of Marshall at these gatherings have come down to us than exist for any other phase of his life. Chester Harding, the artist, when painting Marshall's portrait during the summer of 1826, spent some time in the Virginia Capital, and attended one of the meetings of the Quoit Club. It was a warm day, and presently Marshall, then in his seventy-second year, was seen coming, his coat on his arm, fanning himself with his hat. Walking straight up to a bowl of mint julep, he poured a

[1] Meade, II, 222.
[2] Tyler: *Tyler*, I, 220; and see vol. II, 182-83, of this work.

tumbler full of the liquid, drank it off, said, "How
are you, gentlemen?" and fell to pitching quoits with
immense enthusiasm. When he won, says Harding, "the woods would ring with his triumphant
shout." [1]

James K. Paulding went to Richmond for the
purpose of talking to the Chief Justice and observ-
ing his daily life. He was more impressed by Marshall's gayety and unrestraint at the Quoit Club
than by anything else he noted. "The Chief-Justice
threw off his coat," relates Paulding, "and fell to work
with as much energy as he would have directed to
the decision of . . the conflicting jurisdiction of the
General and State Governments." During the game
a dispute arose between two players "as to the quoit
nearest the meg." Marshall was agreed upon as umpire. "The Judge bent down on one knee and with
a straw essayed the decision of this important question, . . frequently biting off the end of the straw"
for greater accuracy. [2]

The morning play over, the club dinner followed.
A fat pig, roasted over a pit of coals, cold meats,
melons, fruits, and vegetables, were served in the old
Virginia style. The usual drinks were porter, toddy, [3]
and the club punch made of "lemons, brandy, rum,
madeira, poured into a bowl one-third filled with ice

[1] White: *A Sketch of Chester Harding, Artist*, 195-96.
[2] *Lippincott's Magazine*, II, 624. Paulding makes this comment
on Marshall: "In his hours of relaxation he was as full of fun and as
natural as a child. He entered into the spirit of athletic exercises with
the ardor of youth; and at sixty-odd years of age was one of the best
quoit-players in Virginia." (*Ib.* 626.)
[3] *American Turf Register and Sporting Magazine* (1829), I, 41-42;
and see Mordecai, 188-89.

(no water), and sweetened."[1] In addition, champagne and other wines were sometimes provided.[2] At these meals none of the witty company equaled Marshall in fun-making; no laugh was so cheery and loud as his. Not more was John Marshall the chief of the accomplished and able men who sat with him on the Supreme Bench at Washington than, even in his advancing years, he was the leader of the convivial spirits who gathered to pitch quoits, drink julep and punch, tell stories, sing songs, make speeches, and play pranks under the trees of Richmond.

Marshall dearly loved, when at home, to indulge in the giving of big dinners to members of the bench and bar. In a wholly personal sense he was the best-liked man in Richmond. The lawyers and judges living there were particularly fond of him, and the Chief Justice thoroughly reciprocated their regard. Spencer Roane, Judge of the Virginia Court of Appeals, seems to have been the one enemy Marshall had in the whole city. Indeed, Roane and Jefferson appear to have been the only men anywhere who ever hated him personally. Even the testy George Hay reluctantly yielded to his engaging qualities. When at the head of the Virginia bar, Marshall had been one of those leading attorneys who gave the attractive dinners that were so notable and delightful a feature of life in Richmond. After he became Chief Justice, he continued this custom until his "lawyer dinners" became, among men, the principal social events of the place.

---

[1] Recipe for the Quoit Club punch, *Green Bag*, VIII, 482. This recipe was used for many years by the Richmond Light Infantry Blues.

[2] See vol. II, 183, of this work.

Many guests sat at Marshall's board upon these occasions. Among them were his own sons as well as those of some of his guests. These dinners were repetitions within doors of the Quoit Club entertainments, except that the food was more abundant and varied, and the cheering drinks were of better quality — for Marshall prided himself on this feature of hospitality, especially on his madeira, of which he was said to keep the best to be had in America. Wit and repartee, joke, story and song, speech and raillery, brought forth volleys of laughter and roars of applause until far into the morning hours.[1] Marshall was not only at the head of the table as host, but was the leader of the merriment.[2]

His labors as Chief Justice did not dull his delight in the reading of poetry and fiction, which was so keen in his earlier years.[3] At the summit of his career, when seventy-one years old, he read all of Jane Austen's works, and playfully reproved Story for failing to name her in a list of authors given in his Phi Beta Kappa oration at Harvard. "I was a little mortified," he wrote Story, "to find that you had not admitted the name of Miss Austen into your list of favorites. I had just finished reading her novels when I received your discourse, and was so much pleased with them that I looked in it for her name, and was rather disappointed at not finding it. Her flights are not lofty, she does not soar on eagle's wings, but she is pleasing, interesting, equable, and

[1] On these occasions Mrs. Marshall spent the nights at the house of her daughter or sister.

[2] For an extended description of Marshall's "lawyer dinners" see Terhune, 85-87.   [3] See vol. I, 44-45, 153-54, of this work.

yet amusing. I count on your making some apology
for this omission." [1]

Story himself wrote poetry, and Marshall often
asked for copies of his verses.[2] "The plan of life I
had formed for myself to be adopted after my retirement from office," he tells Story, "is to read
nothing but novels and poetry." [3] That this statement genuinely expressed his tastes is supported
by the fact that, among the few books which the
Chief Justice treasured, were the novels of Sir Walter Scott and an extensive edition of the British
poets.[4] While his chief intellectual pleasure was
the reading of fiction, Marshall liked poetry even
better; and he committed to memory favorite passages which he quoted as comment on passing incidents. Once when he was told that certain men had
changed their opinions as a matter of political expediency, he repeated Homer's lines:

"Ye gods, what havoc does ambition make
'Mong all your works." [5]

During the six or eight weeks that the Supreme
Court sat each year, Marshall was the same in manner and appearance in Washington as he was among
his neighbors in Richmond — the same in dress, in
habits, in every way. Once a practitioner sent his
little son to Marshall's quarters for some legal papers.
The boy was in awe of the great man. But the Chief
Justice, detecting the feelings of the lad, remarked:

[1] Marshall to Story, Nov. 26, 1826, Story, i, 506.

[2] Story to his wife, Feb. 26, 1832, ib. ii, 84.

[3] Marshall to Story, Sept. 30, 1829, *Proceedings, Mass. Hist. Soc.*
2d Series, xiv, 341.

[4] Statement of Miss Elizabeth Marshall of Leeds Manor to the
author.   [5] Meade, i, footnote to 99.

"Billy, I believe I can beat you playing marbles; come into the yard and we will have a game." Soon the Chief Justice of the United States and the urchin were hard at play.[1]

If he reached the court-room before the hour of convening court, he sat among the lawyers and talked and joked as if he were one of them;[2] and, judging from his homely, neglected clothing, an uninformed onlooker would have taken him for the least important of the company. Yet there was about him an unconscious dignity that prevented any from presuming upon his good nature, for Marshall inspired respect as well as affection. After their surprise and disappointment at his ill attire and want of impressiveness,[3] attorneys coming in contact with him were unfailingly captivated by his simplicity and charm.

It was thus that Joseph Story, when a very young lawyer, first fell under Marshall's spell. "I love his laugh," he wrote; "it is too hearty for an intriguer, — and his good temper and unwearied patience are equally agreeable on the bench and in the study."[4] And Marshall wore well. The longer and more intimately men associated with him, the greater their fondness for him. "I am in love with his character, positively in love," wrote Story after twenty-four

---

[1] *World's Work*, I, 395.

[2] Gustavus Schmidt in *Louisiana Law Journal* (1841), I, No. 1, 85–86. Mr. Schmidt's description is of Marshall in the court-room at Richmond when holding the United States Circuit Court at that place. Ticknor, Story, and others show that the same was true in Washington.

[3] Quincy: *Figures of the Past*, 242–43.

[4] Story to Fay, Feb. 25, 1808, Story, I, 166–67.

years of close and familiar contact.[1] He "rises . . with the nearest survey," again testified Story in a magazine article.[2]

When, however, the time came for him to open court, a transformation came over him. Clad in the robes of his great office, with the Associate Justices on either side of him, no king on a throne ever appeared more majestic than did John Marshall. The kindly look was still in his eye, the mildness still in his tones, the benignity in his features. But a gravity of bearing, a firmness of manner, a concentration and intentness of mind, seemed literally to take possession of the man, although he was, and appeared to be, as unconscious of the change as he was that there was anything unusual in his conduct when off the bench.[3]

Marshall said and did things that interested other people and caused them to talk about him. He was noted for his quick wit, and the bar was fond of repeating anecdotes about him. "Did you hear what the Chief Justice said the other day?" — and then the story would be told of a bright saying, a quick repartee, a picturesque incident. Chief Justice Gibson of Pennsylvania, when a young man, went to Marshall for advice as to whether he should accept a position offered him on the State Bench. The young attorney, thinking to flatter him, remarked that the Chief Justice had "reached the acme of judicial distinction." "Let me tell you what that

[1] Story to Martineau, Oct. 8, 1835, Story, II, 205.

[2] Ib. I, 522.

[3] Gustavus Schmidt in *Louisiana Law Journal* (1841), I, No. 1, 85–86.

means, young man," broke in Marshall. "The acme of judicial distinction means the ability to look a lawyer straight in the eyes for two hours and not hear a damned word he says." [1]

Wherever he happened to be, nothing pleased Marshall so much as to join a convivial party at dinner or to attend any sort of informal social gathering. On one occasion he went to the meeting of a club at Philadelphia, held in a room at a tavern across the hall from the bar. It was a rule of the club that every one present should make a rhyme upon a word suddenly given. As he entered, the Chief Justice observed two or three Kentucky colonels taking their accustomed drink. When Marshall appeared in the adjoining room, where the company was gathered, he was asked for an extemporaneous rhyme on the word "paradox." Looking across the hall, he quickly answered:

> "In the Blue Grass region,
> A 'Paradox' was born,
> The corn was full of kernels
> And the 'colonels' full of corn." [2]

But Marshall heartily disliked the formal society of the National Capital. He was, of course, often invited to dinners and receptions, but he was usually bored by their formality. Occasionally he would brighten his letters to his wife by short mention of some entertainment. "Since being in this place,"

---

[1] Related to the author by Mr. Sussex D. Davis of the Philadelphia bar.

[2] Related to the author by Thomas Marshall Smith of Baltimore, a descendant of Marshall. Mr. Smith says that this story has been handed down through three generations of his family.

he writes her, " I have been more in company than I wish. . . I have been invited to dine with the President with our own secretaries & with the minister of France & tomorrow I dine with the British minister. . . In the midst of these gay circles my mind is carried to my own fireside & to my beloved wife." [1]

Again: "Soon after dinner yesterday the French Chargé d'affaires called upon us with a pressing invitation to be present at a party given to the young couple, a gentleman of the French legation & the daughter of the secretary of the navy who are lately married. There was a most brilliant illumination which we saw and admired, & then we returned." [2] Of a dinner at the French Legation he writes his wife, it was "rather a dull party. Neither the minister nor his lady could speak English and I could not speak French. You may conjecture how far we were from being sociable. Yesterday I dined with M[r] Van Buren the secretary of State. It was a grand dinner and the secretary was very polite, but I was rather dull through the evening. I make a poor return for these dinners. I go to them with reluctance and am bad company while there. I hope we have seen the last, but I fear we must encounter one more. [3] With the exception of these parties my time was never passed with more uniformity. I rise early, pour [sic] over law cases, go to court and return at

[1] Marshall to his wife, Feb. 14, 1817, MS.
[2] Same to same, Jan. 4, 1823, MS.
[3] For excellent descriptions of Washington society during Marshall's period see the letters of Moss Kent, then a Representative in Congress. These MSS. are in the Library of Congress. Also see Story to his wife, Feb. 7, 1810, Story, I, 196.

the same hour and pass the evening in consultation
with the Judges." [1]

Chester Harding relates that, when he was in
Washington making a full-length portrait of the
Chief Justice,[2] Marshall arrived late for the sitting,
which had been fixed for eight o'clock in the evening.
He came without a hat. Congressman Storrs and
one or two other men, having seen Marshall, bare-
headed, hurrying by their inn with long strides, had
"followed, curious to know the cause of such a strange
appearance." But Marshall simply explained to the
artist that the consultation lasted longer than usual,
and that he had hurried off without his hat. When the
Chief Justice was about to go home, Harding offered
him a hat, but he said, "Oh, no! it is a warm night,
I shall not need one." [3]

No attorney practicing in the Supreme Court was
more unreserved in social conversation than was the
Chief Justice. Sometimes, indeed, on a subject that
appealed to him, Marshall would do all the talking,
which, for some reason, would occasionally be quite
beyond the understanding of his hearer. Of one such
exhibition Fisher Ames remarked to Samuel Dexter:
"I have not understood a word of his argument for

[1] Marshall to his wife, Jan. 30, 1831, MS.

[2] This was painted for the Boston Athenæum. See frontispiece in
vol. III. The other portrait by Harding, painted in Richmond (see
supra, 76), was given to Story who presented it to the Harvard Law
School.

[3] White: *Sketch of Chester Harding*, 194–96.

For the Chief Justice to lose or forget articles of clothing was nothing unusual. "He lost a coat, when he dined at the Secretary of the
Navy's," writes Story who had been making a search for Marshall's
missing garment. (Story to Webster, March 18, 1828, Story MSS.
Mass. Hist. Soc.)

half an hour." "And I," replied the leader of the Massachusetts bar, "have been out of my depth for an hour and a half." [1]

The members of the Supreme Court made life as pleasant for themselves as they could during the weeks they were compelled to remain in "this dismal" place, as Daniel Webster described the National Capital. Marshall and the Associate Justices all lived together at one boarding-house, and thus became a sort of family. "We live very harmoniously and familiarly," [2] writes Story, one year after his appointment. "My brethren are very interesting men," he tells another friend. We "live in the most frank and unaffected intimacy. Indeed, we are all united as one, with a mutual esteem which makes even the labors of Jurisprudence light." [3]

Sitting about a single table at their meals, or gathered in the room of one of them, these men talked over the cases before them. Not only did they "moot every question as" the arguments proceeded in court, but by "familiar conferences at our lodgings often come to a very quick, and . . accurate opinion, in a few hours," relates that faithful chronicler of their daily life, Joseph Story. [4] Story appears to have been even more impressed by the comradery of the members of the Supreme Court than by the difficulty of the cases they had to decide.

None of them ever took his wife with him to Washington, and this fact naturally made the personal relations of the Justices peculiarly close. "The

---

[1] Story, II, 504–05.   [2] Story to Williams, Feb. 16, 1812, ib. I, 214.
[3] Story to Fay, Feb. 24, 1812, ib. 215.   [4] Ib.

Judges here live with perfect harmony," Story reiterates, "and as agreeably as absence from friends and from families could make our residence. Our intercourse is perfectly familiar and unconstrained, and our social hours when undisturbed with the labors of law, are passed in gay and frank conversation, which at once enlivens and instructs." [1]

This "gay and frank conversation" of Marshall and his associates covered every subject — the methods, manners, and even dress of counsel who argued before them, the fortunes of public men, the trend of politics, the incident of the day, the gossip of society. "Two of the Judges are widowers," records Story, "and of course objects of considerable attraction among the ladies of the city. We have fine sport at their expense, and amuse our leisure with some touches at match-making. We have already ensnared one of the Judges, and he is now (at the age of forty-seven) violently affected with the tender passion." [2]

Thus Marshall, in his relation with his fellow occupants of the bench, was at the head of a family as much as he was Chief of a court. Although the discussion of legal questions occurred continuously at the boarding-house, each case was much more fully examined in the consultation room at the Capitol. There the court had a regular "consultation day" devoted exclusively to the cases in hand. Yet, even on these occasions, all was informality, and wit and humor brightened the tediousness. These "consul-

[1] Story to his wife, March 5, 1812, Story, I, 217.
[2] Same to same, March 12, 1812, *ib.* 219.

tations" lasted throughout the day and sometimes
into the night; and the Justices took their meals
while the discussions proceeded. Amusing incidents,
some true, some false, and others a mixture, were related of these judicial meetings. One such story
went the rounds of the bar and outlived the period
of Marshall's life.

"We are great ascetics, and even deny ourselves
wine except in wet weather," Story dutifully informed his wife. "What I say about the wine gives
you our rule; but it does sometimes happen that the
Chief Justice will say to me, when the cloth is removed, 'Brother Story, step to the window and see
if it does not look like rain.' And if I tell him that
the sun is shining brightly, Judge Marshall will sometimes reply, 'All the better, for our jurisdiction extends over so large a territory that the doctrine of
chances makes it certain that it must be raining
somewhere.'" [1]

When, as sometimes happened, one of the Associate Justices displeased a member of the bar, Marshall would soothe the wounded feelings of the lawyer. Story once offended Littleton W. Tazewell of
Virginia by something said from the bench. "On
my return from court yesterday," the Chief Justice
hastened to write the irritated Virginian, "I informed Mr Story that you had been much hurt at an
expression used in the opinion he had delivered in the
case of the Palmyra. He expressed equal surprize
and regret on the occasion, and declared that the

---

[1] *Magazine of American History*, xii, 69; and see Quincy: *Figures
of the Past*, 189–90. This tale, gathering picturesqueness as it was
passed by word of mouth during many years, had its variations.

words which had given offense were not used or understood by him in an offensive sense. He assented without hesitation to such modification of them as would render them in your view entirely unexceptionable." [1]

As Chief Justice, Marshall shrank from publicity, while printed adulation aggravated him. "I hope to God they will let me alone 'till I am dead," he exclaimed, when he had reached that eminence where writers sought to portray his life and character. [2]

He did, however, appreciate the recognition given from time to time by colleges and learned societies. In 1802 Princeton conferred upon him the honorary degree of LL.D.; in 1806 he received the same degree from Harvard and from the University of Pennsylvania in 1815. In 1809, as we have seen, he was elected a corresponding member of the Massachusetts Historical Society; on January 24, 1804, he was made a member of the American Academy of Arts and Sciences; and, in 1830, was elected to the American Philosophical Society. All these honors Marshall valued highly.

This, then, was the man who presided over the Supreme Court of the United States when the decisions of that tribunal developed the National powers of the Constitution and gave stability to our National life. His control of the court was made so easy for the Justices that they never resented it; often, perhaps, they did not realize it. The influence of his strong, deep, clear mind was powerfully aided

[1] Marshall to Tazewell, Jan. 20, 1827, MS.
[2] Wirt to Delaplaine, Nov. 5, 1818, Kennedy: *Memoirs of the Life of William Wirt*, II, 85.

by his engaging personality. To agree with him was a pleasure.

Marshall's charm was as great as his intellect; he was never irritable; his placidity was seldom ruffled; not often was his good nature disturbed. His "great suavity, or rather calmness of manner, cannot readily be conceived," testifies George Bancroft.[1] The sheer magnitude of his views was, in itself, captivating, and his supremely lucid reasoning removed the confusion which more complex and subtle minds would have created in reaching the same conclusion. The elements of his mind and character were such, and were so combined, that it was both hard and unpleasant to differ with him, and both easy and agreeable to follow his lead.

Above all other influences upon his associates on the bench, and, indeed, upon everybody who knew him, was the sense of trustworthiness, honor, and uprightness he inspired.[2] Perhaps no public man ever stood higher in the esteem of his contemporaries for noble personal qualities than did John Marshall.

When reviewing his constructive work and marveling at his influence over his judicial associates, we must recall, even at the risk of iteration, the figure revealed by his daily life and habits — "a man who is tall to awkwardness, with a large head of

---

[1] Bancroft to his wife, Jan. 23, 1832, Howe: *Life and Letters of George Bancroft*, I, 202.

[2] Even Jefferson, in his bitterest attacks, never intimated anything against Marshall's integrity; and Spencer Roane, when assailing with great violence the opinion of the Chief Justice in M'Culloch *vs.* Maryland (see *infra*, chap. VI), paid a high tribute to the purity of his personal character.

hair, which looked as if it had not been lately tied or combed, and with dirty boots," [1] a body that seemed "without proportion," and arms and legs that "dangled from each other and looked half dislocated," dressed in clothes apparently "gotten from some antiquated slop-shop of second-hand raiment .. the coat and breeches cut for nobody in particular." [2] But we must also think of such a man as possessed of "style and tones in conversation uncommonly mild, gentle, and conciliating." [3] We must think of his hearty laughter, his "imperturbable temper," [4] his shyness with strangers, his quaint humor, his hilarious unreserve with friends and convivial jocularity when with intimates, his cordial warm-heartedness, unassuming simplicity and sincere gentleness to all who came in contact with him — a man without "an atom of gall in his whole composition." [5] We must picture this distinctive American character among his associates of the bench in the Washington boarding-house no less than in court, his luminous mind guiding them, his irresistible personality drawing from them a real and lasting affection. We must bear in mind the trust and confidence which so powerfully impressed those who knew the man. We must imagine a person very much like Abraham Lincoln.

[1] Ticknor to his father, Feb. 1, 1815, Ticknor: *Life, Letters, and Journals of George Ticknor*, I, 33.

[2] Description from personal observation, as quoted in Van Santvoord: *Lives and Judicial Services of the Chief Justices*, footnote to 363.

[3] Ticknor to his father, as cited in note 1, *supra*.

[4] *Memoirs of John Quincy Adams*: Adams, IX, 243.

[5] Wirt to Carr, Dec. 30, 1827, Kennedy, 240. For Story's estimate of Marshall's personality see Dillon, III, 363–66.

Indeed, the resemblance of Marshall to Lincoln is striking. Between no two men in American history is there such a likeness. Physically, intellectually, and in characteristics, Marshall and Lincoln were of the same type. Both were very tall men, slender, loose-jointed, and awkward, but powerful and athletic; and both fond of sport. So alike were they, and so identical in their negligence of dress and their total unconsciousness of, or indifference to, convention, that the two men, walking side by side, might well have been taken for brothers.

Both Marshall and Lincoln loved companionship with the same heartiness, and both had the same social qualities. They enjoyed fun, jokes, laughter, in equal measure, and had the same keen appreciation of wit and humor. Their mental qualities were the same. Each man had the gift of going directly to the heart of any subject; while the same lucidity of statement marked each of them. Their style, the simplicity of their language, the peculiar clearness of their logic, were almost identical. Notwithstanding their straightforwardness and amplitude of mind, both had a curious subtlety. Some of Marshall's opinions and Lincoln's state papers might have been written by the same man. The "Freeholder" questions and answers in Marshall's congressional campaign, and those of Lincoln's debate with Douglas, are strikingly similar in method and expression.

Each had a genius for managing men; and Marshall showed the precise traits in dealing with the members of the Supreme Court that Lincoln displayed in the Cabinet.

Both were born in the South, each on the eve of a great epoch in American history when a new spirit was awakening in the hearts of the people. Although Southern-born, both Marshall and Lincoln sympathized with and believed in the North; and yet their manners and instinct were always those of the South. Marshall was given advantages that Lincoln never had; but both were men of the people, were brought up among them, and knew them thoroughly. Lincoln's outlook upon life, however, was that of the humblest citizen; Marshall's that of the well-placed and prosperous. Neither was well educated, but each acquired, in different ways, a command of excellent English and broad, plain conceptions of government and of life. Neither was a learned man, but both created the materials for learning.

Marshall and Lincoln were equally good politicians; but, although both were conservative in their mental processes, Marshall lost faith in the people's steadiness, moderation, and self-restraint; and came to think that impulse rather than wisdom was too often the temporary moving power in the popular mind, while the confidence of Lincoln in the good sense, righteousness, and self-control of the people became greater as his life advanced. If, with these distinctions, Abraham Lincoln were, in imagination, placed upon the Supreme Bench during the period we are now considering, we should have a good idea of John Marshall, the Chief Justice of the United States.

note It is, then, largely the personality of John Marshall that explains the hold, as firm and persistent as it was gentle and soothing, maintained by him upon the Associate Justices of the Supreme Court; and it is this, too, that enables us to understand his immense popularity with the bar — a fact only second in importance to the work he had to do, and to his influence upon the men who sat with him on the bench.

For the lawyers who practiced before the Supreme Court at this period were most helpful to Marshall.[1] Many of them were men of wide and accurate learning, and nearly all of them were of the first order of ability. No stronger or more brilliant bar ever was arrayed before any bench than that which displayed its wealth of intellect and resources to Marshall and his associates.[2] This assertion is strong, but wholly justified. Oratory of the finest quality, though of the old rhetorical kind, filled the courtroom with admiring spectators, and entertained Marshall and the other Justices, as much as the solid reasoning illuminated their minds, and the exhaustive learning informed them.

[1] "He was solicitous to hear arguments, and not to decide causes without hearing them. And no judge ever profited more by them. No matter whether the subject was new or old; familiar to his thoughts or remote from them; buried under a mass of obsolete learning, or developed for the first time yesterday — whatever was its nature, he courted argument, nay, he demanded it." (Story in Dillon, III, 377; and see vol. II, 177–80, of this work.)

[2] See Story's description of Harper, Duponceau, Rawle, Dallas, Ingersoll, Lee, and Martin (Story to Fay, Feb. 16, 1808, Story, I, 162–64); and of Pinkney (notes *supra*); also see Warren: *History of the American Bar*, 257–63. We must remember, too, that Webster, Hopkinson, Emmet, Wirt, Ogden, Clay, and others of equal ability and accomplishments, practiced before the Supreme Court when Marshall was Chief Justice.

Marshall encouraged extended arguments; often demanded them. Frequently a single lawyer would speak for two or three days. No limit of time was put upon counsel.[1] Their reputation as speakers as well as their fame as lawyers, together with the throngs of auditors always present, put them on their mettle. Rhetoric adorned logic; often encumbered it. A conflict between such men as William Pinkney, Luther Martin of Maryland, Samuel Dexter of Massachusetts, Thomas Addis Emmet of New York, William Wirt of Virginia, Joseph Hopkinson of Pennsylvania, Jeremiah Mason of New Hampshire, Daniel Webster, Henry Clay, and others of scarcely less distinction, was, in itself, an event. These men, and indeed all the members of the bar, were Marshall's friends as well as admirers.

The appointment of Story to the Supreme Bench was, like the other determining circumstances in Marshall's career, providential.

Few characters in American history are more attractive than the New England lawyer and publicist who, at the age of thirty-two, took his place at Marshall's side on the Supreme Bench. Hand-

[1] Story relates that a single case was argued for nine days. (Story to Fay, Feb. 16, 1808, Story, I, 162.)

In the Charlestown Bridge case, argued in 1831, the opening counsel on each side occupied three days. (Story to Ashmun, March 10, 1831, ib. II, 51.)

Four years later Story writes: "We have now a case .. which has been under argument eight days, and will probably occupy five more." (Story to Fay, March 2, 1835, ib. 193.)

In the lower courts the arguments were even longer. "This is the fourteenth day since this argument was opened. Pinkney .. promised to speak only two hours and a half. He has now spoken two days, and is, at this moment, at it again for the third day." (Wirt to his wife, April 7, 1821, Kennedy, II, 119.)

some, vivacious, impressionable, his mind was a storehouse of knowledge, accurately measured and systematically arranged. He read everything, forgot nothing. His mental appetite was voracious, and he had a very passion for research. His industry was untiring, his memory unfailing. He supplied exactly the accomplishment and toilsomeness that Marshall lacked. So perfectly did the qualities and attainments of these two men supplement one another that, in the work of building the American Nation, Marshall and Story may be considered one and the same person.

Where Marshall was leisurely, Story was eager. If the attainments of the Chief Justice were not profuse, those of his young associate were opulent. Marshall detested the labor of investigating legal authorities; Story delighted in it. The intellect of the older man was more massive and sure; but that of the youthful Justice was not far inferior in strength, or much less clear and direct in its operation. Marshall steadied Story while Story enriched Marshall. Each admired the other, and between them grew an affection like that of father and son.

Story's father, Elisha Story, was a member of the Republican Party, a rare person among wealthy and educated men in Massachusetts at the time Jefferson founded that political organization. The son tells us that he "naturally imbibed the same opinions," which were so reprobated that not "more than four or five lawyers in the whole state . . *dared* avow themselves republicans. The very name was odious."[1]

---

[1] Story, I, 96.

Joseph Story

Joseph Story was born in Marblehead, Massachusetts, September 18, 1779, one of a family of eighteen
children, seven by a first wife and eleven by a second.
He was the eldest son of the second wife, who had
been a Miss Pedrick, the daughter of a rich merchant and shipowner.[1]

No young member of the Massachusetts bar
equaled Joseph Story in intellectual gifts and acquirements. He was a graduate of Harvard, and few
men anywhere had a broader or more accurate education. His personality was winning and full of charm.
Yet, when he began practice at Salem, he was "persecuted" with "extreme . . virulence" because of his
political opinions.[2] He became so depressed by what
he calls "the petty prejudices and sullen coolness of
New England, . . bigoted in opinion and satisfied in
forms," where Federalism had "persecuted . . [him]
unrelentingly for . . [his] political principles," that
he thought seriously of going to Baltimore to live
and practice his profession. He made headway,
however, in spite of opposition; and, when the growing Republican Party, "the whole" of which he says
were his "warm advocates,"[3] secured the majority
of his district, Story was sent to Congress. "I was
. . of course a supporter of the administration of
Mr. Jefferson and Mr. Madison," although not "a

[1] Story, 1, 2. Elisha Story is said to have been one of the "Indians" who threw overboard the tea at Boston; and he fought at
Lexington. When the Revolution got under way, he entered the
American Army as a surgeon and served for about two years, when
he resigned because of his disgust with the management of the med-
ical department. (Ib.)

[2] Story to Duval, March 30, 1803, ib. 102.

[3] Story to Williams, June 6, 1805, ib. 105–06.

mere slave to the opinions of either." In exercising what he terms his "independent judgment," [1] Story favored the repeal of the Embargo, and so earned, henceforth, the lasting enmity of Jefferson. [2]

Because of his recognized talents, and perhaps also because of the political party to which he belonged, he was employed to go to Washington as attorney for the New England and Mississippi Company in the Yazoo controversy. [3] It was at this period that the New England Federalist leaders began to cultivate him. They appreciated his ability, and the assertion of his "independent principles" was to their liking. Harrison Gray Otis was quick to advise that seasoned politician, Robert Goodloe Harper, of the change he thought observable in Story, and the benefit of winning his regard. "He is a young man of talents, who commenced Democrat a few years since and was much fondled by his party," writes Otis. "He discovered however too much sentiment and honor to go *all lengths* . . and a little attention from the right sort of people will be very useful to him & to us." [4]

The wise George Cabot gave Pickering the same hint when Story made one of his trips to Washington on the Yazoo business. "Though he is a man whom the Democrats support," says Cabot, "I have seldom if ever met with one of sounder mind on the principal points of national policy. He is well worthy the civil attention of the most respectable Federalists." [5]

[1] Story, I, 128.　　[2] At first, Story supported the Embargo.
[3] See vol. III, chap. X, of this work.
[4] Otis to Harper, April 19, 1807, Morison: *Otis*, I, 283.
[5] Cabot to Pickering, Jan. 28, 1808, Lodge: *Cabot*, 377.

It was while in the Capital, as attorney before Congress and the Supreme Court in the Georgia land controversy, that Story, then twenty-nine years old, met Marshall; and impulsively wrote of his delight in the "hearty laugh," "patience," consideration, and ability of the Chief Justice. On this visit to Washington the young Massachusetts lawyer took most of his meals with the members of the Supreme Court.[1] At that time began the devotion of Joseph Story to John Marshall which was to prove so helpful to both for more than a generation, and so influential upon the Republic for all time.

That Story, while in Washington, had copiously expressed his changing opinions, as well as his disapproval of Jefferson's Embargo, is certain; for he was "a very great talker,"[2] and stated his ideas with the volubility of his extremely exuberant nature. "At this time, as in after life," declares Story's son, "he was remarkable for fulness and fluency of conversation. It poured out from his mind . . sparkling, and exhaustless. Language was as a wide open sluice, through which every feeling and thought rushed forth. . . It would be impossible to give an idea of his conversational powers."[3]

It was not strange, then, that Jefferson, who was eager for all gossip and managed to learn everything that happened, or was said to have happened, in Washington, heard of Story's association with the Federalists, his unguarded talk, and especially his admiration for the Chief Justice. It was plain to

[1] Story to Fay, Feb. 16, 1808, Story, I, 162.
[2] Moss Kent to James Kent, Feb. 1, 1817, Kent MSS. Lib. Cong.
[3] Story, I, 140.

Jefferson that such a person would never resist Marshall's influence.

In Jefferson's mind existed another objection to Story which may justly be inferred from the situation in which he found himself when the problem arose of filling the place on the Supreme Bench vacated by the death of Justice Cushing. Story had made a profound study of the law of real estate; and, young though he was, no lawyer in America equaled him, and few in England surpassed him, in the intricate learning of that branch of legal science. This fact was well known to the bar at Washington as well as to that of Massachusetts. Therefore, the thought of Story on the Supreme Bench, and under Marshall's influence, made Jefferson acutely uncomfortable; for the former President was then engaged in a lawsuit involving questions of real estate which, if decided against him, would, as he avowed, ruin him. This lawsuit was the famous Batture litigation. It was this predicament that led Jefferson to try to control the appointment of the successor to Cushing, whose death he declared to be "a Godsend" [1] to him personally; and also to dictate the naming of the district judge at Richmond to the vacancy caused by the demise of Judge Cyrus Griffin.

In the spring of 1810, Edward Livingston, formerly of New York and then of New Orleans, brought suit in the United States Court for the District of Virginia against Thomas Jefferson for damages to the amount of one hundred thousand dollars.

[1] Jefferson to Gallatin, Sept. 27, 1810, *Works:* Ford, XI, footnote to 152–54.

This was the same Livingston who in Congress had
been the Republican leader in the House when Marshall was a member of that body.[1] Afterwards he
was appointed United States Attorney for the District of New York and then became Mayor of that
city. During the yellow fever epidemic that scourged
New York in 1803, Livingston devoted himself to
the care of the victims of the plague, leaving the
administration of the Mayor's office to a trusted
clerk. In time Livingston, too, was stricken. During his illness his clerk embezzled large sums of the
public money. The Mayor was liable and, upon his
recovery, did not attempt to evade responsibility,
but resigned his office and gave all his property to
make good the defalcation. A heavy amount, however, still remained unpaid; and the discharge of
this obligation became the ruling purpose of Livingston's life until, twenty years afterward, he accomplished his object.

His health regained, Livingston went to New
Orleans to seek fortune anew. There he soon became
the leader of the bar. When Wilkinson set up his
reign of terror in that city, it was Edward Livingston
who swore out writs of habeas corpus for those ille-
gally imprisoned and, in general, was the most vigorous as well as the ablest of those who opposed Wilkinson's lawless and violent measures.[2] Jefferson
had been displeased that Livingston had not shown
more enthusiasm for him, when, in 1801, the Federalists had tried to elect Burr to the Presidency,

[1] See vol. II, 461–74, of this work.
[2] See vol. III, chap. VI, of this work.

and bitterly resented Livingston's interference with
Wilkinson's plans to "suppress treason" in New
Orleans.

One John Gravier, a lifelong resident of that city,
had inherited from his brother Bertrand certain real
estate abutting the river. Between this and the
water the current had deposited an immense quantity of alluvium. The question of the title to this
river-made land had never been raised, and everybody used it as a sort of common wharf front. Alert
for opportunities to make money with which fully to
discharge the defalcation in the New York Mayor's
office, Livingston investigated the rightful ownership
of the batture, as the alluvial deposit was termed;
satisfied himself that the title was in Gravier; gave
an opinion to that effect, and brought suit for the
property as Gravier's attorney.[1] While the trial of
Aaron Burr was in progress in Richmond, the Circuit Court in New Orleans rendered judgment in
favor of Gravier,[2] who then conveyed half of his
rights to his attorney, apparently as a fee for the
recovery of the batture.

Livingston immediately began to improve his
property, whereupon the people became excited and
drove away his workmen. Governor Claiborne refused to protect him and referred the whole matter
to Jefferson. The President did not direct the Attorney-General to bring suit for the possession of the
batture — the obvious and the legal form of procedure. Indeed, the title to the property was not so
much as examined. Jefferson did not even take into

[1] Hunt: *Life of Edward Livingston*, 138.　　　　[2] *Ib.* 140.

consideration the fact that, if Livingston was not the rightful owner of the batture, it might belong to the City of New Orleans. He merely assumed that it was National property; and, hastily acting under a law against squatters on lands belonging to the United States, he directed Secretary of State Madison to have all persons removed from the disputed premises. Accordingly, the United States Marshal was ordered to eject the "intruder" and his laborers. This was done; but Livingston told his men to return to their work and secured an injunction against the Marshal from further molesting them. That official ignored the order of the court and again drove the laborers off the batture.

Livingston begged the President to submit the controversy to arbitration or to judicial decision, but Jefferson was deaf to his pleas. The distracted lawyer appealed to Congress for relief.[1] That body ignored his petition.[2] He then brought suit against the Marshal in New Orleans for the recovery of his property. Soon afterward he brought another in Virginia against Jefferson for one hundred thousand dollars damages. Such, in brief outline, was the beginning of the famous "Batture Controversy," in which Jefferson and Livingston waged a war of pamphlets for years.

When he learned that Livingston had begun action against him in the Federal court at Richmond, Jefferson was much alarmed. In anticipation of the death of Judge Cyrus Griffin, Governor John Tyler

[1] *Annals*, 10th Cong. 2d Sess. 702.

[2] *Annals*, 11th Cong. 1st and 2d Sess. 323, 327–49, 418–19, 1373, 1617–18, 1694–1702.

had written Jefferson that, while he "never did apply for an office," yet "Judge Griffin is in a low state of health, and holds my old office." Tyler continues: "I really hope the President will chance to think of me . . in case of accidents, and if an opportunity offers, lay me down softly on a bed of *roses in my latter days*." He condemns Marshall for his opposition to the War of 1812, and especially for his reputed statement that Great Britain had done nothing to justify armed retaliation on our part.[1] "Is it possible," asks Tyler, "that a man who can assert this, can have any true sense of sound veracity? And yet these sort of folks retain their stations and consequence in life."[2]

Immediately Jefferson wrote to President Madison: "From what I can learn Griffin cannot stand it long, and really the state has suffered long enough by having such a cypher in so important an office, and infinitely the more from the want of any counterpoint to the rancorous hatred which Marshall bears to the government of his country, & from the cunning & sophistry within which he is able to enshroud himself. It will be difficult to find a character of firmness enough to preserve his independence on the same bench with Marshall. Tyler, I am certain, would do it. . . A milk & water character . . would be seen as a calamity. Tyler having been the former state judge of that court too, and removed to make way for so wretched a fool as Griffin,[3] has a kind of right of reclamation."

[1] See *supra*, 25, 35–41.
[2] Tyler to Jefferson, May 12, 1810, Tyler: *Tyler*, I, 246–47.
[3] Cyrus Griffin was educated in England; was a member of the

Jefferson gives other reasons for the appointment of Tyler, and then addresses Madison thus: "You have seen in the papers that Livingston has served a writ on me, stating damages at 100,000. D... I shall soon look into my papers to make a state of the case to enable them to plead." Jefferson hints broadly that he may have to summon as witnesses his "associates in the proceedings," one of whom was Madison himself.

He concludes this astounding letter in these words: "It is a little doubted that his [Livingston's] knolege [*sic*] of Marshall's character has induced him to bring this action. His twistifications of the law in the case of Marbury, in that of Burr, & the late Yazoo case shew how dexterously he can reconcile law to his personal biasses: and nobody seems to doubt that he is ready prepared to decide that Livingston's right to the batture is unquestionable, and that I am bound to pay for it with my private fortune." [1]

The next day Jefferson wrote Tyler that he had "laid it down as a law" to himself "never to embarrass the President with any solicitations." Yet, in Tyler's case, says Jefferson, "I .. have done it with all my heart, and in the full belief that I serve him

first Legislature of Virginia after the Declaration of Independence; was a delegate to the Continental-Congress in 1778–81, and again in 1787–88, and was President of that body during the last year of his service. He was made President of the Supreme Court of Admiralty, and held that office until the court was abolished. When the Constitution was adopted, and Washington elected President, one of his first acts, after the passage of the Ellsworth Judiciary Law, was to appoint Judge Griffin to the newly created office of Judge of the United States Court for the District of Virginia. It is thus evident that Jefferson's statement was not accurate.

[1] Jefferson to Madison, May 25, 1810, *Works*: Ford, xi, 139–41.

and the public in urging the appointment." For, Jefferson confides to the man who, in case Madison named him, would, with Marshall, hear the suit, "we have long enough suffered under the base prostitution of the law to party passions in one judge, and the imbecility of another.

"In the hands of one [Marshall] the law is nothing more than an ambiguous text, to be explained by his sophistry into any meaning which may subserve his personal malice. Nor can any milk-and-water associate maintain his own independence, and by a firm pursuance of what the law really is, extend its protection to the citizens or the public. . . And where you cannot induce your colleague to do what is right, you will be firm enough to hinder him from doing what is wrong, and by opposing sense to sophistry, leave the juries free to follow their own judgment." [1]

Upon the death of Judge Griffin in the following December, John Tyler was appointed to succeed him.

On September 13, 1810, William Cushing, Associate Justice of the Supreme Court, died. Only three Federalists now remained on the Supreme Bench, Samuel Chase, Bushrod Washington, and John Marshall. The other Justices, William Johnson of South Carolina, Brockholst Livingston of New York, and Thomas Todd of Kentucky, were Republicans, appointed by Jefferson. The selection of Cushing's successor would give the majority of the court to the Republican Party for the first time since its organization.

[1] Jefferson to Tyler, May 26, 1810, Tyler: *Tyler*, i, 247–48; also *Works:* Ford, xi, footnote to 141–43.

That Madison would fill the vacancy by one of his
own following was certain; but this was not enough
to satisfy Jefferson, who wanted to make sure that
the man selected was one who would not fall under
Marshall's baleful influence. If Griffin did not die in
time, Jefferson's fate in the batture litigation would
be in Marshall's hands.

Should Griffin be polite enough to breathe his
last promptly and Tyler be appointed in season, still
Jefferson would not feel safe — the case might go
to the jury, and who could tell what their verdict
would be under Marshall's instructions? Even Tyler
might not be able to "hinder" Marshall "from wrong
doing"; for nothing was more probable than that,
no matter what the issue of the case might be, it
would be carried to the Supreme Court if any ground
for appeal could be found. Certainly Jefferson would
take it there if the case should go against him. It was
vital, therefore, that the latest vacancy on the Supreme Bench should also be filled by a man on whom
Jefferson could depend.

The new Justice must come from New England,
Cushing having presided over that circuit. Republican lawyers there, fit for the place, were at that
time extremely hard to find. Jefferson had been
corresponding about the batture case with Gallatin,
who had been his Secretary of the Treasury and continued in that office under Madison. The moment
he learned of Cushing's death, Jefferson wrote to
Gallatin in answer to a letter from that able man,
admitting that "the Batture . . could not be within
the scope of the law . . against squatters," under

color of which Livingston had been forcibly ousted from that property. Jefferson adds: "I should so adjudge myself; yet I observe many opinions otherwise, and in defence against a spadassin it is lawful to use all weapons." The case is complex; still no unbiased man "can doubt what the issue of the case ought to be. What it will be, no one can tell.

"The judge's [Marshall's] inveteracy is profound, and his mind of that gloomy malignity which will never let him forego the opportunity of satiating it on a victim. His decisions, his instructions to a jury, his allowances and disallowances and garblings of evidence, must all be subjects of appeal. . . And to whom is my appeal? From the judge in Burr's case to himself and his associate judges in the case of Marbury v. Madison.

"Not exactly, however. I observe old Cushing is dead. . . The event is a fortunate one, and so timed as to be a Godsend to me. I am sure its importance to the nation will be felt, and the occasion employed to complete the great operation they have so long been executing, by the appointment of a decided Republican, with nothing equivocal about him. But who will it be?"

Jefferson warmly recommends Levi Lincoln, his former Attorney-General. Since the new Justice must come from New England, "can any other bring equal qualifications? . . I know he was not deemed a profound common lawyer; but was there ever a profound common lawyer known in one of the Eastern States? There never was, nor never can be, one from those States. . . Mr. Lincoln is . . as learned in their laws as any one they have." [1]

After allowing time for Gallatin to carry this message to the President, Jefferson wrote directly to Madison. He congratulates him on "the revocation of the French decrees"; abuses Great Britain for her "principle" of "the exclusive right to the sea by conquest"; and then comes to the matter of the vacancy on the Supreme Bench.

"Another circumstance of congratulation is the death of Cushing," which "gives an opportunity of closing the reformation [the Republican triumph of 1800] by a successor of unquestionable republican principles." Jefferson suggests Lincoln. "Were he out of the way," then Gideon Granger ought to be chosen, "tho' I am sensible that J.[ohn] R.[andolph] has been able to lessen the confidence of many in him.[2] . . As the choice must be of a New Englander, . . I confess I know of none but these two characters." Of course there was Joseph Story, but he is "unquestionably a tory," and "too young." [3]

Madison strove to follow Jefferson's desires. Cushing's place was promptly offered to Lincoln, who de-

[1] Jefferson to Gallatin, Sept. 27, 1810, *Works:* Ford, xi, footnote to 152–54.

[2] Gideon Granger, as Jefferson's Postmaster-General, had lobbied on the floor of the House for the Yazoo Bill, offering government contracts for votes. He was denounced by Randolph in one of the most scathing arraignments ever heard in Congress. (See vol. iii, 578–79, of this work.)

[3] Jefferson to Madison, Oct. 15, 1810, *Works:* Ford, xi, 150–52. Granger was an eager candidate for the place, and had asked Jefferson's support. In assuring him that it was given, Jefferson tells Granger of his "esteem & approbation," and adds that the appointment of "a firm unequivocating republican" is vital. (Jefferson to Granger, Oct. 22, 1810, *ib.* footnote to 155.)

clined it because of approaching blindness. Granger,
of course, was impossible — the Senate would not
have confirmed him. So Alexander Wolcott, "an
active Democratic politician of Connecticut," of
mediocre ability and "rather dubious . . character," [1]
was nominated; but the Senate rejected him. It
seemed impossible to find a competent lawyer in
New England who would satisfy Jefferson's requirements. John Quincy Adams, who had deserted the
Federalist Party and acted with the Republicans,
and who was then Minister to Russia, was appointed
and promptly confirmed. Jefferson himself had not
denounced Marshall so scathingly as had Adams in
his report to the Senate on the proposed expulsion
of Senator John Smith of Ohio.[2] It was certain that
he would not, as Associate Justice, be controlled
by the Chief Justice. But Adams preferred to continue in his diplomatic post, and refused the appointment.

Thus Story became the only possible choice. After
all, he was still believed to be a Republican by everybody except Jefferson and the few Federalist leaders
who had been discreetly cultivating him. At least
his appointment would not be so bad as the selection
of an out-and-out Federalist. On November 18,
1811, therefore, Joseph Story was made an Associate Justice of the Supreme Court of the United
States. In Massachusetts his appointment "was
ridiculed and condemned." [3]

Although Jefferson afterward declared that he

---

[1] Hildreth: *History of the United States,* vi, 241; and see Adams:
U.S. v, 359–60.

[2] See vol. iii, 541–43, of this work.   [3] Story, i, 212.

"had a strong desire that the public should have been satisfied by a trial on the merits," [1] he was willing that his counsel should prevent the case from coming to trial if they could. Fearing, however, that they would not succeed, Jefferson had prepared, for the use of his attorneys, an exhaustive brief covering his version of the facts and his views of the law. Spencer Roane, Judge of the Virginia Court of Appeals, and as hot a partisan of Jefferson as he was an implacable enemy of Marshall, read this manuscript and gave Tyler "some of the outlines of it." Tyler explains this to Jefferson after the decision in his favor, and adds that, much as Tyler wanted to get hold of Jefferson's brief, still, "as soon as I had received the appointment . . (which I owe to your favor in great measure), it became my duty to shut the door against every observation which might in any way be derived from either side, lest the impudent British faction, who had enlisted on Livingston's side, might suppose an undue influence had seized upon me." [2]

The case aroused keen interest in Virginia and, indeed, throughout the country. Jefferson was still the leader of the Republican Party and was as much beloved and revered as ever by the great majority of the people. When, therefore, he was sued for so large a sum of money, the fact excited wide and lively attention. That the plaintiff was such a man as Edward Livingston gave sharper edge to the general interest. Especially among lawyers, curiosity as to the out-

[1] Jefferson to Wirt, April 12, 1812, *Works* : Ford, xi, 227.
[2] Tyler to Jefferson, May 17, 1812, Tyler: *Tyler*. i, 263.

come was keen. In Richmond, of course, "great expectation was excited."

When the case came on for hearing, Tyler was so ill from a very painful affliction that he could scarcely sit through the hearing; but he persisted because he had "determined to give an opinion." The question of jurisdiction alone was argued and only this was decided. Both judges agreed that the court had no jurisdiction, though Marshall did so with great reluctance. He wished "to carry the cause to the Supreme Court, by adjournment or somehow or other; but," says Tyler in his report to Jefferson, "I pressed the propriety of [its] being decided." [1]

Marshall, however, delivered a written opinion in which he gravely reflected on Jefferson's good faith in avoiding a trial on the merits. If the court, upon mere technicality, were prevented from trying and deciding the case, "the injured party may have a clear right without a remedy"; and that, too, "in a case where a person who has done the wrong, and who ought to make the compensation, is within the power of the court." The situation created by Jefferson's objection to the court's jurisdiction was unfortunate: "Where the remedy is against the person, and is within the power of the court, I have not yet discerned a reason, other than a technical one, which can satisfy my judgment" why the case should not be tried and justice done.

"If, however," continues Marshall, "this technical reason is firmly established, if all other judges respect it, I cannot venture to disregard it," no matter

---

[1] Tyler to Jefferson, May 17, 1812, Tyler: *Tyler*, I, 263-64.

how wrong in principle and injurious to Livingston the Chief Justice might think it. If Lord Mansfield, "one of the greatest judges who ever sat upon any bench, and who has done more than any other, to remove those technical impediments which .. too long continued to obstruct the course of substantial justice," had vainly attempted to remove the very "technical impediments" which Jefferson had thrown in Livingston's way, Marshall would not make the same fruitless effort.

To be sure, the technical point raised by Jefferson's counsel was a legal fiction derived from "the common law of England"; but "this common law has been adopted by the legislature of Virginia"; and "had it not been adopted, I should have thought it in force." Thus Marshall, by innuendo, blames Jefferson for invoking, for his own protection, a technicality of that very common law which the latter had so often and so violently denounced. For the third time Marshall deplores the use of a technicality "which produces the inconvenience of a clear right without a remedy." "Other judges have felt the weight of this argument, and have struggled ineffectually against" it; so, he concluded, "I must submit to it." [1]

Thus it was that Jefferson at last escaped; for it was nothing less than an escape. What a decision on the merits of the case would have been is shown by the opinion of Chancellor Kent, stated with his characteristic emphasis. Jefferson was anxious that the public should think that he was in the right. "Mr. Livingston's suit having gone off on the plea to the

---

[1] 1 Brockenbrough, 206–12.

jurisdiction, it's foundation remains of course unexplained to the public. I have therefore concluded to make it public thro' the . . press. . . I am well satisfied to be relieved from it, altho' I had a strong desire that the public should have been satisfied by a trial on the merits."[1] Accordingly, Jefferson prepared his statement of the controversy and, curiously enough, published it just before Livingston's suit against the United States Marshal in New Orleans was approaching decision. To no other of his documents did he give more patient and laborious care. Livingston replied in an article [2] which justified the great reputation for ability and learning he was soon to acquire in both Europe and America.[3] Kent followed this written debate carefully. When Livingston's answer appeared, Kent wrote him: "I read it eagerly and studied it thoroughly, with a re-examination of Jefferson as I went along; and I should now be as willing to subscribe my name to the validity of your title and to the atrocious injustice you have received as to any opinion contained in Johnson's Reports."[4]

[1] Jefferson to Wirt, April 12, 1812, *Works:* Ford, XI, 226–27. On the Batture controversy see Hildreth, VI, 143–48.

[2] The articles of both Jefferson and Livingston are to be found in Hall's *American Law Journal* (Philadelphia, 1816), vol. V, 1–91, 113–289. A brief but valuable summary of Livingston's reply to Jefferson is found in Hunt: *Livingston*, 143–80. For an abstract of Jefferson's attack, see Randall: *Life of Thomas Jefferson*, III, 266–68.

[3] See Hunt: *Livingston*, 276–80.

[4] Kent to Livingston, May 13, 1814, Hunt: *Livingston*, 181–82. Kent was appointed Chancellor of the State of New York, Feb. 25, 1814. His opinions are contained in *Johnson's Chancery Reports*, to which he refers in this letter.

For twenty years Livingston fought for what he believed to be his .ights to the batture, and, in the end, was successful; but in such

Marshall's attitude in the Batture litigation intensified Jefferson's hatred for the Chief Justice, while Jefferson's conduct in the whole matter still further deepened Marshall's already profound belief that the great exponent of popular government was dishonest and cowardly. Story shared Marshall's views; indeed, the Batture controversy may be said to have furnished that personal element which completed Story's forming antagonism to Jefferson. "Who .. can remember, without regret, his conduct in relation to the batture of New Orleans?" wrote Story many years afterward.[1]

The Chief Justice attributed the attacks which Jefferson made upon him in later years to his opinion in Livingston *vs.* Jefferson, and to the views he was known to have held as to the merits of that case and Jefferson's course in relation to it. "The Batture will never be forgotten," wrote the Chief Justice some years later when commenting on the attacks upon the National Judiciary which he attributed to

fashion that the full value of the property was only realized by his family long after his death.

Notwithstanding Jefferson's hostility, Livingston grew in public favor, was elected to the Louisiana State Legislature and then to Congress, where his work was notable. Later, in 1829, he was chosen United States Senator from that State; and, after serving one term, was appointed Secretary of State by President Jackson. In this office he prepared most of the President's state papers and wrote Jackson's great Nullification Proclamation in 1832.

Livingston was then sent as Minister to France and, by his brilliant conduct of the negotiations over the French Spoliation Claims, secured the payment of them. He won fame throughout Europe and Spanish America by his various works on the penal code and code of procedure. In the learning of the law he was not far inferior to Story and Kent.

Aside from one or two sketches, there is no account of his life except an inadequate biography by Charles H. Hunt.

[1] Story, I, 186.

Jefferson.[1] Again: "The case of the mandamus [2] may be the cloak, but the batture is recollected with still more resentment." [3]

Events thus sharpened the hostility of Jefferson and his following to Marshall, but drew closer the bonds between the Chief Justice and Joseph Story. Once under Marshall's pleasing, steady, powerful influence, Story sped along the path of Nationalism until sometimes he was ahead of the great constructor who, as he advanced, was building an enduring and practicable highway.

[1] Marshall to Story, Sept. 18, 1821, *Proceedings, Mass. Hist. Soc.* 2d series, XIV, 330; and see *infra*, 363–64.

[2] Marbury *vs.* Madison.

[3] Marshall to Story, July 13, 1821, *Proceedings, Mass. Hist. Soc.* 2d series, XIV, 328–29.

CHAPTER III

INTERNATIONAL LAW

It was Marshall's lot in more than one case to blaze the way in the establishment of rules of international conduct. (John Bassett Moore.)

The defects of our system of government must be remedied, not by the judiciary, but by the sovereign power of the people.
(Judge William H. Cabell of the Virginia Court of Appeals.)

I look upon this question as one which may affect, in its consequences, the permanence of the American Union.
(Justice William Johnson of the Supreme Court.)

WHILE Marshall unhesitatingly struck down State laws and shackled State authority, he just as firmly and promptly upheld National laws and National authority. In Marbury *vs*. Madison he proclaimed the power of National courts over Congressional legislation so that the denial of that power might not be admitted at a time when, to do so, would have yielded forever the vital principle of Judiciary supervision.[1] But that opinion is the significant exception to his otherwise unbroken practice of recognizing the validity of acts of Congress.

He carried out this practice even when he believed the law before him to be unwise in itself, injurious to the Nation, and, indeed, of extremely doubtful constitutionality. This course was but a part of Marshall's Nationalist policy. The purpose of his life was to strengthen and enlarge the powers of the National Government; to coördinate into harmonious operation its various departments; and to make it in fact, as well as in principle, the agent of

[1] See vol. III, chap. III, of this work.

a people constituting a single, a strong, and efficient Nation.

A good example of his maintenance of National laws is his treatment of the Embargo, Non-Importation, and Non-Intercourse Acts. The hostility of the Chief Justice to those statutes was, as we have seen, extreme; the political party of which he was an ardent member had denounced them as unconstitutional; his closest friends thought them invalid. He himself considered them to be, if within the Constitution at all, on the periphery of it; [1] he believed them to be ruinous to the country and meant as an undeserved blow at Great Britain upon whose victory over France depended, in his opinion, the safety of America and the rescue of imperiled civilization.

Nevertheless, not once did Marshall, in his many opinions, so much as suggest a doubt of the validity of those measures, when cases came before him arising from them and requiring their interpretation and application. Most of these decisions are not now of the slightest historical importance. [2] His opinions relating to the Embargo are, indeed, tiresome

[1] This is a fair inference from the statement of Joseph Story in his autobiography: "I have ever considered the embargo a measure, which went to the utmost limit of constructive power under the Constitution. It stands upon the extreme verge of the Constitution, being in its very form and terms an unlimited prohibition, or suspension of foreign commerce." (Story, I, 185–86.) When it is remembered that after Story was made Associate Justice his views became identical with those of Marshall on almost every subject, it would seem likely that Story expressed the opinions of the Chief Justice as well as his own on the constitutionality of the Embargo.

[2] See, for instance, the case of William Dixon et al. vs. The United States, 1 Brockenbrough, 177; United States vs. ——, ib. 195; the case of the Fortuna, ib. 299; the case of the Brig Caroline, ib. 384; Thomson and Dixon vs. United States (case of the Schooner Patriot), ib. 407.

and dull, with scarcely a flash of genius to brighten
them. Now and then, but so rarely that search for
it is not worth making, a paragraph blazes with the
statement of a great principle. In the case of the
Ship Adventure and Her Cargo, one such statesman-
like expression illuminates the page. The Non-
Intercourse Law forbade importation of British
goods "from any foreign port or place whatever."
The British ship Adventure had been captured by a
French frigate and given to the master and crew of an
American brig which the Frenchmen had previously
taken. The Americans brought the Adventure into
Norfolk, Virginia, and there claimed the proceeds of
ship and cargo. The United States insisted that ship
and cargo should be forfeited to the Government because brought in from "a foreign place." But, said
Marshall on this point: "The broad navigable ocean,
which is emphatically and truly termed the great
highway of nations, cannot . . be denominated 'a
foreign place.' . . The sea is the common property of
all nations. It belongs equally to all. None can appropriate it exclusively to themselves; nor is it 'foreign' to any." [1]

Where special learning, or the examination of the
technicalities and nice distinctions of the law were required, Marshall did not shine. Of admiralty law in
particular he knew little. The preparation of opinions in such cases he usually assigned to Story who,
not unjustly, has been considered the father of American admiralty law.[2] Also, in knowledge of the intricate law of real estate, Story was the superior of

---

[1] 1 Brockenbrough, 241.   [2] See Warren, 279.

Marshall and, indeed, of all the other members of the court. Story's preëminence in most branches of legal learning was admitted by his associates, all of whom gladly handed over to the youthful Justice more than his share of work. Story was flattered by the recognition. "My brethren were so kind as to place confidence in my researches," [1] he tells his friend Judge Samuel Fay.

During the entire twenty-four years that Marshall and Story were together on the Supreme Bench the Chief Justice sought and accepted the younger man's judgment and frankly acknowledged his authority in every variety of legal questions, excepting only those of international law or the interpretation of the Constitution. "I wish to consult you on a case which to me who am not versed in admiralty proceedings has some difficulty," Marshall writes to Story in 1819. [2] In another letter Marshall asks Story's help on a "question of great consequence." [3] Again and again he requests the assistance of his learned junior associate. [4] Sometimes he addresses Story as though that erudite Justice were his superior. [5] Small wonder that John Marshall should declare that Story's "loss would be irreparable" to the Supreme Bench, if he should be appointed to the place made vacant by the death of Chief Justice Parker of Massachusetts. [6]

[1] Story to Fay, April 24, 1814, Story, i, 261.
[2] Marshall to Story, May 27, 1819, *Proceedings, Mass. Hist. Soc.* 2d Series, xiv, 325. This was the case of the Little Charles.
[3] Same to same, July 13, 1819, *ib.* 326.
[4] Same to same, June 15, 1821, *ib.* 327; Sept. 18, 1821, *ib.* 331; Dec. 9, 1823, *ib.* 334; June 26, 1831, *ib.* 344.
[5] Same to same, July 2, 1823, *ib.* 331–33.
[6] Same to same, Oct. 15, 1830, *ib.* 342.

Only in his expositions of the Constitution did Marshall take supreme command. If he did anything preëminent, other than the infusing of life into that instrument and thus creating a steadying force in the rampant activities of the young American people, it was his contributions to international law, which were of the highest order.[1]

The first two decades of his labors as Chief Justice were prolific in problems involving international relations. The capture of neutral ships by the European belligerents; the complications incident to the struggle of Spanish provinces in South America for independence; the tangle of conflicting claims growing out of the African slave trade — the unsettled questions arising from all these sources made that period of Marshall's services unique in the number, importance, and novelty of cases requiring new and authoritative announcements of the law of nations. An outline of three or four of his opinions in such cases will show the quality of his work in that field of legal science and also illustrate his broad conception of some of the fundamentals of American statesmanship in foreign affairs.

His opinion in the case of the Schooner Exchange lays down principles which embrace much more than was involved in the question immediately before the court [2] — a practice habitual with Marshall and dis-

[1] John Bassett Moore, in his *Digest of International Law*, cites Marshall frequently and often uses passages from his opinions. Henry Wheaton, in his *Elements of International Law*, sometimes quotes Marshall's language as part of the text.

[2] Professor John Bassett Moore, in a letter to the author, says that he considers Marshall's opinion in this case his greatest in the realm of international law.

tinguishing him sharply from most jurists. The vessel in controversy, owned by citizens of Maryland, was, in 1810, captured by a French warship, armed, and taken into the French service. The capture was made under one of the decrees of Napoleon when the war between Great Britain and France was raging fiercely. This was the Rambouillet Decree of March 23, 1810, which because of the Non-Intercourse Act of March 1, 1809, ordered that American ships, entering French ports, be seized and sold.[1] The following year the Exchange, converted into a French national war-craft under the name of the Balaou, manned by a French crew, commanded by a French captain, Dennis M. Begon, put into the port of Philadelphia for repairs of injuries sustained in stress of weather. The former owners of the vessel libeled the ship, alleging that the capture was illegal and demanding their property.

In due course this case came before Marshall who, on March 3, 1812, delivered a long and exhaustive opinion, the effect of which is that the question of title to a ship having the character of a man-of-war is not justiciable in the courts of another country. The Chief Justice begins by avowing that he is "exploring an unbeaten path" and must rely, mainly, on "general principles." A nation's jurisdiction within its own territory is "necessarily exclusive and absolute. It is susceptible of no limitation not imposed by itself." The nation itself must consent to any restrictions upon its "full and complete power . . within its own territories."

---

[1] *Am. State Papers, For. Rel.* III, 384.

Nations are "distinct sovereignties, possessing equal rights and equal independence"; and, since mutual intercourse is for mutual benefit, "all sovereigns have consented" in certain cases to relax their "absolute and complete jurisdiction within their respective territories. . . Common usage, and . . common opinion growing out of that usage" may determine whether such consent has been given. [1] Even when a nation has not expressly stipulated to modify its jurisdiction, it would be guilty of bad faith if "suddenly and without previous notice" it violated "the usages and received obligations of the civilized world."

One sovereign is not "amenable" to another in any respect, and "can be supposed to enter a foreign territory only under an express license, or in the confidence that the immunities belonging to his independent sovereign station, though not expressly stipulated, are reserved by implication, and will be extended to him." From the facts that sovereigns have "perfect equality and absolute independence," and that mutual intercourse and "an interchange of good offices with each other" are to their common advantage, flows a class of cases in which all sovereigns are "understood to waive the exercise of a part of that complete exclusive territorial jurisdiction" which is "the attribute of every nation."

One of these cases "is admitted to be the exemption of the person of the sovereign from arrest or detention within a foreign territory. If he enters that territory with the knowledge and license of its sover-

[1] 7 Cranch, 136.

eign, that license, although containing no stipulation exempting his person from arrest, is universally understood to imply such stipulation." [1] The protection of foreign ministers stands "on the same principles." The governments to which they are accredited need not expressly consent that these ministers shall receive immunity, but are "supposed to assent to it." This assent is implied from the fact that, "without such exemption, every sovereign would hazard his own dignity by employing a public minister abroad. . . Therefore, a consent to receive him, implies a consent" that he shall be exempt from the territorial jurisdiction of the nation to which he is sent. [2]

The armies of one sovereign cannot pass through the territory of another without express permission; to do so would be a violation of faith. Marshall here enters into the reasons for this obvious rule. But the case is far otherwise, he says, as to "ships of war entering the ports of a friendly power." The same dangers and injuries do not attend the entrance of such vessels into a port as are inseparable from the march of an army through a country. But as to foreign vessels, "if there be no prohibition," of which notice has been given, "the ports of a friendly nation are considered as open to the public ships of all powers with whom it is at peace, and they are supposed to enter such ports and to remain in them while allowed to remain, under the protection of the government of the place." [3] Marshall goes into a long examination of whether the rule applies to ships of

[1] 7 Cranch, 137.   [2] *Ib.* 138–39.   [3] *Ib.* 141.

war, and concludes that it does. So the Exchange, now an armed vessel of France, rightfully came into the port of Philadelphia and, while there, is under the protection of the American Government.

In this situation can the title to the vessel be adjudicated by American courts? It cannot, because the schooner "must be considered as having come into the American territory under an implied promise, that while necessarily within it, and demeaning herself in a friendly manner, she should be exempt from the jurisdiction of the country."[1]

Over this general question there was much confusion and wrangling in the courts of various countries, but Marshall's opinion came to be universally accepted, and is the foundation of international law on that subject as it stands to-day.[2]

Scarcely any other judicial act of Marshall's life reveals so clearly his moral stature and strength. He was, as he declared, "exploring an unbeaten path," and could have rendered a contrary decision, sustaining it with plausible arguments. Had he allowed his feelings to influence his judgment; had he permitted his prejudices to affect his reason; had he heeded the desires of political friends — his opinion in the case of the Exchange would have been the reverse of what it was.

In the war then desolating Europe, he was an intense partisan of Great Britain and bitterly hostile to France.[3] He hated Napoleon with all the vigor of his being. He utterly disapproved of what he

[1] 7 Cranch, 147.   [2] See John Bassett Moore in Dillon, i, 521-23.
[3] See *supra*, chap. i.

believed to be the Administration's truckling, or, at least, partiality, to the Emperor. Yet here was a ship, captured from Americans under the orders of that "satanic" ruler, a vessel armed by him and in his service. The emotions of John Marshall must have raged furiously; but he so utterly suppressed them that clear reason and considerations of statesmanship alone controlled him.

In the South American revolutions against Spain, American sailors generally and, indeed, the American people as a whole, ardently sympathized with those who sought to establish for themselves free and independent governments. Often American seamen took active part in the conflicts. On one such occasion three Yankee mariners, commissioned by the insurrectionary government of one of the revolting provinces, attacked a Spanish ship on the high seas, overawed the crew, and removed a large and valuable cargo. The offending sailors were indicted and tried in the United States Court for the District of Massachusetts.

Upon the many questions arising in this case, United States *vs.* Palmer,[1] the judges, Story of the Supreme Court, and John Davis, District Judge, disagreed and these questions were certified to the Supreme Court for decision. One of these questions was: What, in international law, is the status of a revolting province during civil war? [2] In an extended and closely reasoned opinion, largely devoted to the construction of the act of Congress on piracy, the Chief Justice lays down the rule that the relation

[1] 3 Wheaton, 610–44.   [2] *Ib.* 614.

of the United States to parts of countries engaged in internecine war is a question which must be determined by the political departments of the Government and not by the Judicial Department. Questions of this kind "belong . . to those who can declare what the law shall be; who can place the nation in such a position with respect to foreign powers as to their own judgment shall appear wise; to whom are entrusted all its foreign relations. . . In such contests a nation may engage itself with the one party or the other; may observe absolute neutrality; may recognize the new state absolutely; or may make a limited recognition of it.

"The proceeding in courts must depend so entirely on the course of the government, that it is difficult to give a precise answer to questions which do not refer to a particular nation. It may be said, generally, that if the government remains neutral, and recognizes the existence of a civil war, its courts cannot consider as criminal those acts of hostility which war authorizes, and which the new government may direct against its enemy. To decide otherwise, would be to determine that the war prosecuted by one of the parties was unlawful, and would be to arraign the nation to which the court belongs against that party. This would transcend the limits prescribed to the judicial department." [1] So the Yankee "liberators" were set free.

Another instance of the haling of American citizens before the courts of the United States for having taken part in the wars of South American coun-

[1] 3 Wheaton, 634–35.

tries for liberation was the case of the Divina Pastora. This vessel was captured by a privateer manned and officered by Americans in the service of the United Provinces of Rio de la Plata. An American prize crew was placed on board the Spanish vessel which put into the port of New Bedford in stress of weather and was there libeled by the Spanish Consul. The United States District Court awarded restitution, the Circuit Court affirmed this decree, and the case was appealed to the Supreme Court.

Marshall held that the principle announced in the Palmer case governed the question arising from the capture of the Divina Pastora. "The United States, having recognized the existence of a civil war between Spain and her colonies, but remaining neutral, the courts of the Union are bound to consider as lawful those acts which war authorizes." Captures by privateers in the service of the revolting colonies are "regarded by us as other captures, jure belli, are regarded," unless our neutral rights or our laws or treaties are violated.[1]

The liberal statesman and humanitarian in Marshall on matters of foreign policy is often displayed in his international utterances. In the case of the Venus,[2] he dissented from the harsh judgment of the majority of the court, which clearly stated the cold law as it existed at the time, "that the property of an American citizen domiciled in a foreign country became, on the breaking out of war with that country, immediately confiscable as enemy's property, even though it was shipped before he had knowledge of

---

[1] 4 Wheaton, 63–64.   [2] 8 Cranch, 253–317.

the war." [1] Surely, said Marshall, that rule ought not to apply to a merchant who, when war breaks out, intends to leave the foreign country where he has been doing business. Whether or not his property is enemy property depends not alone on his residence in the enemy country, but also on his intention to remain after war begins. But it is plain that evidence of his intention can seldom, if ever, be given during peace and that it can be furnished only "after the war shall be known to him." Of consequence, "justice requires that subsequent testimony shall be received to prove a pre-existing fact." [2]

It is not true that extended residence in a foreign country in time of peace is evidence of intention to remain there permanently. "The stranger merely residing in a country during peace, however long his stay, . . cannot . . be considered as incorporated into that society, so as, immediately on a declaration of war, to become the enemy of his own." [3] Even the ancient writers on international law concede this principle. But modern commerce has sensibly influenced international law and greatly strengthened the common sense and generally accepted considerations just mentioned. All know, as a matter of everyday experience, that "merchants, while belonging politically to one society, are considered commercially as the members of another." [4] The real motives of the merchant should be taken into account.

Of the many cases in which Marshall rendered opinions touching upon international law, however,

[1] John Bassett Moore in Dillon, 1, 524.
[2] 8 Cranch, 289.   [3] Ib. 291-92.   [4] Ib. 293.

that of the Nereid [1] is perhaps the best known. The
descriptions of the arguments in that controversy,
and of the court when they were being made, are the
most vivid and accurate that have been preserved
of the Supreme Bench and the attorneys who practiced before it at that time. Because of this fact an
account of the hearing in this celebrated case will
be helpful to a realization of similar scenes.

The burning of the Capitol by the British in 1814
left the Supreme Court without its basement room
in that edifice; at the time the case of the Nereid
was heard, and for two years afterward,[2] that tribunal held its sessions in the house of Elias Boudinot
Caldwell, the clerk of the court, on Capitol Hill.[3]
Marshall and the Associate Justices sat "inconven-
iently at the upper end" of an uncomfortable room
"unfit for the purpose for which it is used." [4] In the
space before the court were the counsel and other
lawyers who had gathered to hear the argument.
Back of them were the spectators. On the occasion
of this hearing, the room was well filled by members
of the legal profession and by laymen, for everybody
looked forward to a brilliant legal debate.

Nor were these expectations vain. The question

[1] 9 Cranch, 388 et seq.

[2] Until the February session of 1817. This room was not destroyed
or injured by the fire, but was closed while the remainder of the Capitol was being repaired. In 1817, the court occupied another basement
room in the Capitol, where it continued to meet until February,
1819, when it returned to its old quarters in the room where the
library of the Supreme Court is now situated. (Bryan: History of
the National Capital, II, 39.)

[3] Ib., I, 632. Mr. Bryan says that this house still stands and is now
known as 204–06 Pennsylvania Avenue, S.E.

[4] Ticknor to his father, Feb. 1815, Ticknor, I, 38.

was as to whether a certain cargo owned by neutrals, but found in an enemy ship, should be restored. The claimants were represented by J. Ogden Hoffman of New York and the universally known and talked of Thomas Addis Emmet, the Irish patriot whose pathetic experiences, not less than his brilliant talents, appealed strongly to Americans of that day. For the captors appeared Alexander J. Dallas of Pennsylvania and that strangest and most talented advocate of his time, William Pinkney of Maryland, exquisite dandy and profound lawyer,[1] affected fop and accomplished diplomat, insolent as he was able, haughty[2] as he was learned.

George Ticknor gives a vivid description of the judges and lawyers. Marshall's neglected clothing was concealed by his flowing black robes, and his unkempt hair was combed, tied, and "fully powdered." The Associate Justices were similarly robed and powdered, and all "looked dignified." Justice Bushrod Washington, "a little sharp-faced gentleman with only one eye, and a profusion of snuff distributed over his face," did not, perhaps, add to the impressive appearance of the tribunal; but the noble

[1] "His opinions had almost acquired the authority of judicial decisions." (Pinkney: *Life of William Pinkney*, quotation from Robert Goodloe Harper on title-page.)

[2] "He has . . a dogmatizing absoluteness of manner which passes with the million, . . for an evidence of power; and he has acquired with those around him a sort of papal infallibility." (Wirt to Gilmer, April 1, 1816, Kennedy, i, 403.)
Wirt's estimate of Pinkney must have been influenced by professional jealousy, for men like Story and Marshall were as profoundly affected by the Maryland legal genius as were the most emotional spectators. See the criticisms of Wirt's comments on Pinkney by his nephew, Rev. William Pinkney, in his *Life of William Pinkney*, 116–22.

features and stately bearing of William Johnson, the handsome face and erect attitude of young Joseph Story, and the bald-headed, scholarly looking Brockholst Livingston, sitting beside Marshall, adequately filled in the picture of which he was the center.

Opinions were read by Marshall and Story, but evidently they bored the nervous Pinkney, who "was very restless, frequently moved his seat, and, when sitting, showed by the convulsive twitches of his face how anxious he was to come to the conflict. At last the judges ceased to read, and he sprang into the arena like a lion who has been loosed by his keepers on the gladiator that awaited him." This large, stout man wore "corsets to diminish his bulk," used "cosmetics . . to smooth and soften a skin growing somewhat wrinkled and rigid with age," and dressed "in a style which would be thought foppish in a much younger man." [1] His harsh, unmusical voice, grating and high in tone, no less than his exaggerated fashionable attire, at first repelled; but these defects were soon forgotten because of "his clear and forcible manner" of speaking, "his powerful and commanding eloquence, occasionally illuminated with sparkling lights, but always logical and appropriate, and above all, his accurate and discriminating law knowledge, which he pours out with wonderful precision." [2]

Aloof, affected, overbearing [3] as he was, Pinkney

[1] Ticknor to his father, Feb. [day omitted] 1815, Ticknor, i, 38–40.

[2] Story to Williams, Feb. 16, 1812, Story, i, 214; and March 6, 1814, *ib.* 252.

[3] "At the bar he is despotic and cares as little for his colleagues or

overcame prejudice and compelled admiration "by force of eloquence, logic and legal learning and by the display of naked talent," testifies Ticknor, who adds that Pinkney "left behind him . . all the public speaking I had ever heard." [1] Emmet, the Irish exile, "older in sorrows than in years," with "an appearance of premature age," and wearing a "settled melancholy in his countenance," spoke directly to the point and with eloquence as persuasive as that of Pinkney was compelling.[2] Pinkney had insulted Emmet in a previous argument, and Marshall was so apprehensive that the Irish lawyer would now attack his opponent that Justice Livingston had to reassure the Chief Justice.[3]

The court was as much interested in the oratory as in the arguments of the counsel. Story's letters are rich in comment on the style and manner of the leading advocates. At the hearing of a cause at about the same time as that of the Nereid, he tells his wife that Pinkney and Samuel Dexter of Massachusetts "have called crowded houses; all the belles of the city have attended, and have been entranced for hours." Dexter was "calm, collected, and forcible, appealing to the judgment." Pinkney, "vivacious, sparkling, and glowing," although not "as close in his logic as Mr. Dexter," but "step[ping]

adversaries as if they were men of wood." (Wirt to Gilmer, April 1, 1816, Kennedy, i, 403.)
    The late Roscoe Conkling was almost the reincarnation of William Pinkney. In extravagance of dress, haughtiness of manner, retentiveness of memory, power and brilliancy of mind, and genuine eloquence, Pinkney and Conkling were well-nigh counterparts.
    [1] Ticknor to his father, Feb. 21, 1815, Ticknor, i, 40.
    [2] *Ib*. Feb. 1815, 39–40.   [3] Pinkney, 100–01.

aside at will from the path, and strew[ing] flowers of rhetoric around him." [1]

The attendance of women at arguments before the Supreme Court had as much effect on the performance of counsel at this period as on the oratory delivered in House and Senate. One of the belles of Washington jotted down what took place on one such occasion. "Curiosity led me, . . to join the female crowd who throng the court room. A place in which I think women have no business. . . One day Mr. Pinckney [*sic*] had finished his argument and was just about seating himself when Mrs. Madison and a train of ladies enter'd, — he recommenced, went over the same ground, using fewer arguments, but scattering more flowers. And the day I was there I am certain he thought more of the female part of his audience than of the court, and on concluding, he recognized their presence, when he said, 'He would not weary the court, by going thro a long list of cases to prove his argument, as it would not only be fatiguing to them, but inimical to the laws of good taste, which *on the present occasion*, (bowing low) he wished to obey." [2]

---

[1] Story to his wife, March 10, 1814, Story, I, 253.

[2] Mrs. Samuel Harrison Smith to Mrs. Kirkpatrick, March 13, 1814, *First Forty Years of Washington Society:* Hunt, 96.

Pinkney especially would become eloquent, even in an argument of dry, commercial law, if women entered the court-room. "There were ladies present — and Pinkney was expected to be eloquent at all events. So, the mode he adopted was to get into his tragical tone in discussing the construction of an act of Congress. Closing his speech in this solemn tone he took his seat, saying to me, with a smile — 'that will do for the ladies.' " (Wirt to Gilmer, April 1, 1816, Kennedy, I, 404.)

The presence of women affected others no less than Pinkney. "Web-

This, then, is a fairly accurate picture of the Supreme Court of the United States when the great arguments were made before it and its judgments delivered through the historic opinions of Marshall — such the conduct of counsel, the appearance of the Justices, the auditors in attendance. Always, then, when thinking of the hearings in the Supreme Court while he was Chief Justice, we must bear in mind some such scene as that just described.

William Pinkney, the incomparable and enigmatic, passed away in time; but his place was taken by Daniel Webster, as able if not so accomplished, quite as interesting from the human point of view, and almost as picturesque. The lively, virile Clay succeeded the solid and methodical Dexter; and a procession of other eminent statesmen files past our eyes in the wake of those whose distinction for the moment had persuaded their admirers that their equals never would be seen again. It is essential to an understanding of the time that we firmly fix in our minds that the lawyers, no less than the judges, of that day, were publicists as well as lawyers. They were, indeed, statesmen, having deep in their minds the well-being of their Nation even more than the success of their clients.

Briefly stated, the facts in the case of the Nereid were as follows: More than a year after our second war with Great Britain had begun, one Manuel Pinto of Buenos Aires chartered the heavily armed British

ster, Wirt, Taney . . and Emmet, are the combatants, and a bevy of ladies are the promised and brilliant distributors of the prizes," writes Story of an argument in the Supreme Court many years later. (Story to Fay, March 8, 1826, Story, I, 493.)

merchant ship, the Nereid, to take a cargo from London to the South American city and another back
to the British metropolis. The Nereid sailed under
the protection of a British naval convoy. The out-
going cargo belonged partly to Pinto, partly to other
Spaniards, and partly to British subjects. When approaching Madeira an American privateer attacked
the Nereid and, after a brief fight, captured the British vessel and took her to New York as a prize. The
British part of the cargo was condemned without
contest. That part belonging to Pinto and the other
Spaniards was also awarded to the captors, but over
the earnest opposition of the owners, who appealed
to the Supreme Court. The arguments before the
Supreme Court were long and uncommonly able.
Those of Pinkney and Emmet, however, contained
much florid "eloquence." [1]

Space permits no summary of these addresses; the
most that can be given here is the substance of Marshall's very long and tedious opinion which is of no
historical interest, except that part of it dealing with
international law. The Chief Justice stated this capital question: "Does the treaty between Spain and
the United States subject the goods of either party,
being neutral, to condemnation as enemy property,
if found by the other in a vessel of an enemy? That
treaty stipulates that neutral bottoms shall make
neutral goods, but contains no stipulation that enemy bottoms shall communicate the hostile character
to the cargo. It is contended by the captors that the

---

[1] This is illustrated by the passage in Pinkney's argument to which
Marshall in his opinion paid such a remarkable tribute (see *infra*, 141).

two principles are so completely identified that the stipulation of the one necessarily includes the other."

It was, said Marshall, "a part of the original law of nations" that enemy goods in friendly vessels "are prize of war," and that friendly goods in enemy vessels must be restored if captured. The reason of this rule was that "war gives a full right to capture the goods of an enemy, but gives no right to capture the goods of a friend." Just as "the neutral flag constitutes no protection to enemy property," so "the belligerent flag communicates no hostile character to neutral property." The nature of the cargo, therefore, "depends in no degree" upon the ship that carries it.[1]

Unless treaties expressly modified this immemorial law of nations there would, declared Marshall, "seem to be no necessity" to suppose that an exception was intended. "Treaties are formed upon deliberate reflection"; if they do not specifically designate that a particular item is to be taken out of the "ancient rule," it remains within it. "The agreement [in the Spanish treaty] that neutral bottoms shall make neutral goods is . . a concession made by the belligerent to the neutral"; as such it is to be encouraged since "it enlarges the sphere of neutral commerce, and gives to the neutral flag a capacity not given to it by the law of nations."

On the contrary, a treaty "stipulation which subjects neutral property, found in the bottom of an enemy, to condemnation as prize of war, is a concession made by the neutral to the belligerent. It narrows

[1] 9 Cranch, 418-19.

the sphere of neutral commerce, and takes from the neutral a privilege he possessed under the law of nations." However, a government can make whatever contracts with another that it may wish to make. "What shall restrain independent nations from making such a compact" as they please? [1]

Suppose that, regardless of "our treaty with Spain, considered as an independent measure, the ordinances of that government would subject American property, under similar circumstances, to confiscation." Ought Spanish property, for that reason, to be "condemned as prize of war"? That was not a question for courts to decide: "Reciprocating to the subjects of a nation, or retaliating on them its unjust proceedings towards our citizens, is a political, not a legal measure. It is for the consideration of the government, not of its courts. The degree and the kind of retaliation depend entirely on considerations foreign to this tribunal."

The Government is absolutely free to do what it thinks best: "It is not for its courts to interfere with the proceedings of the nation and to thwart its views. It is not for us to depart from the beaten track prescribed for us, and to tread the devious and intricate path of politics." He and his associates had no difficulty, said Marshall, in arriving at these conclusions. "The line of partition" between "belligerent rights and neutral privileges" is "not so distinctly marked as to be clearly discernible." [2] Nevertheless, the neutral part of the Nereid's cargo must "be governed by the principles which would apply to it had

---

[1] 9 Cranch, 419–20.   [2] *Ib.* 422–23.

the Nereid been a general ship." That she was armed, that she fought to resist capture, did not charge the cargo with the belligerency of the ship, since the owners of the cargo had nothing to do with her armed equipment or belligerent conduct.

It is "universally recognized as the original rule of the law of nations" that a neutral may ship his goods on a belligerent vessel. This right is "founded on the plain and simple principle that the property of a friend remains his property wherever it may be found." [1] That it is lodged in an armed belligerent ship does not take it out of this universal rule. The plain truth is, declares Marshall, that "a belligerent has a perfect right to arm in his own defense; and a neutral has a perfect right to transport his goods in a belligerent vessel." Such merchandise "does not cease to be neutral" because placed on an armed belligerent ship, nor when that vessel exercises the undoubted belligerent right forcibly to resist capture by the enemy.

Shipping goods on an armed belligerent ship does not defeat or even impair the right of search. "What is this right of search? Is it a substantive and independent right wantonly, and in the pride of power, to vex and harass neutral commerce, because there is a capacity to do so?" No! It is a right "essential . . to the exercise of . . a full and perfect right to capture enemy goods and articles going to their enemy which are contraband of war. . . It is a mean justified by the end," and "a right . . ancillary to the greater right of capture."

[1] 9 Cranch, 425.

For a neutral to place "his goods in the vessel of an armed enemy" does not connect him with that enemy or give him a "hostile character." Armed or unarmed, "it is the right and the duty of the carrier to avoid capture and to prevent a search." Neither arming nor resistance is "chargeable to the goods or their owner, where he has taken no part" in either.[1] Pinkney had cited two historical episodes, but Marshall waved these aside as of no bearing on the case. "If the neutral character of the goods is forfeited by the resistance of the belligerent vessel, why is not the neutral character of the passengers," who did not engage in the conflict, "forfeited by the same cause?"[2]

In the case of the Nereid, the goods of the neutral shipper were inviolable. Pinkney had drawn a horrid picture of the ship, partly warlike, partly peaceful, displaying either character as safety or profit dictated.[3] But, answers Marshall, falling into something

[1] 9 Cranch, 426–29.   [2] *Ib.* 428–29.

[3] "We .. have Neutrality, soft and gentle and defenceless in herself, yet clad in the panoply of her warlike neighbours—with the frown of defiance upon her brow, and the smile of conciliation upon her lip — with the spear of Achilles in one hand and a lying protestation of innocence and helplessness unfolded in the other. Nay, .. we shall have the branch of olive entwined around the bolt of Jove, and Neutrality in the act of hurling the latter under the deceitful cover of the former. . .
"Call you that Neutrality which thus conceals beneath its appropriate vestment the giant limbs of War, and converts the charter-party of the compting-house into a commission of marque and reprisals; which makes of neutral trade a laboratory of belligerent annoyance; which .. warms a torpid serpent into life, and places it beneath the footsteps of a friend with a more appalling lustre on its crest and added venom in its sting." (Wheaton: *Some Account of the Life, Writings, and Speeches of William Pinkney,* 463, 466.)
Pinkney frankly said that his metaphors, "hastily conceived and hazarded," were inspired by the presence of women "of this mixed and (for a court of judicature) *uncommon* audience." (*Ib.* 464–65.)
Except for this exhibition of rodomontade his address was a wonder-

like the rhetoric of his youth,[1] "the Nereid has not that centaur-like appearance which has been ascribed to her. She does not rove over the ocean hurling the thunders of war while sheltered by the olive branch of peace." Her character is not part neutral, part hostile. "She is an open and declared belligerent; claiming all the rights, and subject to all the dangers of the belligerent character." One of these rights is to carry neutral goods which were subject to "the hazard of being taken into port" in case of the vessel's capture — in the event of which they would merely be "obliged to seek another conveyance." The ship might lawfully be captured and condemned; but the neutral cargo within it remained neutral, could not be forfeited, and must be returned to its owners.[2]

But Marshall anoints the wounds of the defeated Pinkney with a tribute to the skill and beauty of his oratory and argument: "With a pencil dipped in the most vivid colors, and guided by the hand of a master, a splendid portrait has been drawn exhibiting this vessel and her freighter as forming a single figure, composed of the most discordant materials of peace and war. So exquisite was the skill of the artist, so dazzling the garb in which the figure was presented, that it required the exercise of that cold investigating faculty which ought always to belong to those who sit on this bench, to discover its only imperfection; its want of resemblance."[3]

ful display of reasoning and erud'.ion. His brief peroration was eloquence of the noblest order. (See entire speech, Wheaton: *Pinkney*, 455–516.)

[1] See vol. I, 72, 195, of this work.   [2] 9 Cranch, 430–31.   [3] *Ib.* 430.

Such are examples of Marshall's expositions of international law and typical illustrations of his method in statement and reasoning. His opinion in the case of the Nereid is notable, too, because Story dissented [1] — and for Joseph Story to disagree with John Marshall was a rare event. Justice Livingston also disagreed, and the British High Court of Admiralty maintained the contrary doctrine. But the principle announced by Marshall, that enemy bottoms do not make enemy goods and that neutral property is sacred, remained and still remains the American doctrine. Indeed, by the Declaration of Paris in 1856, the principle thus announced by Marshall in 1815 is now the accepted doctrine of the whole world.

Closely akin to the statesmanship displayed in his pronouncements upon international law, was his assertion, in Insurance Co. *vs.* Canter,[2] that the Nation has power to acquire and to govern territory. The facts of this case were that a ship with a cargo of cotton, which was insured, was wrecked on the coast of Florida after that territory had been ceded to the United States and before it became a State of the Union. The cotton was saved, and taken to Key West, where, by order of a local court acting under

[1] "Never in my whole life was I more entirely satisfied that the Court were wrong in their judgment. I hope Mr. Pinkney will . . publish his admirable argument . . it will do him immortal honor." (Story to Williams, May 8, 1815, Story, I, 256.)

Exactly the same question as that decided in the case of the Nereid was again brought before the Supreme Court two years later in the case of the Atalanta. (3 Wheaton, 409.) Marshall merely stated that the former decision governed the case. (*Ib.* 415.)

[2] The American Insurance Company *et al. vs.* David Canter, 1 Peters, 511–46.

a Territorial law, it was sold at auction to satisfy claims for salvage. Part of the cotton was purchased by one David Canter, who shipped it to Charleston, South Carolina, where the insurance companies libeled it. The libelants contended, among other things, that the Florida court was not competent to order the auction sale because the Territorial act was "inconsistent" with the National Constitution. After a sharp and determined contest in the District and Circuit Courts of the United States at Charleston, in which Canter finally prevailed, the case was taken to the Supreme Court.[1]

Was the Territorial act, under which the local court at Key West ordered the auction sale, valid? The answer to that question, said Marshall, in delivering the opinion of the court, depends upon "the relation in which Florida stands to the United States." Since the National Government can make war and conclude treaties, it follows that it "possesses the power of acquiring territory either by conquest or treaty . . Ceded territory becomes a part of the nation to which it is annexed"; but "the relations of the inhabitants to each other [do not] undergo any change." Their allegiance is transferred; but the law "which regulates the intercourse and general conduct of individuals remains in force until altered by the newly created power of the state." [2]

The treaty by which Spain ceded Florida to the United States assures to the people living in that Territory "the enjoyment of the privileges, rights, and immunities" of American citizens; "they do not

[1] 1 Peters, 511–46.   [2] *Ib.* 542.

however, participate in political power; they do not share in the government till Florida shall become a state. In the meantime Florida continues to be a Territory of the United States, governed by virtue of that clause in the Constitution which empowers Congress 'to make all needful rules & regulations respecting the territory or other property belonging to the United States.'" [1]

The Florida salvage act is not violative of the Constitution. The courts upon which that law confers jurisdiction are not "Constitutional Courts; . . they are legislative Courts, created in virtue of the general right of sovereignty which exists in the government, or in virtue of that clause which enables Congress to make all needful rules and regulations respecting the territory belonging to the United States. . . Although admiralty jurisdiction can be exercised, in the States, in those courts only " which are authorized by the Constitution, the same limitation does not extend to the Territories. In legislating for them, Congress exercises the combined powers of the general and of a state government. [2]

Admirable and formative as were Marshall's opinions of the law of nations, they received no attention from the people, no opposition from the politicians, and were generally approved by the bar. At the very next term of the Supreme Court, after the decision in the case of the Nereid, an opinion was delivered by Story that aroused more contention and had greater effect on the American Nation than had all the decisions of the Supreme Court on international

---

[1] 1 Peters, 542.　　　　　　　　　[2] *Ib.* 546.

law up to that time. This was the opinion in the famous case of Martin *vs.* Hunter's Lessee.

It was Story's first exposition of Constitutional law and it closely resembles Marshall's best interpretations of the Constitution. So conspicuous is this fact that the bench and bar generally have adopted the view that the Chief Justice was, in effect, the spiritual author of this commanding judicial utterance.[1] But Story had now been by Marshall's side on the Supreme Bench for four years and, in his ardent way, had become more strenuously Nationalist, at least in expression, than Marshall.[2]

That the Chief Justice himself did not deliver this opinion was due to the circumstance that his brother, James M. Marshall, was involved in the controversy; was, indeed, a real party in interest. This fact, together with the personal hatred of Marshall by the head of the Virginia Republican organization, had much to do with the stirring events that attended and followed this litigation.

[1] Story wrote George Ticknor that Marshall "concurred in every word of it." (Story to Ticknor, Jan. 22, 1831, Story, ii, 49.)

[2] "Let us extend the national authority over the whole extent of power given by the Constitution. Let us have great military and naval schools; an adequate regular army; the broad foundations laid of a permanent navy; a national bank; a national system of bankruptcy; a great navigation act; a general survey of our ports, and appointments of port-wardens and pilots; Judicial Courts which shall embrace the . . justices of the peace, for the commercial and national concerns of the United States. By such enlarged and liberal institutions, the Government of the United States will be endeared to the people . . Let us prevent the possibility of a division, by creating great national interests which shall bind us in an indissoluble chain." (Story to Williams, Feb. 22, 1815, *ib.* i, 254.)

Later in the same year Story repeated these views and added: "I most sincerely hope that a national newspaper may be established at Washington." (Story to Wheaton, Dec. 13, 1815, *ib.* 270–71.)

At the time of the Fairfax-Hunter controversy, Virginia was governed by one of the most efficient party organizations ever developed under free institutions. Its head was Spencer Roane, President of the Court of Appeals, the highest tribunal in the State, an able and learned man of strong prejudices and domineering character. Jefferson had intended to appoint Roane Chief Justice of the United States upon the expected retirement of Ellsworth.[1] But Ellsworth's timely resignation gave Adams the opportunity to appoint Marshall. Thus Roane's highest ambition was destroyed and his lifelong dislike of Marshall became a personal and a virulent animosity.

Roane was supported by his cousin, Thomas Ritchie, editor of the Richmond *Enquirer*, the most influential of Southern newspapers, and, indeed, one of the most powerful journals in the Nation. Another of the Virginia junto was John Taylor of Caroline County, a brilliant, unselfish, and sincere man. Back of this triumvirate was Thomas Jefferson with his immense popularity and his unrivaled political sagacity. These men were the commanding officers of a self-perpetuating governmental system based on the smallest political unit, the County Courts. These courts were made up of justices of the peace appointed by the Governor. Vacancies in the County Courts were filled only on the recommendation of the remaining members.[2] These justices of the peace also named the men to be sent to the State Legislature which appointed the Governor and also chose

---

[1] Professor William E. Dodd, in *Am. Hist. Rev.* xii, 776.

[2] For fuller description of the Virginia County Court system, see chap. ix of this volume.

the members of the Court of Appeals who held office for life.[1] A perfect circle of political action was thus formed, the permanent and controlling center of which was the Court of Appeals.

These, then, were the judge, the court, and the party organization which now defied the Supreme Court of the United States. By one of those curious jumbles by which Fate confuses mortals, the excuse for this defiance of Nationalism by Localism arose from a land investment by Marshall and his brother. Thus the fact of the purchase of the larger part of the Fairfax estate [2] is woven into the Constitutional development of the Nation.

Five years before the Marshall syndicate made this investment,[3] one David Hunter obtained from Virginia a grant of seven hundred and eighty-eight acres of that part of the Fairfax holdings known as "waste and ungranted land." [4] The grant was made under the various confiscatory acts of the Virginia Legislature passed during the Revolution. These acts had not been carried into effect, however, and in 1783 the Treaty of Peace put an end to subsequent proceedings under them.

Denny Martin Fairfax, the devisee of Lord Fairfax, denied the validity of Hunter's grant from the

[1] On the Virginia Republican machine, Roane, Ritchie, etc., see Dodd in *Am. Hist. Rev.* XII, 776–77; and in *Branch Hist. Papers*, June, 1903, 222; Smith in *ib.* June, 1905, 15; Thrift in *ib.* June, 1908, 183; also Dodd: *Statesmen of the Old South*, 70 *et seq.*; Anderson, 205; Turner: *Rise of the New West*, 60; Ambler: *Ritchie*, 27, 82.

[2] Several thousand acres of the Fairfax estate were not included in this joint purchase. (See *infra*, 150.)

[3] 1793–94. See vol. II, 202–11, of this work.

[4] April 30, 1789. See Hunter *vs.* Fairfax's Devisee, 1 Munford, 223.

State on the ground that Virginia did not execute
her confiscatory statutes during the war, and that all
lands and property to which those laws applied were
protected by the Treaty of Peace. In 1791, two years
after he obtained his grant and eight years after the
ratification of the treaty, Hunter brought suit in
the Superior Court at Winchester [1] against Fairfax's
devisee for the recovery of the land. The action was
under the ancient form of legal procedure still practiced, and bore the title of "Timothy Trititle, Lessee
of David Hunter, *vs.* Denny Fairfax," Devisee of
Thomas, Lord Fairfax.[2] The facts were agreed to by
the parties and, on April 24, 1794, the court decided
against Hunter,[3] who appealed to the Court of Appeals at Richmond.[4] Two years later, in May, 1796,
the case was argued before Judges Roane, Fleming,
Lyons, and Carrington.[5] Meanwhile the Jay Treaty
had been ratified, thus confirming the guarantees of
the Treaty of Peace to the holders of titles of lands
which Virginia, in her confiscatory acts, had declared
forfeited.

At the winter session, 1796–97, of the Virginia
Legislature, Marshall, acting for his brother and

[1] For the district composed of Frederick, Berkeley, Hampshire,
Hardy, and Shenandoah Counties.

[2] Order Book, Superior Court, No. 2, 43, Office of Clerk of Circuit
Court, Frederick Co., Winchester, Va.

[3] The judges rendering this decision were St. George Tucker and
William Nelson, Jr. (*Ib.*)

[4] In making out the record for appeal the fictitious name of Timothy Trititle was, of course, omitted, so that in the Court of Appeals
and in the appeals to the Supreme Court of the United States the title
of the case is Hunter *vs.* Fairfax's Devisee, instead of "Timothy Trititle, Lessee of David Hunter," *vs.* Fairfax's Devisee, and Martin *vs.*
Hunter's Lessee.

[5] 1 Munford, 223.

brother-in-law, as well as for himself, agreed to execute deeds to relinquish their joint claims "to the
waste and unappropriated lands in the Northern
Neck" upon condition that the State would confirm
the Fairfax title to lands specifically appropriated [1]
by Lord Fairfax or by his devisee. But for the statement made many years later by Judges Roane and
Fleming, of the Court of Appeals, that this adjustment covered the land claimed by Hunter, it would
appear that Marshall did not intend to include it in
the compromise,[2] even if, as seems improbable, it was
a part of the Marshall syndicate's purchase; for the
decision of the court at Winchester had been against
Hunter, and after that decision and before the compromise, the Jay Treaty had settled the question of
title.

On October 18, 1806, the Marshall syndicate, having finally made the remaining payments for that
part of the Fairfax estate purchased by it — fourteen
thousand pounds in all — Philip Martin, the devisee
of Denny M. Fairfax, executed his warranty to John
and James M. Marshall and their brother-in-law,
Rawleigh Colston; and this deed was duly recorded
in Fauquier, Warren, Frederick, and Shenandoah

---

[1] See vol. II, footnote to 209, of this work.

[2] The adjustment was made because of the memorial of about two
hundred settlers or squatters (mostly Germans) on the wild lands who
petitioned the Legislature to establish title in them. David Hunter was
not one of these petitioners. Marshall agreed to execute deeds "ex-
tinguishing" the Fairfax title "so soon as the conveyance shall be
transmitted to me from Mr. Fairfax." (Marshall to the Speaker of the
House of Delegates, Va., Nov. 24, 1796. See vol. II, footnote to 209,
of this work.) The Fairfax deed to the Marshalls was not executed
until ten years after this compromise. (Land Causes, 1833, 40, Records in Office of Clerk of Circuit Court, Fauquier Co., Va.)

Counties, where the Fairfax lands were situated.[1]
Nearly ten years before this conveyance, James M.
Marshall separately had purchased from Denny
Martin Fairfax large quantities of land in Shenan-
doah and Hardy Counties where the Hunter grant
probably was situated.[2]

[1] Two years later, on October 5, 1808, the Marshall brothers effected a partition of the estate between themselves on the one part
and their brother-in-law on the other part, the latter receiving about
forty thousand acres. (Deed Book 36, 302, Records in Office of Clerk
of Circuit Court, Frederick Co., Va.)

[2] On August 30, 1797, Denny Martin Fairfax conveyed to James M.
Marshall all the Fairfax lands in Virginia "save and except . . the
manor of Leeds." (See Marshall vs. Conrad, 5 Call, 364.) Thereafter
James M. Marshall lived in Winchester for several years and made
many conveyances of land in Shenandoah and Berkeley Counties.
For instance, Nov. 12, 1798, to Charles Lee, Deed Book 3, 634,
Records in Office of Clerk of Circuit Court, Frederick County, Va.;
Jan. 9, 1799, to Henry Richards, ib. 549; Feb. 4, 1799, to Joseph Baker,
Deed Book 25, ib. 561; March 30, 1799, to Richard Miller, Deed
Book 3, ib. 602, etc.

All of these deeds by James M. Marshall and Hester, his wife, re-
cite that these tracts and lots are parts of the lands conveyed to James
M. Marshall by Denny Martin Fairfax on August 30, 1797. John Marshall does not join in any of these deeds. Apparently, therefore, he had
no personal interest in the tract claimed by Hunter.

In a letter to his brother Marshall speaks of the Shenandoah lands
as belonging to James M. Marshall: "With respect to the rents due
Denny Fairfax before the conveyance to you I should suppose a recovery could only be defeated by the circumstance that they passed
to you by the deed conveying the land." (Marshall to his brother,
Feb. 13, 1806, MS.)

At the time when the Fairfax heir, Philip Martin, executed a deed
to the Marshall brothers and Rawleigh Colston, conveying to them the
Manor of Leeds, the lands involved in the Hunter case had been owned
by James M. Marshall exclusively for nearly ten years.

After the partition with Colston, October 5, 1808, John and James
M. Marshall, on September 5, 1809, made a partial division between
themselves of Leeds Manor, and Goony Run Manor in Shenandoah
County, the latter going to James M. Marshall.

These records apparently establish the facts that the "compromise"
of 1796 was not intended to include the land claimed by Hunter; that
James M. Marshall personally owned most of the lands about Win-

It would seem that James M. Marshall continued in peaceful possession of the land, the title to which the Winchester court had decreed to be in the Fairfax devisee and not in Hunter. When Denny M. Fairfax died, he devised his estate to his younger brother [1] Major-General Philip Martin. About the same time he made James M. Marshall his administrator, with the will annexed, apparently for the purpose of enabling him to collect old rents.[2] For thirteen years and six months the case of Hunter *vs.* Fairfax's Devisee slumbered in the drowsy archives of the Virginia Court of Appeals. In the autumn of 1809, however, Hunter demanded a hearing of it and, on October 25, of that year, it was reargued.[3] Hunter was represented by John Wickham, then the acknowledged leader of the Virginia bar, and by another lawyer named Williams.[4] Daniel Call appeared for the Fairfax devisee.

chester; and that John Marshall had no personal interest whatever in the land in controversy in the litigation under review.

This explains the refusal of the Supreme Court, including even Justice Johnson, to take notice of the compromise of 1796. (See *infra*, 157.)

[1] When Lord Fairfax devised his Virginia estate to his nephew, Denny Martin, he required him to take the name of Fairfax.

[2] Order Book, Superior Court of Frederick Co. Va., III, 721.

[3] 1 Munford, 223. The record states that Judge Tucker did not sit on account of his near relationship to a person interested.

[4] It should be repeated that David Hunter was not one of the destitute settlers who appealed to the Legislature in 1796. From the records it would appear that he was a very prosperous farmer and landowner who could well afford to employ the best legal counsel, as he did throughout the entire litigation. As early as 1771 we find him selling to Edward Beeson 536 acres of land in Frederick County. (Deed Book 15, 213, Office of Clerk of Circuit Court, Frederick County, Va.) The same Hunter also sold cattle, farming implements, etc., to a large amount. (Deeds dated Nov. 2, 1771, Deed Book cited above, 279, 280.) These transactions took place eighteen years before Hunter secured

152

JOHN MARSHALL

The following spring[1] the Court of Appeals decided in favor of Hunter, reversing the judgment of the lower court rendered more than sixteen years before. In his opinion Roane, revealing his animosity to Marshall, declared that the compromise of 1796 covered the case. "I can never consent that the appellees,[2] after having got the benefit thereof, should refuse to submit thereto, or pay the equivalent; the consequence of which would be, that the Commonwealth would have to remunerate the appellant for the land recovered from him! Such a course cannot be justified on the principles of justice and good faith; and, I confess, I was not a little surprised that the objection should have been raised in the case before us."[3]

from Virginia the grant of Fairfax lands, twenty-five years before the Marshall compromise of 1796, thirty-eight years before Hunter employed Wickham to revive his appeal against the Fairfax devisee, forty-two years prior to the first arguments before the Supreme Court, and forty-five years before the final argument and decision of the famous case of Martin vs. Hunter's Lessee. So, far from being a poor, struggling, submissive, and oppressed settler, David Hunter was one of the most well-to-do, acquisitive, determined, and aggressive men in Virginia.

[1] April 23, 1810.

[2] By using the plural "appellees," Roane apparently intimates that Marshall was personally interested in the case; as we have seen, he was not. There was of record but one appellee, the Fairfax devisee.

[3] 1 Munford, 232.

The last two lines of Roane's language are not clear, but it would seem that the "objection" must have been that the Marshall compromise did not include the land claimed by Hunter and others, the title to which had been adjudged to be in Fairfax's devisee before the compromise. This is, indeed, probably the meaning of the sentence of Roane's opinion; otherwise it is obscure. It would appear certain that the Fairfax purchasers did make just this objection. Certainly they would have been foolish not to have done so if the Hunter land was not embraced in the compromise.

To this judgment the Fairfax devisee [1] obtained from the Supreme Court of the United States [2] a writ of error to the Virginia court under Section 25 of the Ellsworth Judiciary Act, upon the ground that the case involved the construction of the Treaty of Peace with Great Britain and the Jay Treaty, the Virginia court having held against the right claimed by Fairfax's devisee under those treaties. [3]

The Supreme Court now consisted of two Federalists, Washington and Marshall, and five Republicans, Johnson, Livingston, Story, and Duval; and Todd, who was absent from illness at the decision of this cause. Marshall declined to sit during the arguments, or to participate in the deliberations and

[1] Since James M. Marshall was the American administrator of the will of Denny M. Fairfax, and also had long possessed all the rights and title of the Fairfax heir to this particular land, it doubtless was he who secured the writ of error from the Supreme Court.

[2] 1 Munford, 238.

[3] 7 Cranch, 608–09, 612. The reader should bear in mind the provisions of Section 25 of the Judiciary Act, since the validity and meaning of it are involved in some of the greatest controversies hereafter discussed. The part of that section which was in controversy is as follows:

"A final judgment or decree in any suit, in the highest court of law or equity of a state in which a decision in the suit could be had, where is drawn in question the validity of a treaty or statute of, or an authority exercised under the United States, and the decision is against their validity; or where is drawn in question the validity of a statute of, or an authority exercised under any state, on the ground of their being repugnant to the constitution, treaties or laws of the United States, and the decision is in favor of such their validity; or where is drawn in question the construction of any clause of the constitution, or of a treaty, or statute of, or commission held under the United States, and the decision is against the title, right, privilege or exemption specially set up or claimed by either party, under such clause of the said constitution, treaty, statute or commission, may be re-examined and reversed or affirmed in the supreme court of the United States upon a writ of error."

conclusions of his associates. Indeed, throughout
this litigation the Chief Justice may almost be said
to have leaned backward. It was with good reason
that Henry S. Randall, the biographer and apologist
of Jefferson, went out of his way to laud Marshall's
"stainless private character" and pay tribute to his
"austere public and private virtue." [1]

Eight years before the Hunter-Fairfax controversy was first brought to the Supreme Court, the
case of the Granville heirs against William R. Davie,
Nathaniel Allen, and Josiah Collins, was tried at the
June term, 1805, of the United States Court at
Raleigh, North Carolina. Marshall, as Circuit Judge,
sat with Potter, District Judge. The question was
precisely that involved in the Fairfax title. The
grant to Lord Granville [2] was the same as that to
Lord Fairfax.[3] North Carolina had passed the same
confiscatory acts against alien holdings as Virginia.[4]
Under these statutes, Davie, Allen, and Collins obtained grants to parts of the Granville estate [5] identical with that of Hunter to a part of the Fairfax
estate in Virginia.

Here was an excellent opportunity for Marshall
to decide the Fairfax controversy once and for all.
Nowhere was his reputation at that time higher than
in North Carolina, nowhere was he more admired
and trusted.[6] That his opinion would have been ac-

[1] Randall, II, 35–36.

[2] For a full and painstaking account of the Granville grant, and the
legislation and litigation growing out of it, see Henry G. Connor in
University of Pennsylvania Law Review, vol. 62, 671 *et seq.*

[3] See vol. I, 192, of this work.

[4] Connor in *Univ. of Pa. Law Rev.* vol. 62, 674–75.

[5] *Ib.* 676.   [6] See *supra*, 69.

cepted by the State authorities and acquiesced in by the people, there can be no doubt.[1] But the Chief Justice flatly stated that he would take no part in the trial because of an "opinion . . formed when he was very deeply interested (alluding to the cause of Lord Fairfax in Virginia). He could not consistently with his duty and the delicacy he felt, give an opinion in the cause." [2]

[1] This highly important fact is proved by the message of Governor David Stone to the Legislature of North Carolina in which he devotes much space to the Granville litigation and recommends "early provision to meet the justice of the claim of her [North Carolina's] citizens for remuneration in case of a decision against the sufficiency of the title derived from herself." The "possibility" of such a decision is apparent "when it is generally understood that a greatly and deservedly distinguished member of that [the Supreme] Court, has already formed an unfavorable opinion, will probably enforce the consideration that it is proper to make some eventual provision, by which the purchasers from the State, and those holding under that purchase, may have justice done them." (Connor in *Univ. of Pa. Law Rev.* vol. 62, 690–91.)

From this message of Governor Stone it is clear that the State expected a decision in favor of the Granville heirs, and that the Legislature and State authorities were preparing to submit to that decision.

[2] *Raleigh Register*, June 24, 1805, as quoted by Connor in *Univ. of Pa. Law Rev.* vol. 62, 689.

The jury found against the Granville heirs. A Mr. London, the Granville agent at Wilmington, still hoped for success: "The favorable sentiments of Judge Marshall encourage me to hope that we shall finally succeed," he writes William Gaston, the Granville counsel. Nevertheless, "I think the Judge's reasons for withdrawing from the cause partakes more of political acquiescence than the dignified, official independence we had a right to expect from his character. He said enough to convince our opponents he was unfavorable to their construction of the law and, therefore, should not have permitted incorrect principles to harass our clients and create expensive delays. Mr. Marshall had certainly no interest in our cause, he ought to have governed the proceedings of a Court over which he presided, according to such opinion — it has very much the appearance of shirking to popular impressions."

London ordered an appeal to be taken to the Supreme Court of the United States, remarking that "it is no doubt much in our favor what

The case of Fairfax's Devisee *vs.* Hunter's Lessee
was argued for the former by Charles Lee of Richmond and Walter Jones of Washington, D.C.
Robert Goodloe Harper of Baltimore appeared for
Hunter. On both sides the argument was mainly
upon the effect on the Fairfax title of the Virginia
confiscatory laws; of the proceedings or failure to
proceed under them; and the bearing upon the
controversy of the two treaties with Great Britain.
Harper, however, insisted that the court consider
the statute of Virginia which set forth and confirmed
the Marshall compromise.

On March 15, 1813, Story delivered the opinion
of the majority of the court, consisting of himself and
Justices Washington, Livingston, Todd, and Duval.
Johnson, alone, dissented. Story held that, since
Virginia had not taken the prescribed steps to acquire
legal possession of the land before the Treaty of
Peace, the State could not do so afterward. "The
patent of the original plaintiff [Hunter] . . issued im-

has already dropt from the Chief Justice." (London to Gaston, July 8,
1805, as quoted by Connor in *Univ. of Pa. Law Rev.* vol. 62, 690.)

He was, however, disgusted with Marshall. "I feel much chagrin
that we are put to so much trouble and expense in this business, and
which I fear is in great degree to be attributed to the Chief Justice's
delivery." (Same to same, April 19, 1806, as quoted by Connor in *ib.*
691.)

For more than ten years the appeal of the Granville heirs from the
judgment of the National Court for the District of North Carolina reposed on the scanty docket of the Supreme Court awaiting call for argument by counsel. Finally on February 4, 1817, on motion of counsel
for the Granville heirs, the case was stricken from the docket. The
reason for this action undoubtedly was that William Gaston, counsel
for the Granville heirs, had been elected to Congress, was ambitious
politically, was thereafter elected judge of the Supreme Court of North
Carolina; none of these honors could possibly have been achieved had
he pressed the Granville case.

providently and passed no title whatever." To uphold Virginia's grant to Hunter "would be selling suits and controversies through the whole country." [1] It was not necessary, said Story, to consider the Treaty of Peace, since "we are well satisfied that the treaty of 1794 [2] completely protects and confirms the title of Denny Fairfax." [3]

In his dissenting opinion Justice Johnson ignored the "compromise" of 1796, holding that the grant by the State to Hunter extinguished the right of Fairfax's devisee.[4] He concurred with Story and Washington, however, in the opinion that, on the face of the record, the case came within Section 25 of the Judiciary Act; that, therefore, the writ of error had properly issued, and that the title must be inquired into before considering "how far the . . treaty . . is applicable to it." [5] Accordingly the mandate of the Supreme Court was directed to the judges of the Virginia Court of Appeals, instructing them "to enter judgment for the appellant, Philip Martin [the Fairfax devisee]." Like all writs of the Supreme Court, it was, of course, issued in the name of the Chief Justice.[6]

Hot was the wrath of Roane and the other judges of Virginia's highest court when they received this order from the National tribunal at Washington. At their next sitting they considered whether to obey or to defy the mandate. They called in "the members of the bar generally," and the question

[1] 7 Cranch, 625.
[2] The Jay Treaty. See vol. II, 113–15, of this work.
[3] 7 Cranch, 627.   [4] Ib. 631.
[5] Ib. 632.   [6] For mandate see 4 Munford, 2–3.

"was solemnly argued" at Richmond for six consecutive days.[1] On December 16, 1815, the decision was published. The Virginia judges unanimously declined to obey the mandate of the Supreme Court of the United States. Each judge rendered a separate opinion, and all held that so much of Section 25 of the National Judiciary Act as "extends the appellate jurisdiction of the Supreme Court to this court, is not in pursuance of the constitution of the United States."[2]

But it was not only the Virginia Court of Appeals that now spoke; it was the entire Republican partisan machine, intensively organized and intelligently run, that brought its power to bear against the highest tribunal of the Nation. Beyond all possible doubt, this Republican organization, speaking through the supreme judiciary of the State, represented public sentiment, generally, throughout the Old Dominion. Unless this political significance of the opinions of the Virginia judges be held of higher value than their legal quality, the account of this historic controversy deserves no more than a brief paragraph stating the legal point decided.

The central question was well set forth by Judge Cabell thus: Even where the construction of a treaty is involved in the final decision of a cause by the highest court of a State, that decision being against the title of the party claiming under the treaty, can Congress "confer on the Supreme Court of the United States, a power to *re-examine, by way of appeal or writ of error, the decision of the state Court ; to*

[1] March 31, April 1 to April 6, 1814. (4 Munford, 3.)   [2] *Ib.* 58.

affirm or reverse that decision ; and in case of reversal,
to command the state Court to enter and execute a judg-
ment different from that which it had previously ren-
dered?" [1]

Every one of the judges answered in the negative.
The opinion of Judge Cabell was the ablest, and
stated most clearly the real issue raised by the Virginia court. Neither State nor National Government
is dependent one upon the other, he said; neither can
act *"compulsively"* upon the other. Controversies
might arise between State and National Governments, "yet the constitution has provided no umpire, has erected no tribunal by which they shall be
settled." Therefore, the National court could not
oblige the State court to "enter a judgment not its
own." [2] The meaning of the National "Constitution,
laws and treaties, . . must, in cases coming before
State courts, be decided by the State Judges, *ac-*
cording to their own judgments, and upon their own
responsibility." [3] National tribunals belong to one
sovereignty; State tribunals to a different sovereignty — neither is *"superior"* to the other; neither
can command or instruct the other. [4]

Grant that this interpretation of the Constitution results in conflicts between State and Nation
and even deprives the "general government . . of
the power of executing its laws and treaties "; even
so, "the defects of our system of government must
be remedied, not by the judiciary, but by the sovereign power of the people." The Constitution must
be amended by the people, not by judicial interpre-

[1] 4 Munford, 7.   [2] *Ib.* 8–9.   [3] *Ib.* 11.   [4] *Ib.* 12.

tation;[1] yet Congress, in Section 25 of the Judiciary Act, "attempts, in fact, to make the State Courts *Inferior Federal Courts*." The appellate jurisdiction conferred on the Supreme Court, and the word "*supreme*" itself, had reference to inferior National courts and not to State courts.[2]

Judge Roane's opinion was very long and discussed extensively every phase of the controversy. He held that, in giving National courts power over State courts, Section 25 of the Ellsworth Judiciary Act violated the National Constitution. If National courts could control State tribunals, it would be a "plain case of the judiciary of one government correcting and reversing the decisions of that of another." [3] The Virginia Court of Appeals "is bound, to follow its own convictions . . any thing in the decisions, or supposed decisions, of any other court, to the contrary notwithstanding." Let the court at Winchester, therefore, be instructed to execute the judgment of the State Court of Appeals.[4]

Such was the open, aggressive, and dramatic defiance of the Supreme Court of the United States by the Court of Appeals of Virginia. Roane showed his opinion to Monroe, who approved it and sent it to Jefferson at Monticello. Jefferson heartily commended Roane,[5] whereat the Virginia judge was "very much flattered and gratified." [6]

Promptly Philip Martin, through James M. Marshall, took the case to the Supreme Court by means

---

[1] 4 Munford, 15.   [2] *Ib.* 133.   [3] *Ib.* 38.   [4] *Ib.* 54.

[5] Jefferson to Roane, Oct. 12, 1815, *Works: Ford*, XI, 488–90.

[6] Roane to Jefferson, Oct. 28, 1815, *Branch Hist. Papers*, June, 1905, 131–32.

of another writ of error. It now stood upon the docket of that court as Martin *vs.* Hunter's Lessee. Again Marshall refused to sit in the case. St. George Tucker of Virginia, one of the ablest lawyers of the South, and Samuel Dexter, the leader of the Massachusetts bar, appeared for Hunter.[1] As Harper had done on the first appeal, both Tucker and Dexter called attention to the fact that the decision of the Virginia Court of Appeals did not rest exclusively upon the Treaty of Peace, which alone in this case would have authorized an appeal to the Supreme Court.[2]

Story delivered the court's opinion, which was one of the longest and ablest he ever wrote. The Constitution was not ordained by the States, but "emphatically . . by 'the people of the United States.' [3] . . Its powers are expressed in general terms, leaving to the legislature, from time to time, to adopt its own means to effectuate legitimate objects, and to mold and model the exercise of its powers, as its own wisdom and the public interests should require." [4] Story then quotes Sections 1 and 2 of Article III of the Constitution,[5] and continues: Thus is "the voice

[1] The employment of these expensive lawyers is final proof of Hunter's financial resources.

[2] 1 Wheaton, 317, 318.   [3] *Ib.* 324.   [4] *Ib.* 326–27.

[5] The sections of the Constitution pertaining to this dispute are as follows:

"Article III, Section 1. The judicial Power of the United States, shall be vested in one supreme Court, and in such inferior Courts as the Congress may from time to time ordain and establish. The Judges, both of the supreme and inferior Courts, shall hold their Offices during good Behaviour, and shall, at stated Times, receive for their Services a Compensation, which shall not be diminished during their Continuance in Office.

"Section 2. The judicial Power shall extend to all Cases, in Law

of the whole American people solemnly declared, in
establishing one great department of that government which was, in many respects, national, and in
all, supreme." Congress cannot disregard this Constitutional mandate. At a length which, but for the
newness of the question, would be intolerable, Story
demonstrates that the Constitutional grant of judiciary powers is "imperative." [1]

What, then, is the "nature and extent of the appellate jurisdiction of the United States"? It embraces
"every case . . not exclusively to be decided by way
of original jurisdiction." There is nothing in the
Constitution to "restrain its exercise over state
tribunals in the enumerated cases. . . It is the case,
. . and not the court, that gives the jurisdiction." [2] If
the appellate power does not extend to State courts
having concurrent jurisdiction of specified cases, then
that power does "not extend to all, but to some,
cases" — whereas the Constitution declares that it
extends to all other cases than those over which the
Supreme Court is given original jurisdiction. [3]

With great care Story shows the "propriety" of
this construction. [4] Then, with repetitiousness after
the true Marshall pattern, he reasserts that the

and Equity, arising under this Constitution, the Laws of the United
States, and Treaties made, or which shall be made, under their Authority; — to all Cases affecting Ambassadors, other public Ministers
and Consuls; — to all Cases of admiralty and maritime Jurisdiction
— to Controversies to which the United States shall be a Party; —
to Controversies between two or more States; — between a State and
Citizens of another State; — between Citizens of different States; —
between Citizens of the same State claiming Lands under Grants of
different States, and between a State, or the Citizens thereof, and foreign States, Citizens or Subjects."

[1] 1 Wheaton, 328.   [2] *Ib.* 337-38.   [3] *Ib.* 339.   [4] *Ib.* 341.

Constitution acts on States as well as upon individuals, and gives many instances where the "sovereignty" of the States are "restrained." State judges are not independent "in respect to the powers granted to the United States";[1] and the appellate power of the Nation extends to the State courts in cases prescribed in Section 25 of the Judiciary Act; for the Constitution does not limit this power and "we dare not interpose a limitation where the people have not been disposed to create one."[2]

The case decided on the former record, says Story, is not now before the court. "The question now litigated is not upon the construction of a treaty, but upon the constitutionality of a statute of the United States, which is clearly within our jurisdiction." However, "from motives of a public nature," the Supreme Court would "re-examine" the grounds of its former decision.[3] After such reëxamination, extensive in length and detail, he finds the first decision of the Supreme Court to have been correct.

Story thus notices the Marshall adjustment of 1796: "If it be true (as we are informed)" that the compromise had been effected, the court could not take "judicial cognizance" of it "unless spread upon the record." Aside from the Treaty of Peace, the Fairfax title "was, at all events, perfect under the treaty of 1794."[4] In conclusion, Story announces: "It is the opinion of the whole court that the judgment of the Court of Appeals of Virginia, rendered on the mandate in this cause, be reversed, and the

[1] 1 Wheaton, 343–44.   [2] *Ib.* 351.   [3] *Ib.* 355.   [4] *Ib.* 360.

judgment of the District Court, held at Winchester, be, and the same is hereby affirmed." [1]

It has been commonly supposed that Marshall practically dictated Story's two opinions in the Fairfax-Hunter controversy, and certain writers have stated this to be the fact. As we have seen, Story himself, fifteen years afterwards, declared that the Chief Justice had "concurred in every word of the second opinion"; yet in a letter to his brother concerning the effect of Story's opinion upon another suit in the State court at Winchester, involving the same question, Marshall says: "The case of Hunter & Fairfax is very absurdly put on the treaty of 94." [2]

[1] 1 Wheaton, 362.

[2] Marshall to his brother, July 9, 1822, MS. Parts of this long letter are of interest: "Although Judge White [of the Winchester court] will, of course, conform to the decision of the court of appeals against the appellate jurisdiction of the Supreme court, & therefore deny that the opinion in the case of Fairfax & Hunter is binding, yet he must admit that the supreme court is the proper tribunal for expounding the treaties of the United States, & that its decisions on a treaty are binding on the state courts, whether they possess the appellate jurisdiction or not... The exposition of any state law by the courts of that state, are considered in the courts of all the other states, and in those of the United States, as a correct exposition, not to be reexamined.

"The only exception to this rule is when the statute of a state is supposed to violate the constitution of the United States, in which case the courts of the Union claim a controuling & supervising power. Thus any construction made by the courts of Virginia on the statute of descents or of distribution, or on any other subject, is admitted as conclusive in the federal courts, although those courts might have decided differently on the statute itself. The principle is that the courts of every government are the proper tribunals for construing the legislative acts of that government.

"Upon this principle the Supreme court of the United States, independent of its appellate jurisdiction, is the proper tribunal for construing the laws & treaties of the United States; and the construction of that court ought to be received every where as the right construction. The Supreme court of the United States has settled the con-

Justice Johnson dissented in an opinion as inept and unhappy as his dissent in Fletcher *vs.* Peck.[1] He concurs in the judgment of his brethren, but, in doing so, indulges in a stump speech in which Nationalism and State Rights are mingled in astounding fashion. The Supreme Court of the United States, he says, "disavows all intention to decide on the right to issue compulsory process to the state courts." To be sure, the Supreme Court is "supreme over persons and cases as far as our judicial powers extend," but it cannot assert "any compulsory control over the state tribunals." He views "this question as one . . which may affect, in its consequences, the permanence of the American Union," since the Nation and "one of the greatest states" are in collision. The "general government must cease to exist" if the Virginia doctrine shall prevail, but "so firmly" was he "persuaded that the American people can no longer enjoy the blessings of a free government, whenever the state sovereignties shall be prostrated at the feet of the general government," that he " could borrow the language of a celebrated orator, and exclaim: 'I rejoice that Virginia has resisted.'" [2]

---

struction of the treaty of peace to be that lands at that time held by British subjects were not escheatable or grantable by a state . . I refer particularly to Smith v The State of Maryland 6th Cranch Jackson v Clarke 3 Wheaton & Orr v Hodgson 4 Wheaton. The last case is explicit & was decided unanimously, Judge Johnson assenting.

"This being the construction of the highest court of the government which is a party to the treaty is to be considered by all the world as its true construction unless Great Britain, the other party, should controvert it. The court of appeals has not denied this principle. The dicta of Judge Roane respecting the treaty were anterior to this constitutional construction of it."

[1] See vol. III, chap. X, of this work.   [2] 1 Wheaton, 362-63.

Nevertheless, Johnson agrees with the judgment of his associates and, in doing so, delivers a Nationalist opinion, stronger if possible than that of Story.[1]

The public benefits and the historic importance of the decision was the assertion of the supremacy of the Supreme Court of the Nation over the highest court of any State in all cases where the National Constitution, laws and treaties — "the supreme law of the land" — are involved. The decision of the Supreme Court in Martin *vs.* Hunter's Lessee went further than any previous judicial pronouncement to establish the relation between National courts and State tribunals which now exists and will continue as long as the Republic endures.

When the news of this, the first Constitutional opinion ever delivered by Story, got abroad, he was mercilessly assailed by his fellow Republicans as a "renegade." [2] Congress refused to increase the salaries of the members of the Supreme Court,[3] who found it hard to live on the compensation allowed them,[4] and Story seriously considered resigning from the bench and taking over the Baltimore practice of Mr. Pinkney, who soon was to be appointed Minister

[1] Johnson's opinion was published in the *National Intelligencer*, April 16, 1816, as an answer to Roane's argument. (Smith in *Branch Hist. Papers*, June, 1905, 23.)

[2] Story, I, 277.

[3] *Annals*, 14th Cong. 1st Sess. 194, 231–33.

A bill was reported March 22, 1816, increasing the salaries of all government officials. The report of the committee is valuable as showing the increased cost of living. (*Ib.*)

[4] Nearly three years after the decision of Martin *vs.* Hunter's Lessee, Story writes that the Justices of the Supreme Court are "*starving in splendid poverty.*" (Story to Wheaton, Dec. 9, 1818, Story, I, 313.)

to Russia.[1] The decision aroused excitement and indignation throughout Virginia. Roane's popularity increased from the Tide Water to the Valley.[2] The Republican organization made a political issue of the judgment of the National tribunal at Washington. Judge Roane issued his orders to his political lieutenants. The party newspapers, led by the *Enquirer*, inveighed against the "usurpation" by this distant Supreme Court of the United States, a foreign power, an alien judiciary, unsympathetic with Virginia, ignorant of the needs of Virginians.

This conflict between the Supreme Court of the United States and the Court of Appeals of Virginia opened another phase of that fundamental struggle which war was to decide — a fact without knowledge of which this phase of American Constitutional history is colorless.

Not yet, however, was the astute Virginia Republican triumvirate ready to unloose the lightnings of Virginia's wrath. That must be done only when the whole South should reach a proper degree of emotion. This time was not long to be delayed. Within three years Marshall's opinion in M'Culloch *vs*. Maryland was to give Roane, Ritchie, and Taylor their cue to come upon the stage as the spokesmen of Virginia and the entire South, as the champions, indeed, of Localism everywhere throughout America. Important were the parts they played in the drama of Marshall's judicial career.

[1] Story to White, Feb. 26, 1816, Story, i, 278; and see Story to Williams, May 22, 1816, *ib.* 279.

[2] Ambler: *Sectionalism in Virginia*, 103.

CHAPTER IV

FINANCIAL AND MORAL CHAOS

Like a dropsical man calling out for water, water, our deluded citizens are calling for more banks. (Jefferson.)

Merchants are crumbling to ruin, manufactures perishing, agriculture stagnating and distress universal. (John Quincy Adams.)

If we can believe our Democratic editors and public declaimers it [Bank of the United States] is a Hydra, a Cerberus, a Gorgon, a Vulture, a Viper.
(William Harris Crawford.)

Where one prudent and honest man applies for [bankruptcy] one hundred rogues are facilitated in their depredations. (Hezekiah Niles.)

Merchants and traders are harassed by twenty different systems of laws, prolific in endless frauds, perjuries and evasions. (Harrison Gray Otis.)

THE months of February and March, 1819, are memorable in American history, for during those months John Marshall delivered three of his greatest opinions. All of these opinions have had a determinative effect upon the political and industrial evolution of the people; and one of them [1] has so decisively influenced the growth of the Nation that, by many, it is considered as only second in importance to the Constitution itself. At no period and in no land, in so brief a space of time, has any other jurist or statesman ever bestowed upon his country three documents of equal importance. Like the other fundamental state papers which, in the form of judicial opinions, Marshall gave out from the Supreme Bench, those of 1819 were compelled by grave and dangerous conditions, National in extent.

It was a melancholy prospect over which Marshall's broad vision ranged, when from his rustic

[1] M'Culloch *vs.* Maryland, see *infra*, chap. VI.

bench under his trees at Richmond, during the spring and autumn of 1818, he surveyed the situation in which the American people found themselves. It was there, or in the quiet of the Blue Ridge Mountains where he spent the summer months, that he formed the outlines of those charts which he was soon to present to the country for its guidance; and it was there that at least one of them was put on paper.

The interpretation of John Marshall as the constructing architect of American Nationalism is not satisfactorily accomplished by a mere statement of his Nationalist opinions and of the immediate legal questions which they answered. Indeed, such a narrative, by itself, does not greatly aid to an understanding of Marshall's immense and enduring achievements. Not in the narrow technical points involved, some of them diminutive and all uninviting in their formality; not in the dreary records of the law cases decided, is to be found the measure of his monumental service to the Republic or the meaning of what he did. The state of things which imperatively demanded the exercise of his creative genius and the firm pressure of his steadying hand must be understood in order to grasp the significance of his labors.

When the Supreme Court met in February, 1819, almost the whole country was in grievous turmoil; for nearly three years conditions had been growing rapidly worse and were now desperate. Poverty, bankruptcy, chicanery, crime were widespread and increasing. Thrift, prudence, honesty, and order had seemingly been driven from the hearts and minds of most of the people; while speculation, craft, and unscrupulous devices were prevalent throughout all but one portion of the land. Only New England had largely escaped the universal curse that appeared to have fallen upon the United States; and even that section was not untouched by the economic and social plague that had raged and was becoming more deadly in every other quarter.

While it is true that a genuine democratizing evolution was in progress, this fact does not explain the situation that had grown up throughout the country. Neither does the circumstance that the development of land and resources was going forward in haphazard fashion, at the hands of a new population hard pressed for money and facilities for work and communication, reveal the cause of the appalling state of affairs. It must frankly be said of the conditions, to us now unbelievable, that they were due partly to the ignorance, credulity, and greed of the people; partly to the spirit of extravagance; partly to the criminal avarice of the financially ambitious; partly to popular dread of any great centralized moneyed institution, however sound; partly to that pest of all democracies, the uninformed and incessant demagogue whipping up and then pandering to the passions of the multitude; partly to that scarcely less dangerous creature in a Republic, the fanatical doctrinaire, proclaiming the perfection of government by word-logic and insisting that human nature shall be confined in the strait-jacket of verbal theory. From this general welter of moral and economic debauchery, Localism had once more arisen and was eagerly reasserting its domination.

The immediate cause of the country's plight was an utter chaos in banking. Seldom has such a financial motley ever covered with variegated rags the backs of a people. The confusion was incredible; but not for a moment did the millions who suffered, blame themselves for their tragic predicament. Now praising banks as unfailing fountains of money, now denouncing banks as the sources of poisoned waters, clamoring for whatever promised even momentary relief, striking at whatever seemingly denied it, the people laid upon anything and anybody but themselves and their improvidence, the responsibility for their distress.

Hamilton's financial plans [1] had proved to be as successful as they were brilliant. The Bank of the United States, managed, on the whole, with prudence, skill, and honesty,[2] had fulfilled the expectations of its founders. It had helped to maintain the National credit by loans in anticipation of revenue; it had served admirably, and without compensation, as an agent for collecting, safeguarding, and transporting the funds of the Government; and, more important than all else, it had kept the currency, whether its own notes or those of private banks, on a sound specie basis. It had, indeed, "acted as the general guardian of commercial credit" and, as such, had faithfully and wisely performed its duties.[3]

But the success of the Bank had not overcome the

---

[1] See vol. II, 60, of this work.

[2] Sumner: *History of American Currency*, 63.

[3] See Memorial of the Bank for a recharter, April 20, 1808 (*Am. State Papers, Finance*, II, 301), and second Memorial, Dec. 18, 1810 (*ib.* 451–52). Every statement in these petitions was true. See also Dewey: *Financial History of the United States*, 100, 101.

original antagonism to a great central moneyed institution. Following the lead of Jefferson, who had
insisted that the project was unconstitutional,[1] Madison, in the first Congress, had opposed the bill to
incorporate the first Bank of the United States. Congress had no power, he said, to create corporations.[2]
After twelve years of able management, and in spite
of the good it had accomplished, Jefferson still considered it, potentially, a monster that might overthrow the Republic. "This institution," he wrote in
the third year of his Presidency, "is one of the most
deadly hostility existing, against the principles &
form of our Constitution. . . An institution like this,
penetrating by it's branches every part of the Union,
acting by command & in phalanx, may, in a critical
moment, upset the government. . . What an obstruction could not this bank of the U. S., with all it's
branch banks, be in time of war?"[3]

The fact that most of the stock of the Bank had
been bought up by Englishmen added to the un-
popularity of the institution.[4] Another source of hostility was the jealousy of State banks, much of the
complaint about "unconstitutionality" and "foreign ownership" coming from the agents and friends
of these local concerns. The State banks wished for
themselves the profits made by the National Bank
and its branches, and they chafed under the wise

[1] See vol. II, 70–71, of this work.
[2] *Annals*, 1st Cong. 2d. Sess. 1945. By far the strongest objection
to a National bank, however, was that it was a monopoly inconsistent
with free institutions.
[3] Jefferson to Gallatin, Dec. 13, 1803, *Works:* Ford: x, 57.
[4] "Fully two thirds of the Bank stock . . were owned in England." (Adams: *U.S.* v, 328.)

regulation of their note issues, which the existence of the National system compelled.

For several years these State banks had been growing in number and activity.[1] When, in 1808, the directors of the Bank of the United States asked for a renewal of its charter, which would expire in 1811, and when the same request was made of Congress in 1809, opposition poured into the Capital from every section of the country. The great Bank was a British institution, it was said; its profits were too great; it was a creature of Federalism, brought forth in violation of the Constitution. Its directors, officers, and American stockholders were Federalists; and this fact was the next most powerful motive for the overthrow of the first Bank of the United States.[2]

Petitions to Congress denounced it and demanded its extinction. One from Pittsburgh declared "that your memorialists are 'the People of the United States,'" and asserted that the Bank "held in bondage thousands of our citizens," kept the Government "in duress," and subsidized the press, thus "thronging" the Capital with lobbyists who in general were the "head-waters of corruption."[3] The Legislatures of many States "instructed" their Senators and "earnestly requested" their Representatives in Congress to oppose a new charter for the expiring National institution. Such resolutions came from Pennsylvania, from Virginia, from Massachusetts.[4]

---

[1] Dewey, 127; and Pitkin: *Statistical View of the Commerce of the United States*, 130–32.

[2] Adams: *U.S.* v, 328–29.

[3] *Annals*, 11th Cong. 3d Sess. 118–21.

[4] *Ib.* 153, 201, 308; and see Pitkin, 421.

The State banks were the principal contrivers of all this agitation.[1] For instance, the Bank of Virginia, organized in 1804, had acquired great power and, but for the branch of the National concern at Richmond, would have had almost the banking monopoly of that State. Especially did the Virginia Bank desire to become the depository of National funds[2] — a thing that could not be accomplished so long as the Bank of the United States was in existence.[3] Dr. John Brockenbrough, the relative, friend, and political associate of Spencer Roane and Thomas Ritchie, was the president of this State institution, which was a most important part of the Republican machine in Virginia. Considering the absolute control held by this political organization over the Legislature, it seems probable that the State bank secured the resolution condemnatory of the Bank of the United States.

Certainly the General Assembly would not have taken any action not approved by Brockenbrough, Roane, and Ritchie. Ritchie's *Enquirer* boasted that it "was the first to denounce the renewal of the bank charter."[4] In the Senate, William H. Crawford boldly charged that the instructions of the State Legislatures were "induced by motives of avarice";[5] and Senator Giles was plainly embarrassed in his attempt to deny the indictment.[6]

[1] Adams: *U.S.* v, 327–28. "They induced one State legislature after another to instruct their senators on the subject." Pitkin, 422.

[2] Ambler: *Ritchie*, 26–27, 52.   [3] *Ib.* 67.

[4] *Branch Hist. Papers*, June, 1903, 179.

[5] *Annals*, 11th Cong. 3d Sess. 145.

[6] "It is true, that a branch of the Bank of the United States . . is established at Norfolk; and that a branch of the Bank of Virginia is

Nearly all the newspapers were controlled by the State banks;[1] they, of course, denounced the National Bank in the familiar terms of democratic controversy and assailed the character of every public man who spoke in behalf of so vile and dangerous an institution.[2] It was also an ideal object of assault for local politicians who bombarded the Bank with their usual vituperation. All this moved Senator Crawford, in his great speech for the rechartering of the Bank, to a scathing arraignment of such methods.[3]

In spite of conclusive arguments in favor of the Bank of the United States on the merits of the question, the bill to recharter that institution was de-

also established there. But these circumstances furnish no possible motive of avarice to the Virginia Legislature. . . They have acted . . from the purest and most honorable motives." (*Annals*, 11th Cong. 3d Sess. 200.)

[1] Pitkin, 421.

[2] The "newspapers teem with the most virulent abuse." (James Flint's Letters from America, in *Early Western Travels:* Thwaites, IX, 87.) Even twenty years later Captain Marryat records: "The press in the United States is licentious to the highest possible degree, and defies control. . . Every man in America reads his newspaper, and hardly any thing else." (Marryat: *Diary in America*, 2d Series, 56–59.)

[3] "The Democratic presses . . have . . teemed with the most scurrilous abuse against every member of Congress who has dared to utter a syllable in favor of the renewal of the bank charter." Any member supporting the bank "is instantly charged with being bribed, . . with being corrupt, with having trampled upon the rights and liberties of the people, . . with being guilty of perjury."

According to "the rantings of our Democratic editors . . and the denunciations of our public declaimers," the bank "exists under the form of every foul and hateful beast and bird, and creeping thing. It is an *Hydra*; it is a *Cerberus*; it is a *Gorgon*; it is a *Vulture*; it is a *Viper*. . .

"Shall we tamely act under the lash of this tyranny of the press? . . I most solemnly protest . . To tyranny, under whatever form it may be exercised, I declare open and interminable war . . whether the tyrant is an irresponsible editor or a despotic Monarch." (*Annals*, 11th Cong. 3d Sess. 145.)

feated in the House by a single vote,[1] and in the Senate by the casting vote of the Vice-President, the aged George Clinton.[2] Thus, on the very threshold of the War of 1812, the Government was deprived of this all but indispensable fiscal agent; immense quantities of specie, representing foreign bank holdings, were withdrawn from the country; and the State banks were given a free hand which they soon used with unrestrained license.

These local institutions, which, from the moment the failure of the rechartering of the National Bank seemed probable, had rapidly increased in number, now began to spring up everywhere.[3] From the first these concerns had issued bills for the loan of which they charged interest. Thus banking was made doubly profitable. Even those banks, whose note issues were properly safeguarded, achieved immense profits. Banking became a mania.

"The Banking Infatuation pervades all America," wrote John Adams in 1810. "Our whole system of Banks is a violation of every honest Principle of Banks. . . A Bank that issues Paper at Interest is a Pickpocket or a Robber. But the Delusion will have its Course. You may as well reason with a Hurricane. An Aristocracy is growing out of them, that will be as fatal as The Feudal Barons, if unchecked in Time. . . Think of the Number, the Offices, Stations, Wealth, Piety and Reputations of the Persons in all the States, who have made Fortunes by these Banks, and then you will see how deeply rooted the evil is. The Number of Debtors who hope to pay

---

[1] *Annals*, 11th Cong. 3d Sess. 826.   [2] *Ib.* 347.   [3] Pitkin, 430.

their debts by this Paper united with the Creditors who build Pallaces in our Cities, and Castles for Country Seats, by issuing this Paper form too impregnable a Phalanx to be attacked by any Thing less disciplined than Roman Legions." [1]

Such was the condition even before the expiration of the charter of the first Bank. But, when the restraining and regulating influence of that conservative and ably managed institution was removed altogether, local banking began a course that ended in a mad carnival of roguery, to the ruin of legitimate business and the impoverishment and bankruptcy of hundreds of thousands of the general public.

The avarice of the State banks was immediately inflamed by the war necessities of the National Government. Desperate for money, the Treasury exchanged six per cent United States bonds for the notes of State banks.[2] The Government thus lost five million dollars from worthless bank bills.[3] These local institutions now became the sole depositories of the Government funds which the National Bank had formerly held.[4] Sources of gain of this kind were only extra inducements to those who, by wit alone, would gather quick wealth to set up more local banks. But other advantages were quite enough to appeal to the greedy, the dishonest, and the adventurous.

Liberty to pour out bills without effective restriction as to the amount or security; to loan such

---

[1] Adams to Rush, Dec. 27, 1810, *Old Family Letters*, 272.
[2] Sumner: *Andrew Jackson*, 229.   [3] Dewey, 145.
[4] Twenty-one State banks were employed as Government depositories after the destruction of the first Bank of the United States. (*Ib*. 128.)

"rags" to any who could be induced to borrow; to collect these debts by foreclosure of mortgages or threats of imprisonment of the debtors — these were some of the seeds from which grew the noxious financial weeds that began to suck the prosperity of the country. When the first Bank of the United States was organized there were only three State banks in the country. By 1800, there were twenty-eight; by 1811, they had more than trebled,[1] and most of the eighty-eight State institutions in existence when the first National Bank was destroyed had been organized after it seemed probable that it would not be granted a recharter.

So rapidly did they increase and so great were their gains that, within little more than a year from the demise of the first Bank of the United States, John Adams records: "The Profits of our Banks to the advantage of the few, at the loss of the many, are such an enormous fraud and oppression as no other Nation ever invented or endured. Who can compute the amount of the sums taken out of the Pocketts of the Simple and hoarded in the Purses of the cunning in the course of every year? . . If Rumour speaks the Truth Boston has and will emulate Philadelphia in her Proportion of Bankruptcies." [2]

Yet Boston and Philadelphia banks were the soundest and most carefully conducted of any in the whole land. If Adams spoke extravagantly of the methods and results of the best managed financial institutions of the country, he did not exaggerate

[1] Dewey, 127.
[2] Adams to Rush, July 3, 1812, *Old Family Letters*, 299.

conditions elsewhere. From Connecticut to the Mississippi River, from Lake Erie to New Orleans, the craze for irresponsible banking spread like a contagious fever. The people were as much affected by the disease as were the speculators. The more "money" they saw, the more "money" they wanted. Bank notes fell in value; specie payments were suspended; rates of exchange were in utter confusion and constantly changing. From day to day no man knew, with certainty, what the "currency" in his pocket was worth. At Vincennes, Indiana, in 1818, William Faux records: "I passed away my 20 dollar note of the rotten bank of Harmony, Pennsylvania, for five dollars only!"[1]

The continuance of the war, of course, made this financial situation even worse for the Government than for the people. It could not negotiate its loans; the public dues were collected with difficulty, loss, and delay; the Treasury was well-nigh bankrupt. "The Department of State was so bare of money as to be unable to pay even its stationery bill."[2] In 1814, when on the verge of financial collapse, the Administration determined that another Bank of the United States was absolutely necessary to the conduct of the war.[3] Scheme after scheme was proposed, wrangled over, and defeated.

One plan for a bank[4] was beaten "after a day of the most tumultuous proceedings I ever saw," testi-

---

[1] William Faux's Journal, *E. W. T.*: Thwaites, xi, 207.

[2] Speech of Hanson in the House, Nov. 28, 1814, *Annals*, 13th Cong. 3d Sess. 656.

[3] Catterall: *Second Bank of the United States*, 13–17.

[4] Calhoun's bill.

fies Webster.[1] Another bill passed,[2] but was vetoed
by President Madison because it could not aid in
the rehabilitation of the public credit, nor "provide
a circulating medium during the war, nor . . furnish
loans, or anticipate public revenue."[3] When the war
was over, Madison timidly suggested to Congress the
advisability of establishing a National bank "that
the benefits of a uniform national currency should be
restored."[4] Thus, on April 10, 1816, two years after
Congress took up the subject, a law finally was enacted and approved providing for the chartering
and government of the second Bank of the United
States.[5]

Within four years, then, of the refusal of Congress
to recharter the sound and ably managed first Bank
of the United States, it was forced to authorize
another National institution, endowed with practically the same powers possessed by the Bank which
Congress itself had so recently destroyed.[6] But the
second establishment would have at least one advantage over the first in the eyes of the predominant political party — a majority of the officers
and directors of the Bank would be Republicans.[7]

[1] Webster to his brother, Nov. 29, 1814, Van Tyne, 55.

[2] Webster's bill.

[3] *Annals*, 13th Cong. 3d Sess. 189–91; Richardson, i, 555–57.

[4] Richardson, i, 565–66. Four years afterwards President Monroe
told his Secretary of State, John Quincy Adams, that Jefferson, Madison, and himself considered all Constitutional objections to the Bank
as having been "settled by twenty years of practice and acquiescence
under the first bank." (*Memoirs, J. Q. A.*: Adams, iv, 499, Jan. 8,
1820.)

[5] *Annals*, 14th Cong. 1st Sess. 280–81.

[6] *Annals*, 1st Cong. 2d and 3d Sess. 2375–82; and 14th Cong. 1st
Sess. 1812–25; also Dewey, 150–51.

[7] Catterall, 22.

During their four years of "financial liberty" the number of State banks had multiplied. Those that could be enumerated in 1816 were 246.[1] In addition to these, scores of others, most of them "pure swindles,"[2] were pouring out their paper.[3] Even if they had been sound, not half of them were needed.[4] Nearly all of them extended their wild methods. "The Banks have been going on, as tho' the day of reckoning would never come," wrote Rufus King of conditions in the spring of 1816.[5]

The people themselves encouraged these practices. The end of the war released an immense quantity of English goods which flooded the American market. The people, believing that devastated Europe would absorb all American products, and beholding a vision of radiant prosperity, were eager to buy. A passion for extravagance swept over America;[6] the country was drained of specie by payments for exports.[7] Then came a frenzy of speculation. "The people were wild; . . reason seemed turned topsy turvey."[8]

The multitude of local banks intensified both these manias by every device that guile and avarice could suggest. Every one wanted to get rich at the expense of some one else by a mysterious process, the nature of

[1] Dewey, 144.   [2] Sumner: *Hist. Am. Currency*, 70.

[3] In November, 1818, Niles estimated that there were about four hundred banks in the country with eight thousand "managers and clerks," costing $2,000,000, annually. (Niles, xv, 162.)

[4] "The present multitude of them . . is no more fitted to the condition of society, than a long-tailed coat becomes a sailor on shipboard." (*Ib.* xi, 130.)

[5] King to his son, May 1, 1816, King, vi, 22.

[6] King to Gore, May 14, 1816, *Ib.* 23–25.

[7] Niles, xiv, 109.   [8] *Ib.* xvi, 257.

which was not generally understood beyond the fact
that it involved some sort of trickery. Did any man's
wife and family want expensive clothing — the local
bank would loan him bills issued by itself, but only
on good security. Did any man wish to start some un-
familiar and alluring enterprise by which to make a
fortune speedily — if he had a farm to mortgage, the
funds were his. Was a big new house desired? The
money was at hand — nothing was required to get it
but the pledge of property worth many times the
amount with which the bank "accommodated" him.[1]

Indeed, the local banks urged such "investments,"
invited people with property to borrow, laid traps to
ensnare them. "What," asked Hezekiah Niles, "is
to be the end of such a business? — Mammoth fortunes for the *wise*, wretched poverty for the *foolish*. . . Lands, lots, houses — stock, farming utensils
and household furniture, under custody of the sheriff
— SPECULATION IN A COACH, HONESTY IN THE
JAIL."[2]

Many banks sent agents among the people to
hawk their bills. These were perfectly good, the har-
pies would assure their victims, but they could now
be had at a heavy discount; to buy them was to make
a large profit. So the farmer, the merchant, even the
laborer who had acquired a dwelling of his own, were
induced to mortgage their property or sell it outright in exchange for bank paper that often proved
to be worthless.[3]

Frequently these local banks ensnared prosperous
farmers by the use of "cappers." Niles prints con-

---

[1] Niles, XVI, 257.   [2] *Ib.* XIV, 110.   [3] *Ib.* 195–96.

spicuously as "A True Story"[1] the account of a
certain farmer who owned two thousand acres, well
improved and with a commodious residence and
substantial farm buildings upon it. Through his land
ran a stream affording good water power. He was
out of debt, prosperous, and contented. One day he
went to a town not many miles from his plantation.
There four pleasant-mannered, well-dressed men
made his acquaintance and asked him to dinner,
where a few directors of the local bank were present.
The conversation was brought around to the profits
to be made in the milling business. The farmer was
induced to borrow a large sum from the local bank
and build a mill, mortgaging his farm to secure
the loan. The mill was built, but seldom used because there was no work for it to do; and, in the
end, the two thousand acres, dwelling, buildings,
mill, and all, became the property of the bank directors.[2]

This incident is illustrative of numerous similar
cases throughout the country, especially in the
West and South. Niles thus describes banking
methods in general: "At first they throw out money
profusely, to all that they believe are *ultimately*
able to return it; nay, they wind round some like ser-
pents to tempt them to borrow — .. they then affect
to draw in their notes, .. money becomes scarce,
and notes of hand are *shaved* by them to meet bank
engagements; it gets worse — the *consummation*

---

[1] "Niles' *Weekly Register* is .. an excellent repository of facts and
documents." (Jefferson to Crawford, Feb. 11, 1815, *Works:* Ford, XI,
453.)

[2] Niles, XIV, 426–28.

originally designed draws nigh, and farm after farm,
lot after lot, house after house, are sacrificed." [1]

So terrifying became the evil that the Legislature
of New York, although one of the worst offenders in
the granting of bank charters, was driven to appoint
a committee of investigation. It reported nothing
more than every honest observer had noted. Money
could not be transmitted from place to place, the
committee said, because local banks had "engrossed
the whole circulation in their neighborhood," while
their notes abroad had depreciated. The operations
of the bankers "immediately within their vicinity"
were ruinous: "Designing, unprincipled speculator[s]
.. impose on the credulity of the honest, industrious,
unsuspecting .. by their specious flattery and mis-
representation, obtaining from them borrowed notes
and endorsements, until the ruin is consummated,
and their farms are sold by the sheriff." [2]

Some banks committed astonishing frauds, "such
as placing a partial fund in a distant bank to redeem
their paper" and then "issuing an emission of notes
signed with ink of a different shade, at the same time
giving secret orders to said bank not to pay the notes
thus signed." Bank paper, called "*facility notes,*"
was issued, but "payable in neither money, country
produce, or any thing else that has body or shape."
Bank directors even terrorized merchants who did
not submit to their practices. In one typical case all
persons were denied discounts who traded at a cer-

[1] Niles, XIV, 2-3.

[2] "Report of the Committee on the Currency of this [New York]
State," Feb. 24, 1818, *ib.* 39–42; also partially reproduced in *American History told by Contemporaries:* Hart, III, 441–45.

tain store, the owner of which had asked for bank bills that would be accepted in New York City, where they had to be remitted — this, too, when the offending merchant kept his account at the bank.

The committee describes, as illustrative of banking chicanery, the instance of "an aged farmer," owner of a valuable farm, who, "wishing to raise the sum of one thousand dollars, to assist his children, was told by a director, he could get it out of the bank . . and that he would endorse his note for him." Thus the loan was made; but, when the note expired, the director refused to obtain a renewal except upon the payment of one hundred dollars in addition to the discount. At the next renewal the same condition was exacted and also "a judgment . . in favor of said director, and the result was, his farm was soon after sold without his knowledge by the sheriff, and purchased by the said director for less than the judgment." [1]

Before the second Bank of the United States opened its doors for business, the local banks began to gather the first fruits of their labors. By the end of 1816 suits upon promissory notes, bonds, and mortgages, given by borrowers, were begun. Three fourths of all judgments rendered in the spring of 1818 by the Supreme Court of the State of New York alone were "in favor of banks, against real property." [2] Suits and judgments of this kind grew ever more frequent.

In such fashion was the country hastened toward the period of bankruptcy. Yet the people in general

[1] "Report of Committee on the Currency," New York, *supra*, 184.
[2] Niles, xiv, 108.

still continued to demand more "money." The worse
the curse, the greater the floods of it called for by the
body of the public. "Like a dropsical man calling
out for water, water, our deluded citizens are clamoring for more banks. . . We are now taught to believe
that legerdemain tricks upon paper can produce as
solid wealth as hard labor in the earth," wrote Jefferson when the financial madness was becoming too
apparent to all thoughtful men.[1]

Practically no restrictions were placed upon these
financial freebooters,[2] while such flimsy regulations
as their charters provided were disregarded at will.[3]
There was practically no publicity as to the management and condition of even the best of these
banks;[4] most of them denied the right of any authority to inquire into their affairs and scorned to furnish
information as to their assets or methods.[5] For years
the Legislatures of many States were controlled by
these institutions; bank charters were secured by the
worst methods of legislative manipulation; lobbyists thronged the State Capitols when the General
Assemblies were in session; few, if any, lawmaking
bodies of the States were without officers, directors,
or agents of local banks among their membership.[6]

[1] Jefferson to Yancey, Jan. 6, 1816, *Works: Ford*, xi, 494.

[2] Dewey, 144; and Sumner: *Hist. Am. Currency*, 75.

[3] Niles proposed a new bank to be called "THE RAGBANK OF THE
UNIVERSE," main office at "*Lottery-ville*," and branches at "*Hooks-
town*," "*Owl Creek*," "*Botany Bay*," and "*Twisters-burg*." Directors
were to be empowered also "to put offices on wheels, on ship-board, or
in balloons"; stock to be "one thousand million of old shirts." (Niles,
xiv, 227.)

[4] Dewey, 144.   [5] *Ib*. 153–54.

[6] Flint's Letters, *E. W. T.*: Thwaites, ix, 136; and see " Report of
the Committee on the Currency," New York, *supra*, 184.

Thus bank charters were granted by wholesale and they were often little better than permits to plunder the public. During the session of the Virginia Legislature of 1816–17, twenty-two applications for bank charters were made.[1] At nearly the same time twenty-one banks were chartered in the newly admitted and thinly peopled State of Ohio.[2] The following year forty-three new banks were authorized in Kentucky.[3] In December, 1818, James Flint found in Kentucky, Ohio, and Tennessee a "vast host of fabricators, and venders of base money."[4] All sorts of "companies" went into the banking business. Bridge companies, turnpike companies, manufacturing companies, mercantile companies, were authorized to issue their bills, and this flood of paper became the "money" of the people; even towns and villages emitted "currency" in the form of municipal notes. The City of Richmond, Virginia, in 1815, issued "small paper bills for change, to the amount of $29,948."[5] Often bills were put in circulation of denominations as low as six and one fourth cents.[6]

---

[1] Tyler: *Tyler*, I, 302; Niles, XI, 130.

[2] Niles, XI, 128.

[3] *Ib*. IV, 109; Collins: *Historical Sketches of Kentucky*, 88.

These were in addition to the branches of the Bank of Kentucky and of the Bank of the United States. Including them, the number of chartered banks in that State was fifty-eight by the close of 1818. Of the towns where new banks were established during that year, Burksville had 106 inhabitants; Barboursville, 55; Hopkinsville, 131; Greenville, 75; thirteen others had fewer than 500 inhabitants. The "capital" of the banks in such places was never less than $100,000, but that at Glasgow, with 244 inhabitants, had a capital of $200,000, and several other villages were similarly favored. For full list see Niles, XIV, 109.

[4] Flint's Letters, *E. W. T.*: Thwaites, IX, 133.   [5] Niles, XVII, 85.

[6] John Woods's Two Years' Residence, *E. W. T.*: Thwaites, X, 236.

Rapidly the property of the people became encumbered to secure their indebtedness to the banks.

A careful and accurate Scotch traveler thus describes their methods: "By lending, and otherwise emitting their engravings, they have contrived to mortgage and buy much of the property of their neighbours, and to appropriate to themselves the labour of less moneyed citizens. . . Bankers gave in exchange for their paper, that of *other banks, equally good with their own.* . . The holder of the paper may comply in the barter, or keep the notes . . ; but he finds it too late to be delivered from the snare. The people committed the lapsus, when they accepted of the gew-gaws clean from the press. . . The deluded multitude have been basely duped." [1] Yet, says Flint, "every one is afraid of bursting the bubble." [2]

As settlers penetrated the Ohio and Indiana forests and spread over the Illinois prairies, the banks went with them and "levied their contributions on the first stroke of the axe." [3] Kentucky was comparatively well settled and furnished many emigrants to the newer regions north of the Ohio River. Rough log cabins were the abodes of nearly all of the people [4]

---

[1] Flint's Letters, *E. W. T.*: Thwaites, IX, 133–34.
[2] *Ib.* 136. [3] Niles, XIV, 162.
[4] Woods's Two Years' Residence, *E. W. T.*: Thwaites, X, 274–78; and Flint's Letters, *ib.* IX, 69.

In southwestern Indiana, in 1818, Faux "saw nothing . . but miserable log holes, and a mean ville of eight or ten huts or cabins, sadly neglected farms, and indolent, dirty, sickly, wild-looking inhabitants." (Faux's Journal, Nov. 1, 1818, *ib.* XI, 213–14.) He describes Kentucky houses as "miserable holes, having one room only," where "all cook, eat, sleep, breed, and die, males and females, all together." (*Ib.* 185, and see 202.)

who, for the most part, lived roughly,[1] drank heavily,[2] were poorly educated.[3] They were, however, hospitable, generous, and brave; but most of them preferred to speculate rather than to work.[4] Illness was general, sound health rare.[5] "I hate the prairies. . . I would not have any of them of a gift, if I must be compelled to live on them," avowed an English emigrant.[6]

In short, the settlers reproduced most of the features of the same movement in the preceding generation.[7] There was the same squalor, suspicion,

[1] For shocking and almost unbelievable conditions of living among the settlers see Faux's Journal, *E. W. T.*: Thwaites, xi, 226, 231, 252–53, 268–69.

[2] "We landed for some whiskey; for our men would do nothing without." (Woods's Two Years' Residence, *ib.* x, 245, 317.) "Excessive drinking seems the all-pervading, easily-besetting sin." (Faux's Journal, Nov. 3, 1818, *ib.* xi, 213.) This continued for many years and was as marked in the East as in the West. (See Marryat, 2d Series, 37–41.)

There was, however, a large and ever-increasing number who hearkened to those wonderful men, the circuit-riding preachers, who did so much to build up moral and religious America. Most people belonged to some church, and at the camp meetings and revivals, multitudes received conviction.

The student should carefully read the *Autobiography of Peter Cartwright*, edited by W. P. Strickland. This book is an invaluable historical source and is highly interesting. See also Schermerhorn and Mills: *A Correct View of that part of the United States which lies west of the Allegany Mountains, with regard to Religion and Morals*. *Great Revival in the West*, by Catharine C. Cleveland, is a careful and trustworthy account of religious conditions before the War of 1812. It has a complete bibliography.

[3] Flint's Letters, *E. W. T.*: Thwaites, 153; also Schermerhorn and Mills, 17–18.

[4] "Nature is the agriculturist here [near Princeton, Ind.]; speculation instead of cultivation, is the order of the day amongst men." (Thomas Hulme's Journal, *E. W. T.*: Thwaites, x, 62; see Faux's Journal, *ib.* xi, 227.)

[5] Faux's Journal, *ib.* 216, 236, 242–43.   [6] *Ib.* 214.

[7] See vol. i, chap. vii, of this work.

credulity, and the same combativeness,[1] the same
assertion of superiority over every other people on
earth,[2] the same impatience of control, particularly
from a source so remote as the National Government.[3] "The people speak and seem as if they were
without a government, and name it only as a bugbear," wrote William Faux.[4]

Moreover, the inhabitants of one section knew lit-

---

[1] Flint's Letters, *E. W. T.*: Thwaites, IX, 87; Woods's Two Years
Residence, *ib.* X, 255. "I saw a man this day . . his nose bitten off close
down to its root, in a fight with a nose-loving neighbour." (Faux's
Journal, *ib.* XI, 222; and see Strickland, 24-25.)

[2] The reports of American conditions by British travelers, although
from unsympathetic pens and much exaggerated, were substantially
true. Thus Europe, and especially the United Kingdom, conceived for
Americans that profound contempt which was to endure for generations.

"Such is the land of Jonathan," declared the *Edinburgh Review* in an
analysis in 1820 (XXXIII, 78-80) of a book entitled *Statistical Annals of
the United States*, by Adam Seybert. "He must not . . allow himself to
be dazzled by that galaxy of epithets by which his orators and newspaper scribblers endeavour to persuade their supporters that they are
the greatest, the most refined, the most enlightened, and the most
moral people upon earth. . . They have hitherto given no indications
of genius, and made no approaches to the heroic, either in their morality or character. . .

"During the thirty or forty years of their independence, they have
done absolutely nothing for the Sciences, for the Arts, for Literature,
or even for statesman-like studies of Politics or Political Economy. . .
In the four quarters of the globe, who reads an American book? or
goes to an American play? or looks at an American picture or statue?
What does the world yet owe to American physicians or surgeons?
What new substances have their chemists discovered? or what old
ones have they analyzed? What new constellations have been discovered by the telescopes of Americans? — what have they done in the
mathematics? . . under which of the old tyrannical governments of
Europe is every sixth man a Slave, whom his fellow-creatures may buy
and sell and torture?"

[3] Nevertheless, these very settlers had qualities of sound, clean
citizenship; and beneath their roughness and crudity were noble as-
pirations. For a sympathetic and scholarly treatment of this phase of
the subject see Pease: *Frontier State*, I, 69.

[4] Faux's Journal, *E. W. T.*: Thwaites, XI, 246.

tle or nothing of what those in another were doing. "We are as ignorant of the temper prevailing in the Eastern States as the people of New Holland can be," testifies John Randolph in 1812.[1] Even a generation after Randolph made this statement, Frederick Marryat records that "the United States . . comprehend an immense extent of territory, with a population running from a state of refinement down to one of positive barbarism. . . The inhabitants of the cities . . know as little of what is passing in Arkansas and Alabama as a cockney does of the manners and customs of . . the Isle of Man." [2] Communities were still almost as segregated as were those of a half-century earlier.[3] Marryat observes, a few years later, that "to write upon America *as a nation* would be absurd, for nation . . it is not." [4] Again, he notes in his journal that "the mass of the citizens of the United States have . . a very great dislike to all law except . . the decision of the majority." [5]

These qualities furnished rich soil for cultivation by demagogues, and small was the husbandry required to produce a sturdy and bellicose sentiment of Localism. Although the bills of the Bank of the United States were sought for,[6] the hostility to that National institution was increased rather than diminished by the superiority of its notes over those of the local money mills. No town was too small for a bank. The fact that specie payments were not exacted "indicated every village in the United

[1] Randolph to Quincy, Aug. 16, 1812, Quincy: *Quincy*, 270.
[2] Marryat, 2d Series, 1.   [3] See vol. I, chap. VII, of this work.
[4] Marryat, 1st Series, 15.   [5] Marryat, 2d Series, 176.
[6] Woods's Two Years' Residence, *E. W. T.*: Thwaites, x, 325.

States, where there was a 'church, a tavern and a blacksmith's shop,' as a suitable site for a *bank*, and justified any persons in establishing one who could raise enough to pay the *paper maker* and *engraver*." [1]

Not only did these chartered manufactories of currency multiply, but private banks sprang up and did business without any restraint whatever. Niles was entirely within the truth when he declared that nothing more was necessary to start a banking business than plates, presses, and paper. [2] Often the notes of the banks, private or incorporated, circulated only in the region where they were issued. [3] In 1818 the "currency" of the local banks of Cincinnati was "mere waste paper . . out of the city." [4] The people had to take this local "money" or go without any medium of exchange. When the notes of distant banks were to be had, the people did not know the value of them. "Notes current in one part, are either refused, or taken at a large discount, in another," wrote Flint in 1818. [5]

In the cities firms dealing with bank bills printed

---

[1] Niles, xiv, 2.

[2] See McMaster, iv, 287. This continued even after the people had at last become suspicious of unlicensed banks. In 1820, at Bloomington, Ohio, a hamlet of "ten houses . . in the edge of the prairie . . a [bank] company was formed, plates engraved, and the bank notes brought to the spot." Failing to secure a charter, the adventurers sold their outfit at auction, fictitious names were signed to the notes, which were then put into fraudulent circulation. (Flint's Letters, *E. W. T.*: Thwaites, ix, 310.)

[3] *Ib.* 130–31.

[4] Faux's Journal, Oct. 11, 1818, *E. W. T.*: Thwaites, xi, 171. Faux says that even in Cincinnati itself the bank bills of that town could be exchanged at stores "only 30 or 40 per centum below par, or United States' paper."

[5] Flint's Letters, *E. W. T.*: Thwaites, ix, 132–36.

lists of them with the market values, which changed from day to day.[1] Sometimes the county courts fixed rates of exchange; for instance, the County Court of Norfolk County, Virginia, in March, 1816, decreed that the notes of the Bank of Virginia and the Bank of South Carolina were worth their face value, while the bills of Baltimore and Philadelphia and the District of Columbia were below par.[2] Merchants had to keep lists on which was estimated the value of bank bills and to take chances on the constant fluctuations of them.[3] "Of upwards of a hundred banks that lately figured in Indiana, Ohio, Kentucky, and Tennessee, the money of two is now only received in the land-office, in payment for public lands," testifies Flint, writing from Jeffersonville, Indiana, in March, 1820. "Discount," he adds, "varies from thirty to one hundred per cent."[4] By September, 1818, two thirds of the bank bills sent to Niles in payment for the *Register* could not "be passed for money."[5]

"Chains" of banks were formed by which one member of the conspiracy would redeem its notes only by paying out the bills of another. Thus, if a man presented at the counter of a certain bank the bills issued by it, he was given in exchange those of another bank; when these were taken to this second

---

[1] In Baltimore Cohens's "lottery and exchange office" issued a list of nearly seventy banks, with rates of prices on their notes. The circular gave notice that the quotations were good for one day only. (Niles, xiv, 396.) At the same time G. & R. Waite, with offices in New York, Philadelphia, and Baltimore, issued a list covering the country from Connecticut to Ohio and Kentucky. (*Ib.* 415.) The rates as given by this firm differed greatly from those published by Cohens.
[2] *Ib.* x, 80.   [3] Sumner: *Jackson,* 229.
[4] Flint's Letters, *E. W. T.*: Thwaites, ix, 219.   [5] Niles, xv, 60.

institution, they were exchanged for the bills of a third bank, which redeemed them with notes of the first.[1] For instance, Bigelow's bank at Jefferson-ville, Indiana, redeemed its notes with those of Pi-att's bank at Cincinnati, Ohio; this, in turn, paid its bills with those of a Vincennes sawmill and the saw-mill exchanged its paper for that of Bigelow's bank.[2]

The redemption of their bills by the payment of specie was refused even by the best State banks, and this when the law positively required it. Niles esti-mated in April, 1818, that, although many banks were sound and honestly conducted, there were not "half a dozen banks in the United States that are able to pay their debts *as they are payable*." [3]

All this John Marshall saw and experienced. In 1815, George Fisher [4] presented to the Bank of Virginia ten of its one-hundred-dollar notes for re-demption, which was refused. After several months' delay, during which the bank officials ignored a summons to appear in court, a distringas [5] was secured. The President of the bank, Dr. Brocken-brough, resisted service of the writ, and the "Sheriff then called upon the by-standers, as a *posse comi-tatus*," to assist him. Among these was the Chief Justice of the United States. Fisher had hard work in finding a lawyer to take his case; for months no member of the bar would act as his attorney.[6] For

---

[1] Niles, xiv, 193–96; also xv, 434.   [2] *Ib.* xvii, 164.   [3] *Ib.* xiv, 108.

[4] A wealthy Richmond merchant who had married a sister of Marshall's wife. (See vol. ii, 172, of this work.)

[5] A writ directing the sheriff to seize the goods and chattels of a person to compel him to satisfy an obligation. Bouvier (Rawle's ed.) i, 590.

[6] Richmond *Enquirer*, Jan. 16, 1816.

What was the outcome of this incident does not appear. Professor

in Virginia as elsewhere — even less than in many States — the local banks were the most lucrative clients and the strongest political influence; and they controlled the lawyers as well as the press.

In June, 1818, for instance, a business man in Pennsylvania had accumulated several hundred dollars in bills of a local bank which refused to redeem them in specie or better bills. Three justices of the peace declined to entertain suit against the bank and no notary public would protest the bills. In Maryland, at the same time, a man succeeded in bringing an action against a bank for the redemption of some of its bills; but the cashier, while admitting his own signature on the notes, swore that he could not identify that of the bank's president, who had absented himself.[1]

Counterfeiting was widely practiced and, for a time, almost unpunished; a favorite device was the raising of notes, usually from five to fifty dollars. Bills were put in circulation purporting to have been issued by distant banks that did not exist, and never had existed. In a single week of June, 1818, the country newspapers contained accounts of twenty-eight cases of these and similar criminal operations.[2] Sometimes a forger or counterfeiter was caught; at Plattsburg, New York, one of these had twenty different kinds of fraudulent notes, "well executed."[3]

Sumner says that the bank was closed for a few days, but soon opened and went on with its business. (Sumner: *Hist. Am. Currency*, 74–75.) Sumner fixes the date in 1817, two years after the event.

[1] Niles, xiv, 281.   [2] *Ib.* 314–15.

[3] *Ib.* 333; and for similar cases, see *ib.* 356, 396–97, 428–30. All these accounts were taken from newspapers at the places where criminals were captured.

In August, 1818, Niles estimates that "the notes of at least ONE HUNDRED banks in the United States are counterfeited." [1] By the end of the year an organized gang of counterfeiters, forgers, and distributors of their products covered the whole country. [2] Counterfeits of the Marine Bank of Baltimore alone were estimated at $1,000,000; [3] one-hundred-dollar notes of the Bank of Louisiana were scattered far and wide. [4] Scarcely an issue of any newspaper appeared without notices of these depredations; [5] one half of the remittances sent Niles from the West were counterfeit. [6]

Into this chaos of speculation, fraud, and financial fiction came the second Bank of the United States. The management of it, at the beginning, was adventurous, erratic, corrupt; its officers and directors countenanced the most shameful manipulation of the Bank's stock; some of them participated in the incredible jobbery. [7] Nothing of this, however, was known to the country at large for many months, [8] nor did the knowledge of it, when revealed, afford the occasion for the popular wrath that soon came to be directed against the National Bank. This public hostility, indeed, was largely produced by measures which the Bank took to retrieve the early business blunders of its managers.

These blunders were appalling. As soon as it

[1] Niles, xiv, 428. [2] Ib. xvi, 147–48; also, ib. 360, 373, 390.
[3] Ib. 179. [4] Ib. 210. [5] Ib. 208. [6] Ib. 210.
[7] See Catterall, 39–50.

[8] The frauds of the directors and officers of the Bank of the United States were used, however, as the pretext for an effort to repeal its charter. On Feb. 9, 1819, James Johnson of Virginia introduced a resolution for that purpose. (Annals, 15th Cong. 2d Sess. III, 1140–42.)

opened in 1817, the Bank began to do business on the inflated scale which the State banks had established; by over-issue of its notes it increased the inflation, already blown to the bursting point. Except in New England, where its loans were moderate and well secured, it accommodated borrowers lavishly. The branches were not required to limit their business to a fixed capital; in many cases, the branch officers and directors, incompetent and swayed by local interest and feeling,[1] issued notes as recklessly as did some of the State banks. In the West particularly, and also in the South, the loans made were enormous. The borrowers had no expectation of paying them when due, but of renewing them from time to time, as had been the practice under State banking.

The National branches in these regions showed a faint gleam of prudence by refusing to accept bills of notoriously unsound local banks. This undemocratic partiality, although timidly exercised, aroused to activity the never-slumbering hostility of these local concerns. In the course of business, however, bills of most State banks accumulated to an immense amount in the vaults of the branches of the Bank of the United States. When, in spite of the disposition of the branch officers to extend unending and unlimited indulgence to the State banks and to borrowers generally, the branches finally were compelled by the parent Bank to demand payment of loans and redemption of bills of local banks held by it; and when, in consequence, the State banks were forced to collect debts due them, the catastrophe, so long

[1] See Catterall, 32.

preparing, fell upon sections where the vices of State banking had been practiced most flagrantly.

Suits upon promissory notes, bonds and mortgages, already frequent, now became incessant; sheriffs were never idle. In the autumn of 1818, in a single small county [1] of Delaware, one hundred and fifty such actions were brought by the banks. In addition to this, records the financial chronicler of the period, "their vaults are loaded with bonds, mortgages and other securities, held *in terrorem* over the heads of several hundreds more." [2] At Harrisburg, Pennsylvania, one bank brought more than one hundred suits during May, 1818;[3] a few months later a single issue of one country newspaper in Pennsylvania contained advertisements of eighteen farms and mills at sheriff's sale; a village newspaper in New York advertised sixty-three farms and lots to be sold under the sheriff's hammer.[4] "Currency" decreased in quantity; unemployment was amazing; scores of thousands of men begged for work; throngs of the idle camped near cities and subsisted on charity.[5]

All this the people laid at the doors of the National Bank, while the State banks,[6] of course, encouraged the popular animosity. Another order of the National concern increased the anger of the people and of the State banks against it. For more than a year the parent institution and its branches had redeemed all notes issued by them wherever presented. Since the notes from the West and South

---

[1] New Castle County.　[2] Niles, xv, 162.　[3] *Ib.* 59.　[4] *Ib.* 418.

[5] Flint's Letters, *E. W. T.*: Thwaites, ix, 226.

[6] They, too, asserted that institution to be the author of their woes. (Niles, xvii, 2.)

flowed to the North and East [1] in payment for the manufactures and merchandise of these sections, this universal redemption became impossible. So, on August 28, 1818, the branches were directed to refuse all notes except their own. [2]

Thus the Bank, "like an *abandoned* mother, . . BASTARDIZED its offspring," [3] said the enemies of the National Bank, among them all State banks and most of the people. The enforcement of redemption of State bank bills, the reduction of the volume of "currency," were the real causes of the fury with which the Bank of the United States and its branches was now assailed. That institution was the monster, said local orators and editors; its branches were the tentacles of the Octopus, heads of the Hydra. [4] "The 'branches' are execrated on all hands," wrote an Ohio man. "We *feel* that to the policy pursued by them, we are indebted for all the evils we experience for want of a circulating medium." [5]

The popular cry was for relief. More money, not less, was needed, it was said; and more banks that could and would loan funds with which to pay debts. If the creditor would not accept the currency thus procured, let laws be passed that would compel him to do so, or prevent him from collecting what his contract called for. Thus, with such demands upon their lips, and in the midst of a storm of lawsuits, the people entered at last that inevitable period of bank-

[1] Catterall, 33–37.
[2] *Ib.* 51–53; and see Niles. xv, 25.   [3] Catterall, 33.
[4] Monster, Hydra, Cerberus, Octopus, and names of similar import were popularly applied to the Bank of the United States. (See Crawford's speech, *supra*, 175.)
[5] Niles, xv, 5.

ruptcy to which for years they had been drawing nearer and for which they were themselves largely responsible.

Bankruptcy laws had already been enacted by some States; and if these acts had not been drawn for the benefit of speculators in anticipation of the possible evil day, the "insolvency" statutes certainly had been administered for the protection of rich and dishonest men who wished to escape their liabilities, and yet to preserve their assets. In New York[1] the debtor was enabled to discharge all accounts by turning over such property as he had; if he owed ten thousand dollars, and possessed but fifty dollars, his debt was cancelled by the surrender of that sum. For the honest and prudent man the law was just, since no great discrepancy usually existed between his reported assets and his liabilities. But lax administration of it afforded to the dishonest adventurer a shield from the righteous consequences of his wrongdoing.

The "bankruptcies" of knavish men were common operations. One merchant in an Eastern city "failed," but contrived to go on living in a house for which he "was offered $200,000 in real money."[2] Another in Philadelphia became "insolvent," yet had $7000 worth of wine in his cellar at the very time he was going through "bankruptcy."[3] A merchant tailor in the little town of York, Pennsylvania, resorted to bankruptcy to clear himself of eighty-four thousand dollars of debt.[4]

---

[1] Act of April 3, 1811, *Laws of New York, 1811*, 205–21.
[2] Niles, xvi, 257.   [3] *Ib.*   [4] *Ib.* xvii, 147.

In their speculations adventurous men counted on the aid of these legislative acts for the relief of debtors. "Never . . have any . . laws been more productive of crime than the insolvent laws of Maryland," testifies Niles.[1] One issue of the *Federal Gazette* contained six columns of bankruptcy notices, and these were only about "one-third of the persons" then "'going through our mill.'" Several "bankrupts" had been millionaires, and continued to "*live in splendid affluence*, . . their wives and children, or some kind relative, having been made rich through their swindlings of the people."[2] Many "insolvents" were bankers; and this led Niles to propose that the following law be adopted:

"'Whereas certain persons . . *unknown*, have petitioned for the establishment of a bank at ——:

"'Be it enacted, that . . these persons, . . shall have liberty to become BANKRUPTS, and may legally swindle as much as they can.'"[3]

In a Senate debate in March, 1820, for a proposed new National Bankruptcy Act,[4] Senator Harrison Gray Otis of Massachusetts moderately stated the results of the State insolvency laws. "Merchants and traders . . are harassed and perplexed by twenty

---

[1] "I have known several to *calculate* upon the 'relief' from them, just as they would do on an accommodation at bank, or on the payment of debts due to them! If we succeed in such and such a thing, say they — very well; if not, we can get the benefit of the insolvent laws . . Where one prudent and honest man applies for such benefit, one hundred rogues are facilitated in their depredations." (Niles, XVII, 115.)

[2] *Ib.*   [3] *Ib.* xv, 283.

[4] The bankruptcy law which Marshall had helped to draw when in Congress (see vol. II, 481–82, of this work) had been repealed in 1803. (*Annals*, 8th Cong. 1st Sess. 215, 625, 631. For reasons for the repeal see *ib.* 616–22.)

different systems of municipal laws, often repugnant to each other and themselves; always defective; seldom executed in good faith; prolific in endless frauds, perjuries, and evasions; and never productive of . . any sort of justice, to the creditor. Nothing could be . . comparable to their pernicious effects upon the public morals." [1] Senator Prentiss Mellen, of the same State, described the operation of the bankruptcy mill thus: "We frequently witness transactions, poisoned throughout with fraud . . in which *all* creditors are deceived and defrauded. . . The man *pretends* to be a bankrupt; and having converted a large portion of his property into money . . he . . closes his doors; . . goes through the form of offering to give up all his property, (though secretly retaining thousands,) on condition of receiving a discharge from his creditors. . . In a few months, or perhaps weeks, he recommences business, and finds himself . . with a handsome property at command." [2]

Senator James Burrill, Jr., of Rhode Island was equally specific and convincing. He pictured the career of a dishonest merchant, who transfers property to relatives, secures a discharge from the State bankruptcy courts, and "in a few days . . resumes his career of folly, extravagance, and rashness. . . Thus the creditors are defrauded, and the debtor, in many cases, lives in affluence and splendor." [3] Flint records that "mutual credit and confidence are almost torn up by the roots." [4]

---

[1] *Annals*, 16th Cong. 1st Sess. 505.   [2] *Ib.* 513.   [3] *Ib.* 517–18.
[4] Flint's Letters, *E. W. T.*: Thwaites, ix, 225.

In reviewing *Sketches of America* by Henry Bradshaw Fearon, an Englishman who traveled through the United States, the *Quarterly*

It was soon to be the good fortune of John Marshall to declare such State legislation null and void because in violation of the National Constitution. Never did common honesty, good faith, and fair dealing need such a stabilizing power as at the moment Marshall furnished to the American people. In most parts of the country even insolvency laws did not satisfy debtors; they were trying to avoid the results of their own acts by securing the enactment of local statutes that repealed the natural laws of human intercourse — of statutes that expressed the momentary wish of the uncomfortable, if honest, multitude, but that represented no less the devices of the clever and unscrupulous. Fortunate, indeed, was it for the United States, at this critical time in its development, that one department of the Government could not be swayed by the passion of the hour, and thrice happy that the head of that department was John Marshall.

The impression made directly on Marshall by what took place under his very eyes in Virginia was strengthened by events that occurred in Kentucky. All his brothers and sisters, except two, besides numerous cousins and relatives by marriage, lived there. Thus he was advised in an intimate and personal way of what went forward in that State.[1]

Review of London scathingly denounced the frauds perpetrated by means of insolvent laws. (_Quarterly Review_, xxi, 165.)

[1] None of these letters to Marshall have been preserved. Indeed, only a scant half-dozen of the original great number of letters written him even by prominent men during his long life are in existence. For those of men like Story and Pickering we are indebted to copies preserved in their papers.

Marshall, at best, was incredibly negligent of his correspondence

The indebtedness of Kentucky State banks, and of individual borrowers to the branches of the National Bank located in that Commonwealth, amounted to more than two and one half millions of dollars.[1] "This is the *trifling* sum which the people of Kentucky are called upon to pay in *specie!*"[2] exclaimed a Kentucky paper. The people of that State owed the local banks about $7,000,000 more, while the total indebtedness to all financial institutions within Kentucky was not far from $10,000,000.[3] The sacrifice of property for the satisfaction of mortgages grew ever more distressing. At Lexington, a house and lot, for which the owner had refused $15,000, brought but $1300 at sheriff's sale; another costing $10,000 sold under the hammer for $1500.[4] Even slaves could be sold only at a small fraction of their ordinary market price.

It was the same in other States. Within Marshall's personal observation in Virginia the people were forced to eat the fruits of their folly. "Lands in this State cannot now be sold for a year's rent," wrote Jefferson.[5] A farm near Easton, Pennsylvania, worth $12,500, mortgaged to secure a debt of $2500, was taken by the lender on foreclosure for the amount of the loan. A druggist's stock of the retail value of $10,000 was seized for rent by the landlord and sold for $400.[6] In Virginia a little later a farm

as he was of all other ordinary details of life. Most other important men of the time kept copies of their letters; Marshall kept none; and if he preserved those written to him, nearly all of them have disappeared.

[1] Niles, xv, 385.   [2] *Ib.*   [3] *Ib.* xvi, 261.   [4] *Ib.* xvii, 85.
[5] Jefferson to Adams, Nov. 7, 1819, *Works:* Ford, xii, 145.
[6] Niles, xvii, 85.

of three hundred acres with improvements worth, at the lowest estimate, $1500, sold for $300; two wagon horses costing $200 were sacrificed for $40.

Mines were shut down, shops closed, taxes unpaid. "The debtor . . gives up his land, and, ruined and undone, seeks a home for himself and his family in the western wilderness." [1] John Quincy Adams records in his diary: "Staple productions . . are falling to . . less than half the prices which they have lately borne, the merchants are crumbling to ruin, the manufactures perishing, agriculture stagnating, and distress universal in every part of the country." [2]

During the summer and autumn of 1818, the popular demand for legislation that would suspend contracts, postpone the payment of debts, and stay the judgment of courts, became strident and peremptory. "Our greatest real evil is the question between debtor and creditor, into which the banks have plunged us deeper than would have been possible without them," testifies Adams. "The bank debtors are everywhere so numerous and powerful that they control the newspapers throughout the Union, and give the discussion a turn extremely erroneous, and prostrate every principle of political economy." [3]

This was especially true of Kentucky. Throughout the State great assemblages were harangued by oratorical "friends of the people." "The reign of political quackery was in its glory." [4] Why the

[1] Niles, xvii, 185.
[2] Memoirs, J. Q. A.: Adams, May 27, 1819, iv, 375.
[3] Ib. 391.   [4] Collins, 88.

scarcity of money when that commodity was most needed? Why the lawsuits for the collection of debts, the enforcement of bonds, the foreclosure of mortgages, instead of the renewal of loans, to which debtors had been accustomed? Financial manipulation had done it all. The money power was responsible for the misery of the people. Let that author and contriver of human suffering be suppressed.

What could be easier or more just than to enact legislation that would lift the burden of debt that was crushing the people? The State banks would not resist — were they not under the control of the people's Legislature? But they were also at the mercy of that remorseless creature of the National Government, the Bank of the United States. That malign Thing was the real cause of all the trouble.[1] Let the law by which Congress had given illegitimate life to that destroyer of the people's well-being be repealed. If that could not be done because so many of the National Legislature were corruptly interested in the Bank, the States had a sure weapon with which to destroy it — or at least to drive it out of business in every member of the Union.

That weapon was taxation. Let each Legislature, by special taxes, strangle the branches of the National Bank operating in the States. So came a popular determination to exterminate, by State action, the second Bank of the United States. Na-

---

[1] "The disappointment is altogether ascribed to the Bank of the U. S." (King to Mason, Feb. 7, 1819, King, VI, 205.) King's testimony is uncommonly trustworthy. His son was an officer of the branch of Chillicothe, Ohio.

tional power should be brought to its knees by local authority! National agencies should be made helpless and be dispatched by State prohibition and State taxation! The arm of the National Government should be paralyzed by the blows showered on it when thrusting itself into the affairs of "sovereign" States! Already this process was well under way.

The first Constitution of Indiana, adopted soon after Congress had authorized the second Bank of the United States, prohibited any bank chartered outside the State from doing business within its borders.[1] During the very month that the National Bank opened its doors in 1817, the Legislature of Maryland passed an act taxing the Baltimore branch $15,000 annually. Seven months afterward the Legislature of Tennessee enacted a law that any bank not chartered under its authority should pay $50,000 each year for the privilege of banking in that State. A month later Georgia placed a special tax on branches of the Bank of the United States.

The Constitution of Illinois, adopted in August, 1818, forbade the establishment of any but State banks. In December of that year North Carolina taxed the branch of the National Bank in that State $5000 per annum. A few weeks later Kentucky laid an annual tax of $60,000 on each of the two branches of the Bank of the United States located at Lexington and Frankfort. Three weeks before John Marshall delivered his opinion in M'Culloch *vs.* Maryland, Ohio enacted a statute placing a yearly

[1] See Article x, Section 1, Constitution of Indiana, as adopted June 29, 1816.

tax of $50,000 on each of the two National Bank branches then doing business in that State.[1]

Thus the extinction of the second Bank of the United States by State legislation appeared to be inevitable. The past management of it had well deserved this fate; but earnest efforts were now in operation to recover it from former blunders and to retrieve its fortunes. The period of corruption was over, and a new, able, and honest management was about to take charge. If, however, the States could destroy this National fiscal agency, it mattered not how well it might thereafter be conducted, for nothing could be more certain than that the local influence of State banks always would be great enough to induce State Legislatures to lay impossible burdens on the National Bank.

Such, then, was the situation that produced those opinions of Marshall on insolvency, on contract, and on a National bank, delivered during February and March of 1819; such the National conditions which confronted him during the preceding summer and autumn. He could do nothing to ameliorate these conditions, nothing to relieve the universal unhappiness, nothing to appease the popular discontent. But he could establish great National principles, which would give steadiness to American business, vitality to the National Government; and which would encourage the people to practice honesty, prudence, and thrift. And just this John Marshall did. When considering the enduring work he performed at this time, we must have in our thought

[1] See Catterall, 64–65, and sources there cited.

the circumstances that made that work vitally necessary.

One of the earliest cases decided by the Supreme
Court in 1819 involved the Bankrupt Law of New
York. On November 25, 1817, Josiah Sturges [1] of
Massachusetts sued Richard Crowninshield of New
York in the United States Circuit Court for the
District of Massachusetts to recover upon two promissory notes for the sum of $771.86 each, exe-
cuted March 22, 1811, just twelve days before the
passage, April 3, 1811, of the New York statute
for the relief of insolvent debtors. The defendant
pleaded his discharge under that act. The judges
were divided in opinion on the questions whether
a State can pass a bankrupt act, whether the New
York law was a bankrupt act, and whether it impaired the obligations of a contract. These questions were, accordingly, certified to the Supreme
Court.

The case was there argued long and exhaustively
by David Daggett and Joseph Hopkinson for Sturges
and by David B. Ogden and William Hunter for
Crowninshield. In weight of reasoning and full citation of authority, the discussion was inferior only
to those contests before the Supreme Bench which
have found a place in history.

On February 17, 1819, Marshall delivered the
unanimous opinion of the court. [2] Do the words of
the Constitution, "Congress shall have power . .
to establish . . uniform laws on the subject of

[1] Spelled *Sturgis* on the manuscript records of the Supreme Court.
[2] 4 Wheaton, 192.

bankruptcies throughout the United States" take from the States the right to pass such laws?

Before the adoption of the Constitution, begins Marshall, the States "united for some purposes, but, in most respects, sovereign," could "exercise almost every legislative power." The powers of the States under the Constitution were not defined in that instrument. "These powers proceed, not from the people of America, but from the people of the several states; and remain, after the adoption of the constitution, what they were before, except so far as they may be abridged" by the Nation's fundamental law.

While the "mere grant of a power to Congress" does not necessarily mean that the States are forbidden to exercise the same power, such concurrent power does not extend to "every possible case" not expressly prohibited by the Constitution. "The confusion resulting from such a practice would be endless." As a general principle, declares the Chief Justice, "whenever the terms in which a power is granted to Congress, or the nature of the power, required that it should be exercised exclusively by Congress, the subject is as completely taken from the state legislatures as if they had been expressly forbidden to act on it." [1]

Does this general principle apply to bankrupt laws? Assuredly it does. Congress is empowered to "establish uniform laws on the subject throughout the United States." Uniform National legislation is "incompatible with state legislation" on the same

[1] 4 Wheaton, 192–93.

subject. Marshall draws a distinction between bankrupt and insolvency laws, although "the line of partition between them is not so distinctly marked" that it can be said, "with positive precision, what belongs exclusively to the one, and not to the other class of laws." [1]

He enters upon an examination of the nature of insolvent laws which States may enact, and bankrupt laws which Congress may enact; and finds that "there is such a connection between them as to render it difficult to say how far they may be blended together. . . A bankrupt law may contain those regulations which are generally found in insolvent laws"; while "an insolvent law may contain those which are common to a bankrupt law." It is "obvious," then, that it would be a hardship to "deny to the state legislatures the power of acting on this subject, in consequence of the grant to Congress." The true rule — "certainly a convenient one" — is to "consider the power of the states as existing over such cases as the laws of the Union may not reach." [2]

But, whether this common-sense construction is adopted or not, it is undeniable that Congress may exercise a power granted to it or decline to exercise it. So, if Congress thinks that uniform bankrupt laws "ought not to be established" throughout the country, surely the State Legislatures ought not, on that account, to be prevented from passing bankrupt acts. The idea of Marshall, the statesman, was that it was better to have bankrupt laws of some kind than none at all. "It is not the mere existence

[1] 4 Wheaton, 194.   [2] *Ib.* 195.

of the power [in Congress], but its exercise, which is incompatible with the exercise of the same power by the states. It is not the right to establish these uniform laws, but their actual establishment, which is inconsistent with the partial acts of the states." [1]

Even should Congress pass a bankrupt law, that action does not extinguish, but only suspends, the power of the State to legislate on the same subject. When Congress repeals a National bankrupt law it merely "removes a disability" of the State created by the enactment of the National statute, and lasting only so long as that statute is in force. In short, "until the power to pass uniform laws on the subject of bankruptcies be exercised by Congress, the states are not forbidden to pass a bankrupt law, provided it contain no principle which violates the 10th section of the first article of the constitution of the United States." [2]

Having toilsomely reached this conclusion, Marshall comes to what he calls "the great question on which the cause must depend": Does the New York Bankrupt Law "impair the obligation of contracts"?[3]

What is the effect of that law? It "liberates the person of the debtor, and discharges him from all liability for any debt previously contracted, on his surrendering his property in the manner it prescribes." Here Marshall enters upon that series of expositions of the contract clause of the Constitu-

[1] 4 Wheaton, 196.
[2] "No State shall . . emit Bills of Credit; make any Thing but gold and silver Coin a Tender in Payment of Debts; pass any . . ex post facto Law, or Law impairing the Obligation of Contracts."
[3] 4 Wheaton, 196-97.

tion which, next to the Nationalism of his opinions, is, perhaps, the most conspicuous feature of his philosophy of government and human intercourse.[1] "What is the obligation of a contract? and what will impair it?"[2]

It would be hard to find words "more intelligible, or less liable to misconstruction, than those which are to be explained." With a tinge of patient impatience, the Chief Justice proceeds to define the words "contract," "impair," and "obligation," much as a weary school teacher might teach the simplest lesson to a particularly dull pupil.

"A contract is an agreement in which a party undertakes to do, or not to do, a particular thing. The law binds him to perform his undertaking, and this is, of course, the obligation of his contract. In the case at bar, the defendant has given his promissory note to pay the plaintiff a sum of money on or before a certain day. The contract binds him to pay that sum on that day; and this is its obligation. Any law which releases a part of this obligation, must, in the literal sense of the word, impair it. Much more must a law impair it which makes it totally invalid, and entirely discharges it.

"The words of the constitution, then, are express, and incapable of being misunderstood. They admit of no variety of construction, and are acknowledged to apply to that species of contract, an engagement between man and man, for the payment of money, which has been entered into by these parties."[3]

---

[1] For the proceedings in the Constitutional Convention on this clause, see vol. III, chap. X, of this work.
[2] 4 Wheaton, 197.   [3] *Ib.* 197–98.

What are the arguments that such law does not violate the Constitution? One is that, since a contract "can only bind a man to pay to the full extent of his property, it is an implied condition that he may be discharged on surrendering the whole of it." This is simply not true, says Marshall. When a contract is made, the parties to it have in mind, not only existing property, but "future acquisitions. Industry, talents and integrity, constitute a fund which is as confidently trusted as property itself. Future acquisitions are, therefore, liable for contracts; and to release them from this liability impairs their obligation." [1]

Marshall brushes aside, almost brusquely, the argument that the only reason for the adoption of the contract clause by the Constitutional Convention was the paper money evil; that the States always had passed bankrupt and insolvent laws; and that if the framers of the Constitution had intended to deprive the States of this power, "insolvent laws would have been mentioned in the prohibition."

No power whatever, he repeats, is conferred on the States by the Constitution. That instrument found them "in possession" of practically all legislative power and either prohibited "its future exercise entirely," or restrained it "so far as national policy may require."

While the Constitution permits States to pass bankrupt laws "until that power shall be exercised by Congress," the fundamental law positively for-

[1] 4 Wheaton, 198.

bids the States to "introduce into such laws a clause which discharges the obligations the bankrupt has entered into. It is not admitted that, without this principle, an act cannot be a bankrupt law; and if it were, that admission would not change the constitution, nor exempt such acts from its prohibitions." [1]

There was, said Marshall, nothing in the argument that, if the framers of the Constitution had intended to "prohibit the States from passing insolvent laws," they would have plainly said so. "It was not necessary, nor would it have been safe" for them to have enumerated "particular subjects to which the principle they intended to establish should apply."

On this subject, as on every other dealt with in the Constitution, fundamental principles are set out. What is the one involved in this case? It is "the inviolability of contracts. This principle was to be protected in whatsoever form it might be assailed. To what purpose enumerate the particular modes of violation which should be forbidden, when it was intended to forbid all? . . The plain and simple declaration, that no state shall pass any law impairing the obligation of contracts, includes insolvent laws and all other laws, so far as they infringe the principle the convention intended to hold sacred, and no farther." [2]

At this point Marshall displays the humanitarian which, in his character, was inferior only to the statesman. He was against imprisonment for debt, one of the many brutal customs still practiced.

[1] 4 Wheaton, 199.   [2] *Ib.* 200.

"The convention did not intend to prohibit the passage of all insolvent laws," he avows. "To punish honest insolvency by imprisonment for life, and to make this a constitutional principle, would be an excess of inhumanity which will not readily be imputed to the illustrious patriots who framed our constitution, nor to the people who adopted it... Confinement of the debtor may be a punishment for not performing his contract, or may be allowed as a means of inducing him to perform it. But the state may refuse to inflict this punishment, or may withhold this means and leave the contract in full force. Imprisonment is no part of the contract, and simply to release the prisoner does not impair its obligation." [1]

Following his provoking custom of taking up a point with which he had already dealt, Marshall harks back to the subject of the reason for inserting the contract clause into the Constitution. He restates the argument against applying that provision to State insolvent laws — that, from the beginning, the Colonies and States had enacted such legislation; that the history of the times shows that "the mind of the convention was directed to other laws which were fraudulent in their character, which enabled the debtor to escape from his obligation, and yet hold his property, not to this, which is beneficial in its operation."

But, he continues, "the spirit of .. a constitution" is not to be determined solely by a partial view of the history of the times when it was adopted

[1] 4 Wheaton, 200-01.

— "the spirit is to be collected chiefly from its words." And "it would be dangerous in the extreme to infer from extrinsic circumstances, that a case for which the words of an instrument expressly provide, shall be exempted from its operation." Where language is obscure, where words conflict, "construction becomes necessary." But, when language is clear, words harmonious, the plain meaning of that language and of those words is not "to be disregarded, because we believe the framers of that instrument could not intend what they say."[1]

The practice of the Colonies, and of the States before the Constitution was adopted, was a weak argument at best. For example, the Colonies and States had issued paper money, emitted bills of credit, and done other things, all of which the Constitution prohibits. "If the long exercise of the power to emit bills of credit did not restrain the convention from prohibiting its future exercise, neither can it be said that the long exercise of the power to impair the obligation of contracts, should prevent a similar prohibition." The fact that insolvent laws are not forbidden "by name" does not exclude them from the operation of the contract clause of the Constitution. It is "a principle which is to be forbidden; and this principle is described in as appropriate terms as our language affords."[2]

Perhaps paper money was the chief and impelling reason for making the contract clause a part of the National Constitution. But can the operation of that clause be confined to paper money? "No court

[1] 4 Wheaton, 202. [2] Ib. 203-04.

can be justified in restricting such comprehensive words to a particular mischief to which no allusion is made." The words must be given "their full and obvious meaning." [1] Doubtless the evils of paper money directed the Convention to the subject of contracts; but it did far more than to make paper money impossible thereafter. "In the opinion of the convention, much more remained to be done. The same mischief might be effected by other means. To restore public confidence completely, it was necessary not only to prohibit the use of particular means by which it might be effected, but to prohibit the use of any means by which the same mischief might be produced. The convention appears to have intended to establish a great principle, that contracts should be inviolable. The constitution therefore declares, that no state shall pass 'any law impairing the obligation of contracts.'" [2] From all this it follows that the New York Bankruptcy Act of 1812 is unconstitutional because it impaired the obligations of a contract.

The opinion of the Chief Justice aroused great excitement.[3] It, of course, alarmed those who had been using State insolvent laws to avoid payment of their debts, while retaining much of their wealth. It also was unwelcome to the great body of honest, though imprudent, debtors who were struggling to lighten their burdens by legislation. But the more thoughtful, even among radicals, welcomed Marshall's pronouncement. Niles approved it heartily.[4]

[1] 4 Wheaton, 205.   [2] *Ib*. 206.   [3] Niles, xvi, 76.
[4] "It will probably, make some great revolutions in property, and

Gradually, surely, Marshall's simple doctrine grew in favor throughout the whole country, and is to-day a vital and enduring element of American thought and character as well as of Constitutional law.

As in Fletcher *vs.* Peck, the principle of the inviolability of contracts was applied where a State and individuals are parties, so the same principle was now asserted in Sturges *vs.* Crowninshield as to State laws impairing the obligation of contracts between man and man. At the same session, in the celebrated Dartmouth College case,[1] Marshall announced that this principle also covers charters granted by States. Thus did he develop the idea of good faith and stability of engagement as a life-giving principle of the American Constitution.

raise up many from penury . . and cause others to descend to the condition that becomes *honest men*, by compelling a payment of their debts — as every honest man ought to be compelled to do, if ever able. . . It ought not to be at any one's discretion to say when, or under what *convenient* circumstances, he will *wipe off* his debts, by the benefit of an insolvent law — as some do every two or three years; or, just as often as they can get credit enough to make any thing by it." (Niles, XVI, 2.)

[1] See *infra,* next chapter.

CHAPTER V

THE DARTMOUTH COLLEGE CASE

Such a contract, in relation to a publick institution would be absurd and contrary to the principles of all governments.
(Chief Justice William M. Richardson.)

It would seem as if the state legislatures have an invincible hostility to the sacredness of charters. (Marshall.)

Perhaps no judicial proceedings in this country ever involved more important consequences. (*North American Review*, 1820.)

It is the legitimate business of government to see that contracts are fulfilled, that charters are kept inviolate, and the foundations of human confidence not rudely or wantonly disturbed. (John Fiske.)

JUST before Marshall delivered his opinion in Sturges *vs.* Crowninshield, he gave to the Nation another state paper which profoundly influenced the development of the United States. It was one of the trilogy of Constitutional expositions which make historic the February term, 1819, of the Supreme Court of the United States. This pronouncement, like that in the bankruptcy case, had to do with the stability of contract. Both were avowals that State Legislatures cannot, on any pretext, overthrow agreements, whether in the form of engagements between individuals or franchises to corporations. Both were meant to check the epidemic of repudiatory legislation which for three years had been sweeping over the land and was increasing in virulence at the time when Marshall prepared them. The Dartmouth opinion was wholly written in Virginia during the summer, autumn, or winter of 1818; and it is probable that the greater part of the opinion in

Sturges *vs.* Crowninshield was also prepared when the Chief Justice was at home or on his vacation.

Marshall's economic and political views, formed as a young man,[1] had been strengthened by every event that had since occurred until, in his sixty-fifth year, those early ideas had become convictions so deep as to pervade his very being. The sacredness of contract, the stability of institutions, and, above all, Nationalism in government, were, to John Marshall, articles of a creed as holy as any that ever inspired a religious enthusiast.

His opinion of contract had already been expressed by him not only in the sensational case of Fletcher *vs.* Peck,[2] but far more rigidly two years later, 1812, in the important case of the State of New Jersey *vs.* Wilson.[3] In 1758, the Proprietary Government of New Jersey agreed to purchase a tract of land for a band of Delaware Indians, provided that the Indians would surrender their title to all other lands claimed by them in New Jersey. The Indians agreed and the contract was embodied in an act of the Legislature, which further provided that the lands purchased for the Indians should "not hereafter be subject to any tax, any law, usage or custom to the contrary thereof, in any wise notwithstanding."[4] The contract was then executed, the State purchasing lands for the Indians and the latter relinquishing the lands claimed by them.

After forty years the Indians, wishing to join other Delawares in New York, asked the State of

[1] See vol. I, 147, 231, of this work.
[2] See vol. III, chap. X, of this work.
[3] 7 Cranch, 164.   [4] *Ib.* 165.

New Jersey to authorize the sale of their lands. This
was done by an act of the Legislature, and the lands
were sold. Soon after this, another act was passed
which repealed that part of the Act of 1758 exempting the lands from taxation. Accordingly the lands
were assessed and payment of the tax demanded.
The purchasers resisted and, the Supreme Court of
New Jersey having held valid the repealing act,
took the case to the Supreme Court of the United
States.

In a brief opinion, in which it is worthy of particular note that the Supreme Court was unanimous,
Marshall says that the Constitution protects "contracts to which a state is a party, as well as . .
contracts between individuals. . . The proceedings
[of 1758] between the then colony . . and the Indians . . is certainly a contract clothed in forms of
unusual solemnity." The exemption of the lands
from taxation, "though for the benefit of the Indians,
is annexed, by the terms which create it, to the land
itself, not to their persons." This element of the
contract was valuable to the Indians, since, "in the
event of a sale, on which alone the question could
become material, the value [of the lands] would be
enhanced" by the exemption.

New Jersey "might have insisted on a surrender
of this privilege as the sole condition on which a sale
of the property should be allowed"; but this had
not been done and the land was sold "with the assent
of the state, with all its privileges and immunities.
The purchaser succeeds, with the assent of the state,
to all the rights of the Indians. He stands, with

respect to this land, in their place, and claims the benefit of their contract. This contract is certainly impaired by a law which would annul this essential part of it." [1]

After his opinions in Fletcher *vs.* Peck and in New Jersey *vs.* Wilson, nobody could have expected from John Marshall any other action than the one he took in the Dartmouth College case. [2]

The origins of the Dartmouth controversy are tangled and obscure. When on December 23, 1765, a little ocean-going craft, of which a New England John Marshall [3] was skipper, set sail from Boston Harbor for England with Nathaniel Whitaker and Samson Occom on board, [4] a succession of curious events began which, two generations afterward, terminated in one of the most influential decisions ever rendered by a court. Whitaker was a preacher and a disciple of George Whitefield; Occom was a young Indian, converted to Christianity by one Eleazar Wheelock, and endowed with uncommon powers of oratory.

Wheelock had built up a wilderness school to which were admitted Indian youth, in whom he became increasingly interested. Occom was one product of his labors, and Wheelock sent him to England as a living, speaking illustration of what his school

[1] 7 Cranch, 166–67.

[2] This was true also of the entire court, since all the Justices concurred in Marshall's opinions in both cases as far as the legislative violations of the contract clause were concerned.

[3] He was not at all related to the Chief Justice. See vol. I, footnote to 15–16, of this work.

[4] Chase: *History of Dartmouth College and the Town of Hanover, New Hampshire*, I, 49.

could do if given financial support. Whitaker went
with the devout and talented Indian as the business
agent.[1]

Their mission was to raise funds for the prosecution of this educational and missionary work on the
American frontier. They succeeded in a manner
almost miraculous. Over eleven thousand pounds
were soon raised,[2] and this fund was placed under
the control of the Trustees, at the head of whom
was the Earl of Dartmouth, one of the principal
donors.[3] From this circumstance the name of this
nobleman was given to Wheelock's institution.

On December 13, 1769, John Wentworth, Royal
Governor of the Province of New Hampshire,
granted to Wheelock a charter for his school. It
was, of course, in the name of the sovereign, but it is
improbable that George III ever heard of it.[4] This
charter sets forth the successful efforts of Wheelock,
"at his own expense, on his own estate," to establish
a charity school for Indian as well as white youth,
in order to spread "the knowledge of the great Re-
deemer among their savage tribes"; the contributions to the cause; the trust, headed by Dartmouth
— and all the other facts concerning Wheelock's
adventure. Because of these facts the charter
establishes "DARTMOUTH COLLEGE" for the education of Indians, to be governed by "one body
corporate and politick, . . by the name of the
TRUSTEES OF DARTMOUTH COLLEGE."

---

[1] Chase, 45–48.   [2] Ib. 59.   [3] Ib. 54–55.
[4] Dartmouth and the English Trustees opposed incorporation and
the Bishops of the Church of England violently resisted Wheelock's
whole project. (Ib. 90.)

These Trustees are constituted "forever here-after . . in deed, act, and name a body corporate and politick," and are empowered to buy, receive, and hold lands, "jurisdictions, and franchises, for themselves and their successors, in fee simple, or otherwise howsoever." In short, the Trustees are authorized to do anything and everything that they may think proper. Wheelock is made President of the College, and given power to "appoint, . . by his last will" whomever he chooses to succeed himself as President of the College.

The charter grants to the Trustees and to "their successors forever," or "the major part of any seven or more of them convened," the power to remove and choose a President of the College, and to fill any vacancy in the Board of Trustees occasioned by death, or "removal," or any other cause. All this is to be done if seven Trustees, or a majority of seven, are present at any meeting. Also this majority of seven of the twelve Trustees, if no more attend a meeting, are authorized to make all laws, rules, and regulations for the College. Other powers are granted, all of which the Trustees and their successors are "to have and to hold . . forever." [1] Under this charter, Dartmouth College was established and, for nearly half a century, governed and managed.

Eleazar Wheelock died in 1779, when sixty-eight

[1] Farrar: *Report of the Case of the Trustees of Dartmouth College against William H. Woodward*, 11, 16; also see Charter of Dartmouth College, Chase, 639–49. (Although the official copy of the charter appears in Chase's history, the author cites Farrar in the report of the case; the charter also is cited from his book.)

years of age.[1] By his will he made his son John his successor as President of the College.[2] This young man, then but twenty-five years of age, was a Colonel of the Revolutionary Army.[3] He hesitated to accept the management of the institution, but the Trustees finally prevailed upon him to do so.[4] The son was as strong-willed and energetic as the father, and gave himself vigorously to the work to which he had thus been called.

Within four years troubles began to gather about the College. They came from sources as strange as human nature itself, and mingled at last into a compound of animosities, prejudices, ambitions, jealousies, as curious as any aggregation of passions ever arranged by the most extravagant novelist. It is possible here to mention but briefly only a few of the circumstances by which the famous Dartmouth quarrel may be traced. A woman, one Rachel Murch, complained to the church at Hanover, where Dartmouth College was situated, that a brother of the congregation, one Samuel Haze, had said of her, among other things, that her "character was . . as black as Hell."[5] This incident grew into a sectarian warfare that, by the most illogical and human

---

[1] Chase, 556.   [2] See Wheelock's will, *ib.* 562.

[3] Young Wheelock was very active in the Revolution. He was a member of the New Hampshire Assembly in 1775, a Captain in the army in 1776, a Major the following year, and then Lieutenant-Colonel, serving on the staff of General Horatio Gates until called from military service by the death of his father in 1779. (See Smith: *History of Dartmouth College*, 76.)

[4] Chase, 564.

[5] Rachel Murch "To ye Session of ye Church of Christ in Hanover," April 26, 1783, Shirley: *Dartmouth College Causes and the Supreme Court of the United States*, 67.

processes, eventuated in arraigning the Congrega-
tionalists, or "established" Church, on one side and
all other denominations on the other.[1]

Into this religious quarrel the economic issue entered, as it always does. The property of ministers
of the "standing order," or "State religion," was
exempt from taxation while that of other preachers
was not.[2] Another source of discord arose out of
the question as to whether the College Professor of
Theology should preach in the village church. Coincident with this grave problem were subsidiary ones
concerning the attendance of students at village
worship and the benches they were to occupy. The
fates threw still another ingredient of trouble into
the cauldron. This was the election in 1793, as one
of the Trustees, of Nathaniel Niles, whom Jefferson,
with characteristic exuberance of expression, once
declared to be "the ablest man I ever knew."[3]

Although a lawyer by profession, Niles had taken
a course in theology when a student, his instructor
being a Dr. Joseph Bellamy. Both the elder Wheelock and Bellamy had graduated from Yale and had
indulged in some bitter sectarian quarrels, Bellamy
as a Congregationalist and Wheelock as a Presbyte-
rian. From tutor and parent, Niles and the younger
Wheelock inherited this religious antagonism. Moreover, they were as antipathetic by nature as they
were bold, uncompromising, and dominant. Niles
eventually acquired superior influence over his fel-

[1] Shirley, 66–70.
[2] Ib. 70–75. Only three of the scores of Congregationalist ministers
in New Hampshire were Republicans. (Ib. 70.)
[3] Ib. 82.

low Trustees, and thereafter no friend of President Wheelock was elected to the Board.[1]

An implacable feud arose. Wheelock asked the Legislature to appoint a committee to investigate the conduct of the College. This further angered the Trustees. By this time the warfare in the one college in the State had aroused the interest of the people of New Hampshire and, indeed, of all New England, and they were beginning to take sides. This process was hastened by a furious battle of pamphlets which broke out in 1815. This logomachy of vituperation was opened by President Wheelock who wrote an unsigned attack upon the Trustees.[2] Another pamphlet followed immediately in support of that of Wheelock.[3]

The Trustees quickly answered by means of two pamphlets.[4] The Wheelock faction instantly replied.[5] With the animosity and diligence of political, religious, and personal enemies, the adherents of the hostile factions circulated these pamphlets among the people, who became greatly excited. On August 26, 1815, the Trustees removed Wheelock from the office of President,[6] and thereby increased the public agitation. Two days after Wheelock's removal, the

[1] Shirley, 81, 84–85.

[2] *Sketches of the History of Dartmouth College and Moors' Charity School.*

[3] *A Candid, Analytical Review of the Sketches of the History of Dartmouth College.*

[4] *Vindication of the Official Conduct of the Trustees,* etc., and *A True and Concise Narrative of the Origin and Progress of the Church Difficulties,* by Benoni Dewey, James Wheelock, and Benjamin J Gilbert.

[5] *Answer to the "Vindication,"* etc., by Josiah Dunham.

[6] Lord: *History of Dartmouth College,* 73–77.

Trustees elected as his successor the Reverend Francis Brown of Yarmouth, Maine.[1]

During these years of increasing dissension, political parties were gradually drawn into the controversy; at the climax of it, the Federalists found themselves supporting the cause of the Trustees and the Republicans that of Wheelock. In a general, and yet quite definite, way the issue shaped itself into the maintenance of chartered rights and the established religious order, as against reform in college management and equality of religious sects. Into this issue was woven a contest over the State Judiciary. The Judiciary laws of New Hampshire were confused and inadequate and the courts had fallen in dignity. During the Republican control of the State, Republicans had been appointed to all judicial positions.[2] When, in 1813, the Federalists recovered supremacy, they, in turn, enacted a statute, the effect of which was the ousting of the Republican judges and the appointment of Federalists in their stead.[3] The Republicans made loud and savage outcry against this Federalist " outrage."

Upon questions so absurdly incongruous a political campaign raged throughout New Hampshire

[1] Lord, 78.

[2] In 1811 the salary of Chief Justices of the Court of Common Pleas for four of the counties was fixed at $200 a year; and that of the other Justices of those courts at $180. " The Chief Justice of said court in Grafton County, $180, and the other Justices in that court $160." (Act of June 21, *Laws of New Hampshire, 1811*, 33.)

[3] Acts of June 24 and Nov. 5, *Laws of New Hampshire, 1813*, 6–19; Barstow: *History of New Hampshire*, 363–64; Morison: *Life of Jeremiah Smith*, 265–67. This law was, however, most excellent. It established a Supreme Court and systematized the entire judicial system.

during the autumn and winter of 1815. In March, 1816, the Republicans elected William Plumer Governor,[1] and a Republican majority was sent to the Legislature.[2] Bills for the reform of the Judiciary [3] and the management of Dartmouth College [4] were introduced. That relating to Dartmouth changed the name of the College to "Dartmouth University," increased the number of Trustees from twelve to twenty-one, provided for a Board of twenty-five Overseers with a veto power over acts of the Trustees, and directed the President of the "University" to report annually to the Governor of the State

[1] This was the second time Plumer had been elected Governor. He was first chosen to that office in 1812. Plumer had abandoned the failing and unpatriotic cause of Federalism in 1808 (Plumer, 365), and had since become an ardent follower of Jefferson.

[2] The number of votes cast at this election was the largest ever polled in the history of the State up to that time. (*Ib.* 432.)

[3] See Act of June 27, *Laws of New Hampshire, 1816*, 45–48. This repealed the Federalist Judiciary Acts of 1813 and revived laws repealed by those acts. (See Barstow, 383, and Plumer, 437–38.)

The burning question of equality of religious taxation was not taken up by this Legislature. The bill was introduced in the State Senate by the Reverend Daniel Young, a Methodist preacher, but it received only three votes. Apparently the reform energy of the Republicans was, for that session, exhausted by the Judiciary and College Acts. The "Toleration Act" was not passed until three years later. (McClintock: *History of New Hampshire*, 507–29; also Barstow, 422.) This law is omitted from the published acts, although it is indexed.

[4] In his Message to the Legislature recommending reform laws for Dartmouth College, Governor Plumer denounced the provision of the charter relating to the Trustees as "hostile to the spirit and genius of a free government." (Barstow, 396.) This message Plumer sent to Jefferson, who replied that the idea "that institutions, established for the use of the nation, cannot be touched nor modified, even to make them answer their end .. is most absurd. ... Yet our lawyers and priests generally inculcate this doctrine; and suppose that preceding generations .. had a right to impose laws on us, unalterable by ourselves; .. in fine, that the earth belongs to the dead, and not to the living." (Jefferson to Plumer, July 21, 1816, Plumer, 440–41.)

upon the management and conditions of the institution. The Governor and Council of State were empowered to appoint the Overseers; to fill up the existing Board of Trustees to the number of twenty-one; and authorized to inspect the "University" and report to the Legislature concerning it at least once in every five years.[1] In effect the act annulled the charter and brought the College under the control of the Legislature.

The bitterness occasioned by the passage of this legislation was intense. Seventy-five members of the House entered upon the Journal their formal and emphatic protest.[2] The old Trustees adopted elaborate resolutions, declining to accept the provisions of the law and assigning many reasons for their action. Among their criticisms of the act, the fact that it violated the contract clause of the National Constitution was mentioned almost incidentally. In summing up their argument, the Trustees declared that "if the act . . has its intended operation and effect, every literary institution in the State will hereafter hold its rights, privileges and property, not according to the settled established principles of law, but according to the arbitrary will and pleasure of every successive Legislature."[3]

[1] Act of June 27, *Laws of New Hampshire, 1816*, 48–51; and see Lord, 687–90.

The temper of the Republicans is illustrated by a joint resolution adopted June 29, 1816, denouncing the increase of salaries of Senators and Representatives in Congress, which "presents the most inviting inducements to avarice and ambition," "will introduce a monopolizing power," and "contaminate our elections." (Act of June 27, *Laws of New Hampshire*, 1816, 65–66.)

[2] *Journal*, House of Representatives (N.H.), June 28, 1816, 238–41.

[3] Resolutions of the Trustees, Lord, 690–94.

In later resolutions the old Trustees declined to accept the provisions of the law, "but do hereby expressly refuse to act under the same." [1] The Governor and Council promptly appointed Trustees and Overseers of the new University; among the latter was Joseph Story. The old Trustees were defiant and continued to run the College. When the winter session of the Legislature met, Governor Plumer sharply denounced their action; [2] and two laws were passed for the enforcement of the College Acts, the second of which provided that any person assuming to act as trustee or officer of the College, except as provided by law, should be fined $500 for each offense. [3]

The Trustees of the University "removed" the old Trustees of the College and the President, and the professors who adhered to them. [4] Each side took its case to the people. [5] The new régime ousted the old faculty from the College buildings and the faculty of the University were installed in them. Wheelock was elected President of the State institution. [6] The College faculty procured quarters in

[1] Lord, 96.

[2] "It is an important question and merits your serious consideration whether a law passed and approved by all the constituted authorities of the State shall be carried into effect, or whether *a few individuals* not vested with *any judicial authority* shall be permitted to declare your statutes *dangerous and arbitrary, unconstitutional and void:* whether a *minority* of the trustees of a literary institution formed for the education of your children shall be encouraged to inculcate the doctrine of resistance to the law and their example tolerated in disseminating principles of insubordination and rebellion against government." (Plumer's Message, Nov. 20, 1816, Lord, 103.)

[3] Acts of Dec. 18 and 26, 1816, *Laws of New Hampshire, 1816*, 74-75; see also Lord, 104.)

[4] Lord, 111-12.   [5] *Ib.* 112-15.   [6] *Ib.* 115.

Rowley Hall near by, and there continued their work, the students mostly adhering to them.[1]

The College Trustees took great pains to get the opinion of the best lawyers throughout New Hampshire,[2] as well as the advice of their immediate counsel, Jeremiah Mason, Jeremiah Smith, and Daniel Webster, the three ablest members of the New England bar, all three of them accomplished politicians.[3]

William H. Woodward, who for years had been Secretary and Treasurer of the College, had in his possession the records, account books, and seal. As one of the Wheelock faction he declined to recognize the College Trustees and acted with the Board of the University. The College Trustees removed him from his official position on the College Board;[4] and on February 8, 1817, brought suit against him in the Court of Common Pleas of Grafton County for the recovery of the original charter, the books of record and account, and the common seal — all of the value

[1] Lord, 121. So few students went with the University that it dared not publish a catalogue. (*Ib.* 129.)

[2] *Ib.* 92.

[3] One of the many stories that sprang up in after years about Webster's management of the case is that, since the College was founded for the education of Indians and none of them had attended for a long time, Webster advised President Brown to procure two or three. Brown got a number from Canada and brought them to the river beyond which were the College buildings. While the party were rowing across, the young Indians, seeing the walls and fearing that they were to be put in prison, gave war whoops, sprang into the stream, swam to shore and fled. So Webster had to go on without them. (Harvey: *Reminiscences and Anecdotes of Daniel Webster,* 111–12.) There is not the slightest evidence to support this absurd tale. (Letters to the author from Eugene F. Clark, Secretary of Dartmouth College, and from Professor John K. Lord, author of *History of Dartmouth College.*)

[4] Lord, 99.

of $50,000. By the consent of the parties the case was taken directly before the Superior Court of Appeals, and was argued upon an agreed state of facts returned by the jury in the form of a special verdict.[1]

There were two arguments in the Court of Appeals, the first during May and the second during September, 1817. The court consisted of William M. Richardson, Chief Justice, and Samuel Bell and Levi Woodbury, Associate Justices, all Republicans appointed by Governor Plumer.

Mason, Smith, and Webster made uncommonly able and learned arguments. The University was represented by George Sullivan and Ichabod Bartlett, who, while good lawyers, were no match for the legal triumvirate that appeared for the College.[2] The principle upon which Marshall finally overthrew the New Hampshire law was given a minor place[3] in the plans as well as in the arguments of Webster, Mason, and Smith.

The Superior Court of Appeals decided against the College. The opinion, delivered by Chief Justice Richardson, is able and persuasive. "A corporation, all of whose franchises are exercised for publick purposes, is a publick corporation" — a gift to such a corporation "is in reality a gift to the publick."[4] The

[1] Farrar, 1.

[2] These arguments are well worth perusal. (See Farrar, 28–206; also 65 N.H. Reports, 473–624.)

[3] For instance, Mason's argument, which is very compact, consists of forty-two pages of which only four are devoted to "the contract clause" of the National Constitution and the violation of it by the New Hampshire College Act. (Farrar, 28–70; 65 N.H. 473–502.)

[4] Farrar, 212–13; 65 N.H. 628–29.

corporation of Dartmouth College is therefore public. "Who has any private interest either in the objects or the property of this institution?" If all its "property .. were destroyed, the loss would be exclusively publick." The Trustees, as individuals, would lose nothing. "The office of trustee of Dartmouth College is, in fact, a publick trust, as much so as the office of governor, or of judge of this court." [1]

No provision in the State or National Constitution prevents the control of the College by the Legislature. The Constitutional provisions cited by counsel for the College [2] "were, most manifestly, intended to protect private rights only." [3] No court has ever yet decided that such a charter as that of Dartmouth College is in violation of the contract clause of the National Constitution, which "was obviously intended to protect private rights of property, and embraces all contracts relating to private property." This clause "was not intended to limit the power of the states" over their officers or "their own civil institutions"; [4] otherwise divorce laws would be void. So would acts repealing or modifying laws under which the judges, sheriffs, and other officers were appointed.

Even if the royal charter is a contract, it does not, cannot forever, prevent the Legislature from modifying it for the general good (as, for instance, by increasing the number of trustees) "however strongly the publick interest might require" this to be done. "Such a contract, in relation to a publick institution,

---

[1] Farrar, 214–15; 65 N.H. 630   [2] The contract clause.
[3] Farrar, 216; 65 N.H. 631.   [4] Farrar, 228–29; 65 N.H. 639.

would . . be absurd and repugnant to the principles
of all government. The king had no power to make
such a contract," and neither has the Legislature.
If the act of June 27 had provided that "the twenty-
one trustees should forever have the exclusive controul of this institution, and that no future legislature should add to their number," it would be as
invalid as an act that the "number of judges of this
court should never be augmented." [1]

It is against "sound policy," Richardson affirmed,
to place the great institutions of learning "within
the absolute controul of a few individuals, and out
of the controul of the sovereign power. . . It is a
matter of too great moment, too intimately connected with the publick welfare and prosperity, to
be thus entrusted in the hands of a few." [2] So the
New Hampshire court adjudged that the College
Acts were valid and binding upon the old Trustees
"without acceptance thereof, or assent thereto by
them." And the court specifically declared that
such legislation was "not repugnant to the constitution of the United States." [3]

Immediately the case was taken to the Supreme
Court by writ of error, which assigned the violation
of the National Constitution by the College Acts as
the ground of appeal.[4] On March 10, 1818, Webster
opened the argument before a full bench.[5] Only a
few auditors were present, and these were lawyers [6]

---

[1] Farrar, 231; 65 N.H. 641.   [2] Farrar, 232; 65 N.H. 642.
[3] Farrar, 235.   [4] Ib.
[5] Webster was then thirty-six years of age.
[6] Goodrich's statement in Brown: *Works of Rufus Choate: With
a Memoir of his Life*, I, 515.

who were in Washington to argue other cases.[1] Stirred as New Hampshire and the New England States were by the College controversy, the remainder of the country appears to have taken no interest in it. Indeed, west and south of the Hudson, the people seem to have known nothing of the quarrel. The Capital was either ignorant or indifferent. Moreover, Webster had not, as yet, made that great reputation, in Washington, as a lawyer as well as an orator which, later, became his peculiar crown of glory. At any rate, the public was not drawn to the court-room on that occasion.[2]

The argument was one of the shortest ever made in a notable case before the Supreme Court during the twenty-eight years of its existence up to this time. Not three full days were consumed by counsel on both sides — a space of time frequently occupied by a single speaker in hearings of important causes.[3]

In talents, bearing, and preparation the attorneys

[1] They were Rufus Greene Amory and George Black of Boston, David B. Ogden and "a Mr. Baldwin from New York," Thomas Sergeant and Charles J. Ingersoll of Philadelphia, John Wickham, Philip Norborne, Nicholas and Benjamin Watkins Leigh of Virginia, and John McPherson Berrien of Georgia. (Webster to Sullivan, Feb. 27, 1818, *Priv. Corres.*: Webster, I, 273.)

[2] Brown, I, 515. Story makes no comment on the argument of the Dartmouth case — a pretty sure sign that it attracted little attention in Washington. Contrast Story's silence as to this argument with his vivid description of that of M'Culloch *vs.* Maryland (*infra*, chap. VI). Goodrich attributes the scant attendance to the fact that the court sat "in a mean apartment of moderate size"; but that circumstance did not keep women as well as men from thronging the room when a notable case was to be heard or a celebrated lawyer was to speak. (See description of the argument of the case of the Nereid, *supra*, 133–34.)

[3] For example, in M'Culloch *vs.* Maryland, Luther Martin spoke for three days. (Webster to Smith, Feb. 28, 1819, Van Tyne, 80; and see *infra*, chap. VI.)

for the College were as much superior to those for the University as, in the Chase impeachment trial, the counsel for the defense were stronger than the House managers.[1] Indeed, the similarity of the arguments in the Chase trial and in the Dartmouth case, in respect to the strength and preparation of opposing counsel, is notable; and in both cases the victory came to the side having the abler and better-prepared advocates. With Webster for the College was Joseph Hopkinson of Philadelphia, who had so distinguished himself in the Chase trial exactly thirteen years earlier. Hopkinson was now in his forty-ninth year, the unrivaled leader of the Philadelphia bar and one of the most accomplished of American lawyers.[2]

It would seem incredible that sensible men could have selected such counsel to argue serious questions before any court as those who represented the University in this vitally important controversy. The obvious explanation is that the State officials and the University Trustees were so certain of winning that they did not consider the employment of powerful and expensive attorneys to be necessary.[3] In fact, the belief was general that the contest was practi-

[1] See vol. III, chap. IV, of this work.

[2] The College Trustees at first thought of employing Luther Martin to assist Webster in the Supreme Court (Brown to Kirkland, Nov. 15, 1817, as quoted by Warren in *American Law Review*, XLVI, 665). It is possible that Hopkinson was chosen instead, upon the advice of Webster, who kept himself well informed of the estimate placed by Marshall and the Associate Justices on lawyers who appeared before them. Marshall liked and admired Hopkinson, had been his personal friend for years, and often wrote him. When Peters died in 1828, Marshall secured the appointment of Hopkinson in his place. (Marshall to Hopkinson, March 16, 1827, and same to same [no date, but during 1828], Hopkinson MSS.)

[3] It was considered to be a "needless expense" to send the original counsel, Sullivan and Bartlett, to Washington. (Lord, 140.)

cally over and that the appeal of the College to the Supreme Court was the pursuit of a feeble and forlorn hope.

Even after his powerful and impressive argument in the Supreme Court, Webster declared that he had never allowed himself "to indulge any great hopes of success."[1] It was not unnatural, then, that the State and the University should neglect to employ adequate counsel.

John Holmes, a Representative in Congress from that part of Massachusetts which afterward became the State of Maine, appeared for the University. He was notoriously unfitted to argue a legal question of any weight in any court. He was a busy, agile, talkative politician of the roustabout, hail-fellow-well-met variety, "a power-on-the-stump" orator, gifted with cheap wit and tawdry eloquence.[2]

Associated with Holmes was William Wirt, recently appointed Attorney-General. At that particular time Wirt was all but crushed by overwork, and without either leisure or strength to master the case and prepare an argument.[3] Never in Wirt's life did

[1] Webster to McGaw, July 27, 1818, Van Tyne, 77.

[2] Shirley, 229–32. The fact that Holmes was employed plainly shows the influence of "practical politics" on the State officials and the Trustees of the University. The Board voted December 31, 1817, "to take charge of the case." Benjamin Hale, one of the new Trustees, was commissioned to secure other counsel if Holmes did not accept. Apparently Woodward was Holmes's champion: "I have thought him extremely ready . . [a] good lawyer, inferior to D. W. only in point of oratory." (Woodward to Hall, Jan. 18, 1818, Lord, 139–40.) Hardly had Hale reached Washington than he wrote Woodward: "Were you sensible of the low ebb of Mr. Holmes' reputation here, you would . . be unwilling to trust the cause with him." (Hale to Woodward, Feb. 15, 1818, ib. 139.)

[3] "It is late at night — the fag-end of a hard day's work. My eyes,

he appear in any case so poorly equipped as he was in the Dartmouth controversy.[1]

Webster's address was a combination of the arguments made by Mason and Smith in the New Hampshire court. Although the only question before the Supreme Court was whether the College Acts violated the contract clause of the Constitution, Webster gave comparatively scant attention to it; or, perhaps it might be said that most of his argument was devoted to laying the foundation for his brief reasoning on the main question. In laying this foundation, Webster cleverly brought before the court his version of the history of the College, the situation in New Hampshire, the plight of institutions like Dartmouth, if the College Acts were permitted to stand.

The facts were, said Webster, that Wheelock had founded a private charity; that, to perpetuate this, the charter created a corporation by the name of "The Trustees of Dartmouth College," with the powers, privileges, immunities, and limitations set forth in the charter. That instrument provided for no public funds, but only for the perpetuation and

hand and mind all tired. ... I have been up till midnight, at work, every night, and still have my hands full. ... I am now worn out . . extremely fatigued. . . The Supreme Court is approaching. It will half kill you to hear that it will find me unprepared." (Wirt to Carr, Jan. 21, 1818, Kennedy, II, 73–74.) Wirt had just become Attorney-General. Apparently he found the office in very bad condition. The task of putting it in order burdened him. He was compelled to do much that was not "properly [his] duty." (*Ib.* 73.) His fee in the Dartmouth College case did not exceed $500. (Hale to Plumer, Jan. 1818, Lord, 140.)

[1] "He seemed to treat this case as if his side could furnish nothing but declamation." (Webster to Mason, March 13, 1818, *Priv. Corres.*: Webster, I, 275.)

convenient management of the private charity. For nearly half a century the College "thus created had existed, uninterruptedly, and usefully." Then its happy and prosperous career was broken by the rude and despoiling hands of the Legislature of the State which the College had so blessed by the education of New Hampshire youth.

What has the Legislature done to the College? It has created a new corporation and transferred to it "all the *property, rights, powers, liberties and privileges* of the old corporation." The spirit and the letter of the charter were wholly changed by the College Acts.[1] Moreover, the old Trustees "are to be *punished*" for not accepting these revolutionary laws. A single fact reveals the confiscatory nature of these statutes: Under the charter the president, professors, and tutors of the College had a right to their places and salaries, "subject to the twelve trustees alone"; the College Acts change all this and make the faculty "accountable to new masters."

If the Legislature can make such alterations, it can abolish the charter "rights and privileges altogether." In short, if this legislation is sustained, the old Trustees "have no *rights, liberties, franchises, property or privileges*, which the legislature may not revoke, annul, alienate or transfer to others whenever it sees fit." Such acts are against "common right" as well as violations of the State and National Constitutions.[2]

Although, says Webster, nothing is before the court

[1] Farrar, 241; 65 N.H. 596; 4 Wheaton, 534; and see Curtis, i, 163–66.

[2] Farrar, 242–44; 65 N.H. 597–98; 4 Wheaton, 556–57.

but the single question of the violation of the National Constitution, he will compare the New Hampshire laws with "fundamental principles" in order that the court may see "their true nature and character." Regardless of written constitutions, "these acts are not the exercise of a power properly legislative." They take away "vested rights"; but this involves a "forfeiture . . to . . declare which is the proper province of the judiciary."[1] Dartmouth College is not a civil but "an *eleemosynary* corporation," a "private charity"; and, as such, not subject to the control of public authorities.[2] Does Dartmouth College stand alone in this respect? No! Practically all American institutions of learning have been "established . . by incorporating governours, or trustees. . . All such corporations are . . in the strictest legal sense a private charity." Even Harvard has not "any surer title than Dartmouth College. It may, to-day, have more friends; but to-morrow it may have more enemies. Its legal rights are the same. So also of Yale College; and indeed of all others."[3]

From the time of Magna Charta the privilege of being a member of such eleemosynary corporations "has been the object of legal protection." To contend that this privilege may be "taken away," because the Trustees derive no "pecuniary benefit" from it, is "an extremely narrow view." As well say that if the charter had provided that each Trustee should be given a "commission on the disbursement of the funds," his status and the nature of the cor-

[1] Farrar, 244; 65 N.H. 598–99; 4 Wheaton, 558–59.
[2] Farrar, 248; 65 N.H. 600–01; 4 Wheaton, 563–64.
[3] Farrar, 255–56; 65 N.H. 605–06; 4 Wheaton, 567–68.

poration would have been changed from public to private. Are the rights of the Trustees any the less sacred "because they have undertaken to administer it [the trust] gratuitously? .. As if the law regarded no rights but the rights of money, and of visible tangible property!" [1]

The doctrine that all property "of which the use may be beneficial to the publick, belongs therefore to the publick," is without principle or precedent. In this very matter of Dartmouth College, Wheelock might well have "conveyed his property to trustees, for precisely such uses as are described in this charter" — yet nobody would contend that any Legislature could overthrow such a private act. "Who ever appointed a legislature to administer his charity? Or who ever heard, before, that a gift to a *college*, or *hospital*, or an *asylum*, was, in reality, nothing but a gift to the state?" [2]

Vermont has given lands to the College; was this a gift to New Hampshire? "What hinders Vermont .. from resuming her grants," upon the ground that she, equally with New Hampshire, is "the representative of the publick?" In 1794, Vermont had "granted to the respective towns in that state, certain glebe lands lying within those towns *for the sole use and support of religious worship*." Five years later, the Legislature of that State repealed this grant; "but this court declared [3] that the act of

---

[1] Farrar, 258–59; 65 N.H. 607–08; 4 Wheaton, 571–72.

[2] Farrar, 260–61; 65 N.H. 609; 4 Wheaton, 571.

[3] In Terrett *vs.* Taylor, 9 Cranch, 45 *et seq.* Story delivered the unanimous opinion of the Supreme Court in this case. This fact was well known at the time of the passage of the College Acts; and, in

1794, 'so far as it granted the glebes to the towns, *could not afterwards be repealed by the legislature, so as to divest the rights of the towns under the grant.*'" [1]

So with the Trustees of Dartmouth College. The property entrusted to them was "private property"; and the right to "administer the funds, and . . govern the college was a *franchise* and *privilege*, solemnly granted to them," which no Legislature can annul. "The use being publick in no way diminishes their legal estate in the property, or their title to the franchise." Since "the acts in question violate property, . . take away privileges, immunities, and franchises, . . deny to the trustees the protection of the law," and "are retrospective in their operation," they are, in all respects, "against the constitution of New Hampshire." [2]

It will be perceived by now that Webster relied chiefly on abstract justice. His main point was that, if chartered rights could be interfered with at all, such action was inherently beyond the power of the Legislature, and belonged exclusively to the Judiciary. In this Webster was rigidly following Smith and Mason, neither of whom depended on the violation of the contract clause of the National Constitution any more than did Webster.

Well did Webster know that the Supreme Court of the United States could not consider the violation of a State constitution by a State law. He merely

view of it, there is difficulty in understanding how Story could have been expected to support the New Hampshire legislation. (See *infra*, 257.)

[1] Farrar, 262; 65 N.H. 609–10; 4 Wheaton, 574–75.
[2] Farrar, 273; 65 N.H. 617; 4 Wheaton, 588.

indulged in a device of argument to bring before Marshall and the Associate Justices those "fundamental principles," old as Magna Charta, and embalmed in the State Constitution, which protect private property from confiscation.[1] Toward the close of his argument, Webster discusses the infraction of the National Constitution by the New Hampshire College Acts, a violation the charge of which alone gave the Supreme Court jurisdiction over the case.

What, asks Webster, is the meaning of the words, "no state shall pass any . . law impairing the obligation of contracts"? Madison, in the *Federalist*, clearly states that such laws "'are contrary to the first principles of the social compact, and to every principle of sound legislation.'" But this is not enough. "Our own experience," continues Madison, "has taught us . . that additional fences" should be erected against spoliations of "personal security and private rights." This was the reason for inserting the contract clause in the National Constitution — a provision much desired by the "sober people of America," who had grown "weary of the fluctuating policy" of the State Governments and beheld with anger "that sudden changes, and legislative interferences in cases affecting personal rights, become jobs in the hands of enterprising and influential speculators." These, said Webster, were the words of James Madison in Number 44 of the *Federalist*.

High as such authority is, one still more exalted and final has spoken, and upon the precise point

[1] Farrar, 246–47; 65 N.H. 598–600; 4 Wheaton, 557–59.

now in controversy. That authority is the Supreme
Court itself. In Fletcher *vs.* Peck[1] this very tribunal declared specifically that "a *grant* is a contract, within the meaning of this provision; and that
a grant by a state is also a contract, as much as the
grant of an individual." [2] This court went even
further when, in New Jersey *vs.* Wilson,[3] it decided
that "a grant by a state before the revolution is as
much to be protected as a grant since." [4] The principle announced in these decisions was not new,
even in America. Even before Fletcher *vs.* Peck and
New Jersey *vs.* Wilson, this court denied [5] that a
Legislature "can repeal statutes creating private
corporations, or confirming to them property already acquired under the faith of previous laws, and
by such repeal can vest the property of such corporations exclusively in the state, or dispose of the
same to such purposes as they please, without the
consent or default of the corporators . . ; and we
think ourselves standing upon the principles of
natural justice, upon the *fundamental laws of every
free government,* upon the spirit and letter of the
constitution of the United States, and upon the
decisions of the most respectable judicial tribunals,
in resisting such a doctrine." [6]

From the beginning of our Government until this

---

[1] See vol. III, chap. x, of this work.
[2] Farrar, 273–74; 65 N.H. 618–19; 4 Wheaton, 591–92.
[3] *Supra,* 223.   [4] Farrar, 275; 65 N.H. 619; 4 Wheaton, 591.
[5] In Terrett *vs.* Taylor, see *supra,* footnote to 243.
[6] Farrar, 275; 65 N.H. 619; 4 Wheaton, 591. (Italics the author's.)
It will be observed that Webster puts the emphasis upon "natural
justice" and "fundamental laws" rather than upon the Constitutional
point.

very hour, continues Webster, such has been the uniform language of this honorable court. The principle that a Legislature cannot "repeal statutes creating private corporations" must be considered as settled. It follows, then, that if a Legislature cannot repeal such laws entirely, it cannot repeal them in part — cannot "impair them, or essentially alter them without the consent of the corporators." [1] In the case last cited [2] the property granted was land; but the Dartmouth charter "is embraced within the very terms of that decision," since "a grant of corporate powers and privileges is as much a *contract* as a grant of land." [3]

Even the State court concedes that if Dartmouth College is a private corporation, "its rights stand on the same ground as those of an individual"; and that tribunal rests its judgment against the College on the sole ground that it is a public corporation. [4]

Dartmouth College is not the only institution affected by this invasion of chartered rights. "Every college, and all the literary institutions of the country" are imperiled. All of them exist because of "the inviolability of their charters." Shall their fate depend upon "the rise and fall of popular parties, and the fluctuations of political opinions"? If so, "colleges and halls will . . become a theatre for the contention of politicks. Party and faction will be cherished in the places consecrated to piety and learning."

[1] Farrar, 276; 65 N.H. 619–20; 4 Wheaton, 592.
[2] Terrett *vs.* Taylor.   [3] Farrar, 277; 65 N.H. 620; 4 Wheaton, 592.
[4] Farrar, 280; 65 N.H. 622. The two paragraphs containing these statements of Webster are omitted in *Wheaton's Reports.*

"We had hoped, earnestly hoped," exclaimed Webster, "that the State court would protect Dartmouth College. That hope has failed. It is here, that those rights are now to be maintained, or they are prostrated forever." He closed with a long Latin quotation, not a word of which Marshall understood, but which, delivered in Webster's sonorous tones and with Webster's histrionic power, must have been prodigiously impressive.[1]

Undoubtedly it was at this point that the incomparable actor, lawyer, and orator added to his prepared peroration that dramatic passage which has found a permanent place in the literature of emotional eloquence. Although given to the world a quarter of a century after Webster's speech was delivered, and transmitted through two men of vivid and creative imaginations, there certainly is some foundation for the story. Rufus Choate in his "Eulogy of Webster," delivered at Dartmouth College in 1853, told, for the first time, of the incident as narrated to him by Professor Chauncey A. Goodrich, who heard Webster's argument. When Webster had apparently finished, says Goodrich, he "stood for some moments silent before the Court, while every eye was fixed intently upon him." At length, addressing the Chief Justice, Webster delivered that famous peroration ending: "'Sir, you may destroy this little Institution; it is weak; it is in your hands! I know it is one of the lesser lights in the literary horizon of our country. You may put it out. But if you do so, you must carry through your work!

[1] Farrar, 282-83; 65 N.H. 624; 4 Wheaton, 599.

You must extinguish, one after another, all those great lights of science which, for more than a century, have thrown their radiance over our land!

"'It is, Sir, as I have said, a small College. And yet, *there are those who love it* ——— '" [1]

Then, testifies Goodrich, Webster broke down with emotion, his lips quivered, his cheeks trembled, his eyes filled with tears, his voice choked. In a "few broken words of tenderness" he spoke of his love for Dartmouth in such fashion that the listeners were impressed with "the recollections of father, mother, brother, and all the trials and privations through which he had made his way into life." [2]

Goodrich describes the scene in the court-room, "during these two or three minutes," thus: "Chief Justice Marshall, with his tall and gaunt figure bent over as if to catch the slightest whisper, the deep furrows of his cheek expanded with emotion, and eyes suffused with tears; Mr. Justice Washington at his side, — with his small and emaciated frame, and countenance more like marble than I ever saw on any other human being, — leaning forward with an eager, troubled look; and the remainder of the Court, at the two extremities, pressing, as it were, toward a single point, while the audience below were wrapping themselves round in closer folds beneath the bench to catch each look, and every movement of the speaker's face." Recovering "his

---

[1] Brown, I, 516.

[2] *Ib.* 516–17. This scene, the movement and color of which grew in dignity and vividness through the innumerable repetitions of it, caught the popular fancy. Speeches, poems, articles, were written about the incident. It became one of the chief sources from which the idolaters of Webster drew endless adulation of that great man.

composure, and fixing his keen eye on the Chief
Justice," Webster, "in that deep tone with which
he sometimes thrilled the heart of an audience,"
exclaimed:

"'Sir, I know not how others may feel,' (glancing
at the opponents of the College before him,) 'but,
for myself, when I see my Alma Mater surrounded,
like Cæsar in the senate-house, by those who are
reiterating stab upon stab, I would not, for this
right hand, have her turn to me, and say, *Et tu
quoque, mi fili!*'" [1]

Exclusive of his emotional finish, Webster's whole
address was made up from the arguments of Jeremiah
Mason and Jeremiah Smith in the State court.[2] This
fact Webster privately admitted, although he never
publicly gave his associates the credit.[3]

[1] See Brown, I, 517; Curtis, I, 169–71.

Chauncey Allen Goodrich was in his twenty-eighth year when he
heard Webster's argument. He was sixty-three when he gave Choate the
description which the latter made famous in his "Eulogy of Webster."

[2] Compare their arguments with Webster's. See Farrar 28–70; 104–
61; 238–84.

[3] "Your notes I found to contain the whole matter. They saved
me great labor; but that was not the best part of their service; they
put me in the right path. . . The only new aspect of the argument was
produced by going into cases to prove these ideas, which indeed lie at the
very bottom of your argument." (Webster to Smith, March 14, 1818,
Priv. Corres.: Webster, I, 276–77; and see Webster to Mason, March
22, 1818, *ib.* 278.)

A year later, after the case had been decided, when the question of
publishing Farrar's *Report* of all the arguments and opinions in the
Dartmouth College case was under consideration, Webster wrote
Mason: "My own interest would be promoted by *preventing* the Book.
I shall strut well enough in the Washington Report, & if the 'Book'
should not be published, the world would not know where I borrowed
my plumes — But I am still inclined to have the Book — One reason
is, that you & Judge Smith may have the credit which belongs to you."
(Webster to Mason, April 10, 1819, Van Tyne, 80.)

Farrar's *Report* was published in August, 1819. It contains the

When Farrar's "Report," containing Mason's argument, was published, Story wrote Mason that he was "exceedingly pleased" with it. "I always had a desire that the question should be put upon the broad basis you have stated; and it was a matter of regret that we were so stinted in jurisdiction in the Supreme Court, that half the argument could not be met and enforced. You need not fear a comparison of your argument with any in our annals." [1] Thus Story makes plain, what is apparent on the face of his own and Marshall's opinion, that he considered the master question involved to be that the College Acts were violative of fundamental principles of government. Could the Supreme Court have passed upon the case without regard to the Constitution, there can be no doubt that the decision would have been against the validity of the New Hampshire laws upon the ground on which Mason, Smith, and Webster chiefly relied.

Webster, as we have seen, had little faith in winning on the contract clause and was nervously anxious that the controversy should be presented to the Supreme Court by means of a case which would give that tribunal greater latitude than was afforded by the "stinted jurisdiction" of which Story complained. Indeed, Story openly expressed impatience that the court was restricted to a consideration of the contract clause. Upon his return to Massa-

pleadings and special verdict, the arguments of counsel, opinions, and the judgments in the State and National courts, together with valuable appendices. The Farrar *Report* is indispensable to those who wish to understand this celebrated case from the purely legal point of view.

[1] Story to Mason, Oct. 6, 1819, Story, I, 323.

chusetts after the argument, Story as much as told
Webster that another suit should be brought which
could be taken to the Supreme Court, and which
would permit the court to deal with all the questions
raised by the New Hampshire College Acts. Webster's report of this conversation is vital to an understanding of the views of the Chief Justice, as well
as of those of Story, since the latter undoubtedly
stated Marshall's views as well as his own. "I saw
Judge Story as I came along," Webster reported to
Mason. "He is evidently expecting a case which
shall present all the questions. It is not of great
consequence whether the actions or action, go up at
this term, except that it would give it an earlier
standing on the docket next winter.

"The question which we must raise in one of
these actions, is, 'whether, by the *general principles
of our governments*, the State Legislatures be not
restrained from divesting vested rights?' This, of
course, independent of the constitutional provision
respecting contracts. On this question [the maintenance of vested rights by "general principles"] I
have great confidence in a decision on the right side.
This is the proposition with which you began your
argument at Exeter, and which I endeavored to
state from your minutes at Washington. . . On
general principles, I am very confident the court at
Washington would be with us." [1]

[1] Webster to Mason, April 28, 1818, *Priv. Corres.*: Webster, I, 282–
83. (Italics the author's.) In fact three such suits were brought early
in 1818 on the ground of diverse citizenship. (Shirley, 2–3.) Any one
of them would have enabled the Supreme Court to have passed on
the "general principles" of contract and government. These cases,

Holmes followed Webster. "The God-like Daniel" could not have wished for a more striking contrast to himself. In figure, bearing, voice, eye, intellect, and personality, the Maine Congressman, politician, and stump-speaker, was the antithesis of Webster. For three hours Holmes declaimed "the merest stuff that was ever uttered in a county court." [1] His "argument" was a diffuse and florid repetition of the opinion of Chief Justice Richardson, and was one of those empty and long-winded speeches which Marshall particularly disliked.

Wirt did his best to repair the damage done by Holmes; but he was so indifferently prepared,[2] and

had they arrived on time, would have afforded Story his almost frantically desired opportunity to declare that legislation violative of contracts was against "natural right" — an opinion he fervently desired to give. But the wiser Marshall saw in the case, as presented to the Supreme Court on the contract guarantee of the Constitution, the occasion to declare, in effect, that these same fundamental principles are embraced in the contract clause of the written Constitution of the American Nation.

[1] Webster to Mason, March 13, 1818, *Priv. Corres.*: Webster, I, 275.

"Every body was grinning at the folly he uttered. Bell could not stand it. He seized his hat and went off." (Webster to Smith, March 14, 1818, *ib.* 277; and see Webster to Brown, March 11, 1818, Van Tyne, 75–76.)

Holmes "has attempted as a politician . . such a desire to be admired by *everybody*, that he has ceased for weeks to be regarded by *anybody*. . . In the Dartmouth College Cause, he sunk lower at the bar than he had in the Hall of Legislature." (Daggett to Mason, March 18, 1818, Hillard: *Memoir and Correspondence of Jeremiah Mason*, 199.)

The contempt of the legal profession for Holmes is shown by the fact that in Farrar's *Report* but four and one half pages are given to his argument, while those of all other counsel for Woodward (Sullivan and Bartlett in the State court and Wirt in the Supreme Court) are published in full.

[2] "He made an apology for himself, that he had not had time to study the case, and had hardly thought of it, till it was called on." (Webster to Mason, March 13, 1818, *Priv. Corres.*: Webster, I, 275–76.)

so physically exhausted, that, breaking down in the midst of his address, he asked the court to adjourn that he might finish next day;[1] and this the bored and weary Justices were only too willing to do. Wirt added nothing to the reasoning and facts of Richardson's opinion which was in the hands of Marshall and his associates.

The argument was closed by Joseph Hopkinson; and here again Fate acted as stage manager for Dartmouth, since the author of "Hail Columbia"[2] was as handsome and impressive a man as Webster, though of an exactly opposite type. His face was that of the lifelong student, thoughtful and refined. His voice, though light, had a golden tone. His manner was quiet, yet distinguished.

Joseph Hopkinson showed breeding in every look, movement, word, and intonation.[3] He had a beautiful and highly trained mind, equipped with immense and accurate knowledge systematically arranged.[4] It is unfortunate that space does not permit even a brief *précis* of Hopkinson's admirable argument.[5] He quite justified Webster's assur-

---

[1] "Before he concluded he became so exhausted .. that he was obliged to request the Court to indulge him until the next day." (*Boston Daily Advertiser*, March 23, 1818.)

"Wirt .. argues a good cause well. In this case he said more nonsensical things than became him." (Webster to Smith, March 14, 1818, *Priv. Corres.*: Webster, I, 277.)

[2] Hopkinson wrote this anthem when Marshall returned from France. (See vol. II, 343, of this work.)

[3] This description of Hopkinson is from Philadelphia according to traditions gathered by the author.

[4] Choate says that Webster called to his aid "the ripe and beautiful culture of Hopkinson." (Brown, I, 514.)

[5] The same was true of Hopkinson's argument for Chase. (See vol. III, chap. IV, of this work.)

JOSEPH HOPKINSON

ance to Brown that "Mr. Hopkinson .. will do all that man can do." [1]

At eleven o'clock of March 13, 1818, the morning after the argument was concluded, Marshall announced that some judges were of "different opinions, and that some judges had not formed opinions; consequently, the cause must be continued." [2] On the following day the court adjourned.

Marshall, Washington, and Story [3] were for the College, Duval and Todd were against it, and Livingston and Johnson had not made up their minds. [4] During the year that intervened before the court again met in February, 1819, hope sprang up in the hearts of Dartmouth's friends, and they became incessantly active in every legitimate way. Webster's

[1] Webster to Brown, March 11, 1818, Van Tyne, 75–76.

After Hopkinson's argument Webster wrote Brown: "Mr. Hopkinson understood every part of the cause, and in his argument did it great justice." (Webster to Brown, March 13, 1818, *Priv. Corres.*: Webster, I, 274; and see Webster to Mason, March 13, 1818, *ib.* 275–76.)

"Mr. Hopkinson closed the cause for the College with great ability, and in a manner which gave perfect satisfaction and delight to all who heard him." (*Boston Daily Advertiser*, March 23, 1818.)

It was expected that the combined fees of Webster and Hopkinson would be $1000, "not an unreasonable compensation." (Marsh to Brown, Nov. 22, 1817, Lord, 139.) Hopkinson was paid $500. (Brown to Hopkinson, May 4, 1819, Hopkinson MSS.)

At their first meeting after the decision, the Trustees, "feeling the inadequacy" of the fees of all the lawyers for the College, asked Mason, Smith, Webster, and Hopkinson to sit for their portraits by Gilbert Stuart, the artist to be paid by the Trustees. (Shattuck to Hopkinson, Jan. 4, 1835, enclosing resolution of the Trustees, April 4, 1819, attested by Miles Olcott, secretary, Hopkinson MSS.; also, Webster to Hopkinson, May 9, 1819, *ib.*)

[2] Webster to Smith, March 14, 1818, *Priv. Corres.*: Webster, I, 577.

[3] Many supposed that Story was undecided, perhaps opposed to the College. In fact, he was as decided as Marshall. (See *infra*, 257–58, 275 and footnote.)

[4] Webster to Smith, March 14, 1818, *Priv. Corres.*: Webster, I, 577.

argument was printed and placed in the hands of all influential lawyers in New England.

Chancellor James Kent of New York was looked upon by the bench and bar of the whole country as the most learned of American jurists and, next to Marshall, the ablest.[1] The views of no other judge were so sought after by his fellow occupants of the bench. Charles Marsh of New Hampshire, one of the Trustees of the College and a warm friend of Kent, sent him Webster's argument. While on a vacation in Vermont Kent had read the opinion of Chief Justice Richardson and, "on a hasty perusal of it," was at first inclined to think the College Acts valid, because he was "led by the opinion to assume the fact that Dartmouth College was a public establishment for purposes of a general nature."[2] Webster's argument changed Kent's views.

During the summer of 1818, Justice Johnson, of the National Supreme Court, was in Albany, where Kent lived, and conferred with the Chancellor about the Dartmouth case. Kent told Johnson that he thought the New Hampshire College Acts to be

---

[1] For example, William Wirt, Monroe's Attorney-General, in urging the appointment of Kent, partisan Federalist though he was, to the Supreme Bench to succeed Justice Livingston, who died March 19, 1823, wrote that "Kent holds so lofty a stand everywhere for almost matchless intellect and learning, as well as for spotless purity and high-minded honor and patriotism, that I firmly believe the nation at large would approve and applaud the appointment." (Wirt to Monroe, May 5, 1823, Kennedy, II, 153.)

[2] Kent to Marsh, Aug. 26, 1818, Shirley, 263. Moreover, in 1804, Kent, as a member of the New York Council of Revision, had held that "charters of incorporation containing grants of personal and municipal privileges were not to be essentially affected without the consent of the parties concerned." (Record of Board, as quoted in *ib.* 254.)

against natural right and in violation of the contract clause of the National Constitution.[1] It seems fairly certain also that Livingston asked for the Chancellor's opinion, and was influenced by it.

Webster sent Story, with whom he was on terms of cordial intimacy, "five copies of our argument." Evidently Webster now knew that Story was unalterably for the College, for he adds these otherwise startling sentences: "If you send one of them to each of such of the judges as you think proper, you will of course do it in the manner least likely to lead to a feeling that any indecorum has been committed by the plaintiffs." [2]

In some way, probably from the fact that Story was an intimate friend of Plumer, a rumor had spread, before the case was argued, that he was against the College Trustees. Doubtless this impression was strengthened by the fact that Governor Plumer had appointed Story one of the Board of Overseers of the new University. No shrewder politician than Plumer ever was produced by New England. But Story declined the appointment.[3] He had been compromised, however, in the eyes of both sides. The friends of the College were discouraged, angered, frightened.[4] In great apprehension,

[1] Shirley, 253. Shirley says that Kent "agreed to draw up an opinion for Johnson in this case."

[2] Webster to Story, Sept. 9, 1818, *Priv. Corres.*: Webster. I, 287.

[3] Lord, 143.

[4] "The folks in this region are frightened... It is ascertained that Judge Story .. is the original framer of the law... They suppose that on this account the cause is hopeless before the Sup. Ct. of U.S. This is, however, report." (Murdock to Brown, Dec. 27, 1817, *ib.* 142.)
Murdock mentions Pickering as one of those who believed the

Charles Marsh, one of the College Trustees, wrote
Hopkinson of Story's appointment as Overseer of
the University and of the rumor in circulation. Hopkinson answered heatedly that he would object to
Story's sitting in the case if the reports could be
confirmed.[1]

Although the efforts of the College to get its case
before Kent were praiseworthy rather than repre-
hensible, and although no smallest item of testimony
had been adduced by eager searchers for something
unethical, nevertheless out of the circumstances just
related has been woven, from the materials of eager
imaginations, a network of suspicion involving the
integrity of the Supreme Court in the Dartmouth
decision.[2]

rumors about Story. This explains much. The soured old Federalist
was an incessant gossip and an indefatigable purveyor of rumors concerning any one he did not like, provided the reports were bad enough
for him to repeat. He himself would, with great facility, apply the
black, if the canvas were capable of receiving it; and he could not forget that Story, when a young man, had been a Republican.

[1] Hopkinson to Marsh, Dec. 31, 1817, Shirley, 274–75.

[2] This is principally the work of John M. Shirley in his book *Dartmouth College Causes and the Supreme Court of the United States*. The
volume is crammed with the results of extensive research, strange
conglomeration of facts, suppositions, inferences, and insinuations,
so inextricably mingled that it is with the utmost difficulty that the
painstaking student can find his way.

Shirley leaves the impression that Justices Johnson and Livingston
were improperly worked upon because they consulted Chancellor
Kent. Yet the only ground for this is that Judge Marsh sent Webster's argument to Kent, who was Marsh's intimate friend; and
that the Reverend Francis Brown, President of Dartmouth, went
to see Kent, reported that his opinion was favorable to the College,
and that the effect of this would be good upon Johnson and Livingston.

From the mere rumor, wholly without justification, that Story was
at first against the College — indeed, had drawn the College Acts (for
so the rumor grew, as rumors always grow) — Shirley would have us

Meanwhile the news had spread of the humiliating failure before the Supreme Court of the flamboyant Holmes and the tired and exhausted Wirt as contrasted with the splendid efforts of Webster and Hopkinson. The New Hampshire officials and the University at last realized the mistake they had made in not employing able counsel, and resolved to remedy their blunder by securing the acknowledged leader of the American bar whose primacy no judge or lawyer in the country denied. They did what they should have done at the beginning — they retained William Pinkney of Maryland.

Traveling with him in the stage during the autumn of 1818, Hopkinson learned that the great lawyer had been engaged by the University. Moreover, with characteristic indiscretion, Pinkney told Hopkinson that he intended to request a reargument at the approaching session of the Supreme

believe, without any evidence whatever, that some improper influence was exerted over Story.

Because Webster said that there was something "left out" of the report of his argument, Shirley declares that for a whole hour Webster spoke as a Federalist partisan in order to influence Marshall. (Shirley, 237.) But such an attempt would have been resented by every Republican member of the court and, most of all, by Marshall himself. Moreover, Marshall needed no such persuasion, nor, indeed, persuasion of any kind. His former opinions showed where he stood; so did the views which he had openly and constantly avowed since he was a member of the Virginia House of Burgesses in 1783. The something "left out" of Webster's reported argument was, of course, his extemporaneous and emotional peroration described by Goodrich.

These are only a very few instances of Shirley's assumptions. Yet, because of the mass of data his book contains, and because of the impossibility of getting out of them a connected narrative without the most laborious and time-consuming examination, together with the atmosphere of wrongdoing with which Shirley manages to surround the harried reader, his volume has had a strong and erroneous effect upon general opinion.

Court. In alarm, Hopkinson instantly wrote Webster,[1] who was dismayed by the news. Of all men
the one Webster did not want to meet in forensic
combat was the legal Colossus from Baltimore.[2]

Pinkney applied himself to the preparation of the
case with a diligence and energy uncommon even for
that most laborious and painstaking of lawyers. Apparently he had no doubt that the Supreme Court
would grant his motion for a reargument. It was
generally believed that some of the Justices had
not made up their minds; rearguments, under such
circumstances, were usually granted and sometimes
required by the court; and William Pinkney was
the most highly regarded by that tribunal of all
practitioners before it. So, on February 1, 1819, he
took the Washington stage at Baltimore, prepared at
every point for the supreme effort of his brilliant
career.[3]

Pinkney's purpose was, of course, well advertised
by this time. By nobody was it better understood
than by Marshall and, indeed, by every Justice of

[1] Hopkinson to Webster, Nov. 17, 1818, *Priv. Corres.*: Webster,
I, 288–89. "I suppose he expects to do something very extraordinary
in it, as he says Mr. Wirt 'was not strong enough for it, has not back
enough.'" (*Ib.* 289.)

[2] Both Hopkinson and Webster resolved to prevent Pinkney from
making his anticipated argument. (*Ib.*)

[3] Not only did Pinkney master the law of the case, but, in order to
have at his command every practical detail of the controversy, he kept
Cyrus Perkins, who succeeded Woodward, deceased, as Secretary of
the University Trustees, under continuous examination for an entire
week. Perkins knew every possible fact about the College controversy
and submitted to Pinkney the whole history of the dispute and also
all documents that could illuminate the subject. "Dr. Perkins had
been a week at Baltimore, conferring with Mr. Pinkney." (Webster to
Mason, Feb. 4, 1819, Hillard, 213; and see Shirley, 203.)

the Supreme Court. All of them, except Duval and Todd, had come to an agreement and consented to the opinion which Marshall had prepared since the adjournment the previous year.[1] None of them were minded to permit the case to be reopened. Most emphatically John Marshall was not.

When, at eleven o'clock, February 2, 1819, the marshal of the court announced "The Honorable, the Chief Justice and the Associate Justices of the Supreme Court of the United States," Marshall, at the head of his robed associates, walked to his place, he beheld Pinkney rise, as did all others in the room, to greet the court. Well did Marshall know that, at the first opportunity, Pinkney would ask for a re-argument.

From all accounts it would appear that Pinkney was in the act of addressing the court when the Chief Justice, seemingly unaware of his presence, placidly announced that the court had come to a decision and began reading his momentous opinion.[2] After a few introductory sentences the Chief Justice came abruptly to the main point of the dispute:

"This court can be insensible neither to the magnitude nor delicacy of this question. The validity of a legislative act is to be examined; and the opinion

[1] This fact was unknown to anybody but the Justices themselves. "No public or general opinion seems to be formed of the opinion of any particular judge." (Webster to Brown, Jan. 10, 1819, *Priv. Corres.*: Webster, I, 299.)

[2] "On Tuesday morning, he [Pinkney] being in court, as soon as the judges had taken their seats, the Chief Justice said that in vacation the judges had formed opinions in the College case. He then immediately began reading his opinion, and, of course, nothing was said of a second argument." (Webster to Mason, Feb. 4, 1819, Hillard, 213.)

of the highest law tribunal of a state is to be revised: an opinion which carries with it intrinsic evidence of the diligence, of the ability, and the integrity, with which it was formed. On more than one occasion this court has expressed the cautious circumspection with which it approaches the consideration of such questions; and has declared that, in no doubtful case would it pronounce a legislative act to be contrary to the constitution.

"But the American people have said, in the constitution of the United States, that 'no state shall pass any bill of attainder, *ex post facto* law, or law impairing the obligation of contracts.' In the same instrument they have also said, 'that the judicial power shall extend to all cases in law and equity arising under the constitution.' On the judges of this court, then, is imposed the high and solemn duty of protecting, from even legislative violation, those contracts which the constitution of our country has placed beyond legislative control; and, however irksome the task may be, this is a duty from which we dare not shrink." [1]

Then Marshall, with, for him, amazing brevity, states the essential provisions of the charter and of the State law that modified it; [2] and continues, almost curtly: "It can require no argument to prove that the circumstances of this case constitute a contract." On the faith of the charter "large contributions" to "a religious and literary institution" are conveyed to a corporation created by that charter. Indeed, in the very application it is stated

[1] 4 Wheaton, 625.   [2] *Ib.* 626–27.

that these funds will be so applied. "Surely in this transaction every ingredient of a complete and legitimate contract is to be found." [1]

This being so, is such a contract "protected" by the Constitution, and do the New Hampshire College Acts impair that contract? Marshall states clearly and fairly Chief Justice Richardson's argument that to construe the contract clause so broadly as to cover the Dartmouth charter would prevent legislative control of public offices, and even make divorce laws invalid; and that the intention of the framers of the Constitution was to confine the operation of the contract clause to the protection of property rights, as the history of the times plainly shows. [2]

All this, says Marshall, "may be admitted." The contract clause "never has been understood to embrace other contracts than those which respect property, or some object of value, and confer rights which may be asserted in a court of justice." Divorce laws are not included, of course — they merely enable a court, "not to impair a marriage contract, but to liberate one of the parties because it has been broken by the other."

The "point on which the cause essentially depends" is "the true construction" of the Dartmouth charter. If that instrument grants "political power," creates a "civil institution" as an instrument of government; "if the funds of the college be public property," or if the State Government "be alone interested in its transactions," the Legislature may do

---

[1] 4 Wheaton, 627.   [2] Ib. 627–28.

what it likes "unrestrained" by the National Constitution.[1]

If, on the other hand, Dartmouth "be a private eleemosynary institution," empowered to receive property "for objects unconnected with government," and "whose funds are bestowed by individuals on the faith of the charter; if the donors have stipulated for the future disposition and management of those funds in the manner prescribed by themselves," the case becomes more difficult.[2] Marshall then sets out compactly and clearly the facts relating to the establishment of Wheelock's school; the granting and acceptance of the charter; the nature of the College funds which "consisted entirely of private donations." These facts unquestionably show, he avows, that Dartmouth College is "an eleemosynary, and, as far as respects its funds, a private corporation."[3]

Does the fact that the purpose of the College is the education of youth make it a public corporation? It is true that the Government may found and control an institution of learning. "But is Dartmouth College such an institution? Is education altogether in the hands of government?" Are all teachers public officers? Do gifts for the advancement of learning "necessarily become public property, so far that the will of the legislature, not the will of the donor, becomes the law of donation?"[4]

---

[1] 4 Wheaton, 629–30.   [2] *Ib.* 630.

[3] *Ib.* 631–34. The statement of facts and of the questions growing out of them was by far the best work Marshall did. In these statements he is as brief, clear, and pointed as, in his arguments, he is prolix, diffuse, and repetitious.   [4] *Ib.* 634.

Certainly Eleazar Wheelock, teaching and supporting Indians "at his own expense, and on the voluntary contributions of the charitable," was not a public officer. The Legislature could not control his money and that given by others, merely because Wheelock was using it in an educational charity. Whence, then, comes "the idea that Dartmouth College has become a public institution? . . Not from the source" or application of its funds. "Is it from the act of incorporation?" [1]

Such is the process by which Marshall reaches his famous definition of the word "corporation": "A corporation is an artificial being, invisible, intangible, and existing only in contemplation of law. . . It possesses only those properties which the charter of its creation confers upon it. . . Among the most important are immortality, and . . individuality. . . By these means, a perpetual succession of individuals are capable of acting for the promotion of the particular object, like one immortal being. . . But . . it is no more a state instrument than a natural person exercising the same powers would be." [2]

This, says Marshall, is obviously true of all private corporations. "The objects for which a corporation is created are universally such as the government wishes to promote." Why should a private charity, incorporated for the purpose of education, be excluded from the rules that apply to other corporations? An individual who volunteers to teach is not a public officer because of his personal devotion to

[1] 4 Wheaton, 635-36.   [2] Ib. 636.

education; how, then, is it that a corporation formed for precisely the same service "should become a part of the civil government of the country?" Because the Government has authorized the corporation "to take and to hold property in a particular form, and for particular purposes, has the Government a consequent right substantially to change that form, or to vary the purposes to which the property is to be applied?" Such an idea is without precedent. Can it be supported by reason? [1]

Any corporation for any purpose is created only because it is "deemed beneficial to the country; and this benefit constitutes the consideration, and, in most cases, the sole consideration for the grant." This is as true of incorporated charities as of any other form of incorporation. Of consequence, the Government cannot, subsequently, assume a power over such a corporation which is "in direct contradiction to its [the corporate charter's] express stipulations." So the mere fact "that a charter of incorporation has been granted" does not justify a Legislature in changing "the character of the institution," or in transferring "to the Government any new power over it."

"The character of civil institutions does not grow out of their incorporation, but out of the manner in which they are formed, and the objects for which they are created. The right to change them is not founded on their being incorporated, but on their being the instruments of government, created for its purposes. The same institutions, created for the same objects,

[1] 4 Wheaton, 637.

though not incorporated, would be public institutions, and, of course, be controllable by the legislature. The incorporating act neither gives nor prevents this control. Neither, in reason, can the incorporating act change the character of a private eleemosynary institution." [1]

For whose benefit was the property of Dartmouth College given to that institution? For the people at large, as counsel insist? Read the charter. Does it give the State "any exclusive right to the property of the college, any exclusive interest in the labors of the professors?" Does it not rather "merely indicate a willingness that New Hampshire should enjoy those advantages which result to all from the establishment of a seminary of learning in the neighborhood? On this point we think it impossible to entertain a serious doubt." For the charter shows that, while the spread of education and religion was the object of the founders of the College, the "particular interests" of the State "never entered into the minds of the donors, never constituted a motive for their donation." [2]

It is plain, therefore, that every element of the problem shows "that Dartmouth College is an eleemosynary institution, incorporated for the purpose of perpetuating . . the bounty of the donors, to the specified objects of that bounty"; that the Trustees are legally authorized to perpetuate themselves and that they are "not public officers"; that, in fine, Dartmouth College is a "seminary of education, incorporated for the preservation of its

[1] 4 Wheaton, 638–39.   [2] *Ib.* 639–40

property, and the perpetual application of that prop‹
erty to the objects of its creation." [1]

There remains a question most doubtful of "all
that have been discussed." Neither those who have
given money or land to the College, nor students who
have profited by those benefactions, "complain of
the alteration made in its charter, or think themselves injured by it. The trustees alone complain,
and the trustees have no beneficial interest to be
protected." Can the charter "be such a contract as
the constitution intended to withdraw from the
power of state legislation?" [2]

Wheelock and the other philanthropists who had
endowed the College, both before and after the charter was granted, made their gifts "for something
. . of inestimable value — . . the perpetual application of the fund to its object, in the mode prescribed by themselves. . . The corporation . . stands
in their place, and distributes their bounty, as they
would themselves have distributed it, had they
been immortal." Also the rights of the students
"collectively" are "to be exercised . . by the corporation." [3]

The British Parliament is omnipotent. Yet had it
annulled the charter, even immediately after it had
been granted and conveyances made to the corporation upon the faith of that charter, "so that the
living donors would have witnessed the disappointment of their hopes, the perfidy of the transaction
would have been universally acknowledged." Nevertheless, Parliament would have had the power to

---

[1] 4 Wheaton, 640–41.   [2] *Ib.* 641.   [3] *Ib.* 642–43.

perpetrate such an outrage. "Then, as now, the donors would have had no interest in the property; .. the students .. no rights to be violated; .. the trustees .. no private, individual, beneficial interest in the property confided to their protection." But, despite the legal power of Parliament to destroy it, "the contract would at that time have been deemed sacred by all."

"What has since occurred to strip it of its inviolability? Circumstances have not changed it. In reason, in justice, and in law, it is now what it was in 1769." The donors and Trustees, on the one hand, and the Crown on the other, were the original parties to the arrangement stated in the charter, which was "plainly a contract" between those parties. To the "rights and obligations" of the Crown under that contract, "New Hampshire succeeds." [1] Can such a contract be impaired by a State Legislature?

"It is a contract made on a valuable consideration.

"It is a contract for the security and disposition of property.

"It is a contract, on the faith of which real and personal estate has been conveyed to the corporation.

"It is then a contract within the letter of the constitution, and within its spirit also, unless" the nature of the trust creates "a particular exception, taking this case out of the prohibition contained in the constitution."

It is doubtless true that the "preservation of rights of this description was not particularly in the view of the framers of the constitution when the

[1] 4 Wheaton, 643.

clause under consideration was introduced into that instrument," and that legislative interferences with contractual obligations "of more frequent recurrence, to which the temptation was stronger, and of which the mischief was more extensive, constituted the great motive for imposing this restriction on the state legislatures.

"But although a particular and a rare case may not . . induce a rule, yet it must be governed by the rule, when established, unless some plain and strong reason for excluding it can be given. It is not enough to say that this particular case was not in the mind of the convention when the article was framed, nor of the American people when it was adopted. It is necessary to go farther, and to say that, had this particular case been suggested, the language [of the contract clause] would have been so varied as to exclude it, or it would have been made a special exception." [1]

Can the courts now make such an exception? "On what safe and intelligible ground can this exception stand?" Nothing in the language of the Constitution; no "sentiment delivered by its contemporaneous expounders . . justify us in making it."

Does "the nature and reason of the case itself . . sustain a construction of the constitution, not warranted by its words?" The contract clause was made a part of the Nation's fundamental law "to give stability to contracts." That clause in its "plain import" comprehends Dartmouth's charter. Does public policy demand a construction which

[1] 4 Wheaton, 644.

will exclude it? The fate of all similar corporations is involved. "The law of this case is the law of all." [1] Is it so necessary that Legislatures shall "new-model" such charters "that the ordinary rules of construction must be disregarded in order to leave them exposed to legislative alteration?"

The importance attached by the American people to corporate charters like that of Dartmouth College is proved by "the interest which this case has excited." If the framers of the Constitution respected science and literature so highly as to give the National Government exclusive power to protect inventors and writers by patents and copyrights, were those statesman "so regardless of contracts made for the advancement of literature as to intend to exclude them from provisions made for the security of ordinary contracts between man and man?" [2]

No man ever did or will found a college, "believing at the time that an act of incorporation constitutes no security for the institution; believing that it is immediately to be deemed a public institution, whose funds are to be governed and applied, not by the will of the donor, but by the will of the legislature. All such gifts are made in the pleasing, perhaps delusive hope, that the charity will flow forever in the channel which the givers have marked out for it."

Since every man finds evidence of this truth "in his own bosom," can it be imagined that "the framers of our constitution were strangers" to the same universal sentiment? Although "feeling

[1] 4 Wheaton, 645.   [2] *Ib.* 646–47.

the necessity . . of giving permanence and security to contracts," because of the "fluctuating" course and "repeated interferences" of Legislatures which resulted in the "most perplexing and injurious embarrassments," did the framers of the Constitution nevertheless deem it "necessary to leave these contracts subject to those interferences?" Strong, indeed, must be the motives for making such exceptions.[1]

Finally, Marshall declares that the "opinion of the court, after mature deliberation, is, that this is a contract, the obligation of which cannot be impaired without violating the Constitution of the United States." [2]

Do the New Hampshire College Acts impair the obligations of Dartmouth's charter? That instrument gave the Trustees "the whole power of governing the college"; stipulated that the corporation "should continue forever"; and "that the number of trustees should forever consist of twelve, and no more." This contract was made by the Crown, a power which could have made "no violent alteration in its essential terms, without impairing its obligation."

The powers and duties of the Crown were, by the Revolution, "devolved on the people of New Hampshire." It follows that, since the Crown could not change the charter of Dartmouth without impairing the contract, neither can New Hampshire. "All contracts, and rights, respecting property, remained unchanged by the revolution." [3]

[1] 4 Wheaton, 647–48.   [2] *Ib.* 650.   [3] *Ib.* 651.

As to whether the New Hampshire College Acts radically alter the charter of Dartmouth College, "two opinions cannot be entertained." The State takes over the government of the institution. "The will of the state is substituted for the will of the donors, in every essential operation of the college. . . The charter of 1769 exists no longer " — the College has been converted into "a machine entirely subservient to the will of government," instead of the "will of its founders." [1] Therefore, the New Hampshire College laws "are repugnant to the constitution of the United States." [2]

On account of the death of Woodward, who had been Secretary and Treasurer of the University, and formerly held the same offices in the College against whom the College Trustees had brought suit, Webster moved for judgment *nunc pro tunc;* and judgment was immediately entered accordingly.

Not for an instant could Webster restrain the expression of his joy. Before leaving the court-room he wrote his brother: "All is safe. . . The opinion was delivered by the Chief Justice. It was very able and very elaborate; it goes the whole length, and leaves not an inch of ground for the University to stand on." [3] He informed President Brown that "all is safe and certain. . . I feel a load removed from my shoulders much heavier than they have been accustomed to bear." [4] To Mason, Webster describes Marshall's manner: "The Chief

[1] 4 Wheaton, 652–53.   [2] *Ib.* 654.
[3] Webster "in court" to his brother, Feb. 2, 1819, *Priv. Corres.:* Webster, I, 300.
[4] Webster to Brown, Feb. 2, 1819, *ib.*

Justice's opinion was in his own peculiar way. He reasoned along from step to step; and, not refer-ring to the cases [cited], adopted the principles of them, and worked the whole into a close, connected, and very able argument." [1]

At the same time Hopkinson wrote Brown in a vein equally exuberant: "Our triumph . . has been com-plete. Five judges, only six attending, concur not only in a decision in our favor, but in placing it upon principles broad and deep, and which secure corpora-tions of this description from legislative despotism and party violence for the future. . . I would have an inscription over the door of your building, 'Founded by Eleazar Wheelock, Refounded by Daniel Web-ster.'" [2] The high-tempered Pinkney was vocally indignant. "He talked . . and blustered" ungener-ously, wrote Webster, "because . . the party was in a fever and he must do something for his fees. As he could not talk *in* court, he therefore talked *out* of court." [3]

As we have seen, Marshall had prepared his opin-ion under his trees at Richmond and in the moun-tains during the vacation of 1818; and he had barely time to read it to his associates before the opening of court at the session when it was delivered. But he afterward submitted the manuscript to Story, who made certain changes, although enthusiastically praising it. "I am much obliged," writes Marshall,

[1] Webster to Mason, Feb. 4, 1819, Hillard, 213–14. Webster adds: "Some of the other judges, I am told, have drawn opinions with more reference to authorities." (*Ib.* 214.)

[2] Hopkinson to Brown, Feb. 2, 1819, *Priv. Corres.*: Webster, I, 301.

[3] Webster to Mason, April 13, 1819, Hillard, 223.

"by the alterations you have made in the Dartmouth College case & am highly gratified by what you say respecting it." [1]

Story also delivered an opinion upholding the charter [2] — one of his ablest papers. It fairly bristles with citations of precedents and historical examples. The whole philosophy of corporations is expounded with clearness, power, and learning. Apparently Justice Livingston liked Story's opinion even more than that of Marshall. Story had sent it to Livingston, who, when returning the manuscript, wrote: It "has afforded me more pleasure than can easily be expressed. It was exactly what I had expected from you, and hope it will be adopted without alteration." [3]

At the time of the Dartmouth decision little attention was paid to it outside of New Hampshire and

[1] Marshall to Story, May 27, 1819, *Proceedings, Mass. Hist. Soc.* 2d Series, xiv, 324–25.

[2] 4 Wheaton, 666–713.

[3] Livingston to Story, Jan. 24, 1819, Story, i, 323. This important letter discredits the rumor that Story at first thought the College Acts valid.

Story sent copies of his opinion to eminent men other than his associates on the Supreme Bench, among them William Prescott, father of the historian, a Boston lawyer highly esteemed by the leaders of the American bar. "I have read your opinion with care and great pleasure," writes Prescott. "In my judgment it is supported by the principles of our constitutions, and of all free governments, as well as by the authority of adjudged cases. As one of the public, I thank you for establishing a doctrine affecting so many valuable rights and interests, with such clearness and cogency of argument, and weight of authority as must in all probability prevent its ever being again disturbed. I see nothing I should wish altered in it. I hope it will be adopted without diminution or subtraction. You have placed the subject in some strong, and to me, new lights, although I had settled my opinion on the general question years ago." (Prescott to Story, Jan. 9, 1819, *ib.* 324.)

Massachusetts.[1] The people, and even the bar, were too much occupied with bank troubles, insolvency, and the swiftly approaching slavery question, to bother about a small New Hampshire college. The profound effect of Marshall's opinion was first noted in the *North American Review* a year after the Chief Justice delivered it. "Perhaps no judicial proceedings in this country ever involved more important consequences, . . than the case of Dartmouth College." [2]

Important, indeed, were the "consequences" of the Dartmouth decision. Everywhere corporations were springing up in response to the necessity for larger and more constant business units and because of the convenience and profit of such organizations. Marshall's opinion was a tremendous stimulant to this natural economic tendency. It reassured investors in corporate securities and gave confidence and steadiness to the business world. It is undeniable and undenied that America could not have been developed so rapidly and solidly without the power which the law as announced by Marshall gave to industrial organization.

One result of his opinion was, for the period, of even higher value than the encouragement it gave to private enterprise and the steadiness it brought to business generally; it aligned on the side of Nationalism all powerful economic forces operating through corporate organization. A generation passed before railway development began in Amer-

[1] For instance, the watchful Niles does not even mention it in his all-seeing and all-recording *Register*. Also see Warren, 377.

[2] *North American Review* (1820), **x**, 83.

ica; but Marshall lived to see the first stage of the evolution of that mighty element in American commercial, industrial, and social life; and all of that force, except the part of it which was directly connected with and under the immediate influence of the slave power, was aggressively and most effectively Nationalist.

That this came to be the fact was due to Marshall's Dartmouth opinion more than to any other single cause. The same was true of other industrial corporate organizations. John Fiske does not greatly exaggerate in his assertion that the law as to corporate franchises declared by Marshall, in subjecting to the National Constitution every charter granted by a State "went farther, perhaps, than any other in our history toward limiting State sovereignty and extending the Federal jurisdiction." [1]

Sir Henry Sumner Maine has some ground for his rather dogmatic statement that the principle of Marshall's opinion "is the basis of credit of many of the great American Railway Incorporations," and "has .. secured full play to the economical forces by which the achievement of cultivating the soil of the North American Continent has been performed." Marshall's statesmanship is, asserts Maine, "the bulwark of American individualism against democratic impatience and Socialistic fantasy." [2] Such views of the Dartmouth decision are remarkably similar to those which Story himself expressed soon after it was rendered. Writing to Chancellor Kent

---

[1] Fiske: *Essays, Historical and Literary*, i, 379.
[2] Maine: *Popular Government*, 248.

Story says: "Unless I am very much mistaken the principles on which that decision rests will be found to apply with an extensive reach to all the great concerns of the people, and will check any undue encroachments upon civil rights, which the passions or the popular doctrines of the day may stimulate our State Legislatures to adopt." [1]

The court's decision, however, made corporate franchises infinitely more valuable and strengthened the motives for procuring them, even by corruption. In this wise tremendous frauds have been perpetrated upon negligent, careless, and indifferent publics; and "enormous and threatening powers," selfish and non-public in their purposes and methods, have been created.[2] But Marshall's opinion put the public on its guard. Almost immediately the States enacted laws reserving to the Legislature the right to alter or repeal corporate charters; and the constitutions of several States now include this limitation on corporate franchises. Yet these reservations did not, as a practical matter, nullify or overthrow Marshall's philosophy of the sacredness of contracts.

Within the last half-century the tendency has been strongly away from the doctrine of the Dartmouth decision, and this tendency has steadily become more powerful. The necessity of modifying and even abrogating legislative grants, more freely than is secured by the reservation to do so contained in State constitutions and corporate charters, has further restricted the Dartmouth decision. It is this necessity that has

---

[1] Story to Kent, Aug. 21, 1819, Story, I, 331.
[2] See Cooley: *Constitutional Limitations* (6th ed.), footnote to 335.

produced the rapid development of "that well-known but undefined power called the police power," [1] under which laws may be passed and executed, in disregard of what Marshall would have called contracts, provided such laws are necessary for the protection or preservation of life, health, property, morals, or order. The modern doctrine is that "the Legislature cannot, by any contract, divest itself of the power to provide for these objects. . . They are to be attained and provided for by such appropriate means as the legislative discretion may devise. That discretion can no more be bargained away than the power itself." [2]

Aside from the stability which this pronouncement of the Chief Justice gave to commercial transactions in general, and the confidence it inspired throughout the business world, the largest permanent benefit of it to the American people was to teach them that faith once plighted, whether in private contracts or public grants, must not and cannot be broken by State legislation; that, by the fundamental law which they themselves established for their own government, they as political entities are forbidden to break their contracts by enacting statutes, just as, by the very spirit of the law, private persons are forbidden to break their contracts. If it be said that their representatives may betray the people, the plain answer is that the people must learn to elect honest agents.

For exactly a century Marshall's Dartmouth opin-

[1] Butchers' Union, etc. *vs.* Crescent City, etc. 111 U.S. 750.

[2] Beer Company *vs.* Massachusetts, 97 U.S. 25; and see Fertilizing Co. *vs.* Hyde Park, *ib.* 659.

ion has been assailed and the Supreme Court itself
has often found ways to avoid its conclusions. But
the theory of the Chief Justice has shown amazing
vitality. Sixty years after Marshall delivered it, Chief
Justice Waite declared that the principles it announced are so "imbedded in the jurisprudence of
the United States as to make them to all intents
and purposes a part of the Constitution itself." [1]
Thirty-one years after Marshall died, Justice Davis
avowed that "a departure from it [Marshall's doc-
trine] *now* would involve dangers to society that
cannot be foreseen, would shock the sense of justice
of the country, unhinge its business interests, and
weaken, if not destroy, that respect which has always been felt for the judicial department of the
Government." [2] As late as 1895, Justice Brown asserted that it has "become firmly established as a
canon of American jurisprudence." [3]

It was a principle which Marshall introduced into
American Constitutional law, and, fortunately for
the country, that principle still stands; but to-day
the courts, when construing a law said to impair the
obligation of contracts, most properly require that
it be established that the unmistakable purpose of
the Legislature is to make an actual contract for a
sufficient consideration. [4]

[1] Stone *vs*. Mississippi, October, 1879, 11 Otto (101 U.S.) 816.
[2] The Binghamton Bridge, December, 1865, 3 Wallace, 73.
[3] Pearsall *vs*. Great Northern Railway, 161 U.S. 660.
[4] More has been written of Marshall's opinion in this case than of
any other delivered by him except that in Marbury *vs*. Madison.
For recent discussions of the subject see Russell: "Status and Tendencies of the Dartmouth College Case," *Am. Law Rev.* xxx, 322–56,
an able, scholarly, and moderate paper; Doe: "A New View of the

It is highly probable that in the present state of the country's development, the Supreme Court would not decide that the contract clause so broadly protects corporate franchises as Marshall held a century ago. In considering the Dartmouth decision, however, the state of things existing when it was rendered must be taken into account. It is certain that Marshall was right in his interpretation of corporation law as it existed in 1819; right in the practical result of his opinion in that particular case; and, above all, right in the purpose and effect of that opinion on the condition and tendency of the country at the perilous time it was delivered.

Dartmouth College Case," *Harvard Law Review*, VI, 161–81, a novel and well-reasoned article; Trickett: "The Dartmouth College Paralogism," *North American Review*, XL, 175–87, a vigorous radical essay; Hall: "The Dartmouth College Case," *Green Bag*, XX, 244–47, a short but brilliant attack upon the assailants of Marshall's opinion; Jenkins: "Should the Dartmouth College Decision be Recalled," *Am. Law Rev.* LI, 711–51, a bright, informed, and thorough treatment from the extremely liberal point of view. A calm, balanced, and convincing review of the effect of the Dartmouth decision on American economic and social life is that of Professor Edward S. Corwin in his *Marshall and the Constitution*, 167–72. When reading these comments, however, the student should, at the same time, carefully reëxamine Marshall's opinion.

CHAPTER VI

VITALIZING THE CONSTITUTION

The crisis is one which portends destruction to the liberties of the American people. (Spencer Roane.)

The constitutional government of this republican empire cannot be practically enforced but by a fair and liberal interpretation of its powers.

(William Pinkney.)

The Judiciary of the United States is the subtle corps of sappers and miners constantly working under ground to undermine the foundations of our confederated fabric. (Jefferson.)

The government of the Union is emphatically and truly a government of the people. In form and substance it emanates from them. Its powers are granted by them, and are to be exercised directly on them and for their benefit.

(Marshall.)

ALTHOUGH it was the third of the great causes to be decided by the Supreme Court in the memorable year, 1819, M'Culloch *vs.* Maryland was the first in importance and in the place it holds in the development of the American Constitution. Furthermore, in his opinion in this case John Marshall rose to the loftiest heights of judicial statesmanship. If his fame rested solely on this one effort, it would be secure.

To comprehend the full import of Marshall's opinion in this case, the reader must consider the state of the country as described in the fourth chapter of this volume. While none of his expositions of our fundamental law, delivered in the critical epoch from 1819 to 1824, can be entirely understood without knowledge of the National conditions that produced them, this fact must be especially borne in mind when reviewing the case of M'Culloch *vs.* Maryland.

Like most of the controversies in which Marshall's Constitutional opinions were pronounced, M'Culloch

STORY

JOHNSON

WASHINGTON

DUVAL

LIVINGSTON

TODD

Associate Justices sitting with Marshall in the case of M'Culloch *versus* Maryland

vs. Maryland came before the Supreme Court on an agreed case. The facts were that Congress had authorized the incorporation of the second Bank of the United States; that this institution had instituted a branch at Baltimore; that the Legislature of Maryland had passed an act requiring all banks, established "without authority from the state," to issue notes only on stamped paper and only of certain denominations, or, in lieu of these requirements, only upon the payment of an annual tax of fifteen thousand dollars; that, in violation of this law, the Baltimore branch of the National Bank continued to issue its notes on unstamped paper without paying the tax; and that on May 8, 1818, John James, "Treasurer of the Western Shore," had sued James William M'Culloch, the cashier of the Baltimore branch, for the recovery of the penalties prescribed by the Maryland statute.[1]

The immediate question was whether the Maryland law was Constitutional; but the basic issue was the supremacy of the National Government as against the dominance of State Governments. Indeed, the decision of this case involved the very existence of the Constitution as an "ordinance of Nationality," as Marshall so accurately termed it.

At no time in this notable session of the Supreme Court was the basement room, where its sittings

---

[1] These penalties were forfeits of $500 for every offense — a sum that would have aggregated hundreds of thousands, perhaps millions of dollars, in the case of the Baltimore branch, which did an enormous business. The Maryland law also provided that "every person having any agency in circulating" any such unauthorized note of the Bank should be fined one hundred dollars. (Act of Feb. 11, 1818, *Laws of Maryland*, 174.)

were now again held, so thronged with auditors as
it was when the argument in M'Culloch *vs.* Maryland took place. "We have had a crowded audience
of ladies and gentlemen," writes Story toward the
close of the nine days of discussion. "The hall was
full almost to suffocation, and many went away
for want of room."[1]

Webster opened the case for the Bank. His masterful argument in the Dartmouth College case the
year before had established his reputation as a great
Constitutional lawyer as well as an orator of the first
class. He was attired in the height of fashion, tight
breeches, blue cloth coat, cut away squarely at the
waist, and adorned with large brass buttons, waist-
coat exposing a broad expanse of ruffled shirt with
high soft collar surrounded by an elaborate black
stock.[2]

The senior counsel for the Bank was William Pinkney. He was dressed with his accustomed foppish
elegance, and, as usual, was nervous and impatient.
Notwithstanding his eccentricities, he was Webster's
equal, if not his superior, except in physical presence
and the gift of political management. With Webster and Pinkney was William Wirt, then Attorney-
General of the United States, who had arrived at the
fullness of his powers.

Maryland was represented by Luther Martin, still
Attorney-General for that State, then seventy-five
years old, but a strong lawyer despite his half-

[1] Story to White, March 3, 1819, Story, I, 325.
[2] Webster always dressed with extreme care when he expected to
make a notable speech or argument. For a description of his appearance on such an occasion see Sargent: *Public Men and Events*, I, 172.

century, at least, of excessive drinking. By his side was Joseph Hopkinson of Philadelphia, now fifty years of age, one of the most learned men at the American bar. With Martin and Hopkinson was Walter Jones of Washington, who appears to have been a legal genius, his fame obliterated by devotion to his profession and unaided by any public service, which so greatly helps to give permanency to the lawyer's reputation. All told, the counsel for both sides in M'Culloch *vs.* Maryland were the most eminent and distinguished in the Republic.

Webster said in opening that Hamilton had "exhausted" the arguments for the power of Congress to charter a bank and that Hamilton's principles had long been acted upon. After thirty years of acquiescence it was too late to deny that the National Legislature could establish a bank.[1] With meticulous care Webster went over Hamilton's reasoning to prove that Congress can "pass all laws 'necessary and proper' to carry into execution powers conferred on it."[2]

Assuming the law which established the Bank to be Constitutional, could Maryland tax a branch of that Bank? If the State could tax the Bank at all, she could put it out of existence, since a "power to tax involves . . a power to destroy"[3] — words that Marshall, in delivering his opinion, repeated as his own. The truth was, said Webster, that, in taxing the Baltimore branch of the National Bank, Maryland taxed the National Government itself.[4]

Joseph Hopkinson, as usual, made a superb argu-

[1] 4 Wheaton, 323.   [2] *Ib.* 324.   [3] *Ib.* 327.   [4] *Ib.* 328.

ment — a performance all the more admirable as an
intellectual feat in that, as an advocate for Maryland, his convictions were opposed to his reasoning.[1]
Walter Jones was as thorough as he was lively, but
he did little more than to reinforce the well-nigh perfect argument of Hopkinson.[2] On the same side the
address of Luther Martin deserves notice as the last
worthy of remark which that great lawyer ever made.
Old as he was, and wasted as were his astonishing
powers, his argument was not much inferior to those
of Webster, Hopkinson, and Pinkney. Martin showed
by historical evidence that the power now claimed
for Congress was suspected by the opponents of
the Constitution, but denied by its supporters and
called "a dream of distempered jealousy." So came
the Tenth Amendment; yet, said Martin, now,
"we are asked to engraft upon it [the Constitution]
powers . . which were disclaimed by them [the advocates of the Constitution], and which, if they had
been fairly avowed at the time, would have prevented
its adoption." [3]

Could powers of Congress be inferred as a necessary means to the desired end? Why, then, did the
Constitution *expressly* confer powers which, of necessity, must be implied? For instance, the power
to declare war surely implied the power to raise
armies; and yet that very power was granted in specific terms. But the power to create corporations
"is not expressly delegated, either as an end or a
means of national government." [4]

---

[1] 4 Wheaton, 330 *et seq.* [2] *Ib.* 362 *et seq.*
[3] *Ib.* 272-73. [4] *Ib.* 374.

When Martin finished, William Pinkney, whom Marshall declared to be "the greatest man he had ever seen in a Court of justice," [1] rose to make what proved to be the last but one of the great arguments of that unrivaled leader of the American bar of his period. To reproduce his address is to set out in advance the opinion of John Marshall stripped of Pinkney's rhetoric which, in that day, was deemed to be the perfection of eloquence.[2]

For three days Pinkney spoke. Few arguments ever made in the Supreme Court affected so profoundly the members of that tribunal. Story describes the argument thus: "Mr. Pinkney rose on Monday to conclude the argument; he spoke all that day and yesterday, and will probably conclude to-day. I never, in my whole life, heard a greater speech; it was worth a journey from Salem to hear it; his elocution was excessively vehement, but his eloquence was overwhelming. His language, his style, his figures, his arguments, were most brilliant and sparkling. He spoke like a great statesman and patriot, and a sound constitutional lawyer. All the cobwebs of sophistry and metaphysics about State rights and State sovereignty he brushed away with a mighty besom." [3]

Indeed, all the lawyers in this memorable contest appear to have surpassed their previous efforts at

[1] Tyler: *Memoir of Roger Brooke Taney*, 141.

[2] The student should carefully examine Pinkney's argument. Although the abstract of it given in Wheaton's report is very long, a painstaking study of it will be helpful to a better understanding of the development of American Constitutional law. (4 Wheaton, 377–400.)

[3] Story to White, March 3, 1819, Story, I, 324–25.

the bar. Marshall, in his opinion, pays this tribute
to all their addresses: "Both in maintaining the af-
firmative and the negative, a splendor of eloquence,
and strength of argument seldom, if ever, surpassed,
have been displayed." [1]

After he had spoken, Webster, who at that moment
was intent on the decision of the Dartmouth College
case,[2] became impatient. "Our Bank argument goes
on — & threatens to be long," he writes Jeremiah
Mason.[3] Four days later, while Martin was still
talking, Webster informs Jeremiah Smith: "We are
not yet thro. the Bank question. Martin has been
talking 3 ds. Pinkney replies tomorrow & that
finishes — I set out for home next day." [4] The arguments in M'Culloch *vs*. Maryland occupied nine
days.[5]

Four days before the Bank argument opened in
the Supreme Court, the House took up the resolution offered by James Johnson of Virginia to repeal
the Bank's charter.[6] The debate over this proposal
continued until February 25, the third day of the
argument in M'Culloch *vs*. Maryland. How, asked
Johnson, had the Bank fulfilled expectations and
promises? "What . . is our condition? Surrounded
by one universal gloom. We are met by the tears
of the widow and the orphan." [7] Madison has "cast
a shade" on his reputation by signing the Bank Bill

[1] 4 Wheaton, 426.   [2] See *supra*, chap. v.

[3] Webster to Mason, Feb. 24, 1819, Van Tyne, 78–79.

[4] Webster to Smith, Feb. 28, 1819, *ib*. 79–80.

[5] From February 22 to February 27 and from March 1 to March 3,
1819.

[6] February 18, 1819. See *Annals*, 15th Cong. 2d Sess. 1240.

[7] *Ib*. 1242.

— that "act of usurpation." Under the common law the charter "is forfeited."[1]

The Bank is a "mighty corporation," created "to overawe .. the local institutions, that had dealt themselves almost out of breath in supporting the Government in times of peril and adversity." The financial part of the Virginia Republican Party organization thus spoke through James Pindall of that State.[2]

William Lowndes of South Carolina brilliantly defended the Bank, but admitted that its "early operation" had been "injudicious."[3] John Tyler of Virginia assailed the Bank with notable force. "This charter has been violated," he said; "if subjected to investigation before a court of justice, it will be declared null and void."[4] David Walker of Kentucky declared that the Bank "is an engine of favoritism — of stock jobbing" — a machine for "binding in adamantine chains the blessed, innocent lambs of America to accursed, corrupt European tigers."[5] In spite of all this eloquence, Johnson's resolution was defeated, and the fate of the Bank left in the hands of the Supreme Court.

On March 6, 1819, before a few spectators, mostly lawyers with business before the court, Marshall read his opinion. It is the misfortune of the biographer that only an abstract can be given of this epochal state paper — among the very first of the greatest judicial utterances of all time.[6] It was de-

---

[1] *Annals*, 15th Cong. 2d Sess. 1249–50.   [2] *Ib.* 1254.
[3] *Ib.* 1286.   [4] *Ib.* 1311.   [5] *Ib.* 1404–06.
[6] "Marshall's opinion in M'Culloch *vs.* Maryland, is perhaps the most celebrated Judicial utterance in the annals of the English speaking world." (*Great American Lawyers*: Lewis, II, 363.)

livered only three days after Pinkney concluded his superb address.

Since it is one of the longest of Marshall's opinions and, by general agreement, is considered to be his ablest and most carefully prepared exposition of the Constitution, it seems not unlikely that much of it had been written before the argument. The court was very busy every day of the session and there was little, if any, time for Marshall to write this elaborate document. The suit against M'Culloch had been brought nearly a year before the Supreme Court convened; Marshall undoubtedly learned of it through the newspapers; he was intimately familiar with the basic issue presented by the litigation; and he had ample time to formulate and even to write out his views before the ensuing session of the court. He had, in the opinions of Hamilton and Jefferson,[1] the reasoning on both sides of this fundamental controversy. It appears to be reasonably probable that at least the framework of the opinion in M'Culloch *vs.* Maryland was prepared by Marshall when in Richmond during the summer, autumn, and winter of 1818–19.

The opening words of Marshall are majestic: "A sovereign state denies the obligation of a law . . of the Union. . . The constitution of our country, in its most . . vital parts, is to be considered; the conflicting powers of the government of the Union and of its

---

[1] As the biographer of Washington, Marshall had carefully read both Hamilton's and Jefferson's Cabinet opinions on the constitutionality of a National bank. Compare Hamilton's argument (vol. II, 72–74, of this work) with Marshall's opinion in M'Culloch *vs.* Maryland.

members, . . are to be discussed; and an opinion given, which may essentially influence the great operations of the government." [1] He cannot "approach such a question without a deep sense of . . the awful responsibility involved in its decision. But it must be decided peacefully, or remain a source of hostile legislation, perhaps of *hostility of a still more serious nature.*" [2] In these solemn words the Chief Justice reveals the fateful issue which M'Culloch *vs.* Maryland foreboded.

That Congress has power to charter a bank is not "an open question. . . The principle . . was introduced at a very early period of our history, has been recognized by many successive legislatures, and has been acted upon by the judicial department . . as a law of undoubted obligation. . . An exposition of the constitution, deliberately established by legislative acts, on the faith of which an immense property has been advanced, ought not to be lightly disregarded."

The first Congress passed the act to incorporate a National bank. The whole subject was at the time debated exhaustively. "The bill for incorporating the bank of the United States did not steal upon an unsuspecting legislature, & pass unobserved," says Marshall. Moreover, it had been carefully examined with "persevering talent" in Washington's Cabinet. When that act expired, "a short experience of the embarrassments" suffered by the country "induced the passage of the present law." He must be intrepid, indeed, who asserts that "a measure adopted under

[1] 4 Wheaton, 400.   [2] *Ib.* (Italics the author's.)

these circumstances was a bold and plain usurpation, to which the constitution gave no countenance." [1]

But Marshall examines the question as though it were "entirely new"; and gives an historical account of the Constitution which, for clearness and brevity, never has been surpassed.[2] Thus he proves that "the government proceeds directly from the people; .. their act was final. It required not the affirmance, and could not be negatived, by the state governments. The constitution when thus adopted .. bound the state sovereignties." The States could and did establish "a league, such as was the confed-

[1] 4 Wheaton, 400–02.

[2] "In discussing this question, the counsel for the state of Maryland have deemed it of some importance, in the construction of the constitution, to consider that instrument not as emanating from the people, but as the act of sovereign and independent states. The powers of the general government, it has been said, are delegated by the states, who alone are truly sovereign; and must be exercised in subordination to the states, who alone possess supreme dominion.

"It would be difficult to sustain this proposition. The convention which framed the constitution was indeed elected by the state legislatures. But the instrument, when it came from their hands, was a mere proposal, without obligation, or pretensions to it. It was reported to the then existing Congress of the United States, with a request that it might ' be submitted to a convention of delegates, chosen in each state, by the people thereof, under the recommendation of its legislature, for their assent and ratification.' This mode of proceeding was adopted; and by the convention, by Congress, and by the state legislatures, the instrument was submitted to the people.

" They acted upon it in the only manner in which they can act safely, effectively, and wisely, on such a subject, by assembling in convention. It is true, they assembled in their several states — and where else should they have assembled? No political dreamer was ever wild enough to think of breaking down the lines which separate the states, and of compounding the American people into one common mass. Of consequence, when they act, they act in their states. But the measures they adopt do not, on that account, cease to be the measures of the people themselves, or become the measures of the state governments. From these conventions the constitution derives its whole authority."
(4 Wheaton, 402–03.)

eration. . . But when, 'in order to form a more perfect union,' it was deemed necessary to change this alliance into an effective government, . . acting directly on the people," it was the people themselves who acted and established a fundamental law for their government.[1]

The Government of the American Nation is, then, "emphatically, and truly, a government of the people. In form and in substance it emanates from them. Its powers are granted by them, and are to be exercised directly on them, and for their benefit" [2] — a statement, the grandeur of which was to be enhanced forty-four years later, when, standing on the battle-field of Gettysburg, Abraham Lincoln said that "a government of the people, by the people, for the people, shall not perish from the earth." [3]

To be sure, the States, as well as the Nation, have certain powers, and therefore "the supremacy of their respective laws, when they are in opposition, must be settled." Marshall proceeds to settle that basic question. The National Government, he begins, "is supreme within its sphere of action. This would

---

[1] 4 Wheaton, 403–04.   [2] *Ib.* 405.

[3] The Nationalist ideas of Marshall and Lincoln are identical; and their language is so similar that it seems not unlikely that Lincoln paraphrased this noble passage of Marshall and thus made it immortal. This probability is increased by the fact that Lincoln was a profound student of Marshall's Constitutional opinions and committed a great many of them to memory.

The famous sentence of Lincoln's Gettysburg Address was, however, almost exactly given by Webster in his Reply to Hayne: "It is . . the people's Government; made for the people; made by the people; and answerable to the people." (*Debates*, 21st Cong. 1st Sess. 74; also Curtis, I, 355–61.) But both Lincoln and Webster merely stated in condensed and simpler form Marshall's immortal utterance in M'Culloch *vs.* Maryland. (See also *infra*, chap. x.)

seem to result necessarily from its nature." For "it
is the government of all; its powers are delegated by
all; it represents all, and acts for all. Though any
one state may be willing to control its operations,
no state is willing to allow others to control them.
The nation, on those subjects on which it can act,
must necessarily bind its component parts." Plain
as this truth is, the people have not left the demonstration of it to "mere reason" — for they have, "in
express terms, decided it by saying" that the Constitution, and the laws of the United States which
shall be made in pursuance thereof, "shall be the supreme law of the land," and by requiring all State
officers and legislators to "take the oath of fidelity
to it." [1]

The fact that the powers of the National Government enumerated in the Constitution do not include
that of creating corporations does not prevent Congress from doing so. "There is no phrase in the instrument which, like the articles of confederation,
excludes incidental or implied powers; and which requires that everything granted shall be expressly
and minutely described. . . A constitution, to contain an accurate detail of all the subdivisions of
which its great powers will admit, and of all the
means by which they may be carried into execution,
would partake of a prolixity of a legal code, and
could scarcely be embraced by the human mind.
It would probably never be understood by the
public."

The very "nature" of a constitution, "therefore.

[1] 4 Wheaton, 405–06.

requires, that only its great outlines should be marked, its important objects designated, and the minor ingredients which compose those *objects be deduced from the nature of the objects themselves.*" In deciding such questions "we must never forget," reiterates Marshall, "that it is a *constitution* we are expounding." [1]

This being true, the power of Congress to establish a bank is undeniable — it flows from "the great powers to lay and collect taxes; to borrow money; to regulate commerce; to declare and conduct a war; and to raise and support armies and navies." Consider, he continues, the scope of the duties of the National Government: "The sword and the purse, all the external relations, and no inconsiderable portion of the industry of the nation, are entrusted to its government. . . A government, entrusted with such ample powers, on the due execution of which the happiness and prosperity of the nation so vitally depends, must also be entrusted with ample means for their execution. The power being given, it is the interest of the nation to facilitate its execution. It can never be their interest, and cannot be presumed to have been their intention, to clog and embarrass its execution by withholding the most appropriate means." [2]

At this point Marshall's language becomes as exalted as that of the prophets: "Throughout this vast republic, from the St. Croix to the Gulf of Mexico, from the Atlantic to the Pacific, revenue is to be collected and expended, armies are to be

[1] 4 Wheaton, 406–07. (Italics the author's.)   [2] *Ib.*, 407–08.

marched and supported. The exigencies of the nation may require that the treasure raised in the north should be transported to the south, that raised in the east conveyed to the west, or that this order should be reversed." Here Marshall the soldier is speaking. There is in his words the blast of the bugle of Valley Forge. Indeed, the pen with which Marshall wrote M'Culloch *vs.* Maryland was fashioned in the army of the Revolution.[1]

The Chief Justice continues: "Is that construction of the constitution to be preferred which would render these operations difficult, hazardous, and expensive?" Did the framers of the Constitution "when granting these powers for the public good" intend to impede "their exercise by withholding a choice of means?" No! The Constitution "does not profess to enumerate the means by which the powers it confers may be executed; nor does it prohibit the creation of a corporation, if the existence of such a being be essential to the beneficial exercise of those powers." [2]

Resorting to his favorite method in argument, that of repetition, Marshall again asserts that the fact that "the power of creating a corporation is one appertaining to sovereignty and is not expressly conferred on Congress," does not take that power from Congress. If it does, Congress, by the same reasoning, would be denied the power to pass most laws; since "all legislative powers appertain to sovereignty." They who say that Congress may not select "any appropriate means" to carry out its

[1] See vol. i, 72, of this work.　　　[2] 4 Wheaton, 408–09.

admitted powers, "take upon themselves the burden of establishing that exception." [1]

The establishment of the National Bank was a means to an end; the power to incorporate it is "as incidental" to the great, substantive, and independent powers expressly conferred on Congress as that of making war, levying taxes, or regulating commerce. [2] This is not only the plain conclusion of reason, but the clear language of the Constitution itself as expressed in the "necessary and proper" clause [3] of that instrument. Marshall treats with something like contempt the argument that this clause does not mean what it says, but is "really restrictive of the general right, which might otherwise be implied, of selecting means for executing the enumerated powers" — a denial, in short, that, without this clause, Congress is authorized to make laws. [4] After conferring on Congress all legislative power, "after allowing each house to prescribe its own course of proceeding, after describing the manner in which a bill should become a law, would it have entered into the mind .. of the convention that an express power to make laws was necessary to enable the legislature to make them?" [5]

In answering the old Jeffersonian argument that, [6] under the "necessary and proper" clause, Congress can adopt only those means absolutely "necessary"

---

[1] 4 Wheaton, 409–10.   [2] *Ib.* 411.

[3] "The Congress shall have Power .. to make all Laws which shall be necessary and proper for carrying into Execution the foregoing Powers, and all other Powers vested by this Constitution in the Government of the United States, or in any Department or Officer thereof." (Constitution of the United States, Article i, Section 8.)

[4] 4 Wheaton, 412.   [5] *Ib.* 413.   [6] See vol. ii, 71, of this work.

to the execution of express powers, Marshall devotes an amount of space which now seems extravagant. But in 1819 the question was unsettled
and acute; indeed, the Republicans had again made
it a political issue. The Chief Justice repeats the
arguments made by Hamilton in his opinion to
Washington on the first Bank Bill.[1]

Some words have various shades of meaning, of
which courts must select that justified by "common
usage." "The word 'necessary' is of this description. . . It admits of all degrees of comparison. . .
A thing may be necessary, very necessary, absolutely or indispensably necessary." For instance,
the Constitution itself prohibits a State from "laying
'imposts or duties on imports or exports, except
what may be *absolutely* necessary for executing its
inspection laws'"; whereas it authorizes Congress
to "'make all laws which shall be necessary and
proper'" for the execution of powers expressly
conferred.[2]

Did the framers of the Constitution intend to forbid Congress to employ "*any*" means "which might
be appropriate, and which were conducive to the
end"? Most assuredly not! "The subject is the
execution of those great powers on which the welfare
of a nation essentially depends." The "necessary
and proper" clause is found "in a constitution intended to endure for ages to come, and, consequently, to be adapted to the various crises of human affairs. . . To have declared that the best means
shall not be used, but those alone without which

---

[1] Vol. II, 72–74, of this work.   [2] 4 Wheaton, 414.

the power given would be nugatory, would have been to deprive the legislature of the capacity to avail itself of experience, to exercise its reason, and to accommodate its legislation to circumstances." [1]

The contrary conclusion is tinged with "insanity." Whence comes the power of Congress to prescribe punishment for violations of National laws? No such general power is expressly given by the Constitution. Yet nobody denies that Congress has this general power, although "it is expressly given in some cases," such as counterfeiting, piracy, and "offenses against the law of nations." Nevertheless, the specific authorization to provide for the punishment of these crimes does not prevent Congress from doing the same as to crimes not specified. [2]

Now comes an example of Marshall's reasoning when at his best — and briefest.

"Take, for example, the power 'to establish post-offices and post-roads.' This power is executed by the single act of making the establishment. But, from this has been inferred the power and duty of carrying the mail along the post-road, from one post-office to another. And, from this implied power, has again been inferred the right to punish those who steal letters from the post-office, or rob the mail. It may be said, with some plausibility, that the right to carry the mail, and to punish those who rob it, is not indispensably necessary to the establishment of a post-office and post-road. This right is indeed essential to the beneficial exercise of the power, but not indispensably necessary to its

[1] 4 Wheaton, 415.   [2] *Ib.* 416–17.

existence. So, of the punishment of the crimes of stealing or falsifying a record or process of a court of the United States, or of perjury in such court. To punish these offenses is certainly conducive to the due administration of justice. But courts may exist, and may decide the causes brought before them, though such crimes escape punishment.

"The baneful influence of this narrow construction on all the operations of the government, and the absolute impracticability of maintaining it without rendering the government incompetent to its great objects, might be illustrated by numerous examples drawn from the constitution, and from our laws. The good sense of the public has pronounced, without hesitation, that the power of punishment appertains to sovereignty, and may be exercised whenever the sovereign has a right to act, as incidental to his constitutional powers. It is a means for carrying into execution all sovereign powers, and may be used, although not indispensably necessary. It is a right incidental to the power, and conducive to its beneficial exercise." [1]

To attempt to prove that Congress *might* execute its powers without the use of other means than those absolutely necessary would be "to waste time and argument," and "not much less idle than to hold a lighted taper to the sun." It is futile to speculate upon imaginary reasons for the "necessary and proper" clause, since its purpose is obvious. It "is placed among the powers of Congress, not among the limitations on those powers. Its terms purport

[1] 4 Wheaton, 417–18.

to enlarge, not to diminish the powers vested in the government. . . If no other motive for its insertion can be suggested, a sufficient one is found in the desire to remove all doubts respecting the right to legislate on the vast mass of incidental powers which must be involved in the constitution, if that instrument be not a splendid bauble." [1]

Marshall thus reaches the conclusion that Congress may "perform the high duties assigned to it, in the manner most beneficial to the people." Then comes that celebrated passage — one of the most famous ever delivered by a jurist: "Let the end be legitimate, let it be within the scope of the constitution, and all means which are appropriate, which are plainly adapted to that end, which are not prohibited, but consist with the letter and spirit of the constitution, are constitutional." [2]

Further on the Chief Justice restates this fundamental principle, without which the Constitution would be a lifeless thing: "Where the law is not prohibited, and is really calculated to effect any of the objects entrusted to the government, to undertake here to inquire into the degree of its necessity, would be to pass the line which circumscribes the judicial department, and to tread on legislative ground. The court disclaims all pretensions to such a power." [3]

The fact that there were State banks with whose business the National Bank might interfere, had nothing to do with the question of the power of Congress to establish the latter. The National

[1] 4 Wheaton, 419–21.   [2] *Ib.* 421.   [3] *Ib.* 423.

Government does not depend on State Governments "for the execution of the great powers assigned to it. Its means are adequate to its ends." It can choose a National bank rather than State banks as an agency for the transaction of its business; "and Congress alone can make the election."

It is, then, "the unanimous and decided opinion" of the court that the Bank Act is Constitutional. So is the establishment of the branches of the parent bank. Can States tax these branches, as Maryland has tried to do? Of course the power of taxation "is retained by the states," and "is not abridged by the grant of a similar power to the government of the Union." These are "truths which have never been denied."

With sublime audacity Marshall then declares that "such is the paramount character of the constitution that its capacity to withdraw any subject from the action of even this power, is admitted." [1] This assertion fairly overwhelms the student, since the States then attempting to tax out of existence the branches of the National Bank did not admit, but emphatically denied, that the National Government could withdraw from State taxation any taxable subject whatever, except that which the Constitution itself specifically withdraws.

"The States," argues Marshall, "are expressly forbidden" to tax imports and exports. This being so, "the same paramount character would seem to restrain, as it certainly may restrain, a state from such other exercise of this [taxing] power, as is in

[1] 4 Wheaton, 424–25.

its nature incompatible with, and repugnant to, the constitutional laws of the Union. A law, absolutely repugnant to another, as entirely repeals that other as if express terms of repeal were used."

In this fashion Marshall holds, in effect, that Congress can restrain the States from taxing certain subjects not mentioned in the Constitution as fully as though those subjects were expressly named.

It is on this ground that the National Bank claims exemption "from the power of a state to tax its operations." Marshall concedes that "there is no express provision [in the Constitution] for the case, but the claim has been sustained on a principle which so entirely pervades the constitution, is so intermixed with the materials which compose it, so interwoven with its web, so blended with its texture, as to be incapable of being separated from it without rendering it into shreds." [1]

This was, indeed, going far — the powers of Congress placed on "a principle" rather than on the language of the Constitution. When we consider the period in which this opinion was given to the country, we can understand — though only vaguely at this distance of time — the daring of John Marshall. Yet he realizes the extreme radicalism of the theory of Constitutional interpretation he is thus advancing, and explains it with scrupulous care.

"This great principle is that the constitution and the laws made in pursuance thereof are supreme; that they control the constitution and laws of the respective states, and cannot be controlled by them. From this, which may be almost termed an axiom,

[1] 4 Wheaton, 425–26.

other propositions are deduced as corollaries, on the truth or error of which . . the cause is supposed to depend." [1]

That "cause" was not so much the one on the docket of the Supreme Court, entitled M'Culloch *vs*. Maryland, as it was that standing on the docket of fate entitled Nationalism *vs*. Localism. And, although Marshall did not actually address them, everybody knew that he was speaking to the disunionists who were increasing in numbers and boldness. Everybody knew, also, that the Chief Justice was, in particular, replying to the challenge of the Virginia Republican organization as given through the Court of Appeals of that State.[2]

The corollaries which Marshall deduced from the principle of National supremacy were: "1st. That a power to create implies a power to preserve. 2d. That a power to destroy, if wielded by a different hand, is hostile to, and incompatible with these powers to create and to preserve. 3d. That where this repugnancy exists, that authority which is supreme must control, not yield to that over which it is supreme." [3]

It is "too obvious to be denied," continues Marshall that, if permitted to exercise the power, the States can tax the Bank "so as to destroy it." The power of taxation is admittedly "sovereign"; but the taxing power of the States "is subordinate to, and may be controlled by the constitution of the United States. How far it has been controlled by that instrument must be a question of construction. In

[1] 4 Wheaton, 426.   [2] See *supra*, 158 *et seq.*.   [3] 4 Wheaton, 426.

making this construction, no principle not declared can be admissible, which would defeat the legitimate operations of a supreme government. It is of the very essence of supremacy to remove all obstacles to its action within its own sphere, and so to modify every power vested in subordinate governments as to exempt its own operations from their own influence. This effect need not be stated in terms. It is so involved in the declaration of supremacy, so necessarily implied in it, that the expression of it could not make it more certain. We must, therefore, keep it [the principle of National supremacy] in view while construing the constitution." [1]

Unlimited as is the power of a State to tax objects within its jurisdiction, that State power does not "extend to those means which are employed by Congress to carry into execution powers conferred on that body by the people of the United States . . powers . . given . . to a government whose laws . . are declared to be supreme. . . The right never existed [in the States] . . to tax the means employed by the government of the Union, for the execution of its powers." [2]

Regardless of this fact, however, can States tax instrumentalities of the National Government? It cannot be denied, says Marshall, that "the power to tax involves the power to destroy; that the power to destroy may defeat . . the power to create; that there is a plain repugnance, in conferring on one government a power to control the constitutional measures of another, which other, with respect to

---

[1] 4 Wheaton, 427.   [2] *Ib.* 429–30.

those very measures, is declared to be supreme over that which exerts the control." [1]

Here Marshall permits himself the use of sarcasm, which he dearly loved but seldom employed. The State Rights advocates insisted that the States can be trusted not to abuse their powers — confidence must be reposed in State Legislatures and officials; they would not destroy needlessly, recklessly. "All inconsistencies are to be reconciled by the magic of the word CONFIDENCE," says Marshall. "But," he continues, "is this a case of 'confidence'? Would the people of any one state trust those of another with a power to control the most insignificant operations of their state government? We know they would not."

By the same token the people of one State would never consent that the Government of another State should control the National Government "to which they have confided the most important and most valuable interests. In the legislature of the Union alone, are all represented. The legislature of the Union alone, therefore, can be trusted by the people with the power of controlling measures which concern all, in the confidence that it will not be abused. This, then, is not a case of confidence." [2]

The State Rights theory is "capable of arresting all the measures of the government, and of prostrating it at the foot of the states." Instead of the National Government being "supreme," as the Constitution declares it to be, "supremacy" would be transferred "in fact, to the states"; for, "if the

<hr>

[1] 4 Wheaton, 431.   [2] *Ib.*

states may tax one instrument, employed by the government in the execution of its powers, they may tax any and every other instrument. They may tax the mail; they may tax the mint; they may tax patent-rights; they may tax the papers of the custom-house; they may tax judicial process; they may tax all the means employed by the government, to an excess which would defeat all the ends of government. This was not intended by the American people. They did not design to make their government dependent on the states."

The whole question is, avows Marshall, "in truth, a question of supremacy." If the anti-National principle that the States can tax the instrumentalities of the National Government is to be sustained, then the declaration in the Constitution that it and laws made under it "shall be the supreme law of the land, is empty and unmeaning declamation." [1]

Maryland had argued that, since the taxing power is, at least, "concurrent" in the State and National Governments, the States can tax a National bank as fully as the Nation can tax State banks. But, remarks Marshall, "the two cases are not on the same reason." The whole American people and all the States are represented in Congress; when they tax State banks, "they tax their constituents; and these taxes must be uniform. But, when a state taxes the operations of the government of the United States, it acts upon institutions created, not by their own constituents, but by people over whom they claim no control. It acts upon the measures of a

[1] 4 Wheaton, 432-33.

government created by others as well as themselves,
for the benefit of others in common with themselves.

"The difference is that which always exists, and
always must exist, between the action of the whole
on a part, and the action of a part on the whole —
between the laws of a government declared to be
supreme, and those of a government which, when
in opposition to those laws, is not supreme. . . The
states have no power, by taxation or otherwise, to
retard, impede, burden, or in any manner control
the operations of the constitutional laws enacted by
Congress to carry into execution the powers vested
in the general government." [1]

For these reasons, therefore, the judgment of the
Supreme Court was that the Maryland law taxing
the Baltimore branch of the National Bank was "contrary to the constitution . . and void"; that the judgment of the Baltimore County Court against the
branch bank "be reversed and annulled," and that
the judgment of the Maryland Court of Appeals
affirming the judgment of the County Court also
"be reversed and annulled." [2]

In effect John Marshall thus rewrote the fundamental law of the Nation; or, perhaps it may be more
accurate to say that he made a written instrument a
living thing, capable of growth, capable of keeping
pace with the advancement of the American people
and ministering to their changing necessities. This
greatest of Marshall's treatises on government may
well be entitled the "Vitality of the Constitution."
Story records that Marshall's opinion aroused great

[1] 4 Wheaton, 435-36.　　　　[2] *Ib.* 437.

political excitement;[1] and no wonder, since the Chief Justice announced, in principle, that Congress had sufficient power to "emancipate every slave in the United States" as John Randolph declared five years later.[2]

Roane, Ritchie, Taylor, and the Republican organization of Virginia had anticipated that the Chief Justice would render a Nationalist opinion; but they were not prepared for the bold and crushing blows which he rained upon their fanatically cherished theory of Localism. As soon as they recovered from their surprise and dismay, they opened fire from their heaviest batteries upon Marshall and the National Judiciary. The way was prepared for them by a preliminary bombardment in the *Weekly Register* of Hezekiah Niles.

This periodical had now become the most widely read and influential publication in the country; it had subscribers from Portland to New Orleans, from Savannah to Fort Dearborn. Niles had won the confidence of his far-flung constituency by his honesty, courage, and ability. He was the prototype of Horace Greeley, and the *Register* had much the same hold on its readers that the *Tribune* came to have thirty years later.

In the first issue of the *Register*, after Marshall's opinion was delivered, Niles began an attack upon it that was to spread all over the land. "A deadly blow has been struck at the *sovereignty of the states*, and from a quarter so far removed from the people as to be hardly accessible to public opinion," he

[1] Story to his mother, March 7, 1819, Story, I, 325–26.
[2] See *infra*, 420; also 325–27; 338–39, 534–37.

wrote. "The welfare of the union has received a more dangerous wound than fifty *Hartford* conventions . . could inflict." Parts of Marshall's opinion are "*incomprehensible.* But perhaps, as some people tell us of what *they* call the *mysteries* of religion, the *common people* are not to understand them, such things being reserved only for the *priests ! !*"[1]

The opinion of the Chief Justice was published in full in Niles's *Register* two weeks after he delivered it,[2] and was thus given wider publicity than any judicial utterance previously rendered in America. Indeed, no pronouncement of any court, except, perhaps, that in Gibbons *vs.* Ogden,[3] was read so generally as Marshall's opinion in M'Culloch *vs.* Maryland, until the publication of the Dred Scott decision thirty-eight years later. Niles continues his attack in the number of the *Register* containing the Bank opinion:

It is "more important than any ever before pronounced by that exalted tribunal — a tribunal so far removed from the people, that some seem to regard it with a species of that awful reverence in which the inhabitants of Asia look up to their princes."[4] This exasperated sentence shows the change that Marshall, during his eighteen years on the bench, had wrought in the standing and repute of the Supreme Court.[5] The doctrines of the Chief Justice amount to this, said Niles — "congress may grant *monopolies*" at will, "if the *price* is paid for them, or without any pecuniary consideration at all." As for

---

[1] Niles, xvi, 41–44.   [2] *Ib.* 68–76.   [3] See *infra,* chap. viii.
[4] Niles, xvi, 65.   [5] See vol. iii, 130–31, of this work.

the Chief Justice personally, he "has not added . . to his stock of reputation by writing it — *it is excessively labored.*" [1]

Papers throughout the country copied Niles's bitter criticisms,[2] and public opinion rapidly crystallized against Marshall's Nationalist doctrine. Every where the principle asserted by the Chief Justice became a political issue; or, rather, his declaration, that that principle was law, made sharper the controversy that had divided the people since the framing of the Constitution.

In number after number of his *Register* Niles, pours his wrath on Marshall's matchless interpretation. It is "far more dangerous to the union and happiness of the people of the United States than . . *foreign invasion.*[3] . . Certain nabobs in Boston, New York, Philadelphia and Baltimore, . . to secure the passage of an act of *incorporation*, . . fairly purchase the souls of some members of the national legislature with *money*, as happened in Georgia, or secure the votes of others by making them *stockholders*, as occurred in New York, and the act is passed.[4] . . We call upon the people, the honest people, who hate *monopolies* and *privileged orders*, to arise in their strength and purge our political temple of the *money-changers* and those who sell *doves* — causing a reversion to the original purity of our system of government,

[1] Niles, xvi, 65.

[2] *Ib.* 97. For instance, the *Natchez Press*, in announcing its intention to print Marshall's whole opinion, says that, if his doctrine prevails, "the independence of the individual states . . is obliterated at one fell sweep." No country can remain free "that tolerates incorporated banks, in any guise." (*Ib.* 210.)

[3] *Ib.* 103.   [4] *Ib.* 104.

that the faithful centinel may again say, 'ALL'S
WELL!'" [1]

Extravagant and demagogical as this language of
Niles's now seems, he was sincere and earnest in the
use of it. Copious quotations from the *Register* have
been here made because it had the strongest influence on American public opinion of any publication
of its time. Niles's *Register* was, emphatically, the
mentor of the country editor.[2]

At last the hour had come when the Virginia Republican triumvirate could strike with an effect impossible of achievement in 1816 when the Supreme
Court rebuked and overpowered the State appellate
tribunal in Martin *vs*. Hunter's Lessee.[3] Nobody
outside of Virginia then paid any attention to that
decision, so obsessed was the country by speculation
and seeming prosperity. But in 1819 the collapse
had come; poverty and discontent were universal;
rebellion against Nationalism was under way; and
the vast majority blamed the Bank of the United
States for all their woes. Yet Marshall had upheld
"the monster." The Virginia Junto's opportunity
had arrived.

No sooner had Marshall returned to Richmond
than he got wind of the coming assault upon him.
On March 23, 1819, the *Enquirer* published his
opinion in full. The next day the Chief Justice wrote
Story: "Our opinion in the Bank case has aroused
the sleeping spirit of Virginia, if indeed it ever sleeps.

---

[1] Niles, xvi, 105.

[2] Niles's attack on Marshall's opinion in M'Culloch *vs*. Maryland
ran through three numbers. (See *ib.* 41–44; 103–05; 145–47.)

[3] See *supra*, 161–67.

It will, I understand, be attacked in the papers with some asperity, and as those who favor it never write for the publick it will remain undefended & of course be considered as *damnably heretical.*" [1] He had been correctly informed. The attack came quickly.

On March 30, Spencer Roane opened fire in the paper of his cousin Thomas Ritchie, the *Enquirer*,[2] under the *nom de guerre* of "Amphictyon." His first article is able, calm, and, considering his intense feelings, fair and moderate. Roane even extols his enemy:

"That this opinion is very able every one must admit. This was to have been expected, proceeding as it does from a man of the most profound legal attainments, and upon a subject which has employed his thoughts, his tongue, and his pen, as a politician, and an historian for more than thirty years. The subject, too, is one which has, perhaps more than any other, heretofore drawn a broad line of distinction between the two great parties in this country, on which line no one has taken a more distinguished and decided rank than the judge who has thus expounded the supreme law of the land. It is not in my power to carry on a contest upon such a subject with a man of his gigantic powers." [3]

Niles had spoken to " the plain people "; Roane is now addressing the lawyers and judges of the country. His essay is almost wholly a legal argument.

[1] Marshall to Story, March 24, 1819, *Proceedings, Mass. Hist. Soc.* 2d Series, xiv, 324.

[2] See *supra*, 146.

[3] *Enquirer*, March 30, 1819, as quoted in *Branch Hist. Papers,* June, 1905, 52-53.

It is based on the Virginia Resolutions of 1799 and gives the familiar State Rights arguments, applying them to Marshall's opinion.[1] In his second article Roane grows vehement, even fiery, and finally exclaims that Virginia " never will *employ force to support her doctrines till other measures have entirely failed*." [2]

His attacks had great and immediate response. No sooner had copies of the *Enquirer* containing the first letters of Amphictyon reached Kentucky than the Republicans of that State declared war on Marshall. On April 20, the *Enquirer* printed the first Western response to Roane's call to arms. Marshall's principles, said the Kentucky correspondent, " must raise an alarm throughout our widely extended empire. . . The people must rouse from the lap of Delilah and prepare to meet the Philistines. . . No mind can compass the extent of the encroachments upon State and individual rights which may take place under the principles of this decision." [3]

Even Marshall, a political and judicial veteran in his sixty-fifth year, was perturbed. "The opinion in the Bank case continues to be denounced by the democracy in Virginia," he writes Story, after the second of Roane's articles appeared. "An effort is certainly making to induce the legislature which will meet in December to take up the subject & to pass resolutions not very unlike those which were called forth by the alien & sedition laws in 1799.

[1] *Branch Hist. Papers*, June, 1905, 51–63.
[2] *Enquirer*, April 2, 1819, as quoted in *Branch Hist. Papers*, June, 1905, 76. (Italics the author's.)
[3] *Enquirer*, April 20, 1819, as quoted in *ib.* 76.

SPENCER ROANE

Whether the effort will be successful or not may perhaps depend in some measure on the sentiments of our sister states. To excite this ferment the opinion has been grossly misrepresented; and where its argument has been truly stated it has been met by principles one would think too palpably absurd for intelligent men.

"But," he gloomily continues, "prejudice will swallow anything. If the principles which have been advanced on this occasion were to prevail the constitution would be converted into the old confederation." [1]

As yet Roane had struck but lightly. He now renewed the Republican offensive with greater spirit. During June, 1819, the *Enquirer* published four articles signed "Hampden," from Roane's pen. Ritchie introduced the "Hampden" essays in an editorial in which he urged the careful reading of the exposure "of the alarming errors of the Supreme Court. . . Whenever State rights are threatened or invaded, Virginia will not be the last to sound the tocsin." [2]

Are the people prepared "to give *carte blanche* to our federal rulers"? asked Hampden. Amendment of the Constitution by judicial interpretation is taking the place of amendment by the people. Infamous as the methods of National judges had been during the administration of Adams, "the most abandoned of our rulers," Marshall and his associates have done worse. They have given "a

[1] Marshall to Story, May 27, 1819, *Proceedings, Mass. Hist. Soc.* 2d Series, XIV, 325.

[2] *Enquirer*, June 11, 1819, as quoted in *Branch Hist. Papers*, June, 1905, footnote to 77.

general letter of attorney to the future legislators of the Union. . . That man must be a deplorable idiot who does not see that there is no . . difference" between an "*unlimited* grant of power and a grant limited in its terms, but accompanied with *unlimited* means of carrying it into execution. . . The crisis is one which portends destruction to the liberties of the American people." Hampden scoldingly adds: "If Mason or Henry could lift their patriot heads from the grave, . . they would almost exclaim, with Jugurtha, 'Venal people! you will soon perish if you can find a purchaser.'" [1]

For three more numbers Hampden pressed the Republican assault on Marshall's opinion. The Constitution is a "*compact*, to which the *States* are the parties." Marshall's argument in the Virginia Convention of 1788 is quoted,[2] and his use of certain terms in his "Life of Washington" is cited.[3] If the powers of the National Government ought to be enlarged, "let this be the act of the *people*, and not that of subordinate agents." [4] The opinion of the Chief Justice repeatedly declares "that the general government, though limited in its powers, is supreme." Hampden avows that he does "not understand this jargon. . . The *people* only are supreme.[5] . . Our general government . . is as much a . . 'league' as was the former confederation." Therefore, the

---

[1] *Enquirer*, June 11, 1819, as quoted in *Branch Hist. Papers*, June, 1905, 77–82.

[2] *Enquirer*, June 15, 1819, as quoted in *ib*. 85; also *Enquirer*, June 18, 1819, as quoted in *ib*. 95.

[3] *Enquirer*, June 15, 1819, as quoted in *ib*. 91.

[4] *Ib*. 87; also *Enquirer*, June 18, 1819, as quoted in *ib*. 96–97.

[5] *Ib*. 98.

Virginia Court of Appeals, in Hunter *vs.* Fairfax, declared an act of Congress "unconstitutional, although it had been sanctioned by the opinion of the Supreme Court of the United States." Pennsylvania, too, had maintained its "sovereignty." [1]

Hampden has only scorn for "*some* of the judges" who concurred in the opinion of the Chief Justice. They "had before been accounted republicans. . . Few men come out from high places, as pure as they went in." [2] If Marshall's doctrine stands, "the triumph over our liberties will be . . easy and complete." What, then, could "arrest this calamity"? Nothing but an "appeal" to the people. Let this majestic and irresistible power be invoked. [3]

That he had no faith in his own theory is proved by the rather dismal fact that, more than two months before Marshall "violated the Constitution" and "endangered the liberties" of the people by his Bank decision, Roane actually arranged for the purchase, as an investment for his son, of $4900 worth of the shares of the Bank of the United States, and actually made the investment. [4] This transaction, consummated even before the argument

[1] *Enquirer*, June 22, 1819, as quoted in *Branch Hist. Papers*, June, 1905, 116.

[2] *Ib.* 118.

[3] *Ib.* 121.   Madison endorsed Roane's attacks on Marshall.   (See Madison to Roane, Sept. 2, 1819, *Writings of James Madison :* Hunt, VIII, 447–53.)

[4] See Roane to his son, Jan. 4, 1819, *Branch Hist. Papers*, June, 1905, 134; and same to same, Feb. 4, 1819, *ib.* 135.

Eighteen days before Marshall delivered his opinion Roane again writes his son: "I have to-day deposited in the vaults of the Virga. bank a certificate in your name for 50 shares U. S. bank stock, as per memo., by Mr. Dandridge Enclosed. The shares cost, as you will see, $98 each." (Roane to his son, Feb. 16, 1819, *ib.* 136.)

in M'Culloch *vs.* Maryland, shows that Roane, the able lawyer, was sure that Marshall would and ought to sustain the Bank in its controversy with the States that were trying to destroy it. Moreover, Dr. John Brockenbrough, President of the Bank of Virginia, actually advised the investment.[1]

It is of moment, too, to note at this point the course taken by Marshall, who had long owned stock in the Bank of the United States. As soon as he learned that the suit had been brought which, of a certainty, must come before him, the Chief Justice disposed of his holdings.[2]

So disturbed was Marshall by Roane's attacks that he did a thoroughly uncharacteristic thing. By way of reply to Roane he wrote, under the *nom de guerre* of "A Friend of the Union," an elaborate defense of his opinion and, through Bushrod Washington, procured the publication of it in the *Union* of Philadelphia, the successor of the *Gazette of the United States*, and the strongest Federalist newspaper then surviving.

On June 28, 1819, the Chief Justice writes Washington: "I expected three numbers would have concluded my answer to Hampden but I must write two others which will follow in a few days. If the publication has not commenced I could rather wish

[1] Roane to his son, note 4, p. 317.

[2] The entire transaction is set out in letters of Benjamin Watkins Leigh to Nicholas Biddle, Aug. 21, Aug. 28, Sept. 4, and Sept. 13, 1837; and Biddle to Leigh, Aug. 24 and 25, Sept. 7 and Sept. 15, 1837. (Biddle MSS. in possession of Professor R. C. McGrane of the University of Ohio, to whose courtesy the author is indebted for the use of this material. These letters appear in full in the *Correspondence of Nicholas Biddle:* McGrane, 283–89, 291–92, published in September, 1919, by Houghton Mifflin Company, Boston.)

the signature to be changed to 'A Constitutionalist.'
A Friend of the Constitution is so much like a Friend
of the Union that it may lead to some suspicion of
identity. . . I hope the publication has commenced
unless the Editor should be unwilling to devote so
much of his paper to this discussion. The letters of
Amphyction & of Hampden have made no great
impression in Richmond but they were designed for
the country [Virginia] & have had considerable influence there. I wish the refutation to be in the
hands of some respectable members of the legislature
as it may prevent some act of the assembly [torn —
probably "both"] silly & wicked. If the publication
be made I should ·[like] to have two or three sets of
the papers to hand if necessary. I will settle with
you for the printer." [1]

The reading of Marshall's newspaper effort is
exhausting; a summary of the least uninteresting
passages will give an idea of the whole paper. The
articles published in the *Enquirer* were intended,
so he wrote, to inflict "deep wounds on the constitution," are full of "mischievous errours," and are
merely new expressions of the old Virginia spirit of
hostility to the Nation. The case of M'Culloch *vs.*
Maryland serves only as an excuse "for once more
agitating the publick mind, and reviving those un-
founded jealousies by whose blind aid ambition
climbs the ladder of power." [2]

---

[1] Marshall to Bushrod Washington, June 28, 1819. This letter is
unsigned, but is in Marshall's unmistakable handwriting and is endorsed by Bushrod Washington, "C. Just. Marshall." (Marshall
MSS. Lib. Cong.)

[2] *Union*, April 24, 1819.

After a long introduction, Marshall enters upon his defense which is as wordy as his answer to the Virginia Resolutions. He is sensitive over the charge, by now popularly made, that he controls the Supreme Court, and cites the case of the Nereid to prove that the Justices give dissenting opinions whenever they choose. "The course of every tribunal must necessarily be, that the opinion which is to be delivered as the opinion of the court, is previously submitted to the consideration of all the judges; and, if any part of the reasoning be disapproved, it must be so modified as to receive the approbation of all, before it can be delivered as the opinion of all."

Roane's personal charges amount to this: "The chief justice . . is a federalist; who was a politician of some note before he was judge; and who with his tongue and his pen supported the opinions he avowed." With the politician's skill Marshall uses the fact that the majority of the court, which gave the Nationalist judgment in M'Culloch *vs.* Maryland, were Republicans — "four of whom [Story, Johnson, Duval, and Livingston] have no political sin upon their heads; — who in addition to being eminent lawyers, have the still greater advantage of being sound republicans; of having been selected certainly not for their federalism, by Mr Jefferson, and Mr Madison, for the high stations they so properly fill." For eight tedious columns of diffuse repetition Marshall goes on in defense of his opinion.[1]

When the biographer searches the daily life of a

[1] *Union*, April 24, 1819.

man so surpassingly great and good as Marshall, he hopes in no ungenerous spirit to find some human frailty that identifies his hero with mankind. The Greeks did not fail to connect their deities with humanity. The leading men of American history have been ill-treated in this respect — for a century they have been held up to our vision as superhuman creatures to admire whom was a duty, to criticize whom was a blasphemy, and to love or understand whom was an impossibility.

All but Marshall have been rescued from this frigid isolation. Any discovery of human frailty in the great Chief Justice is, therefore, most welcome. Some small and gracious defects in Marshall's character have appeared in the course of these volumes; and this additional evidence of his susceptibility to ordinary emotion is very pleasing. With all his stern repression of that element of his character, we find that he was sensitive in the extreme; in reality, thirsting for approval, hurt by criticism. In spite of this desire for applause and horror of rebuke, however, he did his duty, knowing beforehand that his finest services would surely bring upon him the denunciation and abuse he so disliked. By such peevishness as his anonymous reply in the *Union* to Roane's irritating attacks, we are able to get some measure of the true proportions of this august yet very human character.

When Marshall saw, in print, this controversial product of his pen, he was disappointed and depressed. The editor had, he avowed, so confused the manuscript that it was scarcely intelligible. At any rate, Marshall did not want his defense reproduced in New England. Story had heard of the article in the *Union*, and wrote Marshall that he wished to secure the publication of it. The Chief Justice replied:

"The piece to which you allude was not published in Virginia. Our patriotic papers admit no such political heresies. It contained, I think, a complete demonstration of the fallacies & errors contained in those attacks on the opinion of the Court which have most credit here & are supposed to proceed from a high source,[1] but was so mangled in the publication that those only who had bestowed close attention to the subject could understand it.

"There were two numbers [2] & the editor of the Union in Philadelphia, the paper in which it was published, had mixed the different numbers together so as in several instances to place the reasoning intended to demonstrate one proposition under another. The points & the arguments were so separated from each other, & so strangely mixed as to constitute a labyrinth to which those only who understood the whole subject perfectly could find a clue." [3]

It appears that Story insisted on having at least Marshall's rejoinder to Roane's first article reproduced in the Boston press. Again the Chief Justice evades the request of his associate and confidant:

---

[1] Marshall means that Jefferson inspired Roane's attacks.

[2] Marshall had written five essays, but the editor condensed them into two numbers.

[3] Marshall to Story, May 27, 1819, *Proceedings, Mass. Hist. Soc.* 2d Series, XIV, 325.

"I do not think a republication of the piece you mention in the Boston papers to be desired, as the antifederalism of Virginia will not, I trust, find its way to New England. I should also be sorry to see it in Mr. Wheaton's [1] appendix because that circumstance might lead to suspicions regarding the author & because I should regret to see it republished in its present deranged form with the two centres transposed." [2]

For a brief space, then, the combatants rested on their arms, but each was only gathering strength for the inevitable renewal of the engagement which was to be sterner than any previous phases of the contest.

Soon after the convening of the first session of the Virginia Legislature held subsequent to the decision of M'Culloch *vs.* Maryland, Roane addressed the lawmakers through the *Enquirer*, now signing himself "Publicola." He pointed out the "absolute disqualification of the supreme court of the U. S. to decide with impartiality upon controversies between the General and State Governments "; [3] and, to " ensure *unbiassed*" decisions, insisted upon a Constitutional amendment to establish a tribunal "(as occasion may require) " appointed partly by the States and partly by the National Government, " with *appellate* jurisdiction from the present supreme court." [4]

Promptly a resolution against Marshall's opinion

[1] Henry Wheaton, Reporter of the Supreme Court.

[2] Marshall to Story, July 13, 1819, *Proceedings, Mass. Hist. Soc.* 2d Series, XIV, 326.

[3] *Enquirer*, Jan. 30, 1821.   [4] *Ib.* Feb. 1, 1821.

was offered in the House of Delegates.[1] This noteworthy paper was presented by Andrew Stevenson,
a member of the "committee for Courts of Justice." [2] The resolutions declared that the doctrines
of M'Culloch *vs.* Maryland would "undermine the
pillars of the Constitution itself." The provision
giving to the judicial power "*all cases* arising *under
the Constitution*" did not "extend to questions which
would amount to a subversion of the constitution
itself, by the usurpation of one contracting party
on another." But Marshall's opinion was calculated
to "change the whole character of the government." [3]

Sentences from the opinion of the Chief Justice
are quoted, including the famous one: "Let the
end be legitimate, . . and all the means which are
appropriate, . . which are not prohibited, . . are
constitutional." Did not such expressions import
that Congress could "conform the constitution to
their own designs" by the exercise of "unlimited
and uncontrouled" power? The ratifying resolution
of the Constitution by the Virginia Convention of
1788 is quoted.[4] Virginia's voice had been heard
to the same effect in the immortal Resolutions of
1799. Her views had been endorsed by the country

---

[1] *Journal*, House of Delegates, Virginia, 1819–20, 56–59.
[2] *Ib.* 9.   [3] *Ib.* 57.
[4] This resolution declared that Virginia assented to the Constitution only on condition that "Every power *not granted*, remains with
the people, and at their will; *that therefore no right of any denomina-
tion can be cancelled, abridged, restrained, or modified*, by the congress,
by the senate, or house of representatives acting in any capacity; by
the President or any department, or officer of the United States, except in those instances in which power is given by the constitution
for those purposes." (*Journal*, House of Delegates, Virginia, 1819–
20, 58.)

in the Presidential election of 1800 — that "great revolution of principle." Her Legislature, therefore, "enter their most solemn protest, against the decision of the supreme court, and of the principles contained in it."

In this fashion the General Assembly insisted on an amendment to the National Constitution "creating a *tribunal*" authorized to decide questions relative to the "powers of the general and state governments, under the compact." The Virginia Senators are, therefore, instructed to do their best to secure such an amendment and "to resist on every occasion" attempted legislation by Congress in conflict with the views set forth in this resolution or those of 1799 "which have been re-considered, and are fully and entirely approved of by this Assembly." The Governor is directed to transmit the resolutions to the other States.[1]

At this point Slavery and Secession enter upon the scene. Almost simultaneously with the introduction of the resolutions denouncing Marshall and the Supreme Court for the judgment and opinion in M'Culloch *vs.* Maryland, other resolutions were offered by a member of the House named Baldwin denouncing the imposition of restrictions on Missouri (the prohibition of slavery) as a condition of admitting that Territory to the Union. Such action by Congress would "excite feelings eminently hostile to the fraternal affection and prudent forbearance which ought ever to pervade the confederated union." [2] Two days later, December 30, the same

---

[1] *Journal*, House of Delegates, Virginia, 1819–20, 59.   [2] *Ib.* 76.

delegate introduced resolutions to the effect that
only the maintenance of the State Rights principle
could "preserve the confederated union," since
"no government can long exist which lies at the
mercy of another"; and, inferentially, that Marshall's opinion in M'Culloch *vs.* Maryland had violated that principle.[1]

A yet sterner declaration on the Missouri question
quickly followed, declaring that Congress had no
power to prohibit slavery in that State, and that
"Virginia will support the good people of Missouri
in their just rights . . and will co-operate with them
in resisting with manly fortitude any attempt
which Congress may make to impose restraints or
restrictions as the price of their admission" to the
Union.[2] The next day these resolutions, strengthened by amendment, were adopted.[3] On February
12, 1820, the resolutions condemning the Nationalist doctrine expounded by the Chief Justice in the
Bank case also came to a vote and passed, 117
ayes to 38 nays.[4] They had been amended and re-
amended,[5] but, as adopted, they were in substance
the same as those originally offered by Stevenson.
Through both these sets of resolutions — that on
the Missouri question and that on the Bank decision — ran the intimation of forcible resistance to
National authority. Introduced at practically the
same time, drawn and advocated by the same men,
passed by votes of the same members, these important declarations of the Virginia Legislature were

---

[1] *Journal*, House of Delegates, Virginia, 1819–20, 85.
[2] *Ib.* 105.   [3] *Ib.* 108–09.   [4] *Ib.* 179.   [5] *Ib.* 175–78.

meant to be and must be considered as a single expression of the views of Virginia upon National policy.

In this wise did the Legislature of his own State repudiate and defy that opinion of John Marshall which has done more for the American Nation than any single utterance of any other one man, excepting only the Farewell Address of Washington. In such manner, too, was the slavery question brought face to face with Marshall's lasting exposition of the National Constitution. For, it should be repeated, in announcing the principles by virtue of which Congress could establish the Bank of the United States, the Chief Justice had also asserted, by necessary inference, the power of the National Legislature to exact the exclusion of slavery as a condition upon which a State could be admitted to the Union. At least this was the interpretation of Virginia and the South.

The slavery question did not, to be sure, closely touch Northern States, but their local interests did. Thus it was that Ohio aligned herself with Virginia in opposition to Marshall's Nationalist statesmanship, and in support of the Jeffersonian doctrine of Localism. In such fashion did the Ohio Bank question become so intermingled with the conflict over Slavery and Secession that, in the consideration of Marshall's opinions at this time, these controversies cannot be separated. The facts of the Ohio Bank case must, therefore, be given at this point.[1]

Since the establishment at Cincinnati, early in 1817, of a branch of the Bank of the United States,

---

[1] For Marshall's opinion in this controversy see *infra*, 347 *et seq.*

Ohio had threatened to drive it from the State by
a prohibitive tax. Not long before the argument of
M'Culloch *vs.* Maryland in the Supreme Court, the
Ohio Legislature laid an annual tax of $50,000 on
each of the two branches which, by that time, had
been established in that State.[1] On February 8, 1819,
only four days previous to the hearing of the Maryland case at Washington, and less than a month before Marshall delivered his opinion, the Ohio lawmakers passed an act directing the State Auditor,
Ralph Osborn, to charge this tax of $50,000 against
each of the branches, and to issue a warrant for the
immediate collection of $100,000, the total amount
of the first year's tax.

This law is almost without parallel in severity,
peremptoriness, and defiant contempt for National
authority. If the branches refused to pay the tax,
the Ohio law enjoined the person serving the State
Auditor's warrant to seize all money or property belonging to the Bank, found on its premises or elsewhere. The agent of the Auditor was directed to
open the vaults, search the offices, and take everything of value.[2]

Immediately the branch at Chillicothe obtained
from the United States District Court, then in

[1] The second branch was established at Chillicothe.

[2] Chap. 83, *Laws of Ohio, 1818–19*, 1st Sess. 190–99.
Section 5 of this act will give the student the spirit of this autocratic law. This section made it the "duty" of the State agent collecting the tax, after demand on and refusal of the bank officers to pay
the tax, if he cannot readily find in the bank offices the necessary
amount of money, "to go into each and any other room or vault ..
and to every closet, chest, box or drawer in such banking house, to
open and search," and to levy on everything found. (*Ib.* 193.)

session at that place, an injunction forbidding
Osborn from collecting the tax;[1] but the bank's
counsel forgot to have a writ issued to stay the
proceedings. Therefore, no order of the court was
served; instead a copy of the bill praying that the
Auditor be restrained, together with a subpœna to
answer, was sent to Osborn. These papers were not,
of course, an injunction, but merely notice that one
had been applied for. Thinking to collect the tax
before the injunction could be issued, Osborn forthwith issued his Auditor's warrant to one John L.
Harper to collect the tax immediately. Assisted by
a man named Thomas Orr, Harper entered the
Chillicothe branch of the Bank of the United States,
opened the vaults, seized all the money to be found,
and deposited it for the night in the local State bank.
Next morning Harper and Orr loaded the specie,
bank notes, and other securities in a wagon and
started for Columbus.[2]

The branch bank tardily obtained an order from
the United States Court restraining Osborn, the
State Auditor, and Harper, the State agent, from delivering the money to the State Treasurer and from
making any report to the Legislature of the collection of the tax. This writ was served on Harper as he
and Orr were on the road to the State Capital with
the money. Harper simply ignored the writ, drove

[1] A private letter to Niles says that when it was found that an injunction had been granted, the friends of the bank rejoiced, "wine
was drank freely and mirth abounded." (Niles, XVII, 85.) This explains the otherwise incredible negligence of the bank's attorneys in
the proceedings next day.

[2] Niles, XVII, 85–87, reprinting account as published in the *Chillicothe Supporter*, Sept. 22, 1819, and the *Ohio Monitor*, Sept. 25, 1819.

on to Columbus, and handed over to the State
Treasurer the funds which he had seized at Chillicothe.

Harper and Orr were promptly arrested and imprisoned in the jail at Chillicothe.[1] Because of technical defects in serving the warrant for their arrest
and in the return of the marshal, the prisoners were
set free.[2] An order was secured from the United
States Court directing Osborn and Harper to show
cause why an attachment should not be issued against
them for having disobeyed the court's injunction not
to deliver the bank's money to the State Treasurer.
After extended argument, the court issued the attachment, which, however, was not made returnable
until the January term, 1821.

Meanwhile the Virginia Legislature passed its
resolutions denouncing Marshall's opinion in M'Culloch vs. Maryland, and throughout the country the
warfare upon the Supreme Court began. The Legislature of Ohio acted with a celerity and boldness
that made the procedure of the Virginia Legislature
seem hesitant and timid. A joint committee was
speedily appointed and as promptly made its report.
This report and the resolutions recommended by it
were adopted without delay and transmitted to the
Senate of the United States.[3]

The Ohio declaration is drawn with notable
ability. A State cannot be sued — the true meaning of the Constitution forbids, and the Eleventh
Amendment specifically prohibits, such procedure.

[1] Niles, xvii, 147.　　　　[2] Ib. 338.
[3] Report of Committee made to the Ohio Legislature and transmitted to Congress. (Annals, 16th Cong. 2d Sess. 1685 et seq.)

Yet the action against Osborn, State Auditor, and Samuel Sullivan, State Treasurer, is, "to every substantial purpose, a process against the State." The decision of the National Supreme Court that the States have no power to tax branches of the Bank of the United States does not bind Ohio or render her tax law "a dead letter." [1]

The Ohio Legislature challenges the *bona fides* of M'Culloch *vs.* Maryland: "If, by the management of a party, and through the inadvertence or connivance of a State, a case be made, presenting to the Supreme Court of the United States for decision important . . questions of State power and State authority, upon no just principle ought the States to be concluded by any decision had upon such a case. . . Such is the true character of the case passed upon the world by the title of McCulloch *vs.* Maryland," which, "when looked into, is found to be . . throughout, an agreed case, made expressly for the purpose of obtaining the opinion of the Supreme Court of the United States. . . This agreed case was manufactured in the summer of the year 1818 " and rushed through two Maryland courts, "so as to be got upon the docket of the Supreme Court of the United States for adjudication at their February term, 1819. . . It is truly an alarming circumstance if it be in the power of an aspiring corporation and an unknown and obscure individual thus to elicit opinions compromitting the vital interests of the States that compose the American Union."

Luckily for Ohio and all the States, this report

[1] *Annals*, 16th Cong. 2d Sess. 1691.

goes on to say, some of Marshall's opinions have
been "totally impotent and unavailing," as, for instance, in the case of Marbury *vs*. Madison. Marbury did not get his commission; "the person appointed in his place continued to act; his acts
were admitted to be valid; and President Jefferson
retained his standing in the estimation of the American people." It was the same in the case of Fletcher
vs. Peck. Marshall held that "the Yazoo purchasers . . were entitled to their lands. But the
decision availed them nothing, unless as a make-
weight in effecting a compromise." Since, in neither
of these cases, had the National Government paid
the slightest attention to the decision of the Supreme Court, how could Ohio "be condemned because she did not abandon her solemn legislative
acts as a dead letter upon the promulgation of an
opinion of that tribunal"? [1]

The Ohio Legislature then proceeds to analyze
Marshall's opinion in M'Culloch *vs*. Maryland. All
the arguments made against the principle of implied
powers since Hamilton first announced that principle,[2] and all the reasons advanced against the doctrine that the National Government is supreme, in
the sense employed by Marshall, are restated with
clearness and power. However, since the object of
the tax was to drive the branches of the Bank out
of Ohio, the Legislature suggests a compromise. If
the National institution will cease business within
the State and "give assurance" that the branches

---

[1] *Annals*, 16th Cong. 2d Sess. 1696–97.
[2] See vol. II, 72–74, of this work.

be withdrawn, the State will refund the tax money it has seized.[1]

Instantly turning from conciliation to defiance, "because the reputation of the State has been assailed," the Legislature challenges the National Government to make good Marshall's assertion that the power which created the Bank "must have the power to preserve it." Ohio should pass laws "forbidding the keepers of our jails from receiving into their custody any person committed at the suit of the Bank of the United States," and prohibiting Ohio judges, recorders, notaries public, from recognizing that institution in any way.[2] Congress will then have to provide a criminal code, a system of conveyances, and other extensive measures. Ohio and the country will then learn whether the power that created the Bank can preserve it.

The Ohio memorial concludes with a denial that the "political rights" and "sovereign powers" of a State can be settled by the Supreme Court of the Nation "in cases contrived between individuals, and where they [the States] are, no one of them, parties direct." The resolutions further declare that the opinion of the other States should be secured.[3] This alarming manifesto was presented to the National Senate on February 1, 1821, just six weeks before Marshall delivered the opinion of the Supreme Court in Cohens vs. Virginia.[4]

Pennsylvania had already taken stronger measures; had anticipated even Virginia. Within seven weeks

[1] *Annals*, 16th Cong. 2d Sess. 1712.   [2] *Ib*. 1713.   [3] *Ib*. 1714.
[4] See *infra*, chap. VII of this work.

from the delivery of Marshall's opinion in M'Culloch
vs. Maryland, the Legislature of Pennsylvania proposed an amendment to the National Constitution
prohibiting Congress from authorizing "any bank
or other monied institution" outside of the District
of Columbia.[1] The action of Ohio was an endorsement of that of Virginia and Pennsylvania. Indiana
had already swung into line.[2] So had Illinois and
Tennessee.[3] For some reason, Kentucky, soon to become one of the most belligerent and persevering of
all the States in her resistance to the "encroachments" of Nationalism as expounded by the Supreme
Court, withheld her hand for the moment.

Most unaccountably, South Carolina actually upheld Marshall's opinion,[4] which that State, within
a decade, was to repudiate, denounce, and defy in
terms of armed resistance.[5] New York and Massachusetts,[6] consulting their immediate interests, were
very stern against the Localism of Ohio, Virginia, and
Pennsylvania.[7] Georgia expressed her sympathy
with the Localist movement, but, for the time being,
was complaisant [8] — a fact the more astonishing that
she had already proved, and was soon to prove
again, that Nationalism is a fantasy unless it is
backed by force.[9]

Notwithstanding the eccentric attitude of various members of the Union, it was only too plain that

---

[1] *State Doc. Fed. Rel.*: Ames, 90; and see Niles, xvi, 97, 132.
[2] Pennsylvania House of Representatives, *Journal, 1819–20*, 537;
State Doc. Fed. Rel.: Ames, footnote to 90–91.
[3] *Ib.*   [4] *Ib.* 91.
[5] See *infra*, chap. x.   [6] *State Doc. Fed. Rel.*: Ames, 92–103.
[7] *Ib.* 92, 101–03.   [8] *Ib.* 91.   [9] See *infra*, chap. x.

a powerful group of States were acting in concert and that others ardently sympathized with them.

At this point, in different fashion, Virginia spoke again, this time by the voice of that great protagonist of Localism, John Taylor of Caroline, the originator of the Kentucky Resolutions,[1] and the most brilliant mind in the Republican organization of the Old Dominion. Immediately after Marshall's opinion in M'Culloch *vs.* Maryland, and while the Ohio conflict was in progress, he wrote a book in denunciation and refutation of Marshall's Nationalist principles. The editorial by Thomas Ritchie, commending Taylor's book, declares that "the crisis has come"; the Missouri question, the Tariff question, the Bank question, have brought the country to the point where a decision must be made as to whether the National Government shall be permitted to go on with its usurpations. "If there is any book capable of arousing the people, it is the one before us."

Taylor gave to his volume the title "Construction Construed, and Constitutions Vindicated." The phrases "exclusive interests" and "exclusive privileges" abound throughout the volume. Sixteen chapters compose this classic of State Rights philosophy. Five of them are devoted to Marshall's opinion in M'Culloch *vs.* Maryland; the others to theories of government, the state of the country, the protective tariff, and the Missouri question. The principles of the Revolution, avows Taylor, "are the keys of construction" and "the locks of liberty.[2]

[1] See vol. II, 397, of this work.
[2] Taylor: *Construction Construed, and Constitutions Vindicated*, 9.

. . No form of government can foster a fanaticism for wealth, without being corrupted." Yet Marshall's ideas establish "the despotick principle of a gratuitous distribution of wealth and poverty by law." [1]

If the theory that Congress can create corporations should prevail, "legislatures will become colleges for teaching the science of getting money by monopolies or favours." [2] To pretend faith in Christianity, and yet foster monopoly, is "like placing Christ on the car of Juggernaut." [3] The framers of the National Constitution tried to prevent the evils of monopoly and avarice by "restricting the powers given to Congress" and safeguarding those of the States; "in fact, by securing the freedom of property." [4]

Marshall is enamored of the word "sovereignty," an "equivocal and illimitable word," not found in "the declaration of independence, nor the federal constitution, nor the constitution of any single state"; all of them repudiated it "as a traitor of civil rights." [5] Well that they had so rejected this term of despotism! No wonder Jugurtha exclaimed, "Rome was for sale," when "the government exercised an absolute power over the national property." Of course it would "find purchasers." [6] To this condition Marshall's theories will bring America.

Whence this effort to endow the National Government with powers comparable to those of a monarchy? Plainly it is a reaction — "many wise and good men, . . alarmed by the illusions of Rousseau

---

[1] Taylor: *Construction Construed*, 11–12. Taylor does not, of course, call Marshall by name, either in this book or in his other attacks on the Chief Justice.

[2] *Ib.* 15.   [3] *Ib.* 16   [4] *Ib.* 18.   [5] *Ib.* 25–26   [6] *Ib.* 28.

John Taylor

and Godwin, and the atrocities of the French revolution, honestly believe that these [democratic] principles have teeth and claws, which it is expedient to draw and pare, however constitutional they may be; without considering that such an operation will subject the generous lion to the wily fox; . . subject liberty and property to tyranny and fraud." [1]

In chapter after chapter of clever arguments, illumined by the sparkle of such false gems as these quotations, Taylor prepares the public mind for his direct attack on John Marshall. He is at a sad disadvantage; he, "an unknown writer," can offer only "an artless course of reasoning" against the "acute argument" of Marshall's opinion, concurred in by the members of the Supreme Court whose "talents," "integrity," "uprightness," and "erudition" are universally admitted.[2] The essence of Marshall's doctrine is that, although the powers of the National Government are limited, the means by which they may be executed are unlimited. But, "as ends may be made to beget means, so means may be made to beget ends, until the co-habitation shall rear a progeny of unconstitutional bastards, which were not begotten by the people." [3]

Marshall had said that "'the creation of a corporation appertains to sovereignty.'" This is the language of tyranny. The corporate idea crept into British law "wherein it hides the heart of a prostitute under the habiliments of a virgin." [4] But since, in America, only the people are "sovereign," and, to use Marshall's own words, the power to create

---

[1] Taylor: *Construction Construed*, 77.   [2] *Ib.* 79.   [3] *Ib.* 84.   [4] *Ib.* 87.

corporations "appertains to sovereignty," it follows that neither State nor National Governments can create corporations.[1]

The Chief Justice is a master of the "science of verbality" by which the Constitution may be rendered "as unintelligible, as a single word would be made by a syllabick dislocation, or a jumble of its letters; and turn it into a reservoir of every meaning for which its expounder may have occasion."

Where does Marshall's "artifice of verbalizing" lead?[2] To an "artificially reared, a monied interest . . which is gradually obtaining an influence over the federal government," and "craftily works upon the passions of the states it has been able to delude" [on the slavery question], "to coerce the defrauded and discontented states into submission." For this reason talk of civil war abounds. "For what are the states talking about disunion, and for what are they going to war among themselves? To create or establish a monied sect, composed of privileged combinations, as an aristocratical oppressor of them all."[3] Marshall's doctrine that Congress may bestow "exclusive privileges" is at the bottom of the Missouri controversy. "Had the motive . . never existed, the discussion itself would never have existed; but if the same cause continues, more fatal controversies may be expected."[4]

[1] Taylor: *Construction Construed*, 89. [2] *Ib.* 161. [3] *Ib.* 233.
[4] *Ib.* 237.

It is interesting to observe that Taylor brands the protective tariff as one of the evils of Marshall's Nationalist philosophy. "It destroys the division of powers between federal and state governments, . . it violates the principles of representation, . . it recognizes a sovereign power over property, . . it destroys the freedom of labour, . . it taxes

Finally Taylor hurls at the Nation the challenge of the South, which the representatives of that section, from the floor of Congress, quickly repeated in threatenings of civil war.[1] "There remains a right, anterior to every political power whatsoever, . . the natural right of self-defence. . . It is allowed, on all hands, that danger to the slave-holding states lurks in their existing situation, . . and it must be admitted that the right of self-defence applies to that situation. . . I leave to the reader the application of these observations." [2]

Immediately upon its publication, Ritchie sent a copy of Taylor's book to Jefferson, who answered that he knew "before reading it" that it would prove "orthodox." The attack upon the National courts could not be pressed too energetically: "The judiciary of the United States is the subtle corps of sappers and miners constantly working under ground to undermine the foundations of our confederated fabric. . . An opinion is huddled up in conclave, perhaps by a majority of one, delivered as if unanimous, and with the silent acquiescence of lazy and timid associates, by a crafty chief judge, who sophisticates the law to his mind, by the turn of his own reasoning." [3]

the great mass of capital and labour, to enrich the few; . . it increases the burden upon the people . . increases the mass of poverty; . . it impoverishes workmen and enriches employers; . . it increases the expenses of government, . . it deprives commerce of the freedom of exchanges, . . it corrupts congress . . generates the extremes of luxury and poverty." (Taylor: *Construction Construed*, 252–53.)

[1] See *infra*, 340–42; and see *infra*, chap. x.

[2] Taylor: *Construction Construed*, 314.

[3] Jefferson to Ritchie, Dec. 25, 1820, *Works*: Ford, xii, 176–78. He declined, however, to permit publication of his endorsement of Taylor's book. (*Ib.*)

CHAPTER VII

THREATS OF WAR

Cannot the Union exist unless Congress and the Supreme Court shall make banks and lotteries?   (John Taylor "of Caroline.")

If a judge can repeal a law of Congress, by declaring it unconstitutional, is not this the exercise of political power?   (Senator Richard M. Johnson.)

The States must shield themselves and meet the invader foot to foot.
(Jefferson.)

The United States . . . form a single nation. In war we are one people. In making peace we are one people. In all commercial regulations we are one and the same people.   (Marshall.)

The crisis has arrived contemplated by the framers of the Constitution.
(Senator James Barbour.)

THE appeals of Niles, Roane, and Taylor, and the defiant attitude toward Nationalism of Virginia, Ohio, Pennsylvania, and other States, expressed a widespread and militant Localism which now manifested itself in another and still more threatening form. The momentous and dramatic struggle in Congress over the admission of Missouri quickly followed these attacks on Marshall and the Supreme Court.

Should that Territory come into the Union only on condition that slavery be prohibited within the new State, or should the slave system be retained? The clamorous and prophetic debate upon that question stirred the land from Maine to Louisiana. A division of the Union was everywhere discussed, and the right of a State to secede was boldly proclaimed.

In the House and Senate, civil war was threatened. "I fear this subject will be an ignited spark, which, communicated to an immense mass of combustion, will produce an explosion that will shake this Union to its centre. . . The crisis has arrived, contemplated

by the framers of the Constitution. . . This portentous subject, twelve months ago, was a little speck
scarcely visible above the horizon; it has already
overcast the heavens, obscuring every other object;
materials are everywhere accumulating with which
to render it darker." [1] In these bombastic, yet serious words Senator James Barbour of Virginia, when
speaking on the Missouri question on January 14,
1820, accurately described the situation.

"I behold the father armed against the son, . . a
brother's sword crimsoned with a brother's blood, . .
our houses wrapt in flames," exclaimed Senator
Freeman Walker of Georgia. "If Congress . . impose the restriction contemplated [exclusion of
slavery from Missouri], . . consequences fatal to the
peace and harmony of this Union will . . result." [2]
Senator William Smith of South Carolina asked "if,
under the misguided influence of fanaticism and
humanity, the impetuous torrent is once put in motion, what hand short of Omnipotence can stay it?" [3]
In picturing the coming horrors Senator Richard
Mentor Johnson of Kentucky declared that "the
heart sickens, the tongue falters." [4]

In the House was heard language even more san-
guinary. "Let gentlemen beware!" exclaimed Robert Raymond Reid of Georgia; for to put limits on
slavery was to implant "envy, hatred, and bitter
reproaches, which

' Shall grow to clubs and naked swords,
To murder and to death.' . .

---

[1] *Annals*, 16th Cong. 1st Sess. 107–08.
[2] *Ib*. 175.   [3] *Ib*. 275.   [4] *Ib*. 359.

Sir, the firebrand, which is even now cast into your society, will require blood .. for its quenching." [1]

Only a few Northern members answered with spirit. Senator Walter Lowrie of Pennsylvania preferred "a dissolution of this Union" rather than "the extension of slavery." [2] Daniel Pope Cook of Illinois avowed that "the sound of disunion .. has been uttered so often in this debate, .. that it is high time .. to adopt measures to prevent it. . . Such declarations .. will have no .. effect upon me. . . Is it .. the intention of gentlemen to arouse .. the South to rebellion?" [3] For the most part, however, Northern Representatives were mild and even hopeful. [4]

Such was the situation concerning which John Marshall addressed the American people in his epochal opinion in the case of Cohens *vs.* Virginia. The noble passages of that remarkable state paper were inspired by, and can be understood only in the light of, the crisis that produced them. Not in the mere facts of that insignificant case, not in the precise legal points involved, is to be found the

[1] *Annals*, 16th Cong. 1st Sess. 1033.

[2] *Ib.* 209. The Justices of the Supreme Court followed the proceedings in Congress with the interest and accuracy of politicians. (See, for example, Story's comments on the Missouri controversy, Story to White, Feb. 27, 1820, Story, I, 362.)

[3] *Annals*, 16th Cong. 1st Sess. 1106–07.

[4] For instance, Joshua Cushman of Massachusetts was sure that, instead of disunion, "the Canadas, with New Brunswick and Nova Scotia, allured by the wisdom and beneficence of our institutions, will stretch out their hands for an admission into this Union. The Floridas will become a willing victim. Mexico will mingle her lustre with the federal constellation. South America .. will burn incense on our .. altar. The Republic of the United States shall have dominion from sea to sea, .. from the river Columbia to the ends of the earth. The American Eagle .. will soar aloft to the stars of Heaven." (*Ib.* 1309.)

inspiration of Marshall's transcendent effort on this occasion. Indeed, it is possible, as the Ohio Legislature and the Virginia Republican organization soon thereafter charged, that Cohens *vs.* Virginia was "feigned" for the purpose of enabling Marshall to assert once more the supremacy of the Nation.

If the case came before Marshall normally, without design and in the regular course of business, it was an event nothing short of providential. If, on the contrary, it was "arranged" so that Marshall could deliver his immortal Nationalist address, never was such contrivance so thoroughly justified. While the legal profession has always considered this case to be identical, judicially, with that of Martin *vs.* Hunter's Lessee, it is, historically, a part of M'Culloch *vs.* Maryland and of Osborn *vs.* The Bank. The opinion of John Marshall in the Cohens case is one of the strongest and most enduring strands of that mighty cable woven by him to hold the American people together as a united and imperishable nation.

Fortunate, indeed, for the Republic that Marshall's fateful pronouncement came forth at such a critical hour, even if technicalities were waived in bringing before him a case in which he could deliver that opinion. For, in conjunction with his exposition in M'Culloch *vs.* Maryland, it was the most powerful answer that could be given, and from the source of greatest authority, to that defiance of the National Government and to the threats of disunion then growing ever bolder and more vociferous. Marshall's utterances did not still those hostile voices, it is true, but they gave strength and courage to Nationalists and furnished to the champions of the Union arguments of peculiar force as coming from the supreme tribunal of the Nation.

Could John Marshall have seen into the future he would have beheld Abraham Lincoln expounding from the stump to the farmers of Illinois, in 1858, the doctrines laid down by himself in 1819 and 1821.

Briefly stated, the facts in the case of Cohens *vs.* Virginia were as follows: The City of Washington was incorporated under an act of Congress [1] which, among other things, empowered the corporation to "authorize the drawing of lotteries for effecting any important improvements in the city which the ordinary funds or revenue thereof will not accomplish," to an amount not to exceed ten thousand dollars, the object first to be approved by the President. [2] Accordingly a city ordinance was passed, creating "The National Lottery" and authorizing it to sell tickets and conduct drawings.

By an act of the Virginia Legislature [3] the purchase or sale within the State of lottery tickets, except those of lotteries authorized by the laws of Virginia, was forbidden under penalty of a fine of one hundred dollars for each offense.

[1] May 3, 1802, *U.S. Statutes at Large.* This act, together with a supplementary act (May 4, 1812, *ib.*), is a vivid portrayal of a phase of the life of the National Capital at that period. See especially Section VI.

[2] Lotteries had long been a favorite method of raising funds for public purposes. As a member of the Virginia House of Delegates, Marshall had voted for many lottery bills. (See vol. II, footnote 1, to 56, of this work.) For decades after the Constitution was adopted, lotteries were considered to be both moral and useful.

[3] Effective January 21, 1820.

On June 1, 1820, "P. J. & M. J. Cohen, . . being evil-disposed persons," violated the Virginia statute by selling to one William H. Jennings in the Borough of Norfolk two half and four quarter lottery tickets "of the National Lottery, to be drawn in the city of Washington, that being a lottery not authorized by the laws of this commonwealth," as the information of James Nimmo, the prosecuting attorney, declared.[1]

At the quarterly session of the Court of Norfolk, held September 2, 1820, the case came on for hearing before the Mayor, Recorder, and Aldermen of said borough and was decided upon an agreed case "in lieu of a special verdict," which set forth the sale of the lottery tickets, the Virginia statute, the act of Congress incorporating the City of Washington, and the fact that the National Lottery had been established under that act.[2] The Norfolk Court found the defendants guilty and fined them in the sum of one hundred dollars. This paltry amount could not have paid one twentieth part of the fees which the eminent counsel who appeared for the Cohens would, ordinarily, have charged.[3] The case was carried to the Supreme Court on a writ of error.

[1] 6 Wheaton, 266–67.   [2] *Ib.* 268–90.

[3] William Pinkney was at this time probably the highest paid lawyer in America. Five years before he argued the case of Cohens *vs.* Virginia, his professional income was $21,000 annually (Story to White, Feb. 26, 1816, Story, I, 278), more than four times as much as Marshall ever received when leader of the Richmond bar (see vol. II, 201, of this work). David B. Ogden, the other counsel for the Cohens, was one of the most prominent and successful lawyers of New York. See Warren, 303–04.

Another interesting fact in this celebrated case is that the Norfolk Court fined the Cohens the minimum allowed by the Virginia statute

On behalf of Virginia, Senator James Barbour of that State [1] moved that the writ of error be dismissed, and upon this motion the main arguments were made and Marshall's principal opinion delivered. In concluding his argument, Senator Barbour came near threatening secession, as he had done in the Senate: "Nothing can so much endanger it [the National Government] as exciting the hostility of the state governments. With them it is to determine how long this government shall endure." [2]

In opening for the Cohens, David B. Ogden of New York denied that "there is any such thing as a sovereign state, independent of the Union." The authority of the Supreme Court "extends . . to all cases arising under the constitution, laws, and treaties of the United States." [3] Cohens vs. Virginia was such a case.

Upon the supremacy of the Supreme Court over State tribunals depended the very life of the Nation, declared William Pinkney, who appeared as the principal counsel for the Cohens. Give up the appellate jurisdiction of National courts "from the decisions of the state tribunals" and "every other branch of federal authority might as well be surrendered. To part with this, leaves the Union a mere league or confederacy." [4] Long, brilliantly, convincingly, did

They could have been fined at least $800, $100 for each offense — perhaps should have been fined that amount had the law been strictly observed. Indeed, the Virginia Act permitted a fine to the extent of "the whole sum of money proposed to be raised by such lottery." (6 Wheaton, 268.)

[1] Barbour declined a large fee offered him by the State. (Grigsby: *Virginia Convention of 1829–30*.)

[2] 6 Wheaton, 344.   [3] *Ib.* 347.   [4] *Ib.* 354.

Pinkney speak. The extreme State Rights arguments were, he asserted, "too wild and extravagant" [1] to deserve consideration.

Promptly Marshall delivered the opinion of the court on Barbour's motion to dismiss the writ of error. The points made against the jurisdiction of the Supreme Court were, he said: "1st. That a state is a defendant. 2d. That no writ of error lies from this court to a state court. 3d. . . that this court . . has no right to review the judgment of the state court, because neither the constitution nor any law of the United States has been violated by that judgment." [2]

The first two points "vitally . . affect the Union," declared the Chief Justice, who proceeds to answer the reasoning of the State judges when, in Hunter *vs.* Fairfax's Devisee, they hurled at the Supreme Court Virginia's defiance of National authority.[3] Marshall thus states the Virginia contentions: That the Constitution has "provided no tribunal for the final construction of itself, or of the laws or treaties of the nation; but that this power may be exercised . . by the courts of every state of the Union. That the constitution, laws, and treaties, may receive as many constructions as there are states; and that this is not a mischief, or, if a mischief, is irremediable." [4]

Why was the Constitution established? Because the "American States, as well as the American people, have believed a close and firm Union to be essential to their liberty and to their happiness. They

---

[1] 6 Wheaton, 375. For a better report of Pinkney's speech see Wheaton: *Pinkney*, 612–16.

[2] *Ib.* 376.   [3] See *supra*, 157–58.   [4] 6 Wheaton, 377.

have been taught by experience, that this Union cannot exist without a government for the whole; and they have been taught by the same experience that this government would be a mere shadow, that must disappoint all their hopes, unless invested with large portions of that sovereignty which belongs to independent states." [1]

The very nature of the National Government leaves no doubt of its supremacy "in all cases where it is empowered to act"; that supremacy was also expressly declared in the Constitution itself, which plainly states that it, and laws and treaties made under it, "' shall be the supreme law of the land; and the judges in every state shall be bound thereby; anything in the constitution or laws of any state to the contrary notwithstanding.'"

This supremacy of the National Government is a Constitutional "principle." And why were "ample powers" given to that Government? The Constitution answers: "In order to form a more perfect union, establish justice, ensure domestic tranquillity, provide for the common defense, promote the general welfare." [2]

The "limitations on the sovereignty of the states" were made for the same reason that the "supreme government" of the Nation was endowed with its broad powers. In addition to express limitations on State "sovereignty" were many instances "where, perhaps, *no other power is conferred on Congress than a conservative power to maintain the principles* established in the constitution. The maintenance of these

---

[1] 6 Wheaton, 380.   [2] *Ib.* 381.

principles in their purity, is certainly among the great duties of the government." [1]

Marshall had been Chief Justice of the United States for twenty years, and these were the boldest and most extreme words that he had spoken during that period. Like all men of the first rank, Marshall met in a great way, and without attempt at compromise, a great issue that could not be compromised — an issue which, everywhere, at that moment, was challenging the existence of the Nation. There must be no dodging, no hedging, no equivocation. Instead, there must be the broadest, frankest, bravest declaration of National powers that words could express. For this reason Marshall said that these powers might be exercised even as a result of "a conservative power" in Congress "to maintain the principles established in the constitution."

The Judicial Department is an agency essential to the performance of the "great duty" to preserve those "principles." "It is authorized to decide all cases of every description, arising under the constitution or laws of the United States." Those cases in which a State is a party are not excepted. There are cases where the National courts are given jurisdiction solely because a State is a party, and regardless of the subject of the controversy; but in all cases involving the Constitution, laws, or treaties of the Nation, the National tribunals have jurisdiction, regardless of parties.[2]

"Principles" drawn from the very "*nature of government*" require that "the judicial power . .

[1] 6 Wheaton, 382. (Italics the author's.)   [2] *Ib*. 382.

must be co-extensive with the legislative, and must
be capable of deciding every judicial question which
grows out of the constitution and laws" — not that
"it is fit that it should be so; but . . that this fit-
ness" is an aid to the right interpretation of the
Constitution.[1]

What will be the result if Virginia's attitude is
confirmed? Nothing less than the prostration of the
National Government "at the feet of every state in
the Union. . . Each member will possess a veto on
the will of the whole." Consider the country's experience. Assumption[2] had been deemed unconstitutional by some States; opposition to excise
taxes had produced the Whiskey Rebellion;[3] other
National statutes "have been questioned partially,
while they were supported by the great majority of
the American people."[4] There can be no assurance
that such divergent and antagonistic actions may
not again be taken. State laws in conflict with National laws probably will be enforced by State
judges, since they are subject to the same prejudices
as are the State Legislatures — indeed, "in many
states the judges are dependent for office and for
salary on the will of the legislature."[5]

The Constitution attaches first importance to the
"independence" of the Judiciary; can it have been
intended to leave to State "tribunals, where this independence may not exist," cases in which " a state
shall prosecute an individual who claims the protection of an act of Congress?" Marshall gives

[1] 6 Wheaton, 384–85. (Italics the author's.)
[2] See vol. II, 66, of this work.
[3] 6 Wheaton, 87.   [4] Ib. 385–86.   [5] Ib. 387.

examples of possible collisions between National and State authority, in ordinary times, as well as in exceptional periods.[1] Even to-day it is obvious that the Chief Justice was denouncing the threatened resistance by State officials to the tariff laws, a fact of commanding importance at the time when Marshall's opinion in Cohens *vs.* Virginia was delivered.

At this point he rises to the heights of august eloquence: "A constitution is framed for ages to come, and is designed to approach immortality as nearly as human institutions can approach it. Its course cannot always be tranquil. It is exposed to storms and tempests, and its framers must be unwise statesmen indeed, if they have not provided it . . with the means of self-preservation from the perils it may be destined to encounter. No government ought to be so defective in its organization as not to contain within itself the means of securing the execution of its own laws against other dangers than those which occur every day."

Marshall is here replying to the Southern threats of secession, just as he rebuked the same spirit when displayed by his New England friends ten years earlier.[2] Then turning to the conflict of courts, he remarks, as though the judicial collision is all that he has in mind: "A government should repose on its own courts, rather than on others." [3]

He recalls the state of the country under the Confederation when requisitions on the States were

---

[1] 6 Wheaton, 386–87.
[2] See U.S. *vs.* Peters, *supra,* 18 *et seq.*   [3] 6 Wheaton, 387–88.

"habitually disregarded," although they were "as constitutionally obligatory as the laws enacted by the present Congress." In view of this fact is it improbable that the framers of the Constitution meant to give the Nation's courts the power of preserving that Constitution, and laws made in pursuance of it, "from all violation from every quarter, so far as judicial decisions can preserve them"? [1]

Virginia contends that if States wish to destroy the National Government they can do so much more simply and easily than by judicial decision — "they have only not to elect senators, and it expires without a struggle"; and that therefore the destructive effect on the Nation of decisions of State courts cannot be taken into account when construing the Constitution.

To this Marshall makes answer: "Whenever hostility to the existing system shall become universal, it will be also irresistible. The people made the constitution, and the people can unmake it. It is the creature of their own will, and lives only by their will. But this supreme and irresistible power to make or to unmake, resides only in the whole body of the people; not in any sub-division of them. The attempt of any of the parts to exercise it is usurpation, and ought to be repelled by those to whom the people have delegated their power of repelling it. The acknowledged inability of the government, then, to sustain itself against the public will, and, by force or otherwise, to control the whole nation, is no sound argument in support of its constitutional

[1] 6 Wheaton, 388.

inability to preserve itself against a section of the nation acting in opposition to the general will." [1]

This is a direct reply to the Southern arguments in the Missouri debate which secessionists were now using wherever those who opposed National laws and authority raised their voices. John Marshall is blazing the way for Abraham Lincoln. He speaks of a "section" instead of a State. The Nation, he says, may constitutionally preserve itself "against a section." And this right of the Nation rests on "principles" inherent in the Constitution. But in Cohens *vs*. Virginia no "section" was arrayed against the Nation — on the record there was nothing but a conflict of jurisdiction of courts, and this only by a strained construction of a municipal lottery ordinance into a National law.

The Chief Justice is exerting to the utmost his tremendous powers, not to protect two furtive peddlers of lottery tickets, but to check a powerful movement that, if not arrested, must destroy the Republic. Should that movement go forward thereafter, it must do so over every Constitutional obstacle which the Supreme Court of the Nation could throw in its way. In Cohens *vs*. Virginia, John Marshall stamped upon the brow of Localism the brand of illegality. If this is not the true interpretation of his opinion in that case, all of the exalted language he used is mere verbiage.

Marshall dwells on "the subordination of the parts to the whole." The one great motive for establishing the National Judiciary "was the pres-

[1] 6 Wheaton, 389–90.

ervation of the constitution and laws of the United
States, so far as they can be preserved by judicial
authority." [1]

Returning to the technical aspects of the controversy, Marshall points out that the Supreme Court
plainly has appellate jurisdiction of the Cohens
case: "If a state be a party, the jurisdiction of this
court is original; if the case arise under a [National]
constitution or a [National] law, the jurisdiction is
appellate. But a case to which a state is a party
may arise under the constitution or a law of the
United States." [2] That would mean a double jurisdiction. Marshall, therefore, shows, at provoking
length,[3] that the appellate jurisdiction of the Supreme
Court "in all cases arising under the constitution,
laws, or treaties of the United States, was not
arrested by the circumstance that a state was a
party"; [4] and in this way he explains that part of
his opinion in Marbury vs. Madison, in which he
reasoned that Section 13 of the Ellsworth Judiciary
Act was unconstitutional.[5]

Marshall examines the Eleventh Amendment
and becomes, for a moment, the historian, a rôle in
which he delighted. "The states were greatly indebted" at the close of the Revolution; the Constitution was opposed because it was feared that
their obligations would be collected in the National
courts. This very thing happened. "The alarm
was general; and, to quiet the apprehensions that
were so extensively entertained, this amendment

[1] 6 Wheaton, 390–91.   [2] Ib. 393.   [3] Ib. 394–404.
[4] Ib. 405.   [5] See vol. III, 127–28, of this work.

was .. adopted." But "its motive was not to maintain the sovereignty of a state from the degradation supposed to attend a compulsory appearance
before the tribunal of the nation." It was to prevent
creditors from suing a State — "no interest could be
felt in so changing the relations between the whole and
its parts, as to strip the government of the means
of protecting, by the instrumentality of its courts,
the constitution and laws from active violation." [1]

With savage relish the Chief Justice attacks and
demolishes the State Rights theory that the Supreme Court cannot review the judgment of a
State court "in any case." That theory, he says,
"considers the federal judiciary as completely foreign to that of a state; and as being no more connected with it, in any respect whatever, than the
court of a foreign state." [2] But "the United States
form, for many, and for most important purposes, a
single nation. . . In war, we are one people. In making peace, we are one people. In all commercial
regulations, we are one and the same people. In
many other respects, the American people are one;
and the government which is alone capable of controlling and managing their interests in all these
respects, is the government of the Union.

"It is their government, and in that character
they have no other. America has chosen to be, in
many respects, and to many purposes, a nation; and
for all these purposes, her government is complete;
to all these objects, it is competent. The people
have declared, that in the exercise of all powers

[1] 6 Wheaton, 406–07.   [2] *Ib.* 413.

given for these objects it is supreme. It can, then, in effecting these objects, legitimately control all individuals or governments within the American territory. The Constitution and laws of a state, so far as they are repugnant to the Constitution and laws of the United States, are absolutely void.

"These states are constituent parts of the United States. They are members of one great empire." [1] The National Court alone can decide all questions arising under the Constitution and laws of the Nation. "The uniform decisions of this court on the point now under consideration," he continues, "have been assented to, with a single exception,[2] by the courts of every state in the Union whose judgments have been revised." [3]

As to the lottery ordinance of the City of Washington, Congress has exclusive power to legislate for the District of Columbia and, in exercising that power, acts "as the legislature of the Union." The Constitution declares that it, and all laws made under it, constitute 'the supreme law of the land." [4] Laws for the government of Washington are, therefore, parts of this "supreme law" and "bind the nation. . . Congress legislates, in the same forms, and in the same character, in virtue of powers of equal obligation, conferred in the same instrument, when exercising its exclusive powers of legislation, as well as when exercising those which are limited." [5]

The Chief Justice gives examples of the exclusive powers of Congress, all of which are binding through-

---

[1] 6 Wheaton, 413–14.   [2] Fairfax's Devisee *vs.* Hunter, *supra*, 157–60.
[3] 6 Wheaton, 420.   [4] *Ib.* 424.   [5] *Ib.* 425–26.

out the Republic. "Congress is not a local legislature, but exercises this particular power [to legislate for the District of Columbia], like all its other powers, in its high character, as the legislature of the Union." [1] The punishment of the Cohens for selling tickets of the National Lottery, created by the City of Washington under authority of an act of Congress, involves the construction of the Constitution and of a National law. The Supreme Court, therefore, has jurisdiction of the case, and the motion to dismiss the writ of error is denied.

Marshall having thus established the jurisdiction of the Supreme Court to hear and decide the case, it was argued "on the merits." Again David B. Ogden appeared for the Cohens and was joined by William Wirt as Attorney-General. For Virginia Webster took the place of Senator Barbour. The argument was upon the true construction of the act of Congress authorizing the City of Washington to establish a lottery; and upon this Marshall delivered a second opinion, to the effect that the lottery ordinance was "only co-extensive with the city" and a purely local affair; that the court at Norfolk had a right to fine the Cohens for violating a law of Virginia; and that its judgment must be affirmed. [2]

So ended, as far as the formal record goes, the famous case of Cohens *vs.* Virginia. On its merits it amounted to nothing; the practical result of the appeal was nothing; but it afforded John Marshall the opportunity to tell the Nation its duty in a crowning National emergency.

[1] 6 Wheaton, 429.   [2] *Ib.* 445–47.

Intense was the excitement and violent the rage in the anti-Nationalist camp when Marshall's opinion was published. Ritchie, in his paper, demanded that the Supreme Court should be abolished.[1] The Virginia Republican organization struck instantly, Spencer Roane wielding its sword. The *Enquirer* published a series of five articles between May 25 and June 8, 1821, inclusive, signed "Algernon Sidney," Roane's latest *nom de plume*.

"The liberties and constitution of our country are .. deeply and vitally endangered by the fatal effects" of Marshall's opinion. "Appointed in one generation it [the Supreme Court] claims to make laws and constitutions for another."[2] The unanimity of the court can be explained only on the ground of "a culpable apathy in the other judges, or a confidence not to be excused, in the principles and talents of their chief." Sidney literally wastes reams of paper in restating the State Rights arguments. He finds a malign satisfaction in calling the Constitution a "compact," a "league," a "treaty" between "sovereign governments."[3]

National judges have "*no* interest in the government or laws of any state but that of which they are citizens," asserts Sidney. "As to every other state but that, they are, completely, aliens and foreigners."[4] Virginia is as much a foreign nation as Russia[5] so far as jurisdiction of the Supreme Court over

[1] Ambler: *Ritchie*, 81.

[2] *Enquirer*, May 25, 1821, as quoted in *Branch Hist. Papers*, June, 1906, 78, 85.

[3] *Enquirer*, May 25 and May 29, 1821, as quoted in *ib.* 89, 100.

[4] *Enquirer*, May 29, 1821, as quoted in *ib.* 101.

[5] *Enquirer*, June 21, 1821, as quoted in *ib.* 110.

the judgments of State courts is concerned. Marshall's doctrine "is the blind and absolute despotism which exists in an army, or is exercised by a tyrant over his slaves." [1]

The apostate Republican Justices who concurred with Marshall are denounced, and with greater force, by reason of a tribute paid to the hated Chief Justice: "How else is it that they also go to all lengths with the ultra-federal leader who is at the head of their court? That leader is honorably distinguished from you messieurs judges. He is true to his former politics. He has even pushed them to an extreme never until now anticipated. He must be equally delighted and *surprised* to find his *Republican* brothers going with him" — a remark as true as it was obvious. "How is it . . that they go with him, not only as to the results of his opinions, but as to all the points and positions contained in the most lengthy, artful and alarming opinions?" Because, answers Sidney, they are on the side of power and of "the government that feeds them." [2]

What Marshall had said in the Virginia Constitutional Convention of 1788 refutes his opinions now. "Great principles then operated on his luminous mind, not hair-splitting quibbles and verbal criticisms." [3] The "artifices" of the Chief Justice render his opinions the more dangerous. [4]

If the anger of John Marshall ever was more aroused than it was by Roane's assaults upon him, no evidence of the fact exists. Before the last number

[1] *Branch Hist. Papers,* June, 1906, 119.   [2] *Ib.* 123–24.
[3] *Enquirer,* June 5, 1821, as quoted in *Branch Hist. Papers,* June, 1906, 146–47.   [4] *Ib.* 182–83.

of the Algernon Sidney essays appeared, the Chief Justice confides his wrathful feelings to the devoted and sympathetic Story: "The opinion of the Supreme Court in the Lottery case has been assaulted with a degree of virulence transcending what has appeared on any former occasion. Algernon Sidney is written by the gentleman who is so much distinguished for his feelings towards the Supreme Court, & if you have not an opportunity of seeing the Enquirer I will send it to you.

"There are other minor gentry who seek to curry favor & get into office by adding their mite of abuse, but I think for coarseness & malignity of invention Algernon Sidney surpasses all party writers who have ever made pretensions to any decency of character. There is on this subject no such thing as a free press in Virginia, and of consequence the calumnies and misrepresentations of this gentleman will remain uncontradicted & will by many be believed to be true. He will be supposed to be the champion of state rights, instead of being what he really is, the champion of dismemberment." [1]

When Roane's articles were finished, Marshall wrote Story: "I send you the papers containing the essays of Algernon Sidney. Their coarseness & malignity would designate the author if he was not avowed. The argument, if it may be called one, is, I think, as weak as its language is violent & prolix. Two other gentlemen [2] have appeared in the papers on this sub-

[1] Marshall to Story, June 15, 1821, *Proceedings, Mass. Hist. Soc.* 2d Series, xiv, 327–28.

[2] Marshall refers to three papers published in the *Enquirer* of May 15 and 22, and June 22, the first two signed "Somers" and the third

ject, one of them is deeply concerned in pillaging the purchasers of the Fairfax estate in which goodly work he fears no other obstruction than what arises

signed "Fletcher of Saltoun." It is impossible to discover who these writers were. Their essays, although vicious, are so dull as not to be worth the reading, though Jefferson thought them "luminous and striking." (Jefferson to Johnson, June 12, 1823, *Works:* Ford, XII, 252, footnote.)

"Somers," however, is compelled to admit the irresistible appeal of Marshall's personality. "Superior talents and address will forever attract the homage of inferior minds." (*Enquirer*, May 15, 1821.)

"The Supreme court . . have rendered the constitution the sport of legal ingenuity. . . . Its meaning is locked up from the profane vulgar, and distributed only by the high priests of the temple." (*Ib.* May 22, 1821.)

"Fletcher of Saltoun" is intolerably verbose: "The victories . . of courts . . though bloodless, are generally decisive. . . The progress of the judiciary, though slow, is steady and untiring as the foot of time."

The people act as though hypnotized, he laments — "the powerful mind of the chief justice has put forth its strength, and we are quiet as if touched by the wand of enchantment; — we fall prostrate before his genius as though we had looked upon the dazzling brightness of the shield of Astolfo. — Triumphant indeed has been this most powerful effort of his extraordinary mind. His followers exult — those who doubted, have yielded; even the faithful are found wavering, and the unconvinced can find no opening in his armor of defense."

This writer points out Marshall's "abominable inconsistencies," but seems to be himself under the spell of the Chief Justice: "I mention not this to the disadvantage of the distinguished individual who has pronounced these conflicting opinions. No man can have a higher respect for the virtues of his character, or greater admiration of the powers of his mind."

Alas for the change that time works upon the human intellect! Consider Marshall, the young man, and Marshall, the Chief Justice! "How little did he, at that early day, contemplate the possibility of his carrying the construction of the constitution to an extent so far beyond even what he then renounced!" [*sic.*]

Thereupon "Fletcher of Saltoun" plunges into an ocean of words concerning Hamilton's theories of government and Marshall's application of them. He announces this essay to be the first of a series; but, luckily for everybody, this first effort exhausted him. Apparently he, too, fell asleep under Marshall's "wand," for nothing more came from his drowsy pen. (*Ib.* June 22, 1821.)

from the appellate power of the Supreme Court, &
the other is a hunter after office who hopes by his
violent hostility to the Union, which in Virginia as-
sumes the name of regard for state rights, & by his
devotion to Algernon Sidney, to obtain one. In support of the sound principles of the constitution & of
the Union of the States, not a pen is drawn. In Virginia the tendency of things verges rapidly to the
destruction of the government & the re-establish-
ment of a league of sovereign states. I look elsewhere for safety." [1]

Another of the "minor gentry" of whom Marshall
complained was William C. Jarvis, who in 1820 had
written a book entitled "The Republicans," in which
he joined in the hue and cry against Marshall because of his opinion in M'Culloch vs. Maryland.
Jarvis sent a copy of his book to Jefferson who, in
acknowledging the receipt of it, once more spoke
his mind upon the National Judiciary. To Jarvis's
statement that the courts are "the ultimate arbiters
of all constitutional questions," Jefferson objected.

It was "a very dangerous doctrine indeed, and one
which would place us under the despotism of an
oligarchy," wrote the "Sage of Monticello." "The
constitution has erected no such single tribunal,
knowing that to whatever hands confided, with the
corruptions of time and party, its members would
become despots. . . If the legislature fails to pass"
necessary laws — such as those for taking of the
census, or the payment of judges; or even if "they

---

[1] Marshall to Story, July 13, 1821, *Proceedings, Mass. Hist. Soc.*
2d Series, XIV, 329.

fail to meet in congress, the judges cannot issue their mandamus to them."

So, concludes Jefferson, if the President does not appoint officers to fill vacancies, "the judges cannot force him." In fact, the judges "can issue their mandamus . . to no executive or legislative officer to enforce the fulfilment of their official duties, any more than the president or legislature may issue orders to the judges. . . When the legislature or executive functionaries act unconstitutionally, they are responsible to the people in their elective capacity. The exemption of the judges from that is quite dangerous enough." [1]

This letter by Jefferson had just been made public, and Story, who appears to have read everything from the Greek classics to the current newspaper gossip, at once wrote Marshall. The Chief Justice replied that Jefferson's view "rather grieves than surprizes" him. But he could not "describe the surprize & mortification" he felt when he learned that Madison agreed with Jefferson "with respect to the judicial department. For Mr Jefferson's opinion as respects this department it is not difficult to assign the cause. He is among the most ambitious, & I suspect among the most unforgiving of men. His great power is over the mass of the people, & this power is chiefly acquired by professions of democracy. Every check on the wild impulse of the moment is a check on his own power, & he is unfriendly to the source from which it flows. He looks of course with ill will at an independent judiciary.

[1] Jefferson to Jarvis, Sept. 28, 1820, *Works:* Ford, xii, 162-63.

"That in a free country with a written constitution any intelligent man should wish a dependent judiciary, or should think that the constitution is not a law for the court as well as for the legislature would astonish me, if I had not learnt from observation that with many men the judgement is completely controuled by the passions." [1]

To Jefferson, Marshall ascribes Roane's attacks upon the Supreme Court: "There is some reason to believe that the essays written against the Supreme Court were, in a degree at least, stimulated by this gentleman, and that although the coarseness of the language belongs exclusively to the author, its acerbity has been increased by his communications with the great Lama of the mountains. He may therefore feel himself . . required to obtain its republication in some place of distinction." [2]

John E. Hall was at that time the publisher at Philadelphia of *The Journal of American Jurisprudence*. Jefferson had asked Hall to reprint Roane's articles, and Hall had told Story, who faithfully reported to Marshall. "I am a little surprized at the request which you say has been made to Mr Hall, although there is no reason for my being so. The settled hostility of the gentleman who has made that request to the judicial department will show itself in that & in every other form which he believes will conduce to its object. For this he has several motives, & it is not among the weakest that the department would never lend itself as a tool to work for his political power. . .

[1] Marshall to Story, July 13, 1821, *Proceedings, Mass. Hist. Soc.* 2d Series, XIV, 328–29.

[2] Same to same, Sept. 18, 1821, *ib.* 330.

"What does Mr Hall purpose to do?" asks Marshall. "I do not suppose you would willingly interfere so as to prevent his making the publication, although I really think it is in form & substance totally unfit to be placed in his law journal. I really think a proper reply to the request would be to say that no objection existed to the publication of any law argument against the opinion of the Supreme Court, but that the coarseness of its language, its personal & official abuse & its tedious prolixity constituted objections to the insertion of Algernon Sidney which were insuperable. If, however, Mr Hall determines to comply with this request, I think he ought, unless he means to make himself a party militant, to say that he published that piece by particular request, & ought to subjoin the masterly answer of Mr Wheaton. I shall wish to know what course Mr Hall will pursue." [1]

Roane's attacks on Marshall did not appear in Hall's law magazine!

Quitting such small, unworthy, and prideful considerations, Marshall rises for a moment to the great issue which he met so nobly in his opinions in M'Culloch *vs.* Maryland and in Cohens *vs.* Virginia. "A deep design," he writes Story, "to convert our government into a mere league of states has taken strong hold of a powerful & violent party in Virginia. The attack upon the judiciary is in fact an attack upon the union. The judicial department is well understood to be that through which the govern-

---

[1] Marshall to Story, July 13, 1821, *Proceedings, Mass. Hist. Soc.* 2d Series, XIV, 329-30.

ment may be attacked most successfully, because it
is without patronage, & of course without power.
And it is equally well understood that every subtraction from its jurisdiction is a vital wound to
the government itself. The attack upon it therefore is a masked battery aimed at the government
itself.

"The whole attack, if not originating with M^r
Jefferson, is obviously approved & guided by him.
It is therefore formidable in other states as well as
in this, & it behoves the friends of the union to be
more on the alert than they have been. An effort will
certainly be made to repeal the 25th sec. of the
judicial act." [1] Marshall's indignation at Roane
exhausted his limited vocabulary of resentment.
Had he possessed Jefferson's resources of vituperation, the literature of animosity would have been
enriched by the language Marshall would have indulged in when the next Republican battery poured
its volleys upon him.

No sooner had Roane's artillery ceased to play
upon Marshall and the Supreme Court than the
roar of Taylor's heavy guns was again heard. In
a powerful and brilliant book, called "Tyranny
Unmasked," he directed his fire upon the newly proposed protective tariff, "this sport for capitalists
and death for the rest of the nation." [2] The theory
of the Chief Justice that there is a "supreme federal
power" over the States is proved false by the proceedings of the Constitutional Convention at Phila-

[1] Marshall to Story, July 13, 1821, *Proceedings, Mass. Hist. Soc*
2d Series, xiv, 330–31.
[2] Taylor: *Tyranny Unmasked*, 89.

delphia in 1787. Certain members then proposed to give the National Government a veto over the acts of State Governments.[1] This proposal was immediately rejected. Yet to-day Marshall proclaims a National power, "infinitely more objectionable," which asserts that the Supreme Court has "a negative or restraining power over the State governments."[2]

A protective tariff is only another monstrous child of Marshall's accursed Nationalism, that prolific mother of special favors for the few. By what reasoning is a protective tariff made Constitutional? By the casuistry of John Marshall, that "present fashionable mode of construction, which considers the constitution as a lump of fine gold, a small portion of which is so malleable as to cover the whole mass. By this golden rule for manufacturing the constitution, a particular power given to the Federal Government may be made to cover all the rights reserved to the people and the States;[3] a limited jurisdiction given to the Federal Courts is made to cover all the State Courts;[4] and a legislative power over ten miles square is malleated over the whole of the United States,[5] as a single guinea may be beaten out so as to cover a whole house."[6] Such is the method by which a protective tariff is made Constitutional.

For one hundred and twenty-one scintillant and learned pages Taylor attacks this latest creation of National "tyranny." The whole Nationalist system

---

[1] This was Madison's idea. See vol. I, 312, of this work.
[2] Taylor: *Tyranny Unmasked*, 33.   [3] M'Culloch *vs.* Maryland.
[4] Martin *vs.* Hunter's Lessee and Cohens *vs.* Virginia.
[5] Cohens *vs.* Virginia.   [6] Taylor: *Tyranny Unmasked*, 132–33.

is "tyranny," which it is his privilege to "unmask,"
and the duty of all true Americans to destroy.[1] Marshall's Constitutional doctrine "amounts to the insertion of the following article in the constitution:
'Congress shall have power, with the assent of the
Supreme Court, to exercise or usurp, and to prohibit the States from exercising, any or all of the
powers reserved to the States, whenever they [Con-
gress] shall deem it convenient, or for the general
welfare.'"[2] Such doctrines invite "civil war."[3]

By Marshall's philosophy "the people are made
the prey of exclusive privileges." In short, under
him the Supreme Court has become the agent of
special interests.[4] "Cannot the Union subsist unless
Congress and the Supreme Court shall make banks
and lotteries?"[5]

Jefferson eagerly read Roane's essays and Taylor's book and wrote concerning them: "The judiciary
branch is the instrument which, working like gravity, without intermission, is to press us at last into
one consolidated mass. Against this I know no one
who, equally with Judge Roane himself, possesses
the power and the courage to make resistance; and
to him I look, and have long looked, as our strongest
bulwark."

At this point Jefferson declares for armed resistance to the Nation in even stronger terms than those
used by Roane or Taylor: "If Congress fails to
shield the States from dangers so palpable and so im-

[1] Taylor: *Tyranny Unmasked*, 133–254. Taylor was the first to state
fully most of the arguments since used by the opponents of protective tariffs.

[2] *Ib.* 260.   [3] *Ib.* 285.   [4] *Ib.* 305.   [5] *Ib.* 341.

minent, the States must shield themselves, and meet
the invader foot to foot. . . This is already half done
by Colonel Taylor's book" which "is the most effectual retraction of our government to its original principles which has ever yet been sent by heaven to our
aid. Every State in the Union should give a copy to
every member they elect, as a standing instruction,
and ours should set the example." [1]

Until his death the aged politician raged continuously, except in one instance,[2] at Marshall and the
Supreme Court because of such opinions and decisions as those in the Bank and Lottery cases. He
writes Justice Johnson that he "considered . . ma-
turely" Roane's attacks on the doctrines of Cohens
vs. Virginia and they appeared to him "to pulverize
every word which had been delivered by Judge Marshall, of the extra-judicial part of his opinion." If
Roane "can be answered, I surrender human reason
as a vain and useless faculty, given to bewilder, and
not to guide us. . . This practice of Judge Marshall,
of travelling out of his case to prescribe what the law

[1] Jefferson to Thweat, Jan. 19, 1821, *Works:* Ford, xii, 196–97.
Wirt, though a Republican, asserted that "the functions to be performed by the Supreme Court . . are among the most difficult and
perilous which are to be performed under the Constitution. They
demand the loftiest range of talents and learning and a soul of Roman
purity and firmness. The questions which come before them frequently involve the fate of the Constitution, the happiness of the
whole nation." (Wirt to Monroe, May 5, 1823, Kennedy, ii, 153.)
Wirt, in this letter, was urging the appointment of Kent to the
Supreme Bench, notwithstanding the Federalism of the New York
Chancellor. "Federal politics are no way dangerous on the bench of
the Supreme Court," adds Wirt. (*Ib.* 155.)
[2] His strange failure to come to Roane's support in the fight, over
the Judiciary amendments to the Constitution, in the Virginia Legislature during the session of 1821–22. (See *infra,* 371.)

would be in a moot case not before the court, is very irregular and censurable." [1]

Again Jefferson writes that, above all other officials, those who most need restraint from usurping legislative powers are "the judges of what is commonly called our General Government, but what I call our Foreign department. . . A few such doctrinal decisions, as barefaced as that of the Cohens," may so arouse certain powerful States as to check the march of Nationalism. The Supreme Court "has proved that the power of declaring what the law is, *ad libitum*, by sapping and mining, slily and without alarm, the foundations of the Constitution, can do what open force would not dare to attempt." [2]

So it came to pass that John Marshall and the Supreme Court became a center about which swirled the forces of a fast-gathering storm that raged with increasing fury until its thunders were the roar of cannon, its lightning the flashes of battle. Broadly speaking, slavery and free trade, State banking and debtors' relief laws were arraigned on the side of Localism; while slavery restriction, national banking, a protective tariff, and security of contract were marshaled beneath the banner of Nationalism. It was an assemblage of forces as incongruous as human nature itself.

The Republican protagonists of Localism did not content themselves with the writing of enraged letters or the publication of flaming articles and books.

[1] Jefferson to Johnson, June 12, 1823, *Works:* Ford, xii, footnote to 255–56.

[2] Jefferson to Livingston, March 25, 1825, Hunt: *Livingston*, 295–97.

They were too angry thus to limit their attacks,
and they were politicians of too much experience
not to crystallize an aroused public sentiment. On
December 12, 1821, Senator Richard M. Johnson
of Kentucky, who later was honored by his party
with the Vice-Presidency, offered an amendment to
the Constitution that the Senate be given appellate
jurisdiction in all cases where the Constitution or
laws of a State were questioned and the State desired to defend them; and in all cases "where the
judicial power of the United States shall be so construed as to extend to any case . . arising under"
the National Constitution, laws, or treaties.[1]

Coöperating with Johnson in the National Senate,
Roane in Virginia, when the Legislature of that State
met, prepared amendments to the National Constitution which, had they been adopted by the States,
would have destroyed the Supreme Court. He declares that he takes this step "with a view to aid"
the Congressional antagonists of Nationalism and
the Supreme Court, "or rather to lead, on this important subject." The amendments "will be copied
by another hand & circulated among the members.
I would not wish to injure the great Cause, by being
known as the author. My name would damn them,
as I believe, nay hope, with the *Tories*." Roane
asks his correspondent to "jog your Chesterfield
Delegates . . and other good republicans," and complains that "Jefferson & Madison hang back too
much, in this great Crisis." [2]

[1] *Annals*, 17th Cong. 1st Sess. 68.
[2] Roane to Thweat, Dec. 24, 1821, Jefferson MSS. Lib. Cong.

On Monday, January 14, 1822, Senator Johnson
took the floor in support of his proposition to reduce
the power of the Supreme Court. "The conflicts between the Federal judiciary and the sovereignty of
the States," he said, "are become so frequent and
alarming, that the public safety" demands a remedy.
"The Federal judiciary has assumed a guardianship
over the States, even to the controlling of their
peculiar municipal regulations." [1] The "basis of encroachment" is Marshall's "doctrine of Federal supremacy . . established by a judicial tribunal which
knows no change. Its decisions are predicated upon
the principle of perfection, and assume the character of immutability. Like the laws of the Medes
and Persians, they live forever, and operate through
all time." What shall be done? An appeal to the
Senate "will be not only harmless, but beneficial."
It will quiet "needless alarms . . restore . . confidence . . preserve . . harmony." There is pressing
need to tranquillize the public mind concerning the
National Judiciary,[2] a department of the government which is a denial of our whole democratic
theory. "Some tribunal should be established, responsible to the people, to correct their [the Judges']
aberrations."

Why should not the National Judiciary be made
answerable to the people? No fair-minded man can
deny that the judges exercise legislative power. "If
a judge can repeal a law of Congress, by declaring
it unconstitutional, is not this the exercise of polit-
cal power? If he can declare the laws of a State

[1] *Annals*, 17th Cong. 1st Sess. 69–70.   [2] *Ib.* 71–72.

unconstitutional and void, and, in one moment, sub-
vert the deliberate policy of that State for twenty-
four years, as in Kentucky, affecting its whole landed
property, .. is not this the exercise of political
power? All this they have done, and no earthly
power can investigate or revoke their decisions."[1]
The Constitution gives the National Judiciary no
such power — that instrument "is as silent as death
upon the subject." [2]

How absurd is the entire theory of judicial independence! Why should not Congress as properly declare the decisions of the National courts unconstitutional as that the courts should do the same thing to
acts of Congress or laws of States? Think of it as a
matter of plain common sense — "forty-eight Senators, one hundred and eighty-eight Representatives,
and the President of the United States, all sworn to
maintain the Constitution, have concurred in the
sentiment that the measure is strictly conformable
to it. Seven judges, irresponsible to any earthly
tribunal for their decisions, revise the measure, declare it unconstitutional, and effectually destroy its
operation. Whose opinion shall prevail? that of the
legislators and President, or that of the Court?" [3]

The Supreme Court, too, has gently exercised the
principle of judicial supervision over acts of Congress; has adjudged that Congress has a free hand
in choosing means to carry out powers expressly
granted to that body. But consider the conduct of
the Supreme Court toward the States: "An irresponsible judiciary" has ruthlessly struck down State

[1] *Annals*, 17th Cong. 1st Sess. 74–75.   [2] *Ib.* 79.   [3] *Ib.* 79–80.

law after State law; has repeatedly destroyed the decisions of State courts. Look at Marshall's opinions in M'Culloch *vs.* Maryland, in the Dartmouth College case, in United States *vs.* Peters, in Sturges *vs.* Crowninshield, in Cohens *vs.* Virginia — smallest, but perhaps worst of all, in Wilson *vs.* New Jersey. The same principle runs through all these pronouncements; — the States are nothing, the Nation everything.[1]

Webster, in the House, heard of Johnson's speech and promptly wrote Story: "Mr. Johnson of Kentucky . . has dealt, they say, pretty freely with the supreme court. Dartmouth College, Sturges and Crowninshield, *et cetera*, have all been demolished. To-morrow he is to pull to pieces the case of the Kentucky betterment law. Then Governor [Senator] Barber [Barbour] is to annihilate Cohens *v.* Virginia. So things go; but I see less reality in all this smoke than I thought I should, before I came here." [2]

It would have been wiser for Webster to have listened carefully to Johnson's powerful address than to have sneered at it on hearsay, for it was as able as it was brave; and, erroneous though it was, it stated most of the arguments advanced before or since against the supervisory power of the National Judiciary over the enactments of State Legislatures and the decisions of State courts.

When the Kentucky Senator resumed his speech the following day, he drove home his strongest weapon — an instance of judicial interference with

[1] *Annals*, 17th Cong. 1st Sess. 84–90.
[2] Webster to Story, Jan. 14, 1822, *Priv. Corres.*: Webster, I, 320.

State laws which, indeed, at first glance appeared to have been arbitrary, autocratic, and unjust. The agreement between Virginia and Kentucky by which the latter was separated from the parent Commonwealth provided that "all private rights and interests of lands" in Kentucky "derived from the laws of Virginia, shall remain valid . . and shall be determined by the laws now existing" in Virginia.[1]

In 1797 the Kentucky Legislature enacted that persons occupying lands in that State who could show a clear and connected title could not, without notice of any adverse title, upon eviction by the possessor of a superior title, be held liable for rents and profits during such occupancy.[2] Moreover, all permanent improvements made on the land must, in case of eviction, be deducted from the value of the land and judgment therefor rendered in favor of the innocent occupant and against the successful claimant. On January 31, 1812, this "occupying claimant" law, as it was called, was further strengthened by a statute providing that any person "seating and improving" lands in Kentucky, believing them "to be his own" because of a claim founded on public record, should be paid for such seating and improvements by any person who thereafter was adjudged to be the lawful owner of the lands.

Against one such occupant, Richard Biddle, the heirs of a certain John Green brought suit in the

[1] Ordinance of Separation, 1789.

[2] Act of Feb. 27, *Laws of Kentucky, 1797:* Littell, 641–45. See also Act of Feb. 28 (*ib.* 652–71), apparently on a different subject; and, especially, Act of March 1 (*ib.* 682–87). Compare Act of 1796 (*ib.* 392–420); and Act of Dec. 19, 1796 (*ib.* 554–57). See also in *ib.* general land laws.

United States Court for the District of Kentucky, and the case was certified to the Supreme Court on a division of opinion of the judges. The case was argued and decided at the same term at which Marshall delivered his opinion in Cohens *vs.* Virginia. Story delivered the unanimous opinion of the court: that the Kentucky "occupying claimant" laws violated the separation "compact" between Virginia and Kentucky, because, "by the *general principles of law*, and from the necessity of the case, titles to real estate can be determined only by the laws of the state under which they were acquired." [1] Unfortunately Story did not specifically base the court's decision on the contract clause of the Constitution, but left this vital point to inference.

Henry Clay, "as *amicus curiæ*," moved for a rehearing because the rights of numerous occupants of Kentucky lands "would be irrevocably determined by this decision," and because Biddle had permitted the case "to be brought to a hearing without appearing by his counsel, and without any argument on that side of the question." [2] In effect, Clay thus intimated that the case was feigned. The motion was granted and Green *vs.* Biddle was awaiting reargument when Senator Johnson made his attack on the National Judiciary.

Johnson minutely examined the historical reasons for including the contract clause in the National Constitution, "in order to understand perfectly well the mystical influence" of that provision. [3] It never

[1] 8 Wheaton, 11–12. (Italics the author's.)   [2] *Ib.* 18.
[3] *Annals*, 17th Cong. 1st Sess. 96–98.

was intended to affect such legislation as the Kentucky land system. The intent and meaning of the contract clause is, that "you shall not declare to-day that contract void, . . which was made yesterday under the sanction of law." [1] Does this simple rule of morality justify the National courts in annulling measures of public policy "which the people have solemnly declared to be expedient"? [2] The decision of the Supreme Court in Green vs. Biddle, said Johnson, "prostrates the deliberate" course which Kentucky has pursued for almost a quarter of a century, "and affects its whole landed interest. The effect is to legislate for the people; to regulate the interior policy of that community, and to establish their municipal code as to real estate." [3]

If such judicial supremacy prevails, the courts can "establish systems of policy by judicial decision." What is this but despotism? "I see no difference, whether you take this power from the people and give it to your judges, who are in office for life, or grant it to a King for life." [4]

The time is overripe, asserts Johnson, to check judicial usurpation — already the National Judiciary has struck down laws of eight States.[5] The career of this judicial oligarchy must be ended. "The

---

[1] *Annals*, 17th Cong. 1st Sess. 102.
[2] *Ib*. 103.   [3] *Ib*. 104.   [4] *Ib*. 108.
[5] Georgia, Fletcher vs. Peck (see vol. III, chap. x, of this work); Pennsylvania, U.S. vs. Peters (*supra*, chap. I); New Jersey, New Jersey vs. Wilson (*supra*, chap. v); New Hampshire, Dartmouth College vs. Woodward (*supra*, chap. v); New York, Sturges vs. Crowninshield (*supra*, chap. IV); Maryland, M'Culloch vs. Maryland (*supra*, chap. VI); Virginia, Cohens vs. Virginia (*supra*, chap. VII); Kentucky, Green vs. Biddle (*supra*, this chapter).

security of our liberties demands it." Let the jurisdiction of National courts be specifically limited; or
let National judges be subject to removal upon address of both Houses of Congress; or let their com-
missions be vacated "after a limited term of service";
or, finally, "vest a controlling power in the Senate . .
or some other body who shall be responsible to the
elective franchise." [1]

The Kentucky Legislature backed its fearless
Senator; [2] but the Virginia Assembly weakened at
the end. Most of the Kentucky land titles, which the
Supreme Court's decision had protected as against
the "occupying claimants," were, of course, held
by Virginians or their assignees. Virginia conservatives, too, were beginning to realize the wisdom of
Marshall's Nationalist policy as it affected all their
interests, except slavery and tariff taxation; and
these men were becoming hesitant about further
attacks on the Supreme Court. Doubtless, also,
Marshall's friends were active among the members
of the Legislature. Roane understood the situation
when he begged friends to "jog up" the apathetic,
and bemoaned the quiescence of Jefferson and Madison. His proposed amendments were lost, though
by a very close vote. [3]

---

[1] *Annals*, 17th Cong. 1st Sess. 113.

[2] Niles, XXI, 404.

[3] *Ib.* The resolutions, offered by John Wayles Eppes, Jefferson's
son-in-law, "*instructed*" Virginia's Senators and requested her Representatives in Congress to "procure" these amendments to the Constitution:

1. The judicial power shall not extend to any power "not expressly
granted . . or *absolutely* necessary for carrying the same into execution."

2. Neither the National Government nor any department thereof

Nevertheless, the Virginia Localists carried the fight to the floors of Congress. On April 26, 1822, Andrew Stevenson, one of Roane's lieutenants and now a member of the National House, demanded the repeal of Section 25 of the Ellsworth Judiciary Act which gave the Supreme Court appellate jurisdiction over the State courts. But Stevenson was unwontedly mild. He offered his resolution "in a spirit of peace and forbearance. . . It was . . due to those States, in which the subject has been lately so much agitated, as well as to the nation, to have it . . decided." [1]

As soon as Congress convened in the winter of 1823, Senator Johnson renewed the combat; but he had become feeble, even apologetic. He did not mean to reflect "upon the conduct of the judges, for he believed them to be highly enlightened and intelligent." Nevertheless, their life tenure and irresponsibility required that some limit should be fixed to their powers. So he proposed that the membership of the Supreme Court be increased to ten, and that at least seven Justices should concur in any opinion involving the validity of National or State laws. [2]

shall have power to bind "*conclusively*" the States in conflicts between Nation and State.

3. The judicial power of the Nation shall never include "*any* case in which a State shall be a party," except controversies between States; nor cases involving the rights of a State "to which such a state shall ask to become a party."

4. No appeal to any National court shall be had from the decisions of any State court.

5. Laws applying to the District of Columbia or the Territories, which conflict with State laws, shall not be enforceable within State jurisdiction. (Niles, XXI, 404.)

[1] *Annals*, 17th Cong. 1st Sess. 1682.
[2] *Ib.*, 18th Cong. 1st Sess. 28.

Four months later, Senator Martin Van Buren reported from the Judiciary Committee, a bill "that no law of any of the States shall be rendered invalid, without the concurrence of at least five Judges of the Supreme Court; their opinions to be separately expressed." [1] But the friends of the Judiciary easily overcame the innovators; the bill was laid on the table; [2] and for that session the assault on the Supreme Court was checked. At the next session, however, Kentucky again brought the matter before Congress. Charles A. Wickliffe, a Representative from that State, proposed that writs of error from the Supreme Court be "awarded to either party," regardless of the decision of the Supreme Court of any State. [3] Webster, on the Judiciary Committee, killed Wickliffe's resolution with hardly a wave of his hand. [4]

After a reargument of Green *vs.* Biddle, lasting an entire week, [5] the Supreme Court stood to its guns and again held the Kentucky land laws unconstitutional. Yet so grave was the crisis that the decision was not handed down for a whole year. This time the opinion of the court was delivered on February 27, 1823, by Bushrod Washington, who held that the contract clause of the National Constitution was violated, but plainly considered that "the principles of law and reason" [6] were of more importance in this case than the Constitutional pro-

---

[1] *Annals*, 18th Cong. 1st Sess. 336.   [2] *Ib.* 419.   [3] *Ib.* 915.

[4] Webster, from the Judiciary Committee, which he seems to have dominated, merely reported that Wickliffe's proposed reform was "not expedient." (*Annals*, 18th Cong. 1st Sess. 1291.)

[5] March 7 to 13, 1822, inclusive.   [6] 8 Wheaton, 75.

vision. Washington's opinion displays the alarm of
the Supreme Court at the assaults upon it: "We
hold ourselves answerable to God, our consciences
and our country, to decide this question according
to the dictates of our best judgment, be the consequences of the decision what they may."[1]

Kentucky promptly replied. In his Message to
the Legislature, Governor John Adair declared that
the Kentucky decisions of the Supreme Court struck
at "the right of the people to govern themselves."
The National authority can undoubtedly employ
force to "put down insurrection," but "that . . day,
when the government shall be compelled to resort
to the bayonet to compel a state to submit to its
laws, will not long precede an event of all others to
be deprecated."[2]

One of Marshall's numerous Kentucky kinsmen,
who was an active member of the Legislature,
stoutly protested against any attack on the Supreme
Court; nevertheless he offered a resolution reciting the grievances of the State and proposing an address "to the supreme court of the United States,
in full session," against the decision and praying for
"its total and definitive reversal."[3] What! exclaimed
John Rowan, another member of the Legislature,
shall Kentucky again petition "like a degraded prov-

---

[1] 8 Wheaton, 93. Johnson dissented. (*Ib.* 94–107.) Todd of Kentucky was absent because of illness, a circumstance that greatly
worried Story, who wrote the sick Justice: "We have missed you
exceedingly during the term and particularly in the Kentucky causes.
. . We have had . . tough business" and "wanted your firm vote
on many occasions." (Story to Todd, March 24, 1823, Story, I,
422–23.)

[2] Niles, xxv, 203–05.   [3] *Ib.* 206.

ince of Rome"? [1] He proposed counter-resolutions
that the Legislature "do .. most solemnly PRO-
TEST .. against the erroneous, injurious, and de-
grading doctrines of the opinion .. in .. Green and
Biddle." [2] When modified, Rowan's resolutions,
one of which hinted at forcible resistance to the
mandate of the Supreme Court, passed by heavy
majorities. [3] Later resolutions openly threatened to
"call forth the physical power of the state, to resist
the execution of the decisions of the court," which
were "considered erroneous and unconstitutional." [4]

In the same year that the Supreme Court decided
the Kentucky land case, Justice Johnson aroused
South Carolina by a decision rendered in the United
States District Court of that State. One Henry
Elkison, a negro sailor and a British subject, was
taken by the sheriff of the Charleston district, from
the British ship Homer; and imprisoned under a
South Carolina law which directed the arrest and
confinement of any free negro on board any ship
entering the ports of that State, the negro to be
released only when the vessel departed. [5] Johnson
wrathfully declared that the "unconstitutionality
of the law .. will not bear argument" — nobody
denied that it could not be executed "without
clashing with the general powers of the United
States, to regulate commerce." Thereupon, one of
the counsel for the State said that the statute must
and would be enforced; and "that if a dissolution [sic]
of the union must be the alternative he was ready

---

[1] Niles, xxv, 205.   [2] Ib. 261.   [3] Ib. 275–76.   [4] Ib. xxix, 228–29.
[5] Ib. xxv, 12; and see Elkison vs. Deliesseline, 8 Federal Cases, 493.

to meet it" — an assertion which angered Johnson who delivered an opinion almost as strong in its Nationalism as those of Marshall.[1]

Throughout South Carolina and other slaveholding States, the action of Justice Johnson inflamed the passions of the white population. "A high state of excitement exists," chronicles Niles.[2] Marshall, of course, heard of the outcry against his associate and promptly wrote Story: "Our brother Johnson, I perceive, has hung himself on a democratic snag in a hedge composed entirely of thorny state rights in South Carolina. . . You . . could scarcely have supposed that it [Johnson's opinion] would have excited so much irritation as it seems to have produced. The subject is one of much feeling in the South. . . The decision has been considered as another act of judicial usurpation; but the sentiment has been avowed that if this be the constitution, it is better to break that instrument than submit to the principle. . . Fuel is continually adding to the fire at which *exaltées* are about to roast the judicial department."[3]

The Governor and Legislature of South Carolina fiercely maintained the law of the State — it was to them a matter of "self-preservation." Niles was distressingly alarmed. He thought that the collision of South Carolina with the National Judiciary threatened to disturb the harmony of the Republic as much as the Missouri question had done.[4]

---

[1] Niles, xxv, 13–16.   [2] *Ib.* 12; and see especially *ib.* xxvii, 242–43.

[3] Marshall to Story, Sept. 26, 1823, Story MSS. Mass. Hist. Soc.

[4] Niles, xxvii, 242. The Senate of South Carolina resolved by a vote of six to one that the duty of the State to "guard against insubordination or insurrection among our colored population . . is para-

This, then, was the situation when the Ohio Bank case reached the Supreme Court.[1] Seven States were formally in revolt against the National Judiciary, and others were hostile. Moreover, the protective Tariff of 1824 was under debate in Congress; its passage was certain, while in the South ever-growing bitterness was manifesting itself toward this plundering device of Nationalism as John Taylor branded it. In the House Southern members gave warning that the law might be forcibly resisted.[2] The first hints of Nullification were heard. Time and again Marshall's Nationalist construction of the Constitution was condemned. To the application of his theory of government was laid most of the abuses of which the South complained; most of the dangers the South apprehended.

Thus again stands out the alliance of the various forces of Localism — slavery, State banking, debtors' relief laws, opposition to protective tariffs — which confronted the Supreme Court with threats of physical resistance to its decrees and with the ability to carry out those threats.

mount to all *laws*, all *treaties*, all *constitutions* . . and will never, by this state, be renounced, compromised, controlled or participated with any power whatever."

Johnson's decision is viewed as "an unconstitutional interference" with South Carolina's slave system, and the State "will, on this subject, . . make common cause with . . other southern states similarly circumstanced in this respect." (Niles, xxvii, 264.) The House rejected the savage language of the Senate and adopted resolutions moderately worded, but expressing the same determination. (*Ib.* 292.)

[1] For the facts in Osborn *vs.* The Bank of the United States, see *supra*, 328-329.

[2] See, for instance, speech of John Carter of South Carolina. (*Annals*, 18th Cong. 1st Sess. 2097 ; and upon this subject, generally, see *infra*, chap. x.)

Two arguments were had in Osborn *vs*. The Bank
of the United States, the first by Charles Hammond
and by Henry Clay for the Bank; [1] the second by
John C. Wright, Governor Ethan Allen Brown, and
Robert Goodloe Harper, for Ohio, and by Clay,
Webster, and John Sergeant for the Bank. Arguments on both sides were notable, but little was
presented that was new. Counsel for Ohio insisted
that the court had no jurisdiction, since the State
was the real party against which the proceedings in
the United States Court in Ohio were had. Clay
made the point that the Ohio tax, unlike that of
Maryland, "was a confiscation, and not a tax. . .
Is it possible," he asked, "that . . the law of the
whole may be defeated . . by a single part?" [2]

On March 19, 1824, Marshall delivered the opinion of the court. All well-organized governments, he
begins, "must possess, within themselves, the means
of expounding, as well as enforcing, their own
laws." The makers of the Constitution kept constantly in view this great political principle. The
Judiciary Article "enables the judicial department
to receive jurisdiction to the full extent of the constitution, laws, and treaties of the United States. . .
That power is capable of acting only when the subject is submitted to it by a party who asserts his
rights in the form prescribed by law. It then becomes a case" over which the Constitution gives
jurisdiction to the National courts. "The suit of
The Bank of the United States *v*. Osborn *et al.*, is a

[1] Who appeared for Ohio on the first argument is not disclosed by
the records.
[2] 9 Wheaton, 795–96.

case, and the question is, whether it arises under a law of the United States." [1]

The fact that other questions are involved does not "withdraw a case" from the jurisdiction of the National courts; otherwise, "almost every case, although involving the construction of a [National] law, would be withdrawn; and a clause in the constitution, relating to a subject of vital importance to the government and expressed in the most comprehensive terms, would be construed to mean almost nothing."

It is true that the Constitution specifies the cases in which the Supreme Court shall have original jurisdiction, but nowhere in the Constitution is there any "prohibition" against Congress giving the inferior National courts original jurisdiction; such a restriction is not "insinuated." Congress, then, can give the National Circuit Courts "original jurisdiction, in any case to which the appellate jurisdiction [of the Supreme Court] extends." [2]

At this particular period of our history this was, indeed, a tremendous expansion of the power of Congress and the National Judiciary. Marshall flatly declares that Congress can invest the inferior National courts with any jurisdiction whatsoever which the Constitution does not prohibit. It marks another stage in the development of his Constitutional principle that the National Government not only has all powers expressly granted, but also all powers not expressly prohibited. For that is just what Marshall's reasoning amounts to during these crucial years.

[1] 9 Wheaton, 818–19.   [2] *Ib.* 819–21.

No matter, continues the Chief Justice, how
many questions, other than that affecting the
Constitution or laws, are involved in a case; if
any National question "forms an ingredient of the
original cause," Congress can "give the circuit
courts jurisdiction of that cause." The Ohio Bank
case "is of this description." All the Bank's powers,
functions, and duties are conferred or imposed by
its charter, and "that charter is a law of the United
States. . . Can a being, thus constituted, have a
case which does not arise literally, as well as substantially, under the law?" [1]

If the Bank brings suits on a contract, the very
first, the "foundation" question is, "has this legal
entity a right to sue? . . This depends on a law of
the United States" — a fact that can never be
waived. "Whether it be in fact relied on or not, in
the defense, it is still a part of the cause, and may be
relied on." [2] Assume, as counsel for Ohio assert, that
"the case arises on the contract"; still, "the validity
of the contract depends on a law of the United
States. . . The case arises emphatically under the
law. The act of Congress is its foundation. . . The
act itself is the first ingredient in the case; is its origin; is that from which every other part arises." [3]

Marshall concedes that the State is directly interested in the suit and that, if the Bank could have
done so, it ought to have made the State a party.
"But this was not in the power of the bank," because the Eleventh Amendment exempts a State
from being sued in such a case. So the "very diffi-

[1] 9 Wheaton, 823.   [2] Ib. 823–24.   [3] Ib. 824–25.

cult question" arises, "whether, in such a case, the
court may act upon the agents employed by the
state, and on the property in their hands." [1]

Just what will be the result if the National courts
have not this power? "A denial of jurisdiction forbids all inquiry into the nature of the case," even of
"cases perfectly clear in themselves; . . where the
government is in the exercise of its best-established
and most essential powers." If the National courts
have no jurisdiction over the agents of a State, then
those agents, under the "authority of a [State] law
void in itself, because repugnant to the constitution, may arrest the execution of any law in the
United States" — this they may do without any to
say them nay. [2]

In this fashion Marshall leads up to the serious
National problem of the hour — the disposition of
some States, revealed by threats and sometimes
carried into execution, to interfere with the officers
of the National Government in the execution of
the Nation's laws. According to the Ohio-Virginia-
Kentucky idea, those officers "can obtain no protection from the judicial department of the government. The carrier of the mail, the collector of the
revenue,[3] the marshal of a district, the recruiting officer, may all be inhibited, under ruinous penalties,
from the performance of their respective duties";
and not one of them can "avail himself of the preventive justice of the nation to protect him in the
performance of his duties." [4]

[1] 9 Wheaton, 846–47.   [2] *Ib.* 847.
[3] Marshall here refers to threats to resist forcibly the execution of
the Tariff of 1824. See *infra,* 535–36.   [4] 9 Wheaton, 847–48.

Addressing himself still more directly to those
who were flouting the authority of the Nation and
preaching resistance to it, Marshall uses stern
language. What is the real meaning of the anti-
National crusade; what the certain outcome of it?
"Each member of the Union is capable, at its will,
of attacking the nation, of arresting its progress at
every step, of acting vigorously and effectually in
the execution of its designs, while the nation stands
naked, stripped of its defensive armor, and incapable of shielding its agent or executing its laws,
otherwise than by proceedings which are to take
place after the mischief is perpetrated, and which
must often be ineffectual, from the inability of the
agents to make compensation."

Once more Marshall cites the case of a State "penalty on a revenue officer, for performing his duty,"
and in this way warns those who are demanding forcible obstruction of National law or authority, that
they are striking at the Nation and that the tribunals
of the Nation will shield the agents and officers of the
Nation: "If the courts of the United States cannot
rightfully protect the agents who execute every law
authorized by the constitution, from the direct action
of state agents in the collecting of penalties, they cannot rightfully protect those who execute any law." [1]

Here, in judicial language, was that rebuke of the
spirit of Nullification which Andrew Jackson was soon
to repeat in words that rang throughout the land and
which still quicken the pulses of Americans. What is the
great question before the court in the case of Osborn

[1] 9 Wheaton, 848–49.

vs. The Bank of the United States; what, indeed, the great question before the country in the controversy between recalcitrant States and the imperiled Nation? It is, says Marshall, "whether the constitution of the United States has provided a tribunal which can peacefully and rightfully protect those who are employed in carrying into execution the laws of the Union, from the attempts of a particular state to resist the execution of those laws."

Ohio asserts that "no preventive proceedings whatever," no action even to stay the hand of a State agent from seizing property, no suit to recover it from that agent, can be maintained because it is brought "substantially against the State itself, in violation of the 11th amendment of the constitution." Is this true? "Is a suit, brought against an individual, for any cause whatever, a suit against a state, in the sense of the constitution?" [1] There are many cases in which a State may be vitally interested, as, for example, those involving grants of land by different States.

If the mere fact that the State is "interested" in, or affected by, a suit makes the State a party, "what rule has the constitution given, by which this interest is to be measured?" No rule, of course! Is then the court to decide the *degree* of "interest" necessary to make a State a party? Absurd! since the court would have to examine the "whole testimony of a cause, inquiring into, and deciding on, the extent of a State's interest, without having a right to exercise any jurisdiction in the case." [2]

[1] 9 Wheaton, 849.   [2] *Ib.* 852-53.

At last he affirms that it may be "laid down as a
rule which admits of no exception, that, in all cases
where jurisdiction depends on the party, it is the
party *named in the record*." Therefore, the Eleventh
Amendment is, "of necessity, limited to those suits
in which a state is a party *on the record*." [1] In the
Ohio Bank case, it follows that, "the state not being
a party on the record, and the court having jurisdiction over those who are parties on the record, the
true question is, not one of jurisdiction, but whether "
the officers and agents of Ohio are "only nominal
parties " or whether "the court ought to make a decree " against them.[2] The answer to this question
depends on the constitutionality of the Ohio tax law.
Although that exact point was decided in M'Culloch
vs. Maryland,[3] "a revision of that opinion has been
requested; and many considerations combine to induce a review of it." [4]

Maryland and Ohio claim the right to tax the
National Bank as an "individual concern . . having
private trade and private profit for its great end and
principal object." But this is not true; the Bank is
a "public corporation, created for public and national purposes"; the fact that it transacts "private
as well as public business" does not destroy its character as the "great instrument by which the fiscal
operations of the government are effected." [5] Obviously the Bank cannot live unless it can do a general business as authorized by its charter. This being
so, the right to transact such business "is necessary

[1] 9 Wheaton, 857. (Italics the author's.)   [2] *Ib.* 858.
[3] See *supra*, chap. vi.   [4] 9 Wheaton, 859.   [5] *Ib.* 859–60.

to the legitimate operations of the government, and was constitutionally and rightfully engrafted on the institution." Indeed, the power of the Bank to engage in general banking is "the vital part of the corporation; it is its soul." As well say that, while the human body must not be touched, the "vivifying principle" which "animates" it may be destroyed, as to say that the Bank shall not be annihilated, but that the faculty by which it exists may be extinguished.

For a State, then, to tax the Bank's "faculties, its trade and occupation, is to tax the Bank itself. To destroy or preserve the one, is to destroy or preserve the other." [1] The mere fact that the National Government created this corporation does not relieve it from "state authority"; but the "operations" of the Bank "give its value to the currency in which all the transactions of the government are conducted." In short, the Bank's business is "inseparably connected" with the "transactions" of the Government. "Its corporate character is merely an incident, which enables it to transact that business more beneficially." [2]

The Judiciary "has no will, in any case" — no option but to execute the law as it stands. "Judicial power, as contradistinguished from the power of the laws, has no existence. Courts are the mere instruments of the law, and can will nothing." They can exercise no "discretion," except that of "discerning the course prescribed by law; and, when that is discerned, it is the duty of the court to follow it.

[1] 9 Wheaton, 861-62.   [2] *Ib.* 862-63.

Judicial power is never exercised for the purpose
of giving effect to the will of the judge; always for
the purpose of giving effect to the will of the legislature." [1] This passage, so wholly unnecessary to
the decision of the case or reasoning of the opinion,
was inserted as an answer to the charges of judicial
"arrogance" and "usurpation."

In conclusion, Marshall holds that the Ohio law
taxing the National Bank's branches is unconstitutional and void; that the State is not a "party on the
record"; that Osborn, Harper, Currie, and Sullivan
are "incontestably liable for the full amount of the
money taken out of the Bank"; that this money may
be pursued, since it "remained a distinct deposit" —
in fact, was "kept untouched, in a trunk, by itself,
. . to await the event of the pending suit respecting it." [2] The judgment of the lower court that the
money must be restored to the Bank was right; but
the judgment was wrong in charging interest against
the State officers, since they "were restrained by
the authority of the Circuit Court from using" the
money, taken and held by them. [3]

So everybody having an immediate personal and
practical interest in that particular case was made
happy, and only the State Rights theorists were dis-
comfited. It was an exceedingly human situation,
such as Marshall, the politician, managed to create
in his disposition of those cases that called for his
highest judicial statesmanship. No matter how
acutely he irritated party leaders and forced upon
them unwelcome issues, Marshall contrived to sat-

[1] 9 Wheaton, 866.   [2] *Ib.* 868–69.   [3] *Ib.* 871.

isfy the persons immediately interested in most of the cases he decided.

The Chief Justice himself was a theorist — one of the greatest theorists America has produced; but he also had an intimate acquaintance with human nature, and this knowledge he rightly used, in the desperate conflicts waged by him, to leave his antagonists disarmed of those weapons with which they were wont to fight.

Seemingly Justice Johnson dissented; but, burning with anger at South Carolina's defiance of his action in the negro sailor case, he strengthened Marshall's opinion in his very "dissent." This is so conspicuously true that it may well be thought that Marshall inspired Johnson's "disagreement" with his six brethren of the Supreme Court. Whether the decision was "necessary or unnecessary originally," begins Johnson, " a *state of things has now grown up, in some of the states*, which renders all the protection necessary, that the general government can give to this bank." [1] He makes a powerful and really stirring appeal for the Bank, but finally concludes, on technical grounds, that the Supreme Court has no jurisdiction.[2]

Immediately the fight upon the Supreme Court was renewed in Congress. On May 3, 1824, Representative Robert P. Letcher of Kentucky rose in the House and proposed that the Supreme Court should be forbidden by law to hold invalid any provision

---

[1] 9 Wheaton, 871–72. (Italics the author's.) In reality Johnson is here referring to the threats of physical resistance to the proposed tariff law of 1824. (See *infra*, chap. x.)

[2] *Ib.* 875–903.

of a State constitution or statute unless five out of the seven Justices concurred, each to give his opinion "separately and distinctly," if the court held against the State.[1] Kentucky, said Letcher, had been deprived of "equal rights and privileges." How? By "*construction*. . . Yes, construction! Its mighty powers are irresistible; . . it creates new principles; . . it destroys laws long since established; and it is daily acquiring new strength."[2] John Forsyth of Georgia proposed as a substitute to Letcher's resolutions that, for the transaction of business, "a majority of the quorum" of the Supreme Court "shall be a majority of the whole court, including the Chief Justice." A long and animated debate[3] ensued in which Clay, Webster, Randolph, and Philip P. Barbour, among others, took part.

David Trimble of Kentucky declared that "no nation ought to submit, to an umpire of minorities.[4] . . If less than three-fourths of the States cannot amend the Constitution, less than three-fourths of the judges ought not to construe it" — for judicial constructions are "explanatory amendments" by which "the person and property of every citizen must stand or fall."[5]

So strong had been the sentiment for placing some restraint on the National Judiciary that Webster,

[1] *Annals*, 18th Cong. 1st Sess. 2514.   [2] *Ib.* 2519–20.

[3] *Ib.* 2527. This debate was most scantily reported. Webster wrote of it: "We had the Supreme Court before us yesterday. . . A debate arose which lasted all day. Cohens *v.* Virginia, Green and Biddle, &c. were all discussed. . . The proposition for the concurrence of five judges will not prevail." (Webster to Story, May 4, 1824, *Priv. Corres.*: Webster, I, 350.)

[4] *Annals*, 18th Cong. 1st Sess. 2538.   [5] *Ib.* 2539.

astute politician and most resourceful friend of the
Supreme Court, immediately offered a resolution
that, in any cause before the Supreme Court where
the validity of a State law or Constitution is drawn
in question "on the ground of repugnancy to the
Constitution, treaties, or laws, of the United States,
no judgment shall be pronounced or rendered until
a majority of all the justices . . legally competent
to sit, . . shall concur in the opinion." [1]

But Marshall's opinion in Gibbons *vs*. Ogden [2]
had now reached the whole country and, for the time
being, changed popular hostility to the Supreme
Court into public favor toward it. The assault in
Congress died away and Webster allowed his soothing resolution to be forgotten. When the attack on
the National Judiciary was again renewed, the language of its adversaries was almost apologetic.

[1] *Annals*, 18th Cong. 1st Sess. 2541.
Throughout this session Webster appears to have been much dis-
turbed. For example, as early as April 10, 1824, he writes Story:
"I am exhausted. When I look in the glass, I think of our old New
England saying, 'As thin as a shad.' I have not vigor enough left,
either mental or physical, to try an action for assault and battery.
. . I shall call up some bills reported by our [Judiciary] committee. . .
The gentlemen of the West will propose a clause, requiring the assent
of a majority of all the judges to a judgment, which pronounces a
state law void, as being in violation of the constitution or laws of the
United States. Do you see any great evil in such a provision? Judge
Todd told me he thought it would give great satisfaction in the West.
In what phraseology would you make such a provision?" (Webster to
Story, April 10, 1824, *Priv. Corres.*: Webster, I, 348-49.)
[2] See next chapter.

CHAPTER VIII

COMMERCE MADE FREE

Marshall's decision involved in its consequences the existence of the Union.
(John F. Dillon.)

Opposing rights to the same thing cannot exist under the Constitution of our country. (Chancellor Nathan Sanford.)

Sir, we shall keep on the windward side of treason, but we must combine to resist these encroachments, — and that effectually. (John Randolph.)

That uncommon man who presides over the Supreme Court is, in all human probability, the ablest Judge now sitting on any judicial bench in the world.
(Martin Van Buren.)

AT six o'clock in the evening of August 9, 1803, a curious assembly of curious people was gathered at a certain spot on the banks of the Seine in Paris. They were gazing at a strange object on the river— the model of an invention which was to affect the destinies of the world more powerfully and permanently than the victories and defeats of all the armies that, for a dozen years thereafter, fought over the ancient battle-fields of Europe from Moscow to Madrid. The occasion was the first public exhibition of Robert Fulton's steamboat.

France was once more gathering her strength for the war which, in May, Great Britain had declared upon her; and Bonaparte, as First Consul, was in camp at Boulogne. Fulton had been experimenting for a long time, and the public exhibition now in progress would have been made months earlier had not an accident delayed it. His activities had been reported to Bonaparte, who promptly ordered members of the Institute [1] to attend the exhibition and report to him on the practicability of the invention, which,

[1] Institut national des sciences et des arts.

he wrote, and in italics, "*may change the face of the world.*" [1] Prominent, therefore, among the throng were these learned men, doubting and skeptical as mere learning usually is.

More conspicuous than Bonaparte's scientific agents, and as interested and confident as they were indifferent or scornful, was a tall man of distinguished bearing, whose powerful features, bold eyes, aggressive chin, and acquisitive nose indicated a character of unyielding determination, persistence, and hopefulness. This was the American Minister to France, Robert R. Livingston of New York, who, three months before, had conducted the Louisiana Purchase. By his side was Fulton himself, a man of medium height, slender and erect, whose intellectual brow and large, speculative eyes indicated the dreamer and contriver.

The French scientists were not impressed, and the French Government dropped consideration of the subject. But Fulton and Livingston were greatly encouraged. An engine designed by Fulton was ordered from a Birmingham manufacturer and, when constructed, was shipped to America.

For many years inventive minds had been at work on the problem of steam navigation. Because of the cost and difficulties of transportation, and the ever-growing demand for means of cheap and easy water carriage, the most active and fruitful efforts to solve the problem had been made in America. [2] Livingston,

---

[1] Dickinson: *Robert Fulton, Engineer and Artist,* 156–57; also see Thurston: *Robert Fulton,* 113.

[2] See Dickinson, 126–32; also Knox: *Life of Robert Fulton,* 72–86; and Fletcher: *Steam-Ships,* 19–24.

then Chancellor of New York, had taken a deep and practical interest in the subject.[1] He had constructed a boat on the Hudson, and was so confident of success that, five years before the Paris experiments of Fulton, he had procured from the New York Legislature an act giving him the exclusive right for twenty years to navigate by steamboats the streams and other waters of the State, provided that, within a year, he should build a boat making four miles an hour against the current of the Hudson.[2] The only difficulty Livingston encountered in securing the passage of this act was the amused incredulity of the legislators. The bill "was a standing subject of ridicule" and had to run the gamut of jokes, jeers, and raillery.[3] The legislators did not object to granting a monopoly on New York waters for a century or for a thousand years,[4] provided the navigation was by steam; but they required, in payment to themselves, the price of derision and laughter.

[1] Dickinson, 134–35; Knox, 90–93.

[2] Act of March 27, 1798, *Laws of New York, 1798*, 382–83. This act, however, was merely the transfer of similar privileges granted to John Fitch on March 19, 1787, to whom, rather than to Robert Fulton, belongs the honor of having invented the steamboat. It was printed in the *Laws of New York* edited by Thomas Greenleaf, published in 1792, i, 411; and also appears as Appendix A to "A Letter, addressed to Cadwallader D. Colden, Esquire," by William Alexander Duer, the first biographer of Fulton. (Albany, 1817.) Duer's pamphlet is uncommonly valuable because it contains all the petitions to, and the acts of, the New York Legislature concerning the steamboat monopoly.

[3] Reigart: *Life of Robert Fulton*, 163. Nobody but Livingston was willing to invest in what all bankers and business men considered a crazy enterprise. (*Ib.* 100–01.)

[4] Knox, 93. It should be remembered, however, that the granting of monopolies was a very common practice everywhere during this period. (See Prentice: *Federal Power over Carriers and Corporations*, 60–65.)

Livingston failed to meet in time the conditions of the steamboat act, but, with Livingston tenacity,[1] persevered in his efforts to build a practicable vessel. When, in 1801, he arrived in Paris as American Minister, his mind was almost as full of the project as of his delicate and serious official tasks.

Robert Fulton was then living in the French Capital, working on his models of steamboats, submarines, and torpedoes, and striving to interest Napoleon in his inventions.[2] Livingston and Fulton soon met; a mutual admiration, trust, and friendship followed and a partnership was formed.[3] Livingston had left his interests in the hands of an alert and capable agent, Nicholas J. Roosevelt, who, in 1803, had no difficulty in securing from the now hilarious New York Legislature an extension of Livingston's monopoly for twenty years upon the same terms as the first.[4] Livingston resigned his office and returned home. Within a year Fulton joined his partner.

The grant of 1803 was forfeited like the preceding one, because its conditions had not been complied with in time, and another act was passed by the Legislature reviving the grant and extending it for two years.[5] Thus encouraged and secured, Fulton and Livingston put forth every effort, and on Monday, August 17, 1807, four years and eight days after the dramatic exhibition on the river Seine in Paris,

[1] Compare with his brother's persistence in the Batture controversy, *supra*, 100–15.

[2] Dickinson, 64–123; Knox, 35–44.

[3] Knox, 93; see also Dickinson, 136.

[4] Act of April 5, 1803, *Laws of New York, 1802–04*, 323–24.

[5] Act of April 6, 1807, *Laws of New York, 1807–09*, 213–14.

the North River,[1] the first successful steamboat, made her voyage up the Hudson from New York to Albany[2] and the success of the great enterprise was assured.

On April 11, 1808, a final law was enacted by the New York Legislature. The period of ridicule had passed; the members of that body now voted with serious knowledge of the possibilities of steam navigation. The new act provided that, for each new boat "established" on New York waters by Livingston and Fulton and their associates, they should be "entitled to five years prolongation of their grant *or contract* with this state," the "whole term" of their monopoly not to exceed thirty years. All other persons were forbidden to navigate New York waters by steam craft without a license from Livingston and Fulton; and any unlicensed vessel, "together with the engine, tackle and apparel thereof," should be forfeited to them.[3]

Obedient to "the great god, Success," the public became as enthusiastic and friendly as it had been frigid and hostile and eagerly patronized this pleasant, cheap, and expeditious method of travel. The profits quickly justified the faith and perseverance of Livingston and Fulton. Soon three boats were running between New York and Albany. The fare each way was seven dollars and proportionate charges were made for intermediate landings, of which there

[1] The North River was afterward named the Clermont, which was the name of Livingston's county seat. (Dickinson, 230.)

[2] The country people along the Hudson thought the steamboat a sea monster or else a sign of the end of the world. (Knox, 110–11.)

[3] Act of April 11, 1808, *Laws of New York, 1807–09*, 407–08. (Italics the author's.)

were eleven.[1] Immediately the monopoly began operating steam ferryboats between New York City and
New Jersey.[2] Having such solid reason for optimism,
Livingston and Fulton, with prudent foresight,
leaped half a continent and placed steamboats on
the Mississippi, the traffic of which they planned to
control by securing from the Legislature of Orleans
Territory the same exclusive privileges for steam
navigation upon Louisiana waters, which included
the mouth of the Mississippi,[3] that New York had
granted upon the waters of that State. Nicholas J.
Roosevelt was put in charge of this enterprise, and
in an incredibly short time the steamboat New
Orleans was ploughing the turgid and treacherous
currents of the great river.[4]

[1] Dickinson, 233–34.

[2] *Ib.* 234–36. The thoroughfare in New York, at the foot of
which these boats landed, was thereafter named Fulton Street. (*Ib.*
236.)

[3] See *infra*, 414.

[4] Dickinson, 230. From the first Roosevelt had been associated
with Livingston in steamboat experiments. He had constructed the
engine for the craft with which Livingston tried to fulfill the conditions
of the first New York grant to him in 1798. Roosevelt was himself
an inventor, and to him belongs the idea of the vertical wheel for propelling steamboats which Fulton afterward adopted with success.
(See J. H. B. Latrobe, in *Maryland Historical Society Fund-Publication,*
No. 5, 13–14.)

Roosevelt was also a manufacturer and made contracts with the
Government for rolled and drawn copper to be used in war-vessels.
The Government failed to carry out its agreement, and Roosevelt became badly embarrassed financially. In this situation he entered into
an arrangement with Livingston and Fulton that if the report he was to
make to them should be favorable, he was to have one third interest
in the steamboat enterprise on the Western waters, while Livingston
and Fulton were to supply the funds.

The story of his investigations and experiments on the Ohio and
Mississippi glows with romance. Although forty-six years old, he had
but recently married and took his bride with him on this memorable

It was not long, however, before troubles came —
the first from New Jersey. Enterprising citizens of

journey. At Pittsburgh he built a flatboat and on this the newly
wedded couple floated to New Orleans; the trip, with the long and
numerous stops to gather information concerning trade, transportation, the volume and velocity of various streams, requiring six months'
time.

Before proceeding far Roosevelt became certain of success. Dis-
covering coal on the banks of the Ohio, he bought mines, set men at
work in them, and stored coal for the steamer he felt sure would be
built. His expectation was justified and, returning to New York from
New Orleans, he readily convinced Livingston and Fulton of the
practicability of the enterprise and was authorized to go back to Pittsburgh to construct a steamboat, the design of which was made by
Fulton. By the summer of 1811 the vessel was finished. It cost
$38,000 and was named the New Orleans.

Late in September, 1811, the long voyage to New Orleans was begun, the only passengers being Roosevelt and his wife. A great crowd
cheered them as the boat set out from Pittsburgh. At Cincinnati the
whole population greeted the arrival of this extraordinary craft. Mr.
and Mrs. Roosevelt were given a dinner at Louisville, where, however, all declared that while the boat could go down the river, it never
could ascend. Roosevelt invited the banqueters to dine with him on
the New Orleans the next night and while toasts were being drunk
and hilarity prevailed, the vessel was got under way and swiftly proceeded upstream, thus convincing the doubters of the power of the
steamboat.

From Louisville onward the voyage was thrilling. The earthquake
of 1811 came just after the New Orleans passed Louisville and this
changed the river channels. At another time the boat took fire and
was saved with difficulty. Along the shore the inhabitants were torn
between terror of the earthquake and fright at this monster of the
waters. The crew had to contend with snags, shoals, sandbars, and
other obstructions. Finally Natchez was reached and here thousands of people gathered on the bluffs to witness this triumph of
science.

At last the vessel arrived at New Orleans and the first steamboat
voyage on the Ohio and Mississippi was an accomplished fact. The
experiment, which began two years before with the flatboat voyage of
a bride and groom, ended at the metropolis of the Southwest in the
marriage of the steamboat captain to Mrs. Roosevelt's maid, with
whom he had fallen in love during this thrilling and historic voyage.
(See Latrobe, in *Md. Hist. Soc. Fund-Pub.* No. 6. A good summary
of Latrobe's narrative is given in Preble: *Chronological History of the
Origin and Development of Steam Navigation*, 77–81.)

that State also built steamboats; but the owners of any vessel entering New York waters, even though acting merely as a ferry between Hoboken and New York City, must procure a license from Livingston and Fulton or forfeit their boats. From discontent at this condition the feelings of the people rose to resentment and then to anger. At last they determined to retaliate, and early in 1811 the New Jersey Legislature passed an act authorizing the owner of any boat seized under the New York law, in turn to capture and hold any steam-propelled craft belonging "in part or in whole" to any citizen of New York; "which boat . . shall be forfeited . . to the . . owner . . of such . . boats which may have been seized" under the New York law.[1]

New York was not slow to reply. Her Legislature was in session when that of New Jersey thus declared commercial war. An act was speedily passed providing that Livingston and Fulton might enforce at law or in equity the forfeiture of boats unlicensed by them, "as if the same had been tortiously and wrongfully taken out of their possession"; and that when such a suit was brought the defendants should be enjoined from running the boat or "removing the same or any part thereof out of the jurisdiction of the court." [2]

Connecticut forbade any vessel licensed by Livingston and Fulton from entering Connecticut waters.[3] The opposition to the New York steamboat monopoly was not, however, confined to other

---

[1] Act of Jan. 25, 1811, *Acts of New Jersey, 1811,* 298–99.
[2] Act of April 9, 1811, *Laws of New York, 1811,* 368–70.
[3] *Laws of Connecticut,* May Sess. 1822, chap. xxviii.

States. Citizens of New York defied it and began to run steam vessels on the Hudson.[1] James Van Ingen and associates were the first thus to challenge the exclusive "contract," as the New York law termed the franchise which the State had granted to Livingston and Fulton. Suit was brought against Van Ingen in the United States Circuit Court in New York, praying that Livingston and Fulton be "quieted in the possession," or in the exclusive right, to navigate the Hudson secured to them by two patents.[2] The bill was dismissed for want of jurisdiction. Thus far the litigation was exclusively a State controversy. Upon the face of the record the National element did not appear; yet it was the governing issue raised by the dispute.

Immediately Livingston and Fulton sued Van Ingen and associates in the New York Court of Chancery, praying that they be enjoined from operating their boats. In an opinion of great ability and almost meticulous learning, Chancellor John Lansing denied the injunction; he was careful, however, not to base his decision on a violation of the commerce clause of the National Constitution by the New York steamboat monopoly act. He merely held that act to be invalid because it was a denial of a natural right of all citizens alike to the free navigation of the waters of the State. In such fashion the National question was still evaded.

[1] Dickinson, 244.

[2] Livingston *et al.* *vs.* Van Ingen *et al.*, 1 Paine, 45–46. Brockholst Livingston, Associate Justice of the Supreme Court, sat in this case with William P. Van Ness (the friend and partisan of Burr), and delivered the opinion.

The Court of Errors[1] reversed the decree of Chancellor Lansing. Justice Yates and Justice Thompson delivered State Rights opinions that would have done credit to Roane.[2] At this point the National consideration develops. The opinion of James Kent, then Chief Justice, was more moderate in its denial of National power over the subject. Indeed, Kent appears to have anticipated that the Supreme Court would reverse him. Nevertheless, his opinion was the source of all the arguments thereafter used in defense of the steamboat monopoly. Because of this fact; because of Kent's eminence as a jurist; and because Marshall so crushingly answered his arguments, a *précis* of them must be given. It should be borne in mind that Kent was defending a law which, in a sense, was his own child; as a member of the New York Council of Revision, he had passed upon and approved it before its passage.

There could have been "no very obvious constitutional objection" to the steamboat monopoly act, began Kent, "or it would not so repeatedly have escaped the notice of the several branches of the government[3] when these acts were under consideration."[4] There had been five acts all told;[5] that of 1798 would surely have attracted attention since it

[1] The full title of this tribunal was the "Court for the Trial of Impeachments and the Correction of Errors." It was the court of last resort, appeals lying to it from the Supreme Court of Judicature and from the Court of Chancery. It consisted of the Justices of the Supreme Court of Judicature and a number of State Senators. A more absurdly constituted court cannot well be imagined.

[2] 9 Johnson, 558, 563.

[3] The State Senate, House, Council of Revision, and Governor.

[4] 9 Johnson, 572.

[5] Those enacted in 1798, 1803, 1807, 1808, and 1811.

was the first to be passed on the subject after the National Constitution was adopted. It amounted to "a legislative exposition" of State powers under the new National Government.

Members of the New York Legislature of 1798 had also been members of the State Convention that ratified the Constitution, and "were masters of all the critical discussions" attending the adoption of that instrument. This was peculiarly true of that "exalted character," John Jay, who was Governor at that time; and "who was distinguished, as well in the *council of revision*, as elsewhere, for the scrupulous care and profound attention with which he examined every question of a constitutional nature." [1] The Act of 1811 was passed after the validity of the previous ones had been challenged and "was, therefore, equivalent to a declaratory opinion of high authority, that the former laws were valid and constitutional." [2]

The people of New York had not "alienated" to the National Government the power to grant exclusive privileges. This was proved by the charters granted by the State to banks, ferries, markets, canal and bridge companies. "The legislative power in a *single, independent government*, extends to every proper object of power, and is limited only by its own constitutional provisions, or by the fundamental principles of all government, and the unalienable rights of mankind." [3] In what respect did the steamboat monopoly violate any of these restrictions? In

[1] 9 Johnson, 573. Jay as Governor was Chairman of the Council of Revision, of which Kent was a member.
[2] *Ib.* 572.   [3] *Ib.* 573. (Italics the author's.)

no respect. "It interfered with no man's property."
Everybody could freely use the waters of New York
in the same manner that he had done before. So
there was "no violation of first principles." [1]

Neither did the New York steamboat acts violate
the National Constitution. State and Nation are
"supreme within their respective constitutional
spheres." It is true that when National and State
laws "come directly in contact, as when they are
aimed at each other," those of the State "must
yield"; but State Legislatures cannot all the time
be on the watch for some possible future collision.
The only "safe rule of construction" is this: "If any
given power was originally vested in this State, if it
has not been exclusively ceded to Congress, or if the
exercise of it has not been prohibited to the States,
we may then go on in the exercise of the power until
it comes practically in collision with the actual exercise of some congressional power." [2]

The power given Congress to regulate commerce is
not, "in express terms, exclusive, and the only prohibition upon the States" in this regard concerns the
making of treaties and the laying of tonnage import or export duties. All commerce within a State
is "exclusively" within the power of that State.[3]
Therefore, New York's steamboat grant to Livingston and Fulton is valid. It conflicts with no act of
Congress, according to Kent, who cannot "perceive
any power which . . can lawfully carry to that extent." If Congress has any control whatever over

---

[1] 9 Johnson, 574.   [2] *Ib.* 575–76.
[3] *Ib.* 577–78.

New York waters, it is concurrent with that of the State, and even then, "no further than may be incidental and requisite to the due regulation of commerce between the States, and with foreign nations." [1]

Kent then plunges into an appalling mass of authorities, in dealing with which he delighted as much as Marshall recoiled from the thought of them. [2] So Livingston and Fulton's steamboat monopoly was upheld. [3]

But what were New York waters and what were New Jersey waters? Confusion upon this question threatened to prevent the monopoly from gathering fat profits from New Jersey traffic. Aaron Ogden, [4] who had purchased the privilege of running ferry-boats from New York to certain points on the New Jersey shore, combined with one Thomas Gibbons, who operated a boat between New Jersey landings, to exchange passengers at Elizabethtown Point in the latter State. Gibbons had not secured the per-

[1] 9 Johnson, 578, 580.   [2] *Ib.* 582–88.

[3] All the Senators concurred except two, Lewis and Townsend, who declined giving opinions because of relationship with the parties to the action. (*Ib.* 589.)

[4] Ogden protested against the Livingston-Fulton steamboat monopoly in a Memorial to the New York Legislature. (See Duer, 94–97.) A committee was appointed and reported the facts as Ogden stated them; but concluded that, since New York had granted exclusive steamboat privileges to Livingston, "the honor of the State requires that its faith should be preserved." However, said the committee, the Livingston-Fulton boats "are in substance the invention of John Fitch," to whom the original monopoly was granted, after the expiration of which "the right to use" steamboats "became common to all the citizens of the United States." Moreover, the statements upon which rested the Livingston monopoly of 1798 "were not true in fact," Fitch having forestalled the claims of the Livingston pretensions. (*Ib.* 103–04.)

mission of the New York steamboat monopoly to navigate New York waters. By his partnership with Ogden he, in reality, carried passengers from New York to various points in New Jersey. In fact, Ogden and Gibbons had a common traffic agent in New York who booked passengers for routes, to travel which required the service of the boats of both Ogden and Gibbons.

So ran the allegations of the bill for an injunction against the offending carriers filed in the New York Court of Chancery by the steamboat monopoly in the spring of 1819. Ogden answered that his license applied only to waters "*exclusively* within the state of *New-York*," and that the waters lying between the New Jersey ports "are within the jurisdiction of *New Jersey*." Gibbons admitted that he ran a boat between New Jersey ports under "a coasting *license*" from the National Government. He denied, however, that the monopoly had "any exclusive right" to run steamboats from New York to New Jersey. Both Ogden and Gibbons disclaimed that they ran boats in combination, or by agreement with each other.[1]

Kent, now Chancellor, declared that a New York statute [2] asserted jurisdiction of the State over "the whole of the river Hudson, southward of the northern boundary of the city of New-York, and the whole of the bay between Staten Island and Long or Nassau Island." He refused to enjoin Ogden because he

[1] 4 Johnson's *Chancery Reports*, 50–51. The reader must not confuse the two series of Reports by Johnson; one contains the decisions of the Court of Errors; the other, those of the Court of Chancery.

[2] Act of April 6, 1808, *Laws of New York, 1807–09*, 313–15.

operated his boat under license of the steamboat
monopoly; but did enjoin Gibbons "from navigating the waters in the bay of New-York, or Hudson
river, between Staten Island and Powles Hook." [1]

Ogden was content, but Gibbons, thoroughly angered by the harshness of the steamboat monopoly
and by the decree of Chancellor Kent, began to run
boats regularly between New York and New Jersey in
direct competition with Ogden.[2] To stop his former
associate, now his rival, Ogden applied to Chancellor
Kent for an injunction. As in the preceding case,
Gibbons again set up his license from the National
Government, asserting that by virtue of this license
he was entitled to run his boats "in the coasting
trade between ports of the same state, or of different
states," and could not be excluded from such traffic
"by any law or grant of any particular state, on any
pretence to an exclusive right to navigate the waters
of any particular state by steam-boats." Moreover,
pleaded Gibbons, the representatives of Livingston
and Fulton had issued to Messrs. D. D. Tompkins,
Adam Brown, and Noah Brown a license to navigate
New York Bay; and this license had been assigned
to Gibbons.[3]

Kent held that the act of Congress,[4] concerning
the enrollment and licensing of vessels for the coasting trade, conferred no right "incompatible with an
exclusive right in Livingston and Fulton" to navigate New York waters.[5] The validity of the steam-

[1] 4 Johnson's *Chancery Reports*, 51, 53.
[2] *Ib.* 152.   [3] *Ib.* 154.
[4] Act of Feb. 18, 1793, *U.S. Statutes at Large*, i, 305–18.
[5] 4 Johnson's *Chancery Reports*, 156.

boat monopoly laws had been settled by the decision
of the Court of Errors in Livingston *vs.* Van Ingen.[1]
If a National law gave to all vessels, "duly licensed"
by the National Government, the right to navigate
all waters "within the several states," despite State
laws to the contrary, the National statute would
"overrule and set aside" the incompatible legislation of the States. "The only question that could
arise in such a case, would be, whether the [Na-
tional] law was constitutional." But that was not
the situation; "there is no collision between the act
of Congress and the acts of this State, creating the
steam-boat monopoly." At least "some judicial decision of the supreme power of the Union, acting
upon those laws, in direct collision and conflict" with
them, is necessary before the courts of New York
"can retire from the support and defence of them."[2]

Undismayed, Gibbons lost no time in appealing to
the New York Court of Errors, and in January, 1820,
Justice Jonas Platt delivered the opinion of that tribunal. Immediately after the decision in Livingston
vs. Van Ingen, he said, many, who formerly had resisted the steamboat monopoly law, acquiesced in
the judgment of the State's highest court and secured
licenses from Livingston and Fulton. Ogden was one
of these. The Court of Errors rejected Gibbons's
defense, followed Chancellor Kent's opinion, and
affirmed his decree.[3]

Thus did the famous case of Gibbons *vs.* Ogden
reach the Supreme Court of the United States; thus

---

[1] 9 Johnson, 507 *et seq.*
[2] 4 Johnson's *Chancery Reports*, 158–59.   [3] 17 Johnson, 488 *et seq.*

was John Marshall given the opportunity to deliver the last but one of his greatest nation-making opinions — an opinion which, in the judgment of most lawyers and jurists, is second only to that in M'Culloch *vs.* Maryland in ability and statesmanship. By some, indeed, it is thought to be superior even to that state paper.

The Supreme Court, the bar, and the public anticipated an Homeric combat of legal warriors when the case was argued, since, for the first time, the hitherto unrivaled Pinkney was to meet the new legal champion, Daniel Webster, who had won his right to that title by his efforts in the Dartmouth College case and in M'Culloch *vs.* Maryland.[1] It was expected that the steamboat monopoly argument would be made at the February session of 1821, and Story wrote to a friend that "the arguments will be very splendid." [2]

But, on March 16, 1821, the case was dismissed because the record did not show that there was a final decree in the court "from which said appeal was made." [3] On January 10, 1822, the case was again docketed, but was continued at each term of the Supreme Court thereafter until February, 1824. Thus, nearly four years elapsed from the time the appeal was first taken until argument was heard.[4]

By the time the question was at last submitted to

[1] See *supra*, 240–50, 284–86.
[2] Story to Fettyplace, Feb. 28, 1821, Story, I, 397.
[3] Records Supreme Court, MS.
[4] The case was first docketed, June 7, 1820, as Aaron Ogden *vs.* Thomas *Gibbins*, and the defective transcript was filed October 17, of the same year. When next docketed, the title was correctly given, Thomas Gibbons *vs.* Aaron Ogden. (*Ib.*)

Marshall, transportation had become the most pressing and important of all economic and social problems confronting the Nation, excepting only that of slavery; nor was any so unsettled, so confused.

Localism had joined hands with monopoly — at the most widely separated points in the Republic, States had granted "exclusive privileges" to the navigation of "State waters." At the time that the last steamboat grant was made by New York to Livingston and Fulton, in 1811, the Legislature of the Territory of Orleans passed, and Governor Claiborne approved, an act bestowing upon the New York monopoly the same exclusive privileges conferred by the New York statute. This had been done soon after Nicholas J. Roosevelt had appeared in New Orleans on the bridge of the first steamboat to navigate the Mississippi. Whoever operated any steam vessel upon Louisiana waters without license from Livingston and Fulton must pay them $5000 for each offense, and also forfeit the boat and equipment.[1]

The expectations of Livingston and Fulton of a monopoly of the traffic of that master waterway were thus fulfilled. When, a few months later, Louisiana was admitted to the Union, the new State found herself bound by this monopoly from which, however, it does not appear that she wished to be released. Thus Livingston and Fulton held the keys to the two American ports into which poured the greatest volume of domestic products for export, and from which the largest quantity of foreign trade found its way into the interior.

[1] Act of April 19, 1811, *Acts of Territory of Orleans, 1811*, 112–18.

Three years later Georgia granted to Samuel Howard of Savannah a rigid monopoly to transport merchandise upon Georgia waters in all vessels "or rafts" towed by steam craft.[1] Anybody who infringed Howard's monopoly was to forfeit $500 for each offense, as well as the boat and its machinery. The following year Massachusetts granted to John Langdon Sullivan the "exclusive rights to the Connecticut river within this Commonwealth for the use of his patent steam towboats for . . twenty-eight years."[2] A few months afterwards New Hampshire made a like grant to Sullivan.[3] About the same time Vermont granted a monopoly of navigation in the part of Lake Champlain under her jurisdiction.[4] These are some examples of the general tendency of States and the promoters of steam navigation to make commerce pay tribute to monopoly by the exercise of the sovereignty of States over waters within their jurisdiction. Retaliation of State upon State again appeared — and in the same fashion that wrecked the States under the Confederation.[5]

But this ancient monopolistic process could not keep pace with the prodigious development of water

[1] Act of Nov. 18, 1814, *Laws of Georgia, 1814*, October Sess. 28–30.

[2] Act of Feb. 7, 1815, *Laws of Massachusetts, 1812–15*, 595.

[3] Act of June 15, 1815, *Laws of New Hampshire, 1815*, ii, 5.

[4] Act of Nov. 10, 1815, *Laws of Vermont, 1815*, 20.

[5] Ohio, for example, passed two laws for the "protection" of its citizens owning steamboats. This act provided that no craft propelled by steam, operated under a license from the New York monopoly, should land or receive passengers at any point on the Ohio shores of Lake Erie unless Ohio boats were permitted to navigate the waters of that lake within the jurisdiction of New York. For every passenger landed in violation of these acts the offender was made subject to a fine of $100. (Chap. xxv, Act of Feb. 18, 1822, and chap. ii, Act of May 23, 1822, *Laws of Ohio, 1822*.)

travel and transportation by steamboat. On every river, on every lake, glided these steam-driven vessels. Their hoarse whistles startled the thinly settled wilderness; or, at the landings on big rivers flowing through more thickly peopled regions, brought groups of onlookers to witness what then were considered to be marvels of progress.[1]

By 1820 seventy-nine steamboats were running on the Ohio between Pittsburgh and St. Louis, most of them from 150 to 650 tons burden. Pittsburgh, Cincinnati, and Louisville were the chief places where these boats were built, though many were constructed at smaller towns along the shore.[2] They carried throngs of passengers and an ever-swelling volume of freight. Tobacco, pork, beef, flour, cornmeal, whiskey — all the products of the West [3] were borne to market on the decks of steamboats which, on the return voyage, were piled high with manufactured goods.

River navigation was impeded, however, by snags, sandbars, and shallows, while the traffic overland was made difficult, dangerous, and expensive by atrocious roads. Next to the frantic desire to unburden themselves of debt by "relief laws" and other

[1] Niles's *Register* for these years is full of accounts of the building, launching, and departures and arrivals of steam craft throughout the whole interior of the country.

[2] See Blane: *An Excursion Through the United States and Canada*, by "An English Gentleman," 119–21. For an accurate account of the commercial development of the West see also Johnson: *History of Domestic and Foreign Commerce*, I, 213–15.

On March 1, 1819, Flint saw a boat on the stocks at Jeffersonville, Indiana, 180 feet long, 40 feet broad, and of 700 tons burden. (Flint's Letters, in *E. W. T.*: Thwaites, IX, 164.)

[3] Blane, 118.

forms of legislative contract-breaking, the thought uppermost in the minds of the people was the improvement of means of communication and transportation. This popular demand was voiced in the second session of the Fourteenth Congress. On December 16, 1816, John C. Calhoun brought the subject before the House.[1] Four days later he reported a bill to devote to internal improvements "the bonus of the National bank and the United States's share of its dividends." [2] It met strenuous opposition, chiefly on the ground that Congress had no Constitutional power to expend money for such purposes.[3] An able report was made to the House based on the report of Secretary Gallatin in 1808. The vital importance of "internal navigation" was pointed out,[4] and the bill finally passed.[5]

The last official act of President James Madison was the veto of this first bill for internal improvements passed by Congress. The day before his second term as President expired, he returned the bill with the reasons for his disapproval of it. He did this, he explained, because of the "insuperable difficulty . . in reconciling the bill with the Constitution." The power "proposed to be exercised by the bill" was not "enumerated," nor could it be deduced "by any just interpretation" from the power of Congress "to make laws necessary and proper" for the execution of powers expressly conferred on Congress.   "The power to regulate com-

---

[1] *Annals*, 14th Cong. 2d Sess. 296.   [2] *Ib.* 361.
[3] See debate in the House, *ib.* 851–923; and in the Senate, *ib.* 166–70.
[4] *Ib.* 924–33.   [5] March 1, 1817, *ib.* 1052.

merce among the several States can not include a
power to construct roads and canals, and to improve
the navigation of water courses." Nor did the
"'common defense and general welfare'" clause
justify Congress in passing such a measure.[1]

But not thus was the popular demand to be silenced. Hardly had the next session convened when
the subject was again taken up.[2] On December 15,
1817, Henry St. George Tucker of Virginia, chairman of the Select Committee appointed to investigate the subject, submitted an uncommonly able
report ending with a resolution that the Bank bonus
and dividends be expended on internal improvements "with the assent of the States." [3] For two
weeks this resolution was debated.[4] Every phase
of the power of Congress to regulate commerce was
examined. And so the controversy went on year
after year.

Three weeks before the argument of Gibbons vs.
Ogden came on in the Supreme Court, a debate began
in Congress over a bill to appropriate funds for sur-
veying roads and canals, and continued during all the
time that the court was considering the case. It was
going on, indeed, when Marshall delivered his opinion and lasted for several weeks. Once more the

[1] Veto Message of March 3, 1817, Richardson, I, 584–85.

[2] Monroe gingerly referred to it in his First Inaugural Address.
(Richardson, II, 8.) But in his First Annual Message he dutifully
followed Madison and declared that "Congress do not possess the
right" to appropriate National funds for internal improvements.
So this third Republican President recommended an amendment to
the Constitution "which shall give to Congress the right in question." (Ib. 18.)

[3] Annals, 15th Cong. 1st Sess. 451–60.

[4] Ib. 1114–1250, 1268–1400.

respective powers of State and Nation over internal improvements, over commerce, over almost everything, were threshed out. As was usual with him, John Randolph supplied the climax of the debate.

Three days previous to the argument of Gibbons *vs.* Ogden before Marshall and his associates, Randolph arose in the House and delivered a speech which, even for him, was unusually brilliant. In it he revealed the intimate connection between the slave power and opposition to the National control of commerce. Randolph conceded the progress made by Nationalism through the extension of the doctrine of implied powers. The prophecy of Patrick Henry as to the extinction of the sovereignty, rights, and powers of the State had been largely realized, he said. The promises of the Nationalists, made in order to secure the ratification of the Constitution, and without which pledges it never would have been adopted, had been contemptuously broken, he intimated. He might well have made the charge outright, for it was entirely true.

Randolph laid upon Madison much of the blame for the advancement of implied powers; and he arraigned that always weak and now ageing man in an effective passage of contemptuous eloquence.[1]

[1] "All the difficulties under which we have labored and now labor on this subject have grown out of a fatal admission" by Madison "which runs counter to the tenor of his whole political life, and is expressly contradicted by one of the most luminous and able State papers that ever was written [the Virginia Resolutions] — an admission which gave a sanction to the principle that this Government had the power to charter the present colossal Bank of the United States. Sir, .. that act, and one other which I will not name Madison's War

When, in the election of 1800, continued Randolph, the Federalists were overthrown, and "the construction of the Constitution according to the Hamiltonian version" was repudiated, "did we at that day dream, .. that a new sect would arise after them, which would so far transcend Alexander Hamilton and his disciples, as they outwent Thomas Jefferson, James Madison, and John Taylor of Caroline? This is the deplorable fact: such is now the actual state of things in this land; .. it speaks to the senses, so that every one may understand it." [1] And to what will all this lead? To this, at last: "If Congress possesses the power to do what is proposed by this bill [appropriate money to survey roads and canals], .. they may *emancipate every slave in the United States* [2] — and with stronger color of reason than they can exercise the power now contended for."

Let Southern men beware! If "a coalition of knavery and fanaticism .. be got up on this floor, I ask gentlemen, who stand in the same predicament as I do, to look well to what they are now doing — to the colossal power with which they are now arm-

Message in 1812], bring forcibly home to my mind a train of melancholy reflections on the miserable state of our mortal being:

> ' In life's last scenes, what prodigies surprise!
> Fears of the brave, and follies of the wise.
> From Marlborough's eyes the streams of dotage flow,
> And Swift expires a driv'ler and a show.'

"Such is the state of the case, Sir. It is miserable to think of it — and we have nothing left to us but to weep over it." (*Annals*, 18th Cong. 1st Sess. 1301.)

Randolph was as violently against the War of 1812 as was Marshall, but he openly proclaimed his opposition.

[1] *Ib.*   [2] Italics the author's.

ing this Government." [1] And why, at the present moment, insist on this "new construction of the Constitution? . . Are there not already causes enough of jealousy and discord existing among us? . . Is this a time to increase those jealousies between different quarters of the country already sufficiently apparent?"

In closing, Randolph all but threatened armed rebellion: "Should this bill pass, one more measure only requires to be consummated; and then we, who belong to that unfortunate portion of this Confederacy which is south of Mason and Dixon's line, . . have to make up our mind to perish . . or we must resort to the measures which we first opposed to British aggressions and usurpations — to maintain that independence which the valor of our fathers acquired, but which is every day sliding from under our feet. . . Sir, this is a state of things that cannot last. . . We shall keep on the windward side of treason — but we must combine to resist, and that effectually, these encroachments." [2]

Moreover, Congress and the country, particularly the South, were deeply stirred by the tariff question; in the debate then impending over the Tariff of 1824, Nationalism and Marshall's theory of Constitutional construction were to be denounced in language almost as strong as that of Randolph on internal improvements. [3] The Chief Justice and his associates were keenly alive to this agitation; they well knew that the principles to be upheld in

---

[1] *Annals*, 18th Cong. 1st Sess. 1308.
[2] *Ib.* 1310-11. The bill passed, 115 yeas to 86 nays. (*Ib.* 1468-69.)
[3] See *infra*, 535-36.

Gibbons *vs.* Ogden would affect other interests and concern other issues than those directly involved in that case.

So it was, then, when the steamboat monopoly case came on for hearing, that two groups of interests were in conflict. State Sovereignty standing for exclusive privileges as chief combatant, with Free Trade and Slavery as brothers in arms, confronted Nationalism, standing at that moment for the power of the Nation over all commerce as the principal combatant, with a Protective Tariff and Emancipation as its most effective allies. Fate had interwoven subjects that neither logically nor naturally had any kinship.[1]

The specific question to be decided was whether the New York steamboat monopoly laws violated that provision of the National Constitution which bestows on Congress the "power to regulate commerce among the several States."

The absolute necessity of a general supervision of commerce was the sole cause of the Convention at Annapolis, Maryland, in 1786, which resulted in the Constitutional Convention in Philadelphia the following year.[2] Since the adoption of uniform

---

[1] See *infra*, chap. x.

[2] See vol. i, 310–12, of this work; also Marshall: *Life of George Washington*, 2d ed. ii, 105–06, 109–10, 125. And see Madison's "Preface to Debates in the Convention of 1787." (*Records of the Federal Convention*: Farrand, iii, 547.) "The want of authy. in Congs. to regulate Commerce had produced in Foreign nations particularly G. B. a monopolizing policy injurious to the trade of the U. S. and destructive to their navigation. . . The same want of a general power over Commerce led to an exercise of this power separately, by the States, wᶜʰ not only proved abortive, but engendered rival, conflicting and angry regulations."

commercial regulations was the prime object of the Convention, there was no disagreement as to, or discussion of, the propriety of giving Congress full power over that subject. Every draft except one [1] of the Committee of Detail, the Committee of Style, and the notes taken by members contained some reference to a clause to that effect. [2]

The earliest exposition of the commerce clause of the Constitution by any eminent National authority, therefore, came from John Marshall. In his opinion in Gibbons *vs.* Ogden he spoke the first and last authoritative word on that crucial subject.

Pinkney was fatally ill when the Supreme Court convened in 1822 and died during that session. His death was a heavy blow to the steamboat monopoly, and his loss was not easily made good. It was finally decided to employ Thomas J. Oakley, Attorney-General of New York, a cold, clear reasoner, and carefully trained lawyer, but lacking imagination,

---

[1] *Records, Fed. Conv.*: Farrand, II, 143. The provision in this draft is very curious. It declares that "a navigation act shall not be passed, but with the consent of (eleven states in) $<\frac{2}{3}$d. of the Members present of$>$ the senate and (10 in) $<$the like No. of$>$ the house of representatives."

[2] *Ib.* 135, 157, 569, 595, 655. Roger Sherman mentioned interstate trade only incidentally. Speaking of exports and imports, he said that "the oppression of the uncommercial States was guarded agst. by the power to regulate trade between the States." (*Ib.* 308.)

Writing in 1829, Madison said that the commerce clause "being in the same terms with the power over foreign commerce, the same extent, if taken literally, would belong to it. Yet it . . grew out of the abuse of the power by the importing States in taxing the non-importing, and was intended as a negative and preventive provision against injustice among the States themselves, rather than as a power to be used for the positive purposes of the General Government, in which alone, however, the remedial power could be lodged." (Madison to Cabell, Feb. 13, 1829, *ib.* III, 478.)

warmth, or breadth of vision.[1] He was not an adequate
substitute for the masterful and glowing Pinkney.

When on February 4, 1824, the argument at last
was begun, the interest in the case was so great that,
although the incomparable Pinkney was gone, the
court-room could hold but a small part of those who
wished to hear that brilliant legal debate. Thomas
Addis Emmet, whose "whole soul" was in the case,
appeared for the steamboat monopoly and made in
its behalf his last great argument. With him came
Oakley, who was expected to perform some mar-
velous intellectual feat, his want of attractive qualities of speech having enhanced his reputation as a
thinker. Wirt reported that he was "said to be one
of the first logicians of the age." [2]

Gibbons was represented by Webster who, says
Wirt, "is as ambitious as Cæsar," and "will not be
outdone by any man, if it is within the compass of
his power to avoid it." [3] Wirt appeared with Webster against the New York monopoly. The argument
was opened by Webster; and never in Congress or
court had that surprising man prepared so carefully
— and never so successfully.[4] Of all his legal argu-

---

[1] See *Monthly Law Reporter*, New Series, x, 177.

[2] Wirt to Carr, Feb. 1, 1824, Kennedy, II, 164.   [3] *Ib.*

[4] "Reminiscence," that betrayer of history, is responsible for the
fanciful story, hitherto accepted, that Webster was speaking on the tariff in the House when he was suddenly notified that Gibbons *vs.* Ogden
would be called for argument the next morning; and that, swiftly concluding his great tariff argument, he went home, took medicine, slept
until ten o'clock that night, then rose, and in a strenuous effort worked
until 9 A.M. on his argument in the steamboat case; and that this was
all the preparation he had for that glorious address. (Ticknor's reminiscences of Webster, as quoted by Curtis, I, 216–17.)

On its face, Webster's argument shows that this could not have
been true. The fact was that Webster had had charge of the case in

ments, that in the steamboat case is incontestably
supreme. And, as far as the assistance of associate
counsel was concerned, Webster's address, unlike
that in the Dartmouth College case, was all his
own. It is true that every point he made had been
repeated many times in the Congressional debates
over internal improvements, or before the New
York courts in the steamboat litigation. But these
facts do not detract from the credit that is rightfully
Webster's for his tremendous argument in Gibbons
vs. Ogden.

He began by admissions—a dangerous method and
one which only a man of highest power can safely employ. The steamboat monopoly law had been "deliberately re-enacted," he said, and afterwards had the
"sanction" of various New York courts, "than which
there were few, if any, in the country, more justly entitled to respect and deference." Therefore he must,
acknowledged Webster, "make out a clear case" if
he hoped to win.[1]

the Supreme Court for three years; and that, since the argument was
twice before expected, he had twice before prepared for it.

The legend about his being stopped in his tariff speech is utterly
without foundation. The debate on that subject did not even begin
in the House until February 11, 1824 (*Annals*, 18th Cong. 1st Sess.
1470), three days after the argument of Gibbons *vs.* Ogden was concluded; and Webster did not make his famous speech on the Tariff Bill
of 1824 until April 1–2, one month after the steamboat case had been
decided. (*Ib.* 2026–68.)

Moreover, as has been stated in the text, the debate on the survey
of roads and canals was on in the House when the argument in Gibbons *vs.* Ogden was heard; had been in progress for three weeks previously and continued for some time afterward; and in this debate
Webster did not participate. Indeed, the record shows that for more
than a week before the steamboat argument Webster took almost no
part in the House proceedings. (*Ib.* 1214–1318.)

[1] 9 Wheaton, 3.

What was the state of the country with respect
to transportation? Everybody knew that the use
of steamboats had become general; everywhere they
plied over rivers and bays which often formed the
divisions between States. It was inevitable that
the regulations of such States should be "hostile"
to one another. Witness the antagonistic laws of
New York, New Jersey, and Connecticut. Surely
all these warring statutes were not "consistent with
the laws and constitution of the United States." If
any one of them were valid, would anybody "point
out where the state right stopped?" [1]

Webster carefully described the New York steamboat monopoly laws, the rights they conferred, and
the prohibitions they inflicted.[2] He contended,
among other things, that these statutes violated
the National Constitution. "The power of Congress
to regulate commerce was complete and entire,"
said Webster, "and to a certain extent necessarily
exclusive." [3] It was well known that the "immediate" reason and "prevailing motive" for adopting
the Constitution was to "rescue" commerce "from
the embarrassing and destructive consequences resulting from the legislation of so many different
states, and to place it under the protection of a
uniform law." [4] The paramount object of establishing the present Government was "to benefit and
improve" trade. This, said Webster, was proved
by the undisputed history of the period preceding
the Constitution.[5]

What commerce is to be regulated by Congress?

[1] 9 Wheaton, 4–5.   [2] Ib. 6–9.   [3] Ib. 9.   [4] Ib. 11.   [5] Ib. 11–12.

Not that of the several States, but that of the Nation as a "unit." Therefore, the regulation of it "must necessarily be complete, entire and uniform. Its character was to be described in the flag which waved over it, *E Pluribus Unum.*" Of consequence, Congressional regulation of commerce must be "exclusive." Individual States cannot "assert a right of concurrent legislation, . . without manifest encroachment and confusion." [1]

If New York can grant a monopoly over New York Bay, so can Virginia over the entrance of the Chesapeake, so can Massachusetts over the bay bearing the name and under the jurisdiction of that State. Worse still, every State may grant "an exclusive right of entry of vessels into her ports." [2]

Oakley, Emmet, and Wirt exhausted the learning then extant on every point involved in the controversy. Not even Pinkney at his best ever was more thorough than was Emmet in his superb argument in Gibbons *vs.* Ogden. [3]

The small information possessed by the most careful and thorough lawyers at that time concerning important decisions in the Circuit Courts of the United States, even when rendered by the Chief Justice himself, is startlingly revealed in all these arguments. Only four years previously, Marshall, at Richmond, had rendered an opinion in which he asserted the power of Congress over commerce as em-

---

[1] 9 Wheaton, 14.   [2] *Ib.* 24.

[3] The student should carefully read these three admirable arguments, particularly that of Emmet. All of them deal with patent law as well as with the commerce clause of the Constitution. (See 9 Wheaton, 33–135.) The argument lasted from February 4 to February 9 inclusive.

phatically as Webster or Wirt now insisted upon it. This opinion would have greatly strengthened their arguments, and undoubtedly they would have cited it had they known of it. But neither Wirt nor Webster made the slightest reference to the case of the Brig Wilson *vs.* The United States, decided during the May term, 1820.

One offense charged in the libel of that vessel by the National Government was, that she had brought into Virginia certain negroes in violation of the laws of that State and in contravention of the act of Congress forbidding the importation of negroes into States whose laws prohibited their admission. Was this act of Congress Constitutional? The power to pass such a law is, says Marshall, "derived entirely" from that clause of the Constitution which "enables Congress, 'to regulate commerce with foreign nations, and among the several States.'" [1] This power includes navigation. The authority to forbid foreign ships to enter our ports comes exclusively from the commerce clause. "If this power over vessels is not in Congress, where does it reside? Does it reside in the States?

"No American politician has ever been so extravagant as to contend for this. No man has been wild enough to maintain, that, although the power to regulate commerce, gives Congress an unlimited power over the cargoes, it does not enable that body to control the vehicle in which they are imported: that, while the whole power of commerce is vested in Congress, the state legislatures may confiscate

[1] 1 Brockenbrough, 430–31.

every vessel which enters their ports, and Congress is unable to prevent their entry."

The truth, continues Marshall, is that "even an empty vessel, or a packet, employed solely in the conveyance of passengers and letters, may be regulated and forfeited" under a National law. "There is not, in the Constitution, one syllable on the subject of navigation. And yet, every power that pertains to navigation has been . . rightfully exercised by Congress. From the adoption of the Constitution, till this time, the universal sense of America has been, that the word commerce, as used in that instrument, is to be considered a generic term, comprehending navigation, or, that a control over navigation is necessarily incidental to the power to regulate commerce." [1]

Here was a weapon which Webster could have wielded with effect, but he was unaware that it existed — a fact the more remarkable in that both Webster and Emmet commented, in their arguments, upon State laws that prohibited the admission of negroes.

But Webster never doubted that the court's decision would be against the New York steamboat monopoly laws. "Our Steam Boat case is not yet decided, but it *can go but one way*," he wrote his brother a week after the argument.[2]

On March 2, 1824, Marshall delivered that opinion which has done more to knit the American people into an indivisible Nation than any other one

---

[1] 1 Brockenbrough, 431–32.
[2] Webster to his brother, Feb. 15, 1824, Van Tyne, 102.

force in our history, excepting only war. In Marbury *vs.* Madison he established that fundamental principle of liberty that a permanent written constitution controls a temporary Congress; in Fletcher *vs.* Peck, in Sturges *vs.* Crowninshield, and in the Dartmouth College case he asserted the sanctity of good faith; in M'Culloch *vs.* Maryland and Cohens *vs.* Virginia he made the Government of the American people a living thing; but in Gibbons *vs.* Ogden he welded that people into a unit by the force of their mutual interests.

The validity of the steamboat monopoly laws of New York, declares Marshall, has been repeatedly upheld by the Legislature, the Council of Revision, and the various courts of that State, and is "supported by great names — by names which have all the titles to consideration that virtue, intelligence, and office, can bestow." [1] Having paid this tribute to Chancellor Kent — for every word of it was meant for that great jurist — Marshall takes up the capital question of construction.

It is urged, he says, that, before the adoption of the Constitution, the States "were sovereign, were completely independent, and were connected with each other only by a league. This is true. But when these allied sovereigns converted their league into a government, when they converted their Congress of Ambassadors, deputed to deliberate on their common concerns, and to recommend measures of general utility, into a legislature, empowered to enact laws . . the whole character" of the States "under-

[1] 9 Wheaton, 186.

went a change, the extent of which must be determined by a fair consideration" of the Constitution.

Why ought the powers "expressly granted" to the National Government to be "construed strictly," as many insist that they should be? "Is there one sentence in the constitution which gives countenance to this rule?" None has been pointed out; none exists. What is meant by "a strict construction"? Is it "that narrow construction, which would cripple the government and render it unequal to the objects for which it is declared to be instituted,[1] and to which the powers given, as fairly understood, render it competent"? The court cannot adopt such a rule for expounding the Constitution.[2]

Just as men, "whose intentions require no concealment," use plain words to express their meaning, so did "the enlightened patriots who framed our constitution," and so did "the people who adopted it." Surely they "intended what they have said." If any serious doubt of their meaning arises, concerning the extent of any power, "the objects for which it was given . . should have great influence in the construction."[3]

Apply this common-sense rule to the commerce clause of the Constitution.[4] What does the word

[1] "WE THE PEOPLE of the United States, in Order to form a more perfect Union, establish Justice, insure domestic Tranquility, provide for the common defence, promote the general Welfare, and secure the Blessings of Liberty to ourselves and our Posterity, do ordain and establish this CONSTITUTION for the United States of America." (Preamble to the Constitution of the United States.)

[2] 9 Wheaton, 187–88.   [3] Ib. 188–89.

[4] "The Congress shall have Power . . to regulate Commerce with foreign Nations, and among the Several States, and with the Indian Tribes." (Constitution of the United States, Article i, Section 8.)

"commerce" mean? Strict constructionists, like
the advocates of the New York steamboat monopoly, "limit it to . . buying and selling . . and do
not admit that it comprehends navigation." But
why not navigation? "Commerce . . is traffic, but
it is something more; it is intercourse." If this is not
true, then the National Government can make no
law concerning American vessels — "yet this power
has been exercised from the commencement of the
government, has been exercised with the consent of
all, and has been understood by all to be a commercial regulation. All America understands . . the
word 'commerce' to comprehend navigation. . .
The power over commerce, including navigation,
was one of the primary objects for which the people
of America adopted their government. . . The attempt to restrict it [the meaning of the word "commerce"] comes too late."

Was not the object of the Embargo, which "engaged the attention of every man in the United
States," avowedly "the protection of commerce? . .
By its friends and its enemies that law was treated
as a commercial, not as a war measure." Indeed, its
very object was "the avoiding of war." Resistance
to it was based, not on the denial that Congress can
regulate commerce, but on the ground that "a perpetual embargo was the annihilation, and not the
regulation of commerce." This illustration proves
that "the universal understanding of the American
people" was, and is, that "a power to regulate navigation is as expressly granted as if that term had been
added to the word 'commerce.'" [1]

[1] 9 Wheaton, 192–93.

Nobody denies that the National Government has unlimited power over foreign commerce — "no sort of trade can be carried on between this country and any other, to which this power does not extend." The same is true of commerce among the States. The power of the National Government over trade with foreign nations, and "among" the several States, is conferred in the same sentence of the Constitution, and "must carry the same meaning throughout the sentence. . . The word 'among' means intermingled with." So "commerce among the states cannot stop at the external boundary line of each state, but may be introduced into the interior." This does not, of course, include the "completely interior traffic of a state." [1]

Everybody knows that foreign commerce is that of the whole Nation and not of its parts. "Every district has a right to participate in it. The deep streams which penetrate our country in every direction, pass through the interior of almost every state in the Union." The power to regulate this commerce "must be exercised whenever the subject exists. If it exists within a state, if a foreign voyage may commence or terminate within a state, then the power of Congress may be exercised within a state."[2]

If possible, "this principle . . is still more clear, when applied to commerce 'among the several states.' They either join each other, in which case they are separated by a mathematical line, or they are remote from each other, in which case other states lie between them. . . Can a trading expedition

[1] 9 Wheaton, 193-94.   [2] *Ib.* 195.

between two adjoining states commence and terminate outside of each?" The very idea is absurd. And must not commerce between States "remote" from one another, pass through States lying between them? The power to regulate this commerce is in the National Government.[1]

What is this power to "regulate commerce"? It is the power "to prescribe the rule by which commerce is to be governed. This power . . is complete in itself, may be exercised to its utmost extent, and acknowledges no limitations, other than are prescribed in the constitution;" and these do not affect the present case. Power over interstate commerce "is vested in Congress as absolutely as it would be in a single government" under a Constitution like ours. There is no danger that Congress will abuse this power, because "the wisdom and the discretion of Congress, their identity with the people, and the influence which their constituents possess at election, are, in this, as in many other instances, as that, for example, of declaring war, the sole restraints on which they [the people] have relied, to secure them from its abuse. They are restraints on which the people must often rely solely, in all representative governments." The upshot of the whole dispute is, declares Marshall, that Congress has power over navigation "within the limits of every state . . so far as that navigation may be, in any manner, connected" with foreign or interstate trade.[2]

Marshall tries to answer the assertion that the power to regulate commerce is concurrent in Con-

[1] 9 Wheaton, 195–96.   [2] *Ib.* 196–97.

gress and the State Legislatures; but, in doing so, he
is diffuse, prolix, and indirect. There is, he insists,
no analogy between the taxing power of Congress
and its power to regulate commerce; the former
"does not interfere with the power of the states to
tax for the support of their own governments." In
levying such taxes, the States "are not doing what
Congress is empowered to do." But when a State
regulates foreign or interstate commerce, "it is exercising the very power . . and doing the very thing
which Congress is authorized to do." However, says
Marshall evasively, in the case before the court the
question whether Congress has exclusive power over
commerce, or whether the States can exercise it until Congress acts, may be dismissed, since Congress
has legislated on the subject. So the only practical
question is: "Can a state regulate commerce with
foreign nations and among the states while Congress is regulating it?" [1]

The argument is not sound that, since the States
are expressly forbidden to levy duties on tonnage,
exports, and imports which they might otherwise
have levied, they may exercise other commercial
regulations, not in like manner expressly prohibited.
For the taxation of exports, imports, and tonnage is
a part of the general taxing power and is not connected with the power to regulate commerce. It is
true that duties on tonnage often are laid "with a
view to the regulation of commerce; but they may be
also imposed with a view to revenue," and, therefore, the States are prohibited from laying such taxes.

[1] 9 Wheaton, 199-200.

There is a vast difference between taxation for the regulation of commerce and taxation for raising revenue. "Those illustrious statesmen and patriots" who launched the Revolution and framed the Constitution understood and acted upon this distinction: "The right to regulate commerce, even by the imposition of duties, was not controverted; but the right to impose a duty for the purpose of revenue, produced a war as important, perhaps, in its consequences to the human race, as any the world has ever witnessed." [1]

In the same way, State inspection laws, while influencing commerce, do not flow from a power to regulate commerce. The purpose of inspection laws is "to improve the quality of the articles produced by the labor of the country. . . They act upon the subject before it becomes an article" of foreign or interstate commerce. Such laws "form a portion of that immense mass of legislation which embraces everything within the territory of a state," and "which can be most advantageously exercised by the states themselves." Of this description are "inspection laws, quarantine laws, health laws . . as well as laws for regulating the internal commerce of a state, and those which respect turnpike-roads, ferries, etc." [2]

Legislation upon all these subjects is a matter of State concern — Congress can act upon them only "for national purposes . . where the power is expressly given for a special purpose, or is clearly incidental to some power which is expressly given."

[1] 9 Wheaton, 202–03.   [2] *Ib.* 203.

Obviously, however, the National Government "in the exercise of its express powers, that, for example, of regulating [foreign and interstate] commerce . . may use means that may also be employed by a state, . . that, for example, of regulating commerce within the state." The National coasting laws, though operating upon ports within the same State, imply "no claim of a direct power to regulate the purely internal commerce of a state, or to act directly on its system of police." State laws on these subjects, although of the "same character" as those of Congress, do not flow from the same source whence the National laws flow, "but from some other, which remains with the state, and may be executed by the same means." Although identical measures may proceed from different powers, "this does not prove that the powers themselves are identical." [1]

It is inevitable in a "complex system" of government like ours that "contests respecting power must arise" between State and Nation. But this "does not prove that one is exercising, or has a right to exercise, the powers of the other." [2] It cannot be inferred from National statutes requiring National officials to "conform to, and assist in the execution of the quarantine and health laws of a state . . that a state may rightfully regulate commerce"; such laws flow from "the acknowledged power of a state, to provide for the health of its citizens." Nevertheless, "Congress may control the state [quarantine and health] laws, so far as it may be necessary to control them, for the regulation of commerce." [3]

[1] 9 Wheaton, 203–04.   [2] *Ib.* 204–05.   [3] *Ib.* 205–06.

Marshall analyzes, at excessive length, National
and State laws on the importation of slaves, on
pilots, on lighthouses,[1] to show that such legislation
does not justify the inference that "the states possess, concurrently" with Congress, "the power to
regulate commerce with foreign nations and among
the states."

In the regulation of "their own purely internal
affairs," States may pass laws which, although in
themselves proper, become invalid when they interfere with a National law. Is this the case with the
New York steamboat monopoly acts? Have they
"come into collision with an act of Congress, and
deprived a citizen of a right to which that act entitles him"?   If so, it matters not whether the State
laws are the exercise of a concurrent power to regulate commerce, or of a power to "regulate their domestic trade and police."   In either case, "the acts
of New York must yield to the law of Congress." [2]

This truth is "founded as well on the nature of the
government as on the words of the constitution."
The theory that if State and Nation each rightfully
pass conflicting laws on the same subject, "they
affect the subject, and each other, like equal opposing
powers," is demolished by the "supremacy" of the
Constitution and "of the laws made in pursuance
of it. The nullity of *any act*, inconsistent with the
constitution, is produced by the declaration that the
constitution is the supreme law." So when a State
statute, enacted under uncontrovertible State powers, conflicts with a law, treaty, or the Constitution

[1] 9 Wheaton, 206–09.   [2] *Ib.* 209–10.

of the Nation, the State enactment "must yield
to it." [1]

It is not the Constitution, but "those laws whose
authority is acknowledged by civilized man throughout the world" that "confer the right of intercourse
between state and state. . . The constitution found
it an existing right, and gave to Congress the power
to regulate it. In the exercise of this power, Congress has passed an act" regulating the coasting
trade. Any law "must imply a power to exercise the
right" it confers. How absurd, then, the contention
that, while the State of New York cannot prevent a
vessel licensed under the National coasting law, when
proceeding from a port in New Jersey to one in New
York, "from enjoying . . all the privileges conferred
by the act of Congress," nevertheless, the State of
New York "can shut her up in her own port, and
prohibit altogether her entering the waters and ports
of another state"![2]

A National license to engage in the coasting trade
gives the right to navigate between ports of different
States.[3] The fact that Gibbons's boats carried passengers only did not make those vessels any the less
engaged in the coasting trade than if they carried
nothing but merchandise — "no clear distinction
is perceived between the power to regulate vessels
employed in transporting men for hire, and property for hire. . . A coasting vessel employed in the
transportation of passengers, is as much a portion
of the American marine as one employed in the

[1] 9 Wheaton, 210–11. (Italics the author's.)
[2] *Ib.* 211–12.   [3] *Ib.* 214.

transportation of a cargo."[1] Falling into his characteristic over-explanation, Marshall proves the
obvious by many illustrations.[2]

However the question as to the nature of the
business is beside the point, since the steamboat
monopoly laws are based solely on the method of
propelling boats — "whether they are moved by
steam or wind. If by the former, the waters of New
York are closed against them, though their cargoes
be dutiable goods, which the laws of the United
States permit them to enter and deliver in New
York. If by the latter, those waters are free to them,
though they should carry passengers only." What
is the injury which Ogden complains that Gibbons
has done him? Not that Gibbons's boats carry passengers, but only that those vessels "are moved by
steam."

"The writ of injunction and decree" of the State
court "restrain these [Gibbons's] licensed vessels,
not from carrying passengers, but from being moved
through the waters of New York by steam, for any
purpose whatever." Therefore, "the real and sole
question seems to be, whether a steam machine, in
actual use, deprives a vessel of the privileges conferred by a [National] license." The answer is easy
— indeed, there is hardly any question to answer:
"The laws of Congress, for the regulation of commerce, do not look to the principle by which vessels
are moved."[3]

Steamboats may be admitted to the coasting trade
"in common with vessels using sails. They are . .

[1] 9 Wheaton, 215–16.   [2] *Ib.* 216–18.   [3] *Ib.* 218–20.

entitled to the same privileges, and can no more be restrained from navigating waters, and entering ports which are free to such vessels, than if they were wafted on their voyage by the winds, instead of being propelled by the agency of fire. The one element may be as legitimately used as the other, for every commercial purpose authorized by the laws of the Union; and the act of a state inhibiting the use of either to any vessel having a license under the act of Congress comes . . in direct collision with that act." [1]

Marshall refuses to discuss the question of Fulton's patents since, regardless of that question, the cause must be decided by the supremacy of National over State laws that regulate commerce between the States.

The Chief Justice apologizes, and very properly, for taking so "much time . . to demonstrate propositions which may have been thought axioms. It is felt that the tediousness inseparable from the endeavor to prove that which is already clear, is imputable to a considerable part of this opinion. But it was unavoidable." The question is so great, the judges, from whose conclusions "we dissent," are so eminent,[2] the arguments at the bar so earnest, an "unbroken" statement of principles upon which the court's judgment rests so indispensable, that Marshall feels that nothing should be omitted, nothing taken for granted, nothing assumed.[3]

Having thus placated Kent, Marshall turns upon

[1] 9 Wheaton, 221.
[2] Marshall is here referring particularly to Chancellor Kent.
[3] 9 Wheaton, 221–22.

his Virginia antagonists: "Powerful and ingenious minds, taking, as postulates, that the powers expressly granted to the government of the Union, are to be contracted, by construction, into the narrowest possible compass, and that the original powers of the States are retained, if any possible construction will retain them, may, by a course of well digested, but refined and metaphysical reasoning, founded on these premises, *explain away the constitution of our country, and leave it a magnificent structure indeed, to look at, but totally unfit for use.*

"They may so entangle and perplex the understanding, as to obscure principles which were before thought quite plain, and induce doubts where, if the mind were to pursue its own course, none would be perceived.

"In such a case, it is peculiarly necessary to recur to safe and fundamental principles to sustain those principles, and, when sustained, to make them the tests of the arguments to be examined." [1]

So spoke John Marshall, in his seventieth year, when closing the last but one of those decisive opinions which vitalized the American Constitution, and assured for himself the grateful and reverent homage of the great body of the American people as long as the American Nation shall endure. It is pleasant to reflect that the occasion for this ultimate effort of Marshall's genius was the extinction of a monopoly.

Marshall, the statesman, rather than the judge, appears in his opinion. While avowing the most determined Nationalism in the body of his opinion,

[1] 9 Wheaton, 222. (Italics the author's.)

he is cautious, nevertheless, when coming to close grips with the specific question of the respective rights of Gibbons and Ogden. He is vague on the question of concurrent powers of the States over commerce, and rests the concrete result of his opinion on the National coasting laws and the National coasting license to Gibbons.

William Johnson, a Republican, appointed by Jefferson, had, however, no such scruples. In view of the strong influence Marshall had, by now, acquired over Johnson, it appears to be not improbable that the Chief Justice availed himself of the political status of the South Carolinian, as well as of his remarkable talents, to have Johnson state the real views of the master of the Supreme Court.

At any rate, Johnson delivered a separate opinion so uncompromisingly Nationalist that Marshall's Nationalism seems hesitant in comparison. In it Johnson gives one of the best statements ever made, before or since, of the regulation of commerce as the moving purpose that brought about the American Constitution. That instrument did not originate liberty of trade: "The law of nations . . pronounces all commerce legitimate in a state of peace, until prohibited by positive law." So the power of Congress over that vital matter "must be exclusive; it can reside but in one potentate; and hence, the grant of this power carries with it the whole subject, leaving nothing for the state to act upon." [1]

Commercial laws! Were the whole of them "repealed to-morrow, all commerce would be lawful."

[1] 9 Wheaton, 227.

The authority of Congress to control foreign commerce is precisely the same as that over interstate commerce. The National power over navigation is not "incidental to that of regulating commerce; . . it is as the thing itself; inseparable from it as vital motion is from vital existence. . . Shipbuilding, the carrying trade, and the propagation of seamen, are such vital agents of commercial prosperity, that the nation which could not legislate over these subjects would not possess power to regulate commerce." [1]

Johnson therefore finds it "impossible" to agree with Marshall that freedom of interstate commerce rests on any such narrow basis as National coasting law or license: "I do not regard it as the foundation of the right set up in behalf of the appellant [Gibbons]. If there was any one object riding over every other in the adoption of the constitution, it was to keep the commercial intercourse among the states free from all invidious and partial restraints. . . If the [National] licensing act was repealed to-morrow," Gibbons's right to the free navigation of New York waters "would be as strong as it is under this license." [2]

So it turned out that the first man appointed for the purpose of thwarting Marshall's Nationalism, expressed, twenty years after his appointment, stronger Nationalist sentiments than Marshall himself was, as yet, willing to avow openly. Johnson's astonishing opinion in Gibbons *vs.* Ogden is conclusive proof of the mastery the Chief Justice had acquired over his Republican associate, or else of

[1] 9 Wheaton, 228–30.   [2] *Ib.* 231–32.

the conquest by Nationalism of the mind of the South Carolina Republican.

For the one and only time in his career on the Supreme Bench, Marshall had pronounced a "popular" opinion. The press acclaimed him as the deliverer of the Nation from thralldom to monopoly. His opinion, records the *New York Evening Post*, delivered amidst "the most unbroken silence" of a "courtroom . . crowded with people," was a wonderful exhibition of intellect — "one of the most powerful efforts of the human mind that has ever been displayed from the bench of any court. Many passages indicated a profoundness and a forecast in relation to the destinies of our confederacy peculiar to the great man who acted as the organ of the court. The steamboat grant is at an end." [1]

Niles published Marshall's opinion in full,[2] and in this way it reached, directly or indirectly, every paper, big and little, in the whole country, and was reproduced by most of them. Many journals contained long articles or editorials upon it, most of them highly laudatory. The *New York Evening Post* of March 8 declared that it would "command the assent of every impartial mind competent to embrace the subject." Thus, for the moment, Marshall was considered the benefactor of the people and the defender of the Nation against the dragon of monopoly. His opinion in Gibbons *vs*. Ogden changed into applause that disfavor which his opinion in M'Culloch *vs*. Maryland had evoked.

[1] *New York Evening Post*, March 5, 1824, as quoted in Warren, 395.
[2] Niles, xxvi, 54–62.

Only the Southern political leaders saw the "danger"; but so general was the satisfaction of the public that they were, for the most part, quiescent as to Marshall's assertion of Nationalism in this particular case.

But few events in our history have had a larger and more substantial effect on the well-being of the American people than this decision, and Marshall's opinion in the announcement of it. New York instantly became a free port for all America. Steamboat navigation of American rivers, relieved from the terror of possible and actual State-created monopolies, increased at an incredible rate; and, because of two decades of restraint and fear, at abnormal speed.[1]

New England manufacturers were given a new life, since the transportation of anthracite coal — the fuel recently discovered and aggravatingly needed — was made cheap and easy. The owners of factories, the promoters of steamboat traffic, the innumerable builders of river craft on every navigable stream in the country, the farmer who wished to send his products to market, the manufacturer who sought quick and inexpensive transportation of his wares — all acclaimed Marshall's decision because all found in it a means to their own interests.

The possibilities of transportation by steam railways soon became a subject of discussion by enterprising men, and Marshall's opinion gave them tre-

[1] For example, steamboat construction on the Ohio alone almost doubled in a single year, and quadrupled within two years. (See table in Meyer-MacGill: *History of Transportation in the United States*, etc., 108.)

mendous encouragement. It was a guarantee that
they might build railroads across State lines and be
safe from local interference with interstate traffic.
Could the Chief Justice have foreseen the development of the railway as an agency of Nationalism, he
would have realized, in part, the permanent and
ever-growing importance of his opinion — in part,
but not wholly; for the telegraph, the telephone, the
oil and gas pipe line were also to be affected for the
general good by Marshall's statesmanship as set
forth in his outgiving in Gibbons *vs*. Ogden.

It is not immoderate to say that no other judicial
pronouncement in history was so wedded to the inventive genius of man and so interwoven with the
economic and social evolution of a nation and a
people. After almost a century, Marshall's Nationalist theory of commerce is more potent than ever;
and nothing human is more certain than that it will
gather new strength as far into the future as forecast can penetrate.

At the time of its delivery, nobody complained of
Marshall's opinion except the agents of the steamboat monopoly, the theorists of Localism, and the
slave autocracy. All these influences beheld, in Marshall's statesmanship, their inevitable extinction.
All correctly understood that the Nationalism expounded by Marshall, if truly carried out, sounded
their doom.

Immediately after the decision was published, a
suit was brought in the New York Court of Equity,
apparently for the purpose of having that tribunal
define the extent of the Supreme Court's holding.

John R. Livingston secured a coasting license for the Olive Branch, and sent the boat from New York to Albany, touching at Jersey and unloading there two boxes of freight. The North River Steamboat Company, assignee of the Livingston-Fulton monopoly, at once applied for an injunction.[1] The matter excited intense interest, and Nathan Sanford, who had succeeded Kent as Chancellor, took several weeks to "consider the question."[2]

He delivered two opinions, the second almost as Nationalist as that of Marshall. "The law of the United States is supreme. . . The state law is annihilated, so far as the ground is occupied by the law of the union; and the supreme law prevails, as if the state law had never been made. The supremacy of constitutional laws of the union, and the nullity of state laws inconsistent with such laws of the union, are principles of the constitution of the United States. . . So far as the law of the union acts upon the case, the state law is extinguished. . . Opposing rights to the same thing, can not co-exist under the constitution of our country."[3] But Chancellor Sanford held that, over commerce exclusively within the State, the Nation had no control.

Livingston appealed to the Court of Errors, and in February, 1825, the case was heard. The year intervening since Marshall delivered his opinion had witnessed the rise of an irresistible tide of public sentiment in its favor; and this, more influential than all arguments of counsel even upon an "in-

---

[1] 1 Hopkins's *Chancery Reports*, 151.
[2] *Ib.* 198.   [3] 3 Cowen, 716–17.

dependent judiciary," was reflected in the opinion
delivered by John Woodworth, one of the judges
of the Supreme Court of that State. He quotes
Marshall liberally, and painstakingly analyzes his
opinion, which, says Woodworth, is confined to
commerce among the States to the exclusion of that
wholly within a single State. Over this latter trade
Congress has no power, except for "national purposes," and then only where such power is "'expressly given . . or is clearly incidental to some
power expressly given.'" [1]

Chief Justice John Savage adopted the same
reasoning as did Justice Woodworth, and examined
Marshall's opinion with even greater particularity,
but arrived at the same conclusion. Savage adds,
however, "a few general remarks," and in these he
almost outruns the Nationalism of Marshall. "The
constitution . . should be so construed as best to
promote the great objects for which it was made";
among them a principal one was "'to form a more
perfect union,'" etc. [2] The regulation of commerce
among the States "was one great and leading in-
ducement to the adoption" of the Nation's fundamental law. [3] "We are the citizens of two distinct,
yet connected governments. . . The powers given to
the general government are to be first satisfied."

To the warning that the State Governments
"will be swallowed up" by the National Government, Savage declares, "my answer is, if such
danger exists, the states should not provoke a
termination of their existence, by encroachments

[1] 3 Cowen, 731–34.   [2] Ib. 750.   [3] Ib.

on their part." [1] In such ringing terms did Savage endorse Marshall's opinion in Gibbons vs. Ogden.

The State Senators "concurred" automatically in the opinion of Chief Justice Savage, and the decree of Chancellor Sanford, refusing an injunction on straight trips of the Olive Branch between New York landings, but granting one against commerce of any kind with other States, was affirmed.

So the infinitely important controversy reached a settlement that, to this day, has not been disturbed. Commerce among the States is within the exclusive control of the National Government, including that which, though apparently confined to State traffic, affects the business transactions of the Nation at large. The only supervision that may be exercised by a State over trade must be wholly confined to that State, absolutely without any connection whatever with intercourse with other States.

One year after the decision of Gibbons vs. Ogden, the subject of the powers and duties of the Supreme Court was again considered by Congress. During February, 1825, an extended debate was held in the Senate over a bill which, among other things, provided for three additional members of that tribunal.[2] But the tone of its assailants had mellowed. The voice of denunciation now uttered words of deference, even praise. Senator Johnson, while still com-

[1] 3 Cowen, 753-54.
[2] This bill had been proposed by Senator Richard M. Johnson of Kentucky at the previous session (Annals, 18th Cong. 1st Sess, 575) as an amendment to a bill reported from the Judiciary Committee by Senator Martin Van Buren (ib. 336).

plaining of the evils of an "irresponsible" Judiciary, softened his attack with encomium: "Our nation has ever been blessed with a most distinguished Supreme Court, . . eminent for moral worth, intellectual vigor, extensive acquirements, and profound judicial experience and knowledge. . . . Against the Federal Judiciary, I have not the least malignant emotion." [1] Senator John H. Eaton of Tennessee said that Virginia's two members of the Supreme Court (Marshall and Bushrod Washington) were "men of distinction, . . whose decisions carried satisfaction and confidence." [2]

Senator Isham Talbot of Kentucky paid tribute to the "wise, mild, and guiding influence of this solemn tribunal." [3] In examining the Nationalist decisions of the Supreme Court he went out of his way to declare that he did not mean "to cast the slightest shade of imputation on the purity of intention or the correctness of judgment with which justice is impartially dispensed from this exalted bench." [4]

This remarkable change in the language of Congressional attack upon the National Judiciary became still more conspicuous at the next session in the debate upon practically the same bill and various amendments proposed to it. Promptly after Congress convened in December, 1825, Webster himself reported from the Judiciary Committee of the House

---

[1] *Debates*, 18th Cong. 2d Sess. 527–33.　　[2] *Ib.* 588.　　[3] *Ib.* 609.
[4] *Ib.* 614.

After considerable wrangling, the bill was reported favorably from the Judiciary Committee (*ib.* 630), but too late for further action at that session.

a bill increasing to ten the membership of the Supreme Court and rearranging the circuits.[1] This measure passed substantially as reported.[2]

When the subject was taken up in the Senate, Senator Martin Van Buren in an elaborate speech pointed out the vast powers of that tribunal, unequaled and without precedent in the history of the world — powers which, if now "presented for the first time," would undoubtedly be denied by the people.[3] Yet, strange as it may seem, opposition has subsided in an astonishing manner, he said; even those States whose laws have been nullified, "after struggling with the giant strength of the Court, have submitted to their fate." [4]

Indeed, says Van Buren, there has grown up "a sentiment . . of idolatry for the Supreme Court . . which claims for its members an almost entire exemption from the fallibilities of our nature." The press, especially, is influenced by this feeling of worship. Van Buren himself concedes that the Justices have "talents of the highest order and spotless integrity." Marshall, in particular, deserves unbounded praise and admiration: "That . . uncommon man who now presides over the Court . . is, in all human probability, the ablest Judge now sitting upon any judicial bench in the world." [5]

[1] *Debates*, 19th Cong. 1st Sess. 845.

[2] Four days after the House adopted Webster's bill (*ib.* 1149), he wrote his brother: "The judiciary bill will probably pass the Senate, as it left our House. There will be no difficulty in finding perfectly safe men for the new appointments. The contests on those constitutional questions in the West have made men fit to be judges." (Webster to his brother, Jan. 29, 1826, *Priv. Corres.*: Webster, i, 401.)

[3] *Debates*, 19th Cong. 1st Sess. 417–18.   [4] *Ib.* 419.   [5] *Ib.* 420–21.

The fiery John Rowan of Kentucky, now Senator from that State, and one of the boldest opponents of the National Judiciary, offered an amendment requiring that "seven of the ten Justices of the Supreme Court shall concur in any judgement or decree, which denies the validity, or restrains the operation, of the Constitution, or law of any of the States, or any provision or enaction in either." [1] In advocating his amendment, however, Rowan, while still earnestly attacking the "encroachments" of the Supreme Court, admitted the "unsuspected integrity" of the Justices upon which "suspicion has never scowled. . . The present incumbents are above all suspicion; obliquity of motive has never been ascribed to any of them." [2] Nevertheless, he complains of "a judicial superstition — which encircles the Judges with infallibility." [3]

This seemingly miraculous alteration of public opinion, manifesting itself within one year from the violent outbursts of popular wrath against Marshall and the National Judiciary, was the result of the steady influence of the conservatives, unwearyingly active for a quarter of a century; of the natural reaction against extravagance of language and conduct shown by the radicals during that time; of the realization that the Supreme Court could be resisted only by force continuously exercised; and, above all, of the fundamental soundness and essential justness

[1] *Debates*, 19th Cong. 1st Sess. 423–24.   [2] *Ib.* 436.
[3] *Ib.* 442. Rowan's amendment was defeated (*ib.* 463). Upon disagreements between the Senate and House as to the number and arrangement of districts and circuits, the entire measure was lost. In the House it was "indefinitely postponed" by a vote of 99 to 89 (*ib.* 2648); and in the Senate the bill was finally laid on the table (*ib.* 784).

of Marshall's opinions, which, in spite of the local and transient hardship they inflicted, in the end appealed to the good sense and conscience of the average man. Undoubtedly, too, the character of the Chief Justice, which the Nation had come to appreciate, was a powerful element in bringing about the alteration in the popular concept of the Supreme Court.

But, notwithstanding the apparent diminution of animosity toward the Chief Justice and the National Judiciary, hatred of both continued, and within a few years showed itself with greater violence than ever. How Marshall met this recrudescence of Localism is the story of his closing years.

When, in Gibbons *vs.* Ogden, Marshall established the supremacy of Congress over commerce among the States, he also announced the absolute power of the National Legislature to control trade with foreign nations. It was not long before an opportunity was afforded him to apply this principle, and to supplement his first great opinion on the meaning of the commerce clause, by another pronouncement of equal power and dignity. By acts of the Maryland Legislature importers or wholesalers of imported goods were required to take out licenses, costing fifty dollars each, before they could sell "by wholesale, bale or package, hogshead, barrel, or tierce." Non-observance of this requirement subjected the offender to a fine of one hundred dollars and forfeiture of the amount of the tax.[1]

Under this law Alexander Brown and his partners,

[1] 12 Wheaton, 420.

George, John, and James Brown, were indicted in
the City Court of Baltimore for having sold a package of foreign dry goods without a license. Judgment against the merchants was rendered; and this
was affirmed by the Court of Appeals. The case was
then taken to the Supreme Court on a writ of error
and argued for Brown & Co. by William Wirt and
Jonathan Meredith, and for Maryland by Roger
Brooke Taney [1] and Reverdy Johnson.[2]

On March 12, 1827, the Chief Justice delivered
the opinion of the majority of the court, Justice
Thompson dissenting. The only question, says
Marshall, is whether a State can constitutionally
require an importer to take out a license "before he
shall be permitted to sell a bale or package" of imported goods.[3] The Constitution prohibits any
State from laying imposts or duties on imports or
exports, except what may be "absolutely necessary
for executing its inspection laws." The Maryland
act clearly falls within this prohibition: "A duty on
imports . . is not merely a duty on the act of importation, but is a duty on the thing imported. . .

"There is no difference," continues Marshall,
"between a power to prohibit the sale of an article
and a power to prohibit its introduction into the
country. . . No goods would be imported if none

[1] Taney, leading counsel for Maryland, had just been appointed
Attorney-General of that State, and soon afterwards was made At-
torney-General of the United States. He succeeded Marshall as Chief
Justice. (See *infra*, 460.)

[2] Johnson was only thirty-one years old at this time, but already
a leader of the Baltimore bar and giving sure promise of the distinguished career he afterward achieved.

[3] 12 Wheaton, 436.

could be sold." The power which can levy a small tax can impose a great one — can, in fact, prohibit the thing taxed: "Questions of power do not depend on the degree to which it may be exercised." [1] He admits that "there must be a point of time when the prohibition [of States to tax imports] ceases and the power of the State to tax commences"; but "this point of time is [not] the instant that the articles enter the country." [2]

Here Marshall becomes wisely cautious. The power of the States to tax and the "restriction" on that power, "though quite distinguishable when they do not approach each other, may yet, like the intervening colors between white and black, approach so nearly as to perplex the understanding, as colors perplex the vision in marking the distinction between them. Yet the distinction exists, and must be marked as cases arise. Till they do arise, it might be premature to state any rule as being universal in its application. It is sufficient for the present, to say, generally, that, when the importer has so acted upon the thing imported that it has become incorporated and mixed up with the mass of property in the country, it has, perhaps, lost its distinctive character as an import, and has become subject to the taxing power of the State; but while remaining the property of the importer, in his warehouse, in the original form or package in which it was imported, a tax upon it is too plainly a duty on imports to escape the prohibition in the constitution." [3]

[1] 12 Wheaton, 437–39.   [2] *Ib.* 441.   [3] *Ib.* 441–42.

It is not true that under the rule just stated, the State is precluded from regulating its internal trade and from protecting the health or morals of its citizens. The Constitutional inhibition against State taxation of imports applies only to "the form in which it was imported." When the importer sells his goods "the [State] law may treat them as it finds them." Measures may also be taken by the State concerning dangerous substances like gunpowder or "infectious or unsound articles" — such measures are within the "police power, which unquestionably remains, and ought to remain, with the States." But State taxation of imported articles in their original form is a violation of the clause of the Constitution forbidding States to lay any imposts or duties on imports and exports.[1]

Such taxation also violates the commerce clause. Marshall once more outlines the reasons for inserting that provision into the Constitution, cites his opinion in Gibbons *vs.* Ogden, and again declares that the power of Congress to regulate commerce "is co-extensive with the subject on which it acts and cannot be stopped at the external boundary of a State, but must enter its interior." This power, therefore, "must be capable of authorizing the sale of those articles which it introduces." In almost the same words already used, the Chief Justice reiterates that goods would not be imported if they could not be sold. "Congress has a right, not only to authorize importation, but to authorize the importer to sell." A tariff law "offers the privilege [of im-

---

[1] 12 Wheaton, 443–44.

portation] for sale at a fixed price to every person
who chooses to become a purchaser." By paying
the duty the importer makes a contract with the
National Government — "he .. purchase[s] the
privilege to sell."

"The conclusion, that the right to sell is connected with the law permitting importation, as an
inseparable incident, is inevitable." To deny that
right "would break up commerce." The power of a
State "to tax its own citizens, or their property
within its territory," is "acknowledged" and is
"sacred"; but it cannot be exercised "so as to obstruct or defeat the power [of Congress] to regulate
commerce." When State laws conflict with National statutes, "that which is not supreme must
yield to that which is supreme" — a "great and
universal truth .. inseparable from the nature of
things," which "the constitution has applied .. to
the often interfering powers of the general and State
governments, as a vital principle of perpetual operation."

The States, through the taxing power, "cannot
reach and restrain the action of the national government .. — cannot reach the administration of justice in the Courts of the Union, or the collection of
the taxes of the United States, or restrain the operation of any law which Congress may constitutionally
pass — .. cannot interfere with any regulation of
commerce." Otherwise a State might tax "goods in
their transit through the State from one port to another for the purpose of re-exportation"; or tax articles "passing through it from one State to another,

for the purpose of traffic"; or tax "the transportation of articles passing from the State itself to another State for commercial purposes." Of what avail the power given Congress by the Constitution if the States may thus "derange the measures of Congress to regulate commerce"?

Marshall is here addressing South Carolina and other States which, at that time, were threatening retaliation against the manufacturers of articles protected by the tariff.[1] He pointedly observes that the decision in M'Culloch *vs.* Maryland is "entirely applicable" to the present controversy, and adds that "we suppose the principle laid down in this case to apply equally to importations from a sister State."[2]

The principles announced by Marshall in Brown *vs.* Maryland have been upheld by nearly all courts that have since dealt with the subject of commerce. But there has been much "distinguishing" of various cases from that decision; and, in this process, the application of his great opinion has often been modified, sometimes evaded. In some cases in which Marshall's statesmanship has thus been weakened and narrowed, local public sentiment as to questions that have come to be considered moral, has been influential. It is fortunate for the Republic that considerations of this kind did not, in such fashion, impair the liberty of commerce among the States before the American Nation was firmly established. When estimating our indebtedness to John Marshall, we must have in mind the state of

[1] See *infra*, 536–38.   [2] 12 Wheaton, 448–49.

the country at the time his Constitutional expositions were pronounced and the inevitable and ruinous effect that feebler and more restricted assertions
of Nationalism would then have had.

Seldom has a triumph of sound principles and of
sound reasoning in the assertion of those principles
been more frankly acknowledged than in the tribute which Roger Brooke Taney inferentially paid to
John Marshall, whom he succeeded as Chief Justice.
Twenty years after the decision of Brown *vs.* Maryland, Taney declared: "I at that time persuaded
myself that I was right. . . But further and more
mature reflection has convinced me that the rule
laid down by the Supreme Court is a just and safe
one, and perhaps the best that could have been
adopted for preserving the right of the United
States on the one hand, and of the States on the
other, and preventing collision between them." [1]

Chief Justice Taney's experience has been that of
many thoughtful men who, for a season and when
agitated by intense concern for a particular cause or
policy, have felt Marshall to have been wrong in
this, that, or the other of his opinions. Frequently,
such men have, in the end, come to the steadfast
conclusion that they were wrong and that Marshall
was right.

[1] 5 Howard, 575.

CHAPTER IX

THE SUPREME CONSERVATIVE

If a judge becomes odious to the people, let him be removed.
                                                    (William Branch Giles.)

Our wisest friends look with gloom to the future. (Joseph Story.)

I have always thought, from my earliest youth till now, that the greatest scourge an angry Heaven ever inflicted upon an ungrateful and a sinning people, was an ignorant, a corrupt, or a dependent judiciary. (Marshall.)

"I WAS in a very great crowd the other evening at Mrs Adams' drawing room, but I see very few persons there whom I know & fewer still in whom I take any interest. A person as old as I am feels that his home is his place of most comfort, and his old wife the companion in the world in whose society he is most happy.

"I dined yesterday with Mr. Randolph. He is absorbed in the party politics of the day & seems as much engaged in them as he was twenty five years past. It is very different with me. I long to leave this busy bustling scene & to return to the tranquility of my family & farm. Farewell my dearest Polly. That Heaven may bless you is the unceasing prayer of your ever affectionate

"J. MARSHALL." [1]

This letter to his ageing and afflicted wife, written in his seventy-second year, reveals Marshall's state of mind as he entered the final decade of his life. While the last of his history-making and nation-building opinions had been delivered, the years still before

---

[1] Marshall to his wife, March 12, 1826, MS.

him were to be crowded with labor as arduous and scenes as picturesque as any during his career on the Bench. It was to be a period of disappointment and grief, but also of that supreme reward for sound and enduring work which comes from recognition of the general and lasting benefit of that work and of the greatness of mind and nobility of character of him who performed it.

For twenty years the Chief Justice had not voted. The last ballot he had cast was against the reëlection of Jefferson in 1804. From that time forward until 1828, he had kept away from the polls. In the latter year he probably voted for John Quincy Adams, or rather against Andrew Jackson, who, as Marshall thought, typified the recrudescence of that unbridled democratic spirit which he so increasingly feared and distrusted.[1]

[1] Nevertheless he watched the course of politics closely. For instance: immediately after the House had elected John Quincy Adams to the Presidency, Marshall writes his brother a letter full of political gossip. He is surprised that Adams was chosen on the first ballot; many think Kremer's letter attacking Clay caused this unexpectedly quick decision, since it "was & is thought a sheer calumny; & the resentment of Clay's friends probably determined some of the western members who were hesitating. It is supposed to have had some influence elsewhere. The vote of New York was not decided five minutes before the ballots were taken."

Marshall tells his brother about Cabinet rumors — Crawford has refused the Treasury and Clay has been offered the office of Secretary of State. "It is meer [sic] common rumor" that Clay will accept. "Mr. Adams will undoubtedly wish to strengthen himself in the west," and Clay is strong in that section unless Kremer's letter has weakened him. The Chief Justice at first thought it had, but "on reflection" doubts whether it will "make any difference." (Marshall to his brother, Feb. 14, 1825, MS.) Marshall here refers to the letter of George Kremer, a Representative in Congress from Pennsylvania. Kremer wrote an anonymous letter to the *Columbian Observer* in which he asserted that Clay had agreed to deliver votes to Adams as the price

JOHN MARSHALL

Yet, even in so grave a crisis as Marshall believed the Presidential election of 1828 to be, he shrank from the appearance of partisanship. The *Marylander*, a Baltimore Democratic paper, published an item quoting Marshall as having said: "I have not voted for twenty years; but I shall consider it a solemn duty I owe my country to go to the polls and vote at the next presidential election — for should Jackson be elected, I shall look upon the government as virtually dissolved." [1]

This item was widely published in the Administration newspapers, including the Richmond *Whig and Advertiser*. To this paper Marshall wrote, denying the statement of the Baltimore publication: "Holding the situation I do .. I have thought it right to abstain from any public declarations on the election; .. I admit having said in private that though I had not voted since the establishment of the general ticket system, and had believed that I never should vote during its continuance, I might probably depart from my resolution in this instance, from the strong sense I felt of the injustice of the

of Clay's appointment to the office of Secretary of State. After much bluster, Kremer admitted that he had no evidence whatever to support his charge; yet his accusation permanently besmirched Clay's reputation. (For an account of the Kremer incident see Sargent, I, 67–74, 123–24.)

Out of the Kremer letter grew a distrust of Clay which he never really lived down. Some time later, John Randolph seized an opportunity to call the relation between President Adams and his Secretary of State "the coalition of Blifil and Black George — the combination, unheard of till then, of the Puritan with the blackleg." The bloodless, but not the less real duel, that followed, ended this quarrel, though the unjust charges never quite died out. (Schurz: *Henry Clay*, I, 273–74.)

[1] Baltimore *Marylander*, March 22, 1828.

charge of corruption against the President & Secretary of State: I never did use the other expressions ascribed to me." [1] This "card" the *Enquirer* reproduced, together with the item from the *Marylander*, commenting scathingly upon the methods of Adams's supporters.

Clay, deeply touched, wrote the Chief Justice of his appreciation and gratitude; but he is sorry that Marshall paid any attention to the matter "because it will subject you to a part of that abuse which is so indiscriminately applied to . . everything standing in the way of the election of a certain individual." [2]

Marshall was sorely worried. He writes Story that the incident "provoked" him, "not because I have any objection to its being known that my private judgement is in favor of the re-election of M[r] Adams, but because I have great objections to being represented in the character of a furious partisan. Intemperate language does not become my age or office, and is foreign from my disposition and habits. I was therefore not a little vexed at a publication which represented me as using language which could be uttered only by an angry party man."

He explains that the item got into the *Marylander* through a remark of one of his nephews "who was on the Adams convention" at Baltimore, to the effect that he had heard Marshall say that, although he had "not voted for upwards of twenty years" he "should probably vote at the ensuing election." His nephew wrote a denial, but it was not published. So, con-

---

[1] *Enquirer*, April 4, 1828.
[2] Meaning Jackson. Clay to Marshall, April 8, 1828, MS.

cludes Marshall, "I must bear the newspaper scurrility which I had hoped to escape, and which is generally reserved for more important personages than myself. It is some consolation that it does not wound me very deeply."[1]

It would seem that Marshall had early resolved to go to any length to deprive the enemies of the National Judiciary of any pretext for attacking him or the Supreme Court because of any trace of partisan activity on his part. One of the largest tasks he had set for himself was to create public confidence in that tribunal, and to raise it above the suspicion that party considerations swayed its decisions. He had seen how nearly the arrogance and political activity of the first Federalist judges had wrecked the Supreme Court and the whole Judicial establishment, and had resolved, therefore, to lessen popular hostility to courts, as far as his neutral attitude to party controversies could accomplish that purpose.

It thus came about that Marshall refrained even from exercising his right of suffrage from 1804 to 1828 — perhaps, indeed, to the end of his life, since it is not certain that he voted even at the election of 1828. Considering the intensity of his partisan feelings, his refusal to vote, during nearly all the long period when he was Chief Justice, was a real sacrifice, the extent of which may be measured by the fact that, according to his letter to Story, he did not even vote against Madison in 1812, notwithstanding the violence of his emotions aroused by the war.[2]

[1] Marshall to Story, May 1, 1828, *Proceedings, Mass. Hist. Soc.* 2d Series, XIV, 336–37.

[2] See chap. I of this volume.

On March 4, 1829, Marshall administered the oath of office to the newly elected President, Andrew Jackson. No two men ever faced one another more unlike in personality and character. The mild, gentle, benignant features of the Chief Justice contrasted strongly with the stern, rigid, and aggressive countenance of "Old Hickory." The one stood for the reign of law; the other for autocratic administration. In Jackson, whim, prejudice, hatred, and fierce affections were dominant; in Marshall, steady, level views of life and government, devotion to order and regularity, abhorrence of quarrel and feud, constancy and evenness in friendship or conviction, were the chief elements of character. Moreover, the Chief Justice personified the static forces of society; the new President was the product of a fresh upheaval of democracy, not unlike that which had placed Jefferson in power.

Marshall had administered the Presidential oath seven times before — twice each to Jefferson, Madison, and Monroe, and once to John Quincy Adams. And now he was reading the solemn words to the passionate frontier soldier from whose wild, undisciplined character he feared so much. Marshall briefly writes his wife about the inauguration: "We had yesterday a most busy and crowded day. People have flocked to Washington from every quarter of the United States. When the oath was administered to the President the computation is that 12 or 15000 people were present — a great number of them ladies. A great ball was given at night to celebrate the election. I of course did not attend it. The affliction of our son [1] would have been sufficient to restrain me had I even felt a desire to go." [2] In a previous letter to his wife he forecast the crowds and commotion: "The whole world it is said will be here. . . I wish I could leave it all and come to you. How much more delightful would it be to me to sit by your side than to witness all the pomp and parade of the inauguration." [3]

Much as he had come to dislike taking part in politics or in public affairs, except in the discharge of his judicial duties, Marshall was prevailed upon to be a delegate to the Virginia Constitutional Convention of 1829–30. He refused, at first, to stand for the place and hastened to reassure his "dearest Polly." "I am told," he continues in his letter describing Jackson's induction into office, "by several that I am held up as a candidate for the convention. I have no desire to be in the convention and do not mean to be a candidate. I should not trouble you with this did I not apprehend that the idea of my wishing to be in the convention might prevent some of my friends who are themselves desirous of being in it from becoming candidates. I therefore wish you to give this information to Mr. Harvie.[4] . . Farewell my dearest Polly. Your happiness is always nearest the heart of your J. Marshall." [5]

He yielded, however, and wrote Story of his disgust at having done so: "I am almost ashamed of

[1] Thomas, whose wife died Feb. 2, 1829. (Paxton, 92.)
[2] Marshall to his wife, March 5 [1829], MS.
[3] Same to same, Feb. 1, 1829, MS.
[4] Jacquelin B. Harvie, who married Marshall's daughter, Mary.
[5] Marshall to his wife, March 5 [1829], MS.

my weakness and irresolution when I tell you that I am a member of our convention. I was in earnest when I told you that I would not come into that body, and really believed that I should adhere to that determination; but I have acted like a girl addressed by a gentleman she does not positively dislike, but is unwilling to marry. She is sure to yield to the advice and persuasion of her friends. . . The body will contain a great deal of eloquence as well as talent, and yet will do, I fear, much harm with some good. Our freehold suffrage is, I believe, gone past redemption. It is impossible to resist the influence, I had almost said contagion of universal example." [1]

For fifty-three years Virginia had been governed under the constitution adopted at the beginning of the Revolution. As early as the close of this war the injustice and inadequacy of the Constitution of 1776 had become evident, and, as a member of the House of Delegates, Marshall apparently had favored the adoption of a new fundamental law for the State.[2] Almost continuously thereafter the subject had been brought forward, but the conservatives always had been strong enough to defeat constitutional reform.

On July 12, 1816, in a letter to Samuel Kercheval, one of the ablest documents he ever produced, Jefferson had exposed the defects of Virginia's constitution which, he truly said, was without "leading principles." It denied equality of representation;

---

[1] Marshall to Story, June 11, 1829, *Proceedings, Mass. Hist. Soc.* 2d Series, xiv, 338–39.

[2] See vol. i, 216–17, of this work.

the Governor was neither elected nor controlled by the people; the higher judges were "dependent on none but themselves." With unsparing severity Jefferson denounces the County Court system.

Clearly and simply he enumerates the constructive reforms imperatively demanded, beginning with "General Suffrage" and "Equal representation," on which, however, he says that he wishes "to take no public share" because that question "has become a party one." Indeed, at the very beginning of this brilliant and well-reasoned letter, Jefferson tells Kercheval that it is "for your satisfaction only, and not to be quoted before the public." [1]

But Kercheval handed the letter around freely and proposed to print it for general circulation. On hearing of this, Jefferson was "alarmed" and wrote Kercheval harshly, repeating that the letter was not to be given out and demanding that the original and copies be recalled.[2] This uncharacteristic perturbation of the former President reveals in startling fashion the bitterness of the strife over the calling of the convention, and over the issues confronting that body in making a new constitution for Virginia.

Of the serious problems to be solved by the Convention of 1829–30, that of suffrage was the most important. Up to that time nobody could vote in Virginia except white owners of freehold estates. Counties, regardless of size, had equal representation

[1] Jefferson to Kercheval, July 12, 1816, *Works:* Ford, XII, 3–15.
[2] Same to same, Oct. 8, 1816, *ib.* footnote to 17.

in the House of Delegates. This gave to the eastern
and southern slaveholding sections of the State, with
small counties having few voters, an immense preponderance over the western and northwestern
sections, with large counties having many voters.
On the other hand, the rich slavery districts paid
much heavier taxes than the poorer free counties.[1]

Marshall was distressed by every issue, to settle
which the convention had been called. The question of the qualification for suffrage especially agitated him. Immediately after his election to the
convention, he wrote Story of his troubles and mis-
givings: "We shall have a good deal of division and
a good deal of heat, I fear, in our convention. The
freehold principle will, I believe, be lost. It will,
however, be supported with zeal. If that zeal should
be successful I should not regret it. If we find that a
decided majority is against retaining it I should prefer making a compromise by which a substantial
property qualification may be preserved in exchange
for it.

"I fear the excessive [torn — probably, democratic
spirit, coin]cident to victory after a hard fought
battle continued to the last extremity may lead to
universal suffrage or something very near it. What
is the prop[erty] qualification for your Senate?
How are your Senators apportioned on the State?
And how does your system work? The question

---

[1] At the time of the convention the eastern part of the State paid,
on the average, more than three times as much in taxes per acre as
the west. The extremes were startling — the trans-Alleghany section
(West Virginia) paid only 92 cents for every $8.43 paid by the Tide-
water. (*Proceedings and Debates of the Virginia State Convention of
1829–30*, 214, 258, 660–61.)

whether white population alone, or white population compounded with taxation, shall form the basis of representation will excite perhaps more interest than even the freehold suffrage. I wish we were well through the difficulty." [1]

The Massachusetts Constitutional Convention had been held nearly a decade before that of Virginia. The problem of suffrage had troubled the delegates almost as much as it now perplexed Marshall. The reminiscent Pickering writes the Chief Justice of the fight made in 1820 by the Massachusetts conservatives against "the conceited innovators." Story had been a delegate, and so had John Adams, fainting with extreme age, but rich with the wisdom of his eighty-five years: "He made a short, but very good speech," begging the convention to retain the State Senate as "the representative of *property;* . . the number of Senators in each district was proportioned to its direct taxes to the State revenue — and not to its population. Some democrats desired that the number of Senators should be apportioned not according to the taxation, but exclusively to the population. This, Mr. Adams and all the most intelligent and considerate members opposed." [2]

Ultra-conservative as Marshall was, strongly as he felt the great body of the people incapable of self-government, he was deeply concerned for the well-being of what he called "the mass of the people." The best that can be done for them, he says in a

---

[1] Marshall to Story, July 3, 1829, *Proceedings, Mass. Hist. Soc.* 2d Series, XIV, 340–41.

[2] Pickering to Marshall, Dec. 26, 1828, Pickering MSS. Mass. Hist. Soc.; see also Story, I, 386–96.

letter to Charles F. Mercer, is to educate them. "In governments entirely popular" general education "is more indispensable . . than in an other." The labor problem troubles him sorely. When population becomes so great that "the surplus hands" must turn to other employment, a grave situation will arise.

"As the supply exceeds the demand the price of labour will cheapen until it affords a bare subsistence to the labourer. The superadded demands of a family can scarcely be satisfied and a slight indisposition, one which suspends labour and compensation for a few days produces famine and pauperism. How is this to be prevented?" Education may be relied on "in the present state of our population, and for a long time to come. . . But as our country fills up how shall we escape the evils which have followed a dense population?" [1]

The Chief Justice went to the Virginia Convention a firm supporter of the strongest possible property qualification for suffrage. On the question of slavery, which arose in various forms, he had not made his position clear. The slavery question, as a National matter, perplexed and disturbed Marshall. There was nothing in him of the humanitarian reformer, but there was everything of the statesman. He never had but one, and that a splendid, vision.

The American Nation was his dream; and to the realization of it he consecrated his life. A full generation after Marshall wrote his last despairing

---

[1] Marshall to Mercer, April 7, 1827, Chamberlain MSS. Boston Pub. Lib.

word on slavery, Abraham Lincoln expressed the
conviction which the great Chief Justice had entertained: "I would save the Union. I would save
it the shortest way under the Constitution. . . If I
could save the Union without freeing any slave, I
would do it; and if I could save it by freeing some
and leaving others alone, I would also do that. What
I do about slavery and the colored race, I do because I believe it helps to save the Union." [1]

Pickering, the incessant, in one of his many and
voluminous letters to Marshall which the ancient
New Englander continued to write as long as he
lived, had bemoaned the existence of slavery — one
of the rare exhibitions of Liberalism displayed by
that adamantine Federalist conservative. Marshall
answered: "I concur with you in thinking that
nothing portends more calamity & mischief to the
Southern States than their slave population. Yet
they seem to cherish the evil and to view with
immovable prejudice & dislike every thing which
may tend to diminish it. I do not wonder that they
should resist any attempt, should one be made, to
interfere with the rights of property, but they have
a feverish jealousy of measures which may do good
without the hazard of harm that is, I think, very
unwise." [2]

Marshall heartily approved the plan of the American Colonization Society to send free negroes back
to Africa. The Virginia branch of that organization

[1] Lincoln to Greeley, Aug. 22, 1862, *Complete Works of Abraham
Lincoln:* Nicolay and Hay, II, 227–28.
[2] Marshall to Pickering, March 20, 1826, *Proceedings, Mass. Hist.
Soc.* 2d Series, XIV, 321.

was formed in 1829, the year of the State Constitutional Convention, and Marshall became a member. Two years later he became President of the Virginia branch, with James Madison, John Tyler, Abel P. Upshur, and other prominent Virginians as Vice-Presidents.[1] In 1831, Marshall was elected one of twenty-four Vice-Presidents of the National society, among whom were Webster, Clay, Crawford, and Lafayette.[2]

The Reverend R. R. Gurley, Secretary of this organization, wrote to the more eminent members asking for their views. Among those who replied were Lafayette, Madison, and Marshall. The Chief Justice says that he feels a "deep interest in the .. society," but refuses to "prepare any thing for publication." The cause of this refusal is "the present state of [his] family"[3] and a determination "long since formed .. against appearing in print on any occasion." Nevertheless, he writes Gurley a letter nearly seven hundred words in length.

Marshall thinks it "extremely desirable" that the States shall pass "permanent laws" affording financial aid to the colonization project. It will be "also desirable" if this legislation can be secured "to incline the people of color to migrate." He had thought for a long time that it was just possible that more negroes might like to go to Liberia than

[1] *Fifteenth Annual Report, Proceedings, American Colonization Society.* The abolitionists, later, mercilessly attacked the Colonization Society. (See Wilson: *Rise of the Slave Power,* i, 208 *et seq.*)

[2] *Fourteenth Annual Report, Proceedings, American Colonization Society.*

[3] His wife's illness. She died soon afterwards. See *infra,* 524-25.

"can be provided for with the funds [of] the Society"; therefore he had "suggested, some years past," to the managers, "to allow a small additional bounty in lands to those who would pay their passage in whole or in part."

To Marshall it appears to be of "great importance to retain the countenance and protection of the General Government. Some of our cruizers stationed on the coast of Africa would, at the same time, interrupt the slave trade — a horrid traffic detested by all good men — and would protect the vessels and commerce of the Colony from pirates who infest those seas. The power of the government to afford this aid is not, I believe, contested." He thinks the plan of Rufus King to devote part of the proceeds from the sale of public lands to a fund for the colonization scheme, "the most effective that can be devised." Marshall makes a brief but dreary argument for this method of raising funds for the exportation of the freed blacks.

He thus closes this eminently practical letter: "The removal of our colored population is, I think, a common object, by no means confined to the slave States, although they are more immediately interested in it. The whole Union would be strengthened by it, and relieved from a danger, whose extent can scarcely be estimated." Furthermore, says the Chief Justice, "it lessens very much . . the objection in a political view to the application of this ample fund [from the sale of the public domain], that our lands are becoming an object for which the States are to scramble, and which threatens to sow

the seeds of discord among us instead of being what
they might be — a source of national wealth." [1]

Marshall delivered two opinions in which the
question of slavery was involved, but they throw
little light on his sentiments. In the case of the
Antelope he held that the slave trade was not prohibited by international law as it then existed; but
since the court, including Story and Thompson,
both bitter antagonists of slavery, was unanimous,
the views of Marshall cannot be differentiated from
those of his associates. Spain and Portugal claimed
certain negroes forcibly taken from Spanish and
Portuguese slavers by an American slaver off the
coast of Africa. After picturesque vicissitudes the
vessel containing the blacks was captured by an
American revenue cutter and taken to Savannah
for adjudication.

In due course the case reached the Supreme Court
and was elaborately argued. The Government insisted that the captured negroes should be given
their liberty, since they had been brought into the
country in violation of the statutes against the importation of slaves. Spain and Portugal demanded

---

[1] Marshall to Gurley, Dec. 14, 1831, *Fifteenth Annual Report, Proceedings, American Colonization Society*, pp. vi–viii.

In a letter even less emotional than Marshall's, Madison favored
the same plan. (*Ib.* pp. v, vi.) Lafayette, with his unfailing floridity,
says that he is "proud . . of the honor of being one of the Vice Presidents of the Society," and that "the progressing state of our Liberia
establishment is . . a source of enjoyment, and the most lively interest" to him. (*Ib.* p. v.)

At the time of his death, Marshall was President of the Virginia
branch of the Society, and his ancient enemy, John Tyler, who succeeded him in that office, paid a remarkable tribute to the goodness and
greatness of the man he had so long opposed. (Tyler: *Tyler,* i, 567–68.)

them as slaves "acquired as property . . in the regular course of legitimate commerce." [1] It was not
surprising that opinion on the slave trade was "unsettled," said Marshall in delivering the opinion of
the court.

All "Christian and civilized nations . . have been
engaged in it. . . . Long usage, and general acquiescence" have sanctioned it.[2] America had been the
first to "check" the monstrous traffic. But, whatever its feelings or the state of public opinion,
the court "must obey the mandate of the law." [3]
He cites four English decisions, especially a recent
one by Sir William Scott, the effect of all being that
the slave trade "could not be pronounced contrary
to the law of nations." [4]

Every nation, therefore, has a right to engage in
it. Some nations may renounce that right sanctioned
by "universal assent." But other nations cannot
be bound by such "renunciation." For all nations,
large and small, are equal — "Russia and Geneva
have equal rights." No one nation "can rightfully
impose a rule on another . . none can make a law
of nations; and this traffic remains lawful to those
whose governments have not forbidden it. . . . It
follows, that a foreign vessel engaged in the African
slave trade, captured on the high seas in time of
peace, by an American cruiser, and brought in for
adjudication, would be restored." [5]

Four months before Marshall was elected a member of the Virginia Constitutional Convention, he

[1] 10 Wheaton, 114.
[2] Ib. 115. Marshall delivered this opinion March 15, 1825.
[3] Ib. 114.   [4] Ib. 118-19.   [5] Ib. 122-23.

delivered another opinion involving the legal status of slaves. Several negroes, the property of one Robert Boyce, were on a steamboat, the Teche, which was descending the Mississippi. The vessel took fire and those on board, including the negroes, escaped to the shore. Another steamboat, the Washington, was coming up the river at the time, and her captain, in response to appeals from the stranded passengers of the burning vessel, sent a yawl to bring them to the Washington. The yawl was upset and the slaves drowned. The owner of them sued the owner of the Washington for their value. The District Court held that the doctrine of common carriers did not apply to human beings; and this was the only question before the Supreme Court, to which Boyce appealed.

"A slave . . cannot be stowed away as a common package," said Marshall in his brief opinion. "The responsibility of the carrier should be measured by the law which is applicable to passengers, rather than by that which is applicable to the carriage of common goods. . . The law applicable to common carriers is one of great rigor. . . It has not been applied to living men, and . . ought not to be applied to them." Nevertheless, "the ancient rule 'that the carrier is liable only for ordinary neglect,' still applies" to slaves. Therefore the District Court was right in its instructions to the jury.[1]

The two letters quoted and the opinions expressing the unanimous judgment of the Supreme Court are all the data we have as to Marshall's views on slav-

[1] 2 Peters, 150–56.

ery. It appears that he regretted the existence of
slavery, feared the results of it, saw no way of getting
rid of it, but hoped to lessen the evil by colonizing in
Africa such free black people as were willing to go
there. In short, Marshall held the opinion on slavery
generally prevailing at that time. He was far more
concerned that the Union should be strengthened,
and dissension in Virginia quieted, than he was
over the problem of human bondage, of which he
saw no solution.

When he took his seat as a delegate to the Virginia
Constitutional Convention of 1829–30, a more determined conservative than Marshall did not live.
Apparently he did not want anything changed —
especially if the change involved conflict — except,
of course, the relation of the States to the Nation.
He was against a new constitution for Virginia;
against any extension of suffrage; against any modification of the County Court system except to
strengthen it; against a free white basis of representation; against legislative interference with
business. His attitude was not new, nor had he
ever concealed his views.

His opinions of legislation and corporate property,
for instance, are revealed in a letter written twenty
years before the Convention of 1829–30. In withdrawing from some Virginia corporation because the
General Assembly of the State had passed a law for
the control of it, Marshall wrote: "I consider the interference of the legislature in the management of
our private affairs, whether those affairs are committed to a company or remain under individual

direction, as equally dangerous and unwise. I have always thought so and I still think so. I may be compelled to subject my property to these interferences, and when compelled I shall submit; but I will not voluntarily expose myself to the exercise of a power which I think so improperly usurped." [1]

Two years before the convention was called, Marshall's unyielding conservatism was displayed in a most conspicuous manner. In Sturges *vs.* Crowninshield,[2] a State law had been held invalid which relieved creditors from contracts made before the passage of that law. But, in his opinion in that case, Marshall used language that also applied to contracts made after the enactment of insolvency statutes; and the bench and bar generally had accepted his statement as the settled opinion of the Supreme Court. But so acute had public discontent become over this rigid doctrine, so strident the demand for bankrupt laws relieving insolvents, at least from contracts made after such statutes were enacted, that the majority of the Supreme Court yielded to popular insistence and, in Ogden *vs.* Saunders,[3] held that "an insolvent law of a State does not

[1] Marshall to Greenhow, Oct. 17, 1809, MSS. "Judges and Eminent Lawyers," Mass. Hist. Soc.

[2] See *supra*, 209-18, of this volume.

[3] 12 Wheaton, 214 *et seq.* John Saunders, a citizen of Kentucky, sued George M. Ogden, a citizen of Louisiana, on bills of exchange which Ogden, then a citizen of New York, had accepted in 1806, but which were protested for non-payment. The defendant pleaded a discharge granted by a New York court under the insolvent law of that State enacted in 1801. (*Ib.*) On the manuscript records of the Supreme Court, Saunders is spelled *Sanders.* After the case was filed, the death of Ogden was suggested, and his executors, Charles Harrod and Francis B. Ogden, were substituted.

impair the obligation of future contracts between its citizens." [1]

For the first time in twenty-seven years the majority of the court opposed Marshall on a question of Constitutional law. The Chief Justice dissented and delivered one of the most powerful opinions he ever wrote. The very "nature of our Union," he says, makes us "one people, as to commercial objects." [2] The prohibition in the contract clause "is complete and total. There is no exception from it.[3] . . Insolvent laws are to operate on a future, contingent unforseen event." [4] Yet the majority of the court hold that such legislation enters into subsequent contracts "so completely as to become a . . part" of them. If this is true of one law, it is true of "every other law which relates to the subject."

But this would mean, contends Marshall, that a vital provision of the Constitution, "one on which the good and the wise reposed confidently for securing the prosperity and harmony of our citizens, would lie prostrate, and be construed into an inanimate, inoperative, unmeaning clause." The construction of the majority of the court would "convert an inhibition to pass laws impairing the obligation of contracts into an inhibition to pass retrospective laws." [5] If the Constitution means this, why is it not so expressed? The mischievous laws which caused the insertion of the contract clause "embraced future contracts, as well as those previously formed." [6]

[1] Washington, Johnson, Thompson, and Trimble each delivered long opinions supporting this view. (12 Wheaton, 254–331, 358–369.)
[2] *Ib*. 334.   [3] *Ib*. 335.   [4] *Ib*. 337.   [5] *Ib*. 356.   [6] *Ib*. 357.

The gist of Marshall's voluminous opinion in Ogden *vs.* Saunders is that the Constitution protects all contracts, past or future, from State legislation which in any manner impairs their obligation.[1] Considering that even the rigidly conservative Bushrod Washington, Marshall's stanch supporter, refused to follow his stern philosophy, in this case, the measure and character of Marshall's conservatism are seen when, in his seventy-fifth year, he helped to frame a new constitution for Virginia.

Still another example of Marshall's rock-like conservatism and of the persistence with which he held fast to his views is afforded by a second dissent from the majority of the court at the same session. This time every one of the Associate Justices was against him, and Story delivered their unanimous opinion. The Bank of the United States had sued Julius B. Dandridge, cashier of the Richmond branch, and his sureties, on his official bond. Marshall, sitting as Circuit Judge, had held that only the written record of the bank's board of directors, that they approved and accepted the bond, could be received to prove that Dandridge had been legally authorized to act as cashier.

The Supreme Court reversed Marshall's judgment, holding that the authorization of an agent by a corporation can be established by presumptive evidence,[2] an opinion that was plainly sound and which stated the law as it has continued to be ever since. But despite the unanimity of his brethren, the clear

[1] Story and Duval concurred with Marshall.
[2] 12 Wheaton, 65–90.

and convincing opinion of Story, the disapproval of his own views by the bench, bar, and business men of the whole country, Marshall would not yield. "The Ch: Jus: I fear will *die hard*," wrote Webster, who was of counsel for the bank.[1]

In a very long opinion Marshall insists that his decision in the Circuit Court was right, fortifying his argument by more than thirty citations. He begins by frank acknowledgment of the discontent his decision in the Circuit Court has aroused: "I should now, as is my custom, when I have the misfortune to differ with this court, acquiesce silently in its opinion, did I not believe that the judgment of the circuit court of Virginia gave general surprise to the profession, and was generally condemned." Corporations, "being destitute of human organs," can express themselves only by writing. They must act through agents; but the agency can be created and proved only by writing.

Marshall points out the serious possibilities to those with whom corporations deal, as well as to the corporations themselves, of the acts of persons serving as agents without authority of record.[2] Powerful as his reasoning is, it is based on mistaken premises inapplicable to modern corporate transactions; but his position, his method, his very style, reveal the stubborn conservative at bay, bravely defending himself and his views.

This, then, was the John Marshall, who, in his old age, accepted the call of men as conservative as

[1] Webster to Biddle, Feb. 20, 1827, *Writings and Speeches of Webster:* (Nat. ed.) XVI, 140.
[2] 12 Wheaton, 90–116.

himself to help frame a new constitution for Virginia.
On Monday, October 5, 1829, the convention met
in the House of Delegates at Richmond. James Madison, then in his seventy-ninth year, feeble and
wizened, called the members to order and nominated James Monroe for President of the convention. This nomination was seconded by Marshall.
These three men, whose careers since before the
Revolution and throughout our formative period,
had been more distinguished, up to that time, than
had that of any American then living, were the most
conspicuous persons in that notable Assembly.
Giles, now Governor of the State, was also a member; so were Randolph, Tyler, Philip P. Barbour,
Upshur, and Tazewell. Indeed, the very ablest men
in Virginia had been chosen to make a new constitution for the State. In the people's anxiety to
select the best men to do that important work,
delegates were chosen regardless of the districts in
which they lived.[1]

To Marshall, who naturally was appointed to the
Judiciary Committee,[2] fell the task of presenting to
the convention the first petition of non-freeholders
for suffrage.[3] No more impressive document was
read before that body. It stated the whole democratic argument clearly and boldly.[4] The first
report received from any committee was made by
Marshall and also was written by him.[5] It provided

[1] Grigsby: *Virginia Convention of 1829–30;* and see Ambler: *Sectionalism in Virginia*, 145. Chapter v of Professor Ambler's book is
devoted exclusively to the convention. Also see preface to *Debates
Va. Conv.* iii; and see Dodd, in *American Journal of Sociology*, xxvi,
no. 6, 735 *et seq.*; and Anderson, 229–36.　　[2] *Debates, Va. Conv.* 23.
[3] *Ib.* 25.　　[4] *Ib.* 25–31.　　[5] Statement of Marshall. (*Ib.* 872.)

for the organization of the State Judiciary, but did not seek materially to change the system of appointments of judges.

Two sentences of this report are important: "No modification or abolition of any Court, shall be construed to deprive any Judge thereof of his office"; and, "Judges may be removed from office by a vote of the General Assembly: but two-thirds of the whole number of each House must concur in such vote." [1] Marshall promptly moved that this report be made the order of the day and this was done.

Ranking next to the question of the basis of suffrage and of representation was that of judiciary reform. To accomplish this reform was one of the objects for which the convention had been called. At that time the Judiciary of Virginia was not merely a matter of courts and judges; it involved the entire social and political organization of that State. No more essentially aristocratic scheme of government ever existed in America. Coming down from Colonial times, it had been perpetuated by the Revolutionary Constitution of 1776. It had, in practical results, some good qualities and others that were evil, among the latter a well-nigh faultless political mechanism. [2]

The heart of this system was the County Courts. Too much emphasis cannot be placed on this fact. These local tribunals consisted of justices of the peace who sat together as County Courts for the hearing and decision of the more important cases. They were almost always the first men of their coun-

[1] *Debates, Va. Conv.* 33.   [2] See *supra*, 146, 147.

ties, appointed by the Governor for life; vacancies were, in practice, filled only on the recommendation of the remaining justices. While the Constitution of 1776 did not require the Governor to accept the nominations of the County Courts for vacancies in these offices, to do so had been a custom long established.[1]

For this acquiescence of the Governor in the recommendation of the County Courts, there was a very human reason of even weightier influence than that of immemorial practice. The Legislature chose the Governor; and the justices of the peace selected, in most cases, the candidates for the Legislature — seldom was any man elected by the people to the State Senate or House of Delegates who was not approved by the County Courts. Moreover, the other county offices, such as county clerks and sheriffs, were appointed by the Governor only on the suggestion of the justices of the peace; and these officials worked in absolute agreement with the local judicial oligarchy. In this wise members of Congress were, in effect, named by the County Courts, and the Legislature dared not and did not elect United States Senators of whom the justices of the peace disapproved.

The members of the Court of Appeals, appointed by the Governor, were never offensive to these minor county magistrates, although the judges of this highest tribunal in Virginia, always able and learned men holding their places for life, had great influence over the County Courts, and, therefore, over the Gover-

[1] See Giles's speech, *Debates, Va. Conv.* 604–05.

ncr and General Assembly also. Nor was this the limit of the powers of the County Courts. They fixed the county rate of taxation and exercised all local legislative and executive as well as judicial power.[1]

In theory, a more oligarchic system never was devised for the government of a free state; but in practice, it responded to the variations of public opinion with almost the precision of a thermometer. For example, nearly all the justices of the peace were Federalists during the first two years of Washington's Administration; yet the State supported Henry against Assumption, and, later, went over to Jefferson as against Washington and Henry combined.[2]

Rigid and self-perpetuating as was the official aristocracy which the Virginia judicial system had created, its members generally attended to their duties and did well their public work.[3] They lived among the people, looked after the common good, composed disputes between individuals; soothed local animosities, prevented litigation; and administered justice satisfactorily when, despite their preventive efforts, men would bring suits. But the whole scheme was the very negation of democracy.[4]

While, therefore, this judicial-social-political plan worked well for the most part, the idea of it was offensive to liberal-minded men who believed in democracy as a principle. Moreover, the official

[1] See Ambler: *Sectionalism in Virginia*, 139.

[2] See vol. II, 62–69, of this work.

[3] Serious abuses sprang up, however. In the convention, William Naylor of Hampshire County charged that the office of sheriff was sold to the highest bidder, sometimes at public auction. (*Debates, Va. Conv.* 486; and see Anderson, 229.)

[4] See Marshall's defense of the County Court system, *infra*, 491.

oligarchy was more powerful in the heavy slave-holding, than in the comparatively "free labor," sections; it had been longer established, and it better fitted conditions, east of the mountains.

So it came about that there was, at last, a demand for judicial reform. Seemingly this demand was not radical — it was only that the self-perpetuating County Court system should be changed to appointments by the Governor without regard to recommendations of the local justices; but, in reality, this change would have destroyed the traditional aristocratic organization of the political, social, and to a great extent the economic, life of Virginia.

On every issue over which the factions of this convention fought, Marshall was reactionary and employed all his skill to defeat, whenever possible, the plans and purposes of the radicals. In pursuing this course he brought to bear the power of his now immense reputation for wisdom and justice. Perhaps no other phase of his life displays more strikingly his intense conservatism.

The conclusion of his early manhood — reluctantly avowed after Washington, following the Revolution, had bitterly expressed the same opinion,[1] that the people, left to themselves, are not capable of self-government — had now become a profound moral belief. It should again be stated that most of Marshall's views, formed as a young lawyer during the riotous years between the achievement of Independence and the adoption of the Constitution, had hardened, as life advanced, into something

[1] See vol. I, 302, of this work.

like religious convictions. It is noteworthy, too, that, in general, Madison, Giles, and even Monroe, now stood with Marshall.

The most conspicuous feature of those fourteen weeks of tumultuous contest, as far as it reveals Marshall's personal standing in Virginia, was the trust, reverence, and affection in which he was held by all members, young and old, radical and conservative, from every part of the State. Speaker after speaker, even in the fiercest debates, went out of his way to pay tribute to Marshall's uprightness and wisdom.[1]

Marshall spoke frequently on the Judiciary; and, at one point in a debate on the removal of judges, disclosed opinions of historical importance. Although twenty-seven years had passed since the repeal of the Federalist Judiciary Act of 1801,[2] Marshall would not, even now, admit that repeal to be Constitutional. Littleton W. Tazewell, also a mem-

[1] For example, Thomas R. Joynes of Accomack County, who earnestly opposed Marshall in the Judiciary debate, said that no man felt "more respect" than he for Marshall's opinions which are justly esteemed "not only in this Convention, but throughout the United States." (*Debates, Va. Conv.* 505.) Randolph spoke of "the very great weight" which Marshall had in the convention, in Virginia, and throughout the Nation. (*Ib.* 500.) Thomas M. Bayly of Accomack County, while utterly disagreeing with the Chief Justice on the County Court system, declared that Marshall, "as a lawyer and Judge, is without a rival." (*Ib.* 510.) Richard H. Henderson of Loudoun County called the Chief Justice his "political father" whose lessons he delighted to follow, and upon whose "wisdom, . . virtue, . . prudence" he implicitly relied. (Henderson's statement as repeated by Benjamin W. Leigh, *ib.* 544.) Charles F. Mercer of the same county "expressed toward Judge Marshall a filial respect and veneration not surpassed by the ties which had bound him to a natural parent." (*Ib.* 563.) Such are examples of the expressions toward Marshall throughout the prolonged sessions of the convention.

[2] See vol. III, chap. II, of this work.

ber of the Judiciary Committee, asserted that, under the proposed new State Constitution, the Legislature could remove judges from office by abolishing the courts. John Scott of Fauquier County asked Marshall what he thought of the ousting of Federalist judges by the Republicans in 1802.

The Chief Justice answered, "with great, very great repugnance," that throughout the debate he had "most carefully avoided" expressing any opinion on that subject. He would say, however, that "he did not conceive the Constitution to have been at all definitely expounded by a single act of Congress." Especially when "there was no union of Departments, but the Legislative Department alone had acted, and acted but once," ignoring the Judicial Department, such an act, "even admitting that act not to have passed in times of high political and party excitement, could never be admitted as final and conclusive." [1]

Tazewell was of "an exactly opposite opinion" — the Repeal Act of 1802 "was perfectly constitutional and proper." Giles also disagreed with Marshall. Should "a public officer .. receive the public money any longer than he renders service to the public"? [2] Marshall replied with spirit. No serious question can be settled, he declared, by mere "confidence of conviction, but on the reason of the case." All that he asked was that the Judiciary Article of the proposed State Constitution should go forth, "uninfluenced by the opinion of any individual: let those, whose duty it was to settle the

---

[1] *Debates, Va. Conv.* 871-72.   [2] *Ib.* 872-74.

interpretation of the Constitution, decide on the Constitution itself." [1] After extended debate [2] and some wrangling, Marshall's idea on this particular phase of the subject prevailed. [3]

The debate over the preservation of the County Court system, for which Marshall's report provided, was long and acrimonious, and a résumé of it is impossible here. Marshall stoutly supported these local tribunals; their "abolition will affect our whole internal police... No State in the Union, has hitherto enjoyed more complete internal quiet than Virginia. There is no part of America, where .. less of ill-feeling between man and man is to be found than in this Commonwealth, and I believe most firmly that this state of things is mainly to be ascribed to the practical operation of our County Courts." The county judges "consist in general of the best men in their respective counties. They act in the spirit of peace-makers, and allay, rather than excite the small disputes .. which will sometimes arise among neighbours." [4]

Giles now aligned himself with Marshall as a champion of the County Court system. In an earnest defense of it he went so far as to reflect on the good sense of Jefferson. Everybody, said Giles,

---

[1] *Debates, Va. Conv.* 873.   [2] See *infra*, 493–501.

[3] Accordingly the following provision was inserted into the Constitution: "No law abolishing any court shall be construed to deprive a Judge thereof of his office, unless two-thirds of the members of each House present concur in the passing thereof; but the Legislature may assign other Judicial duties to the Judges of courts abolished by any law enacted by less than two-thirds of the members of each House present." (Article v, Section 2, Constitution of Virginia, 1830.)

[4] *Debates, Va. Conv.* 505.

knew that that "highly respectable man . . dealt very much in theories." [1]

During the remainder of the discussion on this subject, Marshall rose frequently, chiefly, however, to guide the debate. [2] He insisted that the custom of appointing justices of the peace only on nomination of the County Courts should be written into the constitution. The Executive ought to appoint *all* persons recommended by "a County Court, taken as a whole." Marshall then moved an amendment to that effect. [3]

This was a far more conservative idea than was contained in the old constitution itself. "Let the County Court who now recommended, have power also to appoint: for there it ended at last," said William Campbell of Bedford County. Giles was for Marshall's plan: "The existing County Court system" threw "power into the hands of the middle class of the community," he said; and it ought to be fortified rather than weakened.

Marshall then withdrew his astonishing amendment and proposed, instead, that the advice and "consent of the Senate" should not be required for appointments of county justices, thus utterly eliminating all legislative control over these important appointments; and this extreme conservative proposition was actually adopted without dissent. [4] Thus

---

[1] *Debates, Va. Conv.* 509.

[2] *Ib.* 524, 530, 531, 533, 534.   [3] *Ib.* 604–05.

[4] *Ib.* 605. The provision as it finally appeared in the constitution was that these "appointments shall be made by the Governor, on the recommendation of the respective County Courts." (Article v, Section 7, Constitution of Virginia, 1830.)

the very foundation of Virginia's aristocratic political organization was greatly strengthened.

Concerning the retention of his office by a judge after the court had been abolished, Marshall made an earnest and impressive speech. What were the duties of a judge? "He has to pass between the Government and the man whom that Government is prosecuting: between the most powerful individual in the community, and the poorest and most unpopular. It is of the last importance, that in the exercise of these duties, he should observe the utmost fairness. Need I press the necessity of this? Does not every man feel that his own personal security and the security of his property depends on that fairness?

"The Judicial Department comes home in its effects to every man's fireside: it passes on his property, his reputation, his life, his all. Is it not, to the last degree important, that he should be rendered perfectly and completely independent, with nothing to influence or controul him but God and his conscience?

"You do not allow a man to perform the duties of a juryman or a Judge, if he has one dollar of interest in the matter to be decided: and will you allow a Judge to give a decision when his office may depend upon it? when his decision may offend a powerful and influential man?

"Your salaries do not allow any of your Judges to lay up for his old age: the longer he remains in office, the more dependant he becomes upon his office. He wishes to retain it; if he did not wish to

retain it, he would not have accepted it. And will
you make me believe that if the manner of his decision may affect the tenure of that office, the man
himself will not be affected by that consideration? . .
The whole good which may grow out of this Convention, be it what it may, will never compensate
for the evil of changing the tenure of the Judicial
office."

Barbour had said that to presume that the Legislature would oust judges because of unpopular decisions, was to make an unthinkable imputation.
But "for what do you make a Constitution?"
countered Marshall. Why provide that "no bill of
attainder, or an *ex post facto* law, shall be passed?
What a calumny is here upon the Legislature,"
he sarcastically exclaimed. "Do you believe, that
the Legislature will pass a bill of attainder, or an *ex
post facto* law? Do you believe, that they will pass
a law impairing the obligation of contracts? If not,
why provide against it? . .

"You declare, that the Legislature shall not take
private property for the public use, without just
compensation. Do you believe, that the Legislature
will put forth their grasp upon private property,
without compensation? Certainly I do not. There
is as little reason to believe they will do such an act
as this, as there is to believe, that a Legislature will
offend against a Judge who has given a decision
against some favourite opinion and favourite measure of theirs, or against a popular individual who
has almost led the Legislature by his talents and
influence.

"I am persuaded, there is at least as much danger that they will lay hold on such an individual, as that they will condemn a man to death for doing that which, when he committed it, was no crime. The gentleman says, it is impossible the Legislature should ever think of doing such a thing. Why then expunge the prohibition? . . This Convention can do nothing that would entail a more serious evil upon Virginia, than to destroy the tenure by which her Judges hold their offices." [1]

An hour later, the Chief Justice again addressed the convention on the independence of the Judiciary. Tazewell had spoken much in the vein of the Republicans of 1802.[2] "The independence of all those who try causes between man and man, and between a man and his Government," answered Marshall, "can be maintained only by the tenure of their office. Is not their independence preserved under the present system? None can doubt it. Such an idea was never heard of in Virginia, as to remove a Judge from office." Suppose the courts at the mercy of the Legislature? "What would then be the condition of the court, should the Legislature prosecute a man, with an earnest wish to convict him? . . If they may be removed at pleasure, will any lawyer of distinction come upon your bench?

"No, Sir. I have always thought, from my earliest youth till now, that the greatest scourge an angry Heaven ever inflicted upon an ungrateful and a sinning people, was an ignorant, a corrupt, or a dependent Judiciary. Will you draw down this

[1] *Debates, Va. Conv.* 615–17.   [2] See vol. III, chap. II, of this work.

curse upon Virginia? Our ancestors thought so: we thought so till very lately; and I trust the vote of this day will shew that we think so still." [1]

Seldom in any parliamentary body has an appeal been so fruitful of votes. Marshall's idea of the inviolability of judicial tenure was sustained by a vote of 56 to 29, Madison voting with him.[2]

Lucas P. Thompson of Amherst County moved to strike out the provision in Marshall's Judiciary Article that the abolition of a court should not "deprive any Judge thereof of his office." [3] Thus the direct question, so fiercely debated in Congress twenty-seven years earlier,[4] was brought before the convention. It was promptly decided, and against the views and action of Jefferson and the Republicans of 1802. By a majority of 8 out of a total of 96,[5] the convention sustained the old Federalist idea that judges should continue to hold their positions and receive their salaries, even though their offices were abolished.

Before the vote was taken, however, a sharp debate occurred between Marshall and Giles. To keep judges in office, although that office be destroyed, "was nothing less than to establish a privileged corps in a free community," said Giles. Marshall had said "that a Judge ought to be responsible only to God and to his own conscience." Although "one of the first objects in view, in calling this Convention, was to make the Judges responsible — not nominally, but really responsible," Marshall

---

[1] *Debates, Va. Conv.* 619.   [2] *Ib.* 618–19.   [3] *Ib.* 726.
[4] See vol. III, chap. II, of this work.   [5] *Debates, Va. Conv.* 731.

actually proposed to establish "a *privileged order* of men." Another part of Marshall's plan, said Giles, required the concurrent vote of both Houses of the Legislature to remove a judge from the bench. "This was inserted, for what?" To prevent the Legislature from removing a judge "whenever his conduct had been such, that he became unpopular and odious to the people" — the very power the Legislature ought to have.[1]

In reply, Marshall said that he would not, at that time, discuss the removal of judges by the Legislature, but would confine himself "directly to the object before him," as to whether the abolition of a court should not deprive the judge of his office. Giles had fallen into a strange confusion — he had treated "the office of a Judge, and the Court in which he sat, as being . . indissolubly united." But, asked Marshall, were the words "office and Court synonymes"? By no means. The proposed Judiciary Article makes the distinction when it declares that though the *court* be abolished, the judge still holds his *office*. "In what does the office of a Judge consist? . . in his constitutional capacity to receive Judicial power, and to perform Judicial Duties. . .

"If the Constitution shall declare that when the court is abolished, he shall still hold" his office, "there is no inconsistency in the declaration. . . What creates the office?" An election to it by the Legislature and a commission by the Governor. "When these acts have been performed, the Judges are in office. Now, if the Constitution shall say

[1] *Debates, Va. Conv.* 726-27.

that his office shall continue, and he shall perform
Judicial duties, though his court may be abolished,
does he, because of any modification that may be
made in that court, cease to be a Judge? . .

"The question constantly recurs — do you mean
that the Judges shall be removable at the will of the
Legislature? The gentleman talks of responsibility.
Responsibility to what? to the will of the Legislature? can there be no responsibility, unless your
Judges shall be removable at pleasure? will nothing
short of this satisfy gentlemen? Then, indeed, there
is an end to independence. The tenure during good
behaviour, is a mere imposition on the public belief
— a sound that is kept to the ear — and nothing
else. The consequences must present themselves to
every mind. There can be no member of this body
who does not feel them.

"If your Judges are to be removable at the will of
the Legislature, all that you look for from fidelity,
from knowledge, from capacity, is gone and gone
forever." Seldom did Marshall show more feeling
than when pressing this point; he could not "sit
down," he said, without "noticing the morality" of
giving the Legislature power to remove judges from
office. "Gentlemen talk of sinecures, and privileged
orders — with a view, as it would seem, to cast
odium on those who are in office.

"You seduce a lawyer from his practice, by which
he is earning a comfortable independence, by prom-
ising him a certain support for life, unless he shall be
guilty of misconduct in his office. And after thus
seducing him, when his independence is gone, and

the means of supporting his family relinquished, you will suffer him to be displaced and turned loose on the world with the odious brand of sinecure-pensioner — privileged order — put upon him, as a lazy drone who seeks to live upon the labour of others. This is the course you are asked to pursue."

The provisions of the Judiciary Article before the convention secure ample responsibility. "If not, they can be made [to do] so. But is it not new doctrine to declare, that the Legislature by merely changing the name of a court or the place of its meeting, may remove any Judge from his office? The question to be decided is, and it is one to which we must come, whether the Judges shall be permanent in their office, or shall be dependent altogether upon the breath of the Legislature." [1]

Giles answered on the instant. In doing so, he began by a tribute to Marshall's "standing and personal excellence" which were so great "that he was willing to throw himself into the background, as to any weight to be attached to his [Giles's] own opinion." Therefore, he would "rely exclusively on the merits" of the controversy. Marshall had not shown "that it was not an anomaly to have the court out of being, and an office pertain[ing] to the court in being... It was an anomaly in terms."

Giles "had, however, such high respect" for Marshall's standing, "that he always doubted his own opinion when put in opposition" to that of the Chief Justice. He had not intended, he avowed, "to throw reproach upon the Judges in office." Far be it from

[1] *Debates, Va. Conv.* 727–29.

him to reflect "in the least degree on their honour
and integrity." His point was that, by Marshall's
plan, "responsibility was rather avoided than sought
to be secured." Giles was willing to risk his liberty
thus far — "if a Judge became odious to the people,
let him be removed from office." [1]

The debate continued upon another amendment
by Thompson. Viewing the contest as a sheer struggle of minds, the conservatives were superior to the
reformers,[2] and steadily they gained votes.[3]

Again Marshall spoke, this time crossing swords
with Benjamin W. S. Cabell and James Madison,
over a motion of the former that judges whose courts
were abolished, and to whom the Legislature assigned
no new duties, should not receive salaries: "There
were upwards of one hundred Inferior Courts in Virginia. . . No gentleman could look at the dockets of
these courts, and possibly think " that the judges
would ever have no business to transact.

Cabell's amendment "stated an impossible case,"
said Marshall, — a " case where there should be no
controversies between man and man, and no crimes
committed against society. It stated a case that
could not happen — and would the convention
encounter the real hazard of putting almost every
Judge in the Commonwealth in the power of the
Legislature, for the sake of providing for an impossible case?" [4] But in spite of Marshall's opposition,
Cabell's amendment was adopted by a vote of 59

[1] *Debates, Va. Conv.* 729–30.
[2] See especially the speech of Benjamin Watkins Leigh, *ib.* 733–37.
[3] See *ib.* for ayes and noes, 740, 741, 742, 744, 748.
[4] *Ib.* 764.

to 36.[1] Two weeks later, however, the convention reversed itself by two curious and contradictory votes.[2] So in the end Marshall won.

The subject of the Judiciary did not seriously arise again until the vote on the adoption of the entire constitution was imminent. As it turned out, the constitution, when adopted, contained, in substance, the Judiciary provisions which Marshall had written and reported at the beginning of that body's deliberations.[3]

The other and the commanding problem, for the solution of which the convention had been called, was made up of the associated questions of suffrage, taxation, and representation. Broadly speaking, the issue was that of white manhood suffrage and representation based upon the enumeration of whites, as against suffrage determined by property and taxation, representation to be based on an enumeration which included three fifths of the slave population.[4]

On these complex and tangled questions the State and the convention were divided; so fierce were the contending factions, and so diverse were opinions on various elements of the confused problem, especially among those demanding reform, that at times no solution seemed possible. The friends of reform were fairly well organized and coöperated in a spirit of

[1] *Debates, Va. Conv.* 767.   [2] *Ib.* 880.

[3] Compare Marshall's report (*ib.* 33) with Article v of the constitution (*ib.* 901–02; and see *supra*, 491, note 2.)

[4] Contrast Marshall's resolutions (*Debates, Va. Conv.* 39–40), which expressed the conservative stand, with those of William H. Fitzhugh of Fairfax County (*ib.* 41–42), of Samuel Claytor of Campbell County (*ib.* 42), of Charles S. Morgan of Monongalia (*ib.* 43–44), and of Alexander Campbell of Brooke County (*ib.* 45–46), which state the views of the radicals.

unity uncommon to liberals. But, as generally happens, the conservatives had much better discipline, far more harmony of opinion and conduct. The debate on both sides was able and brilliant.[1]

Finally the convention seemingly became deadlocked. Each side declared it would not yield.[2] Then came the inevitable reaction — a spirit of conciliation mellowed everybody. Sheer human nature, wearied of strife, sought the escape that mutual accommodation alone afforded. The moment came for which Marshall had been patiently waiting. Rising slowly, as was his wont, until his great height seemed to the convention to be increased, his soothing voice, in the very gentleness of its timbre, gave a sense of restfulness and agreement so grateful to, and so desired by, even the sternest of the combatants.

"No person in the House," began the Chief Justice, "can be more truly gratified than I am, at seeing the spirit that has been manifested here today; and it is my earnest wish that this spirit of conciliation may be acted upon in a fair, equal and honest manner, adapted to the situation of the different parts of the Commonwealth, which are to be affected."

The warring factions, said Marshall, were at last

---

[1] See, for instance, the speech of John R. Cooke of Frederick County for the radicals (*Debates, Va. Conv.* 54–65), of Abel P. Upshur of Northampton for the conservatives (*ib.* 65–79), of Philip Doddridge of Brooke County for the radicals (*ib.* 79–89), of Philip P. Barbour of Orange County for the conservatives (*ib.* 90–98), and especially the speeches of Benjamin Watkins Leigh for the conservatives (*ib.* 151–74, 544–48). Indeed, the student cannot well afford to omit any one of the addresses in this remarkable contest.

[2] It is at this point that we see the reason for Jefferson's alarm thirteen years before the convention was called. (*See supra*, 469.)

in substantial accord. "That the Federal numbers [the enumeration of slaves as fixed in the National Constitution] and the plan of the white basis shall be blended together so as to allow each an equal portion of power, seems to be very generally agreed to." The only difference now was that one faction insisted on applying this plan to both Houses of the Legislature, while the other faction would restrict the white basis to the popular branch, leaving the Senate to be chosen on the combined free white and black slave enumeration.

This involves the whole theory of property. One gentleman, in particular, "seems to imagine that we claim nothing of republican principles, when we claim a representation for property." But "republican principles" do not depend on "the naked principle of numbers." On the contrary, "the soundest principles of republicanism do sanction some relation between representation and taxation... The two ought to be connected... This was the principle of the revolution... This basis of Representation is .. so important to Virginia" that everybody had thought about it before this convention was called.

"Several different plans were contemplated. The basis of white population alone; the basis of free population alone; a basis of population alone; a basis compounded of taxation and white population, (or which is the same thing, a basis of Federal numbers:) .. Now, of these various propositions, the basis of white population, and the basis of taxation alone are the two extremes." But, "between the free population, and the white population, there is almost no difference: Between the basis of total population and the basis of taxation, there is but little difference."

Frankly and without the least disguise of his opinions, Marshall admitted that he was a conservative of conservatives: "The people of the East," of whom he avowed himself to be one, "thought that they offered a fair compromise, when they proposed the compound basis of population and taxation, or the basis of the Federal numbers. We thought that we had republican precedent for this — a precedent given us by the wisest and truest patriots that ever were assembled: but that is now past.

"We are now willing to meet on a new middle ground." Between the two extremes "the majority is too small to calculate upon. . . We are all uncertain as to the issue. But all know this, that if either extreme is carried, it must leave a wound in the breast of the opposite party which will fester and rankle, and produce I know not what mischief." The conservatives were now the majority of the convention, yet they were again willing to make concessions. Avoiding both extremes, Marshall proposed, "as a compromise," that the basis of representation "shall be made according to an exact compound of the two principles, of the white basis and of the Federal numbers, according to the Census of 1820." [1]

Further debate ensued, during which animosity seemed about to come to life again, when the Chief Justice once more exerted his mollifying influence. "Two propositions respecting the basis of Representation have divided this Convention almost equally,"

[1] *Debates, Va. Conv.* 497–500.

he said. "The question has been discussed, until discussion has become useless. It has been argued, until argument is exhausted. We have now met on the ground of compromise." It is no longer a matter of the triumph of either side. The only consideration now is whether the convention can agree on some plan to lay before the people "with a reasonable hope that it may be adopted. Some concession must be made on both sides. . . What is the real situation of the parties?" Unquestionably both are sincere. " To attempt now to throw considerations of principle into either scale, is to add fuel to a flame which it is our purpose to extinguish. We must lose sight of the situation of parties and state of opinion, if we make this attempt."

The convention is nearly evenly balanced. At this moment those favoring a white basis only have a trembling majority of two. This may change — the reversal of a single vote would leave the House "equally divided."

The question must be decided "one way or the other"; but, if either faction prevails by a bare majority, the proposed constitution will go to the people from an almost equally divided convention. That means a tremendous struggle, a riven State. Interests in certain parts of the Commonwealth will surely resist "with great force" a purely white basis of representation, especially if no effective property qualification for suffrage is provided. This opposition is absolutely certain "unless human nature shall cease to be what it has been in all time."

No human power can forecast the result of further

contest. But one thing is certain: "To obtain a just compromise, concession must not only be mutual — it must be equal also. . . Each ought to concede to the other as much as he demands from that other. . . There can be no hope that either will yield more than it gets in return."

The proposal that white population and taxation "mixed" with Federal numbers in "equal proportions" shall "form the basis of Representation in both Houses," is equal and just. "All feel it to be equal." Yet the conservatives now go still further — they are willing to place the House on the white basis and apply the mixed basis to the Senate only. Why refuse this adjustment? Plainly it will work well for everybody: "If the Senate would protect the East, will it not protect the West also?"

Marshall's satisfaction was "inexpressible" when he heard from both sides the language of conciliation. "I hailed these auspicious appearances with as much joy, as the inhabitant of the polar regions hails the re-appearance of the sun after his long absence of six tedious months. Can these appearances prove fallacious? Is it a meteor we have seen and mistaken for that splendid luminary which dispenses light and gladness throughout creation? It must be so, if we cannot meet on equal ground. If we cannot meet on the line that divides us equally, then take the hand of friendship, and make an equal compromise; it is vain to hope that any compromise can be made." [1]

The basis of representation does not appear in the

[1] *Debates, Va. Conv.* 561–62.

constitution, the number of Senators and Representatives being arbitrarily fixed by districts and counties; but this plan, in reality, gave the slaveholding
sections almost the same preponderance over the
comparatively non-slaveholding sections as would
have resulted from the enumeration of three fifths
of all slaves in addition to all whites.[1]

While the freehold principle was abandoned, as
Marshall foresaw that it would be, the principle of
property qualification as against manhood suffrage
was triumphant.[2] With a majority against them,
the conservatives won by better management, assisted by the personal influence of the Chief Justice,
to which, on most phases of the struggle, was added
that of Madison and Giles.

Nearly a century has passed since these happen-
ings, and Marshall's attitude now appears to have
been that of cold reaction; but he was as honest as
he was outspoken in his resistance to democratic reforms. He wanted good government, safe government. He was not in the least concerned in the rule
of the people as such. Indeed, he believed that the
more they directly controlled public affairs the worse
the business of government would be conducted.

He feared that sheer majorities would be unjust,
intolerant, tyrannical; and he was certain that they
would be untrustworthy and freakishly changeable.
These convictions would surely have dictated his
course in the Virginia Constitutional Convention of
1829–30, had no other considerations influenced him.

[1] Constitution of Virginia, 1830, Article III, Sections 1 and 2.
[2] *Ib.* Article III, Section 14.

But, in addition to his long settled and ever-petrifying conservative views, we must also take into account the conditions and public temper existing in Virginia ninety years ago. Had the convention reached any other conclusion than that to which Marshall gently guided it, it is certain that the State would have been torn by dissension, and it is not improbable that there would have been bloodshed. All things considered, it seems unsafe to affirm that Marshall's course was not the wisest for that immediate period and for that particular State.

Displaying no vision, no aspiration, no devotion to human rights, he merely acted the uninspiring but necessary part of the practical statesman dealing with an existing and a very grave situation. If Jefferson could be so frightened in 1816 that he forbade the public circulation of his perfectly sound views on the wretched Virginia Constitution of 1776,[1] can it be wondered at that the conservative Marshall in 1830 wished to compose the antagonisms of the warring factions?

The fact that the Nation was then facing the possibility of dissolution [2] must also be taken into account. That circumstance, indeed, influenced Marshall even more than did his profound conservatism. There can be little doubt that, had either the radicals or the conservatives achieved an outright victory, one part of Virginia would have separated from the other and the growing sentiment for disunion would have received a powerful impulse.

[1] See *supra*, 469.   [2] See next chapter.

Hurrying from Richmond to Washington when the convention adjourned, Marshall listened to the argument of Craig *vs.* Missouri; and then delivered one of the strongest opinions he ever wrote — the only one of his Constitutional expositions to be entirely repudiated by the Supreme Court after his death. The case grew out of the financial conditions described in the fourth chapter of this volume.

When Missouri became a State in 1821, her people found themselves in desperate case. There was no money. Banks had suspended, and specie had been drained to the Eastern commercial centers. The simplest business transactions were difficult, almost impossible. Even taxes could not be paid. The Legislature, therefore, established loan offices where citizens, by giving promissory notes, secured by mortgage or pledge of personal property, could purchase loan certificates issued by the State. These certificates were receivable for taxes and other public debts and for salt from the State salt mines. The faith and resources of Missouri were pledged for the redemption of the certificates which were negotiable and issued in denominations not exceeding ten dollars or less than fifty cents. In effect and in intention, the State thus created a local circulating medium of exchange.

On August 1, 1822, Hiram Craig and two others gave their promissory notes for $199.99 in payment for loan certificates. On maturity of these notes the borrowers refused to pay, and the State sued them; judgment against them was rendered in the trial court and this judgment was affirmed by the Supreme Court of Missouri. The case was taken, by writ of error, to the Supreme Court of the United States, where the sole question to be decided was the constitutionality of the Missouri loan office statutes.

Marshall's associates were now Johnson, Duval, Story, Thompson, McLean, and Baldwin; the last two recently appointed by Jackson. It was becoming apparent that the court was growing restive under the rigid practice of the austere theory of government and business which the Chief Justice had maintained for nearly a generation. This tendency was shown in this case by the stand taken by three of the Associate Justices. Marshall was in his seventy-sixth year, but never did his genius shine more resplendently than in his announcement of the opinion of the Supreme Court in Craig *vs.* Missouri.[1]

He held that the Missouri loan certificates were bills of credit, which the National Constitution prohibited any State to issue. "What is a bill of credit?" It is "any instrument by which a state engages to pay money at a future day; thus including a certificate given for money borrowed. . . To 'emit bills of credit' conveys to the mind the idea of issuing paper intended to circulate through the community, for its ordinary purposes, as money, which paper is redeemable at a future day." [2] The Chief Justice goes into the history of the paper money evil that caused the framers of the Constitution to forbid the States to "emit bills of credit."

---

[1] March 12, 1830.   [2] 4 Peters, 432.

Such currency always fluctuates. "Its value is continually changing; and these changes, often great and sudden, expose individuals to immense loss, are the sources of ruinous speculations, and destroy all confidence between man and man." To "cut up this mischief by the roots . . the people declared, in their Constitution, that no state should emit bills of credit. If the prohibition means anything, if the words are not empty sounds, it must comprehend the emission of any paper medium by a state government, for the purpose of common circulation." [1]

Incontestably the Missouri loan certificates are just such bills of credit. Indeed, the State law itself "speaks of them in this character." That the statute calls them certificates instead of bills of credit does not change the fact. How absurd to claim that the Constitution "meant to prohibit names and not things! That a very important act, big with great and ruinous mischief, which is expressly forbidden . . may be performed by the substitution of a name." The Constitution is not to be evaded "by giving a new name to an old thing." [2]

It is nonsense to say that these particular bills of credit are lawful because they are not made legal tender, since a separate provision applies to legal tender. The issue of legal tender currency, and also bills of credit, is equally and separately forbidden: "To sustain the one because it is not also the other; to say that bills of credit may be emitted if they be not made a tender in payment of debts; is . . to expunge that distinct, independent prohibition." [3]

[1] 4 Peters, 432. [2] *Ib.* 433. [3] *Ib.* 434.

In a well-nigh perfect historical summary, Marshall reviews experiments before and during the Revolution in bills of credit that were made legal tender, and in others that were not — all "productive of the same effects," all equally ruinous in results.[1] The Missouri law authorizing the loan certificates, for which Craig gave his promissory note, is "against the highest law of the land, and . . the note itself is utterly void."[2]

The Chief Justice closes with a brief paragraph splendid in its simple dignity and power. In his argument for Missouri, Senator Thomas H. Benton had used violent language of the kind frequently employed by the champions of State Rights: "If . . the character of a sovereign State shall be impugned," he cried, "contests about civil rights would be settled amid the din of arms, rather than in these halls of national justice."[3]

To this outburst Marshall replies: The court has been told of "the dangers which may result from" offending a sovereign State. If obedience to the Constitution and laws of the Nation "shall be calculated to bring on those dangers . . or if it shall be indispensable to the preservation of the union, and consequently of the independence and liberty of these states; these are considerations which address themselves to those departments which may with perfect propriety be influenced by them. This department can listen only to the mandates of law; and can tread only that path which is marked out by duty."[4]

[1] 4 Peters, 434–36.   [2] *Ib*. 437.   [3] *Ib*. 420.   [4] *Ib*. 438.

In this noble passage Marshall is not only re-
buking Benton; he is also speaking to the advocates
of Nullification, then becoming clamorous and threatening; he is pointing out to Andrew Jackson the path
of duty.[1]

Justices Johnson, Thompson, and McLean afterwards filed dissenting opinions, thus beginning the
departure, within the Supreme Court, from the
stern Constitutional Nationalism of Marshall. This
breach in the court deeply troubled the Chief Justice during the remaining four years of his life.

Johnson thought "that these certificates are of
a truly amphibious character." The Missouri law
"does indeed approach as near to a violation of the
Constitution as it can well go without violating its
prohibition, but it is in the exercise of an unquestionable right, although in rather a questionable
form." So, on the whole, Johnson concluded that
the Supreme Court had better hold the statute
valid.[2]

"The right of a State to borrow money cannot be
questioned," said Thompson; that is all the Missouri scheme amounts to. If these loan certificates
are bills of credit, so are "all bank notes, issued either
by the States, or under their authority."[3] Justice
McLean pointed out that Craig's case was only one
of many of the same kind. "The solemn act of a
State .. cannot be set aside .. under a doubtful
construction of the Constitution.[4] .. It would be as
gross usurpation on the part of the federal govern-

[1] See 552-58. [2] 4 Peters, 438-44.
[3] *Ib.* 445-50. [4] *Ib.* 458.

ment to interfere with State rights by an exercise
of powers not delegated, as it would be for a State
to interpose its authority against a law of the
Union." [1]

In Congress attacks upon Marshall and the Supreme Court now were renewed — but they grew
continuously feebler. At the first session after the
decision of the Missouri loan certificate case, a bill
was introduced to repeal the provision of the Judiciary Act upon which the National powers of
the Supreme Court so largely depended. "If the
twenty-fifth section is repealed, the Constitution
is practically gone," declared Story. "Our wisest
friends look with great gloom to the future." [2]

Marshall was equally despondent, but his political vision was clearer. When he read the dissenting
opinions of Johnson, Thompson, and McLean, he
wrote Story: "It requires no prophet to predict
that the 25th section [of the Judiciary Act] is to
be repealed, or to use a more fashionable phrase
to be nullified by the Supreme Court of the United
States." [3] He realized clearly that the great tribunal, the power and dignity of which he had done
so much to create, would soon be brought under
the control of those who, for some years at least,
would reject that broad and vigorous Nationalism which he had steadily and effectively asserted

[1] 4 Peters, 464.

[2] Story to Ticknor, Jan. 22, 1831, Story, II, 49. Nevertheless Story
did not despair. "It is now whispered, that the demonstrations of public opinion are so strong, that the majority [of the Judiciary Commit-
tee] will conclude not to present their report." (Ib.)

[3] Marshall to Story, Oct. 15, 1830, Proceedings, Mass. Hist. Soc.
2d Series, XIV, 342.

during almost a third of a century. One more vacancy on the Supreme Bench and a single new appointment by Jackson would give the court to the opponents of Marshall's views. Before he died, the Chief Justice was to behold two such vacancies.[1]

On January 24, 1831, William R. Davis of South Carolina presented the majority report of the Judiciary Committee favoring the repeal of that section of the Judiciary Act under which the Supreme Court had demolished State laws and annihilated the decisions of State courts.[2] James Buchanan presented the minority report.[3] A few minutes' preliminary discussion revealed the deep feeling on both sides. Philip Doddridge of Virginia declared that the bill was of "as much importance as if it were a proposition to repeal the Union of these States." William W. Ellsworth of Connecticut avowed that it was of "overwhelming magnitude."[4]

Thereupon the subject was furiously debated. Thomas H. Crawford of Pennsylvania considered Section 25 of the Judiciary Act, to be as "sacred" as the Constitution itself.[5] Henry Daniel of Kentucky asserted that the Supreme Court "stops at nothing to obtain power." Let the "States . . prepare for the worst, and protect themselves against the assaults of this gigantic tribunal."[6]

William Fitzhugh Gordon of Virginia, recently elected, but already a member of the Judiciary Com-

[1] See *infra*, 584.   [2] *Debates*, 21st Cong. 2d Sess. 532.
[3] *Ib.* 535.   [4] *Ib.* 534.   [5] *Ib.* 659.   [6] *Ib.* 665.

mittee, stoutly defended the report of the majority: "When a committee of the House had given to a subject the calmest and maturest investigation, and a motion is made to print their report, a gentleman gets up, and, in a tone of alarm, denounces the proposition as tantamount to a motion to repeal the Union." Gordon repudiated the very thought of dismemberment of the Republic — that "palladium of our hopes, and of the liberties of mankind."

As to the constitutionality of Section 25 of the Judiciary Act — "could it be new, especially to a Virginia lawyer"? when the Virginia Judiciary, with Roane at its head, had solemnly proclaimed the illegality of that section. And had not Georgia ordered her Governor to resist the enforcement of that provision of that ancient act of Congress? "I declare to God . . that I believe nothing would tend so much to compose the present agitation of the country . . as the repeal of that portion of the judiciary act." Gordon was about to discuss the nefarious case of Cohens *vs.* Virginia when his emotions overcame him — "he did not wish . . to go into the merits of the question." [1]

Thomas F. Foster of Georgia said that the Judiciary Committee had reported under a "galling fire from the press"; quoted Marshall's unfortunate language in the Convention of 1788; [2] and insisted that the "vast and alarming" powers of the Supreme Court must be bridled. [3]

[1] *Debates*, 21st Cong. 2d Sess. 620–21.
[2] *Ib.* 731, 748; and see vol. I, 454–55, of this work.
[3] *Debates*, 21st Cong. 2d Sess. 739.

But the friends of the court overwhelmed the supporters of the bill, which was rejected by a vote of 138 to 51.[1] It was ominous, however, that the South stood almost solid against the court and Nationalism.

---

[1] *Debates*, 21st Cong. 2d Sess. 542.

This was the last formal attempt, but one, made in Congress during Marshall's lifetime, to impair the efficiency of National courts. The final attack was made by Joseph Lecompte, a Representative from Kentucky, who on January 27, 1832, offered a resolution instructing the Judiciary Committee to "inquire into the expediency of amending the constitution . . so that the judges of the Supreme Court, and of the inferior courts, shall hold their offices for a limited term of years." On February 24, the House, by a vote of 141 to 27, refused to consider Lecompte's resolution, ignoring his plea to be allowed to explain it. (*Debates*, 22d Cong. 1st Sess. 1856–57.) So summary and brusque — almost contemptuous — was the rejection of Lecompte's proposal, as almost to suggest that personal feeling was an element in the action taken by the House.

CHAPTER X

THE FINAL CONFLICT

Liberty and Union, now and forever, one and inseparable. (Daniel Webster.)

Fellow citizens, the die is now cast. Prepare for the crisis and meet it as becomes men and freemen. (South Carolina Ordinance of Nullification.)

The Union has been prolonged thus far by miracles. I fear they cannot continue. (Marshall.)

> It is time to be old,
> To take in sail.   (Emerson.)

THE last years of Marshall's life were clouded with sadness, almost despair. His health failed; his wife died; the Supreme Court was successfully defied; his greatest opinion was repudiated and denounced by a strong and popular President; his associates on the Bench were departing from some of his most cherished views; and the trend of public events convinced him that his labor to construct an enduring nation, to create institutions of orderly freedom, to introduce stability and system into democracy, had been in vain.

Yet, even in this unhappy period, there were hours of triumph for John Marshall. He heard his doctrine of Nationalism championed by Daniel Webster, who, in one of the greatest debates of history, used Marshall's arguments and almost his very words; he beheld the militant assertion of the same principle by Andrew Jackson, who, in this instance, also employed Marshall's reasoning and method of statement; and he witnessed the sudden flowering of public appreciation of his character and services.

During the spring of 1831, Marshall found himself, for the first time in his life, suffering from acute

JOHN MARSHALL
Painted by Robert Matthew Sully

pain. His Richmond physician could give him no relief; and he became so despondent that he determined to resign immediately after the ensuing Presidential election, in case Jackson should be defeated, an event which many then thought probable. In a letter about the house at which the members of the Supreme Court were to board during the next term, Marshall tells Story of his purpose: "Being . . a bird of passage, whose continuance with you cannot be long, I did not chuse to permit my convenience or my wishes to weigh a feather in the permanent arrangements. . . But in addition, I felt serious doubts, although I did not mention them, whether I should be with you at the next term.

"What I am about to say is, of course, in perfect confidence which I would not breathe to any other person whatever. I had unaccountably calculated on the election of P [residen] t taking place next fall, and had determined to make my continuance in office another year dependent on that event.

"You know how much importance I attach to the character of the person who is to succeed me, and calculate the influence which probabilities on that subject would have on my continuance in office. This, however, is a matter of great delicacy on which I cannot and do not speak.

"My erroneous calculation of the time of the election was corrected as soon as the pressure of official duty was removed from my mind, and I had nearly decided on my course, but recent events produce such real uncertainty respecting the future as to create doubts whether I ought not to await the same chances in the fall of 32 which I had intended to await in the fall of 31." [1]

Marshall steadily became worse, and in September he went to Philadelphia to consult the celebrated physician and surgeon, Dr. Philip Syng Physick, who at once perceived that the Chief Justice was suffering from stone in the bladder. His affliction could be relieved only by the painful and delicate operation of lithotomy, which Dr. Physick had introduced in America. From his sick-room Marshall writes Story of his condition during the previous five months, and adds that he looks "with impatience for the operation." [2] He is still concerned about the court's boarding-place and again refers to his intention of leaving the Bench: "In the course of the summer . . I found myself unequal to the effective consideration of any subject, and had determined to resign at the close of the year. This determination, however, I kept to myself, being determined to remain master of my own conduct." Story had answered Marshall's letter of June 26, evidently protesting against the thought of the Chief Justice giving up his office.

Marshall replies: "On the most interesting part of your letter I have felt, and still feel, great difficulty. You understand my general sentiments on that subject as well as I do myself. I am most earnestly attached to the character of the department, and to the wishes and convenience of those with whom it has been my pride and my happiness to be associated for so many years. I cannot be insensible to

[1] Marshall to Story, June 26, 1831, *Proceedings, Mass. Hist. Soc.* 2d Series, XIV, 344-45.

[2] Same to same, Oct. 12, 1831, *ib.* 346-48.

the gloom which lours over us. I have a repugnance to abandoning you under such circumstances which is almost invincible. But the solemn convictions of my judgement sustained by some pride of character admonish me not to hazard the disgrace of continuing in office a mere inefficient pageant." [1]

Had Adams been reëlected in 1828, there can be no doubt that Marshall would have resigned during that Administration; and it is equally certain that, if Jackson had been defeated in 1832, the Chief Justice would have retired immediately. The Democratic success in the election of that year determined him to hold on in an effort to keep the Supreme Court, as long as possible, unsubmerged by the rising tide of radical Localism. Perhaps he also clung to a desperate hope that, during his lifetime, a political reaction would occur and a conservative President be chosen who could appoint his successor.

When Marshall arrived at Philadelphia, the bar of that city wished to give him a dinner, and, by way of invitation, adopted remarkable resolutions expressing their grateful praise and affectionate admiration. The afflicted Chief Justice, deeply touched, declined in a letter of singular grace and dignity: "It is impossible for me . . to do justice to the feelings with which I receive your very flattering address; . . to have performed the official duties assigned to me by my country in such a manner as to acquire the approbation of" the Philadelphia bar, "affords me the highest gratification of which I am capable, and is

[1] Marshall to Story, Oct. 12, 1831, *Proceedings, Mass. Hist. Soc.* 2d Series, XIV, 347. A rumor finally got about that Marshall contemplated resigning. (See Niles, XL, 90.)

more than an ample reward for the labor which those duties impose." Marshall's greatest satisfaction, he says, is that he and his associates on the Supreme Bench "have never sought to enlarge the judicial power beyond its proper bounds, nor feared to carry it to the fullest extent that duty required." [1] The members of the bar then begged the Chief Justice to receive them "in a body" at "the United States Courtroom"; and also to "permit his portrait to be taken" by "an eminent artist of this city." [2]

With anxiety, but calmness and even good humor, Marshall awaited the operation. Just before he went to the surgeon's table, Dr. Jacob Randolph, who assisted Dr. Physick, found Marshall eating a hearty breakfast. Notwithstanding the pain he suffered, the Chief Justice laughingly explained that, since it might be the last meal he ever would enjoy, he had determined to make the most of it. He understood that the chances of surviving the operation were against him, but he was eager to take them, since he would rather die than continue to suffer the agony he had been enduring.

While the long and excruciating operation went on, by which more than a thousand calculi were removed, Marshall was placid, "scarcely uttering a murmur throughout the whole procedure." The

[1] The resolutions of the bar had included the same idea, and Marshall emphasized it by reiterating it in his response.

[2] Hazard's *Pennsylvania Register*, as quoted in Dillon, III, 430–33. The artist referred to was either Thomas Sully, or Henry Inman, who had studied under Sully. During the following year, Inman painted the portrait and it was so excellent that it brought the artist his first general recognition. The original now hangs in the rooms of the Philadelphia Law Association. A reproduction of it appears as the frontispiece of this volume.

physicians ascribed his recovery "in a great degree , . to his extraordinary self possession, and to the calm and philosophical views which he took of his case." [1]

Marshall writes Story about his experience and the results of the treatment, saying that he must take medicine "continually to prevent new formations," and adding, with humorous melancholy, that he "must submit too to a severe and most unsociable regimen." He cautions Story to care for his own health, which Judge Peters had told him was bad. "Without your vigorous and powerful co-operation I should be in despair, and think the 'ship must be given up.'" [2]

On learning of his improved condition, Story writes Peters from Cambridge: "This seems to me a special interposition of Providence in favor of the Constitution. . . He is beloved and reverenced here beyond all measure, though not beyond his merits. Next to Washington he stands the idol of all good men." [3]

While on this distressing visit to Philadelphia, Marshall writes his wife two letters — the last letters to her of which any originals or copies can be found. "I anticipate with a pleasure which I know you will share the time when I may sit by your side by our tranquil fire side & enjoy the happiness of your society without inflicting on you the pain of witnessing my suffering. . . I am treated with the most flattering attentions in Philadelphia. They give me pain,

[1] Randolph: *A Memoir on the Life and Character of Philip Syng Physick*, *M.D.* 97–99.

[2] Marshall to Story, Nov. 10, 1831, *Proceedings, Mass. Hist. Soc.* 2d Series, xiv, 348–49.

[3] Story to Peters, Oct. 29, 1831, Story, ii, 70.

the more pain as the necessity of declining many of them may be ascribed to a want of sensibility." [1]

His recovery assured, Marshall again writes his wife: "I have at length risen from my bed and am able to hold a pen. The most delightful use I can make of it is to tell you that I am getting well .. from the painful disease with which I have been so long affected... Nothing delights me so much as to hear from my friends and especially from you. How much was I gratified at the line from your own hand in Mary's letter.[2].. I am much obliged by your offer to lend me money.[3] I hope I shall not need it but can not as yet speak positively as my stay has been longer and my expenses greater than I had anticipated on leaving home. Should I use any part of it, you may be assured it will be replaced on my return. But this is a subject on which I know you feel no solicitude... God bless you my dearest Polly love to all our friends. Ever your most affectionate J. Marshall." [4]

On December 25, 1831, his "dearest Polly" died. The previous day, she hung about his neck a locket containing a wisp of her hair. For the remainder of his life he wore this memento, never parting with it night or day.[5] Her weakness, physical and mental, which prevailed throughout practically the whole of

---

[1] Marshall to his wife, Oct. 6, 1831, MS.

[2] This is the only indication in any of Marshall's letters that his wife had written him.

[3] Mrs. Marshall had a modest fortune of her own, bequeathed to her by her uncle. She invested this quite independently of her husband. (Leigh to Biddle, Sept. 7, 1837, McGrane, 289.)

[4] Marshall to his wife, Nov. 8, 1831, MS.

[5] Terhune, 98. This locket is now in the possession of Marshall's granddaughter, Miss Emily Harvie of Richmond.

their married life, inspired in Marshall a chivalric adoration. On the morning of the first anniversary of her death, Story chanced to go into Marshall's room and "found him in tears. He had just finished writing out for me some lines of General Burgoyne, of which he spoke to me last evening as eminently beautiful and affecting. . . I saw at once that he had been shedding tears over the memory of his own wife, and he has said to me several times during the term, that the moment he relaxes from business he feels exceedingly depressed, and rarely goes through a night without weeping over his departed wife. . . I think he is the most extraordinary man I ever saw, for the depth and tenderness of his feelings." [1]

[1] Story to his wife, March 4, 1832, Story, II, 86–87.

Soon after the death of his wife, Marshall made his will "entirely in [his] . . own handwriting." A more informal document of the kind seldom has been written. It is more like a familiar letter than a legal paper; yet it is meticulously specific. "I owe nothing on my own account," he begins. (He specifies one or two small obligations as trustee for women relatives and as surety for "considerable sums" for his son-in-law, Jacquelin B. Harvie.) The will shows that he owns bank and railroad stock and immense quantities of land. He equally divides his property among his children, making special provision that the portion of his daughter Mary shall be particularly safeguarded.

One item of the will is curious: "I give to each of my grandsons named John one thousand acres, part of my tract of land called Canaan lying in Randolph county. If at the time of my death either of my sons should have no son living named John, then I give the thousand acres to any son he may have named Thomas, in token for my love for my father and veneration for his memory. If there should be no son named John or Thomas, then I give the land to the eldest son and if no sons to the daughters."

He makes five additions to his will, three of which he specifically calls "codicils." One of these is principally "to emancipate my faithful servant Robin and I direct his emancipation if he *chuses* to conform to the laws on that subject, requiring that he should leave the state or if permission can be obtained for his continuing to reside in it." If Robin elects to go to Liberia, Marshall gives him one hundred dol-

But Marshall had also written something which he did not show even to Story — a tribute to his wife:

"This day of joy and festivity to the whole Christian world is, to my sad heart, the anniversary of the keenest affliction which humanity can sustain. While all around is gladness, my mind dwells on the silent tomb, and cherishes the remembrance of the beloved object which it contains.

"On the 25th of December, 1831, it was the will of Heaven to take to itself the companion who had sweetened the choicest part of my life, had rendered toil a pleasure, had partaken of all my feelings, and was enthroned in the inmost recess of my heart. Never can I cease to feel the loss and to deplore it. Grief for her is too sacred ever to be profaned on this day, which shall be, during my existence, marked by a recollection of her virtues.

"On the 3d of January, 1783, I was united by the holiest bonds to the woman I adored. From the moment of our union to that of our separation, I never ceased to thank Heaven for this its best gift. Not a moment passed in which I did not consider her as a blessing from which the chief happiness of my life was derived. This never-dying sentiment, originating in love, was cherished by a long and close observation of as amiable and estimable qualities as ever adorned

lars. "If he does not go there I give him fifty dollars." In case it should be found "impracticable to liberate" Robin, "I desire that he may choose his master among my sons, or if he prefer my daughter that he may be held in trust for her and her family as is the other property bequeathed in trust for her, and that he may always be treated as a faithful and meritorious servant." (Will and Codicils of John Marshall, Records of Henrico County, Richmond, and Fauquier County, Warrenton, Virginia.)

the female bosom. To a person which in youth was very attractive, to manners uncommonly pleasing, she added a fine understanding, and the sweetest temper which can accompany a just and modest sense of what was due to herself.

"She was educated with a profound reverence for religion, which she preserved to her last moments. This sentiment, among her earliest and deepest impressions, gave a colouring to her whole life. Hers was the religion taught by the Saviour of man. She was a firm believer in the faith inculcated by the Church (Episcopal) in which she was bred.

"I have lost her, and with her have lost the solace of my life! Yet she remains still the companion of my retired hours, still occupies my inmost bosom. When alone and unemployed, my mind still recurs to her. More than a thousand times since the 25th of December, 1831, have I repeated to myself the beautiful lines written by General Burgoyne, under a similar affliction, substituting 'Mary' for 'Anna':

> " ' Encompass'd in an angel's frame,
>   An angel's virtues lay:
> Too soon did Heaven assert its claim
>   And take its own away!
> My Mary's worth, my Mary's charms,
>   Can never more return!
> What now shall fill these widow'd arms?
>   Ah, me! my Mary's urn!
> Ah, me! ah, me! my Mary's urn!' " [1]

After his wife's death, Marshall arranged to live at "Leeds Manor," Fauquier County, a large house

[1] Meade, II, footnote to 222. It would seem that Marshall showed this tribute to no one during his lifetime except, perhaps, to his children. At any rate, it was first made public in Bishop Meade's book in 1857.

on part of the Fairfax estate which he had given to
his son, James Keith Marshall. A room, with very
thick walls to keep out the noise of his son's many
children, was built for him, adjoining the main
dwelling. Here he brought his library, papers, and
many personal belongings. His other sons and their
families lived not far away; "Leeds Manor" was
in the heart of the country where he had grown to
early manhood; and there he expected to spend his
few remaining years.[1] He could not, however, tear
himself from his Richmond home, where he continued to live most of the time until his death.[2]

When fully recovered from his operation, Marshall seemed to acquire fresh strength. He "is in
excellent health, never better, and as firm and ro-
bust in mind as in body," Story informs Charles
Sumner.[3]

The Chief Justice was, however, profoundly depressed. The course that President Jackson was
then pursuing — his attitude toward the Supreme
Court in the Georgia controversy,[4] his arbitrary and
violent rule, his hostility to the second Bank of the
United States — alarmed and distressed Marshall.

The Bank had finally justified the brightest predictions of its friends. Everywhere in the country
its notes were as good as gold, while abroad they
were often above par.[5] Its stock was owned in every

[1] Statements to the author by Miss Elizabeth Marshall of "Leeds
Manor," and by Judge J. K. N. Norton of Alexandria, Va.
[2] Statement to the author by Miss Emily Harvie. Most of Marshall's letters to Story during these years were written from Richmond.
[3] Story to Sumner, Feb. 6, 1833, Story, II, 120.   [4] See *infra*, 540-51.
[5] See Catterall, 407, 421-22, 467; and see especially Parton: *Jackson*, III, 257-58.

nation and widely distributed in America.[1] Up to the time when Jackson began his warfare upon the Bank, the financial management of Nicholas Biddle had been as brilliant as it was sound.[2]

But popular hostility to the Bank had never ceased. In addition to the old animosity toward any central institution of finance, charges were made that directors of certain branches of the Bank had used their power to interfere in politics. As implacable as they were unjust were the assaults made by Democratic politicians upon Jeremiah Mason, director of the branch at Portsmouth, New Hampshire. Had the Bank consented to Mason's removal, it is possible that Jackson's warfare on it would not have been prosecuted.[3]

The Bank's charter was to expire in 1836. In his first annual Message to Congress the President briefly called attention to the question of rechartering the institution. The constitutionality of the Bank Act was doubtful at best, he intimated, and the Bank certainly had not established a sound and uniform currency.[4] In his next Message, a year later, Jackson repeated more strongly his attack upon the Bank.[5]

Two years afterwards, on the eve of the Presidential campaign of 1832, the friends of the Bank in Congress passed, by heavy majorities, a bill extend-

[1] Catterall, Appendix IX, 508.
[2] Ib. chaps. V and VII. Biddle was appointed director of the Bank by President Monroe in 1819, and displayed such ability that, in 1823, he was elected president of the institution. Not until he received information that Jackson was hostile to the Bank did Biddle begin the morally wrong and practically unwise policy of loaning money without proper security to editors and members of Congress.
[3] Parton: *Jackson*, III, 260.   [4] Richardson, II, 462.   [5] *Ib.* 528–29.

ing the charter for fifteen years after March 3, 1836, the date of its expiration.[1] The principal supporters of this measure were Clay and Webster and, indeed, most of the weighty men in the National Legislature. But they were enemies of Jackson, and he looked upon the rechartering of the Bank as a personal affront.

On July 4, 1832, the bill was sent to the President. Six days later he returned it with his veto. Jackson's veto message was as able as it was cunning. Parts of it were demagogic appeals to popular passion; but the heart of it was an attack upon Marshall's opinions in M'Culloch *vs.* Maryland and Osborn *vs.* The Bank.

The Bank is a monopoly, its stockholders and directors a "privileged order"; worse still, the institution is rapidly passing into the hands of aliens —"already is almost a third of the stock in foreign hands." If we must have a bank, let it be "*purely American.*" This aristocratic, monopolistic, un-American concern exists by the authority of an unconstitutional act of Congress. Even worse is the rechartering act which he now vetoed.

The decision of the Supreme Court in the Bank cases, settled nothing, said Jackson. Marshall's opinions were, for the most part, erroneous and "ought not to control the co-ordinate authorities of this Government. The Congress, the Executive, and the Court must each for itself be guided by its own opinion of the Constitution. . . It is as much the

[1] See Catterall, 235. For account of the fight for the Bank Bill see *ib.* chap. x.

duty of the House of Representatives, of the Senate, and of the President to decide upon the constitutionality of any bill or resolution which may be presented to them for passage or approval as it is of the supreme judges when it may be brought before them for judicial decision.

"The opinion of the judges has no more authority over Congress than the opinion of Congress has over the judges, and on that point the President is independent of both. The authority of the Supreme Court must not, therefore, be permitted to control the Congress or the Executive when acting in their legislative capacities, but to have only such influence as the force of their reasoning may deserve." [1]

But, says Jackson, the court did not decide that "all features of this corporation are compatible with the Constitution." He quotes — and puts in italics — Marshall's statement that *"where the law is not prohibited and is really calculated to effect any of the objects intrusted to the Government, to undertake here to inquire into the degree of its necessity would be to pass the line which circumscribes the judicial department and to tread on legislative ground."* This language, insists Jackson, means that "it is the exclusive province of Congress and the President to decide whether the particular features of this act are *necessary* and *proper* .. and therefore constitutional, or *unnecessary* and *improper*, and therefore unconstitutional." [2] Thereupon Jackson points out what he considers to be the defects of the bill.

Congress has no power to "grant exclusive privi-

---

[1] Richardson, II, 580–82.   [2] *Ib.* 582–83.

leges or monopolies," except in the District of Columbia and in the matter of patents and copyrights.
"Every act of Congress, therefore, which attempts,
by grants of monopolies or sale of exclusive privileges
for a limited time, or a time without limit, to restrict
or extinguish its own discretion in the choice of means
to execute its delegated powers, is equivalent to a
legislative amendment of the Constitution, and palpably unconstitutional." [1] Jackson fiercely attacks
Marshall's opinion that the States cannot tax the
National Bank and its branches.

The whole message is able, adroit, and, on its face,
plainly intended as a campaign document.[2] A shrewd
appeal is made to the State banks. Popular jealousy
and suspicion of wealth and power are skillfully
played upon: "The rich and powerful" always use
governments for "their selfish purposes." When laws
are passed "to grant titles, gratuities, and exclusive
privileges, to make the rich richer and the potent
more powerful, the humble members of society —
the farmers, mechanics, and laborers — who have
neither the time nor the means of securing like favors
to themselves, have a right to complain of the injustice of their Government.

"There are no necessary evils in government,"
says Jackson. "Its evils exist only in its abuses. If
it would confine itself to equal protection, and, as

[1] Richardson, II, 584.

[2] Jackson's veto message was used with tremendous effect in the
Presidential campaign of 1832. There cannot be the least doubt that
the able politicians who managed Jackson's campaign and, indeed,
shaped his Administration, designed that the message should be put to
this use. These politicians were William B. Lewis, Amos Kendall,
Martin Van Buren, and Samuel Swartwout.

Heaven does its rains, shower its favors alike on the high and the low, the rich and the poor, it would be an unqualified blessing" — thus he runs on to his conclusion.[1]

The masses of the people, particularly those of the South, responded with wild fervor to the President's assault upon the citadel of the "money power." John Marshall, the defender of special privilege, had said that the Bank law was protected by the Constitution; but Andrew Jackson, the champion of the common people, declared that it was prohibited by the Constitution. Hats in the air, then, and loud cheers for the hero who had dared to attack and to overcome this financial monster as he had fought and beaten the invading British!

Marshall was infinitely disgusted. He informs Story of Virginia's applause of Jackson's veto: "We are up to the chin in politics. Virginia was always insane enough to be opposed to the Bank of The United States, and therefore hurras for the veto. But we are a little doubtful how it may work in Pennsylvania. It is not difficult to account for the part New York may take. She has sagacity enough to see her interest in putting down the present bank. Her mercantile position gives her a controul, a commanding controul, over the currency and the exchanges of the country, if there be no Bank of The United States. Going for herself she may approve this policy; but Virginia ought not to drudge for her benefit." [2]

[1] Richardson, II, 590–91.
[2] Marshall to Story, Aug. 2, 1832, *Proceedings, Mass. Hist. Soc.* 2d Series, XIV, 349–51.

Jackson did not sign the bill for the improvement of rivers and harbors, passed at the previous session of Congress, because, as he said, he had not "sufficient time .. to examine it before the adjournment." [1] Everybody took the withholding of his signature as a veto.[2] This bill included a feasible project for making the Virginia Capital accessible to seagoing vessels. Even this action of the President was applauded by Virginians:

"We show our wisdom most strikingly in approving the veto on the harbor bill also," Marshall writes Story. "That bill contained an appropriation intended to make Richmond a seaport, which she is not at present, for large vessels fit to cross the Atlantic. The appropriation was whittled down in the House of Representatives to almost nothing... Yet we wished the appropriation because we were confident that Congress when correctly informed, would add the necessary sum. This too is vetoed; and for this too our sagacious politicians are thankful. We seem to think it the summit of human wisdom, or rather of American patriotism, to preserve our poverty." [3]

During the Presidential campaign of 1832, Marshall all but despaired of the future of the Republic.

[1] Richardson, II, 638. There was a spirited contest in the House over this bill. (See *Debates*, 22d Cong. 1st Sess. 2438-44, 3248-57, 3286.) It reached the President at the end of the session, so that he had only to refuse to sign it, in order to kill the measure.

[2] In fact Jackson did send a message to Congress on December 6, 1832, explaining his reasons for having let the bill die. (Richardson, II, 638-39.)

[3] Marshall to Story, Aug. 2, 1832, *Proceedings, Mass. Hist. Soc.* 2d Series, XIV, 350.

The autocracy of Jackson's reign; the popular enthusiasm which greeted his wildest departures from established usage and orderly government; the state of the public mind, indicated everywhere by the encouragement of those whom Marshall believed to be theatrical and adventurous demagogues — all these circumstances perturbed and saddened him.

And for the time being, his fears were wholly justified. Triumphantly reëlected, Jackson pursued the Bank relentlessly. Finally he ordered that the Government funds should no longer be deposited in that hated institution. Although that desperate act brought disaster on business throughout the land, it was acclaimed by the multitude. In alarm and despair, Marshall writes Story: "We [Virginians] are insane on the subject of the Bank. Its friends, who are not numerous, dare not, a few excepted, to avow themselves."[1]

But the sudden increase and aggressiveness of disunion sentiment oppressed Marshall more heavily than any other public circumstance of his last years. The immediate occasion for the recrudescence of

[1] Marshall to Story, Dec. 3, 1834, *Proceedings, Mass. Hist. Soc.* 2d Series, xiv, 359.

The outspoken and irritable Kent expressed the conservatives' opinion of Jackson almost as forcibly as Ames stated their views of Jefferson: "I look upon Jackson as a detestable, ignorant, reckless, vain and malignant Tyrant... This American Elective Monarchy frightens me. The Experiment, with its foundations laid on universal Suffrage and an unfettered and licentious Press is of too violent a nature for our excitable People. We have not in our large cities, if we have in our country, moral firmness enough to bear it. *It racks the machine too much.*" (Kent to Story, April 11, 1834, Story MSS. Mass. Hist. Soc.) In this letter Kent perfectly states Marshall's convictions, which were shared by nearly every judge and lawyer in America who was not "in politics."

Localism was the Tariff. Since the Tariff of 1816 the South had been discontented with the protection afforded the manufacturers of the North and East; and had made loud outcry against the protective Tariff of 1824. The Southern people felt that their interests were sacrificed for the benefit of the manufacturing sections; they believed that all that they produced had to be sold in a cheap, unprotected market, and all that they purchased had to be bought in a dear, protected market; they were convinced that the protective tariff system, and, indeed, the whole Nationalist policy, meant the ruin of the South.

Moreover, they began to see that the power that could enact a protective tariff, control commerce, make internal improvements, could also control slavery — perhaps abolish it.[1] Certainly that was "the spirit" of Marshall's construction of the Constitution, they said. "Sir," exclaimed Robert S. Garnett of Virginia during the debate in the House on the Tariff of 1824, "we must look very little to consequences if we do not perceive in the spirit of this construction, combined with the political fanaticism of the period, reason to anticipate, at no distant day, the usurpation, on the part of Congress, of the right to legislate upon a subject which, if you once touch, will inevitably throw this country into revolution — I mean that of slavery. . . Can whole nations be mistaken? When I speak of nations, I mean Virginia, the Carolinas, and other great Southern commonwealths."[2]

John Carter of South Carolina warned the House

[1] See *supra*, 420. [2] *Annals*, 18th Cong. 1st Sess. 2097.

not to pass a law "which would, as to this portion of the Union, be registered on our statute books as a dead letter." [1] James Hamilton, Jr., of the same State, afterwards a Nullification Governor, asked: "Is it nothing to weaken the attachment of one section of this confederacy to the bond of Union? . . Is it nothing to sow the seeds of incurable alienation?" [2]

The Tariff of 1828 alarmed and angered the Southern people to the point of frenzy. "The interests of the South have been . . shamefully sacrificed!" cried Hayne in the Senate. "Her feelings have been disregarded; her wishes slighted; her honest pride insulted!" [3] So enraged were Southern Representatives that, for the most part, they declined to speak. Hamilton expressed their sentiments. He disdained to enter into the "chaffering" about the details of the bill. [4] "You are coercing us to inquire, whether we can afford to belong to a confederacy in which severe restrictions, tending to an ultimate prohibition of foreign commerce, is its established policy. [5] . . Is it . . treason, sir, to tell you that there is a condition of public feeling throughout the southern part of this confederacy, which no prudent man will treat with contempt, and no man who loves his country will not desire to see allayed? [6] . . I trust, sir, that this cup may pass from us. . . But, if an adverse destiny should be ours — if we are doomed to drink 'the waters of bitterness,' in their utmost woe, . . South Carolina will be found on the side of those principles, standing firmly, on the very ground which

[1] *Annals*, 18th Cong. 1st Sess. 2163. [2] *Ib.* 2208.
[3] *Debates*, 20th Cong. 1st Sess. 746. [4] *Ib.* 2431.
[5] *Ib.* 2434. [6] *Ib.* 2435.

is canonized by that revolution which has made us what we are, and imbued us with the spirit of a free and sovereign people." [1]

Retaliation, even forcible resistance, was talked throughout the South when this "Tariff of Abominations," as the Act of 1828 was called, became a law. The feeling in South Carolina especially ran high. Some of her ablest men proposed that the State should tax all articles [2] protected by the tariff. Pledges were made at public meetings not to buy protected goods manufactured in the North. At the largest gathering in the history of the State, resolutions were passed demanding that all trade with tariff States be stopped. [3] Nullification was proposed. [4] The people wildly acclaimed such a method of righting their wrongs, and Calhoun gave to the world his famous "Exposition," a treatise based on the Jeffersonian doctrine of thirty years previous. [5]

A little more than a year after the passage of the Tariff of 1824, and the publication of Marshall's opinions in Osborn vs. The Bank and Gibbons vs. Ogden, Jefferson had written Giles of the "encroachments" by the National Government, particularly by the Supreme Court and by Congress. How should these invasions of the rights of the States be checked? "Reason and argument? You might as well reason

[1] *Debates*, 20th Cong. 1st Sess. 2437.
[2] This was the plan of George McDuffie. Calhoun approved it. (Houston: *A Critical Study of Nullification in South Carolina*, 70–71.)
[3] *Ib.*   [4] *Ib.* 75.
[5] Calhoun's "Exposition" was reported by a special committee of the South Carolina House of Representatives on December 19, 1828. It was not adopted, however, but was printed, and is included in *Statutes at Large of South Carolina*, edited by Thomas Cooper, I, 247–73.

and argue with the marble columns encircling them [Congress and the Supreme Court]. . . Are we then *to stand to our arms?* . . No. That must be the last resource." But the States should denounce the acts of usurpation "until their accumulation shall overweigh that of separation." [1] Jefferson's letter, written only six months before his death, was made public just as the tide of belligerent Nullification was beginning to rise throughout the South. [2]

At the same time defiance of National authority came also from Georgia, the cause being as distinct from the tariff as the principle of resistance was identical. This cause was the forcible seizure, by Georgia, of the lands of the Cherokee Indians and the action of the Supreme Court in cases growing out of Georgia's policy and the execution of it.

By numerous treaties between the National Government and the Cherokee Nation, the Indians were guaranteed protection in the enjoyment of their lands. When Georgia, in 1802, ceded her claim to that vast territory stretching westward to the Mississippi, it had been carefully provided that the lands of the Indians should be preserved from seizure or entry without their consent, and that their rights should be defended from invasion or disturbance. The Indian titles were to be extinguished, however, as soon as this could be done peaceably, and without inordinate expense.

In 1827, these Georgia Cherokees, who were highly civilized, adopted a constitution, set up a

[1] Jefferson to Giles, Dec. 26, 1825, *Works:* Ford, xii, 425–26.
[2] Niles, xxv, 48.

government of their own modeled upon that of the
United States, and declared themselves a sovereign
independent nation.[1] Immediately thereafter the
Legislature of Georgia passed resolutions declaring
that the Cherokee lands belonged to the State "absolutely" — that the Indians were only "tenants
at her will"; that Georgia had the right to, and
would, extend her laws throughout her "conven-
tional limits," and "coerce obedience to them from all
descriptions of people, be they white, red, or black."[2]

Deliberately, but without delay, the State enacted
laws taking over the Cherokee lands, dividing them
into counties, and annulling "all laws, usages and customs" of the Indians.[3] The Cherokees appealed to
President Jackson, who rebuffed them and upheld
Georgia.[4] Gold was discovered in the Indian country, and white adventurers swarmed to the mines.[5]
Georgia passed acts forbidding the Indians to hold
courts, or to make laws or regulations for the tribe.
White persons found in the Cherokee country without a license from the Governor were, upon conviction, to be imprisoned at hard labor for four years.
A State guard was established to "protect" the
mines and arrest any one "detected in a violation
of the laws of this State."[6] Still other acts equally
oppressive were passed.[7]

[1] See Phillips: *Georgia and State Rights*, in *Annual Report, Am. Hist.
Ass'n* (1901), II, 71.

[2] Resolution of Dec. 27, 1827, *Laws of Georgia, 1827*, 249; and
see Phillips, 72.

[3] Act of Dec. 20, *Laws of Georgia, 1828*, 88–89.

[4] Parton: *Jackson*, III, 272.   [5] Phillips, 72.

[6] Act of Dec. 22, *Laws of Georgia, 1830*, 114–17.

[7] Act of Dec. 23, *ib.* 118; Dec. 21, *ib.* 127–43; Dec. 22, *ib.* 145–46.

On the advice of William Wirt, then Attorney-General of the United States, and of John Sergeant of Philadelphia, the Indians applied to the Supreme Court for an injunction to stop Georgia from executing these tyrannical statutes. The whole country was swept by a tempest of popular excitement. South and North took opposite sides. The doctrine of State Rights, in whose name internal improvements, the Tariff, the Bank, and other Nationalist measures had been opposed, was invoked in behalf of Georgia.

The Administration tried to induce the Cherokees to exchange their farms, mills, and stores in Georgia for untamed lands in the Indian Territory. The Indians sent a commission to investigate that far-off region, which reported that it was unfit for agriculture and that, once there, the Cherokees would have to fight savage tribes.[1] Again they appealed to the President; again Jackson told them that Georgia had absolute authority over them. Angry debates arose in Congress over a bill to send the reluctant natives to the wilds of the then remote West.[2]

Such was the origin of the case of The Cherokee Nation *vs.* The State of Georgia.[3] At Wirt's request,

[1] Wirt to Carr, June 21, 1830, Kennedy, ii, 292–93.

[2] See *Debates*, 21st Cong. 1st Sess. 309–57, 359–67, 374–77, 994–1133. For the text of this bill as it passed the House see *ib.* 1135–36. It became a law May 28, 1830. (*U.S. Statutes at Large*, iv, 411.) For an excellent account of the execution of this measure see Abel: *The History of the Events Resulting in Indian Consolidation West of the Mississippi River, Annual Report, Am. Hist. Ass'n*, 1906, i, 381–407. This essay, by Dr. Anne Héloise Abel, is an exhaustive and accurate treatment of the origin, development, and execution of the policy pursued by the National and State Governments toward the Indians. Dr. Abel attaches a complete bibliography and index to her brochure.

[3] 5 Peters, 1.

Judge Dabney Carr laid the whole matter before Marshall, Wirt having determined to proceed with it or to drop it as the Chief Justice should advise. Marshall, of course, declined to express any opinion on the legal questions involved: " I have followed the debate in both houses of Congress, with profound attention and with deep interest, and have wished, most sincerely, that both the executive and legislative departments had thought differently on the subject. Humanity must bewail the course which is pursued, whatever may be the decision of policy." [1]

Before the case could be heard by the Supreme Court, Georgia availed herself of an opportunity to show her contempt for the National Judiciary and to assert her "sovereign rights." A Cherokee named George Tassels was convicted of murder in the Superior Court of Hall County, Georgia, and lay in jail

[1] Marshall to Carr, 1830, Kennedy, II, 296–97.
As a young man Marshall had thought so highly of Indians that he supported Patrick Henry's plan for white amalgamation with them. (See vol. I, 241, of this work.) Yet he did not think our general policy toward the Indians had been unwise. They were, he wrote Story, "a fierce and dangerous enemy whose love of war made them sometimes the aggressors, whose numbers and habits made them formidable, and whose cruel system of warfare seemed to justify every endeavour to remove them to a distance from civilized settlements. It was not until after the adoption of our present government that respect for our own safety permitted us to give full indulgence to those principles of humanity and justice which ought always to govern our conduct towards the aborigines when this course can be pursued without exposing ourselves to the most afflicting calamities. That time, however, is unquestionably arrived, and every oppression now exercised on a helpless people depending on our magnanimity and justice for the preservation of their existence impresses a deep stain on the American character. I often think with indignation on our disreputable conduct (as I think) in the affair of the Creeks of Georgia." (Marshall to Story, Oct. 29, 1829, *Proceedings, Mass. Hist. Soc.* 2d Series, XIV, 337–38.)

until the sentence of death should be executed. A writ of error from the Supreme Court was obtained, and Georgia was ordered to appear before that tribunal and defend the judgment of the State Court.

The order was signed by Marshall. Georgia's reply was as insulting and belligerent as it was prompt and spirited. The Legislature resolved that "the interference by the chief justice of the supreme court of the U. States, in the administration of the criminal laws of this state, . . is a flagrant violation of her rights"; that the Governor "and every other officer of this state" be directed to "disregard any and every mandate and process . . purporting to proceed from the chief justice or any associate justice of the supreme court of the United States"; that the Governor be "authorised and required, with all the force and means . . at his command . . to resist and repel any and every invasion from whatever quarter, upon the administration of the criminal laws of this state"; that Georgia refuses to become a party to "the case sought to be made before the supreme court"; and that the Governor, "by express," direct the sheriff of Hall County to execute the law in the case of George Tassels.[1]

Five days later, Tassels was hanged,[2] and the Supreme Court of the United States, powerless to vindicate its authority, defied and insulted by a "sovereign" State, abandoned by the Administration, was humiliated and helpless.

When he went home on the evening of January 4, 1831, John Quincy Adams, now a member of

[1] Niles, xxxix, 338.   [2] Ib. 353.

Congress, wrote in his diary that "the resolutions
of the legislature of Georgia setting at defiance the
Supreme Court of the United States are published
and approved in the Telegraph, the Administration
newspaper at this place. . . The Constitution, the
laws and treaties of the United States are prostrate
in the State of Georgia. Is there any remedy for
this state of things? None. Because the Executive
of the United States is in League with the State of
Georgia. . . This example . . will be imitated by
other States, and with regard to other national interests — perhaps the tariff. . . The Union is in the
most imminent danger of dissolution. . . The ship is
about to founder." [1]

Meanwhile the Cherokee Nation brought its suit
in the Supreme Court to enjoin the State from executing its laws, and at the February term of 1831 it
was argued for the Indians by Wirt and Sergeant.
Georgia disdained to appear — not for a moment
would that proud State admit that the Supreme
Court of the Nation could exercise any authority
whatever over her.[2]

On March 18, 1831, Marshall delivered the opinion
of the majority of the court, and in it he laid down
the broad policy which the Government has unwa-
veringly pursued ever since. At the outset the Chief
Justice plainly stated that his sympathies were with
the Indians,[3] but that the court could not examine
the merits or go into the moralities of the contro-

---

[1] *Memoirs, J. Q. A.*: Adams, VIII, 262–63.
[2] The argument for the Cherokee Nation was made March 12 and
14, 1831.
[3] 5 Peters, 15.

versy, because it had no jurisdiction. The Cherokees sued as a foreign nation, but, while they did indeed constitute a separate state, they were not a foreign nation. The relation of the Indians to the United States is "unlike that of any other two people in existence." The territory comprises a "part of the United States." [1]

In our foreign affairs and commercial regulations, the Indians are subject to the control of the National Government. "They acknowledge themselves in their treaties to be under the protection of the United States." They are not, then, foreign nations, but rather "domestic dependent nations. . . They are in a state of pupilage." Foreign governments consider them so completely under our "sovereignty and dominion" that it is universally conceded that the acquisition of their lands or the making of treaties with them would be "an invasion of our territory, and an act of hostility." By the Constitution power is given Congress to regulate commerce among the States, with foreign nations, and with Indian tribes, these terms being "entirely distinct." [2]

The Cherokees not being a foreign nation, the Supreme Court has no jurisdiction in a suit brought by them in that capacity, said Marshall. Furthermore, the court was asked "to control the Legislature of Georgia, and to restrain the exertion of its physical force" — a very questionable "interposition," which "savors too much of the exercise of political power to be within the proper province

[1] 5 Peters, 16-17.   [2] *Ib.* 17-18.

of the judicial department." In "a proper case with proper parties," the court might, perhaps, decide "the mere question of right" to the Indian lands. But the suit of the Cherokee Nation against Georgia is not such a case.

Marshall closes with a reflection upon Jackson in terms much like those with which, many years earlier, he had so often rebuked Jefferson: "If it be true that the Cherokee Nation have rights, this is not the tribunal in which those rights are to be asserted. If it be true that wrongs have been inflicted, and that still greater are to be apprehended, this is not the tribunal which can redress the past or prevent the future." [1]

In this opinion the moral force of Marshall was displayed almost as much as in the case of the Schooner Exchange.[2] He was friendly to the whole Indian race; he particularly detested Georgia's treatment of the Cherokees; he utterly rejected the State Rights theory on which the State had acted; and he could easily have decided in favor of the wronged and harried Indians, as the dissent of Thompson and Story proves. But the statesman and jurist again rose above the man of sentiment, law above emotion, the enduring above the transient.

[1] 5 Peters, 20. Justice Smith Thompson dissented in an opinion of immense power in which Story concurred. These two Justices maintained that in legal controversies, such as that between the Cherokees and Georgia, the Indian tribe must be treated as a foreign nation. (*Ib.* 50–80.)

Thompson's opinion was as Nationalist as any ever delivered by Marshall. It well expressed the general opinion of the North, which was vigorously condemnatory of Georgia as the ruthless despoiler of the rights of the Indians and the robber of their lands.

[2] See *supra*, 121–25.

As a "foreign state" the Indians had lost, but the constitutionality of Georgia's Cherokee statutes had not been affirmed. Wirt and Sergeant had erred as to the method of attacking that legislation. Another proceeding by Georgia, however, soon brought the validity of her expansion laws before the Supreme Court. Among the missionaries who for years had labored in the Cherokee Nation was one Samuel A. Worcester, a citizen of Vermont. This brave minister, licensed by the National Government, employed by the American Board of Commissioners for Foreign Missions, appointed by President John Quincy Adams to be postmaster at New Echota, a Cherokee town, refused, in company with several other missionaries, to leave the Indian country.

Worcester and a Reverend Mr. Thompson were arrested by the Georgia guard. The Superior Court of Gwinnett County released them, however, on a writ of habeas corpus, because, both being licensed missionaries expending National funds appropriated for civilizing Indians, they must be considered as agents of the National Government. Moreover, Worcester was postmaster at New Echota. Georgia demanded his removal and inquired of Jackson whether the missionaries were Government agents. The President assured the State that they were not, and removed Worcester from office.[1]

Thereupon both Worcester and Thompson were promptly ordered to leave the State. But they and some other missionaries remained, and were arrested; dragged to prison — some of them with

[1] Phillips, 79.

548 JOHN MARSHALL

chains around their necks;[1] tried and convicted.
Nine were pardoned upon their promise to depart
forthwith from Georgia. But Worcester and one
Elizur Butler sternly rejected the offer of clemency
on such a condition and were put to hard labor in
the penitentiary.

From the judgment of the Georgia court, Worcester and Butler appealed to the Supreme Court of
the United States. Once more Marshall and Georgia
confronted each other; again the Chief Justice faced
a hostile President far more direct and forcible than
Jefferson, but totally lacking in the subtlety and skill
of that incomparable politician. Thrilling and highly
colored accounts of the treatment of the missionaries
had been published in every Northern newspaper;
religious journals made conspicuous display of soul-
stirring narratives of the whole subject; feeling in
the North ran high; resentment in the South rose
to an equal degree.

This time Georgia did more than ignore the Supreme Court as in the case of George Tassels and in
the suit of the Cherokee Nation; she formally refused to appear; formally denied the right of that
tribunal to pass upon the decisions of her courts.[2]
Never would Georgia so "compromit her dignity as
a sovereign State," never so "yield her rights as a
member of the Confederacy." The new Governor,
Wilson Lumpkin, avowed that he would defend
those rights by every means in his power.[3] When
the case of Worcester *vs.* Georgia came on for hearing before the Supreme Court, no one answered for

[1] See McMaster, vi, 47–50.   [2] Phillips, 81.   [3] *Ib.* 80–81.

the State. Wirt, Sergeant, and Elisha W. Chester appeared for the missionaries as they had for the Indians.[1] Wirt and Sergeant made extended and powerful arguments.[2]

Marshall's opinion, delivered March 3, 1832, is one of the noblest he ever wrote. "The legislative power of a State, the controlling power of the Constitution and laws of the United States, the rights, if they have any, the political existence of a once numerous and powerful people, the personal liberty of a citizen, are all involved," begins the aged Chief Justice.[3] Does the act of the Legislature of Georgia, under which Worcester was convicted, violate the Constitution, laws, and treaties of the United States?[4] That act is "an assertion of jurisdiction over the Cherokee Nation."[5]

He then goes into a long historical review of the relative titles of the natives and of the white discoverers of America; of the effect upon these titles of the numerous treaties with the Indians; of the acts of Congress relating to the red men and their lands; and of previous laws of Georgia on these subjects.[6] This part of his opinion is the most extended and exhaustive historical analysis Marshall ever made in any judicial utterance, except that on the law of treason during the trial of Aaron Burr.[7]

Then comes his condensed, unanswerable, brilliant conclusion: "A weaker power does not surrender its independence, its rights to self-govern-

[1] 6 Peters, 534–35.
[2] Story to his wife, Feb. 26, 1832, Story, ii, 84.
[3] 6 Peters, 536.   [4] Ib. 537–42.   [5] Ib. 542.   [6] Ib. 542–61.
[7] See vol. iii, 504–13, of this work.

ment, by associating with a stronger, and taking its protection. A weak state, in order to provide for its safety, may place itself under the protection of one more powerful, without stripping itself of the right of self-government, and ceasing to be a state. . . The Cherokee Nation . . is a distinct community, occupying its own territory . . in which the laws of Georgia can have no force, and which the citizens of Georgia have no right to enter but with the assent of the Cherokees themselves, or in conformity with treaties, and with the acts of Congress. The whole intercourse between the United States and this nation is by our Constitution and laws vested in the government of the United States."

The Cherokee Acts of the Georgia Legislature "are repugnant to the constitution, laws and treaties of the United States. They interfere forcibly with the relations established between the United States and the Cherokee Nation." This controlling fact the laws of Georgia ignore. They violently disrupt the relations between the Indians and the United States; they are equally antagonistic to acts of Congress based upon these treaties. Moreover, "the forcible seizure and abduction" of Worcester, "who was residing in the nation with its permission and by authority of the President of the United States, is also a violation of the acts which authorize the chief magistrate to exercise this authority."

Marshall closes with a passage of eloquence almost equal to, and of higher moral grandeur than, the finest passages in M'Culloch vs. Maryland and in Cohens vs. Virginia. So the decision of the court was that the judgment of the Georgia court be "reversed and annulled." [1]

Congress was intensely excited by Marshall's opinion; Georgia was enraged; the President agitated and belligerent. In a letter to Ticknor, written five days after the judgment of the court was announced, Story accurately portrays the situation: "The decision produced a very strong sensation in both houses; Georgia is full of anger and violence. . . Probably she will resist the execution of our judgement, & if she does I do not believe the President will interfere. . . The Court has done its duty. Let the nation do theirs. If we have a government let its commands be obeyed; if we have not it is as well to know it at once, & to look to consequences." [2]

Story's forecast was justified. Georgia scoffed at Marshall's opinion, flouted the mandate of the Supreme Court. "Usurpation!" cried Governor Lumpkin. He would meet it "with the spirit of determined resistance." [3] Jackson defied the Chief Justice. "John Marshall has made his decision: — *now let him enforce it!*" the President is reported to have said.[4] Again the Supreme Court found itself powerless; the judgment in Worcester *vs.* Georgia came to nothing; the mandate was never obeyed, never heeded.[5]

[1] 6 Peters, 561–63.
[2] Story to Ticknor, March 8, 1832, Story, II, 83.
[3] Lumpkin's Message to the Legislature, Nov. 6, 1832, as quoted in Phillips, 82.
[4] Greeley: *The American Conflict*, I, 106; and see Phillips, 80.
[5] When the Georgia Legislature first met after the decision of the Worcester case, acts were passed to strengthen the lottery and distribution of Cherokee lands (Acts of Nov. 14, 22, and Dec. 24, 1832,

For the time being, Marshall was defeated; Nationalism was prostrate; Localism erect, strong, aggressive. Soon, however, Marshall and Nationalism were to be sustained, for the moment, by the man most dreaded by the Chief Justice, most trusted by Marshall's foes. Andrew Jackson was to astound the country by the greatest and most illogical act of his strange career — the issuance of his immortal Proclamation against Nullification.

Georgia's very first assertion of her "sovereignty" in the Indian controversy had strengthened South Carolina's fast growing determination to resist the execution of the Tariff Law. On January 25, 1830, Senator Robert Young Hayne of South Carolina, in his brilliant challenge to Webster, set forth the philosophy of Nullification: "Sir, if, the measures of the Federal Government were less oppressive, we should still strive against this usurpation. The

Laws of Georgia, 1832, 122–25, 126, 127) and to organize further the Cherokee territory under the guise of protecting the Indians. (Act of Dec. 24, 1832, *ib.* 102–05.) Having demonstrated the power of the State and the impotence of the highest court of the Nation, the Governor of Georgia, one year after Marshall delivered his opinion, pardoned Worcester and Butler, but not without protests from the people.

Two years later, Georgia's victory was sealed by a final successful defiance of the Supreme Court. One James Graves was convicted of murder; a writ of error was procured from the Supreme Court; and a citation issued to Georgia as in the case of George Tassels. The high spirit of the State, lifted still higher by three successive triumphs over the Supreme Court, received the order with mingled anger and derision. Governor Lumpkin threatened secession: "Such attempts, if persevered in, will eventuate in the dismemberment and overthrow of our great confederacy," he told the Legislature. (Governor Lumpkin's Special Message to the Georgia Legislature, Nov. 7, 1834, as quoted in Phillips, 84.)

The Indians finally were forced to remove to the Indian Territory. (See Phillips, 83.) Worcester went to his Vermont home.

South is acting on a principle she has always held sacred — resistance to unauthorized taxation." [1]

Webster's immortal reply, so far as his Constitutional argument is concerned, is little more than a condensation of the Nationalist opinions of John Marshall stated in popular and dramatic language. Indeed, some of Webster's sentences are practically mere repetitions of Marshall's, and his reasoning is wholly that of the Chief Justice.

"We look upon the States, not as separated, but as united under the same General Government, having interests, common, associated, intermingled. In war and peace, we are one; in commerce, one; because the authority of the General Government reaches to war and peace, and to the regulation of commerce." [2]

What is the capital question in dispute? It is this: "Whose prerogative is it to decide on the constitutionality or unconstitutionality of the laws?" [3] Can States decide? Can States "annul the law of Congress"? Hayne, expressing the view of South Carolina, had declared that they could. He had based his argument upon the Kentucky and Virginia Resolu-

---

[1] *Debates*, 21st Cong. 1st Sess. 58. The debate between Webster and Hayne occurred on a resolution offered by Senator Samuel Augustus Foot of Connecticut, "that the Committee on Public Lands be instructed to inquire into the expediency of limiting for a certain period the sales of public lands," etc. (*Ib.* 11.) The discussion of this resolution, which lasted more than three months (see *ib.* 11–302), quickly turned to the one great subject of the times, the power of the National Government and the rights of the States. It was on this question that the debate between Webster and Hayne took place.

[2] *Ib.* 64. Compare with Marshall's language in Cohens *vs.* Virginia, *supra*, 355.

[3] *Debates*, 21st Cong. 1st Sess. 73.

tions — upon the theory that the States, and not
the people, had created the Constitution; that the
States, and not the people, had established the General Government.

But is this true? asked Webster. He answered
by paraphrasing Marshall's words in M'Culloch *vs.*
Maryland: "It is, sir, the people's constitution, the
people's Government; made for the people; made
by the people; and answerable to the people.[1] The
people . . have declared that this Constitution shall
be the supreme law.[2] . . Who is to judge between the
people and the Government?"[3]

The Constitution settles that question by declaring
that "the judicial power shall extend to all cases arising under the Constitution and laws."[4] Because of
this the Union is secure and strong. "Instead of one
tribunal, established by all, responsible to all, with
power to decide for all, shall constitutional questions be left to four and twenty popular bodies, each
at liberty to decide for itself, and none bound to
respect the decisions of others?"[5]

Then Webster swept grandly forward to that
famous peroration ending with the words which in

[1] See Marshall's statement of this principle, *supra*, 293, 355.

[2] *Debates*, 21st Cong. 1st Sess. 74.

This was the Constitutional theory of the Nationalists. As a matter of fact, it was not, perhaps, strictly true. There can be little doubt
that a majority of the people did not favor the Constitution when
adopted by the Convention and ratified by the States. Had manhood
suffrage existed at that time, and had the Constitution been submitted directly to the people, it is highly probable that it would have
been rejected. (See vol. I, chaps. IX–XII, of this work.)

[3] *Debates*, 21st Cong. 1st Sess. 76. See chap. III, vol. III, of this
work.

[4] *Debates*, 21st Cong. 1st Sess. 78.

[5] *Ib.* See Marshall's opinion in Cohens *vs.* Virginia, *supra*, 347–57.

time became the inspiring motto of the whole American people: "Liberty *and* Union, now and forever, one and inseparable!" [1]

Immediately after the debate between Hayne and Webster, Nullification gathered force in South Carolina. Early in the autumn of 1830, Governor Stephen Decatur Miller spoke at a meeting of the Sumter district of that State. He urged that a State convention be called for the purpose of declaring null and void the Tariff of 1828. Probably the National courts would try to enforce that law, he said, but South Carolina would "refuse to sustain" it. Nullification involved no danger, and if it did, what matter! — "those who fear to defend their rights, have none. Their property belongs to the banditti: they are only tenants at will of their own firesides." [2]

Public excitement steadily increased; at largely attended meetings ominous resolutions were adopted. "The attitude which the federal government continues to assume towards the southern states, calls for decisive and unequivocal resistance." So ran a typical declaration of a gathering of citizens of Georgetown, South Carolina, in December, 1830. [3]

In the Senate, Josiah Stoddard Johnston of Louisiana, but Connecticut-born, made a speech denouncing the doctrine of Nullification, asserting the supremacy of the National Government, and declaring that the Supreme Court was the final judge of the constitutionality of legislation. "It has fulfilled the design of its institution; . . it has given form and consistency to the constitution, and uniformity to

[1] *Debates*, 21st Cong. 1st Sess. 80.   [2] Niles, xxxix, 118.   [3] *Ib.* 330.

the laws." [1] Nullification, said Johnston, means "either disunion, or civil war; or, in the language of the times, disunion and blood." [2]

The Louisiana Senator sent his speech to Marshall, who answered that "it certainly is not among the least extraordinary of the doctrines of the present day that such a question [Nullification] should be seriously debated." [3]

All Nullification arguments were based on the Kentucky and Virginia Resolutions. Madison was still living, and Edward Everett asked him for his views. In a letter almost as Nationalist as Marshall's opinions, the venerable statesman replied at great length and with all the ability and clearness of his best years.

The decision by States of the constitutionality of acts of Congress would destroy the Nation, he wrote. Such decision was the province of the National Judiciary. While the Supreme Court had been criticized, perhaps justly in some cases, "still it would seem that, with but few exceptions, the course of the judiciary has been hitherto sustained by the predominant sense of the nation." It was absurd to deny the "supremacy of the judicial power of the U. S. & denounce at the same time nullifying power in a State. . . A law of the land" cannot be supreme "without a supremacy in the exposition & execution of the law." Nullification was utterly destructive of the Constitution and the Union. [4]

This letter, printed in the *North American Re-*

---

[1] *Debates*, 21st Cong. 1st Sess. 287.   [2] *Ib.* 285.
[3] Marshall to Johnston, May 22, 1830. MSS. "Society Collection," Pa. Hist. Soc.
[4] Madison to Everett, Aug. 28, 1830, *Writings*: Hunt, ix, 383–403.

view,[1] made a strong impression on the North, but it only irritated the South. Marshall read it "with peculiar pleasure," he wrote Story: "Mr Madison . . is himself again. He avows the opinions of his best days, and must be pardoned for his oblique insinuations that some of the opinions of our Court are not approved. Contrast this delicate hint with the language Mr Jefferson has applied to us. He [Madison] is attacked . . by our Enquirer, who has arrayed his report of 1799 against his letter. I never thought that report could be completely defended; but Mr Madison has placed it upon its best ground, that the language is incautious, but is intended to be confined to a mere declaration of opinion, or is intended to refer to that ultimate right which all admit, to resist despotism, a right not exercised under a constitution, but in opposition to it." [2]

At a banquet on April 15, 1830, in celebration of Jefferson's birthday, Jackson had given a warning not to be misunderstood except by Nullifiers who had been blinded and deafened by their new political religion. "The Federal Union; — it must be preserved," was the solemn and inspiring toast proposed by the President. Southern leaders gave no heed. They apparently thought that Jackson meant to endorse Nullification, which, most illogically, they always declared to be the only method of preserving the Union peaceably.

Their denunciation of the Tariff grew ever louder; their insistence on Nullification ever fiercer, ever

---

[1] *North American Review* (1830), xxxi, 537-46.

[2] Marshall to Story, Oct. 15, 1830, *Proceedings, Mass. Hist. Soc.* 2d Series, xiv, 342-43.

more determined. To a committee of South Carolina Union men who invited him to their Fourth of
July celebration at Charleston in 1831, Jackson sent
a letter which plainly informed the Nullifiers that if
they attempted to carry out their threats, the National Government would forcibly suppress them.[1]

At last the eyes of the South were opened. At last
the South understood the immediate purpose of that
enigmatic and self-contradictory man who ruled
America, at times, in the spirit of the Czars of
Russia; at times, in the spirit of the most compro-
mising of opportunists.

Jackson's outgiving served only to enrage the
South and especially South Carolina. The Legislature of that State replied to the President's letter
thus: "Is this Legislature to be schooled and rated by
the President of the United States? Is it to legislate
under the sword of the Commander-in-Chief? .. This
is a confederacy of sovereign States, and each may
withdraw from the confederacy when it chooses." [2]

Marshall saw clearly what the outcome was likely
to be, but yielded slowly to the despair so soon to
master him. "Things to the South wear a very
serious aspect," he tells Story. "If we can trust appearances the leaders are determined to risk all the
consequences of dismemberment. I cannot entirely
dismiss the hope that they may be deserted by
their followers — at least to such an extent as to
produce a pause at the Rubicon. They undoubtedly
believe that Virginia will support them. I think they

---

[1] Jackson to the Committee, June 14, 1831, Niles, XL, 351.
[2] *State Doc. Fed. Rel.*: Ames, 167–68.

are mistaken both with respect to Virginia and North Carolina. I do not think either State will embrace this mad and wicked measure. New Hampshire and Maine seem to belong to the tropics. It is time for New Hampshire to part with Webster and Mason. She has no longer any use for such men." [1]

As the troubled weeks passed, Marshall's apprehension increased. Story, profoundly concerned, wrote the Chief Justice that he could see no light in the increasing darkness. "If the prospects of our country inspire you with gloom," answered Marshall, "how do you think a man must be affected who partakes of all your opinions and whose geographical position enables him to see a great deal that is concealed from you? I yield slowly and reluctantly to the conviction that our constitution cannot last. I had supposed that north of the Potowmack a firm and solid government competent to the security of rational liberty might be preserved. Even that now seems doubtful. The case of the south seems to me to be desperate. Our opinions are incompatible with a united government even among ourselves. The union has been prolonged thus far by miracles. I fear they cannot continue." [2]

Congress heeded the violent protest of South Carolina — perhaps it would be more accurate to say that Congress obeyed Andrew Jackson. In 1832 it reduced tariff duties; but the protective policy was retained. The South was infuriated — if the principle were recognized, said Southern men, what could

[1] Marshall to Story, Aug. 2, 1832, *Proceedings, Mass. Hist. Soc.* 2d Series, xiv, 350.

[2] Same to same, Sept. 22, 1832, *ib.* 351-52.

they expect at a later day when this capitalistic, manufacturing North would be still stronger and the unmoneyed and agricultural South still weaker?

South Carolina especially was frantic. The spirit of the State was accurately expressed by R. Barnwell Smith at a Fourth of July celebration: "If the fire and the sword of war are to be brought to our dwellings, . . let them come! Whilst a bush grows which may be dabbled with blood, or a pine tree stands to support a rifle, let them come!" [1] At meetings all over the State treasonable words were spoken. Governor James Hamilton, Jr., convened the Legislature in special session and the election of a State convention was ordered.

"Let us act, next October, at the ballot box — next November, in the state house — and afterwards, should any further action be necessary, let it be where our ancestors acted, *in the field of battle*"; [2] such were the toasts proposed at banquets, such the sentiments adopted at meetings.

On November 24, 1832, the State Convention, elected [3] to consider the new Tariff Law, adopted the famous Nullification Ordinance which declared that the Tariff Acts of 1828 and 1832 were "null, void, and no law"; directed the Legislature to take measures to prevent the enforcement of those acts within South Carolina; forbade appeal to the Supreme Court of the United States from South Carolina courts in any case where the Tariff Law was involved; and required all State officers, civil and military, to

---

[1] Niles, XLII, 387.   [2] *Ib.* 388.
[3] Under Act of Oct. 26, 1832, *Statutes at Large of South Carolina:* Cooper, I, 309–10.

take oath to "obey, execute and enforce this Ordinance, and such act or acts of the Legislature as may be passed in pursuance thereof."

The Ordinance set forth that "we, the People of South Carolina, .. *Do further Declare*, that we will not submit to the application of force, on the part of the Federal Government, to reduce this State to obedience; but that we will consider" any act of the National Government to enforce the Tariff Laws "as inconsistent with the longer continuance of South Carolina in the Union: and that the People of this State .. will forthwith proceed to organize a separate Government, and to do all other acts and things which sovereign and independent States may of right do." [1]

Thereupon the Convention issued an address to the people.[2] It was long and, from the Nullification point of view, very able; it ended in an exalted, passionate appeal: "Fellow citizens, the die is now cast. NO MORE TAXES SHALL BE PAID HERE. . . Prepare for the crisis, and .. meet it as becomes men and freemen. . . Fellow citizens, DO YOUR DUTY TO YOUR COUNTRY, AND LEAVE THE CONSEQUENCES TO GOD."[3]

Excepting only at the outbreak of war could a people be more deeply stirred than were all Americans by the desperate action of South Carolina. In the North great Union meetings were held, fervid speeches made, warlike resolutions adopted. The South, at first, seemed dazed. Was war at hand? This was the question every man asked of his neighbor. A pamphlet on the situation, written by

---

[1] *Statutes at Large of South Carolina:* Cooper, I, 329–31.
[2] *Ib.* 434–45.   [3] *Ib.* 444–45; also Niles, XLIII, 219–20.

some one in a state of great emotion, had been sent
to Marshall, and Judge Peters had inquired about
it, giving at the same time the name of the author.

"I am not surprised," answered Marshall, "that
he [the author] is excited by the doctrine of nullification. It is well calculated to produce excitement in
all. . . Leaving it to the courts and the custom
house will be leaving it to triumphant victory, and
to victory which must be attended with more pernicious consequences to our country and with more
fatal consequences to its reputation than victory
achieved in any other mode which rational men can
devise." [1] If Nullification must prevail, John Marshall preferred that it should win by the sword
rather than through the intimidation of courts.

Jackson rightly felt that his reëlection meant
that the country in general approved of his attitude
toward Nullification as well as that toward the Bank.
He promptly answered the defiance of South Carolina. On December 10, 1832, he issued his historic
Proclamation. Written by Edward Livingston,[2]
Secretary of State, it is one of the ablest of American state papers. Moderate in expression, simple in
style, solid in logic, it might have been composed
by Marshall himself. It is, indeed, a restatement of
Marshall's Nationalist reasoning and conclusions.
Like the argument in Webster's Reply to Hayne,
Jackson's Nullification Proclamation was a repetition of those views of the Constitution and of the
nature of the American Government for which Mar-

---

[1] Marshall to Peters, Dec. 3, 1832, Peters MSS. Pa. Hist. Soc.
[2] See *supra*, footnote to 115.

shall had been fighting since Washington was made President.

As in Webster's great speech, sentences and paragraphs are in almost the very words used by Marshall in his Constitutional opinions, so in Jackson's Proclamation the same parallelism exists. Gently, but firmly, and with tremendous force, in the style and spirit of Abraham Lincoln rather than of Andrew Jackson, the Proclamation makes clear that the National laws will be executed and resistance to them will be put down by force of arms.[1]

The Proclamation was a triumph for Marshall. That the man whom he distrusted and of whom he so disapproved, whose election he had thought to be equivalent to a dissolution of the Union, should turn out to be the stern defender of National solidarity, was, to Marshall, another of those miracles which so often had saved the Republic. His disapproval of Jackson's rampant democracy, and whimsical yet arbitrary executive conduct, turned at once to hearty commendation.

"Since his last proclamation and message," testifies Story, "the Chief Justice and myself have become his warmest supporters, and shall continue so just as long as he maintains the principles contained in them. Who would have dreamed of such an occurrence?"[2] Marshall realized, nevertheless, that even the bold course pursued by the President could not permanently overcome the secession convictions of the Southern people.

---

[1] Richardson, II, 640–56; Niles, XLIII, 260–64.
[2] Story to his wife, Jan. 27, 1833, Story, II, 119.

The Union men of South Carolina who, from the beginning of the Nullification movement, had striven earnestly to stay its progress, rallied manfully.[1] Their efforts were futile — disunion sentiment swept the State. "With . . indignation and contempt," with "defiance and scorn," most South Carolinians greeted the Proclamation [2] of the man who, only three years before, had been their idol. To South Carolinians Jackson was now "a tyrant," a would-be "Cæsar," a "Cromwell," a "Bonaparte." [3]

The Legislature formally requested Hayne, now Governor, to issue a counter-proclamation,[4] and adopted spirited resolutions declaring the right of any State "to secede peaceably from the Union." One count in South Carolina's indictment of the President was thoroughly justified — his approval of Georgia's defiance of Marshall and the Supreme Court. Jackson's action, declared the resolutions, was the more "extraordinary, that he has silently, and . . with entire approbation, witnessed our sister state of Georgia avow, act upon, and carry into effect, even to the taking of life, principles identical with those now denounced by him in South Carolina." The Legislature finally resolved that the State would "repel force by force, and, relying upon the blessing of God, will maintain its liberty at all hazards." [5]

Swiftly Hayne published his reply to the President's Proclamation. It summed up all the arguments for the right of a State to decide the constitu-

---

[1] Niles, XLIII, 266-67.   [2] Ib. 287.   [3] Ib.
[4] Statutes at Large of South Carolina: Cooper, I, 355.   [5] Ib. 356-57.

tionality of acts of Congress, that had been made since the Kentucky Resolutions were written by Jefferson — that "great Apostle of American liberty .. who has consecrated these principles, and left them as a legacy to the American people, recorded by his own hand." It was Jefferson, said Hayne, who had first penned the immortal truth that "NULLIFICATION" of unconstitutional acts of Congress was the "RIGHTFUL REMEDY" of the States.[1]

In his Proclamation Jackson had referred to the National Judiciary as the ultimate arbiter of the constitutionality of National laws. How absurd such a claim by such a man, since that doctrine "has been denied by none more strongly than the President himself" in the Bank controversy and in the case of the Cherokees! "And yet when it serves the purpose of bringing odium on South Carolina, 'his native State,' the President has no hesitation in regarding the attempt of a State to release herself from the controul of the Federal Judiciary, in a matter affecting her sovereign rights, as a violation of the Constitution." [2]

In closing, Governor Hayne declares that "the time has come when it must be seen, whether the people of the several States have indeed lost the spirit of the revolution, and whether they are to become the willing instruments of an unhallowed despotism. In such a sacred cause, South Carolina will feel that she is not striking for her own, but the liberties of the Union and the RIGHTS OF MAN." [3]

[1] *Statutes at Large of South Carolina:* Cooper, I, 362.
[2] *Ib.* 360.   [3] *Ib.* 370.

Instantly [1] the Legislature enacted one law to prevent the collection of tariff duties in South Carolina; [2] another authorizing the Governor to "order into service the whole military force of this State" to resist any attempt of the National Government to enforce the Tariff Acts.[3] Even before Hayne's Proclamation was published, extensive laws had been passed for the reorganization of the militia, and the Legislature now continued to enact similar legislation. In four days fourteen such acts were passed.[4]

The spirit and consistency of South Carolina were as admirable as her theory was erroneous and narrow. If she meant what she had said, the State could have taken no other course. If, moreover, she really intended to resist the National Government, Jackson had given cause for South Carolina's militant action. As soon as the Legislature ordered the calling of the State Convention to consider the tariff, the President directed the Collector at Charleston to use every resource at the command of the Government to collect tariff duties. The commanders of the forts at Charleston were ordered to be in readiness to repel any attack. General Scott was sent to the scene of the disturbance. Military and naval dispositions were made so as to enable the National Government to strike quickly and effectively.[5]

Throughout South Carolina the rolling of drums and blare of bugles were heard. Everywhere was

---

[1] December 20, the same day that Hayne's Proclamation appeared.
[2] *Statutes at Large of South Carolina:* Cooper, I, 271-74.
[3] *Ib.* VIII, 562-64.   [4] *Ib.* 562-98.
[5] Parton: *Jackson,* III, 460-61, 472; Bassett: *Life of Andrew Jackson,* 564; MacDonald: *Jacksonian Democracy,* 156.

seen the blue cockade with palmetto button.[1] Volunteers were called for,[2] and offered themselves by thousands; in certain districts "almost the entire population" enlisted.[3] Some regiments adopted a new flag, a banner of red with a single black star in the center.[4]

Jackson attempted to placate the enraged and determined State. In his fourth annual Message to Congress he barely mentioned South Carolina's defiance, but, for the second time, urgently recommended a reduction of tariff duties. Protection, he said, "must be ultimately limited to those articles of domestic manufacture which are indispensable to our safety in time of war. . . Beyond this object we have already seen the operation of the system productive of discontent."[5]

Other Southern States, although firmly believing in South Carolina's principles and sympathetic with her cause, were alarmed by her bold course. Virginia essayed the rôle of mediator between her warlike sister and the "usurping" National Government. In his Message to the Legislature, Governor John Floyd stoutly defended South Carolina — "the land of Sumpter [sic] and of Marion." "Should force be resorted to by the federal government, the horror of the scenes hereafter to be witnessed cannot now be pictured. . . What surety has any state for her existence as a sovereign, if a difference of opinion should be punished by the sword as treason?" The situation calls for a reference of the whole ques-

[1] Parton: *Jackson*, III, 459. [2] Niles, XLIII, 312. [3] *Ib.* 332.
[4] Parton: *Jackson*, III, 472. [5] Richardson, II, 598-99.

tion to "the PEOPLE of the states. On you depends
in a high degree the future destiny of this republic.
It is for you now to say whether the brand of civil
war shall be thrown into the midst of these states." [1]

Mediative resolutions were instantly offered for the
appointment of a committee "to take into consideration the relations existing between the state of South
Carolina and the government of the United States,"
and the results to each and to Virginia flowing from
the Ordinance of Nullification and Jackson's Proclamation. The committee was to report "such measures as . . it may be expedient for Virginia to adopt
— the propriety of recommending a general convention to the states — and such a declaration of our
views and opinions as it may be proper for her to
express in the present fearful impending crisis, for
the protection of the right of the states, the restoration of harmony, and the preservation of the union." [2]

Only five members voted against the resolution.[3]

The committee was appointed and, on December
20, 1832, reported a set of resolutions — "worlds of
words," as Niles aptly called them — disapproving
Jackson's Proclamation; applauding his recommendation to Congress that the tariff be reduced; re-
gretting South Carolina's hasty action; deprecating
"the intervention of arms on either side"; entreat-
ing "our brethren in S. Carolina to pause in their
career"; appealing to Jackson "to withstay the
arm of force"; instructing Virginia Senators and re-
questing Virginia Representatives in Congress to do
their best to "procure an immediate reduction of the

[1] Niles, XLIII, 275.   [2] Ib.   [3] Ib. 276.

tariff"; and appointing two commissioners to visit South Carolina with a view to securing an adjustment of the dispute.[1]

With painful anxiety and grave alarm, Marshall, then in Richmond, watched the tragic yet absurd procession of events. Much as the doings and sayings of the mediators and sympathizers with Nullification irritated him, serious as were his forebodings, the situation appealed to his sense of humor. He wrote Story an account of what was going on in Virginia. No abler or more accurate statement of the conditions and tendencies of the period exists. Marshall's letter is a document of historical importance. It reveals, too, the character of the man.

It was written in acknowledgment of the receipt of "a proof sheet" of a page of Story's "Commentaries on the Constitution of the United States," dedicating that work to Marshall. "I am .. deeply penetrated," says Marshall, "by the evidence it affords of the continuance of that partial esteem and friendship which I have cherished for so many years, and still cherish as one of the choicest treasures of my life. The only return I can make is locked up in my own bosom, or communicated in occasional conversation with my friends." He congratulates Story on having finished his "Herculean task." He is sure that Story has accomplished it with ability and "correctness," and is "certain in advance" that he will read "every sentence with entire approbation. It is a subject on which we concur exactly. Our opin-

[1] Niles, XLIII, 394-96. The resolutions, as adopted, provided for only one commissioner. (See *infra*, 573.)

ions on it are, I believe, identical. Not so with Virginia or the South generally."

Marshall then relates what has happened in Richmond: "Our legislature is now in session, and the dominant party receives the message of the President to Congress with enthusiastic applause. Quite different was the effect of his proclamation. That paper astonished, confounded, and for a moment silenced them. In a short time, however, the power of speech was recovered, and was employed in bestowing on its author the only epithet which could possibly weigh in the scales against the name of 'Andrew Jackson,' and countervail its popularity.

"Imitating the Quaker who said the dog he wished to destroy was mad, they said Andrew Jackson had become a Federalist, even an ultra Federalist. To have said he was ready to break down and trample on every other department of the government would not have injured him, but to say that he was a Federalist — a convert to the opinions of Washington, was a mortal blow under which he is yet staggering.

"The party seems to be divided. Those who are still true to their President pass by his denunciation of all their former theories; and though they will not approve the sound opinions avowed in his proclamation are ready to denounce nullification and to support him in maintaining the union. This is going a great way for them — much farther than their former declarations would justify the expectation of, and much farther than mere love of union would carry them.

"You have undoubtedly seen the message of our

Governor and the resolutions reported by the committee to whom it was referred — a message and resolutions which you will think skillfully framed had the object been a civil war. They undoubtedly hold out to South Carolina the expectation of support from Virginia; and that hope must be the foundation on which they have constructed their plan for a southern confederacy or league.

"A want of confidence in the present support of the people will prevent any direct avowal in favor of this scheme by those whose theories and whose secret wishes may lead to it; but the people may be so entangled by the insane dogmas which have become axioms in the political creed of Virginia, and involved so inextricably in the labyrinth into which those dogmas conduct them, as to do what their sober judgement disapproves.

"On Thursday these resolutions are to be taken up, and the debate will, I doubt not, be ardent and tempestuous enough. I pretend not to anticipate the result. Should it countenance the obvious design of South Carolina to form a southern confederacy, it may conduce to a southern league — never to a southern government. Our theories are incompatible with a government for more than a single State. We can form no union which shall be closer than an alliance between sovereigns.

"In this event there is some reason to apprehend internal convulsion. The northern and western section of our State, should a union be maintained north of the Potowmack, will not readily connect itself with the South. At least such is the present belief of their most intelligent men. Any effort on their part to separate from Southern Virginia and unite with a northern confederacy may probably be punished as treason. 'We have fallen on evil times.'"

Story had sent Marshall, Webster's speech at Faneuil Hall, December 17, 1832, in which he declared that he approved the "general principles" of Jackson's Proclamation, and that "nullification . . is but another name for civil war." "I am," said Webster, "for the Union as it is; . . for the Constitution as it is." He pledged his support to the President in "maintaining this Union." [1]

Marshall was delighted: "I thank you for Mr Webster's speech. Entertaining the opinion he has expressed respecting the general course of the administration, his patriotism is entitled to the more credit for the determination he expressed at Faneuil Hall to support it in the great effort it promises to make for the preservation of the union. No member of the then opposition avowed a similar determination during the Western Insurrection, which would have been equally fatal had it not been quelled by the well timed vigor of General Washington.

"We are now gathering the bitter fruits of the tree even before that time planted by Mr Jefferson, and so industriously and perseveringly cultivated by Virginia." [2]

Marshall's predictions of a tempestuous debate over the Virginia resolutions were fulfilled. They were, in fact, "debated to death," records Niles.

[1] *Writings and Speeches of Daniel Webster* (Nat. ed.) XIII, 40–42.

[2] Marshall to Story, Dec. 25, 1832, *Proceedings, Mass. Hist. Soc.* 2d Series, XIV, 352–54.

"It would seem that the genuine spirit of 'ancient *dominionism*' would lead to a making of speeches, even in 'the cave of the Cyclops when forging thunderbolts,' instead of striking the hammers from the hands of the workers of iniquity. Well — the matter was debated, and debated and debated. . . The proceedings . . were measured by the *square yard.*" At last, however, resolutions were adopted.

These resolutions "respectfully requested and entreated" South Carolina to rescind her Ordinance of Nullification; "respectfully requested and entreated" Congress to "modify" the tariff; reaffirmed Virginia's faith in the principles of 1798–99, but held that these principles did not justify South Carolina's Ordinance or Jackson's Proclamation; and finally, authorized the appointment of one commissioner to South Carolina to communicate Virginia's resolutions, expressing at the same time, however, "our sincere good will to our sister state, and our anxious solicitude that the kind and respectful recommendations we have addressed to her, may lead to an accommodation of all the difficulties between that state and the general government." [1] Benjamin Watkins Leigh was unanimously elected to be the ambassador of accommodation. [2]

So it came about that South Carolina, anxious to extricate herself from a perilous situation, yet ready to fight if she could not disentangle herself with honor, took informal steps toward a peaceful adjust-

---

[1] Niles, XLIII, 396–97; also *Statutes at Large of South Carolina:* Cooper, I, 381–83.

[2] Niles, XLIII, 397. For the details of Leigh's mission see *ib.* 377–93; also *Statutes at Large of South Carolina:* Cooper, I, 384–94.

ment of the dispute; and that Jackson and Congress, equally wishing to avoid armed conflict, were eager to have a tariff enacted that would work a "reconciliation." On January 26, 1833, at a meeting in Charleston, attended by the first men of the State of all parties, resolutions, offered by Hamilton himself, were adopted which, as a practical matter, suspended the Ordinance of Nullification that was to have gone into effect on February 1. Vehement, spirited, defiant speeches were made, all ending, however, in expressions of hope that war might be avoided. The resolutions were as ferocious as the most bloodthirsty Secessionist could desire; but they accepted the proposed "beneficial modification of the tariff," and declared that, "pending the process" of reducing the tariff, "all . . collision between the federal and state authorities should be sedulously avoided on both sides." [1]

The Tariff Bill of 1833 — Clay's compromise — resulted. Jackson signed it; South Carolina was mollified. For the time the storm subsided; but the net result was that Nullification triumphed [2] — a National law had been modified at the threat of a State which was preparing to back up that threat by force.

Marshall was not deceived. "Have you ever seen anything to equal the exhibition in Charleston and in the far South generally?" he writes Story. "Those people pursue a southern league steadily or they are insane. They have caught at Clay's bill, if their conduct is at all intelligible, not as a real accommoda-

[1] Niles, XLIII, 380-82.   [2] See Parton: *Jackson*, III, 475-82.

tion, a real adjustment, a real relief from actual or supposed oppression, but as an apology for avoiding the crisis and deferring the decisive moment till the other States of the South will unite with them." [1] Marshall himself was for the compromise Tariff of 1833, but not because it afforded a means of preventing armed collision: "Since I have breathed the air of James River I think favorably of Clay's bill. I hope, if it can be maintained, that our manufactures will still be protected by it." [2]

The "settlement" of the controversy, of course, satisfied nobody, changed no conviction, allayed no hostility, stabilized no condition. The South, though victorious, was nevertheless morose, indignant — after all, the principle of protection had been retained. "The political world, at least our part of it, is surely moved *topsy turvy*," Marshall writes Story in the autumn of 1833. "What is to become of us and of our constitution? Can the wise men of the East answer that question? Those of the South perceive no difficulty. Allow a full range to state rights and state sovereignty, and, in their opinion, all will go well." [3]

Placid as was his nature, perfect as was the coordination of his powers, truly balanced as were his intellect and emotions, Marshall could not free his mind of the despondency that had now settled upon him. Whatever the subject upon which he wrote to friends, he was sure to refer to the woeful state of the country, and the black future it portended.

[1] Marshall to Story, April 24, 1833, *Proceedings, Mass. Hist. Soc.* 2d Series, XIV, 356–57.
[2] *Ib.*　　　　　[3] Same to same, Nov. 16, 1833, *ib.* 358.

Story informed him that an abridged edition of his own two volumes on the Constitution would soon be published. "I rejoice to hear that the abridgement of your Commentaries is coming before the public," wrote Marshall in reply, "and should be still more rejoiced to learn that it was used in all our colleges and universities. The first impressions made on the youthful mind are of vast importance; and, most unfortunately, they are in the South all erroneous. Our young men, generally speaking, grow up in the firm belief that liberty depends on construing our Constitution into a league instead of a government; that it has nothing to fear from breaking these United States into numerous petty republics. Nothing in their view is to be feared but that bugbear, consolidation; and every exercise of legitimate power is construed into a breach of the Constitution. Your book, if read, will tend to remove these prejudices." [1]

A month later he again writes Story: "I have finished reading your great work, and wish it could be read by every statesman, and every would-be statesman in the United States. It is a comprehensive and an accurate commentary on our Constitution, formed in the spirit of the original text. In the South, we are so far gone in political metaphysics, that I fear no demonstration can restore us to common sense. The word 'State Rights,' as expounded by the resolutions of '98 and the report of '99, construed by our legislature, has a charm against which all reasoning is vain.

[1] Marshall to Story, June 3, 1833, *Proceedings, Mass. Hist. Soc.* 2d Series, XIV, 358.

"Those resolutions and that report constitute the creed of every politician, who hopes to rise in Virginia; and to question them, or even to adopt the construction given by their author [Jefferson] is deemed political sacrilege. The solemn . . admonitions of your concluding remarks [1] will not, I fear, avail as they ought to avail against this popular frenzy." [2]

He once more confides to his beloved Story his innermost thoughts and feelings. Story had sent the Chief Justice a copy of the *New England Magazine* containing an article by Story entitled "Statesmen: their Rareness and Importance," in which Marshall was held up as the true statesman and the poor quality of the generality of American public men was set forth in scathing terms.

Marshall briefly thanks Story for the compliment paid him, and continues: "It is in vain to lament, that the portrait which the author has drawn of our political and party men, is, in general, true. Lament it as we may, much as it may wound our vanity or our pride, it is still, in the main, true; and will, I fear, so remain. . . In the South, political prejudice is too strong to yield to any degree of merit; and the great body of the nation contains, at least appears to me to contain, too much of the same ingredient.

"To men who think as you and I do, the present is gloomy enough; and the future presents no cheering prospect. The struggle now maintained in every

[1] Story ends his *Commentaries on the Constitution of the United States* by a fervent, passionate, and eloquent appeal for the preservation, at all hazards, of the Constitution and the Union.

[2] Marshall to Story, July 31, 1833, Story, II, 135–36.

State in the Union seems to me to be of doubtful issue; but should it terminate contrary to the wishes of those who support the enormous pretensions of the Executive, should victory crown the exertions of the champions of constitutional law, what serious and lasting advantage is to be expected from this result?

"In the South (things may be less gloomy with you) those who support the Executive do not support the Government. They sustain the personal power of the President, but labor incessantly to impair the legitimate powers of the Government. Those who oppose the violent and rash measures of the Executive (many of them nullifiers, many of them seceders) are generally the bitter enemies of a constitutional government. Many of them are the avowed advocates of a league; and those who do not go the whole length, go great part of the way. What can we hope for in such circumstances? As far as I can judge, the Government is weakened, whatever party may prevail. Such is the impression I receive from the language of those around me." [1]

During the last years of Marshall's life, the country's esteem for him, slowly forming through more than a generation, manifested itself by expressions of reverence and affection. When he and Story attended the theater, the audience cheered him.[2] His sentiment still youthful and tender, he wept over Fanny Kemble's affecting portrayal of Mrs. Haller in "The Stranger."[3] To the very last Marshall per-

[1] Marshall to Story, Oct. 6, 1834, Story, II, 172-73.
[2] Story to his wife, Jan. 20, 1833, *ib.* 116.   [3] *Ib.* 117.

formed his judicial duties thoroughly, albeit with a heavy heart. He "looked more vigorous than usual," and "seemed to revive and enjoy anew his green old age," testifies Story.[1]

It is at this period of his career that we get Marshall's account of the course he pursued toward his malignant personal and political enemy, Thomas Jefferson. Six years after Jefferson's death,[2] Major Henry Lee, who hated that great reformer even more than Jefferson hated Marshall, wrote the Chief Justice for certain facts, and also for his opinion of the former President. In his reply Marshall said:

"I have never allowed myself to be irritated by M[r] Jeffersons unprovoked and unjustifiable aspersions on my conduct and principles, nor have I ever noticed them except on one occasion[3] when I thought myself called on to do so, and when I thought that declining to enter upon my justification might have the appearance of crouching under the lash, and admitting the justice of its infliction."[4]

Intensely as he hated Jefferson, attributing to him, as Marshall did, most of the country's woes, the Chief Justice never spoke a personally offensive word concerning his radical cousin.[5] On the other hand, he never uttered a syllable of praise or appreciation of Jefferson. Even when his great antagonist

---

[1] Story to his wife, Jan. 20, 1833, Story, II, 116.

[2] July 4, 1826.

[3] Jefferson's attacks on Marshall in the X. Y. Z. affair. (See vol. II, 359–63, 368–69, of this work.)

[4] Marshall to Major Henry Lee, Jan. 20, 1832, MSS. Lib. Cong. In no collection, but, with a few unimportant letters, in a portfolio marked "M," sometimes referred to as "Marshall Papers."

[5] *Green Bag*, VIII, 463.

died, no expression of sorrow or esteem or regret or
admiration came from the Chief Justice. Marshall
could not be either hypocritical or vindictive; but
he could be silent.

Holding to the old-time Federalist opinion that
Jefferson's principles were antagonistic to orderly
government; convinced that, if they prevailed, they
would be destructive of the Nation; believing the
man himself to be a demagogue and an unscrupulous if astute and able politician — Marshall,
nevertheless, said nothing about Jefferson to anybody except to Story, Lee, and Pickering; and, even
to these close friends, he gave only an occasional
condemnation of Jefferson's policies.

The general feeling toward Marshall, especially
that of the bench and bar, during his last two years
is not too strongly expressed in Story's dedication
to the Chief Justice of his "Commentaries on the
Constitution of the United States." Marshall had
taken keen interest in the preparation of Story's
masterpiece and warned him against haste. "Pre-
cipitation ought carefully to be avoided. This is a
subject on which I am not without experience." [1]

Story begins by a tribute "to one whose youth was
engaged in the arduous enterprises of the Revolution;
whose manhood assisted in framing and supporting
the national Constitution; and whose maturer years
have been devoted to the task of unfolding its powers,
and illustrating its principles." As the expounder
of the Constitution, "the common consent of your

[1] Marshall to Story, July 3, 1829, *Proceedings, Mass. Hist. Soc.* 2d
Series, xiv, 340.

countrymen has admitted you to stand without a rival. Posterity will assuredly confirm, by its deliberate award, what the present age has approved, as an act of undisputed justice.

"But," continues Story, "I confess that I dwell with even more pleasure upon the entirety of a life adorned by consistent principles, and filled up in the discharge of virtuous duty; where there is nothing to regret, and nothing to conceal; no friendships broken; no confidence betrayed; no timid surrenders to popular clamor; no eager reaches for popular favor. Who does not listen with conscious pride to the truth, that the disciple, the friend, the biographer of Washington, still lives, the uncompromising advocate of his principles?" [1]

Excepting only the time of his wife's death, the saddest hours of his life were, perhaps, those when he opened the last two sessions of the Supreme Court over which he presided. When, on January 13, 1834, the venerable Chief Justice, leading his associate justices to their places, gravely returned the accustomed bow of the bar and spectators, he also, perforce, bowed to temporary events and to the iron, if erratic, rule of Andrew Jackson. He bowed, too, to time and death. Justice Washington was dead,

---

[1] Story to Marshall, January, 1833, Story, ii, 132-33. This letter appears in Story's *Commentaries on the Constitution*, immediately after the title-page of volume i.

Story's perfervid eulogium did not overstate the feeling — the instinct — of the public. Nathan Sargent, that trustworthy writer of reminiscences, testifies that, toward the end of Marshall's life, his name had "become a household word with the American people implying greatness, purity, honesty, and all the Christian virtues." (Sargent, i, 299.)

Johnson was fatally ill, and Duval, sinking under age and infirmity, was about to resign.

Republicans as Johnson and Duval were, they had, generally, upheld Marshall's Nationalism. Their places must soon be filled, he knew, by men of Jackson's choosing — men who would yield to the transient public pressure then so fiercely brought to bear on the Supreme Court. Only Joseph Story could be relied upon to maintain Marshall's principles. The increasing tendency of Justices Thompson, McLean, and Baldwin was known to be against his unyielding Constitutional philosophy. It was more than probable that, before another year, Jackson would have the opportunity to appoint two new Justices — and two cases were pending that involved some of Marshall's dearest Constitutional principles.

The first of these was a Kentucky case [1] in which almost precisely the same question, in principle, arose that Marshall had decided in Craig *vs.* Missouri. [2] The Kentucky Bank, owned by the State, was authorized to issue, and did issue, bills which were made receivable for taxes and other public dues. The Kentucky law furthermore directed that an endorsement and tender of these State bank notes should, with certain immaterial modifications, satisfy any judgment against a debtor. [3] In short, the Legislature had authorized a State currency — had emitted those bills of credit, expressly forbidden by the National Constitution.

Another case, almost equally important, came

[1] Briscoe *vs.* The Commonwealth's Bank of the State of Kentucky, **8** Peters, 118 *et seq.*   [2] See *supra*, 509–13.
[3] Act of Dec. 25, *Laws of Kentucky, 1820*, 183–88.

from New York.[1] To prevent the influx of impover-
ished foreigners, who would be a charge upon the
City of New York, the Legislature had enacted that
the masters of ships arriving at that port should report to the Mayor all facts concerning passengers.
The ship captain must remove those whom the
Mayor decided to be undesirable.[2] It was earnestly
contended that this statute violated the commerce
clause of the Constitution.

Both cases were elaborately argued; both, it was
said, had been settled by former decisions — the
Kentucky case by Craig *vs*. Missouri, the New York
case by Gibbons *vs*. Ogden and Brown *vs*. Maryland.
The court was almost equally divided. Thompson,
McLean, and Baldwin thought the Kentucky and
New York laws Constitutional; Marshall, Story,
Duval, and Johnson believed them invalid. But
Johnson was absent because of his serious illness.
No decision, therefore, was possible.

Marshall then announced a rule of the court,
hitherto unknown by the public: "The practice of
this court is not (except in cases of absolute necessity)
to deliver any judgment in cases where constitutional questions are involved, unless four judges concur in opinion, thus making the decision that of a
majority of the whole court. In the present cases
four judges do not concur in opinion as to the constitutional questions which have been argued. The
court therefore direct these cases to be re-argued at

[1] The Mayor, Aldermen and Commonalty of the City of New York
vs. Miln, 8 Peters, 121 *et seq*.

[2] 11 Peters, 104. This was the first law against unrestricted immi-
gration.

the next term, under the expectation that a larger number of the judges may then be present." [1]

The next term! When, on January 12, 1835, John Marshall for the last time presided over the Supreme Court of the United States, the situation, from his point of view, was still worse. Johnson had died and Jackson had appointed James M. Wayne of Georgia in his place. Duval had resigned not long before the court convened, and his successor had not been named. Again the New York and Kentucky cases were continued, but Marshall fully realized that the decision of them must be in opposition to his firm and pronounced views. [2]

[1] 8 Peters, 122.

[2] These cases were not decided until 1837, when Roger Brooke Taney of Maryland took his seat on the bench as Marshall's successor. Philip Pendleton Barbour of Virginia succeeded Duval. Of the seven Justices, only one disciple of Marshall remained, Joseph Story.

In the New York case the court held that the State law was a local police regulation. (11 Peters, 130–43; 144–53.) Story dissented in a signally able opinion of almost passionate fervor.

"I have the consolation to know," he concludes, "that I had the entire concurrence . . of that great constitutional jurist, the late Mr. Chief Justice Marshall. Having heard the former arguments, his deliberate opinion was that the act of New York was unconstitutional, and that the present case fell directly within the principles established in the case of Gibbons v. Ogden." (Ib. 153–61.)

In the Kentucky Bank case, decided immediately after the New York immigrant case, Marshall's opinion in Craig vs. Missouri was completely repudiated, although Justice McLean, who delivered the opinion of the court (ib. 311–28), strove to show that the judgment was within Marshall's reasoning.

Story, of course, dissented, and never did that extraordinary man write with greater power and brilliancy. When the case was first argued in 1834, he said, a majority of the court "were decidedly of the opinion" that the Kentucky Bank Law was unconstitutional. "In principle it was thought to be decided by the case of Craig v. The State of Missouri." Among that majority was Marshall — "a name never to be pronounced without reverence." (Ib. 328.)

In closing his great argument, Story says that the frankness and

MᶜLEAN   THOMPSON

STORY

WAYNE   BALDWIN

Associate Justices at the last session of the Supreme Court over which John Marshall presided

It is doubtful whether history shows more than a few examples of an aged man, ill, disheartened, and knowing that he soon must die, who nevertheless continued his work to the very last with such scrupulous care as did Marshall. He took active part in all cases argued and decided and actually delivered the opinion of the court in eleven of the most important.[1] None of these are of any historical interest; but in all of them Marshall was as clear and vigorous in reasoning and style as he had been in the immortal Constitutional opinions delivered at the height of his power. The last words Marshall ever uttered as Chief Justice sparkle with vitality and high ideals. In Mitchel *et al. vs.* The United States,[2] a case involving land titles in Florida, he said, in ruling on a motion to continue the case: "Though the hope of deciding causes to the mutual satisfaction of parties would be chimerical, that of convincing them that the case has been fully and fairly considered . . may be sometimes indulged. Even this is not always attainable. In the excite-

fervor of his language are due to his "reverence and affection" for Marshall. "I have felt an earnest desire to vindicate his memory. . . I am sensible that I have not done that justice to his opinion which his own great mind and exalted talents would have done. But . . I hope that I have shown that there were solid grounds on which to rest his exposition of the Constitution. *His saltem accumulem donis, et fungar inani munere.*" (11 Peters, 350.)

[1] Lessee of Samuel Smith *vs.* Robert Trabue's Heirs, 9 Peters, 4–6; U.S. *vs.* Nourse, *ib.* 11–32; Caldwell *et al. vs.* Carrington's Heirs, *ib.* 87–105; Bradley *vs.* The Washington, etc. Steam Packet Co. *ib.* 107–16; Delassus *vs.* U.S. *ib.* 118–36; Chouteau's Heirs *vs.* U.S. *ib.* 137–46; U.S. *vs.* Clarke, *ib.* 168–70; U.S. *vs.* Huertas, *ib.* 171–74; Field *et al. vs.* U.S. *ib.* 182–203; Mayor, etc. of New Orleans *vs.* De Armas and Cucullo, *ib.* 224–37; Life and Fire Ins. Co. of New York *vs.* Adams, *ib.* 571–605.

[2] *Ib.* 711–63.

ment produced by ardent controversy, gentlemen view the same object through such different media that minds, not infrequently receive therefrom precisely opposite impressions. The Court, however, must see with its own eyes, and exercise its own judgment, guided by its own reason." [1]

At last Marshall had grave intimations that his life could not be prolonged. Quite suddenly his health declined, although his mind was as strong and clear as ever. "Chief Justice Marshall still possesses his intellectual powers in very high vigor," writes Story during the last session of the Supreme Court over which his friend and leader presided. "But his physical strength is manifestly on the decline; and it is now obvious, that after a year or two, he will resign, from the pressing infirmities of age. . . What a gloom will spread over the nation when he is gone! His place will not, nay, it cannot be supplied." [2]

As the spring of 1835 ripened into summer, Marshall grew weaker. "I pray God," wrote Story in agonies of apprehension, "that he may long live to bless his country; but I confess that I have many fears whether he can be long with us. His complaints are, I am sure, incurable, but I suppose that they may be alleviated, unless he should meet with some accidental cold or injury to aggravate them. Of these, he is in perpetual danger, from his imprudence as well as from the natural effects of age." [3]

In May, 1835, Kent went to Richmond in order to see Marshall, whom "he found very emaciated,

---

[1] 9 Peters, 723.   [2] Story to Fay, March 2, 1835, Story, ii, 193.
[3] Story to Peters, May 20, 1835, *ib.* 194.

feeble & dangerously low. He injured his Spine by
a Post Coach fall & oversetting. . . He . . made me
Promise to see him at Washington next Winter." [1]

Kent wrote Jeremiah Smith of New Hampshire
that Marshall must soon die. Smith was overwhelmed with grief "because his life, at this time
especially, is of incalculable value." Marshall's
"views . . of our national affairs" were those of
Smith also. "Perfectly just in themselves they now
come to us confirmed by the dying attestation of
one of the greatest and best of men." [2]

Marshall's "incurable complaint," which so distressed Story, was a disease of the liver.[3] Finding
his health failing, he again repaired to Philadelphia
for treatment by Dr. Physick. When informed that
the prospects for his friend's recovery were desperate, Story was inconsolable. "Great, good and
excellent man!" he wrote. "I shall never see his
like again! His gentleness, his affectionateness, his
glorious virtues, his unblemished life, his exalted
talents, leave him without a rival or a peer." [4]

At six o'clock in the evening of Monday, July 6,
1835, John Marshall died, in his eightieth year,
in the city where American Independence was proclaimed and the American Constitution was born —
the city which, a patriotic soldier, he had striven to
protect and where he had received his earliest national recognition. Without pain, his mind as clear
and strong as ever, he "met his fate with the forti-

[1] Kent's Journal, May 16, 1835, Kent MSS. Lib. Cong.
[2] Smith to Kent, June 13, 1835, Kent MSS. Lib. Cong.
[3] Randolph: *Physick*, 100–01.
[4] Story to Peters, June 19, 1835, Story, II, 199–200.

tude of a Philosopher, and the resignation of a Christian," testifies Dr. Nathaniel Chapman, who was
present.[1] By Marshall's direction, the last thing
taken from his body after he expired was the locket
which his wife had hung about his neck just before
she died.[2] The morning after his death, the bar of
Philadelphia met to pay tribute to Marshall, and at
half-past five of the same day a town meeting was
held for the same purpose.[3]

Immediately afterward, his body was sent by boat
to Richmond. The bench, bar, and hundreds of citizens of Philadelphia accompanied the funeral party
to the vessel. During the voyage a transfer was
made to another craft.[4] A committee, consisting of
Major-General Winfield Scott, of the United States
Army, Henry Baldwin, Associate Justice of the Supreme Court, Richard Peters, formerly Judge for the
District of Pennsylvania, John Sergeant, Edward D.
Ingraham, and William Rawle, of the Philadelphia
bar, went to Richmond.

In the late afternoon of July 9, 1835, the steamboat
Kentucky, bearing Marshall's body, drew up at the
Richmond wharf. Throughout the day the bells had
been tolling, the stores were closed, and, as the vessel
came within sight, a salute of three guns was fired.

---

[1] Chapman to Brockenbrough, July 6, 1835, quoted in the Richmond
Enquirer, July 10, 1835. Marshall died "at the Boarding House of Mrs.
Crim, Walnut street below Fourth." (Philadelphia Inquirer, July 7,
1835.) Three of Marshall's sons were with him when he died. His
eldest son, Thomas, when hastening to his father's bedside, had been
killed in Baltimore by the fall upon his head of bricks from a chimney
blown down by a sudden and violent storm. Marshall was not informed of his son's death.

[2] Terhune, 98.

[3] Philadelphia Inquirer, July 7, 1835.   [4] Niles, XLVIII, 322.

All Richmond assembled at the landing. An immense procession marched to Marshall's house,[1] where he had requested that his body be first taken, and then to the "New Burying Ground," on Shockoe Hill. There Bishop Richard Channing Moore of the Episcopal Church read the funeral service, and Jchn Marshall was buried by the side of his wife.

When his ancient enemy and antagonist, the Richmond *Enquirer*, published the news of Marshall's death, it expressed briefly its true estimate of the man. It would be impossible, said the *Enquirer*, to over-praise Marshall's "brilliant talents." It would be "a more grateful incense" to his memory to say "that he was as much beloved as he was respected. . . There was about him so little of 'the insolence of office,' and so much of the benignity of the man, that his presence always produced . . the most delightful impressions. There was something irresistibly winning about him." Strangers could hardly be persuaded that "in the plain, unpretending . . man who told his anecdote and enjoyed the jest — they had been introduced to the Chief Justice of the United States, whose splendid powers had filled such a large space in the eye of mankind." [2]

The Richmond *Whig and Public Advertiser* said that "no man has lived or died in this country, save its father George Washington alone, who united such a warmth of affection for his person, with so deep and unaffected a respect for his character, and admiration for his great abilities. No man ever bore

[1] Richmond *Enquirer*, July 10, 1835.   [2] *Ib.*

public honors with so meek a dignity... It is hard
.. to conceive of a more perfect character than his,
for who can point to a vice, scarcely to a defect —
or who can name a virtue that did not shine conspicuously in his life and conduct?"[1]

The day after the funeral the citizens of Richmond
gathered at and about the Capitol, again to honor the
memory of their beloved neighbor and friend. The
resolutions, offered by Benjamin Watkins Leigh, declared that the people of Richmond knew "better
than any other community can know" Marshall's
private and public "virtues," his "wisdom," "simplicity," "self-denial," "unbounded charity," and
"warm benevolence towards all men." Since nothing
they can say can do justice to "such a man," the
people of Richmond "most confidently trust, to
History alone, to render due honors to his memory,
by a faithful and immortal record of his wisdom, his
virtues and his services."[2]

All over the country similar meetings were held,
similar resolutions adopted. Since the death of
Washington no such universal public expressions
of appreciation and sorrow had been witnessed.[3]
The press of the country bore laudatory editorials
and articles. Even Hezekiah Niles, than whom no
man had attacked Marshall's Nationalist opinions
more savagely, lamented his death, and avowed
himself unequal to the task of writing a tribute to

[1] Richmond *Whig and Public Advertiser*, July 10, 1835.
[2] Richmond *Enquirer*, July 14, 1835.
[3] See Sargent, I, 299. If the statements in the newspapers and mag-
azines of the time are to be trusted, even the death of Jefferson called
forth no such public demonstrations as were accorded Marshall.

Marshall that would be worthy of the subject. "'A great man has fallen in Israel,'" said Niles's *Register*. "Next to WASHINGTON, only, did he possess the reverence and homage of the heart of the American people." [1]

One of the few hostile criticisms of Marshall's services appeared in the *New York Evening Post* over the name of "Atlantic." [2] This paper had, by now, departed from the policy of its Hamiltonian founder. "Atlantic" said that Marshall's "political doctrines . . were of the ultra federal or aristocratic kind. . . With Hamilton" he "distrusted the virtue and intelligence of the people, and was in favor of a strong and vigorous General Government, at the expense of the rights of the States and of the people." While he was "sincere" in his beliefs and "a good and exemplary man" who "truly loved his country . . he has been, all his life long, a stumbling block . . in the way of democratic principles. . . His situation . . at the head of an important tribunal, constituted in utter defiance of the very first principles of democracy, has always been . . an occasion of lively regret. That he is at length removed from that station is a source of satisfaction." [3]

The most intimate and impressive tributes came, of course, from Virginia. Scarcely a town in the State that did not hold meetings, hear orations, adopt resolutions. For thirty days the people of Lynchburg

[1] Niles, XLVIII, 321.

[2] Undoubtedly William Leggett, one of the editors. See Leggett: *A Collection of Political Writings*, II, 3–7.

[3] As reprinted in Richmond *Whig and Public Advertiser*, July 14, 1835.

wore crape on the arm.[1]   Petersburg honored "the Soldier, the Orator, the Patriot, the Statesman, the Jurist, and above all, the good and virtuous man."[2] Norfolk testified to his "transcendent ability, perfect integrity and pure patriotism."[3]   For weeks the Virginia demonstrations continued.   That at Alexandria was held five weeks after his death. "The flags at the public square and on the shipping were displayed at half mast; the bells were tolled . . during the day, and minute guns fired by the Artillery"; there was a parade of military companies, societies and citizens, and an oration by Edgar Snowden.[4]

The keenest grief of all, however, was felt by Marshall's intimates of the Quoit Club of Richmond. Benjamin Watkins Leigh proposed, and the club resolved, that, as to the vacancy caused by Marshall's death, "there should be no attempt to fill it ever; but that the number of the club should remain one less than it was before his death."[5]

Story composed this "inscription for a cenotaph":

"To Marshall reared — the great, the good, the wise;
Born for all ages, honored in all skies;
His was the fame to mortals rarely given,
Begun on earth, but fixed in aim on heaven.
Genius, and learning, and consummate skill,
Moulding each thought, obedient to the will;
Affections pure, as e'er warmed human breast,
And love, in blessing others, doubly blest;

---

[1] Richmond *Enquirer*, July 21, 1835.   [2] *Ib.*   [3] *Ib.* July 17, 1835.
[4] Alexandria *Gazette*, Aug. 13, 1835, reprinted in the Richmond *Enquirer*, Aug. 21, 1835.
[5] Magruder: *John Marshall*, 282.

> Virtue unspotted, uncorrupted truth,
> Gentle in age, and beautiful in youth; —
> These were his bright possessions. These had power
> To charm through life and cheer his dying hour.
> Are these all perished? No! but snatched from time,
> To bloom afresh in yonder sphere sublime.
> Kind was the doom (the fruit was ripe) to die,
> Mortal is clothed with immortality." [1]

Upon his tomb, however, were carved only the words he himself wrote for that purpose two days before he died, leaving nothing but the final date to be supplied:

JOHN MARSHALL

The son of Thomas and Mary Marshall
Was born on the 24th of
September, 1755; intermarried
with Mary Willis Ambler
the 3d of January, 1783;
departed this life the 6th day
of July, 1835.

---

[1] Story, ii, 206.

THE END

WORKS CITED IN THIS VOLUME

WORKS CITED IN THIS VOLUME

The material given in parentheses and following certain titles indicates the form in which those titles have been cited in the footnotes.

ABEL, ANNIE HÉLOISE. The History of Events resulting in Indian Consolidation west of the Mississippi. [Volume 1 of *Annual Report of the American Historical Association* for 1906.]

ADAMS, HENRY. History of the United States of America from 1801 to 1817. 9 vols. New York. 1889–93. (Adams: *U.S.*)

—— Life of Albert Gallatin. Philadelphia. 1879. (Adams: *Gallatin.*)

ADAMS, HENRY, *editor*. Documents relating to New England Federalism, 1800–15. Boston. 1877. (*N.E. Federalism:* Adams.)

—— *See also* Gallatin, Albert. Writings.

ADAMS, JOHN. *See* Old Family Letters.

ADAMS, JOHN QUINCY. Memoirs. Edited by Charles Francis Adams. 12 vols. Philadelphia. 1874–77. (*Memoirs, J. Q. A.*: Adams.)

AMBLER, CHARLES HENRY. Sectionalism in Virginia, from 1776 to 1861. Chicago. 1910.

—— Thomas Ritchie: A Study in Virginia Politics. Richmond. 1913. (Ambler: *Ritchie.*)

AMBLER, CHARLES HENRY, *editor. See* John P. Branch Historical Papers.

American Colonization Society. Annual Reports, 1–72. 1818–89.

American Historical Review. Managing Editor, J. Franklin Jameson. Vols. 1–24. New York. 1896–1919. (*Am. Hist. Rev.*)

American Jurist and Law Magazine. 28 vols. Boston. 1829–43.

American Law Journal. Edited by John E. Hall. 6 vols. Baltimore. 1808–17.

American State Papers. Documents, Legislative and Executive, of the Congress of the United States. Selected and edited under the Authority of Congress. 38 vols. Wash-

ington.   1832–61.   [Citations in this work are from "Foreign Relations" (*Am. State Papers, For. Rel.*); and "Finance" (*Am. State Papers, Finance*).]

American Turf Register and Sporting Magazine. Edited by
J. S. Skinner. 7 vols. Baltimore. 1830–40.

AMES, FISHER. Works. Edited by Seth Ames. 2 vols. Boston.
1854. (*Ames:* Ames.)

AMES, HERMAN VANDENBURG, *editor.* State Documents on
Federal Relations: The States and the United States.
Philadelphia. 1906. (*State Doc. Fed. Rel.*: Ames.)

ANDERSON, DICE ROBINS. William Branch Giles: A Study in
the Politics of Virginia and the Nation, from 1790–1830.
Menasha, Wis. 1914. (Anderson.)

BABCOCK, KENDRIC CHARLES. Rise of American Nationality,
1811–1819. New York. 1906. [Volume 13 of *The American Nation: A History.*]   (Babcock.)

BANCROFT, GEORGE. *See* Howe, M. A. DeWolfe.

BARSTOW, GEORGE. History of New Hampshire. Concord,
1842. (Barstow.)

BASSETT, JOHN SPENCER. Life of Andrew Jackson. 2 vols.
New York. 1911.

BAYARD, JAMES ASHETON. Papers from 1796 to 1815. Edited
by Elizabeth Donnan. [Volume 2 of *Annual Report of
the American Historical Association* for 1913.] (*Bayard
Papers:* Donnan.)

BIDDLE, ALEXANDER. *See* Old Family Letters.

BIDDLE, NICHOLAS. Correspondence. Edited by Reginald
C. McGrane. Boston. 1919.

BLANE, WILLIAM NEWNHAM. An Excursion through the United
States and Canada during the Years 1822–23. By an
English Gentleman. London. 1824.

Branch Historical Papers. *See* Dodd, W. E.

BROCKENBROUGH, JOHN W., *reporter.* Reports of Cases decided by the Honourable John Marshall, in the Circuit
Court of the United States, for the District of Virginia
and North Carolina, from 1802 to 1833 inclusive. 2 vols.
Philadelphia. 1837. (Brockenbrough.)

BROWN, SAMUEL GILMAN. Life of Rufus Choate. Boston.
1870. (Brown.)

BRYAN, WILHELMUS BOGART. A History of the National Capital. 2 vols. New York. 1914–16. (Bryan.)

CABOT, GEORGE. *See* Lodge, Henry Cabot.

CALL, DANIEL. Reports of the Court of Appeals, Virginia [1779–1818]. 6 vols. Richmond. 1801–33.

CARTWRIGHT, PETER. Autobiography of Peter Cartwright, the Backwoods Preacher. Edited by W. P. Strickland. New York. 1856.

CATTERALL, RALPH CHARLES HENRY. Second Bank of the United States. Chicago. 1903. [Decennial Publications of the University of Chicago.] (Catterall.)

CHANNING, EDWARD. A History of the United States. Vols. 1–4. New York. 1905–17. (Channing: *U.S.*)

—— Jeffersonian System, 1801–1811. New York. 1906. [Volume 12 of *The American Nation: A History*.] (Channing: *Jeff. System*.)

CHASE, FREDERICK. A History of Dartmouth College, and the Town of Hanover, New Hampshire. Edited by John King Lord. 2 vols. [Vol. 2: A History of Dartmouth College, 1815–1909. By John King Lord.] Cambridge. 1891. 1913.

CHOATE, RUFUS. *See* Brown, Samuel Gilman.

CLAY, HENRY. *See* Schurz, Carl.

CLEVELAND, CATHERINE CAROLINE. Great Revival in the West, 1797–1805. Chicago. 1916.

COLLINS, LEWIS. Historical Sketches of Kentucky. Cincinnati. 1847. (Collins.)

CONNECTICUT. Public Statute Laws of the State of Connecticut. May Sessions 1822, 1823, 1825, 1826. Hartford. n. d.

COOLEY, THOMAS MCINTYRE. A Treatise on the Constitutional Limitations which rest upon the Legislative Power of the States of the American Union. Boston. 1868.

COOPER, THOMAS, *editor*. Statutes at Large of South Carolina. Vols. 1–5. Columbia, S.C. 1836.

CORWIN, EDWARD SAMUEL. John Marshall and the Constitution. New Haven. 1919.

COTTON, JOSEPH P., JR., *editor*. Constitutional Decisions of John Marshall. 2 vols. New York. 1905.

COWEN, EZEKIEL, *reporter*. Reports of Cases argued and determined in the Supreme Court .. of the State of New York. 9 vols. Albany. 1824–30. (Cowen.)

CRANCH, WILLIAM, *reporter*. Reports of Cases argued and adjudged in the Supreme Court of the United States. 9 vols. New York. 1812–17. (Cranch.)

CURTIS, GEORGE TICKNOR.   Life of Daniel Webster.   2 vols. New York.   1870.   (Curtis.)

DEWEY, DAVIS RICH.   Financial History of the United States. New York.   1903.   [American Citizen Series.]   (Dewey.)

DICKINSON, H. W.   Robert Fulton, Engineer and Artist: His Life and Works.   London.   1913.   (Dickinson.)

DILLON, JOHN FORREST, *compiler and editor*.   John Marshall: Life, Character and Judicial Services, as portrayed in the Centenary Proceedings throughout the United States on Marshall Day.   1901.   3 vols.   Chicago.   1903.   (Dillon.)

DODD, WILLIAM EDWARD, *editor*.   See John P. Branch Historical Papers.

—— Statesmen of the Old South.   New York.   1911.

DONNAN, ELIZABETH, *editor*.   See Bayard, James A.   Papers.

DUER, WILLIAM ALEXANDER.   A Letter addressed to Cadwallader D. Colden, Esquire.   In Answer to the Strictures contained in his "Life of Robert Fulton," etc.   Albany 1817.

Edinburgh Review.

EMBARGO LAWS, with the Message from the President, upon which they were founded.   Boston.   1809.

FARMER, JOHN.   Sketches of the Graduates of Dartmouth College.   Concord.   1832.   1834.   [In *New Hampshire Historical Society*.   Collections.   Volumes 3 and 4.]

FARRAND, MAX, *editor*.   See Records of the Federal Convention of 1787.

FARRAR, TIMOTHY, *reporter*.   Report of the Case of the Trustees of Dartmouth College against William H. Woodward. Portsmouth, N.H.   1819.   (Farrar.)

Federal Cases: Cases, Circuit and District Courts, United States [1789–1880].   St. Paul.   1894–97.

First Forty Years of Washington Society.   See Hunt, Gaillard.

Fiske, John.   Essays Historical and Literary.   2 vols.   New York.   1902.

FLANDERS, HENRY.   Lives and Times of the Chief Justices of the Supreme Court of the United States.   2 vols.   Philadelphia.   1881.

FLETCHER, R. A.   Steam-Ships.   The Story of Their Development to the Present Day.   Philadelphia.   1910.

FORD, PAUL LEICESTER, *editor*. *See* Jefferson, Thomas. Works.

FULTON, ROBERT. *See* Dickinson, H. W.; Knox, Thomas W.; Reigart, J. Franklin; Thurston, Robert H.

GALLATIN, ALBERT. Writings. Edited by Henry Adams. 3 vols. Philadelphia. 1879. (*Writings:* Adams.)
> *See also* Adams, Henry.

GEORGIA. Acts of the General Assembly of the State of Georgia, at an Annual Session, in October and November, 1814. Milledgeville, Ga. 1814.

GILES, WILLIAM BRANCH. *See* Anderson, Dice Robins.

Great American Lawyers. *See* Lewis, William Draper.

GREELEY, HORACE. The American Conflict. 2 vols. Hartford. 1864. 1867.

Green Bag, The: An Entertaining Magazine for Lawyers. Edited by Horace W. Fuller. Boston. 1889–1914. (*Green Bag*.)

GRIGSBY, HUGH BLAIR. The Virginia Convention of 1829–1830. Richmond. 1854.

HARDING, CHESTER. A Sketch of Chester Harding, Artist. Drawn by his own Hand. Edited by Margaret Eliot White. Boston. 1890.

Harper's Magazine.

HART, ALBERT BUSHNELL, *editor*. American History told by Contemporaries. 4 vols. New York. 1897–1901.

—— The American Nation: A History. 27 volumes. New York. 1904–1908.

Harvard Law Review.

HARVEY, PETER. Reminiscences and Anecdotes of Webster. Boston. 1877.

HAY, GEORGE. A Treatise on Expatriation. Washington. 1814.

HILDRETH, RICHARD. History of the United States of America. 6 vols. New York. 1854–55. (Hildreth.)

HILLARD, GEORGE STILLMAN. Memoir and Correspondence of Jeremiah Mason. Cambridge. 1873. (Hillard.)

HOPKINS, SAMUEL M., *reporter*. Reports of Cases argued and determined in the Court of Chancery of the State of New York. Albany. 1839.

HOUSTON, DAVID FRANKLIN. A Critical Study of Nullification in South Carolina. New York. 1896. [Harvard Historical Studies.] (Houston.)

HOWARD, BENJAMIN CHEW. Reports of Cases argued and adjudged in the Supreme Court of the United States, 1843–60. 24 vols. Philadelphia. 1852–[61].

HOWE, HENRY. Historical Collections of Virginia. Charleston, S.C. 1845. (Howe.)

HOWE, MARK ANTONY DeWOLFE, JR. Life and Letters of George Bancroft. 2 vols. New York. 1908.

HUNT, CHARLES HAVENS. Life of Edward Livingston. New York. 1864. (Hunt: *Livingston*.)

HUNT, GAILLARD, *editor*. First Forty Years of Washington Society, portrayed by the Family Letters of Mrs. Samuel Harrison Smith. New York. 1906.

—— *See* Madison, James. Writings.

INDIANA. Revised Laws of Indiana, adopted and enacted by the General Assembly at their Eighth Session. Corydon. 1824.

INGERSOLL, CHARLES JARED. History of the Second War between the United States of America and Great Britain. (Second Series.) 2 vols. Philadelphia. 1853.

JACKSON, ANDREW.   *See* Bassett, John Spencer; Parton, James; Sumner, William Graham.

JEFFERSON, THOMAS. Works. Edited by Paul Leicester Ford. 12 vols. New York. 1904–05. [Federal Edition.] (*Works:* Ford.)
        See Randall, Henry Stephens.

John P. Branch Historical Papers, issued by the Randolph-Macon College. Vols. 1–5. [Edited by W. E. Dodd and C. H. Ambler.] Ashland, Va. 1901–18. (Branch Historical Papers.)

JOHNSON, EMORY RICHARD, *and others*. History of Domestic and Foreign Commerce of the United States. 2 vols. Washington. 1915. [Carnegie Institution of Washington. Publications.]

JOHNSON, WILLIAM, *reporter*. Reports of Cases adjudged in the Court of Chancery of New-York, 1814–23. 7 vols. Albany. 1816–24. (Johnson's *Chancery Reports*.)

—— Reports of Cases argued and determined in the Supreme Court . . in the State of New-York (1806–22). 20 vols. New York and Albany. 1808–23. (Johnson.)

KENNEDY, JOHN PENDLETON. Memoirs of the Life of William Wirt. 2 vols. Philadelphia. 1849. (Kennedy.)

KING, RUFUS. Life and Correspondence. Edited by Charles R. King. 6 vols. New York. 1894–1900. (King.)

KNOX, THOMAS W. Life of Robert Fulton and a History of Steam Navigation. New York. 1896.

LANMAN, CHARLES. Private Life of Daniel Webster. New York. 1852.

LEGGETT, WILLIAM. A Collection of Political Writings. 2 vols. New York. 1840.

LEWIS, WILLIAM DRAPER, editor. Great American Lawyers: A History of the Legal Profession in America. 8 vols. Philadelphia. 1907–09.

LINCOLN, ABRAHAM. Complete Works. Edited by John G. Nicolay and John Hay. 12 vols. New York. 1894–1905.

Lippincott's Magazine of Literature, Science and Education.

LITTELL, WILLIAM. The Statute Law of Kentucky: with Notes, Prælections, and Observations on the Public Acts. 3 vols. Frankfort (Ky.), 1809.

LIVINGSTON, EDWARD. *See* Hunt, Charles Havens.

LODGE, HENRY CABOT. Daniel Webster. Boston. 1883. [American Statesmen.]

—— Life and Letters of George Cabot. Boston. 1877. (Lodge: *Cabot.*)

LORD, JOHN KING. A History of Dartmouth College, 1815–1909. Being the second volume of History of Dartmouth College and the Town of Hanover, New Hampshire, begun by Frederick Chase. Concord, N.H. 1913. (Lord.)

LOSHE, LILLIE DEMING. The Early American Novel. New York. 1907. [Columbia University. Studies in English.]

Louisiana Law Journal. Edited by Gustavus Schmidt. Volume 1, nos. 1–4. New Orleans. 1841.

LOWELL, JOHN. Mr. Madison's War. By a New England Farmer (*pseud.*). Boston. 1812.

—— Peace Without Dishonour — War Without Hope. By a Yankee Farmer (*pseud.*). Boston. 1807.

—— Review of a Treatise on Expatriation by George Hay, Esquire. By a Massachusetts Lawyer (*pseud.*). Boston. 1814.

McClintock, John Norris. History of New Hampshire. Boston. 1888.

McCord, David James, *editor*. Statutes at Large of South Carolina. Vols 6 to 10. Columbia, S.C. 1839–41.

MacDonald, William. Jacksonian Democracy, 1829–1837. New York. 1906. [Volume 15 of *The American Nation: A History.*]

McGrane, Reginald C., *editor*. *See* Biddle, Nicholas. Correspondence.

McHenry, James. *See* Steiner, Bernard Christian.

McMaster, John Bach. A History of the People of the United States from the Revolution to the Civil War. 8 vols. New York. 1883–1913. (McMaster.)

Madison, James. Writings. Edited by Gaillard Hunt. 9 vols. New York. 1900–1910. (*Writings:* Hunt.)

Magazine of American History.

Magruder, Allan Bowie. John Marshall. Boston. 1885. [American Statesmen.]

Maine, *Sir* Henry. Popular Government. London. 1885.

Manuscripts:

Chamberlain MSS. Boston Public Library.

Dreer MSS. Pennsylvania Historical Society.

Frederick Co., Va., Deed Book; Order Book.

Jefferson MSS. Library of Congress.

"Judges and Eminent Lawyers" Collection. Massachusetts Historical Society.

Kent MSS. Library of Congress.

Marshall MSS. Library of Congress.

Monroe MSS. Library of Congress.

Peters MSS. Pennsylvania Historical Society.

Pickering MSS. Massachusetts Historical Society.

Plumer MSS. Library of Congress.

"Society Collection." Pennsylvania Historical Society.

Story MSS. Massachusetts Historical Society.

Supreme Court Records.

Marryat, Frederick. A Diary in America, with Remarks on its Institutions. 2 vols. Philadelphia. 1839.

—— Second Series of A Diary in America, with Remarks on its Institutions. Philadelphia. 1840.

Marshall, John. Letters of Chief Justice Marshall to Timothy Pickering and Joseph Story. [From Pickering Papers and Story Papers. *Massachusetts Historical Society.*

Proceedings. Second Series. Vol. xiv, pp. 321–360.]
(*Proceedings, Mass. Hist. Soc*).

See Corwin, Edward Samuel; Cotton, Joseph P., Jr.;
Dillon, John Forrest; Magruder, Allan Bowie.

MARTINEAU, HARRIET. Retrospect of Western Travel. 2 vols.
London. 1838.

MARYLAND. Laws made and passed by the General Assembly
of the State of Maryland. Annapolis, Md. 1818.

Maryland Historical Society Fund-Publications. Baltimore.
(*Md. Hist. Soc. Fund-Pub.*)

MASON, JEREMIAH. *See* Hillard, George S.

MASSACHUSETTS. Laws of the Commonwealth of Massa-
chusetts, passed at the several Sessions of the General
Court, beginning 26th May, 1812, and ending on the 2d
March, 1815. Boston. 1812–15.

Massachusetts Historical Society. Proceedings. *See* Marshall,
John. Letters.

MEADE, *Bishop* WILLIAM. Old Churches, Ministers, and
Families of Virginia. 2 vols. Richmond. 1910. (Meade.)

Monthly Law Reporter. Edited by John Lowell. Vol. xx. New
Series, vol. x. Boston. 1858.

MOORE, JOHN BASSETT. Digest of International Law. 8 vols.
Washington. 1906.

MORDECAI, SAMUEL. Richmond in By-Gone Days, being the
Reminiscences of an old Citizen. Richmond. 1856.
(Mordecai.)

MORISON, JOHN HOPKINS. Life of the Hon. Jeremiah Smith.
Boston. 1845.

MORISON, SAMUEL ELIOT. Life and Letters of Harrison Gray
Otis, Federalist, 1765–1848. 2 vols. Boston. 1913.
(Morison: *Otis*.)

MORRIS, GOUVERNEUR. Diary and Letters. Edited by Anne
Cary Morris. 2 vols. London. 1888. (Morris.)

MORSE, JOHN TORREY, JR., *editor*. American Statesmen. 40
vols. Boston. 1882–1917.

MUNFORD, WILLIAM, *reporter*. Report of Cases argued and
determined in the Supreme Court of Appeals of Virginia
[1810–1820]. 6 vols. New York. 1812–21. (Munford.)

NELSON, JAMES POYNTZ. Address: The Chesapeake and Ohio
Railway. [Before the Railway Men's Improvement Society, New York City, January 27, 1916.] n. p., n. d.

NEW HAMPSHIRE. Journal of the House of Representatives of the State of New-Hampshire, at their session begun and holden at Concord, on the first Wednesday of June, A.D. 1816. Concord. 1816.

—— Laws of the State of New Hampshire. Exeter. 1815–16.

—— Public Laws of the State of New-Hampshire passed at a session of the General Court begun and holden at Concord on the fifth day of June, 1811. Concord. 1811.

—— Public Laws of the State of New-Hampshire passed at a session of the General Court begun and holden at Concord on the first Wednesday of June, 1813. Concord. 1813.

—— Public Laws of the State of New-Hampshire passed at a session of the General Court begun and holden at Concord on Wednesday the 27th day of October, 1813. Concord. 1813.

NEW JERSEY. Acts of the Thirty-fifth General Assembly of the State of New-Jersey. Trenton. 1811.

NEWSPAPERS:

Baltimore, Md.   *Marylander*, March 22, 1828.

Boston, Mass.   *Columbian Centinel*, January 11, 1809.
                    Daily Advertiser, March 23, 1818.
                    Spirit of Seventy-Six, July 17, 1812.

Philadelphia, Pa.   *Inquirer*, July 7, 1835.
                    The Union: The United States Gazette and True American, April 24, 1819.

Richmond, Va.   *Enquirer*, January 16, 1816; January 30, February 1, May 15, 22, June 22, 1821; April 4, 1828; July 10, 14, 17, 21, August 21, 1835.
                    Whig and Public Advertiser, July 10, 14, 1835.

NEW YORK. Laws of the State of New-York, passed at the Twenty-first and Twenty-second Sessions of the Legislature. Albany. 1798.

—— Laws of the State of New-York, passed at the Twenty-fifth, Twenty-sixth, and Twenty-seventh Sessions of the Legislature. Albany. 1804.

—— Laws of the State of New-York passed at the Thirtieth, Thirty-first, and Thirty-second Sessions of the Legislature. Albany. 1809.

—— Laws of the State of New-York, passed at the Thirty-fourth Session of the Legislature. Albany. 1811.

NICOLAY, JOHN GEORGE *and* HAY, JOHN, *editors.   See* Lincoln, Abraham.   Works.

Niles's Weekly Register.   Baltimore.   1811–1849.

North American Review.

OHIO.   Acts of the State of Ohio, passed at the First Session of the Seventeenth General Assembly.   Chillicothe.   1819.

—— Acts passed at the First Session of the Twentieth General Assembly of the State of Ohio.   Columbus.   1822.

—— Acts passed at the Second Session of the Twentieth General Assembly of the State of Ohio; and . . at the First Session of the Twenty-first General Assembly.   Columbus.   1822–23.

Old Family Letters.   Copied from the Originals for Alexander Biddle.   Philadelphia.   1892.

ORLEANS TERRITORY.   Acts passed at the Second Session of the Third Legislature of the Territory of Orleans.   New Orleans, La.   1811.

OTIS, HARRISON GRAY.   *See* Morison, Samuel Eliot.

PARTON, JAMES.   Life of Andrew Jackson.   3 vols.   Boston.   1861.   (Parton: *Jackson.*)

PAXTON, WILLIAM MCCLUNG.   Marshall Family.   Cincinnati.   1885.

PEASE, THEODORE CALVIN.   The Frontier State, 1818–1848.   Springfield.   1918.   [Volume 2 of *Centennial History of Illinois.*]

PECQUET DU BELLET, KATE LOUISE NOÉMIE.   Some Prominent Virginia Families.   4 vols.   Lynchburg, Va.   1907.   (Pecquet du Bellet.)

PETERS, RICHARD, JR., *reporter.*   Reports of Cases argued and adjudged in the Supreme Court of the United States, 1828–43.   17 vols.   Philadelphia.   1828–43.   (Peters.)

PHILLIPS, ULRICH BONNELL.   Georgia and State Rights.   Washington.   1902.   [Volume 2 of *Annual Report of the American Historical Association* for 1901.]

PHYSICK, PHILIP SYNG.   *See* Randolph, Jacob.

PICKERING, OCTAVIUS, *and* UPHAM, CHARLES WENTWORTH.   Life of Timothy Pickering.   4 vols.   Boston.   1867–73.

PICKERING, TIMOTHY.   A Letter . . to James Sullivan, Governor of Massachusetts.   Boston.   1808.

—— Life.   *See* Pickering, Octavius, and Upham, Charles W.

PINKNEY, WILLIAM.   *See* Pinkney, William; Wheaton, Henry.

PINKNEY, WILLIAM.   Life of William Pinkney.   New York.   1853.

PITKIN, TIMOTHY.   A Statistical View of the Commerce of the United States of America.   New Haven.   1835.   (Pitkin.)

PLUMER, WILLIAM, *Governor*.   *See* Plumer, William, Jr.

PLUMER, WILLIAM, JR.   Life of William Plumer, edited, with a Sketch of the Author's Life, by A. P. Peabody.   Boston. 1857.   (Plumer.)

PREBLE, GEORGE HENRY.   A Chronological History of the Origin and Development of Steam Navigation.   Philadelphia. 1895.

PRENTICE, EZRA PARMALEE.   Federal Power over Carriers and Corporations.   New York.   1907.

Quarterly Review.   London.

QUINCY, EDMUND.   Life of Josiah Quincy of Massachusetts. Boston.   1867.   (Quincy: *Quincy*.)

QUINCY, JOSIAH, *d.* 1864.   *See* Quincy, Edmund.

QUINCY, JOSIAH, *d.* 1882.   Figures of the Past, from the Leaves of Old Journals.   Boston.   1883.

RANDALL, HENRY STEPHENS.   Life of Thomas Jefferson.   3 vols.   New York.   1858.   (Randall.)

RANDOLPH, JACOB.   A Memoir on the Life and Character of Philip Syng Physick, M.D.   Philadelphia.   1839.   (Randolph: *Physick*.)

Records of the Federal Convention of 1787.   Edited by Max Farrand.   3 vols.   New Haven.   1911.   (*Records Fed. Conv.*: Farrand.)

REIGART, J. FRANKLIN.   Life of Robert Fulton.   Philadelphia. 1856.

RICHARDSON, JAMES DANIEL, *compiler*.   A Compilation of the Messages and Papers of the Presidents, 1789–1897.   10 vols.   Washington.   1900.   (Richardson.)

RITCHIE, THOMAS.   *See* Ambler, Charles Henry.

ROOSEVELT, THEODORE.   Naval War of 1812.   New York. 1882.   (Roosevelt.)

SARGENT, NATHAN.   Public Men and Events, from 1817 to 1853.   2 vols.   Philadelphia.   1875.   (Sargent.)

SCHERMERHORN, JOHN F., *and* MILLS, SAMUEL J.   A Correct View of that Part of the United States which lies west of the Allegany Mountains, with regard to Religion and Morals. Hartford. 1814.

SCHURZ, CARL. Henry Clay. 2 vols. Boston. 1887. [American Statesmen.]

SHIRLEY, JOHN M. The Dartmouth College Causes and the Supreme Court of the United States. St. Louis. 1879. (Shirley.)

SMITH, BAXTER PERRY. The History of Dartmouth College. Boston. 1878.

SMITH, ROBERT. An Address to the People of the United States. London. 1811.

SMITH, *Mrs.* SAMUEL HARRISON. *See* Hunt, Gaillard.

SOUTH CAROLINA. Statutes at Large. *See* McCord, David James.

Southern Literary Messenger. Richmond, Va. 1834–64.

STEINER, BERNARD CHRISTIAN. Life and Correspondence of James McHenry. Cleveland. 1907. (Steiner.)

STORY, JOSEPH. Life and Letters. Edited by William Wetmore Story. 2 vols. Boston. 1851. (Story.)

STRICKLAND, WILLIAM PETER, *editor.* *See* Cartwright, Peter. Autobiography. (Strickland.)

SUMNER, WILLIAM GRAHAM. Andrew Jackson. As a Public Man. Boston. 1882. [American Statesmen.] (Sumner: *Jackson.*)

—— A History of American Currency. New York. 1875. (Sumner: *Hist. Am. Currency.*)

TANEY, ROGER BROOKE. *See* Tyler, Samuel.

TAYLOR, JOHN. Construction Construed and Constitutions Vindicated. Richmond. 1820. (Taylor: *Construction Construed.*)

—— New Views of the Constitution of the United States. Washington. 1823.

—— Tyranny Unmasked. Washington. 1822. (Taylor: *Tyranny Unmasked.*)

TERHUNE, MARY VIRGINIA HAWES. Some Colonial Homesteads and their Stories. By Marion Harland (*pseud.*). 2 vols. New York. 1912. (Terhune.)

THOMAS, DAVID. Travels through the Western Country in 1816. Auburn, N.Y. 1819.

THURSTON, ROBERT HENRY. Robert Fulton: His Life and its Results. New York. 1891.

THWAITES, REUBEN GOLD, *editor*. Early Western Travels. 32 vols. Cleveland, 1904–07. (*E. W. T.*: Thwaites.)

TICKNOR, GEORGE. Life, Letters, and Journals. Edited by Anna Ticknor and George S. Hillard. 2 vols. Boston. 1876. (Ticknor.)

TURNER, FREDERICK JACKSON. Rise of the New West, 1819–1829. New York. 1906. [Volume 14 of *The American Nation: A History.*]

TYLER, LYON GARDINER. Letters and Times of the Tylers. 2 vols. Richmond. 1884. (*Tyler*: Tyler.)

TYLER, SAMUEL. Memoir of Roger Brooke Taney, Chief Justice of the Supreme Court of the United States. Baltimore. 1872.

UNITED STATES CONGRESS. Debates and Proceedings in the Congress of the United States. First Congress, First Session, to eighteenth Congress, First Session; Mar. 3, 1789 to May 27, 1824. [Known as the Annals of Congress.] 42 vols. Washington. 1834–56. (*Annals.*)

—— Register of Debates. Eighteenth Congress, Second Session — Twenty-fifth Congress, First Session. 29 vols. Washington. 1825–37. (*Debates.*)

—— Laws of the United States of America. 5 vols. Washington. 1816.

—— Statutes at Large.

UNITED STATES SUPREME COURT. Reports of Cases adjudged. *University of Pennsylvania Law Review and American Law Register.*

VAN SANTVOORD, GEORGE. Sketches of the Lives and Judicial Services of the Chief-Justices of the Supreme Court of the United States. New York. 1854.

VAN TYNE, CLAUDE HALSTEAD, *editor*. *See* Webster, Daniel. Letters.

VERMONT. Laws passed by the Legislature of the State of Vermont at their Session at Montpelier on the second Thursday of October, 1815. Windsor. n. d.

VIRGINIA. Journals of the House of Delegates. Richmond. 1819.

—— Proceedings and Debates of the Virginia State Convention of 1829–30. Richmond. 1830. (*Debates, Va. Conv.*)

—— Report of the Commissioners appointed to view certain

Rivers within the Commonwealth of Virginia, John Marshall, Chairman. Printed, 1816.

VIRGINIA. Reports of Cases argued and decided in the Court of Appeals. Richmond. 1833.

Virginia Branch Colonization Society. Report. 1832.

Virginia Magazine of History and Biography. 25 vols. Richmond. 1893–1917.

WALLACE, JOHN WILLIAM. Cases argued and adjudged in the Supreme Court of the United States, 1863–74. 23 vols. Washington, 1870–76.

WARREN, CHARLES. History of the American Bar. Boston. 1911. (Warren.)

WEBSTER, DANIEL. Letters of Daniel Webster, from Documents owned principally by the New Hampshire Historical Society. Edited by Claude H. Van Tyne. New York. 1902. (Van Tyne.)

—— Private Correspondence. Edited by Fletcher Webster. 2 vols. Boston. 1857. (*Priv. Corres.*: Webster.)

—— *See* Curtis, George Ticknor; Harvey, Peter; Lanman, Charles; Lodge, Henry Cabot; Wilkinson, William Cleaver.

WENDELL, JOHN LANSING, *reporter.* Reports of Cases argued and determined in the Supreme Court of Judicature . . of the State of New York. 26 vols. Albany. 1829–42.

WHEATON, HENRY. A Digest of the Decisions of the Supreme Court of the United States from 1789 to February Term, 1820. New York. 1821.

—— Elements of International Law, with a Sketch of the History of the Science. Philadelphia. 1836.

—— Some Account of the Life, Writings, and Speeches of William Pinkney. Philadelphia. 1826. (Wheaton: *Pinkney.*)

WHEATON, HENRY, *reporter.* Reports of Cases argued and adjudged in the Supreme Court of the United States, 1816–27. 12 vols. Philadelphia. 1816–27. (Wheaton.)

WILKINSON, WILLIAM CLEAVER. Daniel Webster: A Vindication. New York. 1911.

WILSON, HENRY. Rise and Fall of the Slave Power in America. 3 vols. Boston. 1872.

WIRT, WILLIAM. *See* Kennedy, John Pendleton.

World's Work.

GENERAL INDEX

GENERAL INDEX

Abel, Anne H., monograph on Indian consolidation, **4**, 541 *n*.

Adair, John, and Burr Conspiracy, **3**, 291, 292, 314; career, 292 *n*., 336 *n*.; Wilkinson's letter to, 314, 336; arrested by Wilkinson, 335, 336, 337 *n*.; suit against Wilkinson, 336 *n*.; brought to Baltimore, released, 344; statement, 488 *n*.; and Green *vs.* Biddle, **4**, 381.

Adams, Abijah, trial, **3**, 44–46.

Adams, Henry, on M. in Jonathan Robins case, **2**, 458; on Pickering impeachment, **3**, 143; on isolation of Burr, 280; on Burr and Merry, 289; on American law of treason, 401 *n*.; on impressment, **4**, 8 *n*.; on causes of War of 1812, 29 *n*.

Adams, John, on drinking, **1**, 23 *n*.; library, 25; on Philadelphia campaign, 102; belittles Washington (1778), 123 *n*.; story of expected kingship, 291; on American and French revolutions, **2**, 2 *n*.; and title for President, 36; on Hamilton's financial genius, 61 *n*.; and policy of neutrality, 92; M. on, 214; on M., 218; address to Congress on French affairs (1797), French demand of withdrawal of it, 225, 226, 316; appointment of X. Y. Z. Mission, 226–29; and X. Y. Z. dispatches, 336, 338; offers M. Associate Justiceship, 347, 378, 379; Federalist toast to, 349 *n*.; statement of French policy (1798), 351; and M.'s journal of mission, 366; M. on foreign policy, 403; and prosecutions under Sedition Law, 421; reopening of French negotiations, political result, 422–28; pardons Fries insurrectionists, political effect, 429–31, **3**, 36; absence from Capital, **2**, 431, 493; address to Congress (1799), 433; M.'s reply of House, 433–36; Jonathan Robins case, 458–75; disruption of Cabinet, 485–88; temperament contrasted with Washington's, 486, 488; appointment of M. as Secretary of State, 486, 489–93; Republican comment on reorganized Cabinet, 491, 494; pardon of Williams, 495; and Bowles in Florida, 497; and British debts dispute, 503, 505; and possible failure of new French negotiations, 522; M. writes address to Congress (1800), 530, 531; eulogy by *Washington Federalist*, 532 *n*.; and enlargement of Federal Judiciary, 547; and Chief Justiceship, appointment of M., 552–54, 558; continues M. as Secretary of State, 558; midnight appointments, 559–62, **3**, 57, 110; magnanimous appointment of Wolcott, **2**, 559, 560; Jefferson and midnight appointments, **3**, 21; Republican seditious utterances, 30, 33, 37, 42 *n*.; and subpœna,

33, 86; and partisan appointments, 81; on Bayard's Judiciary speech (1802), 82; on John Randolph, 171; and Chase, 211 *n*.; and M.'s biography of Washington, 257; on his situation as President, 258 *n*.; biography of Washington on, 263 *n*.; on Embargo controversy, **4**, 15; on banking mania, 176, 178; in Massachusetts Constitutional Convention (1820), 471. *See also* Elections (*1800*).

Adams, John Q., Publicola papers, **2**, 15–19; on vandalism of French Revolution, 32 *n*.; on American support of French Revolution, 39; on economic division on policy of neutrality, 97 *n*.; on dangers of war with England (1795), 110 *n*., 112 *n*.; on necessity of neutrality, 119 *n*.; Minister to Prussia, 229 *n*.; on France and American politics, 279 *n*.; on Washington streets (1818), **3**, 5; on Federalist defeat, 12; on impeachment plans (1804), 157–60, 173; on impeachment of Pickering, 166, 167; on articles of impeachment against Chase, 172; on Chase trial, 190 *n*., 191 *n*.; on Randolph's speech at trial, 216 *n*.; votes to acquit Chase, 218; on Burr's farewell address, 274 *n*.; on Wilkinson, 341 *n*.; on Eaton's story on Burr, 345; on Swartwout and Bollmann trial, 346; report on Burr conspiracy and trial, 541–44; report and courtship of administration, 541 *n*.; later support of M., **4**, 542 *n*.; on Giles's speech on report, 544; and Yazoo claims, attorney in Fletcher *vs.* Peck, 582, 585, 586; and Justiceship, **4**, 110; on crisis of 1819, 205; M. and election of 1828, 462–65; on Georgia-Cherokee controversy, 543.

Adams, Mrs. John Q., drawing room, **4**, 461.

Adams, Samuel, and Ratification, **1**, 348.

Adams, Thomas, sedition, **3**, 44.

Addison, Alexander, charge on Sedition Act, **2**, 385 *n*.; and British precedents, **3**, 28 *n*.; as judge, denounces Republicans, 46; on the stump, 47; on declaring acts void, 117; impeachment, 164.

Admiralty, M. on unfairness of British courts, **2**, 511, 512; Story as authority, **4**, 119; jurisdiction in Territories, 142–44. *See also* International law; Prize.

Adventure and Her Cargo case, **4**, 119.

Agriculture, M. on French (1797), **2**, 267; M.'s interest, **4**, 63.

Albany Plan, **1**, 9 *n*.

Alexander, James, and Burr conspiracy, arrested, **3**, 334; freed, 343.

Alexandria, Va., tribute to M., **4**, 592.

standing of M.'s opinion, 350, 414 n., 484, 493, 496, 502, 504–13, 540, 619–26; lack of evidence of treasonable design, 353–56, 377–79, 388; Judiciary and Administration and public opinion, 357, 376, 388; House debate on Wilkinson's conduct, 358–60; Burr's assembly on island at mouth of Cumberland, 361; boats, 361 n.; Burr in Mississippi, grand jury refuses to indict him, 363–65; release refused, flight and military arrest, 365–68, 374; taken to Richmond, 368–70; M.'s warrant for civil arrest, 370; preliminary hearing before M., 370, 372, 379; Burr and M. contrasted, 371, 372; bail question, 372, 379, 380, 423, 424, 429, 516; Burr's statement at hearing, 374; M.'s opinion, commits for high misdemeanor only, 375–79; M.'s conduct and position at trials, 375, 397, 404, 407, 408, 413 n., 421, 423, 480, 494, 517, 526; public opinion, appeal to it, Jefferson as prosecutor, 374, 379–91, 395–97, 401, 406, 411, 413, 414, 416–22, 430–32, 435, 437, 439, 441, 471, 476, 477, 479, 480, 497 n., 499, 499 n., 503, 516 n.; M.'s reflection on Jefferson's conduct, 376; collection of evidence, time question, 378, 385–90, 415, 417, 418, 425, 473; Wilkinson's attendance awaited, 383, 393, 415, 416, 429, 431, 432, 440; supposed overt acts, 386 n.; money spent by Administration, 391, 423; Jefferson's violation of faith with Bollmann, 391, 392; pardons for informers, 392, 393; Dunbaugh's evidence, 393, 427, 462, 463; development of Burr support at Richmond, 393, 415, 470, 478, 479; M. and Burr at Wickham's dinner, 394–97; appearance of court, crowd, 398–400; M. on difficulty of fair trial, 401; Jackson's denunciation of Jefferson and Wilkinson, 404, 405, 457; Burr's conduct and appearance in court, 406, 408, 456, 457, 479, 481, 499, 518; Burr's counsel, 407, 428; prosecuting attorneys, 407; M. and counsel, 408; selection of grand jury, 408–13, 422; Burr's demand for equal rights, 413, 414, 418; instruction of grand jury, 413–15, 442, 451; Hay's reports to Jefferson, 415, 431; new motion to commit for treason, 415–29; Jefferson and publication of evidence, 422, 515; legal order of proof, 424, 484–87; conduct of Eaton at Richmond, 429; Bollmann and pardon, 430, 431, 450–54; demand for Wilkinson's letter to Jefferson, subpœna duces tecum, 433–47, 450, 454–56, 518–22; M.'s admonition to counsel, 439; M.'s statement on prosecution's expectation of conviction, 447–49; Wilkinson's arrival, conduct and testimony, just escapes indictment, 456, 457, 463, 464; testimony before grand jury, 458–65; indictment of Burr and Blennerhassett for treason and misdemeanor, 465, 466; other indictments, 466 n.; attacks on Wilkinson, 471–75, 477; confinement of Burr, 474, 478, 479; selection of petit jury, 475, 481–83; M. seeks advice of Justices on treason, 480; Hay's opening statement, 484; testimony on Burr's expressions, 487, 488; on

overt act, 488–91; argument of proof of overt act, 491–504; unprecedented postponement, 494; Wirt's famous passage, 497, 616–18; poison hoax, 499 n.; irrelevant testimony, 512, 515, 542; attacks on M., threats of impeachment, Jefferson's Message, 500, 501, 503, 516, 525, 530–35, 540; judgment of law and fact, 500, 531; irregular verdict of not guilty, 513, 514; prosecution's advances to Blennerhassett and others, 514, 515 n.; nolle prosequi, 515, 524; reception of verdict in Richmond, 517; trial for misdemeanor, 522–24; commitment for trial in Ohio, 524, 527, 528, 531 n.; Burr's anger at M., 524, 528; and Daveiss's pamphlet, 525; Burr on drawn battle, 527; prosecution dropped, 528; M. on trial, 530; Baltimore mob, 535–40; bibliography, 538 n.; attempt to amend law of treason, 540; attempt to expel Senator Smith, Adams's report, 540–44.

Burrill, James, Jr., on bankruptcy frauds, 4, 202.

Burwell, Rebecca, and Jefferson, 1, 149.

Burwell, William A., and attempt to suspend habeas corpus (1807), 3, 348.

Butchers' Union vs. Crescent City, 4, 279 n.

Butler, Elizur, arrest by Georgia, 4, 548; pardoned, 552 n. See also Worcester vs. Georgia.

Byrd, William, library, 1, 25.

Cabell, Benjamin W. S., in Virginia Constitutional Convention, 4, 500.

Cabell, Joseph, at William and Mary, 1, 159.

Cabell, Joseph C., grand juror on Burr, 3, 413 n.; on Swartwout, 465.

Cabell, William, at William and Mary, 1, 159; in the Legislature, 203; and Henry-Randolph quarrel, 407 n.

Cabell, William H., opinion in Martin vs. Hunter's Lessee, 4, 158–60.

Cabinet, dissensions in Washington's, 2, 82; changes in Washington's, his offers to M., 122–25, 147; disruption of Adams's, 485–88; M.'s appointment as Secretary of State, 486, 489–91, 493; Republican comment on Adams's reorganized, 491; salaries (1800), 539 n.

Cabot, George, on democratic clubs, 2, 38; on policy of neutrality, 94 n.; and M. (1796), 198; on Gerry, 364, 366; on M.'s views on Alien and Sedition Acts, 391–93; on reopening of French negotiations, 424, 426; on M. in Congress, 432; on Adams and Hamiltonians, 488; on M. as Secretary of State, 492; opposition to Adams, 517 n.; in defeat, 3, 11; on Republican success, 11; political character, 11 n.; on attack on Judiciary, 98; on protest on repeal of Judiciary Act, 123 n.; on Louisiana Purchase, 150; and secession, 152; and Hartford Convention, 4, 52; and Story, 98.

Calder vs. Bull, 3, 612.

Caldwell, Elisha B., Supreme Court sessions in house, 4, 130.

Calhoun, John C., and War of 1812, 4, 29; Bonus Bill, 417; Exposition, 538; and nonintercourse with tariff States, 538 n.

INDEX

Government; Separation of powers; Union.

Cherokee Indians, power, **3**, 553; origin of Georgia contest, **4**, 539, 540; Jackson's attitude, 540, 541, 547, 548, 551; first appeal to Supreme Court, 541; popular interest and political involution, 541, 548; and removal, 541; monograph on contest, 541 *n.*; Tassels incident, Georgia's defiance of Supreme Court, 542–44; Cherokee Nation *vs.* Georgia, Georgia ignores, 544; M.'s opinion, Cherokees not a foreign nation, 544–46; M.'s rebuke of Jackson, 546; dissent from opinion, 546 *n.*; origin of Worcester *vs.* Georgia, arrest of missionaries, 547, 548; Georgia refuses to appear before Court, 548; counsel, 549; M.'s opinion, no State control over Indians, 549–51; mandate of Court ignored, 551; final defiance of Court, Graves case, 552 *n.*; removal of Indians, 552 *n.*

Cherokee Nation *vs.* Georgia. *See* Cherokee Indians.

Chesapeake-Leopard affair, Jefferson and, **3**, 475–77, **4**, 9.

Chester, Elisha W., counsel in Worcester *vs.* Georgia, **4**, 549.

Cheves, Langdon, and War of 1812, **4**, 29.

Children, M.'s fondness for, **4**, 63.

Chisholm *vs.* Georgia, **2**, 83 *n.*, **3**, 554 *n.*

Choate, Rufus, on Marbury *vs.* Madison, **3**, 101; on Webster's tribute to Dartmouth, **4**, 248.

Choctaw Indians, power, **3**, 553.

Christie, Gabriel, and slavery, **2**, 450.

Church ——, and X. Y. Z. Mission, **2**, 254.

Cincinnati, first steamboat, **4**, 403 *n.*

Cincinnati, Order of the, popular prejudice against, **1**, 292–94.

Cipher, necessity of use, **1**, 266 *n.*

Circuit Courts, Supreme Court Justices in, **3**, 55, 56; rights of original jurisdiction, **4**, 386. *See also* Judiciary; Judiciary Act of 1801.

Circuit riders, work, **4**, 189 *n.*

Citizenship, Virginia bill (1783), **1**, 208. *See also* Naturalization.

Civil rights, lack, **3**, 13 *n. See also* Bill of Rights.

Civil service, M. and office-seekers, **2**, 494; Adams and partisan appointments, **3**, 81; Jefferson's use of patronage, 81 *n.*, 208. *See also* Religious tests.

Claiborne, William C. C., and election of Jefferson, reward, **3**, 81 *n.*; and Wilkinson and Burr conspiracy, 326, 331, 363, 366; and Livingston, **4**, 102; and steamboat monopoly, 414.

Clark, Daniel, and Burr, **3**, 294, 295; and disunion rumors, 296.

Clark, Eugene F., acknowledgment to, **4**, 233 *n.*

Clark, George Rogers, surveyor, **1**, 210 *n.*; Indiana Canal Company, **3**, 291 *n.*

Classes, in colonial Virginia, **1**, 25–28; after the Revolution, 277, 278.

Clay, Charles, in Virginia Ratification Convention, **1**, 472.

Clay, Henry, duelist, **3**, 278 *n.*; and Burr conspiracy, 296, 318, 319 *n.*; on Daveiss and Burr, 317 *n.*; as exponent of Nationalism, **4**, 28, 29; as practitioner before M., 95, 135; and Green *vs.* Biddle, 376; counsel in Osborn *vs.* Bank, 385; in debate on Supreme Court, 395; Kremer's attack, 462 *n.*; Randolph duel, 463 *n.*; and report on M. and election of 1828, 464; and American Colonization Society, 474; and recharter of Bank of the United States, 530; Compromise Tariff, 574.

Clayton, Philip, and Yazoo lands act, **3**, 547, 548.

Clayton, Samuel, in Virginia Constitutional Convention, **4**, 501 *n.*

Clermont, Fulton's steamboat, **4**, 401 *n.*

Clinton, De Witt, presidential candidacy (1812), **4**, 47.

Clinton, George, letter for second Federal convention, **1**, 379–81, 477, **2**, 49, 57 *n.*; elected Vice-President, **3**, 197; defeats recharter of Bank of the United States, **4**, 176.

Clopton, John, deserts Congress (1798), **2**, 340 *n.*; candidacy (1798), 414.

Clothing. *See* Dress.

Cobbett, William, on American enthusiasm over French Revolution, **2**, 5 *n.*; as conservative editor, 30 *n.*

Cockade, black, **2**, 343.

Cocke, William, on Judiciary Act of 1801, **3**, 57 *n.*; at Chase trial, 194.

Cohens *vs.* Virginia, conditions causing opinion, its purpose, **4**, 342–44, 353; facts, 344, 345; as moot case, 343; counsel, argument, 346; M.'s opinion on appellate power, 347–57; statement of State Rights position, 347; supremacy of National Government, 347–49; Federal Judiciary as essential agency in this supremacy, 349–52; resistance of disunion, 352, 353; State as party, Eleventh Amendment, 354–56; hearing on merits, 357; Roane's attack on, 358, 359; rebuke of concurring Republican Justices, 358, 359; M. on attacks, 359–62; other Virginia attacks, 361 *n.*; Jefferson's attack on principles, M. on it, 362–66, 368–70; attack as one on Union, 365; Taylor's attack on principles, 366–68.

Coleman, *vs.* Dick and Pat, **2**, 180 *n.*

Colhoun, John E., and repeal of Judiciary Act, **3**, 62 *n.*, 72 *n.*

College charters as contracts. *See* Dartmouth College *vs.* Woodward.

Collins, Josiah, Granville heirs case, **4**, 154.

Collins, Minton, on economic division on Ratification, **1**, 313; on opposition to Ratification, 322.

Colston, Rawleigh, purchase of Fairfax estate, **2**, 203 *n.*, 204, **4**, 149, 150 *n.*; M.'s debt, **3**, 224.

Columbian Centinel, on Republicans (1799),

Duché, Jacob, beseeches Washington to apostatize, **1**, 105.

Duckett, Allen B., and Swartwout and Bollmann, **3**, 346.

Dueling, prevalence, **3**, 278 *n.*

Dunbar, Thomas, in Braddock's defeat, **1**, 5.

Dunbaugh, Jacob, and trial of Burr, evidence, **3**, 393, 459, 462, 463; credibility destroyed, 523.

Dunmore, Lord, Norfolk raid, **1**, 74–79.

Dutrimond, ——, and X. Y. Z. Mission, **2**, 326.

Duval, Gabriel, appointed Justice, **4**, 60; and Dartmouth College case, 255; dissent in Ogden *vs.* Saunders, 482 *n.*; resigns, 582, 584; and Briscoe *vs.* Bank and New York *vs.* Miln, 583.

Dwight, Theodore, on Republican rule (1801), **3**, 12.

Early, Peter, argument in Chase trial, **3**, 197.

Eaton, John H., on Supreme Court, **4**, 451.

Eaton, William, on Jefferson, **3**, 149 *n.*; antagonism to Jefferson, 302; career in Africa, 302 *n.*, 303 *n.*; conference with Burr, report of it, 303–05, 307; affidavit on Burr's statement, 345, 352; claim paid, 345 *n.*; at trial of Burr, testimony, 429, 452, 459, 487; loses public esteem, 523.

Economic conditions, influence on Federal Convention and Ratification, **1**, 241, 242, 310, 312, 429 *n.*, 441 *n.*; prosperity during Confederation, 306; influence on attitude towards French Revolution, **2**, 42; and first parties, 75, 96 *n.*, 125 *n. See also* Banking; Commerce; Contracts; Crisis of 1819; Land; Prices; Social conditions.

Edinburgh Review, on M.'s biography of Washington, **3**, 271; on United States (1820), **4**, 190 *n.*

Education, of colonial Virginia women, **1**, 18 *n.*, 24 *n.*; in colonial Virginia, 24; M.'s, 42, 53, 57; condition under Confederation, 271–73; M. on general, **4**, 472. *See also* Dartmouth College *vs.* Woodward; Social conditions.

Eggleston, Joseph, grand juror on Burr, **3**, 412.

Egotism, as National characteristic, **3**, 13.

Eighteenth Fructidor *coup d'état*, **2**, 230, 245 *n.*, 246 *n.*; M. on, 232, 236–44; Pinckney and, 246 *n.*

Elections, Federal, in Virginia (1789), **2**, 49, 50; (1794), 106; State, in Virginia (1795), 129–30; Henry and presidential candidacy (1796), 156–58; M.'s campaign for Congress (1798), 374–80, 401, 409–16; issues in 1798, 410; methods and scenes in Virginia, 413.

1800: Federalist dissensions, Hamiltonian plots, **2**, 438, 488, 515–18, 521, 526; issues, 439, 520; influence of campaign on Congress, 438; Federalist bill to control, M.'s defeat of it, 452–58; effect of defeat of bill, 456; effect of Federalist dissensions, 488; Adams's attack on Hamiltonians, 518, 525; Adams's advances to Jefferson, 519; Republican ascendancy, 519, 521; and new French negotiations, 522, 524; M.'s efforts for Federalist harmony, 526; Hamilton's attack on Adams, 527–29; campaign virulence, 529; size of Republican success, 531; Federalist press on result, 532 *n.*; Jefferson-Burr contest in Congress, 532–47; Jefferson's fear of Federalist intentions, 533; reasons for Federalist support of Burr, 534–36; Burr and Republican success, 535 *n.*; M.'s neutrality, 536–38; his personal interest in contest, 538, 539; influence of his neutrality, 539; Burr's refusal to favor Federalist plan, 539 *n.*; *Washington Federalist's* contrast of Jefferson and Burr, 541 *n.*; question of deadlock and appointment of a Federalist, 541–43; Jefferson's threat of armed resistance, 543; Federalists ignore threat, 544, 545 *n.*; effect of Burr's attitude and Jefferson's promises, 545–47, **3**, 18; election of Jefferson, **2**, 547; rewards to Republican workers, **3**, 81 *n.*

1804: Campaign and attacks on Judiciary, **3**, 184. — *1812:* M.'s candidacy, **4**, 31–34; Clinton as candidate, 47; possible victory if M. had been nominated, 47. — *1828:* M. and, 462–65. — *1832:* Bank as issue, 532 *n.*, 533; M.'s attitude, 534.

Electoral vote, counting in open session, **3**, 197.

Eleventh Amendment, origin, **2**, 84 *n.*, **3**, 554; purpose and limitation, **4**, 354; and suits against State officers, 385, 387–91.

Elkison, Henry, case, **4**, 382.

Elliot, James, on Wilkinson's conduct, **3**, 358.

Elliot, Jonathan, inaccuracy of *Debates*, **1**, 388 *n.*

Ellsworth, Oliver, and presidential candidacy (1800), **2**, 438; on Sedition Law, 451; resigns Chief Justiceship, 552; and common-law jurisdiction on expatriation, **3**, 27, **4**, 53; and Judiciary Act of 1789, **3**, 53, 128; on obligation of contracts, 558 *n.*

Ellsworth, William W., and attack on Supreme Court, **4**, 515.

Emancipation, as involved in Nationalist development, **4**, 370, 420, 536.

Embargo Act, **4**, 11; effect, opposition, 12–16; M.'s opinion, 14, 118; Force Act, 16; repeal, 202. *See also* Neutral trade.

Emmet, Thomas A., as practitioner before M., **4**, 95, 135 *n.*; counsel in *Nereid* case, 131; appearance, 133; counsel in Gibbons *vs.* Ogden, 424, 427.

Eppes, John W., and attempt to suspend habeas corpus (1807), **3**, 348; and amendment on Judiciary, 378 *n.*

Eppes, Tabby, M.'s gossip on, **1**, 182.

Equality, demand for division of property, **1**, 294, 298; lack of social (1803), **3**, 13.

2, 109; depredations on American commerce, 496; intrigue in West, Wilkinson as agent, **3**, 283, 284; resentment of West, expectation of war over West Florida, 284, 285, 295, 301, 306, 312, 383 n.; treaty of 1795, 550 n.; intrigue and Yazoo grant, 554.

Spanish America, desire to free, **3**, 284, 286; Miranda's plans, 286, 300, 301, 306; revolt and M.'s contribution to international law, **4**, 126–28. See also Burr Conspiracy.

Speculation, after funding, **2**, 82, 85; in land, 202; as National trait, **3**, 557; after War of 1812, **4**, 169, 181–84. See also Crisis of 1819.

Speech, freedom, and sedition trials, **3**, 42. See also Press.

Stamp Act, opposition in Virginia, **1**, 61–65.

Standing army. See Army.

Stanley, John, in Judiciary debate (1802), **3**, 74 n., 75.

Stark, John, Ware vs. Hylton, **2**, 188.

State Rights and Sovereignty, effect on Revolutionary army, **1**, 82, 88–90, 100; in American Revolution, 146; and failure of the Confederation, 308–10; union with democracy, **3**, 48; and declaring Federal acts void, 105; M. on, as factor under Confederation, 259–62; compact, **4**, 316; strict construction and reserved rights, 324 n.; Taylor's exposition, 335–39; forces (c. 1821), 370; M. on effect of strict construction, 442; and Georgia-Cherokee contest, 541; incompatible with federation, 571. See also Contracts; Eleventh Amendment; Implied powers; Government; Kentucky Resolutions; Nationalism; Nullification; Secession; Virginia Resolutions.

States, Madison on necessity of Federal veto of acts, **1**, 312; suits against, in Federal courts, 454, **2**, 83. See also Government.

Stay and tender act in Virginia, **1**, 207 n. See also Debts.

Steamboats, Fulton's experiments, Livingston's interest, **4**, 397–99; Livingston's grants of monopoly in New York, 399; first on the Mississippi, grant of monopoly in Louisiana, 402, 402 n., 403 n., 414; other grants of monopoly, 415; interstate retaliation, 415; great development, 415, 416. See also Gibbons vs. Ogden.

Steele, Jonathan, witness against Pickering, reward, **3**, 181 n.

Stephen, Adam, in Ratification Convention, characterized, **1**, 465; on Indians, 465.

Steuben, Baron von, on Revolutionary army, **1**, 84; training of the army, 88 n., 133.

Stevens, Edward, officer of minute men, **1**, 69.

Stevens, Thaddeus, as House leader, **3**, 84 n.

Stevens vs. Taliaferro, **2**, 180 n.

Stevenson, Andrew, resolution against M'Culloch vs. Maryland, **4**, 324; and repeal of appellate jurisdiction of Supreme Court, 379.

Stewart, Dr. ——, and Jay Treaty, **2**, 121.

Stirling, William, Lord, intrigue against, **1**, 122.

Stith, Judge, and Yazoo lands, **3**, 555.

Stoddert, Benjamin, Aurora on, **2**, 492; at Burr trial, **3**, 458; as Secretary of the Navy, 458 n.; proposes M. for President, **4**, 31–34.

Stone, David, and Granville heirs case, **4**, 155 n.

Stone vs. Mississippi, **4**, 279 n.

Stony Point, assault, **1**, 138–42.

Story, ——, on Ratification in Virginia, **1**, 445.

Story, Elisha, Republican, **4**, 96; children, 97; in Revolution, 97 n.

Story, Joseph, on M. and his father, **1**, 43; on M. in Jonathan Robins case, **2**, 473; on Washington (1808), **3**, 6; and common-law jurisdiction, 28 n., **4**, 30 n.; on Chase, **3**, 184 n.; on Jefferson's Anas, 230 n.; and Yazoo claims, 583, 586; on conduct of Minister Jackson, **4**, 23; on conduct of Federalists (1809), 23 n.; on Federalists and War of 1812, 30, 40; on Chief Justiceship, 59 n.; appointed Justice, history of appointment, 60, 106–10; compared and contrasted with M., 60; on M.'s attitude toward women, 71; and poetry, 80; on M.'s charm, 81; on life of Justices, 86, 87; on M.'s desire for argument of cases, 94 n., 95 n.; character, 95; as supplement to M., 96, 120, 523; Republican, 96; birth, education, 97; antipathy of Federalists, 97; in Congress, Jefferson's enmity, 97, 99; cultivated by Federalists, 98; devotion to M., 99, 523; authority on law of real estate, 100; and Nationalism, 116, 145; on constitutionality of Embargo, 118 n.; authority on admiralty, 119; United States vs. Palmer, 126; appearance, 132; on oratory before Supreme Court, 133, 135 n.; dissent in Nereid case, 142; opinions in Martin vs. Hunter's Lessee, 144, 145, 156, 161–64; assailed for opinion, contemplates resignation, 166; and Dartmouth College case, 232, 243 n., 251, 255, 257, 259 n., 274, 275; opinion in Terrett vs. Taylor, 243; on Dartmouth decision, 277; on M'Culloch vs. Maryland, 284, 287; and M.'s reply to Roane, 322; omnivorous reader, 363; and Jefferson's attack on Judiciary, 363, 364; opinion in Green vs. Biddle, 376; on Todd's absence, 381 n.; in Massachusetts Constitutional Convention, 471; on slave trade and law of nations, 476; opinion in Bank vs. Dandridge, 482; dissent in Ogden vs. Saunders, 482 n.; on proposed repeal of appellate jurisdiction, 514; and M.'s suggested resignation, 520; on M.'s recovery, 528; dissent in Cherokee Nation vs. Georgia, 546 n.; on Worcester vs. Georgia, 551; on Nullification movement, 559; on Jackson's Proclamation, 563; M. and Commentaries and its dedication, 569, 576, 580, 581; on Webster's speech against Nullification, 572; article on statesmen, 577; on

362, 377 n., 382 n.; on campaign for Anti-Constitutionalist delegates, 366, 367; on opposition of leaders in State politics, 366 n.; on detailed debate in Virginia Convention, 370 n.; influence on Ratification Convention, 476; on the contest in Virginia, 478; and opposition after Ratification, 248; as distiller, 2, 86 n.; on West and Union, 3, 282 n.

As President and after: hardships of travel, 1, 255, 259; influence of French Revolution, 2, 3; and beginning of French Revolution, 10; and Genêt, 28; and imprisonment of Lafayette, 33; on democratic clubs, 38, 88, 89; Virginia address (1789), 57; on Virginia's opposition (1790), 68 n.; opposes partisanship, 76; and antagonism in Cabinet, 82; and Whiskey Insurrection, 87, 89; and neutrality, 92; on attacks, 93 n., 164; and attacks on M.'s character, 102, 103; and British crisis (1794), 112; attacks on, over Jay Treaty, 116–18; J. Q. Adams on policy, 119 n.; on attacks on treaty, 120; M. refuses Cabinet offices, 122, 123, 147; M. advises on Cabinet positions, 124–26, 132; virtual censure by Virginia Legislature, 137–40; offers French mission to M., 144–46; and support of Jay Treaty, 149, 150; final Republican abuse, 158, 162–64; address of Virginia Legislature (1796), 159–62; and M.'s appointment to X. Y. Z. Mission, 216; Monroe's attack, 222; M.'s letters during X. Y. Z. mission, 229, 233–44, 267–72, 320–23; on hopes for X. Y.'Z. Mission, 244; on X. Y. Z. dispatches and French partisans, 340, 359, 360; Federalist toast to (1798), 349 n.; accepts command of army, 357; does not anticipate land war, 357; on Gerry, 365; persuades M. to run for Congress (1798), 374–78; Langhorne letter, 375 n.; and M.'s election, 416; and M.'s apology for statement by supporters, 416, 417; death, M.'s announcement in Congress, 440–43; House resolutions, authorship of "first in war" designation, 443–45; and slavery petitions, 450 n.; temperament contrasted with Adams's, 487 n.; Jefferson's Mazzei letter on, 537 n.; Weems's biography, 3, 231 n.; and French War, 258 n.; M.'s biography on Administration, 263–65; and Yazoo lands, 569. *See also* Biography.

Washington, D.C., Morris's land speculation, 2, 205 n.; condition when first occupied, 494 n.; aspect (1801), 3, 1–4; lack of progress, 4–6; malaria, 6; absence of churches, 6; boarding-houses, 7; population, 9; drinking, 9; factions, 10; Webster on, 4, 86. *See also* District of Columbia.

Washington Federalist, on Hamilton's attack on Adams, 2, 528; campaign virulence, 530 n.; eulogism of Adams, 532 n.; M.'s reputed influence over, 532 n., 541, 547 n.; and Jefferson-Burr contest, 534 n., 540;

on Hay's attack on M., 543 n.; on Republican armed threat, 544 n., 545 n.; sentiment after Jefferson's election, 547 n., on Judiciary debate (1802), and secession, 3, 72; on Bayard's speech on Judiciary, 82; on Randolph's speech, 87 n.; on repeal of Judiciary Act, 92, 93; on Burr's farewell address, 274 n.

Washington's birthday, celebration abandoned (1804), 3, 210 n.; Burr's toast, 280.

Washita lands, Burr's plan to settle, 3, 292 n., 303, 310, 312, 313, 314 n., 319, 324 n., 361 n, 362, 461, 462, 523, 527.

Water travel, hardships, 1, 259, 3, 55 n. *See also* Steamboat.

Watkins, John, and Burr, 3, 295; and Wilkinson and Adair, 337 n.

Watson, Elkanah, on army at Valley Forge, 1, 111 n.; on hardships of travel, 263 n.; on Virginia social conditions, 277 n.; on dissipation, 283 n.

Wayne, Anthony, discipline, 1, 88; in Brandywine campaign, 93, 95, 96; in Philadelphia campaign, 100; Germantown, 102; Monmouth campaign, 135; Stony Point, 139–41; and supplies, 139 n.; on military smartness, 139 n.

Wayne, C. P., negotiations to publish M.'s biography, 3, 225–27; agreement, 227, 228; and political situation, 230; solicitation of subscriptions, 230, 235; and M.'s delays and prolixity, 235, 236, 239, 241; and financial problem, 236, 250; payment of royalty, 247, 248, 251; and revised edition, 272.

Wayne, James M., appointment to Supreme Court, 4, 584.

Webb, Foster, and Tabby Eppes, 1, 182.

Webster, Daniel, on Yazoo claims, 3, 602; opposes new Western States, 4, 28 n.; and War of 1812, 48; opposes conscription, 51 n., 52 n.; on M., 59 n.; on Washington, 86; as practitioner before M., 95, 135; on bank debate, 180; counsel in Dartmouth College case, 233, 234, 260, 273; and story of Indian students, 233 n.; on the trial, 237, 240 n., 250 n., 253 n., 254 n., 261 n., 273, 274; argument in case, 240–52; tribute to Dartmouth, 248–50; fee and portrait, 255 n.; and success in case, 273; counsel in M'Culloch *vs.* Maryland, appearance, 284; argument, 285; on the case, 288; debt to M. in reply to Hayne, 293 n., 552–55; counsel in Cohens *vs.* Virginia, 357; in and on debate on Supreme Court, 379, 380, 395, 395 n., 452 n.; counsel in Osborn *vs.* Bank, 385; resolution on regulating power to declare State acts void, 396, 451; counsel in Gibbons *vs.* Ogden, 413, 424; argument, 424–27; fanciful story on it, 424 n.; overlooks M.'s earlier decision on question, 427–29; and American Colonization Society, 474; and re-charter of the Bank, 530; on Nullification, M.'s commendation, 572.

Webster, Ezekiel, on War of 1812, 4, 46 n.